WALKING WITH ARCHANGELS

The Angelic Way of Ascension:
a handbook for self-transformation
and personal growth.

WALKING WITH ARCHANGELS
Copyright © Hilary Jane Hargreaves 2017
HB ISBN 978-0-9957518-0-4

ALL RIGHTS RESERVED
No part of this publication may be reproduced, stored in a retrieval system,
or transmitted in any form or by any means – electronic, mechanical, photocopying,
scanning, recording or otherwise, without the prior written permission of the publisher and the author;
nor be otherwise circulated in any form of binding or cover other than which it is published –
and without similar conditions being imposed upon any subsequent purchaser.

Author: Hilary Jane Hargreaves
All material original © Hilary Hargreaves / School of Inner Light 2005-2017.
For more details (or for other publications from 'Unity Consciousness Books')
visit www.unityconsciousnessbooks.com
and/or visit the on-line shop at www.innerlightcrystals.co.uk

Picture (front cover) 'Archangel Metatron'
gifted to Mark of 'Inner Light' by the artist.
Picture (back cover) 'The Stranger'
given into the guardianship of Hilary and Mark of 'Inner Light' by the artist.
Both artworks © Alison Knox (artist) of EVERYDaY ANGeLS,
whose inspired artworks enabled me to deepen my connections with the Angelic Realm.
(find her at www.everydayangelsart.com)

Published by 'Unity Consciousness Books'.
Printed and bound in Wales by Gomer Press, Llandysul, SA44 4JL.

This book is firstly dedicated to my Earthly 'three Ms':

♥♥♥

Maggie, my first spiritual teacher,
who opened my eyes to other realities;
Mollie, my wonderful friend,
whose generous spirit and radiant Light has always been there for me;
and Mark, my soul partner, husband and twin flame,
who always supports, accepts and loves me unconditionally.

♥♥♥

Without them I would not be on this path,
and this book would never have been written.

Secondly, this book is dedicated to my Heavenly 'three Ms':

♥♥♥

Metatron, Michael and Melchisadek –
and to all my Angelic teachers and mentors, family and friends (real and unreal),
who are such an important part of my journey;

♥♥♥

and to ALL the members of the mineral, plant and animal Kingdoms of Earth,
who truly understand the interconnectedness of all things
and without whom humankind could not exist.

And finally, this book is dedicated to you, dear reader:

♥♥♥

*Reach out to embrace all with love and compassion,
and see yourself reflected in another's eyes – and know that you are Divine:
then, being Divine, you will know and see ALL to be Divine,
and act at all times with wisdom and without ego in service to the Light.*

♥♥♥

May you walk this world with an open mind and a heart full of love,
and Become all you truly wish to BE.

Disclaimer:
The material in this book is intuitively derived.
The author's intent is only to offer the material to aid the reader or user in their personal spiritual quest, and should be evaluated in the light of the reader or user's own experiences.
It is not intended to be a replacement for medical care from a qualified doctor or health practitioner.
The publisher and author assume no responsibility for the reader or user's choices, or their actions and/or their outcomes.

INDEX OF CONTENTS

BEFORE YOU START TO READ OR WORK WITH THIS BOOK ...	1
THE WRITER'S TALE... and how it all began	2
THE SEVEN GREAT KINGDOMS OF EARTH	4
WHAT'S IN A NAME?... everything IS simply Light!	5
ASCENSION AND THE MULTIDIMENSIONAL SOUL	7
THE UNDERLYING OBJECTIVE OF THIS BOOK	8
USING THIS BOOK AS AN AID TO SELF-MASTERY	8
CONNECTING WITH THE ARCHANGELS AND ARCHEIA	9
UNDERSTANDING THE TEACHINGS	10
A FEW FINAL WORDS	11

THE ARCHANGELS AND ARCHEIA:

(The index that follows shows:
THE ARCHANGEL / ARCHEIA'S NAME AND 'THEME';
Their three Teachings ['The'...] – one of which includes their Gift ['The Gift of...];
Their three Crystal Champions;
Their three Creature Companions;
Their two Greenwood Guardians.)

TZADKIEL: 'POTENTIAL FOR CHANGE' 15
    The Violet Ray and The Cloak of Immaculate Illumination
    The Gift of The Violet Flame of Transmutation
    The All-seeing Eye and The Communion of The Grail
    Sugilite, Lepidolite, Golden Labradorite;
    Jay, Vulture, Goose;
    Larch and Tamarisk.

AMETHYSTIA: 'PROGRESS THROUGH LEARNING' 29
    The Gift of The Amethyst Flame of Transformation
    The Spiral of Transformation – Perspective and Choice
    The Sacred Purpose of Sigils, Symbols and Signs
    Amethyst, Honey Calcite, Clear Selenite;
    Crab, Deer, Mouse;
    Aspen and Scots Pine.

METATRON: 'RESTRUCTURE YOUR LIFE' 43
    The Power of the Rainbow and The Light Within
    The Gift of The Lightning Bolt of Divine Inspiration
    The Star-borne Hammer of Dissolution and Creation
    Flame Aura Quartz, Yellow Jasper, Haematoid Quartz;
    Peacock, Lion, Donkey;
    Chile Pine (Monkey Puzzle Tree) and Redwood.

SOPHIA: 'BALANCE THROUGH BRAVERY' 57
    The Gift of The Absolute Light of The Illumined Heart
    The Crucible and The Alchemy of The Silver-Violet Flame
    The Tau Key of Perfected Manifestation
    Tiger Eye, Charoite, Blue Lace Agate;
    Squirrel, Rabbit, Mountain Lion;
    Robinia (False Acacia) and Beech.

SERAPHINA: 'LOVE YOURSELF FIRST' 71
    The Lyre of Light and The Charitable Heart
    The Healing Power of Love Without Limits
    The Gift of The Pink Flame of Divine Love
    Clear Optical Calcite, Prehnite, Pink Girasol;
    Merlin, Wren, Lovebird;
    Poplar and Ash.

CHAMUEL: 'SELF-ACCEPTANCE' 85
    The Gift of The Rose-pink Flame of Divine Compassion
    The Sword of Divine Justice and the True Meaning of Power
    The Blessing of Mercy and the Promise of Karmic Freedom
    Rose Quartz, Rhodocrosite, Ruby;
    Turtledove, Horse, Dog;
    Birch and Cherry.

MARYLLISA: 'LIFE IS BEAUTIFUL' 99
    The Light of The Star of Venus and The Beauty Within
    The Rose of Peace and The Dynamic Duality of Absolute Balance
    The Gift of The Mirror of The Soul
    Angelite, Malachite, Carnelian;
    Chameleon, Glow-worm, Great Grey Owl;
    Apple and Rowan.

HANIEL: 'WALK YOUR WALK – TALK YOUR TALK' 113
    The Book of Illumined Truths and The Waters of The Diamond Light
    The Flame of Truth and Light and The Serpents of Creation
    The Gift of The Quill of Quetzalcoatl
    Clear Apophyllite, Blue Celestite, Bronzite;
    Black Jaguar, Cicada, Golden Eagle;
    Tamarisk and Oak.

MICHAEL: 'KNOW YOUR TRUTHS' 127
    The Light of The Sun and The Sword of Truth
    The Unicorns of Ultimate Purity and The Spiral of Contemplation
    The Gift of The Sapphire Flame of Divine Expression
    Indigo Kyanite, Sodalite, Blue Sapphire;
    Snow Leopard, Praying Mantis, Crow;
    Holly and Larch.

MIKAELA: 'WALK THE LABYRINTH WITH ME' 141
    The Circle of Life – the Labyrinth and the Maze
    The Holographic Universe and the Multifaceted Nature of Divine Truth
    The Gift of The Blue Flame of Divine Will and Power
    Labradorite, Azurite, Blue Chalcedony;
    Tiger, Cobra, Bat;
    Myrrh and Weeping Willow.

LUCIDA: 'FIND THE CHRIST WITHIN' 155
    The Grounding of The Christ-Light through the Cedar and the Rose
    The Gift of The Yellow Flame of Divine Wisdom
    The Art of Balance through Focused Self-awareness
    Tiger Iron, Natural Citrine, Tree Agate;
    Egret, Jaguar, Tree Creeper;
    Pomegranate and Fig.

JOPHIEL: 'SHINE YOUR LIGHT'   169
    The Gift of The Golden-yellow Flame of Illumined Wisdom
    The Circle of Learning – the Jasmine and the Rose
    The Secret Garden and The Gold Flame of Joy
    Heat-treated Citrine, White Phantom Quartz, Ametrine;
    Locust, Kestrel, Wolf;
    Sweet Chestnut and Bamboo.

ANNUNCIATA: 'HOPE SHINES THROUGH'   183
    The Knowledge of Perfected Balance and The 'I' of The Pearl
    The Knowledge of Perfected Creation and The Songs of the Whales
    The Gift of The Pearl-white Flame of Hope
    Pearl, Fire Opal, Rainbow Moonstone;
    Stork, Whale, White Dove;
    Linden (Lime) and Magnolia.

GABRIEL: 'JOYFUL JOURNEYS'   197
    The Crystal Ray and The Staff of Awakening
    The New Dawn Flame and the Baptism of Fire
    The Gift of The Crystal-clear Flame of First Consciousness
    Herkimer Diamond, Lapis Lazuli, White Selenite (Satin Spar);
    Honeybee, Golden Pheasant, Griffon;
    Hornbeam and Horse Chestnut.

URIEL: 'CREATE WHAT YOU DESIRE'   211
    The Sacred Flames of Resurrection and Rebirth
    The Keys of Understanding and The Scroll of Akasha
    The Gift of The Divine Templates of Creation
    Amber, Green Jade, Red Jasper;
    Phoenix, Swan, Spider;
    Mulberry and Sycamore.

RAINBOW AURORA: 'OPEN YOUR HEART'   225
    The 'Tao' of the Open and Balanced Heart
    The Seal of Embedded Creation and The Dragons of the Rainbow Realm
    The Gift of The Rainbow Key of Light
    Morganite, Preseli Bluestone, Rainbow (Angel / Opal) Aura Quartz;
    Snowy Owl, Rose Dragon, White Stag;
    Sycomore Fig and Mimosa.

SHEKHINAH: 'LOOK FOR ME WITHIN'   **239**
    The Gift of The Holon of Universal Balance
    The Diamond Light that IS Within and Without
    The Light of Universal Consciousness and The Holon of Infinity
    Hematite, Zircon, Magnesite;
    Dolphin, Magpie, Cat;
    Juniper and Amelanchier (Snowy Mespil).

SANDALPHON: 'BALANCE AND GROWTH'   **253**
    The Alignment of The Lotus of the Heart with the Linear Bodies
    The Alignment of the Heart of the Lotus with the Unified Body
    The Gift of The Sacred Seeds of Limitless Potential
    Petrified (Fossilised) Wood, Tourmalinated Quartz, Gaia (Polychrome) Jasper;
    Turtle, Crane, White Peacock;
    Oak and Coconut.

MAREIA: 'RETURN THE LIGHT TO YOUR LIFE'   **267**
    The Emerald Key of Modification and Balance
    The Evolution of Life and the Perfection of Divine Creation
    The Gift of The Infinity Cross of Multidimensional Reality
    Seraphinite, Scolecite, Turquoise;
    White Eagle, Puffin, Hummingbird;
    Baobab and Yew.

RAPHAEL: 'WHOLENESS THROUGH TRANSFORMATION'   **281**
    The Key to Wholeness and Health – Self-awareness and Love
    The Mastery of Balance through the Still-point Within
    The Gift of The Enlightened Lotus of Divinity
    Pink Optical Calcite, Green Aventurine, Watermelon Tourmaline;
    Little Owl, Green Woodpecker, Hornet;
    Yew and Maple.

MAGDALENA: 'THE BLESSING OF MERCY'   **295**
    The Merciful Freedom of Living in The NOW
    The Fearless Heart and The Glory of The Grail
    The Gift of The Magdalene Flame of Innocence, Purity and Love
    White Moonstone, White Girasol, Aqua Aura Quartz;
    Butterfly, Ocelot, Firebird;
    Hawthorn and Eucalyptus.

AZRAEL: 'CHANGE AND TRANSITION'   309
    The Obsidian Mirror – Truth, Trust and Transformation
    The Diamond Lantern – Surrender, Sacrifice and Self-mastery
    The Gift of The Merkaba of The Ascension
    Black Obsidian, Clear Danburite, Moldavite;
    Dragonfly, Adder, Raven;
    Gingko Biloba and Corkscrew Hazel.

RATZIEL: 'OPEN TO THE LIGHT'   323
    The Knowledge and Wisdom of The Ancient Ones
    The Book of Ratziel – Love, Light and The Word
    The Gift of The Black Light of The Alpha and Omega
    Apache Tear, Snowflake Obsidian, Jet;
    Cheetah, Ostrich, Elephant;
    Maple and Acacia.

JOCHARA: 'SWEET SURRENDER'   337
    The Fundamental Forces of Air and Water
    The Fundamental Forces of Earth and Fire
    The Gift of The White Light of The Alpha and Omega
    Aquamarine, Tibetan (Black) Tektite, Snow (White) Quartz;
    Condor, Mountain Goat, Polar Bear;
    Rowan and Date Palm.

OKINA: 'WHAT IS CONSCIOUSNESS?'   351
    The Ray of Revelation and The Mind of The Divine
    The Gift of The Golden Halo of Universal Awareness
    The Magenta Ray and The Cosmic Seeds of Light
    Cobalt Aura Quartz, Pyrite, Chrysanthemum Stone;
    Otter, Scarab Beetle, Skunk;
    Wych Hazel and Elm.

TZAPHKIEL: 'KNOW YOURSELF – KNOW ALL THINGS'   365
    The Alignment of Personal Will and Divine Will
    The Gift of The Spear of Divine Enlightenment
    The Enlightenment of The Platinum Star of Illumined Truth
    Hawks (Falcons / Blue Tiger) Eye, Rainbow Obsidian, Clear Quartz;
    Peregrine Falcon, Octopus, Sparrow;
    Cypress and Baobab.

REFERENCE SECTION:

AN OVERVIEW OF THE HUMAN ENERGY BODY   381
   1: The Linear Energy Body and the Linear Chakras   *381*
   2: The Unified Energy Body (the Unified Chakra and Unified Body)   *383*
   3: The Lotus of the Heart   *385*
   4: The Lotus of the Soul   *385*

THE DIVINE LIGHT AND THE SACRED RAYS   386

INDEXES:

ALPHABETICAL INDEX OF CREATURE COMPANIONS   388

ALPHABETICAL INDEX OF CRYSTAL CHAMPIONS   390

ALPHABETICAL INDEX OF GREENWOOD GUARDIANS   392

ALPHABETICAL INDEX OF TEACHINGS   394

BEFORE YOU START TO READ OR WORK WITH THIS BOOK ...
please read all of this page.

The objective of this book is to offer and present a systematic and comprehensive programme of Archangelic mentoring that (through guided processes of self-reflection and self-understanding) has the potential to result in profound transformation and growth on many levels. Accordingly, I was directed to construct this book exactly as you see it, simply because every chapter, Teaching and Gift has a specific purpose and function – each adding to, and building upon, the material in the pages preceding it: therefore, if you choose to embrace the aim of this book by using and following it as an all-encompassing aid to your self-healing and spiritual growth, it is very important that you carefully read, address and work through all of the chapters and Teachings one at a time, AND in the order in which they are presented – i.e. starting at the beginning of Tzadkiel's chapter, and finishing at the end of Tzaphkiel's chapter.

Within the pages of this book you will find that each Archangel and Archeia will offer you three Teachings (mentoring sessions). One of these Teachings presents you with a 'Gift' that is designed to augment your energies and deepen the work that you can undertake on the topics and Themes presented by them – both now, and in the future: the heading of these always begins with the words 'The Gift of...'. Each Gift takes the form of an etheric template (subtle energy structure) that will be 'placed' at a specific location within your energy field as you read the words and follow them in your mind's eye; and, chapter by chapter, each will build upon those that have been given before – ultimately creating a cohesive Higher-Dimensional construct that (IF you follow and complete the full programme of Teachings offered) is designed and intended to promote the grounding of your Lightbody. Therefore it is also very important to understand that:

- ♥ If you read *any* of the 'Gift of...' Teachings in full* it will be assumed that you have elected to receive that Archangel or Archeia's Gift, and accordingly its etheric energy structure will become a permanent part of your energy field. If you do NOT wish this to happen, please do NOT read those particular Teachings.
  (* If curiosity causes you to have a look at any of those sections, please ensure that you only skim through the material, and engage with it on a very superficial level.)

- ♥ You cannot pick and choose which Gifts to receive: if you wish to receive one Gift, you must be willing to receive them all*. Moreover, you MUST work through all the material in the book from start to finish, so that each Gift is given and received at the appropriate time.
  (* The ONLY exception to this rule is Tzadkiel's Gift: as his is the first Gift offered, you may accept it even if you choose to accept no others – in fact you will find his Gift of The Violet Flame to be very useful as you read and work with the other material in this book!)

Lastly, because the Archangels and Archeia appreciate that not everyone will want to undertake the full programme of work offered within these pages, the wisdoms presented may also be used more 'lightly': so, if you simply want to know more about a particular Archangelic, crystal, animal or tree – or are drawn to a particular Teaching – you may dip into the material as you please (apart from 'The Gift of....' Teachings, of course!).

THE WRITER'S TALE... and how it all began

I had a fairly conventional English 'middle-class' upbringing, and from an early age I was sent to Sunday-school each week: subsequently, throughout my teens I became a regular church-goer, and – although not particularly devout – over time I came to value the peaceful and serene atmosphere of the church, and found comfort in the music and rituals associated with Christian practice. I also enjoyed wandering the wild tranquillity of the churchyard, and was often drawn to talk to a large white marble Angel that stood sentinel over one of the graves, although I never questioned why! Life passed: I survived school, and found myself on the treadmill of a predictable and mundane office job; got married, and experienced many of the ups and downs that life – and relationships – often generates. Eventually, having found that conventional medicine was of no lasting help in dealing with the mental and emotional fallout of the worst of the 'downs', I sought an alternative solution and a different approach.

My journey began with essential oils: their effectiveness astonished me and led me to train as an aromatherapist, which in turn led to my first exploratory steps into other aspects of the esoteric and 'alternative' world, as I strived to understand myself and discover my 'reason for being'. Classes were taught in rooms above a 'New Age' shop (where my love of crystals was kindled over many a wet lunch break!); and here too the fates brought me a tutor who had a deeply spiritual and intuitive side. She introduced me to the delights of guided visualisations and to Angel Cards, both of which opened doorways in my consciousness as I connected with the unseen world around me. My awakening was furthered by a wonderful friend (and great Light and dear Soul) I met on the same course, who persuaded me to learn Reiki – and later supported and encouraged me through a time when I was tempted to give it all up after experiencing another 'dark night of the soul'.

During my seven-year spiritual 'wake-up' process, I got divorced; moved home to a new location; changed my job; and found (and married) my twin-flame and soul-partner, Mark. He provided the secure foundation I needed to have the courage and strength to explore my place in the world, and later supported and facilitated my journey of self-understanding and healing as I sought to lay my inner demons to rest. As I grew, I found that exploring the subtle world in an attempt to understand it (and my Self) enthused me more than the 'hands-on' work did; and as a relentless seeker of knowledge, I consumed a wide-ranging diet of esoteric books and attended many different workshops and courses to experience and learn as much as I could.

As part of this, I dabbled in various tomes on Angels – and then soon after the Millennia I attended a workshop that brought one of them in particular into my life with a bang. I still recall the experience vividly.... I was enjoying a 'journey' immersed in a guided visualisation, when I suddenly felt a vast presence rise up through the floor just behind me (we were on the top floor of the building): then a *very* powerful masculine energy enveloped me, and a commanding voice announced very clearly – so clearly, in fact, I opened my eyes for a peek! – "*I am Metatron, Angel of Light and Mercy....*" Back then I did not have a clue who 'Metatron' was, but our 'close encounter' was rapidly followed by other encounters with Uriel and Michael – then the floodgates opened and these awesome Beings simply poured into my awareness, and the Archangels (and later the Archeia) became a constant and powerful presence in my life.

In the meantime, my love of crystals had led me to complete a graduate diploma course in Crystal and Gem Therapy; and this, coupled with Mark's innate clairvoyance, enabled us to create crystal layouts to help us connect with, and learn from, a variety of archetypal energies – including (of course!) some of the Archangels. We were then asked to teach and share what we had learnt and experienced, and so in 2002 we established the 'School of Inner Light' and began to research, write, compile and lead workshops and courses, whilst also continuing with our individual research, learning and growth in the mind-body-spirit field. Seven years later Mark left the 'corporate' world behind him, and now shares his skills as a therapist, channel, teacher, healer and etheric surgeon, allowing us to make 'Inner Light' our full-time vocation.

As we learned and grew we established four websites to broadcast and disseminate our work, one of which ('Inner Lightworkers') included some information extracted from material we had channelled and explored when writing our 'The Way of the Archangels' course in 2005/6. At that time we had been asked to include the Archeia in our teaching (about whom not much was generally known), and as a consequence we had worked with the masculine *and* feminine aspects of thirteen Archangelics in great depth. This enabled us to glean some significant understandings from our encounters, and led to us compiling a unique set of 'Archangelic Messages' and publishing them on our websites by means of an interactive randomly-generated 'pick-a-card' facility. This feature gave rise to many positive responses from people all over the world, and led (over a series of events) to the creation of this book, which I actually began writing in 2011.

Back then, I thought – in hindsight perhaps rather naively – it would be a relatively simple task, perhaps involving the extraction and compilation of insightful material from courses that we had already researched and taught over the previous decade. However, as soon as I 'put pen to paper' (or rather 'fingers to keyboard') my Archangelic mentors made it quite clear that was *not* how it was to be done! They told me to get ready to work in a way I had never worked before, and to prepare myself to write every word from a totally new and original perspective, so that their Archangelic presences could become exactly that: *present*. It is time, they told me, for a completely fresh approach, so that everyone truly understands that they – the Archangels *and* the Archeia – are real and approachable. They also stressed how vital it is that *everyone,* from those who are just awakening to the reality of their innate spirituality, to those who are much further down their path, is able to access their guidance much more clearly and effectively. Indeed, throughout my writing the Archangels and Archeia have proved to me that they are not some 'lofty presence' far too removed from our world to help us unless we beg. Instead, they have proved to be ever-present, kind and compassionate; infinitely knowledgeable and wise; and (above all) loving and non-judgmental companions, who can simply see, perceive and understand *everything* from a much Higher perspective than our own.

Thus, I spent over a year in near-constant communion with the Archangels and Archeia completing a first (very substantial!) draft. Then, totally unexpectedly, I was told that what I had thought to be the finished product merely laid the groundwork for a series of books, each of which was to hold different aspects of the material. Some were to offer ways in which the 'messages' they gave me could be used to catalyse understanding and growth; but one was to be a more substantial book presented as a series of Teachings designed to guide and support a self-led programme of profound spiritual transformation and inner healing. The Archangelics also stressed their wish for me to include wisdoms contributed by the mineral, plant and animal Kingdoms alongside these 'Teachings', so that (as humans) we recognise, appreciate and truly *know* how we are eternally supported from both above *and* below. Hence several more years of yet deeper and more complex communion with them all followed – and this book is that end product.

Now, over time I have developed enough faith and trust in myself (and my abilities) to 'take dictation': indeed, at times those I work with are very specific about what they wish to get across *and* how they want it to read. On such occasions I hear and convey their words as clearly as I can (any text *"italicised in quote marks"* is 'as given'). When this is not the case, I usually 'see' the concepts that are being conveyed to me in my minds eye like a snapshot or impression; or sense them as a feeling or an emotion; or receive them as an intuitive thought or inner 'knowing'. Here then is my dilemma: much of what I 'see', 'feel' or 'know' is energy without form, which I have to *give* form by means of my 'imagination', and then *define* through words, in such a way that anyone who reads them can recreate that image, feeling or sense of understanding for himself or herself. This necessitates me finding the right words and phrases to describe, sum up and convey whatever that is, until the resonances of what I 'see' and what I write marry. Needless to say, in the process of writing this book I have learnt that words don't always exist that will impart what I am being shown satisfactorily enough to meet my own (self-imposed) rather high standards, and so there have been many times when I have stomped off in a major strop in sheer frustration at not being able to articulate exactly what I need and want to convey. Yet at other times I have laughed myself silly, or found myself crying uncontrollable tears of bliss, as the power and energy of certain concepts or of certain presences have been so incredibly pure or amazingly profound that they have completely overwhelmed me.

So, here's the thing: *anyone* can sense the presence of Angels; *anyone* can hear and talk with them. All it takes is faith and trust – in your Self, and in them. To connect with their love and receive their guidance you need only to be willing to open your heart and mind to their presence, and ask them to draw closer to you – in whatever world you live. For my part, I have done the best I can to facilitate this for you, and now I simply trust that 'they' will do the rest. May they Bless *your* life just as they eternally Bless mine!

THE SEVEN GREAT KINGDOMS OF EARTH

In my Archangelic encounters I was lovingly (and repeatedly!) shown how taking time out to appreciate the wonders of the natural world, and learning to value *everything* that exists on Earth, truly helps heal body, mind and Soul, and aids balance and growth. Indeed, when first working with Archangel Raphael he explained why, saying:

"Many see my 'healing' role from a rather limited viewpoint, often restricting it to a very human, personal level. Yet I address healing – and view wholeness – from a much

wider perspective at both Cosmic and planetary levels, for my Galactic duties include anchoring the Divine Plan for the evolution of the Seven Great Kingdoms of Earth, whilst facilitating ecological health and balance within and between them. I have found that it is not always appreciated that Earth was specifically designed with the capacity to promote and support humankind's health and balance through its minerals and crystals, flora and fauna. Indeed, within the aforementioned hierarchy, the first three Kingdoms – mineral, plant and animal – unfailingly support the fourth Kingdom, that of humanity, which has been granted dominion over them. Note, however, it is imperative to recognise that 'dominion over' is not an 'entitlement', whereby you simply take without care, consideration or due respect; but must be interpreted and enacted in its true sense as 'wise and compassionate stewardship'. Know then that humankind's place in the world carries both power and *responsibility – for the Earth offers many means to wholeness and health to those that have the wit to recognise her myriad gifts so freely given, and who have the wisdom to understand and work in harmony with her ordained and innate capacity for self-regulated evolution and growth."*

Gradually it became clear to me that I was being asked to highlight the essential role that minerals, plants and animals play in making human life on Earth possible; and so I was guided to include wisdoms from some 'Crystal Champions' of the mineral Kingdom and 'Creature Companions' of the animal Kingdom, each of whom asked to support you in working with the Archangelic Teachings; and from some 'Greenwood Guardians' of the plant Kingdom, who asked to aid you in understanding and assimilating the Archangelic 'Gifts' (if you choose to accept them), and to support you in integrating and grounding any shifts and changes that might occur as a consequence of *all* your endeavours.

On a personal note, I was lucky enough to be given the time and space to complete the first drafts of this book whilst living in a tranquil spot overlooking the western slopes of the Brecon Beacons in Wales (thank you to Peter and Jemima!). Here I was immersed in the beauty of the natural world and surrounded by woodland and trees, and over time I became filled with wonder at the profound and enlightened wisdom that they were prepared to share with me. I was, of course, already used to the companionship and inspiration of the mineral Kingdom, who are a constant and important part of my life – and although I cannot claim to have encountered any 'real' dragons, all the spirits of the animal Kingdom I called upon were happy to walk (or fly, swim or crawl) the Earth with me. Moreover, despite the fact that humankind still has so much to learn about respecting and taking proper care of the myriad resources of the natural world – and about living harmoniously with *all* sentient life forms (including our fellow humans!) who share that world with us – they all volunteered their aid unconditionally, and readily shared their insightful observations and the many secrets of their worlds. I was truly awed by the amount of support that was so freely given, and for this I thank them, with all my heart.

WHAT'S IN A NAME?... everything IS simply Light!

To begin with, I did not feel comfortable using the word 'God' in my re-awakened spiritual life – perhaps because I connected it with more conventional spiritual practices. This was not to say that I rejected the concept of there being an Ultimate Power, but it took me quite a while to accept that the word 'God' was a title that still held meaning for me – and which was at least quick to type! Still, because I did not wish to imply that the Angelics only interact with those who have a specific set of beliefs, I gave a great deal of thought about what word(s) to use for the purposes of this book. Eventually I decided to use 'The Divine' in most of the text, but you can choose to substitute this with 'Allah', 'All That Is', 'Creator', 'Great Spirit', 'Source', 'Yahweh' – or whatever feels right and comfortable to you, and suits your own path and personal beliefs and practices. This is because, as a physical Being, you are designed to function in a third-Dimensional reality, making your *conscious* connections on a tangible level by means of your physical senses of sight, sound, touch, smell and taste; and your *subconscious* connections by means of your non-physical Bodies and Higher senses of intuition and inner-knowing. You then instinctively interpret and process whatever you see, know or sense; and use the language with which you are the most familiar to apply words, names, labels and titles to what you identify and explore in order to make everything meaningful to you. So, when you think about the many different languages and dialects spoken around the world, and consider the countless number of words (and the multitudinous symbols and scripts) that we use to define it, it makes perfect sense that the actual *word* used for something is not important, *as long as* it holds a specific meaning for the user, and its usage is clear and consistent.

As my personal understanding has grown, I might now choose to define 'God' as All That IS – an Omni-dimensional multi-faceted and limitless Light and Potential – yet 'he' remains an *indefinable* presence that I simply know: the word I choose to use merely serves as an identifier for that presence, enabling me to 'file' it in my consciousness and access it as I need. Furthermore, I am pretty sure 'God' doesn't mind or care what name or gender 'he' is given – and I *know* the Archangelics take the same view, because in our encounters over the years I have found that they use a variety of descriptives and titles for 'him' themselves. Likewise, the names and titles I use for the Archangels and Archeia are those given to Mark and I *by* them as we encountered, worked with and experienced their energies: however, you may find that these names differ from those given by other authors, and so if you already know any of them by a different name, it is fine to use whichever you feel comfortable with. It really does not matter whether you name an Archangel or Archeia 'Fred' 'Fauriel' 'Faith' or 'Freda' – as long as the name or title has meaning for you, *and* you can relate it to their particular presence.

Regardless then of how you choose to name them, in their *true* form the Archangels and Archeia are simply Light* that has a multidimensional energy presence and a unique energy signature. This can be 'tuned into', decoded and identified, simply by expanding your awareness and engaging your 'Higher' senses – making it possible to know 'who' and 'what' they are, even if (as may happen, according to your needs and expectations at the time) they present themselves in different forms. In fact, as your perspective shifts, you will find that *every* Being – including you! – has a unique identifier 'written' in the 'Language of Light', which is universally recognised, regardless of Time or Dimension.

(* 'Light' – with a capital 'L' – is a massive concept to understand! To help shed a little light – with a small 'l' – on the matter, I have included a separate section headed 'The Divine Light and the Sacred Rays' in the reference section at the back of this book.)

ASCENSION AND THE MULTIDIMENSIONAL SOUL

Throughout this book you will come across terminology (such as 'chakra' 'energy field' and 'aura') that relates to the subtle – non-physical – human energy Body and/or its evolution. You may already be very familiar with some or all of these terms, but if you are not, the section headed 'An Overview of the Human Energy Body' in the reference section at the back of this book may help you understand more. It may also help you put material into an appropriate context when you are given 'Gifts' or assisted with 'energy shifts', at which time it may be particularly useful and beneficial for you to understand the significance of what is occurring.

You will also come across the term 'Ascension', which many envisage as being an event that entails moving 'up' or 'away from' physical existence; or as being a rather nebulous 'something' that will 'take' or 'transport' them to a new or different place. Yet Ascension is essentially an extension of the frequency at which the atoms that comprise your physical body vibrate, enabling you to switch your conscious awareness within and between the third- and sixth-Dimensions; and when you understand that *all* Dimensions occupy the same 'space', you will realise that in fact it is your *perception* and *conscious awareness* that determine the nature of your reality and Planes of experience.

As an integral part of the Ascension process, the state of 'Unified Body' facilitates this necessary change of perception and awareness by aiding and supporting a gradual shift from the 'physical' to the 'non-physical' Dimensions. This helps you release your hold on what, until then, has been the reality of your Linear energy-Body matrix (the subtle anatomy and third-Dimensional physical structure of your human body) and create a *new* reality that holds the Light-frequency and matrices of your fifth-Dimensional (and Higher) 'Lightbody'. This increases your ability to hold and carry an increasing quantum of Light, offering the potential to transform your physical body into a Body of Light, and thus freeing your Soul from the cycle of physical birth and death. In turn this will enable you to merge fully with your Higher Selves, allowing you to recall and draw upon all you have ever experienced, learned and understood throughout your many different planes of existence: in effect your 'past' and 'future' become your 'now'.

Ascension is not, therefore, some weird mystical event, but is a *process* that occurs as a consequence of the evolution and expansion of your multidimensional Body, mind and spirit. This requires you to develop the ability to *consistently* hold Higher frequencies of energy whilst simultaneously maintaining appropriate equilibrium within all aspects of your Linear Body and physical existence, *at all times*. This will eventually enable you to become an 'Ascended (or Illumined) Master' – this title designating one who has literally 'mastered' their body, mind and spirit, and thus accomplished their Ascension to BE 'in' their Body of Light. Hence, if *you* wish to hold a greater and finer quantum of Light, you will have to clarify or transform the 'denser' aspects of your physical and energy Bodies. You will appreciate this can *only* happen with hard work and self-discipline, and not by indulging in ego-led 'enlightenment' processes; or (unfortunately!) by simply waving a magic wand: if the glass of the lantern is dirty, it is irrelevant how bright the light within it is. Luckily then (!) this book has been written to offer such a process of self-mastery to those who choose to follow and complete the full programme of Teachings offered.

THE UNDERLYING OBJECTIVE OF THIS BOOK

In essence, this book has been written to help you connect with the Love, Light and Wisdom of the Archangels and Archeia, regardless of your existing belief system and spiritual practices. In the Angelic Kingdom, *all* are unconditionally welcome – you need only to be open and willing to ask for, and accept, their presence and their love. Yet at the end of the day you may realise that in so doing you are *actually* connecting with the Love, Light and Wisdom of The Divine: the Archangels and Archeia seek only to present themselves to you in their Divinely appointed stations as aspects and emissaries *of* that Light. Hence, as you read (and hopefully work through) all the material in this book, you may also come to realise that every Theme underpins the same fundamental objective – which is to BE Love.

Although this sounds simple, attaining (and retaining) the state whereby you *are* Love at *all* times is not easy – especially when human thoughts, feelings and emotions come into play! Accordingly, you will find that each Theme, discourse and Teaching is offered from a different perspective, in order to help you perfect your self-mastery and achieve your ultimate objective of embodying your Divinity and BEing Love. To do this, each Archangelic 'holds up a mirror' so that you may focus upon and recognise different aspects of yourself in isolation: this will help you discern your Light and your many component parts independently – for to see all that you are (and all that IS The Divine) at once might present a picture too complex to make sense of, and make accomplishing your objective seem too daunting to attempt. Hence the Archangelics' preference is to mentor and support you through a series of smaller and more manageable steps, so that you may hone and perfect each part with more ease – thus enabling you to move towards becoming ONE with The Divine by *progressively* recognising, accepting and embodying the Truth of your own Divine nature.

The Archangelics seek also to remind you that, as a Soul in human form, you have been born with one of the most valued gifts in the Universe, which is the Gift of Free Will. This gives you the opportunity to encounter diverse experiences and challenges from the widest breadth of perspectives possible, each and any of which can help you truly understand the Laws of cause and effect, and so appreciate the consequences of all the choices and actions open to you here on Earth. The ultimate objective of this is to teach you to recognise the Divine Light in all things ('good' and 'bad'), whilst achieving *total* mastery of your 'lower-self' – i.e. of your human body, mind and emotions.

USING THIS BOOK AS AN AID TO SELF-MASTERY

Each Archangelic's chapter covers the main issues they wish to address with you, but please bear in mind that it is important to be open and flexible in your approach, as they may need you to work with a topic that is not specifically mentioned, covered or explored in depth within these pages: the 'Meeting…' sections will help you form deep bonds with each Archangel and Archeia, so that you are safely supported and monitored as you identify and address whatever you need to master. My own experiences over the years lead me to *strongly* recommend that you keep a written record of your insights and experiences as you interact with your mentors and helpers: this is particularly useful if something you experience does not make sense, as review of your notes further down the line often brings clarity and understanding.

When working on a chapter it is a good idea to start by reading quickly through the whole chapter *(NB: see page 1),* and then go back and work through each section in turn, slowly and in detail – maybe even a paragraph at a time. You may find that some aspects need more attention and take longer to work through, whilst others can be resolved more quickly. You may also discover that the text holds a great deal of subtext: indeed, I soon realised that something that is *not* obvious tends to be particularly important! Re-reading sections is always beneficial, as this may reveal a fresh (and maybe polar) perspective on something you *thought* you had already addressed and dealt with. Alternatively it might highlight or bring to your attention something you might have not noticed before, or that you had dismissed as being irrelevant or inapplicable to you or your situation at that time. The same applies if you are guided or drawn to re-visit earlier pages, chapters or Teachings: this is because you may be required to shift your viewpoint to see or address something from a fresh or different perspective as you gain a greater understanding of your Self and your needs as you progress; or may need to re-address a Theme or topic that is especially important for you to master. My own experience has shown that the material presented is both multi-layered and multi-faceted, and so can be viewed and addressed from many different viewpoints: moreover, *what* you notice, perceive and/or interpret within the text will vary according to your needs, perspective and degree of understanding at the time, which will be constantly changing and evolving.

Lastly, it is anticipated that you will probably need to spend a number of weeks with the Archangel or Archeia who is mentoring and guiding you through all that you need to understand and resolve within their chapter: so if you choose to undertake the full programme of work within this book, please do not try to rush through it – true Mastery is rarely a swift or easy process! It is also essential that *all* the work that you can (or need to) address and undertake at that time has been completed and fully assimilated before you move on to the next chapter and start to work with your next Archangelic mentor. I would also advise you to take a complete break from working on the material for *at least* a week between chapters, even if you consider yourself to be 'experienced' in this type of work: pacing yourself sensibly (and taking a little time out for some well-deserved rest and relaxation) will not only help you assimilate any energetic shifts and changes more comfortably, but will also help you to move through and complete the programme more easily – remember the tale of the tortoise and the hare?!

CONNECTING WITH THE ARCHANGELS AND ARCHEIA

As *two* aspects (Archangel and Archeia) of *one* energy, twin flames' chapters are always 'paired': this is because whatever you undertake and accomplish with one will always have some bearing on what you do (or did) with the other. Sometimes the 'male' aspect's chapter precedes the 'female' aspect's chapter; sometimes the reverse applies: this is solely to do with the order in which their material is the most easily and logically assimilated, and never implies that one is 'more important' than the other. The same statement applies to the order in which the 'pairs' appear in this book.

Because they want to become as real for you as possible, all the Archangels and Archeia asked me to write each chapter in a very particular way, so that it feels as if they are truly at your side – showing and telling *you* what they feel you really need to know and understand. Their physical appearance and environmental setting as described in each 'Meeting...' section are how each chose to appear for the specific purpose of mentoring and guiding you through the processes in this book. Hence, *everything* detailed was very explicitly shown for a purpose and a reason, and/or to support their Theme, Gift and/or Teaching: this includes their physical appearance, attire, personal adornments and anything they carry or hold; their setting, surroundings and environment; all colours, shapes and forms; and all specified minerals, flora and fauna.

Much of what they showed me I have described in detail, especially where it had significant core symbolism that demanded identification and interpretation – either under their very specific guidance; or through my own experiences, given from a very personal perspective: however you may discover more (or other) than this in your own encounters, and arrive at some interesting, unique and equally valid realisations of your own. Thus it is important that you allow the images formed by the words you read to become real and substantial to you by means of your *own* imagination or personal vision; and that you are willing to expand your awareness and open your mind, so that you may identify anything that has significance or meaning for you at that time. If any detail or any item stands out within the text – or indeed differs from what you read within the text – it is important that you research it and explore it. You may also find it illuminating to consider and explore why objects, colours, minerals, flora or fauna appear in more than one chapter, as this usually hints at some intriguing links between Archangelics and/or their Themes – twin flames in particular often sharing (or mirroring) certain characteristics that offer subtle pointers as to how they share their duties and tasks.

UNDERSTANDING THE TEACHINGS

You may find that the Teachings in each chapter have a connection to something that you have already observed in the 'Meeting…' section for that Archangel or Archeia, or to something they bring your attention to during the course of their dialogue. At times this gives you further insight into the purpose or function of an aspect of their adornment, or an item they hold or carry with them; and sometimes it tells you something about an aspect of their environment that may be important for you to understand. Occasionally a Teaching may also guide you through a *process* to aid your self-understanding and/or contribute to your self-healing and growth: here four dots (....) – usually at the end of a paragraph or line – indicates when you may need to pause in your reading in order to contemplate or 'do' something described within the text.

As you go through the book, you will also find that each Archangel and Archeia's chapter begins with an affirmation: this appears on the back of their title page, adjacent to the start of the 'Meeting...' section. Each emphasises something they consider key to the Teachings and Theme of their chapter – and you may find it helpful to work with these at intervals as you go through the material. As with all affirmations (if you choose to use them) you should always repeat the words three times, with sincere intent.

As you work through this book you may sometimes find aspects of the material difficult to read or follow, and you may not *consciously* understand everything the first time you read it – especially if this sort of thing is new to you. Please don't worry if you do not 'get' something straight away (there were many times when writing this book that I felt the same!): if this happens, just allow yourself time to *subconsciously* process it (maybe overnight), and then return to it later and read it through again. Additionally, if you choose to use this book as it was intended and work through it in its entirety, you may find that the subject matter increases in complexity the further through the book you travel: this is because each chapter builds on the understandings of the ones preceding it, a little like a pyramid. Gabriel also reminds me that the written word carries great power, for the mind 'hears' and *knows* what it reads – so it is important to allow your intuitive mind to absorb *whatever* it needs to, without undue interference from your 'logical' mind. He also assures me that the Love, Light and Power of the Archangels and Archeia is held within the words on every page, and at some point all will become clear. Please do not be discouraged: the harder the climb, the more amazing the view!

A FEW FINAL WORDS

Lastly, before you 'get stuck in' and begin to get to know your Archangelic mentors and guides, I want to emphasise that there is nothing special about me *or* my abilities: if I can walk and talk with the Archangels and Archeia, then so can you! After all, all the information that is 'out there' has to come from somewhere – there IS no singular or definitive truth, just as no one person owns an exclusive hotline to the Angelic Realm. There is also no reason why the processes and information given in this book (or written or offered by any other person) is any more 'right' or valid than what *you* think, see, sense or feel. Indeed, I personally believe that anything and everything we might need or want to know is accessible to us, so long as we have the courage, trust and self-belief to look for it. Furthermore, I know that it is vital that each of us follows our own heart first and foremost, having the astuteness to understand – and the faith to accept – that *we* are our own wisest teacher and brightest guiding light!

This was made clear to me some years ago when I was on a course and trying to understand how something I believed to be 'true' could possibly be 'false', when (having awoken very early with this on my mind) I found myself having a conversation with a Guiding Collective that I now know as Unity Consciousness, who said something very pertinent that I would like to share with you now: they told me...

> *"...Divinity is in all places and has many guises, that you may discern how that which is presented resonates with your Soul. So be guided, but not led, and let the Light of your Heart illuminate the Way – for Oneness is a point of realisation: it cannot be taught; it cannot be learnt; it can only be found. Thus take all into your Heart – for there are neither falsehoods nor truths: indeed, there IS no singular truth; there IS no singular fact, save one – that The Divine is Love..."*

May many Blessings Light your Way....

YOUR ARCHANGELIC TEACHERS AND GUIDES

LOVE is ALL.

♥ ♥ ♥

HERE IN THE NOW
lies your TRUE POTENTIAL.

♥ ♥ ♥

BE ALL:
RELEASE what does not serve you;
CHANGE what does not affirm you;
and EMPOWER yourself
through SELF-KNOWLEDGE,
so that through REBIRTH of your Spirit
you SURRENDER to your own Divinity
and REVEAL yourself for what you truly are.

♥ ♥ ♥

And then, with us, in UNITY,
you will BE FREE.

The lines above hold words given by thirteen 'Illumined Ones' during the grounding of their Light in August 2009. (The Illumined Ones are aspects of 'Unity Consciousness' – a Collective Consciousness of Higher life-streams that encompasses the "I AM" presence of all self-realised Cosmic and Ascended Masters, Angelics and Elohim.) They gave stress to the words that are capitalised – I believe for a reason!

ARCHANGEL TZADKIEL

'POTENTIAL FOR CHANGE'

CRYSTAL CHAMPIONS:

Sugilite ♥ Lepidolite ♥ Golden Labradorite

CREATURE COMPANIONS:

Jay ♥ Vulture ♥ Goose

GREENWOOD GUARDIANS:

Larch ♥ Tamarisk

*I am the Violet Flame.
I stand fully in my Perfected Body of Light.
I AM perfect Harmony.*

MEETING TZADKIEL

It is a fine day in late spring, and you find yourself walking down a narrow path that is winding its way through a copse of young birch and beech trees, which lies at the heart of an ancient oak forest. Carpets of bluebells spread out around you as far as the eye can see, laying in waxy blue-violet swathes that blanket the ground beneath the trees' slender sun-dappled trunks and arching branches, each nodding head crowning a bright-green stem that springs from the shelter of bladelike leaves. Here and there you come across clusters of wild violets nestling shyly in mossy nooks and crannies sheltered by the roots of the trees, and as you stroll onwards, you feel yourself begin to relax – your perception shifting to allow your subtle senses to expand and come to the fore, and making you truly aware of the life force present in the woodland. With every step you can feel the potential for growth in the earth beneath your feet – and, as you reach out to touch the life that surrounds you, you sense the vigour of fresh sap rising in the young trees and the vital energy that fills and imbues every leaf and flower, branch and bud. You also intuit their eagerness to fulfil the promise of new life brought by every spring dawn and recognise their joy in reawakening, which cheers your heart with a feeling of hopeful anticipation.

After a while your path ends at the shores of a wide lake, which is set in a clearing that is open to the spring sky. The lake reflects the blue and white of the sky above, its surface rippling in silvery waves where it is touched by a cool and gentle breeze, and all is silent and still, calm and serene. As you rest and soak up the atmosphere, you find your attention suddenly drawn to a black swan that is gliding serenely across the lake towards you – its curling white-tipped wing feathers arched elegantly over its back, its head and scarlet beak held proudly high.... Reaching the shore, the swan climbs onto the bank and stands in front of you, holding your gaze with a rare intelligence in its startlingly clear violet eyes: then, amazingly, it begins to grow larger and taller, until eventually its head towers high above your own. Turning, the swan crouches down and opens its wings, and you understand that it is inviting you to get onto its back: so you climb carefully up, settling onto the swan's broad downy back and tucking your knees over its wing joints, before gently grasping the ruff of feathers that graces its neck. Once you are settled the swan turns to face the open water and strides into the shallows: then, opening its wings, it begins to run across the surface of the lake, and with a few powerful beats of its massive wings, it springs into the air and you are airborne – cresting the trees and soaring into the sky, where you are swiftly surrounded by puffy white clouds.

You fly for what seems like forever, the white clouds slowly turning pinker and pinker, until you are finally enveloped in a billowing magenta mass that is oddly both dark and light: at this point you feel the swan losing height – and, as you drop, you exit the clouds to find yourself in a strange new world. Here the sun is a soft pale violet, although the sky itself is still pale blue, and you note that there are two moons hovering in the sky above you – one a purple so deep that it almost seems black; the other a cool reflective silvery-white.

Landing softly on the ground the swan crouches and allows you to alight, before swiftly taking off again and disappearing over the horizon. Left alone, you look around and find that you are standing on the rim of a wide-open crater that crowns what you assume to be a mountaintop, whose sides fall gently away below you. The depths beyond are obscured by layers of mist, whilst the cup-shaped crater itself appears to be lined with a massive bed of deep-purple crystals, as if a giant amethyst geode has been sliced in half and opened to the sky above. In front of you a series of roughly cut steps seem to offer a way down to the floor of the crater, and so – deciding to follow where they lead – you carefully descend them one at a time. Each deep step clings to the steep crystalline walls and gives off a warming purple glow that clears your mind and sharpens all your senses; and as you continue your descent, you realise that the crater is much larger than you first thought, and has two wide, yet shallow, smoothly rounded depressions polished into its base. These are separated by a flat ridge of amethyst, in the middle of which stands a tall man robed in violet, wearing a cloak made of long curling black feathers that brush the ground around his feet: this is Archangel Tzadkiel. He is holding a tall spiralling wooden staff topped with a large silver sphere in his left hand, and holding his other hand out towards you in welcome; and, as you make your way carefully along the ridge towards him, he greets you, declaring:

"I am Tzadkiel – Keeper of the Flames of Freedom, Overseer of the Communion of the Grail, High-Priest of the Sacred Fire and twin flame of Amethystia, the Lady Purity. I offer you my hand, and would guide you to find the Light at your heart: the guiding light that is the beacon for your journey home to reunion with your greater Self. For at the heart of all things that live is a spark of Light – that first Element, which was once part of something much greater; a Divine thought and inspiration, sent out on wings of love to be nourished and sustained by the Light of hope, faith and trust. Remember, all is never as it might seem, for each embodied spark rides the endless loop of infinity, which holds the current of life and all of existence from black through to white and all stations in-between. For only thus may the widest experience possible be acquired – not just for one, but for all, that all may know both greatness and smallness and truly understand the nature of both cause and effect; and thence choose wisely what they wish to Be."

As you reach him, you realise Tzadkiel is standing at the mid-point of a long 'S'-shaped pathway, which has been etched into the surface of the amethyst so that it spirals into (and links) the two polished depressions in the crater's floor. Each path leads towards the centre of one of the 'bowls' – one end terminating at a large square structure that appears to be solid and black, the other at a hearth where it looks as if a fire is burning. It is towards the latter that he directs you, and so you follow him down the spiralling path to its centre: here you find a flickering mass of purple and violet flames encircled by a bench made of polished crystal, which is so clear it looks like ice – although it is warm to the touch. Laying his staff down, Tzadkiel removes his feathered cloak and invites you to sit on the bench, so that you may take your time to examine him and become accustomed to his energies: then, taking a seat opposite you, he rests his hands lightly on his knees and squares his shoulders.

This enables you to see how his upright posture emphasises his height and shows off his long flowing robe: this is made of a soft material that glimmers as it catches the light of the flames, revealing its different hues and tones of purple and violet, highlighted by the creases and folds of the velvety pile. In style the robe resembles an old-fashioned dressing gown, overlapping high on his chest to wrap snugly around his body, and with a simple knotted cord plaited from long threads of purple silk to secure it just above his waist. Ribbons of violet silk bind its edges – the wide generous sleeves falling loosely around his wrists revealing tanned slender hands, which have long elegant fingers that are free of any adornment.

Shifting his stance, Tzadkiel takes his hands from his knees and leans back on the bench, supporting himself on his open arms and casually crossing his ankles. This causes his robe to fall open, revealing a long-sleeved knee-length violet linen shift and exposing his feet, which are long tanned and bare, like his hands. His movement also causes the material of his robe to spark with light, and – as you look at it more closely – you realise this is because its velvety nap is randomly dotted with tiny six-pointed stars that have been stitched in fine silver thread.

Lifting your gaze, you note that Tzadkiel has well-defined high cheekbones and a long straight nose, centred in a square face framed by long jet-black hair, which falls over his shoulders in a sleek and silky curtain. He also has dense black eyebrows, and wears a closely-cropped dark beard that emphasises his strong jaw line and firm-lipped mouth, and (although his hair is dark and his tanned skin is smooth and unlined) you sense that he is mature in years: even so, he has a youthful, almost hypnotic, magnetism that attracts and draws you in – perhaps, in part, because of his eyes, which have vibrant violet irises and very dark pupils.

Tzadkiel's only – and very obvious – adornment comprises a simple circlet of solid silver that rests on his brow and encircles his head. This has a large silver disc affixed to its centre, which spans his third eye and Soma centre and bears a crystal of exceptionally clear deep-violet amethyst that has been cut and faceted into a six-pointed star – and, noting your interest, Tzadkiel smiles and explains that this star holds The Violet Flame, and denotes his role as High Priest of the Sacred Fire.

TZADKIEL'S TEACHINGS
The Violet Ray and The Cloak of Immaculate Illumination:

Satisfied that your inspection is complete, Tzadkiel tells you that the world you are now experiencing is an anchor point for the Violet Ray and its multifaceted Light, which condenses as the Sacred Fire that you see in the hearth before you. He points out that the Power of the Light held within the deep purple crystals that lined your path has already illuminated you, enabling you to begin to sense and experience these energies as you walked to join him – explaining that the Violet Ray (which he oversees and directs) rules both Spiritual and Cosmic Law. He adds that *this* is the Ray of the Adept and Spiritual Alchemist, who knows the true nature of Power, and understands the Divine organisation and structure underpinning the vastness of the Universe; and who bears responsibility for its construction and deconstruction, through the righteous manipulation of matter and form. He reminds you that *everything* that exists is simply Divine Light made manifest, whether tangible to the physical senses or not; hence, *nothing* can ever be eradicated: it can only be transmuted (changed) from one state of being to another.

Smiling, Tzadkiel informs you that facilitating and enabling said 'construction' and 'deconstruction' is his speciality! He explains that this is because the Light of the Violet Ray on which he serves has the Power to reveal the patterns and truths that underlie all things that exist (or have the potential to exist); *and* has the Power to transmute anything that cloaks the true Light, so that its fundamental (Divine) state may be clearly seen. He says that, hence, if you call upon its Light it can help you see things more clearly – and even show you all that you are, and all that you have the potential to become! Tzadkiel adds that, furthermore, its Light can also help you to recognise and accept that *everything* you choose to be or do is within your *own* power, enabling you to take control of your life and determine with more certainty how you wish to direct its course.

Emphasising that this is but one step, Tzadkiel expounds that the Violet Light is also a powerful transformer and refiner of energy, and tells you that calling upon the Ray may then help you change, shift and adjust your energies to fit the patterns that best align you with those choices. With another smile he adds that the High resonance of the Ray intrinsically promotes selflessness, whereby the choices you make embrace not simply yourself and your own desires, but also your world and *all* other sentient life, which helps ensure that you make your choices with your search for your Inner Light and Truth clearly in mind, *and* in accordance with The Divine Plan.

As you think about this, Tzadkiel says that he understands how life can sometimes seem cruel or hard, and how it is easy to become mired in your own troubles – but he reminds you that *every single day* many miracles happen, big and small; and many great deeds of selflessness and innumerable small acts of kindness take place all around the world. With a wry smile he observes that, sadly, such things tend to pass unnoticed; and so you often hear only of that which perhaps serves to make you believe that the world in which you live is intrinsically unsafe or unkind: yet the bigger picture shows that most of the people who share your world are kind and caring at heart. With this in mind, he asks you to recall times when individuals, communities and countries have opened their hearts (and often their pockets) to give support to others who have suffered grievous loss; or have pulled together to help effect real change – stressing that he knows *everyone* has the potential for living with both humanity and compassion, and therefore, even if you think you cannot directly affect what is happening around you, it is important to remember that you always have unlimited power over *yourself* and your actions.

Moving to your side, Tzadkiel takes your hand and counsels that to dwell on any emotionally destructive or 'negative' happenings around you (or in the world) reinforces their energies – whereas focusing on all that is 'positive' counteracts them: consequently, for every act of kindness you perform; for every blessing you give to the world; and for every iota of Violet Light you call upon, the balance shifts – until ultimately evils cannot be sustained. Assuring you that he will always answer your call if you need his support in finding the energy and focus to be positive and strong, Tzadkiel then takes his cloak and spreads it out to reveal its violet lining. He explains that this holds the Light of the Violet Ray and enrobes him in its Power; whilst the black feathers of its outer side hold Black Light in a state of Divine Grace, giving him immediate and profound access to *any and all* Powers and Potentials he requires in the performance of his duties as Overseer of the

Violet Ray. He tells you that, if you ask, he will bring *you* a violet-lined cloak that will enrobe *you* in Violet Light, enabling you to stand fully in your own Power and live in alignment with the truths of your own heart, which will ensure that the words or actions of others will not influence or unbalance you. With a smile, he adds that the nature (and colour) of your cloak's outer side will always be appropriate for your needs at that time: therefore, if you wish to understand how the cloak will support you (and thus know how to use it), you will find it helpful to explore the symbolism of its form, materials, colour and design, which may not always remain the same.

Returning his cloak to his shoulders, he gives a low whistle – at which a jay appears over the horizon and flies to his side. Tzadkiel explains that **Jay** is a member of the Crow family and hence can teach you much about the correct application of Sacred Law – and in particular about the Right and proper use of Magic: this will help you understand more about spiritual alchemy and the work of the Seventh Order of Melchizedek, which is especially relevant to the tasks he, Tzadkiel, undertakes with those who choose to enrobe themselves in Violet Light. Hence Jay can help you claim and wear your cloak *and* aid you in discovering its unique properties, so that you may understand how and why it will support you; whilst also teaching you about the Right use of your Power, so that you may identify and use your innate talents and abilities with wisdom and discernment. Drawing your attention to its peachy-brown plumage and black and white markings, Tzadkiel tells you that the name 'jay' derives from 'Gaia' (another name for Earth): accordingly Jay may also help you learn more about the realms of physicality and the planet on which you live, and show you how to keep grounded if difficulties in the world about you make it hard for you to keep your emotional balance. Furthermore, Jay can offer you a strong connection between Earth and the Higher Realms, which will aid you in accessing further knowledge and attaining greater understanding, giving you the confidence and strength to be able to stand up for yourself in contentious situations, and/or stand by what you truly believe in. Pointing to the turquoise flashes on its wings, Tzadkiel adds that Jay can also open your mind to receive intuitive flashes of inspiration that will help you speak with conviction and authority, whilst its raucous call will make sure that your voice is always heard. With a chuckle, he advises that (last, but not least) Jay's fondness for acorns and sweet apples highlights its ability to seek out the wisdom and sweetness at the heart of everything that truly nourishes the body and spirit – which is probably the most valuable lesson he can teach you!

Giving you a small polished stone that is darkly mottled in shades of purple pink and magenta, Tzadkiel says that this is **Sugilite**, his first Crystal Champion – explaining:

> *"Sugilite will help clear your mind, whilst activating your Higher energy centres and aligning you with your Higher-self and its wisdom. It strongly carries and directs the Violet, Purple and Magenta Rays, and will project the Violet Flame for you to use in clearing and purifying your physical (and non-physical) Bodies of negativity, and/or in dismantling or transmuting anything that is preventing you from reaching your full potential or realising your innermost dreams in this lifetime. Sugilite can, therefore, be a very protective crystal and – if you intend it to be so – it can erect and maintain a shield of Violet Light around you, enabling you to open yourself fully in order to work*

at the deepest and most profound levels possible. This is because the Violet Ray has the ability and Power to create and establish multidimensional gateways, which permit access to Higher, Cosmic and Universal energies that exist outside those in which your normal perceptions and feelings operate. Furthermore, Sugilite's sweet yet penetrating resonance can help you connect with finer levels of reasoning and knowing, thus aiding you in viewing and understanding your Self and your needs from a fresh perspective, and supporting you in learning and growing with appropriate discernment – and with greater confidence and determination."

With a smile, Tzadkiel affirms that Sugilite may therefore help you in truly knowing the Light of the Violet Ray, and in addressing all issues of personal power and direction.

The Gift of The Violet Flame of Transmutation:

Reminding you that he and Amethystia, his twin flame, are Divine Directors (High Priest and Priestess), Guardians and Overseers of the Sacred and Holy Fire, Tzadkiel takes up his staff and touches the silver sphere at its head to the flames that are burning in the hearth before you. At its touch, they flare up higher and higher, gradually coalescing to take on the form of a tall and fiery winged Being, whose body is composed of a mass of feather-like tongues of violet, purple, gold and silver fire. This is the Angel of the Sacred Fire, who speaks to you, saying:

"Beloved, call I, as I call thee. Let my Divine fire burn away all hurts, all pains; so that thee may be at ease with whom thou truly art: for in that bless-ed release, you will know and be sure of all that connects thee to I, and I to thee; and in that connection you will find your Self...."

You understand you have the opportunity to step into the cool heat of the fire and enter the Angel's embrace – but Tzadkiel suggests that, before you do, you consider whether there is anything within your body, mind or spirit that you would like to change and/or illuminate, and allows you a while to think....

Once you have done so, Tzadkiel stands and moves opposite you, before reaching through the flames to take your hands and support you as you step within the hearth....

As the Flames that *are* the Angel of the Sacred Fire embrace you, they concentrate on your heart and surround it in a deep mauve Light shot through with silver – at which Tzadkiel explains that the Angel is offering you the Light of dispassionate compassion, allowing self-review and self-judgement in its Highest and purest form.... He asks that you now bring to mind what you wanted to understand, improve or refine about yourself, and allow the Light to illuminate it in order to see your true motivations with clarity, and understand how you may change or transform whatever is preventing you from growing and evolving....

As you do so, Tzadkiel releases your hands and tells you that the Sacred Fire blends the Violet Flames of Transmutation with the Amethyst Flames of Transformation, thus enabling all that withholds the Truth or suppresses the Divine Light within you to be powerfully burned away whilst the presence of the Gold and Silver Rays illuminates your Soul – allowing you to see the root of the issue you are contemplating, and enabling you to understand how to move forwards and fulfil your true potential....

As his words penetrate your mind, the Flames around you burn more brightly – and as the Power of the Sacred Fire gradually brings about the illumination you need and the change you desire, you feel your heart become stronger and stronger as the power you have over your Self is slowly refreshed and restored....

Eventually, when you have seen and done all you can understand and accomplish at this time, the Light around your heart slowly fades; and the Flames shrink back down into the hearth.... As this happens, Tzadkiel plucks a small violet flame from their midst, and gently places it within the Hara centre of your energy Body – then, stepping back, he gently rests his hands on your shoulders, saying:

"This is my Gift of The Violet Flame of Transmutation, which is given to help you keep your body, mind and emotions clear of negativity, and to make ready the space wherein your 'Lotus of the Soul' may eventually dwell. The flame burns brightly within you now – so, as its Light and Power fills your body and expands your Soul, let it bring with it the Order and Grace that is your birthright and give you the strength that you need to succeed in everything that you bring forth under the True Light of your Divine-self."

Gift given, Tzadkiel steps back, and tells you that to use his Gift for personal clearing, you need simply see or imagine its violet fire growing to fill your entire physical body from the very top of your head to the ends of your fingers and toes: and then – once your physical body is full – you need simply see or imagine its violet fire expanding out through your aura, until its Light fills your entire body *and* energy field.

Once your Flame has found the right balance, Tzadkiel helps you back to your seat on the bench and settles at your side: here he adds that you can also use the Violet Flame to illuminate and transmute anything you wish to change within yourself – including unconstructive feelings such as anger, frustration or jealousy; harmful attitudes such as indolence, self-indulgence or self-pity; or physical pains or discomforts and their root causes, if you know them. Furthermore, because its violet Fire transmutes such 'lower' energies, feelings, actions and deeds into a Higher form, the (maybe unexpected!) bonus is that these 'new' energies will enhance your clarity and strengthen your positivity and purpose, supporting you in becoming a more perfect channel for the Light as you move towards union with your Christed-self.

Reaching into the fire, he picks out a lilac-coloured stone whose polished surface is dotted with silvery metallic speckles and gives it to you, saying that this is **Lepidolite**, his second Crystal Champion – explaining:

"Lepidolite is a stone of profound peace and transformation that can calm your mind and ease your Spirit, helping to return both to their true and innate state of tranquil and open acceptance. Despite its soft gentle energy and delicate appearance, Lepidolite offers you the fortitude and will to change and grow, understanding that the potential gains from such a process always outweighs any initial pains: this is because Lepidolite carries the pink and purple Light of the Violet and Amethyst Rays, enabling all that it works upon to become compassionately transformed and so BE all that it is meant to be. Furthermore, the effervescent sparks of the Silver Ray that it bears may supply you with the Will and inspiration to move forwards, whilst holding all that you are in the Light of Grace – enabling you to become more perfectly aligned with your Highest purpose, and

know peace. Know then, that to be at peace within your heart is to understand and know the Power and Love of The Divine, which inspires and fires the deepest and dearest desires of your Soul: and it is this that is probably Lepidolite's greatest gift!"

With a smile, Tzadkiel affirms that Lepidolite may therefore help you work with your Violet Flame, and support you in transmuting anything that hides your Light – stressing that you can *always* call upon himself or the Angel of the Sacred Fire if you need help to work with your Violet Flame; and/or want to clear the energetic residue of past traumas; and/or need to transmute karmic issues that you have been released from resolving in this lifetime or others.

Sitting back, Tzadkiel lifts his gaze to the skies and points to a large black and white bald-headed vulture circling overhead: sensing your interest the bird glides down and alights nearby, where it begins to preen its breast feathers with its large hooked beak. Tzadkiel comments that vultures fulfil an important role in the natural world – yet (sadly) they are commonly disliked for their appearance, and reviled for their apparent relish for dead flesh. He explains that vultures' strong constitution enables them to consume rotten and decaying flesh, which not only provides them with sustenance but also prevents the spread of disease through other life forms. With a smile, he points out that this affirms the axiom 'from death comes life' – the vulture mirroring the role that the Violet Flame performs in transmuting something negative or unwanted into something that is positive or desired: accordingly, you may choose to call upon **Vulture** if you want to understand how to change or transform something from one state to another, or convert something old into something new; and/or if you need help to change any negativity you hold within into attributes that can promote and support your growth. Observing that the vulture was revered and held sacred by the Ancient Egyptians, for whom it symbolised rebirth and the shifting of consciousness from one level to another, Tzadkiel tells you that Vulture also has symbolic links with the Goddess Nephthys – the counterpart of the Goddess Isis (Isis representing light and generation; Nephthys representing darkness and dissolution). He explains that therefore, because Nephthys and Isis together define the cycle of life, death and rebirth, and exemplify the miraculous act of Creation – whereby 'something' seemingly miraculously comes from 'nothing', you may also ask Vulture for help if you wish to know more about the wheel of birth, death and rebirth – and the purpose behind your Soul's desire to experience different states of Being; or if you want to understand more about the nature and purpose of (and the attributes that define) the 'polar states' of White Light and Black Light, darkness and light, 'being' and 'non-being'.

The All-seeing Eye and The Communion of The Grail:

After a while Tzadkiel stands and, asking you to join him, he leads you back down the path that spirals away from the fire.... As you walk, he reminds you that your etheric 'soul Body' is the energy vehicle that carries the essence of your Divinity, which has chosen to separate from Source in order to experience and learn. He explains that as soon as your Spark individualised from Divine Source, it lowered its vibrational frequency and took on density – the degree to which it continues to do so depending on the choices you make, and the energies thus drawn to you, which in turn determines how far your essence travels away from the Truth of your pure nature. Stressing that Free Will allows you the Right to choose that degree of density, Tzadkiel says that it is important to understand that *you* create your own life-path through the choices you make, which (as you fully experience and understand their consequences) provide you with limitless opportunities to truly know yourself *and* know The Divine. Smiling, he adds that this eventually will lead you to realise that only when your soul Bodies are 100% pure Love (the Highest possible frequency of Light) can your Divine Spark return to Unity with Source!

As you reach the ridge that defines the centre of the amethyst crater, Tzadkiel says that at one time you would have had to work very hard to understand and reconcile the consequences of all your choices, actions and deeds and achieve such clarity: however now, by Divine dispensation, you may call for the Violet Flame to help you transmute your density and raise your frequency, without the need for constant karmic planning and balancing. With another smile, he tells you that this does not mean you will no longer acquire karmic debt, but means that acknowledging the issue and addressing it with the aid of the Violet Flame reduces the need for you to experience it actively from all sides. Assuring you that the Violet Flame works in harmony with any belief system or spiritual practice, Tzadkiel confirms that you may call upon its Power at any time (even if you did not choose to accept his Gift), for its access is open to *all* – but stresses you may only use the Violet Flame to transmute and clear anything that affects your *personal* density; or use it in your own defence to protect yourself against the imposition of density upon you by others. After a short pause, he adds that the only exception to this arises if and when you identify density that has been *imposed* upon the world of matter (or other Souls) in direct or indirect contravention of the Spiritual Laws that govern personal Sovereignty and Free Will. Clarifying this, Tzadkiel expounds that some Souls *knowingly* choose a path that leads them to acquire density, but others may have been forced or persuaded to take a path that they have *not* freely chosen – perhaps because they have come under the mal-intentioned influence of someone who has imposed a distorted perception of reality upon them. Tzadkiel counsels you that, in such cases, you have the Right to defend Free Will by using the Violet Flame to transmute the negativity that is at the root of the issue, thus reinstating the clarity that will enable Souls to reclaim their personal Sovereignty and exercise their own Divine Right of Freedom of Choice.

Whilst he has been talking you have reached the other end of the spiralling path, and now stand in front of the small square building you noticed earlier. Closer inspection reveals it to have walls made of highly polished black obsidian, fronted by a bench made of the same super-clear crystal as the one that encircles the Sacred Fire. Here Tzadkiel sits and asks you to join him, before passing you his staff and giving you permission to examine it.... This enables you to see that the shaft is made from a long spiralling length of dark wood that looks very old – and, as you run your fingers over its smooth surface, you can feel that it is subtly pulsing with what feels like a low-voltage electrical current. Explaining that the staff is a symbol of his authority and position within the Seventh Order of Melchizadek (that of the Order of the Violet Robe), Tzadkiel tells you that the corkscrew-hazel shaft channels Black and White Light, and gives him the ability to connect with deep and ancient hidden wisdoms that are beyond Time and Dimension.

Reaching up with your other hand, you touch the silver sphere that surmounts the shaft, and note that it is unexpectedly warm: recognising your surprise, Tzadkiel reaches over and somehow opens it, revealing the huge eight-pointed star-tetrahedron (merkaba) that lies hidden within. He explains that this has been cut and polished from a brilliantly clear diamond, which is the gem that links him with Amethystia, his twin flame; and tells you that its shape symbolises the Body of Light that enrobes all those who have attained their goal of absolute Self-mastery – what some refer to as 'Ascension'. As you watch, you notice that the diamond is beginning to emit tiny sparks of rainbow light – and then, as you sit mesmerised by the light that is now dancing around you, you realise the crystal is humming with a low sound that rises and falls in rhythm with the pulses of energy you can feel spiralling up and down the wooden shaft.

Recognising what you have felt, Tzadkiel closes the sphere with a satisfied smile and, reclaiming his staff, he taps it twice on the ground: at this a large greylag goose with grey-brown plumage and an orange beak appears as if from nowhere, and waddles over to lay her head on Tzadkiel's knee. Gently stroking her neck, he remarks that goose (like jay) is a mediator between the realms of Heaven and Earth, and laughingly tells you that she makes a faithful 'watchdog' who is always alert to the presence of new or different energies. Hence **Goose** can always be relied upon to warn you if danger or negativity is near, so that you may react quickly and appropriately in a threatening situation. Drawing your attention to her bright eyes, he says that Goose can also remind you to 'look before you leap', and can help you remain true to yourself if presented with a new, unusual or incomprehensible situation that might require you to make a difficult decision. Observing that geese undertake long flights during migration, requiring them to have great strength and stamina, Tzadkiel says that Goose is always willing to help you increase and refine your physical *and* spiritual energy and endurance by helping you work with the Violet Flame and other transformative techniques: furthermore, their willingness to share the task of 'flight leader' indicates that Goose can also show you the benefits of working as a team as you strive to reach new heights and achieve your goals; and/or encourage you to share the burdens and responsibilities of leadership between all those who can manage them, so that *all* may have the opportunity to learn and grow – thus making their Divine potential an everyday reality. With a smile, he counsels that if Goose ever appears to you in dreams or meditation and presents you with a 'golden egg', this will be a sign that the action you are contemplating will help strengthen your connection to your Christed-self, and enable you to ground your Christ-consciousness more clearly and effectively.

Standing, Tzadkiel turns and touches the head of his staff to the glassy-black wall of the building behind you: at this the wall shimmers and turns crystal-clear, allowing you to see through it to the large square chamber within.... In stark contrast to the black of the exterior, all the inner surfaces are clad in highly polished white jade; and a large square, outlined in gold, is inscribed on the floor: this is spanned diagonally by a wide-open eye (intricately etched and layered in gold) that has a very large golden disc set at its centre to define its pupil.

Tzadkiel tells you that what you are looking at is the All-seeing Eye of The Divine, which can show all that are ready, able and willing to stand within its Light exactly who (and what) they truly are – and, with a gesture of his staff, he creates a cylinder of Light that connects the pupil of the eye to the chamber's ceiling above, which slowly fills with gold light from below and silver light from above. These come together and blend into a silvery-gold Light that has a translucent reflective quality; and, as you watch, he explains how the essence of the one standing in this Light will be held within the Diamond Light reflected from the heart of The Divine – strengthening their link with their Divine-self, and aligning them with the Highest frequencies of Light they can absorb and assimilate at that time. Tzadkiel adds that this process is known as 'The Communion of the Grail', which is given so that – through Truth and Vision – anyone who stands in its Light may be reminded of the Divine patterning that underlies the four cornerstones of existence (those of Liberty, Life, Light and Love), whose objectives are at the heart of all you are. With a smile, he taps the wall with his staff again, at which the cylinder of Light simply vanishes, and the wall shimmers and becomes solidly black again.

Returning to sit beside you on the bench Tzadkiel tells you that, as a Master of the Heart and a 'Tzaddik' (one who is always at a point of perfect harmony), he oversees the 'Eye' and directs its processes – for one of his joys is to help Souls attain their Highest possible potential through perfecting their form and perfecting their nature: hence he is always willing to help you become ready to receive the 'Communion of the Grail'. Giving you a small transparent golden-yellow polished stone, Tzadkiel says that this is **Golden Labradorite**, his third Crystal Champion – explaining:

> *"Golden Labradorite carries the Gold Ray of The Divine Masculine, which holds all that is made manifest through its Light in stability and balance; and IS the warp and weft of the tapestry of Universal Life, allowing the spiritual threads of all existences to weave the magnificent images that tell the stories of every lifetime. Golden Labradorite thus holds the attributes of strength, courage, stability, structure and clear thought; whilst supporting your inner strength and outward focus, enabling you to view life from a holographic perspective, and so see that what is 'without' is also 'within' – just as what is 'within' is also 'without'! Golden Labradorite also links with the golden-yellow Flame of Divine Wisdom, helping you to discover and recognise the Love, Mind and Intelligence of the Divine Creator in all that you see and experience: by definition this includes discovering and recognising your own Divinity – your 'I AM' presence. In this way Golden Labradorite's joyful and brilliant Light will illuminate you and all that you are, whilst holding you safely within its compassionate and accepting embrace: this will enable you to recognise and embrace the hand and the heart of The Divine in all things and all Beings that are external to your 'Self'; and accordingly release anything held within your thoughts, feelings and beliefs that does not allow you to define pure Love."*

With a smile, Tzadkiel affirms that Golden Labradorite may therefore help you know and understand much more about what it means to 'BE' in the Light of The Divine.

The Greenwood Guardians – Larch and Tamarisk:

His *personal* mentoring complete for now, Tzadkiel affirms he is always available to aid and support you: you need only bring him to mind and ask for his presence, and he will attend you. Furthermore, he tells you that two great Tree Beings of the Plant

Kingdom have also asked to support you in addressing his Theme of 'POTENTIAL FOR CHANGE', adding that you need only request *their* presence, and they will be with you.

He explains that the first of these Greenwood Guardians is the Masculine essence of Larch, who has asked to overlight and help you ground whatever work you undertake within *any* aspect of his chapter. The second is the Feminine essence of Tamarisk, who has expressly asked to help you understand and assimilate his Gift of The Violet Flame of Transmutation (if you have chosen to accept it).

When you are ready to connect with Tzadkiel's first Greenwood Guardian, you need simply call for the presence of **Larch** (*).... Larch envelops you in a spring-green Light, and the Masculine spirit essence of Larch speaks to you, saying:

"Although my physical presence may be short-lived, my essence speaks of the rocky mountains of my first birth, and of the wide starry skies that fill me with gladness in the simple act of Being, glorying in my sure and steady growth towards the heavens. Beauty and grace are my inspiration and my delight, and even in the face of setbacks and obstacles, my heart and strength will always prevail. Know then that my tall and slender body will always support you and hold you in perfect balance, as you allow my affinity with the Elements of air and water to help you clarify and make whole all the diverse and wondrous aspects of your mind, emotions and spirit. For I have the will to calm and strengthen you within – and empower and uphold all that you are – as you strive to embody your own beauty, strength and grace; and the charity to show you how to truly value and embrace the life that you have been given...."

(* Bronzite will help you ground and connect with the energies and wisdom of Larch, if you wish to enhance your experience using crystals.)

If you have chosen to accept and work with Tzadkiel's Gift, and when you are ready to connect with his second Greenwood Guardian, you need simply call for the presence of **Tamarisk** (*) .... Tamarisk envelops you in a deep Oxford-blue Light, and the Feminine spirit essence of Tamarisk speaks to you, saying:

"I carry the Light of the whole and balanced heart of The Divine Feminine, and am a Master of flexibility and adaptability. Let me provide the loving protection and shelter that you need to survive the winds of change, and show you how to find and use your many strengths that lie within, whilst knowing and accepting your limitations. For I can help you learn how to adapt your skills without compromising your truths; and aid you in understanding that true mastery comes from asserting Power over your Self, and not over anything – or anyone – else. Then together we may work to refine and polish all that you are, spreading the seeds of Light that are within your heart freely and compassionately for all those who share your path. So connect with the free-flowing luminous form of my body, and feel me reinforce and deepen your roots; then let me help cleanse, purify and heal your heart, so that you may accept your own Sovereignty and understand how to attain true freedom, thus knowing both abundance and peace...."

(* Purpurite and Green Jade will help you ground and connect with the energies and wisdom of Tamarisk, if you wish to enhance your experience using crystals.)

ARCHEIA AMETHYSTIA

'PROGRESS THROUGH LEARNING'

CRYSTAL CHAMPIONS:

Amethyst ♥ Honey Calcite ♥ Clear Selenite

CREATURE COMPANIONS:

Crab ♥ Deer ♥ Mouse

GREENWOOD GUARDIANS:

Aspen ♥ Scots Pine

*I am thankful for all that I learn,
and all that I teach,
in every moment of every day.*

MEETING AMETHYSTIA

You find yourself standing alone, enveloped in a swirling cloud of purple and white mist that spirals and spins all about you. It is an odd sensation, but not uncomfortable; and even though your logical mind tells you that there is no solid ground beneath your feet, you feel safe and secure. Your mind merely observes the misty light with calm attentiveness, and you simply watch the colours as they shift through all possible hues and tones of violet and purple: blending and separating, brightening and fading – like stirring purple paint through cream. Everything is silent and still (apart from the colours moving around you), yet you somehow know that you are being swiftly and efficiently transported through Time and space....

After a while the coloured mist clears from your immediate vicinity, enabling you to see that you are standing in front of an ornate and imposing throne-like chair, which has been crafted from white marble – as has the highly polished floor. Sitting in it is a tall and slender woman who has an upright regal bearing and a commanding presence: this is Archeia Amethystia. She is clad in formal regalia, because she has chosen to appear to you here in her persona of Holy Amethyst, High Priestess of the Sacred Fire: hence her attire is relatively plain and austere, comprising a floor-length white linen robe with long flowing sleeves and a close-fitting neckline, over which she wears a knee-length tabard of amethyst-coloured linen hemmed and bound in silver. A large 'Cross of Saint John' has been embroidered on the front of the tabard in silver thread – a tiny silver six-pointed star adorning the centre of each quadrant delineated by its four arms; and the same (but much smaller) pattern is clearly visible on the tops of her purple felt slippers, which are peeping out from beneath the hem of the robe.

Amethystia's head is covered by a starched white linen cloth that mirrors the style of the 'Nemes' headdress, as worn by Ancient Egyptian Pharaohs: this frames her face and shoulders, and is secured by a plain silver circlet that holds a dark purple amethyst crystal centred over her third eye. This amethyst has been cut and faceted into the shape of a flame, indicating her status as High Priestess of the Sacred Fire; and also links her with Tzadkiel through the amethyst he (likewise) wears to denote his status.

Beneath the headdress you can see that Amethystia's skin is very pale, – her heart-shaped face having a delicately pointed chin and neatly defined features; her long-lashed eyes having astonishingly vibrant violet irises with unusual almond-shaped pupils, rather like a cat's. Oddly she has no eyebrows – and, as you are puzzling over this, she reaches up with pale slender hands and lifts her headdress and circlet from her head, revealing a bare scalp covered with black tattoos of randomly sized and orientated curly 'S'-shaped spirals. Smiling gently at your reaction, Amethystia steps forwards, declaring:

"I am Amethystia, the Lady Purity – Master Cryptographer and Inscriber of the Divine Light, High-Priestess of the Sacred Fire and twin flame of Tzadkiel. I have come from the heart of the Violet Star, whose Light is given to aid the Beings of this Galaxy in their search for their own truths and Inner Light. Hence, within and through me you will find a Fire so bright, that to gaze upon it would blind mortal sight: yet, in spirit, you can see clearly the imprint that it leaves upon your Soul, marking you as one of the Creator's children – a son or daughter of the Divine Light. All that I AM I hold hallowed, and I

ask that you do likewise: for you and I are each seeking the essential truth and purity of our nature, and the ultimate prize of absolute union with all our many aspects that have dispersed throughout the Universe in order to live, learn and grow greater in wisdom and understanding. And so, I would take your hand and offer to be your mentor and guide, as you endeavour to attain the same goal as I...."

With these words, Amethystia reaches out and takes your hand – and you are again enveloped in swirling clouds of violet and purple light.... Once more you experience a vague sense of disorientation, and know that you are travelling both swiftly and far: then suddenly the light dissipates, and you find yourself standing in a field of sun-ripened golden wheat, which spans the floor of a valley nestling amongst chalky ridges of rolling green downland.

It is mid-morning on a perfect day in late summer, and the sky above you is clear and blue. A gold-white sun is climbing slowly into the sky – and, as the ground beneath you warms beneath its gaze, you smell the earthy tang of the soil releasing its moisture to the day. Unsure of where to go, you look around and note that a copse of beech trees stands at the far side of the field, which is otherwise hedged with clusters of hawthorn, blackthorn, elder and box. Just as you are debating whether to seek out their shade, a cool breeze stirs around you, the long stems of wheat rustling and whispering as they ripple in undulating golden waves at its touch, and a woman materialises, hovering over the centre of the field: you know this is Archeia Amethystia, and so you make your way to join her as she alights on the ground....

As you draw closer, you note that the ground where she stands is in the middle of an area of flattened wheat that bears the imprint of a crop circle – and, as you approach, she lowers herself to the ground and tucks her bare feet beneath her. With a smile, she invites you to settle opposite her, so that you may accustom yourself to her energies and examine her appearance – which is somewhat different than it was before.

Once you are comfortably settled, you note that Amethystia's eyes have retained their long dark lashes and deep and mesmerising violet irises, although her pupils are now 'normal' – round and black. Her face has also changed shape, and is now an elegant oval that displays a well-defined bone structure, smooth ivory skin, and a long narrow nose set over full lips. The greatest difference, however, is that her face is now framed by a lustrous mane of dark-brown hair, which ripples in glossy waves to her waist.

Amethystia's attire is also different, as she is now clad in a loose-fitting gown made of deep-violet velvet, whose dense nap glitters with silvery sparkles as the light catches its gathers and folds. The gown has a low scooped neckline and long flowing sleeves that drape softly around her wrists; and full skirts that pile in soft folds on the ground around her ankles and legs. The colour of the material is so dark that it almost appears black – and as you inspect it more closely, you see it is dotted with tiny stars embroidered in dark purple silk, making them hard to spot against the deep colour of the velvet.

The scooped neck of the gown reveals a long slender neck and a pale and creamy expanse of skin: this draws your eye to the pendant that lies suspended over Amethystia's heart, where a strong silver chain suspends a large star tetrahedron that has been cut from a crystal-clear diamond. As you look at this more closely, you note that it gives off tiny rainbow flashes of light as the sunlight sparks off its points, and recognise it as the gem that links her with Tzadkiel, her twin flame.

Noting your interest, Amethystia lifts her hands to hold the diamond between her fingertips, enabling you to see that each of her long slender fingers bears a wide silver ring: the ring on the middle finger of her left hand differs from the others, however, as it holds a dark purple amethyst that has been intricately cut into the shape of a flame, which looks identical to the one on the circlet she wore in her persona as 'Holy Amethyst'.

AMETHYSTIA'S TEACHINGS
The Gift of The Amethyst Flame of Transformation:

Recognising that your examination is complete, Amethystia holds out her hand to show you that the amethyst on her ring has a living flame flickering in its depths. She tells you that what you see is an Amethyst Flame, which is an aspect of the Sacred Fire and an aspect of the Violet Ray on which she serves; and explains that it holds the Light of Spiritual Purification and Divine Potential in perfect balance, enabling her to see all things in their True light. She adds that she also uses it to facilitate perfected Creation by applying the catalytic Power of its Fire to whatever she is addressing (be this a person, a 'thing' or a situation), in order that it might be transformed into the Highest Light of its essential and fundamental Purity. Reaching forwards, Amethystia briefly touches her ring to the top of your brow – at which you become aware of a gentle warmth establishing itself in the upper part of your head....

Sitting back, she tells you that her Gift of The Amethyst Flame of Transformation (which was so swiftly given) has been placed within your energy Body so that it spans the root of your brow chakra and your Soma centre. She explains that this will help bring about purity of mind and clarity of thought on all levels, thus allowing you to see and understand your Self and other people and any situation you encounter truly and clearly – and so ensuring that whatever thoughts and beliefs you hold about your world, yourself and others are true. Gently touching your forehead again, she tells you that whenever you wish to use the Gift she has given you, you need simply remind yourself of its presence; and then see or imagine your head being filled with a clear amethyst Light. With a smile, she adds that, because the Amethyst Flame aids clear sight, its Light will help you to see where (and what) you are – and hence understand where you need to go (and what you can become): in this way you can be sure that whatever you plan (and however you move forwards) is both clear and in perfect alignment with your Highest purpose at that time.

Reminding you that the precursor of all things is thought, Amethystia observes that the mind is where brilliant and inspirational ideas begin: yet it is also where incorrect or distorted beliefs may be fledged – and the Amethyst Flame is particularly useful for identifying and correcting these! Suggesting that you might like to experience this now, Amethystia instructs you to take your attention to the Flame she had given you, simply accepting its Light and its transformative Power, and allowing it to fill your head and clear your mind of extraneous thoughts, feelings, emotions or physical sensations, until your mind is open, quiet, calm and still....

After allowing time for this to happen, she asks you to bring to mind any thought, belief, attitude, feeling or situation that you instinctively know may be preventing you from fulfilling your true potential – reminding you that holding on to *anything* that interferes with your inner balance prevents you from seeing clearly, and so restricts your growth. As you begin to consider this, she reminds you to call upon the Amethyst Flame to help you identify whatever you need to see and address now with absolute clarity and compassionate understanding....

When she is happy that you have decided upon something, Amethystia directs you to use the Flame to help you release or transform whatever no longer serves your greater purpose by seeing, feeling or imagining the Flame expanding to encompass all of your physical body and aura, until you are completely filled and surrounded with its amethyst Light – advising you to concentrate its Light in any area that appears to be dark; or where you feel (or know) you are holding physical, emotional, mental or spiritual imbalance, pain or trauma....

As you follow her instructions, she counsels you that, if you choose, you may also add the Light of the *Violet* Flame (the Gift given by Tzadkiel, her twin flame) to aid you in this, because combining them 'as one' will help transmute any negativity you hold into clear Light, offering you the potential for even greater self-transformation and growth. With a gentle smile she adds:

> *"Be not afraid to look closely at those parts of your Self that are now revealed, for what needs to be revealed is revealed; what needs to be released is released; what needs to be cleansed is cleansed. There is no fear; there is no shame; there is no blame, no guilt or denial attached to releasing these things from your energy field...."*

Time passes; and when Amethystia is happy you have achieved everything you can at this time, the Light around you fades; and you feel yourself reach a new state of clarity and inner balance, as the Amethyst Flame dies away to the merest flicker....

Reassuring you that the Flame will re-awaken if you need it, Amethystia gives you a purple crystal and tells you this is **Amethyst**, her first Crystal Champion – explaining:

> *"Amethyst unwaveringly holds the resonance of the Amethyst Flame, which is an aspect of the alchemical Violet Ray of Transmutation and Transformation. It shines a clear and refined Spiritual Light upon all that it touches, revealing its true nature and highlighting anything that is not of its original consciousness, in order that it may be returned to the purity of how it was first created or made manifest. Amethyst has a high vibration that can facilitate the awakening of your upper energy centres and aid your connection to Higher Planes of awareness, making it easier to detach yourself from lower ego-based emotional reactions and responses: this allows you to look at situations and events from a more dispassionate – and compassionate – perspective. Viewing things in this manner makes it easier for you to transmute, release, accept or assimilate whatever is seen, in the way that is the most appropriate for the highest good of* all *concerned. Moreover, by connecting you with your Higher nature, Amethyst can help you see and understand why and how you are responsible for creating the reality that you choose to experience in every moment of every day – and, therefore, reminds you that you also have the power to change or transform that reality, if you truly want or choose to. Above all, Amethyst is a highly evolved yet gentle crystal that is both*

balanced and complete, making it an ideal choice for all new starts in life, and an ideal companion for all stages of your journey – indeed, it is an interesting fact that Amethyst is the first crystal many people choose to buy, which is proof of its simple ability to be 'all things to all people'."

With a smile, Amethystia affirms that Amethyst may therefore help you connect with your Amethyst Flame and the Light of its Fire: and then, with each tie you release; each negative event you clear; and each karmic debt you settle, you will move one step closer towards your goal – for without attaining that absolute state of purity, total reunion with All that you ARE and All that IS cannot be achieved.

Leaning forwards, Amethystia places a second amethyst on the ground between you and touches it with her ring, at which it grows and grows – shaping itself into a wide bowl as it does so. Peering in, you see that somehow it has filled with water, and observe that its bottom is covered with pebbles and fronds of seaweed, which are sheltering a small purple-shelled crab. Amethystia chuckles, and points out that although crabs have a very strong exoskeleton **Crab** can teach you a great deal about how to achieve the right balance between protecting yourself with so much 'armour' that it weighs you down and prevents easy movement, and using other more subtle or adaptable forms of camouflage or defence. Scooping the crab from the water, she places it on the ground and suggests you observe how (although it can walk forwards) it moves fastest when going sideways. Pointing out that crabs use whatever method best suits the terrain and the situation, she tells you that Crab can guide you to find solutions to problems in a subtle or indirect way, proving that 'full-steam ahead' is not always the most effective, nor the wisest, option; whilst also helping you see how best to avoid or circumvent an obstacle in your path, rather than struggle over it! Reminding you that crabs can survive on land as well as in water, she adds that Crab can also teach you how to be more flexible and open-minded when making decisions; or show you how to let go and 'go with the flow' so that you move in accordance with the natural tides and cycles of your life without limitation or fear; and/or help you to remain physically and emotionally focused and grounded during times of turmoil or change. Returning it to the water, Amethystia explains that all crabs need to shed their shells in order to grow: hence you may also call upon Crab to support you through times of change if you feel vulnerable or scared – or if you are dreading the thought of having to discard the 'old' to make way for the 'new'. With a smile, she adds that Crab may also come to *you* if it knows it is time for you to discard something that has shielded you (or made you feel safe) in the past, but which is now constricting or preventing your growth: then, touching her ring to the bowl, it – and the crab – are gone!

The Spiral of Transformation – Perspective and Choice:

Moving so that you sit knee-to-knee, Amethystia pulls up her right sleeve and rotates her arm, revealing the black tattoo that spans the underside of her forearm from elbow to wrist: this resembles a reversed 'S' with spiralling ends, just like those you saw on her bared scalp when you first encountered her. She explains that this mark is known as the Spiral of Transformation, which is a sacred symbol that promotes and empowers movement, growth and change whilst upholding the Universal principles that guide and direct involution and evolution, perspective, choice and discernment. Using the index finger of her left hand, she then slowly traces the mark from one end to the other, before holding out her arm and asking you to trace it in the same way....

After tracing it once, you find yourself pausing at the end of a spiral, and (quickly placing her finger over yours to hold it still) Amethystia gives a smile. She tells you that *this* is the eye – the 'I AM' – of the spiral: a calm centre of balance, where all movement ceases – whether just for a moment, or an eternity. Here, she says, is a place of stillness and rest from which all can be viewed and reviewed from a pure point of wisdom – and, as you consider this, you realise that your mind has stilled, and all your focus is now simply on the point of the spiral....

After a while Amethystia releases your finger, and asks you to begin to mindfully trace out the symbol from one end to the other. As you do as she asks, she observes that it is the nature of the spiral to promote movement and change, because Universal energy (Divine Light) instinctively seeks to grow and evolve: then, directing you to continue to track the spiral with your finger, she asks you to think about whether moving out from an eye of the spiral requires conscious choice to do so.... to consider the amount of effort it takes for you to change direction each time.... and to decide if spiralling *into* an eye feels any different from spiralling *out* of an eye – and if so, in what way....

Once you have considered each of these things, Amethystia invites you to sit back and relax, pointing out that – even though the eye is a still-point, without it there can *be* neither expansion nor contraction! With a smile, she tells you that the double spiral also demonstrates how diametrically opposed and/or extreme experiences (even those that are potentially painful or hard) enable you to develop your understanding of Free Will and its consequences – reminding you that this teaches discernment, leading ultimately to the attainment of true Wisdom. Tapping the eye of the spiral on her arm, she counsels you that the knack to handling such experiences lies in finding the still-point at the 'end of the spiral', in order to have the focus to clearly identify all the choices open to you, and so consider and plan the best way to return to equilibrium.

Settling back, Amethystia explains that the double spiral also teaches the value of perspective within the totality of life-experience; and, asking you to close your eyes, she directs you to imagine that you are walking down a path shaped like the double spiral: this can be situated in any landscape of your choosing – the most important thing is the path itself.... she then asks you to make your way towards the eye of the spiral, looking all around you as you walk; and asks you to observe how your path – where you have come from, as well as where you are going – can be viewed from different viewpoints and perspectives as you follow its curves....

Once you reach the eye of the spiral, Amethystia tells you to stop. She asks you to think about how pausing at the still-point of the eye helps you see the path you have just taken from a calm and focused standpoint, enabling you to review your journey and plan when and how to move next – whilst also allowing you 'breathing space' to gather your energies before moving on again....

After allowing you time to experience this, Amethystia tells you to open your eyes again. She reminds you that the still eye of the spiral lies at its heart; and points out that, likewise, *your* heart is the centre of (and balance point for) your energy Body: hence it is important to keep your heart as clear as you can, so that you always make well-reasoned and appropriate choices and decisions.

Suddenly a pair of turtle-doves flies swiftly over the field towards you: one of them is holding a twig in its beak, which it drops in Amethystia's lap. She shows you that the bird's gift is a sprig of hawthorn bearing a cluster of dewy white blossoms; and leaning over, she rests it on your heart chakra: at its touch, you feel your heart ease and slowly begin to open; and, after a few moments, you sense that your heart is starting to release ancient hurts and pains, allowing some of the negativity that you have held within to dissipate and clear.... Gradually you feel your heart move to a new and improved state of balance, and you feel your mind strengthen and your emotions calm – each in greater harmony with the other.... Somehow you know that in this state it is possible for you to be more open, trusting and accepting of all that you see, sense, hear and know – and recognising this, Amethystia smiles and sits back, tucking the twig into her hair.

Taking your attention back to the turtle-doves, who are now looping and swooping through the air above you, it seems to you that their focus in this moment is on the sheer pleasure of flying and nothing more. Amethystia laughs with delight as she watches them testing the air currents and using their tail and wing feathers to dexterously manoeuvre with superb agility and skill; and admits that one of her own greatest joys is to be found in the freedom of flight. She counsels you that doing something that gives you joy (even if it serves no apparent purpose) is an essential part of living – for being carefree and happy strengthens your heart and promotes inner peace and harmony, enabling you to make the well-balanced and considered choices that will support you in joyfully dancing on the winds of change!

Her eye caught by a sudden movement, Amethystia draws your attention to a small group of deer resting in the shade of the trees at the far side of the field. They are well camouflaged in the dappled light, and she points out how their colouring helps them to remain invisible when still, whilst their unassuming demeanour and delicate tread means that others do not easily hear them, or see them as a threat: hence, you might call **Deer** to teach you how to keep a low profile, or remain still, or move in an unobtrusive manner if you need to avoid attracting unwanted attention. She adds that deer have keen senses of hearing, sight and smell that help alert them to any signs of danger; whilst their speed and agility enables them to move quickly if they need to evade anything that threatens their safety: thus, Deer can be called upon if you need to increase your awareness of your Self, or your environment, and/or those around you; and/or to help you understand when and how to change direction fast – whether for self-protection or personal advancement. Amethystia remarks that gentle Deer can also show you how to accomplish things quietly and calmly – for you do not always need a sledgehammer to crack a nut: she then gives a low call, at which a small hind steps out from the shelter of the trees to meet your gaze. You are amazed to see that this little female has an unusual coat that is the exact colour of clotted cream, and that she has a small but beautifully formed set of golden antlers, which glint and gleam in the sunlight. Amethystia announces that this rare and beautiful beast is a Golden Hind, whose presence symbolises the gift of empowered Wisdom: so if you encounter her (maybe in dreams, journeying or in meditation) you should be aware that you are being asked to understand and master something that has the potential to advance your personal understanding and growth ten-fold. With a smile, she adds that a Golden Hind may also appear if it is time to walk 'the dark or hidden pathways of the forest', when you may be assured of her wise guidance and counsel – although this does not mean that the paths she will lead you down will be easy: and then, as silently as she appeared, the hind fades back into the trees....

Holding out her hand, Amethystia gives you a honey-coloured waxy stone, telling you that this is **Honey Calcite**, her second Crystal Champion – explaining:

"Honey Calcite has an appropriate name, for this stone possesses a soft sweetness and gentle innocence that aids a return to the purity and integrity of your innate (and True) Self, whilst making the trials and tribulations of everyday life easier to bear. Honey Calcite emits a gentle and warming energy that has the potential to strengthen you on many levels, and is particularly useful to work with if you have any 'raw' wounds (physical, mental, emotional or *spiritual) that need a comforting balm to help remove trauma or pain and promote thorough and complete healing. Honey Calcite may also be used as a general support if you are recovering from a long illness or need a shoulder to lean on, for it has a profound and generous inner strength that enables it to 'keep on giving'. All the various members of the colourful calcite family can be of great value in helping heal and strengthen your energy Bodies, but Honey Calcite is especially useful in healing, supporting and balancing your sacral and solar plexus chakras, which govern your mind and your emotions. Nonetheless, Honey Calcite may also be used to help support your heart, brow and throat chakras, as it attracts and holds the Yellow and Golden-yellow Rays of Divine and Illumined Wisdom, which will empower your heart and focus your mind so that you can make all your choices and decisions with both wisdom and love."*

Smiling, Amethystia affirms that Honey Calcite may therefore help you in healing your chakras and subtle energy centres, which in turn will help you find inner balance.

The Sacred Purpose of Sigils, Symbols and Signs:

Scooting round to sit at your side, Amethystia pulls up her left sleeve to reveal her forearm, which is bound round with two leather straps: these secure a small holder (a bit like a miniature scabbard) to its underside, from which she draws a stylus that resembles an old-fashioned pen and nib. This has a slender shaft made of polished beech wood; and a nib-like blade made of silver, with a brilliantly clear faceted diamond in its centre. A wider strap secures a square block of what looks like solidified black ink to the upper side of her wrist: this, she informs you, is *not* in fact ink, but is a condensation of Black Light, which provides the 'space' that enables all things to become manifest through the Power of the Diamond Light that flows through the 'nib' of her pen. She explains that she uses these tools in much the same way as a tattoo artist works on skin – for, in her role as Master Cryptographer and Inscriber of the Divine Light, she is required to define, delineate and seal Divine energies throughout the Universe in their purest form possible, by using the Diamond Light to mark out and construct the sacred blueprints that underlie shape and form; and to design and inscribe sacred symbols or sigils that encapsulate all acts of Divine Creation.

Pulling her sleeve down again, Amethystia says that many cultures and civilisations (both on Earth and much farther afield!) choose to permanently mark the skin with sigils, symbols and/or patterns that create a visible record of personal allegiances, attainments, mastery or status. She explains that such marks span space, Time and Dimension – each one carrying Divine Light that has been shaped by thought and word; and each holding a unique Power that may be known to any that look, as long as they are ready and prepared to sense or understand their meaning. This is because *all* symbols (as with sacred shape and form) are tangible expressions of Universal language – the Light made manifest, if you like – and hence the merest imprint of them confers that Divine Light and Power, transforming thought and word into action and deed. Looking into your eyes, Amethystia stresses that such marks create a permanent addition to the bearer's energy field and adjust its Light signature accordingly: therefore she strongly counsels that you *always* employ discernment, care and thought before requesting (or accepting) the placement of any symbol, sign, mark or sigil upon your physical *or* non-physical Bodies – including energy 'Gifts' such as she and the other Archangels and Archeia are offering you!

Giving you a clear and slender crystal, Amethystia tells you this is **Clear Selenite**, her third Crystal Champion – explaining:

"Selenite is one of the finest and most dependable carriers of the crystal-white Light. Despite its relative softness it has an inner strength within its rather delicate exterior: indeed, Selenite in this clear form has a particularly refined and penetrating resonance that can powerfully shift energy blocks and clear away negativity, making it useful for clarifying and energising your chakras – and, if placed vertically above your Soul Star chakra, and likewise below your Earth Star chakra, may also clear your pranic core. Clear Selenite resonates especially well with the Elements of water and ether, and thus has an innate affinity with the sacral and heart chakras, where it may help you balance your emotional and spiritual Bodies with greater clarity and ease, whilst helping remove negative attitudes and feelings that might interfere with expressing your spirituality through your heart. Additionally, Clear Selenite's ability to ground the full spectrum of Light within any physical body (whether your own, or the Earth's) can quickly and safely activate and open your Higher energy centres and 'inner eye', facilitating clearer and more reliable psychic insights, and helping you develop a finer level of intuitive connection and understanding: this is because Divine Light IS energy and information; and when you are able to draw down and fully ground it throughout your entire energy field it becomes easier to access information (on any level), and identify whatever you see, hear, sense or feel with much greater clarity and reliability. Most importantly, Clear Selenite is able to modify its energies in accordance with your changing and evolving needs and capabilities, making it a useful companion at any – and all – stages of your journeys of self-healing and self-growth."

With a smile, Amethystia affirms that Clear Selenite may therefore bring you greater clarity and awareness – and thus true understanding – of any issue or situation, enabling you to be more objective and discerning in your decision-making processes.

Sitting back and holding out her hands, Amethystia invites you to look at the rings on her fingers: as you have already seen and experienced, one holds an amethyst, but the plain silvered surfaces of the other seven appear somewhat dull. On closer inspection you realise this is because they are covered with minute engravings, whose intricate details are invisible to the naked eye. With a smile, she informs you that these hold the patterns with which she works, requiring her to not only have clear vision but absolute mental focus and pure spiritual intent as well (which is why the Amethyst Flame dwells in her other ring!): furthermore, although her skills are mostly called upon at Universal level, they may also be required at Galactic or planetary level, especially if shifts or changes at 'grass roots' level are required.

Reminding you that you are currently sitting in a 'crop circle', she laughs and says that 'grass roots level' is a particularly apt expression – for, although they are often the source of speculation, crop circles are in fact *natural* formations that are simply external expressions of energies grounded within the planet: as such, they are wittingly designed to adjust planetary resonances and/or redress planetary imbalances; at the same time as (consciously *or* subconsciously) illuminating and edifying those that observe them.

Asking for your trust, Amethystia stands and helps you to your feet, before taking your hands and lifting you up into the air – supporting you high enough above the ground so that you may clearly see the pattern that this particular crop circle makes.... As you look down, she explains that whatever you see or sense holds symbolic meaning and/or a message that you will find useful to research and meditate upon later – reassuring you that, even if you cannot *consciously* discern a pattern, your subconscious mind will have recognised and understood its significance, and will apply it in whatever way is relevant and appropriate for you now....

When she knows you have perceived enough, Amethystia returns you to the ground and comments that you may also find it illuminating to seek out images of crop circles as and when they appear each year – for their symbolic significance (from both a personal *and* a planetary point of view) can be very enlightening!

Catching a sudden movement from the corner of her eye, Amethystia swoops down and plucks something from the ground: opening her hand, she reveals she has caught a small harvest mouse that had been gathering up stray grains of wheat. Unconcerned, the little mouse begins to nose around her fingers for any 'edibles' she may be hiding – at which she chuckles, observing that mice are great opportunists and always on the lookout for sources of food that, if plentiful, they can stockpile for leaner times: thus you can always ask **Mouse** for advice if you need to plan ahead; and/or if you wish to make sure you have planned for all possible eventualities. With a smile, she adds that, conversely, if you are 'all talk and no do', or have a tendency to over-plan or prevaricate, Mouse can also be called upon to help you identify whatever fears are preventing you from moving forwards, enabling you to get to the heart of the issue so that you may take appropriate, positive and productive action. After a while the mouse realises there is no food to be found, and settles down to fastidiously groom its long whiskers. As it does, Amethystia explains that mice have relatively poor eyesight, and so tend to 'see' by using their nose, paws and the sensitivity of their whiskers to feel vibrations and disturbance in the air around them – accordingly you may ask Mouse to be your teacher if you want to expand your senses and understand how to utilise subtle vibrational energies to develop your awareness of your Self or the world about you: furthermore, because mice are painstaking and organised in their habits, you may also call upon Mouse to show you how to examine a situation carefully from all angles, especially if you need to define or plan something in great detail; or if you need to make sure you have thought about, and considered, all your available options and choices. Returning the little mouse to the ground, Amethystia draws your attention to how swiftly and dexterously it weaves through the 'forest' of wheat, remarking that it is amazing the tiny spaces a mouse can squeeze through: therefore you might also call upon Mouse if you need to get to the root of a seemingly impossible problem or situation; or want help accessing knowledge or information that appears to be beyond your grasp; or if you simply cannot see 'the wood for the trees'!

The Greenwood Guardians – Aspen and Scots Pine:

Her *personal* mentoring complete for now, Amethystia affirms she is always available to aid and support you: you need only bring her to mind and ask for her presence, and she will attend you. Furthermore, she tells you that two great Tree Beings of the Plant Kingdom have also asked to support you in addressing her Theme of 'PROGRESS THROUGH LEARNING', adding that you need only request *their* presence, and they will be with you.

She explains that the first of these Greenwood Guardians is the unified (Masculine *and* Feminine) essence of Aspen, who has asked to overlight and help you ground whatever work you undertake within *any* aspect of her chapter. The second is the Feminine essence of Scots Pine, who has specifically asked to help you understand and assimilate her Gift of The Amethyst Flame of Transformation (if you have chosen to accept it).

When you are ready to connect with Amethystia's first Greenwood Guardian, you need simply call for the presence of **Aspen** (*) .... Aspen surrounds your aura in a steel-blue Light, and the unified (Masculine *and* Feminine) spirit essence of Aspen speaks to you, saying:

"Feel my energy surround you, so that you may have the space in which to find yourself and come to balance – centred, calmed and relaxed.... then simply allow your worries and cares to fall away, and free yourself from whatever confines you in fear: for I have come as the spiritual warrior, to shield you in my essence and support you as you work to attain purity, knowing that you have the Light within that has the power to conquer all ills that might beset you.... Then I would share with you my key wisdom, which is that true strength comes through flexibility and the ability to adapt and BE as you need to be, in any situation: hence my bark holds the multifaceted 'diamonds' of Universal Wisdom; my heart holds the pure white rainbow Light of Source, without which nothing can be made manifest; and my leaves channel the light of the Silver Ray, which holds all that is required for movement and growth.... So let me help you connect with all that you are through the wisdom of the Earth and the Cosmos – that you may see everything

with clarity and compassion, and so recognise and accept that you have the potential for anything you choose to Be within your grasp...."

(* Snow [White] Quartz and Hawks [Blue Tiger] Eye will help you ground and connect with the energies and wisdom of Aspen, if you wish to enhance your experience using crystals.)

If you have chosen to accept and work with Amethystia's Gift, and when you are ready to connect with her second Greenwood Guardian, you need simply call for the presence of **Scots Pine** (*) .... Scots Pine envelops you in a pale blue Light, and the Feminine spirit essence of Scots Pine speaks to you, saying:

"My spirit is wide-rooted, enabling me to draw upon the energies that fill and span the Earth from pole to pole: this grounds me fully to the Cosmos and to the knowledge of all that I AM, and fills me at all times with the love and inspiration of the Creator – so feel the open strength of my roots and stability of my body support you; and expand your senses to recognise that the love and inspiration of the Creator (and of your Divine-self) is always there for you.... Then allow me to help you connect with the dragon-power of the Earth, so that you may draw upon the fire and determination that you need in order to transform every aspect of your Self into the Highest possible Light.... Those who know me well recognise that I have the Will to survive in almost any environment, knowing how to stand in water and sand, ice and rock, without allowing my strength to fade: thus have I learned to find the best in any situation, and take comfort in the loving embrace of the Earth in all her multifaceted manifestations – and this too you may come to learn and understand through me, as we stand As One at the heart of the world. Understand too that, as I grow taller, I have no hesitation in shedding my attachment to my lower branches: thus I can likewise teach you how to shed all that confines you in smallness and holds you to your lower ego-self, so that you may learn to master your body, mind and emotions through the power of all the Elements of earth, wind and water, regardless of the place in which you find yourself – for only thus may you move to live fully within your heart, and truly embrace the totality of your Spirit...."

(* Preseli Bluestone and White Selenite will help you ground and connect with the energies and wisdom of Scots Pine, if you wish to enhance your experience using crystals.)

ARCHANGEL METATRON

'RESTRUCTURE YOUR LIFE'

CRYSTAL CHAMPIONS:

Flame Aura Qtz ♥ Yellow Jasper ♥ Haematoid Qtz

CREATURE COMPANIONS:

Peacock ♥ Lion ♥ Donkey

GREENWOOD GUARDIANS:

Chile Pine ♥ Redwood

*I am ready and willing
to make change happen
NOW.*

MEETING METATRON

It is late afternoon on a hot summer's day, and you find yourself standing on a high rocky cliff that has a breathtaking view over the azure ocean below. Where you stand is open to the elements and seemingly devoid of life – the ochre ground beneath your feet dusty and bare – yet somehow the starkness complements the raw elemental power you sense swirling about you, and tells of the formidable forces that shape your world. As you turn to survey the area behind you, you note that the barren landscape slopes gently up and away from you towards a large square open-fronted building that has a pitched roof made of red clay tiles. The entrance to the building is fronted by seven deep stone steps, which lead down to a paved courtyard below; and is sheltered by an overhanging portico supported by ten ornamental columns, which runs the whole width of the facade. The grand and once white edifice is heavily weathered and encrusted with pale green-grey lichens and some of the tiles are missing or cracked – yet, despite the apparent dilapidation, it retains an atmosphere of grandeur that hints of an intriguing past.

With a mounting feeling of anticipation, you decide to make your way towards it – but just as you are getting into your stride, a sharp breeze picks up.... Rooted to the spot, you shut your eyes tightly as the dust begins to swirl around you, afraid to move in any direction in case you fall – hearing only the plaintive cries of seabirds wheeling and soaring overhead, and the sound of waves crashing against the rocks tumbled at the foot of the cliffs. As your senses sharpen, you become aware of the grittiness of the sandy dust peppering your skin, and can smell the seaweed-salt tang of the ocean and taste the dusty heat spiralling about you. Then, as your physical senses fade and your non-physical awareness expands, you sense the ancient spiritual energies of this place, and feel them reaching out to touch your Soul: and, as you acknowledge their presence, the wind drops; the dust settles; and a loud and sudden rumble of thunder causes you to open your eyes....

Turning seawards, you see the cloudless blue sky lower, darkening rapidly to an angry grey; and a vast roiling mass of dark clouds starts to boil across the sky towards you. As they draw closer your nostrils become filled with the scents of ozone and brine, and your skin starts to prickle as it senses the electrical energies mounting in the air: then all of a sudden the sullen black clouds are pierced by jagged bolts of lightning, which arc through the sky and fork down to the sea below, illuminating everything about you with crackling flares of blue-white light.... Inexorably the storm draws closer and closer, bombarding your senses in thundering reverberations that grow louder and louder, until the storm is finally crashing all about you, making your whole body vibrate with its energy: then, just as you are thinking you cannot take any more, a fiery ball of golden light rips through the heart of the clouds and streaks across the sky like a giant shooting star, tearing a vast rent in the darkness. Brilliant shafts of sunlight begin to flood through the opening thus created – and as the ball of light zigzags through the sky, rippling curtains of white-gold light forming in its wake, the dark clouds fade; the thunder and lightning slowly die away; and the sun is once again visible, shining with ever increasing brilliance in its rightful place in the heavens....

Calm restored the ball of light shimmers and fades, revealing its source to be a golden chariot drawn by a team of six pure-white winged horses that are harnessed to it in two / four formation. Illuminated in radiant shafts of sunlight and standing on the platform at the rear of the chariot you see a tall and commanding figure of a man dressed in the style of a Roman centurion, complete with a golden helmet plumed with white horsehair; and who is wearing a long white cloak that is streaming and billowing behind him in the wind: this is Archangel Metatron. As the chariot approaches, you note that a small black myna bird is perched atop the chariot's curving prow, whistling and calling encouragement as the chariot draws nearer and – landing in a cloud of dust – rolls to a halt nearby. Stepping down, Metatron removes his helmet and stows it in the chariot: he then whistles back to the bird; shakes free his mop of curly black hair; and wraps his cloak around his body, before striding over (legs and feet bare) and greeting you with a strong handshake, declaring:

"I am Metatron of the Light – Guardian of the Threshold and Keeper of the Gate, Assigner of the Measures of the Universal Light, and twin flame of Sophia, the Lady Constance. I greet you with much love in my heart, for I recognise you in the clear Light of The Divine as a spark sent out from His hand. Thus, I have come to aid you as you endeavour to define your true needs and ascertain whatsoever within your life requires change – supporting you with my strong arms, and holding you in the Light of my love, that you might have the courage to see and do what you know, at heart, must be done. Know that the masterpiece we will then craft together will be a thing of beauty indeed, with both wisdom and understanding at its heart: for I am a Master Smith who works the fires and forges of the Heavens with strength and vigour, with the Divine Plan that IS for all things always in my heart and mind. Remember: all that you are – and all that you can become – simply awaits your touch. So let me aid you in moulding and shaping your future, for your heart already knows *what it is to be – and knows too that, in its making, it will sing to you all the glorious and harmonious notes of your Soul!"*

Inviting you to follow him, Metatron then strides away towards the distant building with his cloak billowing around his legs. As you hurry after him, you can see that the cloak bears the image of a Pegasus in flight: this has been embroidered using fine gold thread – more of which binds the edges and secures the tightly-woven white wool outer-side to its gold silk lining. Drawing closer, you realise that every aspect of the Pegasus has been intricately and lovingly detailed – especially its features and its eyes, whose pupils are defined by two large and fiery cut and faceted diamonds.

Reaching the building, Metatron takes a seat on the lowest of the steps – immediately relaxing and allowing his cloak to fall open as he casually crosses his tanned muscular legs and clasps them about the knees with square capable hands. As you catch up, he invites you to join him; and, as you settle at his side, you cannot help but notice that these are the hands of a person accustomed to hard manual work – the fingers unadorned, with close-trimmed nails; the palms calloused and scarred. In complete contrast to this, however, Metatron wears a pair of white leather braces strapped around his wrists and well-muscled forearms, each of which is edged in gold and (again) adorned with the image of a golden Pegasus in flight.

Whilst musing on this paradoxical blend of functional and flamboyant you lift your gaze to scan Metatron's face, which is broad and tanned a deep golden-brown. His strong jaw sports a closely-cropped dark beard, which outlines a full, rather sensual, mouth; whilst deep laughter-lines radiate out from the corners of his deep-set eyes, bracketing a 'roman' nose that has a high and prominent bridge set below bushy black eyebrows. Meeting his gaze, you are surprised to note that the irises of his long-lashed eyes are an unusual tawny-gold, with very deep and reflective black pupils – and, as you survey each other, you sense that he already sees and knows all there is to know about you: yet you find that you are not uncomfortable with his scrutiny, which holds both humour and love.

Continuing your inspection, you scan Metatron's rather minimal apparel, and note that his well-muscled chest is covered with a moulded breastplate made of gold, which is secured by brown leather straps that buckle over his shoulders and round his torso. A pendant that holds a large double-terminated phenacite crystal, which is the crystal that links him with Sophia, his twin flame, rests over his heart – a wide gold band embossed with the image of a rearing Pegasus (which is a recurring theme!) encircling its mid-point and securing it horizontally to the long gold chain that he wears around his neck.

Below the breastplate Metatron is wearing a knee-length white linen underskirt: over this he wears a 'kilt' made of lappets (long tongues) of stiff white leather, each of which has been tooled and edged in gold and embossed with a tiny image of a golden Pegasus in flight in the same style as his wrist braces. Once more a paradoxical mix of function and fashion, the lappets are secured to a brown leather belt that is well-worn and very plain: this fastens with a simple iron buckle, hinting of its utilitarian nature – and noting your interest, Metatron folds back his cloak to show you that (somewhat weirdly) there is what looks like a golden lightning bolt tucked into it on the right-hand side.

The belt itself looks like a workman's tool-belt, with long loops of leather holding a 'tool' of some sort at each hip: the one on his right side holds a square-headed hammer; whilst the one on his left side holds what looks like a bolas (or boleadoras). Examining this more closely, you see that it comprises three different-sized metallic spheres – the smallest being gold, the largest silver, the other bronze – each connected to a large gold ring by long threads of finely-woven iridescent fibres, which are so transparent they are barely visible. Noting your puzzlement, Metatron explains that (very simply) these are strands of 'solidified' Light, which create a device that allows him to bring down and restrain any who deliberately seek to disrupt the Divine flow of Light throughout the Universe – for, as a warrior *of* and *for* that Light, he will not tolerate anything (or anyone) that seeks to interfere with the Divine Laws that regulate its use and application, or meddle with the Divine Rights and Freedoms that the Light confers, explaining:

> "They spin a web of energy, fine, to entangle and entrap – preventing flight and holding fast until I may deal with them – the Light and metals, three, possessing all that is required for combat regardless of space, Time or Dimension..."

METATRON'S TEACHINGS
The Power of the Rainbow and The Light Within:

Recognising you have seen all you need to for now, Metatron stands and – with just a wave of his hand – he creates a luminous rainbow that spans the sky above you in an arc of radiant colour. Smiling, he says that rainbows are one of nature's beautiful gifts that never fail to move the heart and uplift the spirit – for they are symbols of optimism and hope that carry the promise that calm always follows the storm: furthermore, whenever you see a rainbow you may be sure that he is at hand, overseeing the Divine Flow of Light and its regulation, adjustment and balance. Removing his phenacite pendant from around his neck, Metatron then holds it up and points it towards the rainbow, which divides into seven individual arcs of colour (red through to violet) each of which is drawn down into the crystal one by one....

Showing you the crystal, which glows and sparks with a clear white light, Metatron explains that each of your primary chakras (energy centres) innately resonates with the tones of the rainbow of Light that is held with the crystal; and asks you to stand in front of him on the first step: he then holds the crystal in front of your base chakra, and asks you to simply allow the appropriate resonance and quantum of red Light to flow into it, until it is filled and fully charged.... Once this is done, he asks you to move up onto the next step: here he holds the crystal in front of your sacral chakra, asking you to once again allow the appropriate resonance and quantum of Light (this time orange) to flow into it, until it is filled and fully charged....

This done, Metatron guides you up the remainder of the seven steps one by one – each time pausing to allow you to fill and fully charge each of your chakras with the appropriate resonance and quantum of Light in turn, continuing with yellow at your solar plexus chakra on the third step.... with green at your heart chakra on the fourth step.... with blue at your throat chakra on the fifth step.... with indigo at your brow chakra on the sixth step.... and lastly with violet at your crown chakra on the seventh (and final) step....
Once all seven chakras are fully charged, Metatron turns the crystal to lie vertically in front of your heart chakra and tells you that he is always happy to aid and support those who are willing to accept the Light with an open and honest heart: at his words, you feel your heart begin to open and expand, slowly connecting and aligning with each of your other chakras in turn....

This done, your whole energy field starts to expand; and you become aware of all your senses being heightened and sharpened.... somehow you know that you are being completely filled with Divine Light; and you feel a renewed sense of purpose and determination as you connect with your Soul and start to sense the vastness and magnificence of your True Self. In this state too you realise that you innately *know* what is truly you, and what is not – and you begin to appreciate your potential, and understand the worth of working to transform your lower-self into its true Glory....

Once you have reached this point of realisation, Metatron suggests that you sit on the top step to allow time for your energy field to find the state of balance that is right for you at this time, and returns his pendant to his neck. Wrapping his cloak around him, he sits beside you and tells you that clarifying and charging your whole energy field with Light aligns you with the potential of your Highest Being, aiding you in connecting with your Divine spark or Inner Light: this is because the Divine Light that lies at the heart of your Soul holds that which is most in alignment with your True nature, whose innate purity and integrity cannot become tainted or tarnished by any of your life experiences.

Giving you a small crystal with a vivid and intense multicoloured sheen, Metatron tells you that this is **Flame Aura Quartz**, his first Crystal Champion – explaining:

> *"This clear quartz crystal has been bonded with titanium under the application of heat and pressure, such that this element has become part of its structure. As such, the Light that Flame Aura Quartz holds has many diverse and multifaceted applications in both the physical and the non-physical worlds, for titanium powerfully aids connection and communication between worlds and Dimensions. Accordingly, you may use Flame Aura Quartz to help you journey within and without, and/or to support you in connecting with many wise sources of Guidance, especially with those Angelics and Masters who oversee or direct the various spectrum resonances of Light. Close inspection will also allow you to observe that the three most prominent colours in Flame Aura Quartz are magenta, blue and gold – signifying its ability to ignite and empower the three-fold flames of the Lotus of your Heart: those of Divine Love, Power and Wisdom. Yet you will also find that Flame Aura Quartz has more hues and tones than these, signifying that it has the vibrancy to awaken and energise all aspects of any chakra or energy centre, especially those concerned with the establishment of your fifth- and sixth-Dimensional Lightbody. Thus, it is important to apply Flame Aura Quartz with care and discernment, taking time to adjust to its energies gradually, and allowing yourself plenty of time for assimilation of any energy shifts or adjustments between applications – for as its name suggests, it may be somewhat 'fiery' in its nature and effects!"*

With a smile, Metatron affirms that Flame Aura Quartz may therefore, through the full spectrum of Divine and Universal Light, aid you in reconnecting with your Inner Light.

Relaxing back and casually crossing his legs, Metatron tells you that regularly allowing yourself time out to rest and regroup your energies is enormously beneficial to body, mind and spirit: in fact, it is named recreation ('re-creation'!) for good reason – for having some light-hearted fun is one of the most constructive things you can do to aid your self-healing and balance. Smiling again, he adds that, although he can be a tough taskmaster, he has a great sense of humour and greatly values laughter and lightness of heart: indeed, some call him 'The Cosmic Joker'! – yet it is these very characteristics that gives him the fortitude and resolve he needs to carry out his duties, for humour augments the ability to carry and hold the purest Light: hence, if *you* ever feel that life is getting too intense (or you know that you are taking yourself, others, or a situation more seriously than is really warranted) then maybe it is time to take a break and give him a call!

Suddenly you hear something rustling behind you; and turn to see a peacock strutting along beneath the portico – his tail open and erect to show off its beautiful patterning and colours. Metatron laughs, and remarks that the male peacock is a showy bird (a bit like him!) whose power is often overlooked because of the eye-catching splendour of his plumage and what is perceived perhaps to be self-obsessed vanity (and more than a little dim-wittedness): yet in reality the peacock holds the all-embracing Light of the Great Central Sun, and carries the blazing transformative resonances of the lineage of Angels known as the Seraphim; and has simply chosen to hide his intelligence and power through misdirection. Calling the peacock closer, Metatron says that you may, therefore, choose to call upon **Peacock** to teach you how to create the illusion of being less than you are, and/or to stand in front of you if you need a fiery shield of protection;

or to be your guide when it is time to use the fires of transformation to clear and refine your energies, so that you may merge more fully with the Divine Light that IS within you. Asking you to look closely at the peacock's tail feathers, Metatron points out how their 'eyes' display the same iridescent colours of Light as the Flame Aura Quartz he gave you, adding that you can also call Peacock if you simply wish to bring more Light into your life; or want help to work with your crystal to connect with the Ray-Masters of Light; or to come to your aid if you need to add or restore brilliance, colour or beauty to any aspect of your life. Suddenly closing and lowering his tail, the peacock gives a raucous cry, before strutting even closer.... then, with an attention-seeking rattle, he opens and fans it out again: laughing appreciatively at his blatant display of self-importance, Metatron says that you may also call upon Peacock if you need to bolster your self-esteem; or if you want to have more self-confidence and self-assurance during times of personal or spiritual evolution or change, when he may arrive to facilitate and guide your transition from one stunningly beautiful state to another! With a knowing wink, Metatron looks you in the eye, and adds that whenever you see a peacock fan open its tail you may be confident that your alchemical process of self-transformation is on track, and that an end to your current phase of hard work is in sight.

The Gift of The Lightning Bolt of Divine Inspiration:
Getting to his feet, Metatron casually plucks the lightning bolt from his belt and hurls it into the sky: as it rockets away from you, it takes on the blue-white hue of super-heated metal; before plummeting to the ground in the distance, leaving a metallic trail of silver-gold sparks in its wake. In the instant that it strikes the ground, everything is illuminated by an explosion of blindingly-white light; and you hear the familiar 'crack' of a lightning strike: for a moment everything around you loses its colour and becomes starkly black and white – and you have to blink a few times to restore and clear your sight. As you do, Metatron returns to sit at your side, explaining that his lightning bolt is charged with the Metatronic Light of Illumination – and thus it has both the power to reveal all things fully, completely, truthfully and accurately; and the purity to illuminate all darkness, highlight all extremes, and expose whatever is hidden: this means that its Light always shows the true nature of whatever it touches upon – revealing anything that hides in the shadows, and showing up anything that attempts to conceal or disguise what is truly there. With a smile, he says that it can therefore help you to identify, understand and reconcile any extreme or contradictory thoughts and behaviours you harbour, by helping you recognise what is real and unreal; safe and unsafe; true and false; valid and invalid – which, in turn, will help you decide what you want (and don't want) to 'be' or 'have' in your present and future reality. Holding out his hand Metatron chuckles, adding that Metatronic energy is also dynamic and adaptable, with the ability to travel 'from A to B' faster than the blink of an eye – and, as if by magic, his lightning bolt is once more there in his hand....

Balancing it on his left palm, and using his right index finger to slowly trace its zigzags from one end to the other, Metatron explains that the lightning bolt defines the descent of the Divine Light through the Tree of Life – passing down from the realm of

Divine Light and Will; through the realms of Wisdom, Understanding and Reason – and then onwards. At the end of the bolt he pauses, before slowly repeating the action very deliberately: this reveals a line of arcane glyphs, which momentarily glow with a bright silver-blue Light before fading from view. With another smile he says that thus, in addition to offering illumination and catalysing change, his lightning bolt has the power to fire and inspire the mind – enabling all knowledge gained to be applied with genuine wisdom, with the ultimate objective of self-realisation and Enlightenment.

Metatron moves to kneel in front of you, reminding you that humankind's ultimate goal is to seek out and find the truth of their nature and their reason for existence, which may only be found through inner illumination and by making a conscious connection to the Divine Source of Truth and Light itself. He then traces his finger down the length of the lightning bolt for a third time, before repeating the movement in the air in front of your head: this leaves an energetic imprint of the golden lightning bolt hovering between you – and, with a gentle touch to your brow, Metatron directs this into your body so that it comes to rest within your pranic core, spanning the root of your crown, brow and throat chakras....

Telling you that you have received his Gift of The Lightning Bolt of Divine Inspiration to aid your understanding, progress and growth, Metatron rests a hand reassuringly on your shoulder and says he will always support you in accepting and opening to its Light – giving you the strength and courage to see the truth; and the self-belief and determination to do whatever is necessary to bring about positive transformation, change and growth. Returning to your side, he explains that such self-empowerment is possible because (as in the physical world) his lightning bolt's strike may ignite a potent fire that compellingly promotes and motivates change – and, if you choose to yield to its power, you will recognise with greater ease and certainty why (and how) to demolish the outmoded and unwanted to make way for the fresh and the new.

Directing you to now take your attention back to his Gift, Metatron asks you to become aware of its gentle warmth and subtle light; and suggests that you allow its Light to reveal anything you want (or need) to change in or about yourself or your life – reminding you that you can also call upon Amethystia's Gift of The Amethyst Flame for added clarity, if you feel this would be helpful....

After allowing you a little time to identify something that you know requires (or would benefit from) change, Metatron instructs you to ask the lightning bolt to help you recognise or know the solution or path that will enable you to bring about the change you need (or desire) with the greatest ease. He emphasises that it is important you do not try too hard, but that you relax and simply *allow* your mind to be open to receive what might (at first) seem to be random thoughts; and reminds you that you can also use Tzadkiel's Gift of The Violet Flame to help you transmute any unwanted, detrimental or obstructive thoughts or feelings you encounter as you work things through....

After a while, you find your thoughts return to more commonplace matters; and, with a smile, Metatron observes that sometimes you need to allow time for 'muddied waters' to settle and clarify before knowing how to proceed – adding that it is important to remember that every 'problem' has more than one solution, and hence the straightest and/or most obvious path is not always the easiest – or the most effective, which is why it is vital to keep an open mind and think things through carefully and methodically.

Giving you a small and opaque butter-yellow polished stone, Metatron tells you that this is **Yellow Jasper**, his second Crystal Champion – explaining:

> *"Yellow Jasper carries the Light of the Gold and Yellow Rays of Divine Wisdom and Illumination, making it a valuable and useful companion at any stage of your journey. It is a stone of discernment and contentment that knows and understands both its role and purpose in BEing, and fulfils both with patience and steely resolve: this fortitude and tenacity can assist and support you when times are difficult or hard – encouraging the state of mind that promotes a willingness to learn; whilst offering the inner strength that will help you to accept and grow from what you might view as your 'mistakes'. Yellow Jasper also grounds the full Light of the Sun, enabling you to assimilate its life-giving energies, regardless of hour or season: this makes it a perfect support for your solar plexus chakra and mental Body, aiding and balancing logical, well-ordered thought and clarity of mind. Yellow Jasper's energy is forthright, honest and frank – yet it also has a laid back and 'sunny' disposition that can help cheer you on dark days, showing you how to retain (or find!) your sense of humour if you need to relax and enjoy life more."*

With a smile, Metatron affirms that Yellow Jasper may therefore help you in working with his Gift – lighting the way if things are unclear, and giving you greater insight, wisdom or courage if your path is difficult or demanding.

Turning, Metatron gives a low whistle, at which a large lion in his prime, with a solid well-muscled body and dense shaggy mane, emerges from the doorway of the building behind you. He pads assuredly over to lie at Metatron's feet, who strokes its head (producing a contented rumble as he does so) and tells you that the lion is a noble and regal animal that embodies Solar qualities like strength, courage, endurance and wise leadership: accordingly you may call upon **Lion** to be your guide if it is time to claim the sovereignty of your 'inner king'; or if you need help to strengthen or balance your 'masculine' side – including any of the energies or attributes of your base, solar plexus and throat chakras; or if you need your left-brain and logical mind to take the lead. Metatron smiles and remarks that – like all cats – lions innately know the exact amount of energy required to launch, perform and accomplish any action with precision and ease: therefore Lion may also teach you a great deal about the wise use, direction and conservation of energy and power within body, mind and/or spirit. Watching him begin to relax and doze, Metatron chuckles and observes that all cats value rest and sleep, when (in dream state) they travel far: thus Lion, being a strong protector and infinitely wise counsellor, is an excellent choice of companion when travelling – whether in physicality or in spirit. With a knowing look, he adds that Lion can also be asked to be your guide when travelling out-of-body with the express purpose of exploring other worlds or Dimensions, when he will support you in interacting with those that inhabit them: this can be of particular help in connecting you with some of the Galactic Masters linked with Earth's ancient past, including those of the Lion People (or Lionel); the Paschats; the Hathors and the ones known as the Crystal People.

The Star-borne Hammer of Dissolution and Creation:
Asking you to accompany him, Metatron leads you back down the steps, and draws his hammer from its loop on his belt. Encouraging you to sit, he lays it across your lap, inviting you to feel and sense its energies: to the eye it resembles nothing more than a short-handled sledgehammer; but as you run a hand over the hammer's head, you feel the metal warm to your touch, and sense it begin to spark with vitality. Metatron explains that the head is made of meteorite iron, which is the Cosmic aspect of hematite; and which has the power to awaken, anchor and ground the Kundalini energy that sleeps at the base of your spine. Smiling again, he adds that this energy has been given many interpretations – yet, at its most simple, the awakening of the Kundalini is about raising your consciousness through your pranic core to your heart and crown, in order to attain Union with your Christed-self and thus engender a heightened state of awareness and clarity: this means his hammer can bring about significant awakenings and initiate substantial change – if you are ready and willing to accept its catalytic actions.

Encouraging you to rest your hands on the hammer's oak handle, Metatron asks you to feel its solidity and strength of purpose: indeed, you can tell how years of handling have polished it smooth; and, as you connect with its energy, you feel your spine straighten and your body fill with resolute strength. Recognising this, Metatron tells you that he wants you to understand more about how his hammer serves him in his role as a Forge-Master and Smith – before lifting it from your hands and striking it on the ground in front of you: at this there is a loud thunderclap of energy, and everything goes white....

As the dust clears, you find yourself standing in front of a long open-fronted building that has whitewashed walls and a low terracotta tiled roof. Metatron is at your side, and he explains that this is his smithy: inviting you to step inside, he shows you how the centre of the building is occupied by the fiery hearth of the forge, in front of which a large anvil sits beside a wide bench holding various tools. To the right, the walls and floor are covered with metal objects in various stages of completion; whilst to the left a large wheel-like wooden structure of posts and cogs sits beside a fenced-off enclosure and a straw-filled stall: this is home to a small brown donkey, who senses your presence and ambles across to the fence.

Bending down, Metatron strokes her creamy muzzle and explains that this humble little beast drives the wheel that powers the bellows of his forge, making the fiery process of transformation possible. With a smile, he comments that donkeys are said to be stubborn, but he sees them as determined and persistent, which are two very valuable traits to have! He adds that donkeys are also willing and intelligent workers who very quickly understand what is required of them: hence **Donkey** may help you learn how to absorb and retain useful knowledge, information and instructions; or aid you in developing and trusting your intuitive or instinctive 'knowing'. Gently rubbing her long fuzzy ears, Metatron remarks that donkeys have excellent hearing, so Donkey can also help you develop your clairaudient skills, and enhance your awareness of all forms of inner and outer communication. Moving his hand down to rest on the darker cross-shape on her shoulders and back, he explains that this mark honours the donkey's humble willingness to be of service to others by bearing and sharing their burdens – thus you can be sure that Donkey will be a faithful and dedicated companion when you are in need of a friend. After a final pat, he leads the donkey to the wheel, where it takes its place and begins to walk.... as Metatron watches, he muses that often work can be monotonous or boringly repetitive – but by calling upon Donkey you can learn to value every aspect of what you do, and appreciate what those (often mundane) tasks produce in the longer term – both for yourself, and for others. With a chuckle he remarks that such work is interestingly sometimes referred to as 'donkey-work' – yet without someone willing to do it, nothing of value or consequence would ever be achieved!

As the donkey continues its slow steady pace, you become aware of the creaking and whistling of the giant bellows that it powers; and watch as the fire of the furnace glows with increasing depth, until it eventually turns golden-white: noting this, Metatron strides over to his work table; removes his cloak and breastplate; dons a large leather apron; and picks up a dull black bar of metal.... plunging this into the heart of the fire, he watches the metal change colour until it glows deep golden-yellow, and then removes it with a pair of tongs: placing it on the flat of his anvil, he then wields his hammer in a seamless series of swift but steady strokes, striking and turning it repeatedly. With every hammer-strike black dust and impurities fall away, and the colour of the metal slowly fades to a dull red glow – at which point Metatron returns it to the fire, before repeating the processes of heating, turning, folding, hammering and shaping....

As he works, he explains that he is using his hammer firstly to strike away anything that is not of the pure substance of the metal (pointing out how each time it is returned to the fire the metal emerges stronger and purer); and, secondly, to mould and transform the metal, in order to make manifest the concept or ideal that he has in mind in the most efficient and effective way.... Time passes, and Metatron continues to craft the metal until he is finally satisfied with the result, at which he quenches it in a trough of water, before calling the donkey from her wheel and thanking her for her work. Giving you the item he has made, he says that he has created it to help you shape your future with more skill – suggesting that you research its symbolism later, in order to understand more.

After removing his apron and washing himself off in a nearby barrel of cool water, Metatron shows you some of the items that line the walls and floor of the forge: you notice that some pieces are obviously still 'work in progress', whilst others are finished, albeit in different ways – some are simply burnished; some ornately enamelled; some very intricately embossed or engraved – yet all are superbly fit for purpose. Noting your surprise at some of the artistry and complex detailing, Metatron smiles and points out that it *is* possible for anything you create to be both functional *and* beautiful – although it is acceptable to make compromises as you work towards that outcome, if that is the best (or most) you can achieve at that time. With a laugh, he says that sometimes you simply have to get on with it and 'make do and mend' – although, in his experience, the best and most effective construction and creation follows a series of well-ordered steps, whereby you address, refine and perfect each stage in turn – constantly reviewing and considering your progress and hammering out imperfections, before planning and moving on to the next. Often, he muses, it helps to stand back and take time to think – and ask yourself: is this right and fit for purpose?... is this what I meant to create?... is there a better way to do this?... would something other than this be more appropriate or more effective, or offer greater precision or greater strength?... (and so on). With a wry smile, he adds that sometimes 'deconstruction' is the only way forwards – and if this is the case it is vital to be willing to recognise it, and to be prepared to demolish or take it apart, and start again.

Returning to the forge, Metatron plucks a small crystal from its heart with a pair of tongs, and quenches its heat in the water trough before giving it to you. You find that it is a polished piece of clear crystal, dotted with tiny orange streaks; and Metatron tells you that this is **Haematoid Quartz**, his third Crystal Champion – explaining:

> *"This quartz crystal has been marked by minute traces of hematite, which is the mineral that resonates most strongly with the Earth's molten iron core. Yet despite its earthing qualities, hematite has a unique vibration that can clearly connect you with the wisdom of Higher-frequency planetary and Cosmic energies, whilst simultaneously helping you to fully ground and integrate whatever information or knowledge you access. In this way Haematoid Quartz may help you connect with your Self that IS throughout all Times and Planes of Dimension, and so aid you in understanding how all your aspects are simply facets of a much greater whole. The clear quartz that embraces the markings within allows Haematoid Quartz to amplify and focus your attributes like a mirror, powerfully highlighting your 'perfections' and 'imperfections' and enabling you to examine each aspect in detail, in order that you may recognise and appreciate the many positive and constructive qualities that every part brings you. Haematoid Quartz can then help you identify any part or aspect that, after due consideration, you decide you no longer want or require; before attracting the might of my hammer to help you break and reform it into something else, that is hopefully more positive and productive! Lastly (on a subtle energy level), Haematoid Quartz has an affinity with your lower three chakras and the Omega centre of your Unified Body, through which it has the facility to rouse the power of the Kundalini from its slumbers – thus aiding and supporting you in the grounding and integration of your Christed-self and your Lightbody."*

Smiling, Metatron affirms that Haematoid Quartz may therefore bring you the Cosmic Power and Wisdom that will support you in restructuring your Self (and your life!) – pointing out that everything you have observed here is a metaphor for your personal growth and spiritual evolution; and reassuring you that (even though change can be difficult and/or uncomfortable) the future consequence of whatever restructuring you choose to undertake will be more precious than gold, and more valuable than diamonds!

The Greenwood Guardians – Chile Pine and Redwood:

His *personal* mentoring complete for now, Metatron affirms he is always available to aid and support you: you need only bring him to mind and ask for his presence, and he will attend you. Furthermore, he tells you that two great Tree Beings of the Plant Kingdom have also asked to support you in addressing his Theme of 'RESTRUCTURE YOUR LIFE', adding that you need only request *their* presence, and they will be with you.

He explains that the first of these Greenwood Guardians is the Masculine essence of Chile Pine (Monkey Puzzle Tree), who has asked to overlight and help you ground whatever work you undertake within *any* aspect of his chapter. The second is the Masculine essence of Redwood, who has specifically asked to help you understand and assimilate his Gift of The Lightning Bolt of Divine Inspiration (if you have chosen to accept it).

When you are ready to connect with Metatron's first Greenwood Guardian, you need simply call for the presence of **Chile Pine** (*) .... Chile Pine envelops you in a deep jade-green Light, and the Masculine spirit essence of Chile Pine speaks to you, saying:

"All that I AM I would share with you, for despite my physical body's short-lived existence, my Soul is ancient beyond knowing and my spirit embraces the Heavens. Over aeons I have come to appreciate Earth's many and varied life-giving blessings that nourish and inspire me, and am ever aware of her Illumined Wisdom and the Christed-Light that enfolds her. Thus, through the riches of that gold at my core I can offer you both strength and wisdom: so let me help you ground yourself fully, that you too may know the blessings of the Earth, and thence find balance and healing in our embrace. Then let me connect you with the Trinity of Love, Wisdom and Power that guides, inspires and protects you in every moment; and with the Highest Realms of Spirit that empower your Soul to recognise and know the beauty and intricate design that is at the purposeful heart of all things. Then you may understand the true nature and purpose of 'black' and 'white' and know *the steps you need to take in order to fulfil the promise of immortality, and BE in the diamond-clear Light of Divine Mind...."*

(* Tiger Iron and Scolecite will help you ground and connect with the energies and wisdom of Chile Pine, if you wish to enhance your experience using crystals.)

If you have chosen to accept and work with Metatron's Gift, and when you are ready to connect with his second Greenwood Guardian, you need simply call for the presence of **Redwood** (*) .... Redwood envelops you in a diffuse scarlet Light, and the Masculine spirit essence of Redwood speaks to you, saying:

"As one of the tallest living Beings on Earth I offer you the benefit of my insightful wisdom and my dispassionate strength, acquired through countless centuries of growth. I have watched seasons come and go – and seen empires and civilisations rise and fall – and yet still the Earth turns, and her nurture and love prevails. Hence, I can help you understand the reasoning behind the many varied seasons of your life, and thus aid you in identifying the patterns that underlie your own strength and wisdom, which is held within your core. So allow yourself to sink into the gentle softness of my bark, and become as ONE with me.... allow me to help you extend your awareness down through the roots that lie far below your feet, so that you may sense and know that the Earth fires and feeds the growth of your heart and the love that it holds.... then let me help you reach up, so that you may sense and know that the Heavens fire and feed the growth of your mind and the wisdom that it holds. Then simply allow my peace and light to fill and ground you; and let my steadfastness give you the courage and determination to clarify and balance yourself heart, mind and Soul, so that ALL you truly are may fire and inspire all creation...."

(* Hematite and Kambala Jasper will help you ground and connect with the energies and wisdom of Redwood, if you wish to enhance your experience using crystals.)

ARCHEIA SOPHIA

'BALANCE THROUGH BRAVERY'

CRYSTAL CHAMPIONS:

Tiger Eye ♥ Charoite ♥ Blue Lace Agate

CREATURE COMPANIONS:

Squirrel ♥ Rabbit ♥ Mountain Lion

GREENWOOD GUARDIANS:

Robinia ♥ Beech

*I am an Alchemical Master of Balance.
I maintain perfect and appropriate
equilibrium at all times.*

MEETING SOPHIA

It is dusk on a fine summer's evening, and you find yourself sitting on the grassy bank of a slow-running river, which is meandering through the lush heart of a remote and peaceful valley. The river is generously wide, and (although deep in parts) is dotted with sandbars – their shallows lined with rocks and rounded pebbles, around which the waters eddy and swirl. As you listen to the river's burbling song, you contentedly dangle your bare feet in the water, which cools and soothes them; and enjoy the last warm and gentle caresses of the sun as it drops ever lower in the sky – its lengthening rays reflecting off the gently rippling surface of the river in sparkles of silvery light. The floor of the valley where you rest is carpeted in meadow grass, which also contours the slopes that lie in the shelter of an ancient oak woodland that densely clads the valley's crown; and, as your gaze absorbs the majestic splendour of the mass of trees, you find yourself captivated by their beauty, and begin to sense their ancient and wise energies calling you to them.

Feeling a tingle of anticipation (and comprehending that this is a sacred and magical place where – perhaps – anything is possible), you lift your feet from the water and hurry through the meadow. Ascending the slope as quickly as you can, you finally reach the trees: here, a little breathless, you take a rest and look back over the valley, surprised at how far you have climbed. All around you is still – and so, feeling relaxed and at peace, you close your eyes and listen to the sweet melodious sound of a blackbird singing its farewells to the day. Gradually you sense how the dry warmth of the day is giving way to a moist coolness you can feel on your skin and on the flattened grass beneath your feet; and you become aware of the many subtly sweet and earthy scents that surround you: these seem to grow in complexity and profundity with each breath you take, as if you are breathing-in and absorbing the very essence of this place – and so, for a while, you allow yourself to just 'be' in the energies....

Eventually you open your eyes, and see that the last rays of the sun are kissing the fading outline of the trees that silhouette the opposite side of the valley. Enthralled, you stand awhile and enjoy the stillness and solitude as the stars emerge and multiply – the night sky gradually darkening and filling with silvery pinpricks of light, as if a giant hand has randomly scattered millions of tiny diamonds across a vast expanse of deep-indigo velvet. Finally the clarity of your vision begins to fade, and all colours turn to grey – a solitary barn owl gliding over the meadow below you nothing more than a soundless drift of spectral white: then suddenly you hear a rustling behind you, and turn to see a rabbit hopping through the trees towards you. This is illuminated by a nimbus of bright silvery light, which appears to be following in its footsteps, and which (as it draws closer) you realise surrounds and encircles the tall and imposing figure of a woman: this is Archeia Sophia. She opens her arms to you in welcome, declaring:

"I am Sophia, the Lady Constance – Keeper of the Alchemical Mysteries, Wielder of the Key of Tau, and twin flame of Metatron of the Light. I am the Stars to his Sun; the night to his day; the Silver to his Gold. Know then that I have the grace, nobility and stamina to work tirelessly with him, partnering him as he works ceaselessly to carry out the Will of The Divine. And so, I extend to you my hands in friendship and offer you the love of my heart and the light of my Soul, that your heart may be steady and your mind strong

and wise as you walk your path in the human world. For in my role I fully understand and embrace the nature of perfect balance, and I would aid you in your search for the Holy Grail: the Light and essence of The Divine that has the Power to open you to the reality of your True nature, which in truth lies within. Accordingly I will encourage your endeavours to be the best that you can, as you work to reveal your Light to the world – so walk with me now, and let us move forwards as ONE into a complete and balanced state of Being, to fearlessly face the New Dawn together with impassioned hearts full of Love and illumined minds full of the Light of Grace."

Sophia then stoops and lifts the rabbit into her arms, before turning to lead you down a narrow track that winds its way into the dark woodland behind her – the soft whispering of the oak leaves and the arching embrace of their ancient branches welcoming you as you pass within.

As you follow Sophia's silvery outline the woodland seems to come alive – your route marked out by the tiny glimmers of light being emitted by hundreds of glow-worms that adorn the branches of the trees lining your way, like delicate strands of fairy-lights. Their soft glow illuminates a black-and-white masked racoon that (rather oddly) seems to be following in your footsteps; whilst the spectral barn owl you noticed before drifts like white mist through the trees at your side....

After a while the track widens, finally ending at a mossy glade set within a clearing that is open to the night sky above: here Sophia gently places the rabbit on the ground – and, once the creatures that accompanied you have all returned to the shelter of the forest, beckons you forwards to stand at her side. This enables you to see the eight tall standing stones that form an open circle in the centre of the clearing: the circle is about sixteen paces wide; and each standing stone is just a little larger than a fully grown person. In the centre of the circle a mass of silvery flames blazes in a wide bronze bowl, their light illuminating the eight stones that encircle it – each stone seemingly both absorbing *and* enhancing this with a subtle light and energy of their own, which causes them each to softly glow, as if lit from within.

Directing you to pass between two of the stones and enter the stone circle, Sophia stands aside and lets you choose your way in.... this done, you step forwards and walk towards the fire – glancing at the glowing stones as you pass: this reveals that they seem to be covered with glyphs; and, although you do not understand their meaning or their significance, you realise that these give the stones their power, and you gain a sense of their ancient and wise protection, which simultaneously strengthens and grounds you....

Once you reach the fire, Sophia too passes into the circle: as she does so, the stones absorb the silvery nimbus that surrounded her, until it appears as if you are now encircled by eight shimmering Beings of Light – and, as this happens and the diaphanous glimmer around her fades, her form is fully revealed.... With a smile, Sophia settles on the ground next to the hearth, and invites you to sit at her side so that you may take a little time to examine her and become comfortable with her energies – and those of this special place.

As you join her, the firelight falls on her heart-shaped face so that the first thing you notice are her eyes: these are blessed with long lush dark lashes and astonishingly vivid violet irises; and, as she meets your gaze, you become drawn into their depths and realise that they hold incredible Power and wisdom – yet you also perceive the calm practical nature (and wry sense of humour) that is at the heart of who she is. Dragging your attention away to examine the rest of her face, you find that she has a well-defined bone structure, with paradoxically strong – almost masculine – features that reflect the strength that lies within. All is framed by a lustrous mass of thick and wavy dark brown hair, which she wears simply brushed back from her face and over her shoulders, from where it ripples unconfined to her waist.

Sitting with her back regally erect, Sophia is resting her hands in the lap of her gown, which is fashioned from a heavy midnight-blue silk shot through with threads of shimmering silver. The full-length gown fits her snugly to the waist, and has a low scooped neckline that shows off her womanly figure and pale flawless skin to perfection; whilst its sleeves fit her upper arms closely to her elbows, before flaring out to drape in soft folds around her wrists. The full skirt billows around her and falls in folds around her tucked up legs, revealing her long and slender feet, which are clad in silver dancing slippers dotted with hundreds of tiny sparkling diamonds: these catch the firelight to give off multitudinous sparks of rainbow light, which flicker and dance all around you.

Looking up, you realise that some of the sparks are being reflected by two metallic-looking objects that are resting in Sophia's lap; whilst (rather oddly) a third object, which is matte-black, palm-sized, flat and rectangular appears to be absorbing them. Closer inspection reveals that each of the first two objects is attached to opposite ends of a long plaited silver cord that is stitched securely to her gown from elbow to elbow – running up the back of each arm and spanning her shoulders below the nape of her neck: the cord itself continues on past her elbows and hangs freely to her wrists, so that the objects it secures (a small silver cup-shaped bowl; and something that looks like a T-shaped 'key') can be accessed quickly and easily. Intriguingly, the third object, which hangs on the right-hand side, dangles from a separate cord made of the same light-absorbing material as the object itself – and, noting your interest, Sophia simply smiles.

Your curiosity satisfied for the time being, you shift your attention to the pendant that is suspended from a heavy silver chain around her neck: this holds a superbly clear double-terminated phenacite crystal, which is the crystal that links Sophia with Metatron, her twin flame. The crystal sits vertically over her heart – a wide band of silver embossed with an image of a Pegasus in flight encircling its centre point, and serving to secure it to the chain. Noting your gaze, Sophia lifts her left hand to touch the crystal with her long and slender fingers, enabling the firelight to illuminate the ring that adorns her middle finger – its wide silver band and inset oval cabochon of highly-polished silvery-grey meteorite iron giving off hundreds of tiny silver and gold sparks, which dance with the sparks of rainbow light created by the diamonds on her slippers, before being drawn into the crystal in her pendant, causing it to fill with a luminous inner fire.

SOPHIA'S TEACHINGS
The Gift of The Absolute Light of The Illumined Heart:
Recognising that you have seen all you need to for now, Sophia helps you to your feet, and leads you over to take a closer look at one of the eight standing stones.... Here,

she encourages you to examine its blue-grey surface, whose depths have a greenish cast, spotted with creamy star-like flecks; and tells you that this ancient stone is known as a 'Bluestone'. She explains that each of these stones holds information concerning Earth's history, and acts rather like a radio antenna to connect the planet with the rest of the Solar System – adding that, in this way wisdom and understanding can be shared, not only for the benefit of humankind, but for *all* sentient life-forms that exist in this small part of the Galaxy. Sophia then runs her hands over a few of the glyphs engraved on the stone, at which they flicker and spark with a silvery-grey light; and tells you that as you come to understand and truly know who you are, and accept *all* that is within your heart (both dark and light), then you may be able to sense and interpret the stones' vibrations, and read the histories and records that they hold – not just of Earth, but of *all* the planets and bodies that comprise the Solar System.

With a smile, she stresses that it would be folly to assume that Earth stands alone in her evolution and growth – then turns to face the fire and gestures to the bowl that holds the silvery flames in the centre of the stone circle. Sophia explains that the bronze that forms it is an alloy of copper and tin, which (alchemically) relate to three other planets of the Solar System: *copper* aligning Earth with Venus (the source of the Flame of Truth and Light) and aiding the multidimensional transmission of information and knowledge; and *tin* aligning Earth with Jupiter (the local base for the Healing Academies of Light of this Galactic quadrant) and Neptune (the distribution point for the Ten Sacred Rays of the Solar System), and aiding the processes of evolution and change through dissolution and expansion.

Guiding you to stand between two of the standing stones, and reassuring you that what she is about to do is quite safe, Sophia smiles and adds that she has found bronze to have an inherent strength that will not tarnish or wear – for it is both the metal of the Warrior, forged before time, with the power to shield and support, whilst opening you to all potentials; *and* the metal of the Seeker, with the alchemical power to help transform the 'lead' of your lower nature into the 'gold' of your perfected Self. She then walks to the centre of the circle, and steps into the bowl: at this the flames flare and absorb all that she is, merging into a single silver flame that grows taller and taller, until it is three times as tall as the standing stones around you; and then, with a flash of light, the bronze bowl vanishes – and your vision blurs....

As your sight clears, you can see that nine beams of light (each one a different colour) have converged in a halo around the flame: one beam has been projected up from the ground beneath the flame and is gold in colour; the others have each been projected out from one of the eight stones that form the circle – one red, one orange, one yellow, one green, one blue, one indigo, one violet and one pearlescent-white, so that it seems as if the silver flame is at the very heart of a circular rainbow wheel.... then slowly all the beams merge with the flame, gradually coalescing into a single column of blazing white light that is so bright you have to shield your eyes.... Eventually you sense the light dimming, and (taking a swift peek) see Sophia – now standing beside a very tall standing stone that appears to be made of snow-white quartz, its shimmering light illuminating the ground around her – beckoning you forwards....

As you reach her, Sophia lifts her pendant from around her neck, and touches one end of it to the glowing white pillar: using the crystal, she draws out a fist-sized sphere of clear light, which is held within a translucent shell of rainbow light that makes it look a little like a soap bubble, and manoeuvres it until it floats in front of your body.... Telling you that this is her Gift of The Absolute Light of the Illumined Heart, she says that it is her hope that its Light will help you know yourself fully, so that you may come to accept and value all that you are, all that you learn, and all that you know. Smiling, she adds that its Rainbow Light will be boosted each time you call upon the power of her twin flame's Gift, because the Lightning Bolt will act as a conduit that can channel even more Light down through your pranic core, enabling you to more fully ground it into the heart of who you are.

Sophia now directs the sphere into your chest so that it encompasses your Gaia centre; and waits for it to settle and come to a balance.... Once she is satisfied, she bows and returns her pendant to her neck – telling you that it is her dearest wish that your Gaia centre is henceforth always filled with the clear Light of Divine Source, and your heart always held in its Rainbow Light; before leading you out of the circle of standing stones towards a mossy cluster of tree roots that offer a resting place beneath the wide-spread branches of an ancient oak tree at the edge of the clearing.

Here she invites you to take your ease, before conjuring up a new fire and settling at your side. Drawing your attention to a red squirrel that (oddly) is busily gathering fallen acorns, even though autumn has not yet arrived, Sophia chuckles and reminds you that, here, anything is possible! As you both watch the squirrel dart about collecting, hiding and burying his finds, she says that **Squirrel** can teach you a great deal about flexibility, resourcefulness and quick change of direction – all of which may help you in planning and implementing your programme of self-transformation. She adds that squirrels have excellent spatial awareness, which not only helps them remember where they had stashed their booty when they need to retrieve it but also aids their surefooted agility when leaping from tree to tree: hence, you may ask Squirrel to help you if you want to recall facts or retrieve information that is stored in your memory or subconscious; or if you need to make 'lightning quick' decisions – logically or intuitively – with greater ease and clarity. Smiling, Sophia says that she admires squirrel's determination and perseverance, and its intelligent ability to try out a variety of approaches to achieve its goals – thus, you may also find Squirrel's guidance useful if you have reached a dead end and want a fresh perspective, or need encouragement to keep on going. Furthermore, she tells you that squirrels understand how to go with the ebb and flow of the seasons and cycles of the natural world, and innately know when the time is right to rest, work and play: hence, Squirrel may also teach you how to choose between action or deliberation, gathering in or giving out, applying logic and reason or trusting on your 'gut feelings' and intuition; as well as helping you recognise the importance of holding the appropriate degree of balance in the many aspects of your life – including in and between your work-life, home-life and spiritual life – so that you may learn how to differentiate between what you *want* and what you *need*.

Reaching down, Sophia picks up an acorn that the squirrel has dropped by her feet:

splitting it open, she extracts from it a small polished stone with a chatoyancy that shifts between golden-yellow and brown in the light of the fire; and, with a smile, she gives it to you, saying that this is **Tiger Eye**, her first Crystal Champion – explaining:

> *"Tiger Eye has a well-grounded, stable energy that is nonetheless somewhat fiery: this means that it can strengthen your mental and emotional determination and commitment, and inspire you to take positive and effective action in response to the daily demands and challenges of everyday life. Tiger Eye resonates especially strongly with the solar plexus chakra and mental (thinking) Body, and so can help activate and clarify your intellect and logical mind, whilst bringing you into alignment with Divine Wisdom: hence, it can be of great help as you seek to understand more about yourself, your path and your place in the world. Tiger Eye is born into the world as indigo-blue Hawks Eye, and only changes into this golden-brown form upon exposure to oxygen, offering a metaphor for your ability to attain the state of Christ-consciousness through connecting with the Light and Wisdom of the Universe. Therefore, because it evolved in this way, Tiger Eye can also connect you with the power of your intuitive mind, and help you accept that sometimes simply innately knowing something is enough! Moreover, as Tiger Eye helps ground the Golden Light of Christed-consciousness, it can promote an open-minded attitude that embraces compassion and balance, encouraging you to see all the aspects of an issue or situation in order to find the best possible solution that is both wise and non-judgmental; whilst its Gold Ray aspect strengthens and grounds the Wisdom of your Higher-self, and makes BEing in the everyday world a more joyful, exciting and fulfilling experience."*

With a smile, Sophia affirms that (as a stone that links Heaven to Earth) Tiger Eye may therefore aid your growth by helping you to access, ground and assimilate Higher knowledge and information.

The Crucible and The Alchemy of The Silver-Violet Flame:
Sitting back, Sophia explains that all processes of inner and outer transformation are triggered in accordance with subconscious needs and desires, and so are a natural process of personal and spiritual evolution: however, where this comes about without conscious volition or awareness; or where it is resisted or avoided (commonly because of the fears people naturally have about undertaking the potentially difficult or painful processes that self-directed transformation often necessitates and requires – or of its consequences) the process is slow, and frequently a struggle.

Taking your hand, Sophia acknowledges that all life-experiences can, of course, be testing (sometimes almost unbearably so), and so require both courage and determination to endure and overcome: yet when you choose to immerse yourself in the processes of transformation – and actively and willingly direct them – you will find that *consciously* working upon yourself (body, mind, emotions and spirit) to address and resolve such testing issues or situations will enable you to initiate many positive shifts and changes. Smiling again, she adds that this in turn will allow you to accept and assimilate many new energies and potentials, speeding you towards your ultimate goal of Enlightenment more efficiently and effectively.

Affirming that she will help you find the courage you need to conquer your fears and so bring about the profound transformation you seek, Sophia detaches the tiny silver bowl from the silver cord that hangs from her left elbow. Showing you that this is just a simple – yet sturdy – bowl, she explains that this serves her as a 'crucible', which (from an alchemists perspective) is simply an open vessel that is a suitable (and safe) container to use when there is need to transform or change something from one state of being to another. With a smile, she adds that her twin flame is very familiar with this one's use, as it may be used to collect or hold molten metals – although, esoterically, it fundamentally provides a discrete space where anything (or anyone!) may be exposed to (or experience) any force or forces that promote change.

Then, asking only for your trust in return, she places her tiny crucible in your open palms.... slowly it grows until it fills your cupped hands; and then its outside warms with a gentle heat, as waves of silver light begin to pulse around its inner surface.... observing this, Sophia asks you to use the Light of your heart (enhanced by her Gift, if you chose to accept it) to help you identify whatever you know you *need* to change most about your life or your Self as a priority now – considering, perhaps, your lifestyle; or your personal situation; or your long-term aims and ambitions; or your thoughts and thinking processes; or your feelings and reactions to something that is affecting you at this time....

After allowing you enough time to isolate something you know is vital to address, Sophia asks you to determine what you fear most about the processes or consequences of dealing with and making that change.... as you consider this, she asks you to instinctively allocate whatever arises a shape and a colour....

As you begin to give your fears form, the exterior of the crucible shimmers, and a line of glyphs materialises just below its outer rim: seeing this, Sophia encourages you to make your fears yet more tangible, suggesting that you also give them a texture – and maybe even a sound and an aroma – reassuring you that whatever is taking form cannot harm you; and stressing that whatever it is does not need to make any logical sense....

After a while, the glyphs round the rim of the bowl start to glow with a silvery-gold light – and then, when she is happy you have made your fears 'real' enough – Sophia directs you to imagine you are placing whatever your mind has given form into the bowl of the crucible, releasing it *fully* from your mind as you do so....

This done, Sophia leans over the bowl, and projects two beams of violet-coloured Light from her eyes towards the object you placed there – explaining, as she does so, that she is using the alchemical power of the Violet and Silver Rays to penetrate, dissolve and transmute the fears you chose to give form. As you watch, you become aware that the waves of silver light circling the interior of the crucible are getting brighter; and sense that the bowl is growing warmer in your hands: then all of a sudden you witness the fears you had made manifest being completely enveloped in a mass of silver and violet flames, before exploding in a shower of violet and silver sparks, leaving just the crucible – now empty and cool – in your hands.

Taking this from you, Sophia explains that you have observed just one of the many possible alchemical acts of transmutation, and witnessed the power of the Silver-Violet Flame. She tells you that this may be used to transform all forms of 'negative energy' into pure Light – emphasising that whatever you see or define as 'negativity' always, and *without exception*, comes into being through fear: thus, if you can identify and transmute those fears at their root, that negativity can no longer exist! With a smile, she stresses that *everyone* has the ability to change the 'lead' of their fears into the 'gold' of their Higher Being – and using the Silver-Violet Flame to bring about positive transformation and lasting change will always benefit your growth and self-understanding.

Sophia passes her hand over the crucible – and, as it shrinks down to its previous size, you see that it now holds a small polished stone that is beautifully streaked in silver, purple, pink and violet: giving this to you, she tells you that this is **Charoite**, her second Crystal Champion – explaining:

> *"Charoite is a carrier of the Silver-Violet Flame, which combines the transmutative properties of the Violet Flame with the spark that animates all that is created or formed. Together they can change stagnation and negativity into action and positivity, and can be used to create a robust and infinitely adaptable shield of High-frequency Light to help keep your energy field strong and clear. Charoite's fine resonance also harmonises with your innate spiritual nature to generate greater clarity within your whole energy field, which can help you identify and understand the root causes of your fears, and/or assist you in pinpointing any damaging behaviours or patterns you need to address. As Charoite also attracts the Pink Ray of Divine Compassion, it enables you to have more love for yourself and for others, thus actively encouraging and promoting all acts of forgiveness and mercy, which are powerful means for healing the Soul and balancing karma. To aid this, Charoite can open and empower your Soul Star, heart and crown chakras, assisting you in connecting with Higher Guidance with greater precision and purpose; whilst its red and blue Light simultaneously act to help ground you firmly in the Truth behind the reason for your physical being. Likewise, Charoite will resonate intensely with your Unified Body for similar purposes (but at Divine and Universal levels), to awaken and align your High Heart, Soma and Universal centres so that you may connect more powerfully and decisively with your Divine nature."*

Smiling, Sophia affirms that Charoite may therefore help you conquer your fears and master the (sometimes painful) practices of self-reflection, self-transformation and self-realisation, which, ultimately, will lead to Enlightenment.

Reattaching the crucible to its silver cord, Sophia gives a low call – at which the rabbit that heralded her arrival earlier appears from behind the tree and hops over to sit by her feet. Lifting it into her lap, she explains that rabbits are usually creatures of dawn and dusk, and most at ease when their predators (of which there are many!) are asleep. Gently stroking its ears, she says that some perceive rabbits as exemplifying anxiety and fear, but she prefers to view them as careful, quiet and cautious – for they have learnt to survive and thrive despite their vulnerabilities. She states that therefore **Rabbit** can be your guide and advisor if you need to confront your fears in order to identify what risks or dangers are real, and which are perhaps false or only imagined – and then be asked to help you understand what triggers your fearful or anxious thoughts or feelings, and to aid and support you in addressing them, in order to achieve a more confident and balanced state of being. Reminding you that rabbits are always alert and aware of what is going on around them, Sophia adds that you may also ask Rabbit to teach you how to become more aware of the state of your own (or others') energies and/or of those within your environment, so that you may understand how to positively change or transform them in a constructive manner – enabling you to move forwards without fear, and so manifest and create the future that you truly want. With a smile, she remarks that rabbits also have the good sense to give their burrows several entrances and exits, so that they always have a choice of routes to take (as well as some handy bolt holes in case of emergency): hence, you may also ask Rabbit to teach you how to plan your future moves, aims and ambitions with an eye to flexibility and choice; or to help you determine the path that is best suited to your needs; or to show you how to recognise the possibilities within all the choices and options open to you; or to help you re-evaluate your position and change direction if you think you are going the wrong way.

The Tau Key of Perfected Manifestation:
Hearing a sudden rustling in the woodland behind you, you turn to see a tawny-coloured mountain lion padding towards you through the trees: with a lithe and powerful bound he hops over the tree roots, and sits down at your feet. You are surprised that this does not scare the rabbit away, but as Sophia reaches across to gently stroke his head, she explains that **Mountain Lion** has come to assist Rabbit in helping you to address and conquer your fears; for he is a powerful, intelligent and confident animal that knows how to develop the attributes and skills that lead to self-reliance and self-assertion. She adds that, because Mountain Lion is quick, agile and skilled at moving over difficult terrain, he can help you find a sure and safe path that will guide you through whatever challenges your fears present. With a smile, Sophia says that, like her, Mountain Lion has perfected the art of balance – not just physically, but also in his decision-making processes: thus, he knows when the time is right to be still and when to move fast, when to be gentle and when to be forceful, when to roar and when to stay quiet, when to attack and when to retreat – all attributes you might learn to emulate! As you watch him, he yawns and sinks belly down into the moss – at which Sophia chuckles, observing that because Mountain Lion is very at home with all the Elements, and understands the importance of regulation and balance within the natural world, you may also choose to call upon him if you want to understand more about working harmoniously with the Elements of earth, air, fire and water and/or the seasons and cycles of life; or if you need to recognise and appreciate the varied benefits that diverse states of be-ing offer you, and so choose the most appropriate point of equilibrium for you at that time; or if you would like aid and support if you feel out of balance with the energies around you, or need help interpreting what you sense in your environment during times of planetary change or shift.

Sitting back, Sophia detaches the 'T-shaped' device from the silver cord that hangs from her right elbow, and shows it to you: you can see that it seems to be made from some type of silvery metal that has been polished smooth by constant handling; and see too that it has a rounded handle (rather like that of a corkscrew) and a wide cylindrical shaft. As she turns it in her hand, you note that the handle is slightly indented to aid grip; whilst the end of the shaft has been milled into an equilateral three-sided shape that has a circular hollow core. Sophia informs you that what you see is a tool that she uses in much the same way as a tuning key is used to adjust the tension of the wires in a harp in order to return them to the correct pitch; although, in this case, its purpose is to 'test' and 'tune' the Light so that it attains and retains the appropriate resonances that needs dictate.

Balancing the 'key' across her palm, Sophia explains that, like Metatron's hammer, it is made of meteorite iron; and likewise holds Galactic and Universal energies: she then touches it to the crystal on her pendant, at which the key grows bigger – thus enabling you to see it in much more detail.... As she turns it so that you can see the handle from all angles, you note that each blunt end is etched with a pattern: one resembles a dandelion 'clock', defined with slivers of gypsum that hold tiny bronzite 'seeds'; the other portrays a cluster of stars, defined with tiny diamonds.

You can also see that there are some thin metallic-looking wires inset around each side of the handle: three on one side, two on the other. Noting your interest, Sophia explains that she and Metatron both command the interface of the Diamond Light with the Gold and Silver Rays: thus, the set of three wires embody and define the threefold manifestation of the Diamond Light (The Light itself, its movement and direction, and the space within which it is held and focused); whilst the other set embody and channel the Gold and Silver Rays (the masculine and feminine expressions of The Divine, which together enable and allow the fundamental matter of Creation to take on both form and life) – therefore she quite *literally* holds the Key to perfected manifestation!

Shifting her position, Sophia returns the 'key' to its cord, informing you as she does so that its 'T' shape also represents two more important concepts that are integral to her work: the first of which is the 'Tau', whose philosophies concern humankind's search for 'spiritual treasure' within the confines of earthly existence. Smiling again, she explains that hence it may also be a Key to your Enlightenment, if you have the courage to ask for and accept its presence – aiding you in opening and aligning your upper chakras and Higher energy centres, whilst she helps you learn how to *consciously* regulate the resonance and flow of Divine Light throughout your bodies: then, as you learn how to integrate and balance 'all that you are' – and understand how to retain inner and outer balance and equilibrium – you may also learn how to create and empower the reality you wish for. She stresses that the ability to control Light with clarity and precision is a fundamental requirement for all acts of manifestation and creation; and counsels that endeavouring to learn, understand and perfect this ability will eventually enable you to attain a state of absolute Enlightenment and Unity, whereby masculine is unified with feminine; Soul with Spirit; darkness with light; and the world of physicality with the worlds of Higher form – what some refer to as Ascension.

Taking your attention back to the 'key', Sophia tells you that the second concept represented by the 'T' is the 'Tav', which is the kabbalistic pathway on the 'Tree of Life' that channels and grounds the Divine Light of Kether (Heaven). She explains that she oversees the pathway of Tav, whilst Metatron oversees the sphere of Kether – thus she 'is' the lightning rod that grounds his lightning bolts! With a chuckle Sophia remarks that some find her a bit of an enigma – for she is always still, yet in constant motion; always solidly grounded, yet aware of *everything* throughout all Times and Realities; always stable, yet continuously shifting to embrace all potentials (each of which might *seem* to be contradictory, yet *are* in fact complementary!): therefore, despite her name, you should never mistake her 'constancy' for inactivity – for her strength and dynamic vigour coupled with her ability to hold polar energies whilst maintaining perfect balance (what she prefers to see as a constant state of flexible equilibrium) can initiate great change and transformation in you, if you have the courage to seek it. With a smile, she points out that it is these attributes that make her the ideal 'anvil' for Metatron's 'hammer', upon which anything may be shaped or refined; and the ideal 'flint' to ignite the 'fires' of his forge, which catalyse all works of transformation. Touching her pendant, she adds that working with phenacite (the crystal they share) will call *both* of them to you, which you may find especially helpful if you are working with any particularly deep transformative processes.

Reaching into the fire, Sophia pulls out a blue and white banded stone: giving this to you, she says that this is **Blue Lace Agate**, her third Crystal Champion – explaining:

"Blue Lace Agate calms, cools, soothes and relaxes the body, mind and emotions; helps activate the intuition; and enhances Higher levels of communication: this can aid you in recognising and accepting whatever you need to do to address and release your fears, and so know harmony and peace. In everyday life Blue Lace Agate can support you in expressing your Self, through words both spoken and written: hence it can aid you in building and maintaining positive relationships with family and friends; and support you when inner (or outer) communication is an important part of your work. Blue Lace Agate's pale blue colour also sustains the loving, wise and co-creative energies of The Divine Feminine and the catalytic energy of the Silver Ray as ONE, helping you clarify and actively realise your Soul's purpose and inherent desires whilst retaining inner calm and equilibrium; whilst its layers of white chalcedony and clear quartz embrace the full spectrum of Light and the absolute peace and clarity of Source, supplying all that you might ever need to draw upon to effect both dissolution and creation. Then, as you learn how to control the resonance and flow of Light into and through your bodies (both physical and etheric) you will be more able to attain and retain the appropriate state of balance – no matter what assails you or affects the world about you: in turn this will give you the courage and resolve that will enable you to fulfil your quest for the Holy Grail of your Soul's True Light."

With a smile, Sophia affirms that Blue Lace Agate may therefore help you gain the clarity you need to always BE 'in the flow' of the balanced Light of your own Spirit.

The Greenwood Guardians – Robinia and Beech:

Her *personal* mentoring complete for now, Sophia affirms she is always available to aid and support you: you need only bring her to mind and ask for her presence, and she will attend you. Furthermore, she tells you that two great Tree Beings of the Plant Kingdom have also asked to support you in addressing her Theme of 'BALANCE THROUGH BRAVERY', adding that you need only request *their* presence, and they will be with you.

She explains that the first of these Greenwood Guardians is the Masculine essence of Robinia (False Acacia or Locust Tree), who has asked to overlight and help you ground whatever work you undertake within *any* aspect of her chapter. The second is the Masculine essence of Beech, who has specifically asked to help you understand and assimilate her Gift of The Absolute Light of the Illumined Heart (if you have chosen to accept it).

When you are ready to connect with Sophia's first Greenwood Guardian, you need simply call for the presence of **Robinia** (*) .... Robinia envelops you in a pale apricot-pink Light, and the Masculine spirit essence of Robinia speaks to you, saying:

> *"The essence of my Soul is like a flowing river born of a sparkling spring that rises from the ground – cool, clear and full of life-giving energies. Find me in spring, as my leaves unfurl in feathery cascades of fresh yellow-green, and my branches grow laden with hopeful tumbles of sweet white flowers: then, as the seasons progress, see how my riches embrace the earth in falls of red and orange, and bless her with seeds that are as deeply dark and mysterious as the outmost reaches of space. Then allow a seed to take root within your mind and fill you with its Light, that you may understand the totality of your Self and your true power and potential; and then let the love of my heart and the compassionate peace of my Being embrace you, that I may clarify your core and enable you to see yourself, mirrored in my Truth.... for, thus, you may identify how to heal and balance your mind and emotions, and gain the courage and strength that will help you acquire the wisdom to accept the purity and sweetness of your heart – and so transform all that you are into the Highest possible Light...."*

(* Blue Aquamarine and Labradorite will help you ground and connect with the energies and wisdom of Robinia, if you wish to enhance your experience using crystals.)

If you have chosen to accept and work with Sophia's Gift, and when you are ready to connect with her second Greenwood Guardian, you need simply call for the presence of **Beech** (*) .... Beech envelops you in a diffuse golden-yellow Light, and the Masculine spirit essence of Beech speaks to you, saying:

> *"In majesty I greet you; in strength I honour you; in peace I find you.... My wisdom is ancient, and that of which the elders speak as they tell their stories and sing their songs that hold the history and knowledge of the Earth in permanency and grace: for over years too many to number I have learned that the only way to* have *all is to* give *all. And thus, I live in a constant state of communion with the Earth, sharing of her gifts and giving of the bounty of my silver, gold and bronze, in order to nurture, uplift and inspire humankind and all sentient life-forms that live within my sphere: so stand with me now, and feel my solidity at your back shielding you from harm.... then know my resilience and peace, as you align yourself with the ancient wisdoms of the Earth, as my spreading branches shelter your Soul, and teach you how to grow ever closer to Heaven.... For thus you may touch the golden threads that bind the Universe in stability and Joy; thus you may thrill with the Light of Life that is to be found within the heart of ALL; and thus you may encounter the Platinum Light of Stellar Enlightenment and Illumined Truth, which truly knows the Love and bounteous Wisdom of the Divine Creator...."*

(* Carnelian and Blue Lace Agate will help you ground and connect with the energies and wisdom of Beech, if you wish to enhance your experience using crystals.)

ARCHEIA SERAPHINA

'LOVE YOURSELF FIRST'

CRYSTAL CHAMPIONS:

Clear Optical Calcite ♥ Prehnite ♥ Pink Girasol

CREATURE COMPANIONS:

Merlin ♥ Wren ♥ Lovebird

GREENWOOD GUARDIANS:

Poplar ♥ Ash

*I allow Divine Love to flow through me
without limit.
I AM limitless Love.*

MEETING SERAPHINA

It is morning in early autumn, and you find yourself standing in the middle of a wild and windswept moor, surrounded by a ring of misty grey mountains that rise starkly into a washed out sky. The sky is scattered with high scudding clouds, through which the sun is doing its best to shine with a watery brilliance; and all is quiet, save for the rustling of brackens and ferns as they are stirred by the wind. Slowly scanning your surroundings in search of life, you observe that the gently rolling terrain is randomly crisscrossed by a series of narrow tracks and trails that look to have been made by animals of some kind, although none are immediately visible. You also note that many of the trails seem to lead towards a rounded hill that is shrouded in mist – and, as this is not too far away, it seems as good a destination as any, so you choose one of the tracks that heads in that direction and begin to make your way along it.

The compacted path leads you over close-cropped expanses of grass and through rugged mounds of bracken and heather, winding its way around solitary windblown trees and denser patches of undergrowth that shadow small clearings, or hide darkly reflective pools of black peaty water. As you follow the trail you realise that this place is not as barren as you first thought – the sparkling dew-clad cobwebs that festoon infant pines and ground-hugging junipers providing homes for spiders of all shapes and sizes; the chattering alarm calls of birds (and their darting flight across your path) leading you to wonder how many creatures thrive in this seemingly desolate environment. At one point, having stopped to admire the small pink flowers that garland a white-berried snowberry bush like fairy bells, you even come across a silver-furred chinchilla curled up in a sleepy ball of warm contentment, confirming your growing belief that this place is probably not as it first seemed. As you draw closer to the hill that is your destination, the path snakes around higher banks of shrubs and ferns; and you find yourself dawdling as you pick and taste tiny sweetly-sharp wild strawberries that lie hidden in sheltered hollows; or inhale the warmly aromatic scent of coconut, as you amble past thickets of golden gorse that offer bright splashes of colour and provide refuge for warblers and wrens. Eventually the track ends; and you find yourself at the foot of the hill, where a white billy-goat, sporting a straggly beard and a pair of long curving horns, bars your way forward.

Just as you are wondering what to do next, you hear the drumming of rapid hoof beats – and turn to see a magnificent pure-white Arab stallion gallop into view.... He is carrying a tall and slender woman on his back, her long grey cloak streaming out behind her in the wind of their passage as the horse charges towards you, where – rearing to an abrupt halt, his head held proudly high – he takes your measure with keen and intelligent eyes. Although he quickly settles and now stands calmly, you can sense his great power and strength, which his rider is holding expertly contained, despite the lack of saddle and bridle: this is Archeia Seraphina. Smiling, she springs lightly to the ground to greet you, declaring:

"I am Seraphina, the Lady Charity – Keeper of the Pink Heart-Flame of Divine Love, Bearer of the Lyre of Light, and twin flame of Chamuel. I have come to show you the comfort to be found when you are bathed in the Light of The Divine, resting at ease within an embrace that is at all times both secure and absolute in its Love; and to show

you the inner peace you may find when you have the courage to open your heart and release all self-hurts, and then bless yourself for being the wonderful and whole person that you are, in truth, at heart. For I would have you experience the joy of such a wondrous state of Being, whilst my fingers play the notes and harmonies of Love's Light for you, soothing and comforting you and bringing solace and balm to the hurts and pains that life has bestowed upon you: then, as you allow your heart to be healed, you will come to know and understand the true Power of Love; and you – and your love – will be freed."

Then, leaving the stallion to graze under the watchful eye of the goat, Seraphina takes the ruby-red blanket that covered the stallion's back, and invites you to accompany her to the top of the hill....

Tucking the blanket under her arm, she leads the way up a well-trodden path that spirals up the hillside, which is carpeted with emerald-green grass and dotted with scarlet pimpernel, as if strewn with rubies. As you climb, the mists that shroud the hilltop slowly fade and dissipate, allowing you to see that the hill is crowned with a high and forbidding tor – almost as if a giant hand has randomly piled a towering mass of granite rocks and boulders on its peak: one side is open to the elements; the other is sheltered by an arc of seven mature larch trees, whose slender needles are just turning golden-yellow. After a while, you are close enough to see that the tor's weatherworn rocks are peppered with feathery silver lichens; and note how clumps of white and purple heather have taken root in its nooks and crannies, softening its starkness and providing shelter and cover for small animals and birds. Rather worryingly you also spot a snow leopard with some cubs resting in the shelter of an overhang on a ledge high above you – but, with a reassuring smile, Seraphina tells you that you have nothing to fear, and guides you towards a flat rock near the base of the tor: here she lays out the red blanket, and (patting it invitingly) invites you to take a little time to rest and study her, so that you may become at ease with her energies and those of this place.

Once you are settled, Seraphina sweeps her cloak back to mantle her shoulders and sits beside you, regarding you with a calm and even gaze. As you survey her in return you are immediately drawn to meet her clear and wide-set eyes, which have intense emerald-green irises and unusual dark – almost purple – pupils with a strange cat-like opacity. These are set below elegantly arched pale eyebrows in a perfectly symmetrical oval face, whose ivory translucent skin is faintly glowing as if lit from within – its fine bone structure, delicate features and dainty tip-tilted nose complementing her graceful bearing. Turning her head, Seraphina reveals neat and tiny ears that are slightly pointed and elfin-like: these give her a somewhat other-worldly appearance that is echoed in her white-blonde hair, which is long and straight, and so fine it seems almost transparent. She wears this drawn up and away from her face, passing it through a delicately wrought silver filigree tube that secures it at the back of her crown, from which it spills like a waterfall of silk to her waist. Examining the finger-sized tube more closely, you note that it is held in place by six silver pins topped with small white pearls; and also observe that its filigree pattern portrays a galloping horse, whose long flowing mane and tail is curling and streaming in the wake of its passage.

Turning back, Seraphina smoothes down her outfit, which is obviously designed both for warmth and for riding astride. The outer layers are made of dove-grey cashmere wool, and worn over a shell-pink silk 'vest' that softly moulds itself to her slender body: the 'vest' has a close-fitting turtleneck collar and long sleeves, and is embellished at the neck and wrists with deep frills of cream lace that – on closer inspection – you note to be interwoven with silver thread and studded with tiny cream seed-pearls; whilst the dove-grey outer layer comprises a wrap-around sleeveless bolero and matching softly-pleated culottes, which at first glance look like a full-length gathered skirt. Seraphina's feet are just visible below their hem, and she lifts one up to show you her knee-high riding boots made of supple grey leather. Her hands are clad in fingerless gloves made of the same soft leather, and fasten around her delicate wrists with a strap secured by a cream pearl button. Flexing her slender fingers, she shows you how the gloves allow great freedom of movement; before turning them to show you how their palms are made of grey suede to provide grip, whilst their backs are covered with tiny links of white gold studded with more seed-pearls, which protects the backs of her hands, like miniature chain mail.

With a smile, Seraphina loosens the simple plaited grey cord that secures her long dove-grey cashmere cloak round her shoulders, revealing the large heart-shaped brooch that is pinned in the hollow beneath her collarbone, just above her heart: this brooch is made of silver and inset with a large heart-shaped cut and faceted pink sapphire, which is the gem that links her with Chamuel, her twin flame. Removing her cloak, Seraphina quickly pleats it, and shows you how the brooch can be used to anchor her cloak so that it covers one shoulder and fans out behind her, in the manner of a Scottish plaid: then, with another quick smile, she plucks a fresh sprig of white heather from a fissure in the rocks behind you, and secures it at a jaunty angle through the pin of her brooch.

Now that her back is no longer concealed by her cloak, you can see that Seraphina is wearing what looks like a large white satchel: this is firmly secured by a pair of white leather shoulder straps, ensuring that it is comfortably and evenly balanced across her back, regardless of whether she is riding or on foot. Noting your curiosity, she shrugs the satchel from her shoulders and lifts it into her lap, allowing you to see that it is made of plain white canvas – the top folding over to create a deep flap, which is held closed by a heart-shaped toggle carved from ivory whalebone threaded through a simple canvas loop.

SERAPHINA'S TEACHINGS
The Lyre of Light and The Charitable Heart:

Recognising that your inspection is complete, Seraphina undoes the satchel's toggle and lifts the flap, revealing that it hides an intricate heart-shaped design that has been embroidered on the canvas body of the satchel in gold thread. A tear-drop-shaped blood-red ruby, glowing with an inner fire, sits in the very centre of this heart; and she explains that this gem holds the Ruby Ray, which is the fundamental creative energy of Source – the elemental *expression* of Divine Love. She expounds that this Ray fires and inspires the Pink Ray upon which she serves (which incorporates the pearl-white rainbow Light that guides and directs Divine Manifestation) and governs the *action* of Divine Love through resonant compassion. After thinking for a moment, Seraphina tells you:

> "Love is not about 'doing', but about 'allowing'. It cannot be forced or created: it can only be allowed to flow. And it can only flow freely and boundlessly from a clear and open heart, which neither judges nor condones, but simply allows with unconditional compassion, accepting all as being perfect and right for that moment: hence, BEing in a clear state of open-hearted acceptance has the power to invoke the boundlessness of Divine Love, and enables the Divine attribute of Charity – which IS Compassion in Action – to be embraced and upheld."

Opening her satchel, Seraphina lifts out a small 'U'-shaped stringed instrument: lovingly caressing its creamy frame, whose curves are inlaid and embellished with a line of ruby-red hearts, she tells you that this is her 'Lyre of Light', which has been crafted from the trunk of an ash tree, and inlaid with wood given from the heartwood of a larch tree. She explains that this has created an instrument of great beauty, harmony and power, which upholds the free-flow of Light (and Love!); and promotes the release of anything that might block or stifle it.... Seraphina explains that (apart from its body) her lyre has three main parts, comprising an ebony rod that spans the top of the lyre's 'U', which secures the 'strings' and maintains the instrument's integrity; a clear sheet of glass-like material made of a compound of silica and rare-earth elements that spans its base and forms what might be called a 'light-board' (rather than a 'sound-board'); and ten 'strings', which run between the ebony rod at one end and the glass-like board at the other.

Shifting so that she sits cross-legged, Seraphina settles the lyre in her lap so that one side rests against her heart, and gently places her hands on the strings. At her touch they shimmer and seemingly disappear; and, noting your puzzlement, she counsels you to take a closer look: doing so, you find that the strings have not vanished, but have turned into something that looks like strands of crystal-clear shimmering water. Seraphina explains that what you see might be described as Liquid Light, which can be 'played' to create whatever resonances are required to return absolute clarity and balance to any*thing* or any*one*. With a smile, she adds that one of her specialties focuses on facilitating clarity and balance within the mind and emotions, because she knows that such changes or shifts in mood or intent can bring about a more harmonious state of being that supports truth, understanding and genuine accord.

Gently she plucks a few of the 'strings' – and, as they vibrate, they momentarily flush through with shifting hues and tones of colour, before once more fading into near invisibility: then, saying that she wants you to experience the clarity of consciousness that her Lyre of Light can bring, Seraphina asks you to relax and close your eyes....

As you allow your eyes to close, she begins to gently pluck the strings of her lyre: to begin with, you hear nothing but the sounds of the natural world around you – yet, as your body, mind and emotions still, you feel the air around you stir; and find yourself relaxing, becoming peaceful, calm and at ease.... at this, the air stills – and the sounds of the lyre (at once both beautiful and profound) envelop and embrace you; and you hear Seraphina say:

> "Allow the full spectrum of Light to penetrate your consciousness. Let its truth become a part of who you are, and know that you are a warrior for that truth: because its truth is Unity, and where there is Unity there can be only Love."

As you recognise the truth in her words, you become aware that your heart is opening – and gradually all your energy centres and chakras come into gentle alignment through your pranic core, and your heart becomes the centre of all that you are....

As Seraphina continues to play, the sounds encompass and fill you – until it feels as if you are expanding to vastness: then suddenly you are overwhelmed with an immense feeling of gratitude for your life; and your heart fills and swells with a profound and unconditional love for everyone and everything that shares your world – and for the world itself.... slowly your mind acknowledges the wonder, love and joy that you are feeling – and, recognising this, Seraphina gently points out that *this* is what you have been seeking, even though you may not have been aware of your search; and you hear the smile in her voice, as she reminds you that you do not have to look far for love, for it is literally at the heart of all things and with you at all times....

As you continue to enjoy the moment, Seraphina asks if you can begin to appreciate how transforming and empowering love is; and if you can now see how it has the power to bring both grace and harmony to *all* lives and existences, not simply your own – and as you allow the love to completely fill and surround you, you feel your heart expand and your mind open to acknowledge the true meaning of Unity with ALL things....

After a while Seraphina plays a final melodic chord – and as your energies slowly return to a comfortable state of balance, you open your eyes to see her watching you with loving regard. Laying her lyre aside, she tells you that every time someone endeavours to open their heart and live within the compassionate Light of Love and understanding, the balance of Power within the world shifts, and the advent of Paradise on Earth draws closer: then, giving a gentle smile, she asks if you can imagine giving and sharing love without limits in a world where *every* thought, feeling, action, word and deed were coloured with love and expressed through an open and compassionate heart, and consider how wonderful that might be!

Reaching into her satchel, Seraphina pulls out a small rhomboid of clear crystal that has a rainbow-like transparency: giving this to you, she says that this is **Clear Optical Calcite**, her first Crystal Champion – explaining:

> *"Clear Optical Calcite offers exceptional clarity and brings a high and fine resonance to your personal energy field, aiding in the removal of blocks and the release of negative thoughts, feelings or beliefs. Its clear pure Light helps you see the truth behind all that you give out or endure and enables you to look into the depths of your own Soul with honesty and openness. Clear Optical Calcite also carries the full rainbow spectrum of Light and so is infinitely versatile, having a strong yet balanced energy that can inspire and support all manner of internal shifts and changes. Moreover, Clear Optical Calcite's reflective surface can aid you in identifying any self-destructive attitudes that make you cling to anything that, in truth, does not serve you; and help you acknowledge anything that restricts and confines you in the 'smallness' of your embodied human experience. Then, as you learn to surrender your hold upon those things, Clear Optical Calcite will help you open your heart and free your spirit, encouraging it to soar and align with your Highest nature, which knows Unity and unconditionally accepts and loves ALL."*

Smiling, Seraphina affirms that Clear Optical Calcite may therefore help you overcome the conditioning of your lower ego-self, so that you may see the world (and everything within it) in the pure Light of compassionate understanding.

As she returns the lyre to its satchel, Seraphina brushes against the strings with her fingers, at which a small bird with grey speckled plumage swoops down from the sky to perch on her left shoulder. She explains that this nimble, swift and tenacious little bird is a falcon known as a merlin, which was traditionally carried by ladies when hunting on horseback: symbolically he links her with the Druid Journeyman and Master 'Merlin Magus' – a Walker between Worlds, who works with the five Elements of earth, air, fire, water and ether to bring about movement and change for all that has been created. She says that accordingly you may find it of use to call **Merlin** to you during times of rapid shift or change on a personal *or* global level, especially if you need help assimilating or adjusting to the energies with more speed. With a sharp cry the little merlin takes flight again and starts quartering the hillside in search of prey: observing this, Seraphina remarks that Merlin's mastery in the air also means that he can be of great help if you want to understand how to navigate the twists and turns of your life with more agility, clarity or focus; or to attend you if you need to see something from a fresh perspective. With a smile, she adds that you may also ask Merlin to open your mind to Higher vision and wisdoms to help you strategise or deal with pressing problems – perhaps by inner journeying in meditation or in visualisation; or to bolster your determination and will, so that you may meet your goals with greater speed or positivity; or to teach you how to boost or recharge your energies if you need extra fortitude or forbearance to make (or manage) any quick or sudden changes within your life. With another smile, she says that Merlin may also come to *you* if it is time for you to 'step up to the plate' and accept and/or acknowledge the responsibilities that, as an inhabitant of this world, you have agreed to undertake as a part of your Soul's journey in this lifetime!

The Healing Power of Love Without Limits:

Placing her satchel aside, Seraphina tilts her head and listens intently to a loud and insistent chirring sound, then points out a tiny russet-brown bird that is flitting around the rocks searching for food. Explaining that it is a wren, she smilingly observes that it has an incredibly loud voice for such a small bird – pausing in admiration as a trilling stream of clear and brilliantly pure notes cascade from its wide-open beak. She tells you that the Druids revere the wren, understanding that its voice channels great power and wisdom: hence, you might call for **Wren** if you need insightful guidance or direction; or if you are working on any project connected with the bardic arts of poetry, song or ceremonial magics; or if you want to connect with the wisdoms of the natural world – especially those of the Tree-beings of Ancient Earth; or if it is time to 'make your voice heard' and you need a boost to your courage, strength, confidence and/or determination to succeed. Seraphina then recounts the tale of when wren entered a contest to decide the bird who could fly closest to the sun: it craftily hid itself on the back of the high-flying eagle; then, as the eagle thought it had won and begun its descent, it fluttered up from its hiding place to claim the prize! Smiling, she says that this gained wren the reputation of being clever and resourceful – and as being fearless of fire: hence Wren can also be asked to show you how to master the 'fires' of transformation; or to support you in addressing and resolving conflicts of your heart or spirit; or to teach you how to balance your needs with your desires; or to help you heal your heart and calm your emotions by taking a different (and maybe even unconventional) view of the issues involved – perhaps by adopting a more flexible approach to their resolution.

As the wren flutters away, Seraphina remarks that, although it can be aggressively territorial, wrens recognise the worth of kinship and collective cooperation in enabling its survival and growth, frequently sharing its roost with others of its kind for both warmth and protection. She adds that, likewise, at Soul level humans also recognise the value of 'family', and so (usually prior to their embodiment) tend to create most common learning situations within their immediate planned circle of family and friends. Seraphina points out that therefore it is common to find that those who teach you the most powerful lessons are likely to be of your own soul family, who will have agreed at Soul level to embody with you at that time for that very purpose. She adds that those who are closest to you will often be your strictest teachers; and, with a wry smile, acknowledges that the lessons they teach you might be easy or hard – and thus perceived as either a blessing or a curse: yet *all* will have been lovingly designed between you (before embodiment) to promote your understanding and growth. Seraphina tells you that, even though it may be hard, it will further free your heart when you are willing and able to recognise the great gifts given to you in this way by your family and friends; and are prepared to accept and acknowledge the unique part that each has played in your life – and be thankful for them! She emphasises that in this way, as you come to recognise the much greater reality of your life and its purpose, you will learn to apply wisdom with understanding (and justice with mercy) in *every* situation you meet: for *this* is the true nature of the Divine Light, which is LOVE without limits!

Turning to face you, Seraphina asks you to look at her eyes again: as you do so, you see her pupils expand, and the iris of each eye flares with intense sparks of emerald-green Light. With a smile, she tells you that the nature of her eyes allow her to see as easily in the dark as she can in the light, hence it matters not to her whether it is day or night! She adds that this ability is equally relevant to her aptitude to see into 'spiritual darkness', as a result of which she can aid humankind in releasing sorrow, pain and emotional traumas associated with all hurts of the heart, so that all hearts may be freed to become healed and whole. Drawing your attention to the sparks of Light, which now encircle her pupils in a ring of emerald fire, Seraphina explains that she uses the Light of the Emerald Ray of Profound Truths to see whatever is revealed within the darkness with absolute clarity and from all perspectives, with unbiased and merciful eyes. She points out that, in this way, anything that is not as it should be will be accurately identified and fully understood, enabling her to plan its resolution in the most appropriate and effective way. Seraphina then draws your attention to her pupils, explaining that their deep purple colour blends the power and passion of the Ruby Ray with the Sapphire Ray of Truth and Higher wisdom, enabling her to dismiss and remove anything that withholds or suppresses The Divine Light (and Love).

Taking your hands, Seraphina says that, by casting the Light of her eyes upon your 'inner darkness', she can help you identify memories, thoughts, feelings or emotions that have a negative impact on your heart; and aid you in releasing them or transforming them into something positive and constructive, in turn creating the potential for profound self-healing – and asks you to have the courage to look deeply into her eyes. Reassured by her touch, you do as she asks – and gradually her eyes expand to fill your entire vision; their vivid emerald irises rimmed with an emerald ring of fire that casts a beautiful green Light over the deep and reflective translucency of their centres: then, in the mirrors of her eyes, you see your Self – yet you find that this holds no fears, and feel nothing but a sense of calm serenity; connected and aware of everything you see, yet filled with a dispassionate, non-judgmental detachment....

Slowly you feel yourself relax, becoming centred and balanced with effortless ease; and, recognising the point you have reached, Seraphina asks you to call to mind an issue or situation that has hurt you, and which you find hard to forgive or release.... As you begin to think about this she gently squeezes your hands, stressing that holding on to grievances takes energy and is unproductive – blocking change and growth, and stifling your Light; whereas releasing them and letting them go will set you free, allowing and enabling healing to occur (for yourself *and* for others)....

As she waits, Time and space stand still; and you find you are able to consider and review the issue or situation with great clarity and from all perspectives. You begin to see yourself as part of *everything* and *everyone* – united not separate; and can also see how, over many lifetimes, you have experienced different sides of the same coin, *and* see how you – as well as any others involved – experienced and lived with the consequences of the choices you made (and indeed how you made those choices possible) as you sought to understand the true nature of balance and choice....

Eventually, Seraphina asks you to deepen and slow your breathing, and engage in honest introspection by seeing yourself through her eyes.... refocusing, you observe your reflection, and watch as it gently pulses with pale green light – then suddenly you see yourself encompassed by a deep purple light, which focuses on your heart; and you find you can see the issue or situation for what it truly is....

Slowly the burdens and hurts you held within begin to disintegrate and dissolve, and, observing this, Seraphina asks you to repeat this affirmation:

"I release everything within my heart that holds me back and does not serve my life purpose.... I release everything within my heart that holds me back and does not serve my life purpose.... I release everything within my heart that holds me back and does not serve my life purpose...."

Gradually you become aware that your heart feels lighter, and Seraphina releases your hands and your gaze: she advises you that repeating this affirmative statement often and regularly will help you detach from unproductive and harmful thoughts and emotions – thus freeing your heart, and supporting you in moving forwards with positivity and hope.

Reaching into her satchel, Seraphina produces a pale-green translucent stone: giving this to you, she says that it is **Prehnite**, her second Crystal Champion – explaining:

"Prehnite in tumbled form, like this one, is more energetically comfortable to use than in crystalline form, having a gentler yet (unusually) rarer and finer resonance. Prehnite carries the pale green Light of profound transformational change, balance and healing; and has a well-balanced and well-rounded energy that is capable of connecting your heart and Soul Star chakras, whilst grounding all energies down your pranic core and out through your Earth Star chakra. Prehnite's translucency signifies that it also resonates with the Element of Water, and so has the ability to purify and cleanse (as well as balance) many aspects of your energy Body – but especially your heart chakra and spiritual Body, and your sacral chakra and emotional Body. Furthermore, Prehnite may help link your spirit, mind and emotions whilst promoting a sense of calm and peace that aids restful sleep. Interestingly, Prehnite's hue tends to vary depending on the angle of light within which it is held: one that is faintly yellow signifies that it may be of benefit to your mental Body and solar plexus, where it may help put the 'ego-self' in its rightful place by aiding you in seeing the bigger picture within any situation from a much Higher perspective; whilst one that is faintly blue signals its ability to make clear connections with other-worldly Elemental energies – and in this you may discover it to prove surprisingly powerful and enlightening!"

With a smile, Seraphina affirms that Prehnite may therefore help you to shed unwanted burdens, enabling you to move forwards unencumbered by old hurts and pains.

The Gift of The Pink Flame of Divine Love:

Shifting her position, Seraphina tells you that 'unconditional love' means 'loving without expectation': hence, *BEing* unconditional love requires you to see things with absolute honesty and dispassion, and to be accepting *and* forgiving of your own and others' faults or failings – real or perceived. She explains that being willing to *ask for* and *give* forgiveness where forgiveness is due serves to balance or resolve karmic debts: thus, whenever you have the courage to acknowledge any wrongs you have done and say 'sorry' (or, conversely, freely offer forgiveness if you are the one who has been wronged) you are set free to move on. Touching your hand, Seraphina tells you she understands that to love unconditionally and to sincerely ask for or impart forgiveness can be difficult to do, but stresses that unresolved karmic debts burden both the Soul and the heart – and thus it is impossible for *either* party to attain proper balance within their heart, mind and spirit until such debts are addressed and dealt with. Smiling again, she adds that all is not lost, however, because she can help you fill your heart with love so that you will find this *easy* to do: then, taking the sprig of white heather from her brooch, she touches it to the centre of your chest. Slowly your heart opens, and becomes at one with your High Heart centre; and you become aware of the presence of the Lotus of your Heart within....

You gradually become aware of its protective layer of outer petals unfurling, to reveal a tightly closed pink bud within.... Seraphina now unpins the heart-shaped brooch at her shoulder; and touches the pink sapphire that it holds gently to the bud: at this, the gem flares with an intense Light; and all the pink petals of your Heart Lotus slowly open and begin to flush through with pink Light.... then, one by one, each petal ignites – until eventually a cluster of bright pink flames is glowing within your heart....

Returning the brooch to her shoulder, Seraphina tells you that she has given you her Gift of the Pink Flame of Divine Love, so that everything you are and everything you do may be influenced by its fiery presence at your heart, enabling you to truly embrace LOVE, in all its glorious and wondrous forms. Placing one hand over your heart, she then asks you if there is anyone to whom you find it hard to show unconditional love, and to think about why this might be so – and, as you ponder this, she tells you:

"When your heart is full of love you will find that it is easy to accept and forgive – both yourself and others. So let me help you see the greater picture; and as you do so, allow your heart to fill with pink Light and soften: then all your concerns can be seen for what they truly are, and you will find that it becomes easy to let go.... Remember: by freeing others you too will be freed...."

As her words penetrate your consciousness you shift your awareness to your heart, and see the pink flames of Divine Love you hold within generate a sphere of pale pink Light: this slowly expands to fill your whole energy field; and in your mind's eye you see the person you had been thinking of surrounded in its Light....

Seraphina encourages you to share with her whatever you know needs to be said or acknowledged to put things right and restore harmony and balance to the situation: so take as much time as you need to do as she suggests, simply allowing the pink Light to saturate everything and everyone that needs to be held in its loving Light; and accepting that Seraphina is your go-between in this matter....

Once she knows that the situation has found an appropriate point of balance, Seraphina lifts her hand and touches the sprig of white heather to your chest again: at this the pink Light fades; the pink flames settle, and all the petals of your Heart Lotus find balance, as they are once more enfolded in their outer protective layers....

Returning the brooch to her shoulder, and the heather to her brooch, Seraphina tells you that she is always willing to be your mediator in such matters, and reminds you that you can always call upon the Light of Divine Love that is now burning within your heart to help you recognise The Divine that IS within everyone, including yourself, *and* within every situation. With a smile, she adds that spending time expanding its Light will help you acknowledge and accept the truth of your own innate loving nature, and support you in loving yourself fully and completely *exactly* as you are.

Helping you to your feet, Seraphina leads you to the other side of the tor, and draws your attention to a tiny wild cherry tree that stands in the shelter of the seven larch trees. A pair of lovebirds is perched in its branches; and, as they become aware of your gaze, they take flight and circle around you, proudly showing off their delicate pink and green colouring. Reminding you that these are the perfected colours of the heart, signifying happiness and harmony, Seraphina tells you that **Lovebird** can be called upon whenever you need to open your heart to allow yourself to feel, give or receive love more freely; or if you need to achieve a better balance within any of your heart-centred relationships. With another smile, she adds that lovebirds exemplify faithfulness and fidelity, for their loving bond is one made for life: therefore, you can also ask Lovebird to aid you if you need help in 'keeping faith' – perhaps within a personal or familial relationship, or if you are finding it hard to remain true to a cause that is dear to your heart. Seraphina laughs as one of the birds settles upon your shoulder, swiftly joined by its mate – observing that, 'as one', they exemplify the unbreakable bonds to be found in true love situations: thus you may call upon Lovebird if you need aid in finding true love, or if you are sincerely seeking your soul-mate or a life-partner; or (in the case of twin souls and twin flames) to help you understand the true nature and realities of such relationships. She points out that lovebirds also share tasks involved in rearing their young, and make gentle and devoted parents – hence, Lovebird may also be your guide if you have any difficult situations that require resolution within your family; or if you have concerns connected with parenting skills – whether as a parent or a child!

Leaving you as swiftly as they arrived, one of the lovebirds drops a small polished stone into your lap: this feels cool, and has a pale-pink translucent lustre; and Seraphina tells you that this is **Pink Girasol**, her third Crystal Champion – explaining:

"Pink Girasol is in many ways similar to Rose Quartz, both in its composition and in its uses and effects. Yet it has within it a refined resonance and delicate watery quality that makes it ideally suited to attracting the Light of Love into your thought processes and emotions: this can help dissolve away grief, fear and/or anger-based emotions; and aid you in cleansing your emotional Body of any long-held hurts or negativity that might be preventing its expansion or balance. Pink Girasol's gentle quality also supports all compassionate and altruistic endeavours, whether of a personal, familial or planetary nature – encouraging genuine and open-hearted generosity and leading you to reach a state of profound inner peace and harmony: in turn this may help you truly know the Divine Unity that lies at the heart of the Universe, of which all things are a part; and eventually to you aligning your Self with the blissful state of 'Samadhi', which is your ultimate goal and purpose for Being. Indeed, Pink Girasol truly demonstrates that Love is the greatest force in the Universe, by attracting the presence of the Pink-flame Angels who will, if asked, support your emotional needs and aid your self-healing, whatever your age or degree of spiritual development. Pink Girasol also has an innocence that resonates wonderfully with the energies of young children and babies, reconnecting them with the Light of innocence and love that is their birthright, and supporting them as they begin a new life in this physical (and often bewildering) world – just as it will support the newly-reborn Spiritual Seeker as they take their first steps exploring (and reconnecting with) the wisdoms they left hidden behind the Veils of Forgetfulness!"

With a smile, Seraphina affirms that Pink Girasol may therefore help you recognise and acknowledge the presence of Love in your life, whilst compassionately boosting your confidence and faith in yourself, your path and/or your abilities.

The Greenwood Guardians – Poplar and Ash:

Her *personal* mentoring complete for now, Seraphina affirms she is always available to aid and support you: you need only bring her to mind and ask for her presence, and she will attend you. Furthermore, she tells you that two great Tree Beings of the Plant Kingdom have also asked to support you in addressing her Theme of 'LOVE YOURSELF FIRST', adding that you need only request *their* presence, and they will be with you.

She explains that the first of these Greenwood Guardians is the Feminine essence of Poplar, who has asked to overlight and help you ground whatever work you undertake within *any* aspect of her chapter. The second is the Feminine essence of Ash, who has specifically asked to help you understand and assimilate her Gift of The Pink Flame of Divine Love (if you have chosen to accept it).

When you are ready to connect with Seraphina's first Greenwood Guardian, you need simply call for the presence of **Poplar** (*) .... Poplar envelops you in a royal-blue Light, and the Feminine spirit essence of Poplar speaks to you, saying:

> *"Stand with me, and feel the cheery joy of my Being flow through you, lifting your heart and feeding your Soul and spirit with my optimism and love – for I know the pleasure of service, and love the adventure of striving to always Be the best that I can BE. And thus, on even the dullest of days and through the most testing of times, I may support you and show you how to find the Light and Love that is within yourself and within all things. So see how my heart reaches to the heart of the Sun and glories in its warmth and succour, even when its face is hidden from view and the winds of change blow strong (for my heart knows always what my eye might not see, and is in constant communion with the Light and Power that flows through the Web of Life!); and let me help bring you to a still place of calm, where you may see life as if through the heart and eyes of The Divine, and thence cease in your struggles and release your pain to my transformative heart: for though my roots may take in the waters of your emotions, my heart holds the light of one thousand suns, and has the power to bring the One Light to your world...."*

(* Yellow Jasper and Sugilite will help you ground and connect with the energies and wisdom of Poplar, if you wish to enhance your experience using crystals.)

If you have chosen to accept and work with Seraphina's Gift, and when you are ready to connect with her second Greenwood Guardian, you need simply call for the presence of **Ash** (*) .... Ash envelops you in an intense red-pink Light, and the Feminine spirit essence of Ash speaks to you, saying:

> *"I hold and channel the Black and White Light of pure potential, which together hold the means whereby all that you wish for and design may be brought into existence. So be as one with my backbone – a spear of Light, flexible yet strong; and let my roots connect you with the power and passion of the Earth, that you may know her Light and feel her zest and passion for Being.... then let that Light surround you – lifting your spirits, firing your heart and mind, and inspiring your imagination, so that you recognise and connect with the infinite potentials and possibilities that are opened to you in every moment of every day.... Seize the moment! And let your Soul dance in the rainbow light that empowers the majesty of Creation, and brings all that is and can be made manifest to full and glorious completion. For YOU are Master of your own life, and I can assist you in finding the keys that will allow you to access the mystic and ancient wisdoms of the Earth, which in turn will connect you with the absolute Love that is the awe-inspiring Power behind All That IS, was and ever will BE...."*

(* Jet and Clear Quartz will help you ground and connect with the energies and wisdom of Ash, if you wish to enhance your experience using crystals.)

ARCHANGEL CHAMUEL

'SELF-ACCEPTANCE'

CRYSTAL CHAMPIONS:

Rose Quartz ♥ Rhodocrosite ♥ Ruby

CREATURE COMPANIONS:

Turtledove ♥ Horse ♥ Dog

GREENWOOD GUARDIANS:

Birch ♥ Cherry

*I have the honesty to see myself,
and the courage to accept myself,
fully and completely.*

MEETING CHAMUEL

It is soon after dawn on a fine day in early summer, and you find yourself standing alone in a grassy meadow. This sits in a wide open plain that is surrounded on all sides by rolling green hills, and has been left to run wild – leaving you knee-deep in a mass of slender grasses, many of whose heads are beginning to ripen and swell with seed. Above you the sun is slowly rising in a china-blue sky, its high layered clouds flushed through with traces of pink and edged in silver; and the morning air is cool crisp and clear. There are no signs of habitation, and all is silent and still: then, just as you are wondering where to go, a soft breeze begins to whisper all around you – and the grasses begin to bend and sway in a rippling sea of silver, gold and bronze, revealing a host of wild poppies (their scarlet heads open-hearted to the sky, like rubies scattered in their midst); and a narrow track, which you are drawn to follow....

After threading your way carefully through the long grasses, you eventually reach the edge of the meadow: here the track continues on across a field, which is bisected in the distance by a low spectral drift of mist: this veils what lies beneath, yet you can hear the sound of running water, and assume it marks the course of a river or stream. There seems to be no reason to hurry, so you amble through the dew-laden grass towards the mist, enjoying the sensation of the sun warming your skin as it slowly gains in strength. Gradually the mist rolls away downstream, enabling you to see that you are approaching a fast-flowing river: here the track converges with a path that leads alongside the water; and something encourages you to go with the flow, and follow its course.

As you walk further down the path the river widens – and, as the current slows, the sound of it changes, becoming sweeter and more melodious as it flows over and around the pebbles and rocks that now define its path and line its bed. Here the ground becomes more soft and springy underfoot – the river's moss-damp banks brightened with creeping masses of bright yellow celandine and pale-blue water-forget-me-not; its marshy margins more loosely defined by deep stands of rushes, reeds and water-loving flag iris. The field to the other side of the path also boasts more colour – its greenness now lushly scattered with tall golden meadow-buttercups, entwined with silvery stems of white moon daisies; and dotted with pink and purple-hued orchids and ground-hugging blue speedwell, whose petals are shyly opening to the sun.

Absorbed in the variety of plant life around you, you are surprised to suddenly find a snow-white peacock in front of you – his magnificent tail fanned open to bar your way. Looking up, you find that you are near the end of the path; and see a tall man standing beneath a willow tree that stands near the water's edge. Both are lightly shrouded in mist, hence his grey-clad form is almost invisible – yet, when he steps forwards, his features become clearer; and you know that this is Archangel Chamuel. As he walks towards you, his arms folded self-assuredly in front of him, you admire his upright bearing and lithe athletic physique, which is apparent even though his face is lined with age. Interestingly, his features are like those of a Mongolian elder, with weather-beaten skin and nut-brown almond-shaped eyes, which are bracketed by deep laughter lines and set beneath jutting white eyebrows: his most startling feature, however, is his exceptionally long hair, which ripples back over his shoulders and cascades to the ground, like a waterfall in full spate.

As Chamuel draws near, you can sense the aura of raw power he holds firmly in check, yet despite his rather stern and disciplined bearing he is smiling warmly at you in welcome, and greets you, declaring:

"I am Chamuel – Keeper of the Rose-pink Flame of Compassionate Action, Wielder of the Sword of Justice, and twin flame of Seraphina, the Lady Charity. In me you see a gentle warrior – a hand of The Divine, bathed in Divine Love and with grace and infinite compassion at my heart. Yet know that I fiercely defend the Right of ALL to know the eternal presence of the Love of the Divine Creator, which is the most powerful force in the Universe, binding foes together and healing rifts or divisions through its warm embrace; and softening even the hardest of hearts, that it may reveal its true strength that lies within. I understand and appreciate that to show love; to accept love; to BE love is not an easy option and takes courage – for to do and be this you must surrender all resistance and open your heart to live at all times fully and purely in the Light of Love. However, then (and only then) will you understand that nothing *can hurt you, and* know *yourself to be truly and totally invincible."*

Inviting you to inspect his attire and adornments – and accustom yourself to his energies; Chamuel turns slowly on the spot, whilst reaching up to bind his hair into a shorter braid using a long leather thong: this braid is obviously much more practical, and you can see that this practicality extends his functional clothing, which is clearly made for riding on horseback. His torso is encased in a thickly padded sleeveless V-necked jerkin made of dove-grey felted wool, edged and bound in white linen, which fastens invisibly down the front – its shoulders reinforced for protection, and anchoring his long grey hooded cloak: this is made of densely-woven grey wool, and attaches to his jerkin at each shoulder, where its pleats are secured by long golden 'kilt-pins' shaped like arrows.

Under the jerkin Chamuel wears a full-length sleeveless grey linen robe, edged and bound in grey silk; and – as he turns – you can see that this is slit to the groin at the front and back, allowing him excellent freedom of movement, and making it comfortable for riding astride. Beneath the robe his legs are clad in soft grey suede leggings, which are bound tightly to his calves with brown leather straps that criss-cross his legs from ankle to knee; whilst his feet are comfortably shod in short flat-soled boots fashioned from supple brown leather.

Pausing with his back to you, allowing you to note that his cloak gapes open at the nape, Chamuel sweeps his cloak aside to show you that this allows him easy access to the items hidden beneath, both of which are held in a leather harness that loops around his shoulders in a 'figure-8'. The first of these is a leather-bound bamboo sheath, from which juts a long straight handle (presumably of a sword) that is bound in grey suede; the other is a stiff leather frame that holds a short bow and a quiver of arrows, each fletched with rainbow-grey feathers.

Recognising that your examination of his apparel is complete, Chamuel holds out his arms, which are well-muscled tanned and bare: this enables you to see that he has an ivory bracer and wrist-guard (designed to support and protect his arm when using a bow) laced around his left forearm – and, inspecting this closely, you can see that it has been decoratively edged with silver, and engraved with the image of a herd of running horses.

You also see that his right hand is encased in a fingerless glove, which is secured to a wide gold band at his wrist: the underside of the glove is made of thick, yet supple, grey suede that protects his fingers when drawing his bow, and provides grip when wielding his sword; whilst its back is covered with a fine gold mesh, which protects the back of his hand and his knuckles: the mesh bears an octagonal gold filigree mount, inset with a flat ruby cabochon (the gem that grounds and activates the Ruby Ray upon which he serves), which has been polished to reveal its intense blood-red colour and fiery depths.

Lastly your gaze is drawn by the large deep-pink sapphire nestling in the open 'V' of his jerkin: this is the gem that links him with Seraphina, his twin flame. The sapphire has been cut and faceted in the shape of a heart, and hangs from the end of a short silver chain, which in turn hangs from a flat silver collar that sits snugly around the base of his neck – and, looking at the gem more closely, you realise there is a flame flickering at its core, which is emitting a subtle, yet constant, deep rose-pink Light.

CHAMUEL'S TEACHINGS
The Gift of The Rose-pink Flame of Divine Compassion:

Chamuel leads you to the willow tree where you first saw him, which is larger than you first thought – the mist that had shrouded it now lifted; and asks you to lean against its trunk: he then directs you to relax and close your eyes, so that you can focus on what you can feel; and, as you do, you feel your limbs grow heavy; and sense yourself beginning to merge in consciousness with the tree....

Gradually, with an expanding sense of awareness, you find you can sense the water and sap circulating through the tree's body; and feel the energy and life-force that fills and surrounds it.... this somehow both cools and enlivens you – at which Chamuel points out that the willow has a reputation for absorbing 'dis-ease', reminding you that its bark has long been valued as a cooling and pain-relieving remedy. With a smile in his voice, he explains that you may therefore allow the tree to help you release any hurts or pains that you hold within your body, mind and emotions that eclipse or burden your spirit, so that you are freed to move forwards with a mind that is more open and a heart that is free: hearing his words, somehow everything that IS the willow becomes a part of you; and you feel yourself become grounded and rooted, calm and still.... you understand too how the tree draws on the elements that nurture it; and *know* that the waters of the river and the life-blood of the willow are lovingly cleansing all that you are – all pains lessening, your burdens somehow lifted from you....

Chamuel waits until he feels you are ready to continue, before guiding you down the riverbank to a wide bend in the river, where a curving wooden bench sits overlooking the water: here the river runs slow and deep – its flat, mirror-like surface reflecting the sky above. Inviting you to take a seat, Chamuel produces a small creamy-white wooden bowl, and fills it with water from the river: he passes this to you, then sits at your side, explaining that the mirror-like clarity of the water in the bowl can show you the masks that you wear to hide or disguise your True Self from yourself – or others. He points out that 'masks' are often adopted as a means of protection, whereby the 'wearer' can appear to be more than – or less than – they really are; or can present themselves in a way that is inconsistent with, or uncharacteristic of, their true character. He adds that whatever the waters reveal may be instantly recognisable; or may appear to you in symbolic form; or may manifest as concepts, thoughts or feelings: yet whatever their form, the willow tree (from which this bowl is made) will help you identify it and recognise its purpose, so that you may understand why you have chosen to wear it....

Asking you to look into the bowl, Chamuel instructs you to allow your awareness to expand, just as you did before: and, as you do as he asks, you feel your solar plexus, throat and brow chakras slowly come into alignment and balance with each other.... then gradually you understand that you have the clarity and honesty to see yourself revealed, in all your glory and pain; and understand too that it is important to accept whatever the waters show you; in order to discover the True worth and value hidden away beneath....

As you look into the water, you are aware of the spirit of the willow helping you connect with the wisdoms of your Higher-self, whilst encouraging the intrinsic love and respect you have for your Self and your path to come to the fore; and are able to see past any 'false personas' you have created to the complex human that lies beneath....

Gradually you see how the 'masks' that are being shown to you actually hinder your growth; and realise that adopting different coping strategies or ways of being will enable you to be true to your Self, and accept the validity of who and what you truly are: at this point, Chamuel directs you to ask the spirit of the willow to temporarily lift these masks from you – because later you will be asked to decide if you *truly* need them, and if you are now ready and willing to discard some or all of them....

Once this is done, Chamuel takes the bowl from you and places it aside: he then points to the sky, where a plump pair of turtledoves are circling above you. He tells you that these beautiful birds supply the feathers that fletch his 'arrows of love', with which he penetrates ignorance to bring about awareness within any and all levels of body, mind and spirit: accordingly you may call upon **Turtledove** if you want to 'get to the heart' of a matter; or wish to extend your awareness multidimensionally; or need to understand the truth behind something you think, or have been told. As you watch the birds he remarks that the gift of flight is a wonderful thing, enabling great freedom of movement and offering a huge range of perspectives: thus, you may call Turtledove if you need help seeing or interpreting anything from a new or Higher perspective; or if you feel 'stuck' and wonder if it is time for you to change direction, and want aid recognising the options and choices open to you. Swooping closer, the birds loop through the air, sensing the air currents and riding them with great agility and dexterity: it seems that their focus in this moment is on the sheer pleasure of flying and nothing more, at which Chamuel remarks that play is an essential part of life – for, although it may seem to have no purpose, it has the power to banish fear and sorrow and fill you with joy, which can promote inner peace and harmony. With a smile, he adds that Turtledove is always willing to help you find the space in which you may relax and 'be' yourself; or teach you how to fly (metaphorically and spiritually!) without fear, so that you may master the 'winds of change' with ease: furthermore, as turtledoves pair for life, they epitomise the unbreakable bonds of true love: hence Turtledove may also come to *you* if you need to strengthen (or mend) your bonds with family and friends – whether within the worlds of physicality or spirit.

After a while, Chamuel stands and gives a whistle; at which the birds begin to circle over the river in front of you.... faster and faster they fly, tightening their circle as they do so – then, all of a sudden, a pure-white lotus flower appears on the surface of the water: skilfully the turtledoves lift and guide the lotus to Chamuel's outstretched hand, before flying away, their task done.

Chamuel now turns to you, and touches the ruby on his glove to the white petals of the lotus: at this, they momentarily flush through with pink light, and the tight bud at the flower's centre unfurls, revealing the deep rose-pink flame burning at its heart.... Lifting the lotus up to your crown, Chamuel encourages it to merge with your crown chakra: then, as they settle into a harmonious state of equilibrium, he steps back, declaring:

> *"My Gift of The Rose-pink Flame of Divine Compassion now rests within the centre of the thousand petalled Lotus that sits within your crown. It tinges its petals of white with the power of the Ruby Ray, and grounds the Pink Ray of Divine Love and Mercy, which is born of the Infinite Fire and Compassion of Divine Source. From this point forwards, all that descends from the Higher Realms and from your Divine and Christed Selves will be inspired with the Fires of Divine Love and Mercy – flowing down through your core, and diffusing throughout your body to fill your entire Being, so that your every thought, word and deed may be founded upon compassion."*

Retaking a seat at your side, Chamuel advises you that simply taking your attention to his Flame whenever you need to make a decision or review a situation or event will ensure that your Soul's compassion always guides your humanity. Smiling, he adds that his Gift is etherically linked with the Pink Flame in your heart (the Gift of *his* twin flame), and so 'As One' they will enable you to more fully embody and BE Love. He then asks you to take your attention to both Flames; and take a little time to consider whether you wish to have any of the masks you shed earlier returned to you – in which case the spirit of the willow will reinstate and/or permanently remove them, as appropriate....

Once you have made your decision, Chamuel gives you a palm-sized rose-pink stone, telling you that this is **Rose Quartz**, his first Crystal Champion – explaining:

> *"Rose Quartz carries the Pink Ray of Divine Love and Mercy, which has the purity and power to bring about change through the alchemy of limitless and resonant compassion. This is because Rose Quartz holds the vibration of pure untainted love, whose innate innocence can help restore purity and strength to a 'broken' or damaged heart. The red spectrum of Light within Rose Quartz also supplies the passion and courage to help you release lower or denser thoughts, feelings and memories; and opens you to the Highest possible resonances that support and enhance open-hearted compassion, for yourself and for others. This can help your heart and emotional Body heal their wounds and recover from old hurts, pains and traumas; whilst the white Light with which it merges embraces, calms and purifies your body and mind – and works to re-establish your elemental patterns of faith, hope and trust. Thus, Rose Quartz connects Heaven and Earth, and aligns, balances and centres all energy centres through your heart – which, in turn, is effectively connected to the heart of The Divine: this makes it easier for you to 'BE' in greater harmony with your Soul, whilst recognising and appreciating how Love in its fullest and purest form empowers growth and healing on all levels."*

With a smile, Chamuel affirms that Rose Quartz may therefore help you engage in the honest self-reflection that will help you identify and manage your fears (which tend to create your masks!) in a positive and constructive way; thus enabling you to transform all your fears into love!

The Sword of Divine Justice and the True Meaning of Power:
Chamuel tells you that, in folklore, willow has a reputation for being a conductor for lightning, its love of water being believed to attract lightning towards it, and so away from habitation. Smiling, he remarks that all myths often conceal truths; and drawing his sword from its sheath on his back, he shows it to you – warning that it is very sharp. The straight, double-edged sword looks oriental in style, with a long handle whose grip is plainly bound in grey suede; and with a simple oval hilt and guard delicately filigreed in gold. As he turns it round, you can see that the end of the handle is inset with a ruby disc engraved with a stalk of cherries; and that the long tapering blade has been traditionally forged from multiple folds and layers of metal.

Carefully running the gloved palm of his right hand down the flat of the blade, Chamuel tells you that his sword grounds the Lightning Power of Divine Justice: thus (as a warrior for The Light) he wields it to blaze trails and clear pathways that will enable Divine Light – and Divine Love – to flow freely and without hindrance. At his words, the subtle waves in the layered metal flash with blue-white light, and the blade begins to hum with an electrical-type energy.... With another smile, Chamuel explains that he uses the Light of his sword to illuminate the many polarities and extremes of existence, and to highlight and challenge anything that is false or unjust; before using the Power of its blade to penetrate, dissect or separate whatever is revealed, and to cut away anything that prevents or inhibits clear sight. He expounds that thence, by exposing the Truth that lies beneath, everything is free to realign with their true core essence, and make choices in accordance with their Soul's innate desire for harmony and growth – ultimately leading to a return to Divine perfection.

Gently tapping its blade, Chamuel affirms that, if asked, he will bring his sword to aid you in identifying and understanding what influences or motivates you; or to help you become aware of any negative attitudes, expectations or behaviours that you hold; or to reveal any inconsistencies in your thoughts and beliefs. After thinking for a moment, he says that, ultimately, his sword has the power to strip you back to Soul level, by cutting away *all* masks, artifices, pretences or disguises that bind or confine you – thus freeing you to see yourself fully and completely. Taking your hand, he promises that therefore he will always answer your call if you ask him to help you understand, accept, value and love *all* of your Self without judgement or condemnation; and will aid and support you in whatever endeavours you choose to undertake, in order to return you to a state of perfect harmony and peace.

Giving you a polished stone banded in creamy hues of apricot and pink, Chamuel tells you that this is **Rhodochrosite**, his second Crystal Champion – explaining:

"Rhodochrosite is a serene, loving and joyful stone that carries the pure and clear energies of Divine Love and Compassion. Working with its many-layered structure can

aid the recall and recovery of early or past-life memories of any trauma held within your body, mind or spirit; and support you in releasing, clearing and healing whatever is revealed: this has the power and potential to free you beyond recognition! Yet you may be assured that Rhodochrosite's powerful energy will keep you fully supported throughout whatever processes of self-healing and self-transformation you choose to undertake; whilst being a constant reminder to you of the infinite, all-encompassing and eternal Love and Compassion of The Divine. Rhodochrosite's Light may also serve to bring you hope, and remind you of the true purpose of each embodied lifetime and of the many learning opportunities they offer – each of which you have chosen *to experience. Then – when you have truly addressed whatever holds you back, and acknowledged and assimilated or released your past – you will be empowered to know and own your innate talents, gifts and Inner Light; and BE the person you were born to be, without being disempowered by your own fears, or troubled by the thoughts, words or deeds of others."*

Smiling, Chamuel affirms that Rhodochrosite may therefore give you the strength and courage to align with your Highest potential, enabling you to create clearer and more positive connections with your Divine-self and your Inner Light.

Placing the sword carefully aside, Chamuel observes that Power can, of course, be directed to any ends; and in the best of hands it will be wielded with fairness and with the Highest of intentions to bring about equality, harmony and peace: yet, in the worst of hands, it may be wielded with self-interest, bias and discrimination; leading to inequality, discord and conflict. He adds that, for this reason, those in any position of Power must have the clarity and perspicacity to examine their motivations truthfully; the courage and honesty to fully consider all the possible consequences of their actions; and the Higher focus to be certain that the way in which they exercise their Power is both Just and Right – and in absolute harmony with their Soul. With a smile, he gently points out that anyone who has responsibility for something or someone is in a position of power – and asks you to consider if *you* treat others fairly, just as you would wish them to treat you; and if you do your best to see things from all perspectives and viewpoints – whilst also reflecting about how the faults you see in others are often reflections of those you have yourself!...

After allowing you time to mull this over Chamuel gives a trilling whistle, and you hear a whinnying reply as a snow-white mare gallops over the fields to his side. He tells you that his mare is the mate of Seraphina's stallion, and his constant companion and friend – carrying him wherever he needs to go, guided by the merest of thoughts. He explains that the stallion's energy augments Seraphina's power, particularly in situations where *personal* control or energy is required; whilst his mare's energy augments his power, especially when *situational* control or initiation is required. Observing that a horse's powerful stride and stamina offers the freedom and ability to respond instantly in any situation, Chamuel suggests that you call **Horse** if you need robust support during times of forward movement or sudden change; and (reminding you of the image on his wrist guard) adds that their flowing movement and innate intelligence also makes Horse a useful teacher or guide if your natural flow is being stifled or blocked and you need to move an idea or plan forwards; or if you need support in planning, creating or designing something effectively; or if you want to move more swiftly, or with greater flexibility. Patting the mare as she wanders away to graze, he adds that, whenever you see a *white* horse, it is one of the signs of the presence of the Divine Mother, and the mark of refined and perfected action through the wise and reasoned use of Power: thus, you might want to specifically call upon a *white* Horse if you need to see anything with greater clarity and compassion; or want to understand the consequences of something you are planning, making or doing; or to help you deal with a situation or event with calm considered wisdom, rather than reacting impetuously through your emotions. Smiling, he adds that Horse may also appear to *you*, to remind you to treat yourself – and others – fairly, and to have tolerance for all your own – and others' – weaknesses and mistakes!

The Blessing of Mercy and the Promise of Karmic Freedom:

Once more warning you not to touch the blade, Chamuel lifts his sword, and rests it across his knees: this time using his left palm, he traces a line down the centre of the blade; revealing a line of glyphs you had not noticed before, which glitter with a strange fiery Light as his hand passes over them. He explains that, in addition to the Power and Light of Divine Justice, his sword also carries the Power and Light of Divine Mercy – for either one may not be dispensed without the other: hence, through the Power of his 'double-edged sword' he brings the promise of Karmic Freedom – championing the concept that whatever you do to another, you do to your Self, just as (likewise) whatever you do to your Self, you do to another. Smiling, he adds that, in essence, when you truly understand this, and have made this truth a part of your reality, you will have grasped the fundamental Truth that All are One: and then it is not so hard to understand and accept that – if All are Divine, and The Divine IS Love – it is impossible to BE anything other than Love!

Gently tapping his sword, Chamuel goes on to explain that what you call 'karma' is a very important facet of any learning experience – even though when you achieve self-mastery you will no longer need to accrue it. After thinking, he explains that, basically, karma teaches about balancing justice and mercy with fairness and accountability, through learning and understanding all possible consequences of Free Will and choice. He adds that the insight thus gained can promote profound realisations about the true nature of Love; and, through compassionate action, enable sincere acts of forgiveness to take place. With a gentle smile Chamuel emphasises that true judgement is therefore *not* about punishment, but about considering whatever is being judged from all perspectives with an open and compassionate heart – and thus it is about being both just *and* merciful. He adds that, therefore, justice and mercy must *always* be even-handed: for even though admitting fault and yielding recompense is an essential part of equitable judgement; to withhold mercy with the other hand is as detrimental to the withholder's Soul, as it is to those to whom forgiveness is being denied.

Taking your hand, Chamuel says he understands that to have compassion for others – especially those who have hurt you – is not easy: yet, if you do your best to view things with an open heart from a dispassionate and objective perspective, this will help you to see The Divine in others, and make it easier to act with wisdom, mercy and compassion.

He stresses that then, through forgiveness and sincere acts of atonement (a word that actually means being 'at one-ment' with your Soul), you can heal the wounds of the past and make yourself whole and complete again. With another gentle smile he says that in this way you are *empowered* to free yourself – and others – from Karmic ties that may have prevented you from moving forwards; and *enabled* to balance and release karmic debts arising in this lifetime and others.

Chamuel tells you that he wishes to use his sword to channel the Light of Mercy for you, in order that you may see events, situations, and/or people and your interactions with them clearly and honestly – for in this way you may see any wrongdoings (yours or others'; real or imagined) in their true Light; and so identify and understand the reasons behind, and natural consequences of, all your (and other associated) actions....

Standing, and walking behind you, he gently touches the tip of his sword to the rear of each chakra in turn – starting with your base chakra, and working up to your crown chakra.... When he reaches this point, he turns his sword so that the blade is pointing to the sky, with the pommel resting lightly on your crown chakra; and asks you to think of an issue, event or situation in your life that has hurt you, or from which you are finding it hard to move on....

After allowing you time to identify anything that is important for you to understand at this time, he asks you to replay the experience in your mind – seeing it from every side and all points of view, not just your own.... and, as you comply, you become aware that you are being surrounded in an electric-blue Light; and you find your emotional reactions to whatever you are contemplating fading – your reasoning processes become focused, clear and concise....

Recognising this, Chamuel directs you to pinpoint anything you learned (*and* what you may have enabled others to learn) because of the experience.... and, as your mind explores this, you become aware that the Light surrounding you has turned golden-yellow – and you find that you are able to see all aspects of what your experienced with profound insight and understanding....

Once he is happy that you have achieved a balanced perspective, Chamuel asks you to forgive yourself, and any others concerned, for any transgressions – real or perceived; and to thank all those concerned for what has been taught and learned.... and, as you open your heart, the Light surrounding you changes to a deep rose-pink; and your heart is filled with unconditional love for all concerned....

In this state you are truly ready to forgive *and* forget.... and, as you recognise and accept this, the Light around you shifts one last time, and becomes a bright silver.... Observing this, Chamuel asks you to repeat the following affirmation:

> *"I am ready and willing to release and discharge any and all karmic debts and ties connected with this event. I invoke the Divine Light of Grace to free me NOW....*
> *I am ready and willing to release and discharge any and all karmic debts and ties connected with this event. I invoke the Divine Light of Grace to free me NOW....*
> *I am ready and willing to release and discharge any and all karmic debts and ties connected with this event. I invoke the Divine Light of Grace to free me NOW...."*

Gradually you realise that your heart and mind feel lighter and more free – and, as the

Light around you fades, Chamuel returns his sword to its sheath, asking that (once you have practised it for yourself), you share this process with others, so that they too may move forwards less burdened.

Strolling a little way down the bank, Chamuel reaches out to a cluster of purple iris growing near the water's edge, and carefully plucks one: then, returning to sit beside you, he uses a finger to outline its three curving petals – drawing your attention to the deep-purple fluted edges and white centres, and the tight cluster of golden stamens at its heart. He tells you that the purple of the flower melds the Ruby Ray of the Passion and Power of Divine Love (on which he and his twin flame serve) with the Indigo Ray of Cosmic Wisdom and Insight; and focuses them on the white centre and golden core, which holds the purity and totality of Divine Source, anchored through supremely wise and focused intent. Gently touching the petals of the flower again, one-by-one, Chamuel adds that the three petals also symbolise the three-fold Flames of the heart – those of Will, Wisdom and Love – held in perfect balance. With a smile, he tells you that the iris serves him as a symbol of hope *and* as a reminder of the Absolute Light, reunion with which can only be accomplished through total surrender to the Power of Love – adding that, whenever you see an iris of any colour, it is a sign of his presence; and a reminder of the Love that he carries for you: furthermore, if you research the meaning or principles behind its colour, this will give you insight into the purpose of (or reason for) his presence at that time.

Having tucked the flower into his braid, he gives you a deep-red hexagonal crystal, and tells you that this is **Ruby**, his third Crystal Champion – explaining:

> *"Rubies are the primary carriers of the Ruby Ray, which governs the Transformative Passion and Power of The Divine. Hence Ruby is energising and warming on all levels, and can provide you with the courage and determination to move forwards in life with greater faith and trust in your Self – and in the future. Ruby can also help you in being merciful and kind to yourself and to others, and will support you in recognising that* nothing *is more important than living freely through your heart in the Light of Love. Ruby achieves this by, firstly, opening your heart to the Divine Presence and aligning you with your Highest potential; and secondly – and most importantly – by helping you ground the Light of Divine Love and Compassion fully into your Bodies – physical and energetic. Ruby's innate Fire may then give you the courage to identify, locate and reveal any traumatic memories held within your body, mind and/or emotions; and the strength to fully release their karmic imprint from All that you ARE, freeing you on all levels to embrace your innately loving and forgiving nature, whilst revelling in every opportunity that life has to offer. Then, as your heart is freed, you will find that Ruby is the gem of the spiritual warrior, supporting you in aiding others with your merciful insight and compassion."*

Smiling, Chamuel affirms that Ruby may therefore aid you in surrendering to the Love that IS within you, firing and inspiring you with Divine Passion!

Turning his head, Chamuel gives a low whistle, at which a pair of fawn and white dogs bound out from where they have been resting in the shade of the willow tree. As they come to lie calmly at his feet, Chamuel tells you that these are Saluki – an ancient breed of hunting dog that has a keen sense of smell and excellent eyesight. He explains that this pair guard and protect the entrances to the Temple of the Ruby Ray in which he serves, and – if you ever decide to visit him in that Temple – they will let you pass, as long as your heart and mind are open and ready to accept his Teachings. Stroking their silky fur, he remarks that dogs are intensely loyal companions, who show both devotion and unconditional love to all who treat them with kindness and respect: accordingly you might choose to call upon **Dog** whenever you need a loyal and trustworthy companion to walk by your side; or if you need to understand how to give (or earn) loyalty and trust; or if you want to learn how to expand your heart, and love yourself and others without condition. With a smile, he points out that Dog's keen senses may also help guide you back to the right path if you have become lost or confused; whilst their ability to 'see' the world in different ways (and through other Dimensions) can be called upon if you wish to learn how to hone your own senses, and shift or extend your awareness in (or out of) the physical world – perhaps if you would like to be more in tune with the natural world around you; or when you are journeying, meditating or in an otherwise altered state. With a chuckle, he points out that dogs are also excellent guards, and good judges of character: hence you may also call upon Dog to teach you discernment in your dealings with other people; or ask that these particular animals draw close to attend you if you feel unsafe or vulnerable on any level – adding that Dog may also appear to *you* to warn you if danger is near, or if something you are contemplating doing is unsafe or unwise (or, in the case of this pair) to lead you to his Temple, if it is time to expand your learning.

The Greenwood Guardians – Birch and Cherry:

His *personal* mentoring complete for now, Chamuel affirms he is always available to aid and support you: you need only bring him to mind and ask for his presence, and he will attend you. Furthermore, he tells you that two great Tree Beings of the Plant Kingdom have also asked to support you in addressing his Theme of 'SELF-ACCEPTANCE', adding that you need only request *their* presence, and they will be with you.

He explains that the first of these Greenwood Guardians is the Masculine essence of Birch, who has asked to overlight and help you ground whatever work you undertake within *any* aspect of his chapter. The second is the Feminine essence of Cherry, who has specifically asked to help you understand and assimilate his Gift of The Rose-pink Flame of Divine Compassion (if you have chosen to accept it).

When you are ready to connect with Chamuel's first Greenwood Guardian, you need simply call for the presence of **Birch** (*) .... Birch envelops you in a misty silver-grey Light, and the Masculine spirit essence of Birch speaks to you, saying:

> *"I am the flexibility that you need in all situations where you find yourself challenged by the words or deeds of others – or even just through the simple act of being in this world. For I have the fullness and generosity of spirit to simply* allow*: and, in that act of allowing, I offer you my peace, serenity and soft and gentle tranquillity.... So simply rest awhile in my embrace and enjoy the beauty that surrounds you.... Then know that in my arms may be found rest; in my arms may be found peace; and in my arms may be discovered the courage such as is found in the heart of a lion, and the innocence such*

as is found in the heart of the lamb. Then let the soft whispers of my leaves calm your mind, and let my bark draw forth your pains and sorrows, that they may be returned to the Earth, purified by my touch.... For, in learning to accept all, whilst still fighting to clarify and uphold your own truths above all else, you will discover the true beauty that you hold within – that of a pure and loving heart that bleeds always for the Divine within all things. Know, however, that for every drop that is shed so you will come to find the peace that allows you to BE: and in that BEing so you may find yourself, and truly understand your reason for being...."

(* Dalmation Stone and Blue Chalcedony will help you ground and connect with the energies and wisdom of Birch, if you wish to enhance your experience using crystals.)

If you have chosen to accept and work with Chamuel's Gift, and when you are ready to connect with his second Greenwood Guardian, you need simply call for the presence of **Cherry** (*) .... Cherry envelops you in a deep rose-pink Light, and the Feminine spirit essence of Cherry speaks to you, saying:

"Let me fill your heart with brightness and good cheer, suffusing you with the sweetness that lies at my heart, so that you may recognise and appreciate the bountiful beauty of the world around you, which has been so perfectly designed to meet every need in every moment.... Then may the strength and Light at my heart provide you with renewed hope and determination, given through the fruits of my being – their sweet flesh offering pleasure and comfort to the Soul; their seeds offering new life and new beginnings.... See too how every aspect of me honours all those that share my world, through an open heart and a generosity of spirit that understands there is abundance and plenty for all, freely and lovingly given: for my grace and joy in giving knows that a gift freely given is a gift shared – and so my heart swells with love for all that I give and all that I see within the hearts of others. Thus I would help you *give of* your *Self, that you might lovingly reveal the bitter-sweetness at your heart, that it may become transformed in the Divine Light and so mirror the sweet perfection of my own...."*

(* Malachite and Scolecite will help you ground and connect with the energies and wisdom of Cherry, if you wish to enhance your experience using crystals.)

ARCHEIA MARYLLISA

'LIFE IS BEAUTIFUL'

CRYSTAL CHAMPIONS:

Angelite ♥ Malachite ♥ Carnelian

CREATURE COMPANIONS:

Chameleon ♥ Glow-worm ♥ Great Grey Owl

GREENWOOD GUARDIANS:

Apple ♥ Rowan

*I recognise and appreciate
the beauty and munificence of the Universe.
ALL is right and perfect!*

MEETING MARYLLISA

You find yourself standing alone enveloped in something that appears to be a dense white mist – yet it is neither cold nor wet. Whatever it is has no substance that you can sense; and totally obscures your vision, so you cannot see the ground – even though you can feel it is reassuringly present beneath your feet. You feel somewhat disorientated, yet you are not afraid: instead you feel strangely peaceful and calm as the intense whiteness slowly fills your mind, stilling all your senses. After a while the mist starts swirling about you, thinning and fading just enough to enable you to see the bent and twisted figure of an old woman, sitting on a rough wooden bench in front of you – the white mist eddying all around her.

The garment she is wearing is ragged and dirty, its original form and colour long gone, and her deeply lined face sags in misshapen creases and folds of grime-encrusted skin. Unkempt bristly eyebrows protrude over pouched eyelids and gauntly-hollow eye sockets, drawing your attention to her long hooked nose, which bears a particularly repulsive dewdrop on its tip; whilst a wild tangle of straggly grey hair, matted with grease, completes the image of a truly ugly old crone. Lifting a wrinkled hand spotted with age, she beckons to you to come closer with a gnarled and clawed finger that ends in a yellowing talon-like nail, which is also caked in some sort of filth whose origin you have no wish to contemplate – and so, despite your outer revulsion at what you see (and smell!) you step closer. As you do, the old crone suddenly lifts her head – and you find yourself gazing into a pair of the most beautiful emerald-green eyes you have ever seen: these seem to draw you hypnotically in, and so when she asks you to sit beside her, you simply do as she asks.

Once you are settled, the woman speaks to you with a voice that is cracked with age and disuse. She asks you to close your eyes, and then use the power of your imagination to create a beautiful scene or landscape in your mind – somewhere that brings you close to nature, and where you feel especially at ease: this might be an actual place that you already love and know well, or be one created solely within your mind that – for you – encapsulates beauty and peace. So, closing your eyes, you lose yourself in the enjoyment and fun of this task, observing and adding as much detail as possible to your rendering – including the location's atmosphere and environment; its flora and fauna; and its colours, aromas, textures and sounds....

Once you have included all the aspects you can think of or imagine, the woman tells you to open your eyes – and you discover that the white mist has vanished; the scene you imagined made manifest *here*, down to every last perfect detail!

The old woman is still there in all her forsaken glory, however, (the only thing that mars the perfection of the scene!) – and, noting your thought, she gives a small smile: she then asks you to close your eyes again, and use your imagination once more – this time to create in your mind an image of whatever you define as womanly perfection. Again you close your eyes, and lose yourself in this task – observing and considering every single tiny feature of the face you wish to create, along with every possible aspect of her figure and form; before clothing and adorning her in whatever way you wish, again in as much detail as you possibly can....

Once you have included all the elements you can think of or imagine, she again tells you to open your eyes – at which you discover that the ugly old crone has been remade in the image you have just created in your mind's eye: this beautiful woman is Archeia Maryllisa. With a gentle smile she lovingly embraces you; and greets you in a light and musical voice, declaring:

> *"I am Maryllisa, the Lady Radiant – Archangelic Mirror of the Divine Light, Keeper of the Flame of Truth and Light, and twin flame of Haniel. In me you see your feminine, (and perhaps Angelic!) perfected ideal revealed in all its glory and magnificence – even if in this lifetime you have chosen the human, and perhaps masculine, form of Be-ing. Yet the beauty you see here truly IS in the eye (I) of the beholder, for in the splendour of nature and in the perfection of me you see yourself; and through my Light you see and know the pure, brilliant and beautiful Being you truly are – for Truth is beauty, as indeed beauty is Truth! And when you realise that Truth is the offspring of the Union of Divine Wisdom and Love, you will understand that, through the Divine Creator Unified as ONE, comes the Power of Oneness over all things.... So surrender to that ultimate peace, and embrace the bliss of Being within the Light of the One True Self – Creation and Creator; where there* is *no separation.... no division.... no disharmony. For it is only in Union that we see and know the whole, perfect and complete beauty, harmony and peace that exists at the heart of all we are – in this lifetime and state of Being, and in others – and thence* know *all and BE all."*

The form you have created for Maryllisa then shimmers, and she momentarily fades from sight; before reappearing bathed in soft golden light, like the glow of candlelight. She smiles again, and suggests that you take a little time to note anything that has changed about her or her environment, whilst accustoming yourself to her energies.

As your eyes quickly scan Maryllisa's face and form, you find that her appearance remains much as you imagined it: the only obvious exceptions appear to be her skin, which is now translucent and glowing – as if lit from within by the same soft gold Light that surrounds her; her eyes, which are now an even deeper emerald-green than they were when she first held your gaze; and two additions to her personal adornment.

The first (and most striking) of these is a close-fitting gold collar that encircles the base of her neck: this collar has a small loop affixed at its centre, from which two fine gold chains suspend a delicate cage-like gold pendant over her heart. The 'cage' has been fashioned in such a way that it secures a large brilliant-cut diamond on the horizontal plane – face up; point down: this is the gem that links her with Haniel, her twin flame. A large gold ring creates the top of the 'cage', and holds the upper face of the diamond in its correct orientation; whilst a much smaller gold ring creates the base of the 'cage', and supports and protects the diamond's point. The rings are joined by ten perpendicular gold wires (like the bars of a birdcage), which hold the diamond securely and safely in place. When you examine the diamond more closely, you observe that its face has a mirror-like sheen and is highly reflective; whilst the body of the gem appears to hold a living flame, which flickers and flares with rainbow Light.

The only other addition that is obvious is the ring that Maryllisa is wearing on the middle finger of her right hand: this has a wide gold band, and bears a dark-red ruby set in a plain gold surround. The ruby has been polished into an oval domed cabochon – and, noting your interest, Maryllisa tilts her hand, showing how the highly-polished surface of the gem diffracts the light, creating a radiant five-rayed star; and explaining that, for obvious reasons, this type of ruby is known as a 'Star Ruby'.

Your scrutiny of Maryllisa complete, you shift your attention to your surroundings, which again remain much as you had imagined them. The main difference is that the bench you are both sitting on is now both functional *and* beautiful – the sturdy seat of the bench being made from a wide plank of seasoned oak that has been polished to a soft sheen, set within an arching frame that has been delicately wrought from a silvery-grey metal. The frame has open-latticed side panels that are decorated with insects and birds – one side being intricately embellished with tiny flowers, bees and lacewing beetles, which have been fashioned from silver, bronze and gold and painstakingly gilded and enamelled in exquisite detail, so that they seem almost to be alive; whilst the other is covered with equally amazing renditions of multi-coloured Birds of Paradise, central to which is an emerald-green quetzal bird, whose eyes are depicted by orange fire opals.

The only other changes are within your immediate environment, where an old apple tree now stands behind the bench, its ancient twisted branches supporting a rambling rose whose creamy-white blossoms are emitting a sweet yet subtle perfume; whilst in front of you a low rockery hosts a mass of tall slender-stemmed white amaryllis lilies, which are swaying to and fro as they are stirred by a gentle breeze.

MARYLLISA'S TEACHINGS
The Light of The Star of Venus and The Beauty Within:

Recognising your interest, Maryllisa reaches down to carefully extract an amaryllis from the ground: gently cradling the tear-shaped bulb at the base of the stem, she tells you that bulbs are designed to absorb nourishment during each leafing period, supplying the energy that allows the plant to grow with vigour and blossom anew, year upon year; and then storing everything needed to sustain the plant through its periods of dormancy. She observes that some call these particular plants 'naked ladies' because they flower after their foliage has died down – yet their proper name is 'Amaryllis Belladonna', which is a name that she identifies closely with! Holding it out, she directs your attention to the plant's leafless bronze stem, and the cluster of twelve trumpet-shaped flowers at its tip, each of which has three outer and three inner snow-white petals: these are delicately veined in the deepest crimson; and, as she tilts the flower from side to side, you see that each petal has an iridescent shimmer, which is visible only as it catches the light. At this, Maryllisa smiles, explaining that the name is very apt, as 'Amaryllis' means 'to sparkle'; whilst 'Belladonna' means 'beautiful lady'.

Maryllisa tells you that – in their wild and natural state – amaryllis grow and bloom the most prolifically following a wildfire: this is because fire burns away environmental negativity and disease and clears the way to allow more light to reach the ground beneath – thus providing the ideal environment for vigorous and productive growth. She muses that this shows the plants' innate resilience and ability to conquer adversity; and serves as a metaphor for human embodiment, whereby you undergo the 'trials of fire' created by life's lessons and experiences, using the clarity and knowledge thus gained to grow and blossom anew with greater wisdom and strength; before finally casting off your physical beauty and shedding your form.

Gently stroking the petals of the amaryllis, Maryllisa remarks that their stunning beauty is only present for a relatively short part of the plant's life-cycle: yet, to her, *all* of the plant is beautiful *all* of the time, because she understands that true beauty is not about the superficial appearance of physical perfection, shape or form, but is about the inner beauty and radiance of the spirit within. With a smile, she adds that therefore, if you truly wish to grow (and sparkle!), one of the most valuable things you can do is to recognise, own and appreciate *your* inner beauty, especially if it is currently masked or obscured. Wryly she observes that, sadly, some people seek to hide, suppress or alter who they truly are beneath fake facades or layers of camouflage – perhaps because they fear that who and what they are is somehow 'not good enough'; or in the misguided belief that hiding their true Self makes them less vulnerable.

Taking your hand, Maryllisa holds your gaze with her fabulous eyes, and stresses that *true* beauty is founded upon how you choose to live your life, and the daily choices you make; in the love and respect you have for yourself and *all* of your world; and in the honesty and integrity you demonstrate in every moment of every single day. With a gentle smile she emphasises that *everyone* has a beautiful and gifted Soul, and declares that you will find *your* inner Light and beauty by believing in your strengths, attributes and innate gifts and talents; and living them with every beat of your heart: after all, if your Light is camouflaged or veiled, how can others possibly hope to see and emulate your reality?

Releasing your hand and getting to her feet, Maryllisa tells you that she wants to help the beautiful truth of your Divinity (which IS within) blossom; so that it may sparkle and shine throughout all of your Being – and with these words she gently touches the amaryllis to your Soul Star chakra and crown, before circling it once in the air above you.... as she does so, you sense your crown chakra gently opening; and you feel yourself becoming connected to the wisdom and guidance of your Higher-self with greater clarity and strength: then somehow you see, feel or simply know that you are being showered in a multitude of iridescent sparks of rainbow Light, which are pouring down through your auric field and saturating you to your very core....

As you immerse yourself in the blissful sensations of the moment, Maryllisa urges you to allow your energies to shift and adjust; and to engage with whatever new state of Being is right for you at this time – explaining that the beauty and glory of the Divine Light (which is now within *and* without you) will help you to become more at ease with your true Self, supporting you in refining and polishing all your many positive aspects – until they spill, like stars, to surround you in a sparkling halo of Light....

After allowing you time for your energies to rebalance and settle, Maryllisa rests her hand on your head in Blessing, reminding you that – in that Light – nothing can be hidden; and thus you will be seen and acknowledged as the beautiful spirit and spark of The Divine that, in truth, you are: she then returns the amaryllis carefully to its earthy bed, thanking it for its gift.

Looking down, Maryllisa draws your attention to a small lizard with bug eyes and a coiled up tail resting on the rockery near the lilies. It is so well camouflaged, with dull fawn and brown markings, that you had not noticed it before; and, with a chuckle, she lifts it and places it near the quetzal bird on the lattice panel, where you watch its skin morph into hues of silver, grey and green. Telling you that this clever little lizard is a chameleon, and a master of the art of camouflage, she remarks that (even though she has asked you to shed your disguises) **Chameleon** can teach you to recognise the merits of utilising camouflage if and when circumstances truly warrant it, and/or to understand the disadvantages of employing camouflage when it is not really necessary or appropriate. With a smile, she adds that Chameleon can also help you identify the reasons behind any perceived need you might have to project a certain image if it is not truly necessary, and show you how to create the image you really need to convey in a more appropriate form, whilst still remaining true to your Self. Maryllisa explains that Chameleon may also help you see behind any falsehoods, disguises or facades that others might erect to hide the truth from you; or aid you in sensing the true nature of anything that you encounter in visualisation or meditation, or when journeying out-of-body in other Dimensions. She points out that, as you can see, chameleons can adjust the different wavelengths of light that they reflect, and shift through an amazingly varied colour palette: thus, Chameleon is an ideal teacher to call upon if you would like to know more about the complexity and attributes of colour, in all its hues, tones and textures (perhaps to understand how using or wearing certain colours in your environment can enhance, change or adjust your energies – and thus influence or reinforce the image that you convey); or if you would like to comprehend more about the properties and purpose of Light, in all its frequencies and vibrational forms, so that you may discover how to use it to support your growth and development. Returning the chameleon to its original location, Maryllisa chuckles as it stretches out to soak up the warmth of the rock and changes colour again; and retakes her seat beside you on the bench....

Lifting her hand, Maryllisa draws your attention back to her ruby ring, pointing out the five-rayed star that it bears at its heart. She tells you that what you see is the Star of Venus, which anchors another aspect of her persona – that of Ishtar, Goddess 'Venus Morning Star', in which role she bears the Light of Truth for Earth and all the planetary bodies of the Solar System; and through which she upholds the Light of The Divine Feminine, by means of the Madonna-blue Light of the Mother and the Silver Light of The Ray of Illumination and Inspiration. Then, with a quick movement of her hand that leaves an impression of a silvery-blue five-rayed star hovering in the air between you, Maryllisa smiles – reaching out and closing her hand around the star, before opening her fingers to reveal a small soft-blue polished stone.

Giving this to you, she tells you that this is **Angelite**, her first Crystal Champion – explaining:

"Angelite has a high fine resonance and is the stone that can most easily connect you with the spiritual attributes of the planet Venus, which are those of the Highest Spiritual Love. Angelite holds the Blue and Silver Rays in perfect balance and harmony, carrying both Truth and Grace at its heart; and resonates strongly with the throat, brow, crown

and Soul Star chakras to promote open, honest and trustworthy communication between your lower-self and Higher-self – and between (and within) all Planes and Dimensions of Being, including (as its name suggests) the Realms of the Angels. Angelite innately promotes a feeling of inner peace, making it a useful support for meditation or inner work; whilst its cooling and calming energies make it useful to hold or carry if you have a tendency to be impetuous or outspoken, helping you think with care and consideration before you speak or act. Angelite is especially good to work with if you are truly serious about your spiritual growth, and have (or are willing to have) the determination to shine your Light and BE true to your Self – for, despite its aura of stillness and calm, Angelite also has the ability to 'light the fires' of transformation and growth within you, if and when you are truly ready to move forwards."

With a smile, Maryllisa affirms that Angelite may therefore help you connect with the Star of Venus and embody the Truth of your Being – thus accepting your inner beauty and perfection, and finding inner peace.

The Rose of Peace and The Dynamic Duality of Absolute Balance:

Reaching out, Maryllisa plucks a tightly closed bud from the climbing rose behind you and caresses its pale peachy-pinkness: then, placing it on her palm, she asks you to watch as it slowly unfurls – revealing each perfect petal one by one, until eventually a flawless creamy-white bloom, tinged with pink and gold, lies fully open in her hand.... With a smile, she tells you that the rose is a rich symbol of many things, including all that is of The Divine Feminine and the eternal spark of the Soul. Showing how the creamy-white pink-blushed petals grow from the golden heart of the flower, which is tinged with red, Maryllisa remarks that this rose is well-named, 'Peace' – for it bears the passion of The Divine Father (red), which flows through the heart of Divine Wisdom (gold) and is given life through the purity and love of The Divine Mother (white and pink). Touching you over your heart, Maryllisa reminds you that, just like the rose, beauty comes through your heart: for this is where you connect to your Christed-self through your three-fold heart-flames of Divine Will, Wisdom and Love – explaining that the rose therefore offers a metaphor for the advent of Christ-consciousness, whereby (as the Wisdom of your Christed-self becomes As One with your Being) you embody Divine Love, and know both perfect balance and true Peace.

Taking your attention back to the climbing rose, Maryllisa points out how all its stems and flowers come from just one root – the same principle of which may be applied to you: for you will have chosen to play many roles over many lifetimes in a wide range of situations – some of which will have been on Earth; some of which may not even have been human, or of this world. She explains that, nonetheless, all will have been designed to help you learn about and understand the qualities of personal power and sovereignty, tolerance and acceptance, compassion and unconditional love, so that you may come to recognise and know the beauty and glory of the Divine Light that is within (and a part of) all things: then – once more holding your gaze with her emerald eyes – she stresses that therefore attaining and retaining 'perfect balance' – whilst grounding and holding Love within your heart – is key to your Ascension.

After thinking, Maryllisa says that one of the main reasons for earthly embodiment is to experience the duality of human nature, in order to understand your strengths and know your weaknesses – and thus learn and grow: one aspect of this means being able to recognise and appreciate your 'masculine' and 'feminine' sides in order to utilise them harmoniously and effectively, which is extremely important if you wish to BE in balance. With a chuckle she points out that this has nothing to do with the gender in which you embody; but concerns the varied aspects, attributes and characteristics that *everyone* possesses and can draw upon, which tend to be classed either as 'masculine' (such as physical presence, structure, form and logic) or 'feminine' (such as emotional presence, creativity, change and intuition). Maryllisa expounds that being able to recognise that different situations require different strengths and skills is, therefore, vital: for example, if you wanted to build something like a house or a car, in order to construct the best possible product you would need to draw on your creativity and imagination *as well as* your logic and attention to detail – ideally bringing your 'masculine' or 'feminine' aspects to the fore as each situation required. Smiling, she adds that, regardless of the body you have chosen now, you *will* have taken both male and female forms in other lifetimes and existences, which will have served to let you experience things from their very different perspectives – and so (amongst other things) enabled you to learn about honour, integrity and respect and the right and proper use of power. She points out that this in turn helps you understand how to be balanced in heart, mind and spirit, so that you may then more fully embody the Reality of 'Unity of Self' – whereby 'masculine' and 'feminine'; the many and the one, are simply aspects of one being and *not* separate entities; and through which you will ultimately be able to embrace the Divine state of Unity Consciousness, where *all* is simply held in absolute balance and is *always* at the point of perfect harmony.

Reminding you that it is only through accepting and recognising all as being equal in the eyes and heart of The Divine that you will know balance and be at peace, she gives you a small polished stone that is banded in shades of emerald green and black; and tells you that this is **Malachite**, her second Crystal Champion – explaining:

"Malachite, as you can see, forms in beautiful layers that carry the Emerald Ray of Profound Truths and Perfected Manifestation, along with the Green Ray of Balance and the Black Light of Potential. Malachite is an excellent transmitter of a deep and intense energy that has the power to break down density and shift blockages in the energy field, making it especially good at 'un-earthing' anything that needs to be addressed and resolved in order for you to move forwards unburdened. Accordingly, Malachite can (and will) catalyse change within anything that tests your heart balance on any level of mind, body and spirit; whilst strengthening your resolve and giving you the self-belief and confidence to overcome your inner fears and accept whatever change will enable your heart to truly blossom. Although working with Malachite can be demanding and even testing at times, it is without peer in encouraging and supporting all efforts of transformation that require refinement, change and/or transition from a 'lower' to a 'Higher' state. Malachite is also the stone that can most closely connect you with the spiritual attributes of the Earth – and, if used together with Angelite, it will powerfully

and lovingly support you through all times of change and transformation, whilst helping you to clear and balance yourself on all levels, so that you hold more Light (and Love) in your heart."

Smiling, Maryllisa affirms that Malachite may therefore help you identify and clear anything that prevents you from having an open heart, whilst also giving you the inner strength to balance opposing forces and hold them in harmony.

Settling back in her seat, Maryllisa tells you that if *you* want to know balance, it is also important to accept and acknowledge that you have (and are capable of expressing) many different aspects of your Self, including those that perhaps you perceive as 'bad' – appreciating and respecting the strengths *and* weaknesses that each contributes to your life experiences and makes you the person that you are in this lifetime. Emphasising that every aspect has more than one side, Maryllisa stresses that, hence, it is useful and wise to understand the divergent qualities of each: for instance, you might view the emotion of anger as 'bad' – yet it can rouse you to appropriately-focused acts of physical strength and honourable behaviour, by boosting your determination, fierceness or courage; *or* (conversely) initiate intolerant, inflexible, out-of-control or inappropriate behaviours that are hazardous to the body, mind and Soul. Smiling, she adds that recognising that true 'balance' is therefore not static, but is dynamic and open to instantaneous change depending on the circumstance or situation you find yourself in, may help you see that how you choose to *label* the different aspects of your Self is not important, but how you choose to *apply* them is!

Reaching up towards a tiny source of light that glows at the very top of the arbour, Maryllisa captures it in her hands: she tells you that this is a female glow-worm, which despite its name is actually a type of beetle. As you look at it, you realise how strong and effective its light is and how far it carries, even though it is very small: at this, Maryllisa smiles and tells you that calling upon **Glow-worm** can help you make connections to the vast repositories of Spiritual Wisdom and Enlightenment held within the Universal Web, and assist you in comprehending the mysteries behind your reason for Being – including those that inspired your choices for your current cycle of death and rebirth, and/or your 'past', 'future' or 'other' existences. She adds that, because Glow-worm is a master at creating light, she can also be asked to assist you in balancing the flow of Light within your heart, helping you fulfil your purpose for Being with more confidence and ease; or to show you how to shift the balance of light you hold, so that in every moment you instinctively know the most appropriate aspect of your Self to call upon; or to help you recognise and appreciate the value of who you are and what you have to contribute to the world; or support you in understanding and/or learning ways of making your own light shine more brightly. Returning the glow-worm to her home on the arbour with a knowing smile, Maryllisa remarks that Glow-worm also knows the best way to attract a mate over a long distance: hence, you could also call upon her guidance if you want to do the same(!) – or if you simply wish to attract new friends or companions into your life, whether this is to aid your learning at that time, or if you just want to lift your spirits and have some fun.

The Gift of The Mirror of The Soul:
With a smile, Maryllisa morphs back into the form in which you first met her – for it is of little importance to her what shape or form she takes; and, now you know who and what she truly is, you find it is of less consequence to you as well.... she then asks you to close your eyes and open your heart and mind, as you did before; and focus on simply feeling and sensing *her* heart and *her* innate essence....

As you do as she asks, you sense the beauty that is you and that is her – the beauty of an open heart and an open mind filled with acceptance and love; and realise the joy and ecstasy of just simply Being.... and then, as your heart expands, you feel yourself connecting with Maryllisa's strength and grace; and hear her ask if you are willing to accept her presence.... Your Soul immediately says 'yes' – at which you feel your energy field expand to twice its usual size, strengthening around your pranic core and grounding you firmly to the ground below your feet.... at some level you realise that you have experienced BEing like this before, and recognise too that, in this state, you *know* what it is to be at absolute peace....

After waiting to allow you time to assimilate and enjoy this feeling, Maryllisa tells you not to doubt what you are thinking – emphasising that *knowing* and *feeling* the power and inner strength of who and what you truly are draws you ever closer to your true Divine nature – for *that* is truly you, not your human third-Dimensional Self, which so often becomes mired in the trivia that holds you back from BEcoming your Reality.... then, after allowing you a little longer in the bliss of the moment, Maryllisa withdraws her immediate presence, and you feel your energy field gradually return to normal....

Opening your eyes you are aware that your heart feels more open and balanced, even though most of the sensations have faded; and with a smile, Maryllisa tells you that you have just experienced merely a taste of what it is to be your Christed-self. Gently taking your hand, she says that if you wish to always BE in that state, you have to learn to master your 'lower' nature, which necessitates being able to attain and retain balance within your mind, body and spirit at all times. With a sympathetic smile she says that she knows that this is not easy, but reminds you that the first steps in accomplishing it lie in, firstly, recognising when you are out of balance and then, secondly, doing something about it – which entails identifying *what* has unbalanced you, and *why*; and proactively making whatever changes are necessary in order to help you return to balance and regain your centre.

Saying that her Gift is designed to aid you with this, Maryllisa's outline blurs and shimmers, and she returns to the 'perfect' form you created for her.... then, standing in front of you, she takes her pendant and presses the upper face of the diamond to her right palm – and, holding out her hand, shows you that this has made an impression of a small silvered lens-shaped disc, which – as you watch – slowly takes on etheric shape and form.... Explaining that this is her Gift of The Mirror of the Soul, Maryllisa now rests her left hand on your shoulder, and turns her right hand palm down over your crown: this allows the disc to pass through your crown and down the pranic core of your energy Body, until it finally comes to rest on the horizontal plane, spanning your pranic core level with your heart....

You then feel Maryllisa's hand rest on your head in Blessing, and hear her say:

"Be open.... Be free.... Be true to your Self and proud of who you are and what you bring to the world. Acknowledge and accept the role you have to play, and be secure in the truth and perfection of your inner nature and Soul essence that enables this to be so. This, above all things, I ask of you; and, in return, I promise my love and support whenever you have need of it."

Her words complete, Maryllisa retakes her seat by your side and explains that her Gift reflects and focuses the Diamond Light, and has a threefold purpose: firstly, it will show you your true reflection (not only that of your embodied 'lower-self', but that of the Self that IS you, regardless of the path you choose or the nature of your Reality); secondly, it will allow you to see the reflection of The Divine (in whatever form it chooses to show itself), that you may never be without hope or purpose; and thirdly, it will help you to magnify your magnificence and shine your Light more radiantly to the world. Smiling, she adds that the mirror allows no pretence, no masks, no lies – and hence you may also use it to help you discern the true essence of a person, a place or a situation, rather than relying on your sense of sight alone – which can sometimes lead you astray, if it is not fully engaged with your heart and Soul.

Maryllisa now gives you a translucent orange stone, telling you that it is **Carnelian**, her third Crystal Champion – explaining:

"Carnelian is one of the prime carriers of the Orange Ray, on which I am honoured to serve. Its Light resonates with the fiery core of the Earth, and defines the passion which you experience through human embodiment, and the zest you have for the life you are able to live: thus, to work with Carnelian is to connect with your inner power, giving you the self-confidence and self-belief to BE in your own truth and proudly say 'This is who I am', undaunted by – and unconcerned about – the reactions and responses of others. Carnelian is also well-regarded as a stone for the warrior, offering you a fiery yet stable support when times are difficult or hard; and providing a boost of power when you need the energy and determination to be (or do) what you truly have to. Along the way, as you search for your True Self and your place in the world, Carnelian will do its best to inspire you to look deeper within and around you, whilst reminding you of the importance of discernment and discretion in all that you think, say and do. Carnelian is also an ideal choice for helping you connect with the Elemental Beings of Earth, that you may understand how ALL life forms – visible and invisible – have a part to play in the Planetary Sphere of Life."

With a smile, Maryllisa affirms that Carnelian may therefore give you the courage to see yourself with honesty and clarity, and the strength to enable you to shine your Light brightly upon the world.

Gesturing at the landscape you created, she remarks that humankind rarely takes enough time to stop and truly look in detail at the world in which they live – reminding you that everything that has been created through the hand of The Divine has its own beauty and purpose (and hence is capable of engendering a sense of wonder within you, if you examine it with an open heart and mind). She adds that it is only through opening your eyes to see the wondrous design and purpose behind everything that surrounds you that you will *truly* understand your connection to Source – and to all life, sentient and non-sentient; and will *truly* appreciate that everything IS an infinite part of you, just as you too are an infinite part of the Creator: beautiful in your Light, and perfectly created for your purpose.

Maryllisa then gives a whistle, and a large grey owl glides silently over the ground towards her.... As he lands on her outstretched arm, she tells you that this is a Great Grey owl, who is also perfectly created for his purpose, being one of the most skilled, swift and silent hunters of the night – able to track his prey, even when it is hidden beneath layers of snow. She says that, accordingly, you might call upon **Great Grey Owl** if you need to see below the surface – of yourself, another person, or a situation; or if you want to get to the root of an issue or concern, which may be hidden or hard to see or define. Gently lifting one of the owl's talons, Maryllisa remarks upon their flexibility and strength, observing that you may also call upon Great Grey Owl if you need to get to grips with something (or simply 'get a grip'!), or want help in pinning something down; or if you are having difficulties getting to the root, or heart, of a problem. Directing your attention to his golden eyes and the feathered discs that amplify and focus his hearing, she suggests that Great Grey Owl may also teach you how to utilise all your senses, by helping you develop clairvoyant, clairaudient or clairsentient skills; or show you how to survey a situation, issue or problem with greater clarity and wisdom. Smiling, Maryllisa adds that – as a fearless creature of the night – Great Grey Owl may be a particularly helpful guide if you choose to confront and address your shadow-side, or when you need to conquer your fears of the dark – literal or metaphorical, physical or spiritual; or to show you how to identify, interpret and understand anything you encounter in dreams, visualisations or meditations, or when working or journeying multidimensionally.

The Greenwood Guardians – Apple and Rowan:

Her *personal* mentoring complete for now, Maryllisa affirms she is always available to aid and support you: you need only bring her to mind and ask for her presence, and she will attend you. Furthermore, she tells you that two great Tree Beings of the Plant Kingdom have also asked to support you in addressing her Theme of 'LIFE IS BEAUTIFUL', adding that you need only request *their* presence, and they will be with you.

She explains that the first of these Greenwood Guardians is the Feminine essence of Apple, who has asked to overlight and help you ground whatever work you undertake within *any* aspect of her chapter. The second is the Masculine essence of Rowan, who has specifically asked to help you understand and assimilate her Gift of The Mirror of the Soul (if you have chosen to accept it).

When you are ready to connect with Maryllisa's first Greenwood Guardian, you need simply call for the presence of **Apple** (*) .... Apple envelops you in a pale rust-red Light, and the Feminine spirit essence of Apple speaks to you, saying:

> *"Know that I carry the Light of the Rose and the Hope of the World, which lives within the heartwood at my core. Therefore, through me you may draw upon all possibilities and potentials that Life has to offer you, and experience the infinite ways in which the*

wisdom of the Creator manifests for you. So let me help you open to this now, and aid you in cleansing and clearing all that is not of the Highest order.... then feel yourself slowly come to balance within your centre and become filled with optimistic expectation, as my own inner Light fires and inspires you.... It is true that I know intense sweetness, and I know profound bitterness – yet through the star that is held at the heart of my fruits I know too the nature of eternity and immortality. Thus, within me all IS in balance – and, within that balance, you will encounter knowledge so great that you may tremble as you merge with its Power.... So let me guide you to find the sweetness of life and know the power of true and enlightened wisdom, which is your birthright as an embodied Soul and spark of the Divine Light; that you may come to know yourself truly, and BE certain of your place within the beautiful world that is currently yours...."

(* Smoky Quartz and Red Jasper will help you ground and connect with the energies and wisdom of Apple, if you wish to enhance your experience using crystals.)

If you have chosen to accept and work with Maryllisa's Gift, and when you are ready to connect with her second Greenwood Guardian, you need simply call for the presence of **Rowan** (*) .... Rowan envelops you in a rose-gold Light, and the Masculine spirit essence of Rowan speaks to you, saying:

"The Light that surrounds you now is anchored within the jewel-like fruits of my heart, which know stability, grace and presence. Yet (if you choose to look deeply) you will find inspiration and flexibility too, and experience the joy that can be found when you open yourself – heart, mind and Soul – to the Greater good that underlies all creation. For, in every ruby-red droplet you will find courage and strength; in every orange-fire droplet you will find inspiration and zest; and in every golden-yellow droplet you will find wisdom and learning. Thus, through me, you may learn to ground the Divine Light within, and so experience stability regardless of where your feet are rooted.... through me, you may learn to give and receive with an open and balanced heart, regardless of what assails you.... and, through me, you may understand how to achieve vast spiritual and energetic expansion, limited only by your own beliefs and self-imposed illusions.... So open your heart, and know my protection, which is as old as Time itself: then release your fears and all that holds you confined in smallness, and let me help you live every moment of every day as if it were your last, grasping each and every opportunity with courage, and joyfully taking advantage of all that human life and Earthly embodiment blesses you with...."

(* Bronzite and Green Aventurine will help you ground and connect with the energies and wisdom of Rowan, if you wish to enhance your experience using crystals.)

ARCHANGEL HANIEL

'WALK YOUR WALK – TALK YOUR TALK'

CRYSTAL CHAMPIONS:
Clear Apophyllite ♥ Blue Celestite ♥ Bronzite

CREATURE COMPANIONS:
Black Jaguar ♥ Cicada ♥ Golden Eagle

GREENWOOD GUARDIANS:
Tamarisk ♥ Oak

*I open my heart and freely share
all that inspires and enlightens me.*

MEETING HANIEL

It is midnight on a warm evening in midsummer; and a silvery crescent moon hangs low in the sky, casting just a hint of light that paints your surroundings in shadowy tones of charcoal-black and graphite-grey. Judging by the dark and uninterrupted horizon that stretches away below and all around you, you deduce that you are sitting on the summit of a high rounded hill, which is bare of any discernable features and seemingly far from civilisation. All is silent; all is still, with barely a breath of wind; and there is absolutely nothing to see, except for the magnificent indigo sky that arches overhead and fills your vision – its dark velvety depths teeming with countless silvery pinpricks of light. So, with nothing to do and nowhere to go, you lie back on the grass and relax into the peaceful solitude, simply gazing at the stars....

Little by little all tension drains from your physical body – and, as you become one with the ground beneath you, you feel your energy field begin to expand, until eventually it seems as if you embrace both earth and sky.... and in that moment, you *know* that you are touching upon the infinite wisdom and mystery of the Cosmos, and comprehend the paradox that is simultaneously both your insignificance and your magnificence. As you begin to contemplate this notion, your attention is taken by one of the far-away stars, which appears to be getting bigger: after a moment you realise this is because its once distant light is moving rapidly towards you, drawing ever closer, until you recognise that what you had thought was a star is, in fact, a massive Angel!

Its wings are huge, and with every powerful beat it speeds nearer and nearer, finally landing on the hilltop a short distance away. Startled, you jump to your feet – but the light emanating from the Angel's body is so dazzling that you can only clearly see its outspread wings, which are marked like those of a golden eagle in rich hues and tones of brown, buff and gold: then, with a loud snap, they are folded away and – blinded by the brilliance of the light – you momentarily shield your eyes.

Sensing movement, you decide to chance a peek, and see the Angel adjust its size and sweep a cloak around its shoulders, veiling its light and dimming it to a more tolerable level. In the softened light you now see a human-sized figure of a man who has glowing white skin, which appears to be lit from within: this is Archangel Haniel. He is simply clad in a white knee-length robe, over which he has thrown a magnificent high-collared cloak made from hundreds of feathers of all sorts and sizes – mostly subtle in colour, but some being gloriously vibrant and colourful. Other than this, the only thing of note that you see is a large gold-bound book, which is tucked under his right arm. Haniel greets you, declaring:

"I am Haniel – Guardian of the Flame of Truth and Light, Keeper of the Book of Illumined Truths, and twin flame of Maryllisa, the Lady Radiant. You see within me a Light so great that my body shines like the stars, for it cannot confine it; just as I see the same Light within you, as yet fully veiled. Know that my love and commitment to the Earth and all sentient life she bears is infinite and pure, for it is my proud task and eternal joy to assist this planet, and all that are embraced by her love, to learn and grow, until they too shed their current reality and transmute into Bodies of Light like my own. For this I have worked for aeons, and so I will continue – aided by Souls, like your

own perhaps, who are ready to pledge with whole and joyful hearts to be part of the unique process that is bringing a planet to Light. So feel my Light shine upon your face, and look upon the Book that I carry, for this bears words that are written in Light, penned by your own hand: these show your pledge. And if you connect with the Book through your heart, you will know deep within your Soul what it holds – and who, and what, in truth you are; and then too you may understand the choices you make in moving forwards, as you work to BE that which you designed yourself to be."

With a gentle smile, Haniel steps forwards and touches the book that he carries briefly to your lips, brow and heart; before removing his cloak and draping it carefully around your shoulders: as he does so his light flares, then shimmers and dims as he veils and modifies his form so that you can see and discern him more clearly – at which, the sky around you simply absorbs his Light, and (incredibly) night turns into day.

With a gesture of his hand, Haniel creates a grassy hollow where you both may be at ease: here an orange-berried rowan tree stands behind a low stone bench, which in turn is set beside a still pool of water that reflects the now clear blue sky above. The bench offers somewhere shady to sit – and it is here that Haniel leads you, inviting you to make yourself comfortable so that you may study him and accustom yourself to his energies.

As you settle, you notice that the smoothly polished surface of the bench bears an oriental-style engraving depicting a crane in flight; and (oddly) that a golden tamarind monkey is dozing in the tree above you: Haniel, meanwhile, has settled effortlessly in the lotus position, cross-legged and with his hands resting on the book, which now rests in his lap. Quickly scanning him, you cannot help but notice that his skin remains white and translucent – and, although the light he emits now projects a softer and more subtle aura of Power, you realise you feel safe and secure in his presence, in spite of his slight stature and relatively small physical size.

Taking your gaze to Haniel's face, you observe that his features are classically neat and refined; and note that their delicate (almost androgynous) appearance is reflected in his hands and feet, which are long slim and elegant – and unadorned. He has small ears and a long straight nose, which is set over full lips that hold a gentle smile; and his skin is smooth and unlined, giving the impression of youthfulness. His pure-white close-cropped hair draws the attention to his somewhat sharp bone structure and the paleness of his skin – although you also notice that he has surprisingly dense white eyebrows and lashes, the latter framing a pair of deep-set eyes that have ice-blue irises and deep dark pupils. Their responding gaze seems to penetrate you to the core; yet, even though you know he sees everything you are, you are not unnerved, and you somehow *know* your encounter will be of great benefit to you. You are also becoming aware that his calm demeanour is having a soothing effect on your own energies, and you find yourself reassured by his unassuming – yet profound – air of compassionate wisdom, which makes you eager to learn more.

Turning your attention to his apparel, you see that Haniel is now wearing a simple full-length round-necked robe made of saffron-gold linen: this is gathered round his waist by a belt made from tiny interlocking silver plates that resemble the shield-shaped scales of a snake, which fastens with a figure-eight clasp made of silver, fashioned in the form of two intertwined snakes. A large purse hangs on the right-hand side of his belt: this is shaped like a truncated triangle, and is made of the same saffron linen as his robe. Closer inspection shows that it closes with a flap that is secured by a silver clasp fashioned in the form of a crane, which has a tiny faceted ruby inset to its crown. Noting your interest, Haniel lifts the flap, revealing that the purse bears a symbol embroidered in gold thread, depicting a circle within which a many-rayed Sun is rising over a flat horizon.

Lifting your gaze, your eye is caught by the collar Haniel wears around his neck: this sits just above the neckline of his robe; and is made of a thick 'rope' of solid gold. This holds a large round golden disc (engraved with the same many-rayed sun symbol as his purse) centred over the sternal notch at his throat; and has a long golden cord attached to its lower edge: this cord comprises three fine chains fashioned from tiny oval scales of gold, which have been braided into a single cord that spans his throat and solar plexus chakras. At the midway point of the cord two large eagle's claws – intricately fashioned from gold again – are grasping a large octagonal cut and faceted diamond, which flickers and flares with an inner fire: this rests over his High Heart centre, and is the gem that links him with Maryllisa, his twin flame.

Tearing your gaze away, you note how Haniel's robe has exceptionally long sleeves that are very loose and flowing – and, observing your curiosity, he hitches them up: this reveals that each bicep is encircled by a spiralling torc shaped like a long slender snake. These are similar to those that form the clasp on his belt – although, here, one is made of silver and one of gold: on closer inspection you are amazed by how each is fashioned in exquisite detail – one appearing to be banded, one plain; and you can also see how each has eyes that are inset with tiny cut and faceted deep-orange fire opals, which flicker as if holding tiny living flames.

HANIEL'S TEACHINGS
The Book of Illumined Truths and The Waters of The Diamond Light:

Recognising that your inspection is complete, Haniel lifts the book that is resting in his lap and tells you that this is the Book of Illumined Truths, which contains a record of all the life-path agreements and contracts, sacred commitments, oaths, vows and pledges that you have made over the course of all your existences, in all your many – and varied – states of Being. He explains that all such agreements and commitments are made as you yourself determine it to be appropriate, which is usually – but not necessarily only – at the start of every lifetime or embodiment. Haniel expounds that it is normal practice for you to receive guidance about the exact nature, content and wording of each entry from your Teachers, Guides and your Higher-selves before they are made; emphasising that whatever is eventually written down is binding under Spiritual Law – although entries *can* be added to or amended in exceptional circumstances. With a comical waggle of his eyebrows, he adds that half the 'fun' of Earthly embodiment is that you cannot automatically recall what you have written: this, he explains (on a more serious note) is so you may truly operate with absolute Free Will and choice – even though your apparent lack of direction may feel frustrating, to say the least! Haniel smiles, and tells you that he can empathise with this, for aspects of his Being have experienced Earthly embodiment – and so he understands the dichotomy that this involves.

Putting your Book to one side, Haniel reveals that he has some understanding of the ancient civilisations of the South Americas; and of the spiritual belief system you know as Buddhism. He tells you that the latter system, in particular, has shown him that there is great merit in undertaking the discipline of regular meditation – adding that, even if you choose not to follow its strictest observances, you will find that setting aside daily 'quiet time' for inner contemplation and self-review can be immensely helpful. He explains that this is because mindful practices like this can aid you in reviewing, questioning, planning and navigating your life-path with greater ease – and in recognising and fulfilling your contracts and commitments more effectively: moreover, taking time for inner review and self-contemplation will offer you the clarity and perspective that will enable you to dispel falsehoods and untruths – helping to prevent the accumulation of negativity that might confuse or cloud your mind; and making it easier to address and resolve any issues more quickly, and with greater dispassion.

Haniel now gives a high whistle – at which a lithe and sleek black jaguar appears over the crest of the hill, and bounds across to settle at his side, turning its head to gaze at you with deep topaz-coloured eyes. Haniel tells you that **Black Jaguar** loves to run with the night, and is an experienced guide and powerful protector for anyone who chooses to confront their innermost fears and darkest thoughts, feelings or beliefs. With a smile, he reminds you that you often face your toughest spiritual challenges in the darkness – but if you have the courage to run with Black Jaguar he will fiercely guard you, whilst helping you to identify whatever hides or cloaks the true clear Light of your Soul; and will be your guide if it is time to explore the deepest and darkest depths of your Self: moreover, because Black Jaguar has the power to catalyse and empower positive transformation and growth, you may then ask him to help you understand and deal with whatever you find; and/or aid you in your endeavours to reveal your absolute Light. Guiding you to look closely at the jaguar's coat, Haniel points out its underlying markings and patterns, which are only visible when light shines upon it – adding that you may also choose to call upon Black Jaguar if you want aid to interpret and understand the subtle messages or wisdoms of dreams, signs or patterns that you encounter in your meditations or journeying; or if you need additional energy or support to help shed light upon that which is hidden (or as yet unknown), as you endeavour to make sense of everyday life.

With another small smile, Haniel observes that the heart and truth of a matter may be hard to see because it has been muddied by the assumptions, expectations, beliefs or judgements you hold about yourself or others, or about the world about you; or because it has become distorted by unjustified, unrealistic or false thoughts, feelings and emotions. Gesturing towards the pool, he explains that its waters can help you see through whatever obscures your vision or prevents you from clearly seeing the truth – enabling you to see any problematic situation or difficult issue (or something that worries or concerns you, or annoys or irritates you) for what it truly is – and, at another gesture of his hand, the water of the pool becomes infused with a silvery Light, and its surface turns flat and reflective, like a mirror. Haniel explains that he has cast his Illuminating Light upon the waters; and asks you bring to mind anything that is troubling you – being open to seeing whatever is at its heart that requires a fresh perspective and/or a different approach....

After waiting to allow your mind to settle and your thoughts to clarify, Haniel asks you to kneel by the pool and allow your heart (and his twin flame's Gift of the Mirror of the Soul, if you have it) to show you the facts behind the matter you have brought to mind.... he then directs you to look into the pool, and allow the reflective waters to help you see how, when and why the Truth has become clouded or distorted by any erroneous thoughts, beliefs or feelings you might have....

Having isolated something that is troubling you, you consider what you see.... then, when he knows that you have found something that does not resonate fully with your heart – or that no longer serves your purpose, Haniel withdraws his Light, and allows the waters of the pool to return to normal....

Asking you to hold your thoughts in your mind, Haniel explains that the waters of the pool may also be used to transmute, transform or refine the resonant energies of your thoughts, feelings and emotions; and asks you to consider whether you wish to discard, change or revise any of the thoughts or feelings (or assumptions, expectations, beliefs or judgments) that you hold in your mind – and, if you do, to bring it (or them) to the fore....

After pausing for a short while to allow you time to do so, Haniel gestures towards the pool again, which this time becomes infused with the same radiant fiery-white Light as the diamond in his pendant. He then instructs you to use both hands to scoop a little water from the pool; and directs you to touch it to your heart, lips and brow three times – whilst asking that (whatever thoughts or feelings you wish to discard, change or revise) are cleansed and transformed by the waters of the Diamond Light as appropriate for your Highest good now....

Composedly you follow his instructions – and with every touch of the water upon your skin, you feel your heart, mind and spirit become lighter.... and, as your perspective shifts, you slowly become aware that your whole energy Body is clarifying, calming and settling into a new, and more appropriate, balance....

Finally, recognising that you have done enough for now, Haniel affirms that you may return here under his guidance any time you need to review and resolve anything that requires similar action; before helping you to your feet, and guiding you back to your seat. He then takes a small clear pyramidal crystal from the waters of the pool and gives it to you, before retaking his seat at your side: this, he tells you, is **Clear Apophyllite**, his first Crystal Champion – explaining:

"Clear Apophyllite carries high resonances of Light that can clarify, activate and align your crown, Soul Star and Higher chakras, enhancing spiritual insight and helping you ground the frequencies of your Divine-self more easily, which will aid you in accepting and processing all life's learning experiences – and in understanding your thoughts, feelings and emotions – from a new and Higher perspective. Clear Apophyllite can also shine a powerful silver-white Light, which will illuminate all darkness and help you get to the 'heart' of a matter – thus revealing openings or potentials that have previously been cloaked by self-generated illusions or fears, and enabling you to identify or plan new and constructive ways forwards if your path is blocked or unclear; whilst its serene clarity will boost your inner certainty, faith and trust in the Divine Process and the direction of your own Life Plan, making you more positive about yourself and whatever

> *you choose to think, say or do. Clear Apophyllite can also reflect your innermost truths, whilst showing you the connectedness of all things throughout the Universe: thus, it may help you identify and understand commitments you have already made that currently affect your life so that you may review or plan your future goals, aims or life-path agreements and contracts accordingly."*

With a smile Haniel affirms that Clear Apophyllite may therefore give you the clarity and strength to be true to yourself – reminding you that taking time to consciously reflect upon yourself and your path will help you understand yourself more fully, which in turn will help you flow through life with greater faith and trust in your path and your purpose.

The Flame of Truth and Light and The Serpents of Creation:
Opening the purse that hangs from his belt, Haniel brings out a kernel of maize: he tells you that this single seed will grow into a plant that has many kernel-bearing cobs, which can either be harvested and consumed, perhaps feeding one family for a day; or be replanted to give a greater bounty in the following season. With a smile, he says that the wise person would consume a small amount, *and* put some aside to plant, thus ensuring future harvests year upon year – adding that, in this way, the precious natural resource is utilised to its maximum potential, and a sustainable balance is maintained.

Emphasising that, thus, a single seed has the power to nourish not just one life, but many; Haniel places it on his palm, and gently blows upon it – at which the maize kernel vanishes, and a tiny blue-white flame springs up in its place. He tells you that this is the Flame of Truth and Light, which has the power to feed your Soul and sustain its growth; and which can help you embrace and BEcome your full potential, by enabling you to stay true to yourself, and true to the ultimate Truth: moreover, as the Flame grows within you, its Fire can be passed on to others, so that they too may be nourished by its Light.

Haniel tells you that – if you choose – he can plant this Flame within you now; but stresses that (if he does so) the *only* thing that will be important to you from that point on will be the Truth: everything else will become meaningless! He then allows you time to decide if you wish to accept the Flame (and to choose where you want it to be planted, which can be anywhere within your physical body or subtle Bodies).... then, if you *have* chosen to receive it, he gently plants it in the location of your choice, saying:

> *"Whenever you feel that untruths are being presented to you, call upon and bring forth the Light of the Flame, so that you may realise the true message that lies behind any falsehoods you hear. Then allow its Truth to guide you at all times, and dress it not in your own ego – simply expressing it purely and cleanly as you find it, for all to see and experience: for only in this way will the Light and Power of the Flame multiply, so that all may become as ONE once more"*

Gradually you become aware of a gentle warmth as the Flame takes root; and you feel your entire energy field clarifying and strengthening, as it is permeated by its Light....

Stepping back, Haniel takes another kernel of maize from his purse, and softly blows on it as before – however, this time when the kernel vanishes it leaves a small blue crystal in its place: giving this to you he tells you it is **Blue Celestite**, his second Crystal Champion – explaining:

"Blue Celestite can help open your eyes to the Truth that lies at the heart of all things, enabling you to trust in your inner Light and in your innate wisdom and Higher-knowing. Blue Celestite can also give you the honesty to see through any expectations and self-illusions that may be making you 'set the bar' too high for yourself or others, or be making you unrealistic about what is and is not possible within the parameters of human existence. Furthermore, as Blue Celestite carries both the Blue and the Platinum Rays, it may aid you in manifesting the reality you truly need, whilst strengthening your perception of your place in the Universe – on all *Planes of awareness: this can give you the determination to discover and explore all your gifts and talents, so that you may employ them more effectively – trusting in your Self, and all that you can accomplish for yourself and for others. Blue Celestite has a High resonance that can open and align your throat, third eye and Soul Star chakras – so heightening your awareness of the true nature of your Self, the world, the Cosmos and ultimately the Universe: in this way, as you see the 'bigger picture', you will recognise your connection to everything and understand the greater purpose behind all of Creation, and so more willingly surrender to the Light of Divine Will and Cosmic Wisdom."*

Smiling, Haniel affirms that Blue Celestite grounds the Flame of Truth and Light, and so may therefore aid you in finding *your* truths and joyfully sharing them with others.

Drawing your attention to a rasping chirruping noise coming from a branch on the tree, Haniel tells you that this (perhaps slightly annoying!) sound is made by a male insect called a cicada. He explains that each cicada transitions through different stages of growth – egg; nymph; adult – and as such they are potent symbols of rebirth, change and transformation: hence **Cicada** can be called upon if you need help in making changes in any aspect of your life; or if you need the courage to try something new and would like additional guidance or help. Pointing out that cicadas utilise trees for food; the earth for protection; and the air for movement and communication, Haniel adds that Cicada may also help you connect with the Wisdoms of the Tree-beings; or teach you how to use the subtle energies of the planet for grounding and protection, and/or for support in aligning with Cosmic energies; or to show you how to balance your mind and its logical thought processes with greater clarity and grace. As you listen to its sound, Haniel remarks that what you hear is a series of very rapid vibrations, amplified within its body – each of which has a distinct pattern: hence, Cicada can help you hear and understand the patterns and meanings within all forms of subtle vibration and resonance; or show you how to make your voice heard (figuratively and literally) and communicate with confidence and dynamism, especially by means of the rhythmic mediums of music or song – but also through the spoken and written word. With a chuckle he adds that Cicada is a persistent (but cheerful!) supporter during times of change: hence he may come to persuade you to unfurl your wings and find your voice – empowering you to take flight and call your destiny to you, whilst encouraging you to define and speak your truth clearly and concisely, having pride in who you are, and in all you think, say and do. Furthermore, if you unexpectedly hear Cicada's repetitive chirruping, this brings the message that you need to be more patient or still, because it is time for you to focus and look within for the answers or solutions you seek, and so recognise the right direction to take.

Moving to sit cross-legged on the ground in front of you, Haniel lifts his left sleeve to reveal the silver torc, fashioned like a snake, that spirals around his bicep: at his gentle touch it comes to life, and twines sinuously down his arm to coil contentedly in the lap of his robe.... Lifting his other sleeve, Haniel does likewise with the golden torc – at which the gold snake also comes to life, and spirals down his arm to entwine itself with the other snake in his lap. With a smile, he touches both again – and this time they shimmer, and become real: one (now a pretty mottled-green) slips from his lap and coils in the grass, perfectly camouflaged; the other (now striped coral white and black) remains coiled in his lap. Haniel explains that each is demonstrating the virtues of different forms of self-protection – one by merging into the background; the other by mimicking a snake that is much more deadly. He chuckles and tells you that both know the virtues of action and stillness, camouflage and misdirection – understanding when the time is right to take positive action, and when it is not. Adding that the same principles apply when you want to communicate your truths or utilise your talents, Haniel says that there may be times when you will simply be wasting your energies to press forwards; and other times when your actions will be truly productive: therefore, it is important to always find the right balance between having the courage to act or speak, and knowing when it is better to remain still or silent – whilst exercising discernment over when, why, what, where and how you choose to communicate your truths.

Lifting each snake in turn, Haniel returns them to his upper arms, where they once more become solid coils of silver and gold; and explains that, in this form, they balance and hold the feminine and masculine sides of the creative process – those of inspiration and activation; structure and form. Pointing to their orange fire opal eyes, he expounds that these gems ground the Orange Ray (which he is tasked with regulating and directing) through the Light of the Silver and Gold Rays – firing the impulses that follow each act of Creation; and empowering the momentum that inspires and encourages the evolution and progression of whatever has been made manifest. He emphasises that 'Creation' does not therefore merely define the *initial* formation or establishment of something, but also includes the active advancement of its growth and development. Reminding you that, on some level, *you* actively create your reality in every moment, he stresses that the right and appropriate balance of 'masculine' and 'feminine'; stasis and motion; inaction and action is crucial at every step, if you want to have effective growth and ensure that what you are creating 'meets the brief' of your Higher-self and Soul.

The Gift of The Quill of Quetzalcoatl:
Haniel says that there are many Ancient Toltec myths about the 'God' Quetzalcoatl, who was often depicted as a snake with feathers (hence the title of 'Great Feathered Serpent), and who was said to have the power of flight – symbolising light (and life) emerging from the darkness, reborn and renewed with each new dawn. With a chuckle Haniel remarks that there is often fact within myth: for Quetzalcoatl supposedly came from Venus with the power to join the Realms of 'Heaven' and 'Earth'; and was said to have brought the staple food of maize to the native Toltecs, and created a form of writing that enabled them to record and communicate their history.

Tapping his biceps, Haniel says that snakes are powerful symbols of regeneration, and of the same lineage as the serpents and dragons of Ancient history, whose nature has become sadly misinterpreted and maligned over the years – for they are, in fact, some of the greatest Masters of Creation referred to in some Creation myths, declaiming:

"...The serpent opened its mouth, and from within the darkness a Great Light appeared, consum-ed not by the shadows but sheltered within, until the time was right for it to be made known in all its Glory. And the Light Illuminated the darkness, so that all *was revealed – the serpent stark in its nakedness and simplicity, accepted and embraced in the Light, no longer a thing rejected and reviled. And by the Light was also revealed the Truth – that the serpent is cloaked in feathers, that it may take flight to return home, Illuminated in the Light of its own Spirit..."*

Smiling, Haniel observes that many people loathe or fear snakes: for, just as they might fear the darkness of night for what it might conceal, they can see only the danger within them – yet without knowing 'night' you could not know 'day'; just as without knowing darkness you could not know light! Furthermore, as Masters of Creation, snakes truly know the value of darkness, understanding that, above all, Creation must be undertaken with great care and forethought, emphasising:

"Do not confuse darkness with negativity! Darkness is NOT negativity, it is merely the template against which the Light may be drawn; whereas negativity seeks to corruptly cloak the Light – and this is worse than darkness. Darkness is not to be feared, and it is something that all hold within – for if all was light, then nothing could be seen: indeed, the light needs *the darkness, for there must be balance between light and dark to bring about Creation, and allow experience to be gained."*

Moving to your side, Haniel stresses how important it is to expose your fears to the Light and explore the root of your thoughts and feelings on all that you deem dark, so that you may more clearly see and accept that – without that darkness – you could not create, experience and appreciate the choices that Free Will offers you. He says that, ultimately, this will reveal the Truth: which is that the 'serpent' of your own darkness is cloaked in feathers, giving *you* the power to 'take flight and return home' Illuminated in the Light of your own Spirit. With a smile, he reminds you that you *are* an aspect of The Divine, simply learning to embrace everything that is *of* The Divine, whilst travelling the long road back to Unity with All That You Are.

Suddenly a magnificent golden eagle appears over the crest of the hill, and flies to perch at Haniel's side. Gently stroking the honey-brown feathers of its breast, he declares that nothing can exist that is *not* of The Divine: for, at the moment of First Creation, The Divine spoke and created Light, from which ALL that is made is made – and it is the *application* of that Light that brings about 'negativity' or 'positivity', and *not* the Light (or its absence) itself. Drawing your attention to the eagle's fierce eyes that are constantly scanning its surroundings, Haniel says that **Golden Eagle** may come to help you see the Reality within all things, enabling you to perceive the difference between falsehoods and truths, darkness and negativity; or to support you in viewing whatever you need to address from all directions and from the highest perspective possible; or even (perhaps) to aid you in mastering the many possible applications of the Divine Light with righteous and conscious awareness. Pointing to the eagle's powerful talons and large hooked beak, Haniel explains that these make it a very powerful and efficient hunter: hence, you can call upon Golden Eagle if you need to 'get a grip' on a situation that may be getting out of control (especially if your fears are at its root); or to show you how to get to the heart of any issue or situation that you need to address, in order to prosper or progress. Adding that this regal eagle is a superb flier, skilfully mastering the ever-shifting currents of the skies with ease, Haniel says that you might also choose to call upon Golden Eagle if you want help to master your thinking processes or thoughts, or need to bring your logical reasoning skills to the fore – perhaps if you are in the planning or development stages of something; or to bolster your determination and reinforce your self-belief as you learn to connect with the limitless and profound Wisdom that underlies Universal existence. Just then you notice the eagle sizing you up – and, with a laugh, Haniel remarks that eagles have an instinctive intelligence, with little patience for prevarication: this means that Golden Eagle may come and make it very clear to *you* if it is time to stop 'faffing about'!

Suddenly the eagle gives a shrill cry and leaps into the air, rapidly rising higher with every powerful beat of its wings.... as you watch it climb, you suddenly realise that the eagle has left a single feather floating in front of you: this is deep brown, and appears to be a primary wing feather, used for forward movement and balance. With a smile, Haniel plucks this from the air, and moves to stand in front of you: then, telling you to hold your head still and erect, he gently places it in front of your throat chakra, where it simply dissipates into Light and is absorbed into your energy Body – at which, your spirit strengthens; and you are filled with a renewed sense of purpose and determination.

Haniel tells you that this is his Gift of The Quill of Quetzalcoatl, whose Light and Power has a threefold purpose: firstly, it will illuminate all darkness, so that you may understand the difference between darkness and negativity, and so learn to deal with all your fears appropriately; secondly, it will aid you in identifying your skills and talents, and encourage you in valuing all your qualities and capabilities, so that you make the most of the life you have chosen to live; and thirdly, it will empower you to walk within the Light of Truth at all times, and so 'communicate your truths' accordingly.

Resting his hands on your shoulders, Haniel assures you that he will always support you in standing in your own authority, and assist you in communicating your core values and truths as clearly and accurately as possible – adding that you may choose to express these in whatever way suits you and your innate skills and aptitudes; but emphasising that this must *always* be done with an open heart that empowers others to live according to their own Truths, and *never* to force, coerce, dictate to or dominate others.

Reaching into his purse again, Haniel produces a small brown stone that is streaked with metallic hues of bronze and gold – reminding you of the eagle's breast feathers. Giving this to you, he says that this is **Bronzite**, his third Crystal Champion – explaining:

> *"Bronzite is a stone for the warrior-knight, promoting wisdom and judgement in equal measures. Its base colour indicates its connection with the very fabric of the Earth, and shows that Bronzite is stabilising and grounding; whilst its bronze-gold metallic streaks indicate its capacity to activate, align and strengthen all that links your mind and spirit,*

aiding Higher reasoning and enhancing all your powers of discernment. Bronzite can also armour and shield your emotional Body during times of upheaval or trial, boosting and reinforcing your mental resilience and improving your inner balance: this can help you view situations or issues with calm composure, making it easier to make clear and effective decisions, and enabling positive forward movement on all levels. Bronzite may also be used to restore energy levels if your body is depleted through ill-health; or to lift your mind or spirit if they are low. Last, but not least, Bronzite connects the Earthly and Higher Realms, aiding you in identifying and owning your Truths whilst having the courage and conviction to stand up for the Divine Rights of all who are, for whatever reason, unable to do the same for themselves."

Smiling, Haniel affirms that (like Eagle) Bronzite may therefore be a strong support that will strengthen your heart and guide your arm as you move forwards with positivity, always practising what you preach.

Haniel finally takes his cloak from around your shoulders – and, with a gesture, it is gone, leaving one more lone feather floating in the air before you.... With another smile Haniel says that this is an extra gift to support and encourage your efforts at this time. He advises you to take note of its colours and form – for you should find it illuminating to identify the bird that supplied it, and research its symbolic significance, as this will be relevant for you in understanding both your inner Truths and your purpose for Being.

The Greenwood Guardians – Tamarisk and Oak:

His *personal* mentoring complete for now, Haniel affirms he is always available to aid and support you: you need only bring him to mind and ask for his presence, and he will attend you. Furthermore, he tells you that two great Tree Beings of the Plant Kingdom have also asked to support you in addressing his Theme of 'WALK YOUR WALK – TALK YOUR TALK', adding that you need only request *their* presence, and they will be with you.

He explains that the first of these Greenwood Guardians is the Masculine essence of Tamarisk, who has asked to overlight and help you ground whatever work you undertake within *any* aspect of his chapter. The second is the Masculine essence of Oak, who has specifically asked to help you understand and assimilate his Gift of The Quill of Quetzalcoatl (if you have chosen to accept it).

When you are ready to connect with Haniel's first Greenwood Guardian, you need simply call for the presence of **Tamarisk** (*) .... Tamarisk envelops you in a deep blue Light, and the Masculine spirit essence of Tamarisk speaks to you, saying:

"I help hold the emotional balance of the Earth, and know the Cosmic Wisdom that constantly embraces and supports all sentient life as we journey into the unknown. I know too the thoughts and feelings of all those who have lived and experienced polar extremes of Earthly existence, and known both the darkest of the dark, and the lightest of the light – for their lives are written in the very fabric of the rocks and minerals that nourish and support me, and have shown me that it is often only by knowing what you do not want within your world that you can decide what you do, enabling undesirable beliefs and practises to be refined in the pure light of understanding. Know then that

this is where I would aid you; for I can align you with your Soul, and help you read the histories that founded your birth, as well as the words that you have penned in your own hand, which record your hopes and fears, wishes and dreams.... So stand with me now, and allow me to help you review and refine your world and all that you are, whilst connecting you with the infinite and wise counsel – both of this Earth, and not – that is there for all those that ask for support...."

(* Purpurite and Green Jade will help you ground and connect with the energies and wisdom of Tamarisk, if you wish to enhance your experience using crystals.)

If you have chosen to accept and work with Haniel's Gift, and when you are ready to connect with his second Greenwood Guardian, you need simply call for the presence of **Oak** (*) .... Oak envelops you in a reflective silver Light, and the Masculine spirit essence of Oak speaks to you, saying:

"I understand the nature of sacrifice, and know the dread of facing fear – yet still I stand, resilient and strong, determined to continue to shelter and protect all that rely on me, whilst growing always towards the light of the Sun. For by its limitless power and infinite Light, the Sun encompasses and nurtures me, telling me of the eternal and compassionate wisdom that fires and inspires all life, and giving me the courage to BE all that the Creator designed me to be. Thus, I can support you in knowing and living your purpose.... so stand in my Light and see yourself and your world truly.... and let my strength fill you, as you sink your roots deep into the ground with mine, allowing yourself to feel the fire and passion that will feed and inspire your Soul to transform and grow.... And then, allow that fire to flow into you, balancing and aligning you body, mind and Soul, and clarifying the innate connection that links the Earth with your heart.... for, as you recognise and embrace the Light that is yours, you will then feel yourself fill with joy – empowered and impassioned, and reborn into a new way of BEing...."

(* Bloodstone and Green Aventurine will help you ground and connect with the energies and wisdom of Oak, if you wish to enhance your experience using crystals.)

ARCHANGEL MICHAEL

'KNOW YOUR TRUTHS'

CRYSTAL CHAMPIONS:

Indigo Kyanite ♥ Sodalite ♥ Blue Sapphire

CREATURE COMPANIONS:

Snow Leopard ♥ Praying Mantis ♥ Crow

GREENWOOD GUARDIANS:

Holly ♥ Larch

I align myself with the purity of my Soul.
I remember who I am.
I AM Divine.

MEETING MICHAEL

It is midday in high summer, and you find yourself climbing steadily up a narrow path that is zigzagging its way up the steeply-sloping sides of a mountain. As you pause for breath, you look back and see that you have already climbed a long way to get to this point; and see how your journey to the foothills led you through a range of terrains: cold; hot; arid; wet; barren; lush – each one distinct, and each typifying a different region of the Earth. However, here and now the air is clear, dry and warm, and so you continue your journey....

As you climb higher, the air around you turns cooler and damper – and then, as you enter a layer of cloud, you are enveloped in a soft white mist: as a result you can only see a short distance around you, but everything that you *can* see has a crystal-like clarity that enables you to make out every minute detail of the moss-clad rocks that define your path, and the lichen-clad shrubs festooned with condensed droplets of water, which shimmer in the diffuse sunlight, and set rainbow sparks of light dancing around you as you walk. A little way further on, the cloud cloaking you thins and the light brightens – and at last you emerge into warm and dazzling sunlight beneath a cloudless china-blue sky; and find you have reached the end of the path.

Here a large circular plateau has been carved into the side of the mountain close to its peak, cutting deeply into the rock so that it is sheltered from the prevailing winds by the high curves of the peak. Even so, it is open to the sky above – and the side where you stand offers stunning views over the tops of the clouds mantling the mountain below, where a majestic black and white condor is effortlessly mastering the constantly-shifting air currents and thermals.

Stepping onto the plateau itself, you find that it has been paved in black and white cobbles, which have been laid out so that they spiral around a circular plinth that sits at the very centre of the plateau. The plinth has been polished from a large piece of white alabaster, and bears a life-sized statue of a rearing unicorn sculpted from the same stone: this has a horse-like head and a spiralling horn (as you would expect); but its body is like that of a stag, and it has a very long coat of hair that skirts its body almost to its knees. Closer scrutiny of the cobbles then reveals that they have been laid to portray a tightly coiled snake – a slumbering adder, by the look of its black and white diamond patterning! The head, where you stand, is wonderfully detailed; and the body seems almost alive – the black cobbles absorbing and reflecting the sunlight in swirls of rainbow light, like oil on water; the white cobbles gleaming with a silvery-blue iridescence: then, just as you are marvelling at its lifelike rendering, everything suddenly goes dark....

It is as if night has suddenly fallen; and, looking up at the sky, which is now a deep indigo-black and filled with a multitude of stars, your attention is grabbed by a radiant blue light haloed in gold that is emerging from the heart of one of the constellations. This light speeds swiftly towards you, reducing in intensity as the dark sky gradually absorbs its light – until eventually it resolves into the form of a magnificent Angel robed in royal-blue, who is holding aloft a golden sword wreathed in a dazzling nimbus of silvery-blue flames: this is Archangel Michael.

Alighting on the plateau, he momentarily blazes with Light – at which the darkness

Michael

fades as abruptly as it came, and daylight takes over once more: this reveals him standing proudly erect, with his stunningly beautiful kingfisher-blue wings mantling his shoulders, and his sword extended towards the sun that is again high in the sky – and, with a smile, he strides over and greets you, declaring:

> *"I am Michael – Knight Defender and Archangel of the Sun, Wielder of the Sword of Truth, and twin flame of Mikaela, the Lady Faith. I am here to give you the courage to live your life freely and honestly; and to aid you in discovering the truth of your own nature – so feel the strength of my Being embrace you, and see my sword held aloft, to guide you with its fiery Light and hold you securely within its brilliant protection. For I know that every Soul has the Divine Right to BE always in the Truth and Light of their own nature – and so I fight until the end of Time to uphold the Light of Truth, whilst maintaining the Spiritual Laws that govern the application of Free Will. This I do for you and for all, that none may be forced against their Will to bend to the will of another, thus upholding the Right of every individual to have and hold sovereignty over their own Being. Know then that in finding freedom you will find your Truth: and then, as your nature becomes clear, so will your Light shine forth with brightness and vigour, and* all *will be bathed in its Glory."*

With a shimmer, Michael swiftly blurs his Angelic Self and takes human form – furling his wings and sheathing his sword, before leading you across to the unicorn statue: here he briefly examines the top of the plinth, which is etched with an intricate labyrinthine design that has a large faceted diamond set at its centre; before turning to settle himself beneath the unicorn's rearing hooves. Smiling, he invites you to sit at his left-hand side, and suggests that you take time to examine him more closely, and become accustomed to his energies.

Settling beside him, you can sense the aura of vigour and vitality that he exudes, and see that he is in his physical prime, with the taut and finely-honed body of an athlete. His skin is fair and lightly tanned, and all his features are well-balanced and elegantly refined – his clean-shaven heart-shaped face haloed by a mass of golden-yellow hair, which curls softly around his head and shoulders. Michael's cornflower-blue eyes are set below arching brows and are piercing in their brilliance – and as he surveys you with an open and honest gaze, you realise that he knows *all* that you are: yet here, in his eyes, you see and sense only unconditional love, and genuine care and kindness.

Turning your attention to his apparel, you note that he is clad in a long sleeveless vest of silvery chain mail, which he wears over a long-sleeved knee-length shift made of white linen that forms a protective layer between the mail and his skin. Over these very functional layers he wears a slightly shorter full-sleeved tunic made of a very fine velvety royal-blue fabric, which drapes softly around his body: its style is comfortably loose and flowing, allowing plenty of room for movement; whilst its flared cuffs and hem and wide scooped neck are embellished with a design known as the 'Hellenic (or Greek) Key', which has been embroidered in crystal-white spider-silk.

A narrow belt made of indigo-blue dragon skin sits low on his waist: this is secured with a grey-white iridium buckle, fashioned in the form of a coiled and sleeping dragon; and gathers the tunic loosely about his hips. The belt also holds the scabbard that houses his sword so that it rests on his left hip: this scabbard is covered in indigo-blue dragon skin, like his belt; and has been reinforced at throat, tip and sides with bands of meteorite iron, whose silvery-grey surfaces are etched with tiny lines and runic symbols. Drawn to inspect the scabbard more closely, you can see that its outer-side is inlaid with strands of gold wire to portray a vine of ivy entwined with a stem of holly – the latter embellished with small cabochons of ruby-red garnets to depict its berries.

Resting his right arm casually across his knee, Michael pushes up his sleeve, so that you can see the armoured glove and chain mail sleeve that sheathes it from fingertips to elbow: this looks to be made of the same silvery metal as that of his chain mail tunic; and with a smile he lifts his other hand, showing you a workmanlike (yet graceful) hand that bears multiple calluses and scars, which look to have been gained in battle. Recognising this, you realise that Michael presents a study in absolute contrasts – his softly elegant clothing at odds with his practical armour and weaponry; his delicate almost feminine grace and loose relaxed stance belied by his commanding and watchful manner and his obvious experience with combat.

Dropping your gaze, you note that Michael's finely-muscled tanned legs are shod in calf-length riding boots made of soft black leather: tucked into the top of the right-hand one is a small dagger, whose hilt has a plain black haft bound in silver, with a large oval emerald (which has been fashioned into the shape of a shield-beetle) inset to its pommel.

Finally your eyes are drawn to the only seemingly non-purposeful item Michael wears, which is a large, round (and rather ornamental) pendant, which is suspended over his heart on a sturdy silvery chain. Close examination reveals that the pendant comprises several layered iridium discs, which have been etched with tiny glyphs and symbols that look a little like those on his scabbard. These discs are 'stepped' – the widest forming the pendant's back; the smallest surrounding a round cut and faceted deep-blue sapphire, which is set at the pendant's very centre: this gem affirms Michael's role as co-overseer of the Sapphire Ray; and is the gem that links him with Mikaela, his twin flame.

MICHAEL'S TEACHINGS
The Light of The Sun and The Sword of Truth:

Recognising that your inspection is complete, Michael grins, and remarks that you may already be familiar with him in his role as an Archangelic Guardian – yet he is also the Knight Defender of the Faith, protecting the Divine Rights of all those who choose to live within the Light: this means that he seeks always to uphold the Divine Laws and edicts that are the foundation upon which individualisation is built, including all personal rights and freedoms – thus, you can always call upon him if you are in need of his protection or support.

Drawing his sword, Michael rests it across his knees so that you may see it, warning you not to touch it, as it is very sharp! You can see that the long straight silver-grey blade has a yellow-gold sheen; and, noting your interest, Michael explains that the blade has been forged from a mix of meteorite iron and iridium (a rare metal element that is highly resistant to heat and pressure). You can also see that the sword has a simple cross-guard made of bronze; and, as Michael runs his gloved finger over it, he reveals a line of ornate glyphs – explaining that these create a sacred bond that unites him with his sword, so that he may freely bear and wield its Powers for the Light. Tilting the sword, he shows you that the hilt's grippe has been 'barrel-cut' from a large blade of indigo kyanite and bound with rings of bronze; before showing you the pommel at the top of the hilt, which is inset with a magnificent round cushion-cut emerald – informing you that this carries and holds the brilliant and catalytic energy of the Emerald Ray, which augments and enhances the sword's Power, and sustains him in perfect heart-centred balance.

Rising to his feet, he leads you to stand a little distance away from the plinth, and turns to face you: placing his left hand on your right shoulder, he raises his sword above his head, as if in salute – declaring:

"See me with armoured hand and glove, sword aloft held to the Sun: yet soft and gentle be my garb, for with the unicorn I do run. Thus, I stand on cusp of night, to guard the balance of the black, the white – and that of darkness and of light..."

As he speaks, his sword flushes through with light as it is charged with the Light of the Sun – the blade filling with its light, and becoming wreathed in silvery-blue flames; and you watch as his aura glows with a bright golden light, which slowly turns silvery-blue as he draws the energies of the flames down through his arm and into his body....

Carefully channelling their Power down his left arm and into both your physical and subtle Bodies, Michael explains that he is clearing and charging you with the Light of the Sun – and, as you feel the (surprisingly cool) energy filter through you, you realise that some of the Light is being absorbed – cleansing and purifying you on all levels; whilst the remainder is strengthening and reinforcing the natural defences of your aura....

Once this is complete, Michael lofts his sword again – and this time a brilliant Light erupts from the cutting edges of the blade; and a mass of tiny blue flames begin to flicker and burn across its surface.... mesmerised by their glimmering patterns, you listen as Michael explains that the Light of the Great Central Sun also charges his sword, giving it the Power to cut away negativity and falsehoods that conceal or bind something's – or someone's – original (True and Pure) nature.... Asking for your full attention, he looks deeply into your eyes, and declares that he can help you to find your Truths by giving you the ability to identify any misperceptions or untruths that taint your feelings or cloud your judgement. With a smile, he adds that he will then help you decide whether you are ready and willing to discard whatever you no longer wish to be a part of your essence, before wielding his sword to cut you free of whatever restricts, confines or binds you.

Michael emphasises that this will demand that you have the courage and honesty to examine the roots of your core belief systems (and whatever thoughts or feelings they provoke within you) in order to understand what *is* truly a part of who you are – and what is not: then, reassuring you that he will support you throughout, he explains that he will now charge his sword, and direct its Light to fall upon anything that cloaks or conceals whatever you need to contemplate and address at this time.

Asking you to close your eyes, Michael again lofts his sword, and asks you to think about any belief you have about yourself that you *know* in your heart is not (or cannot be) true: this may be something that someone else has told you, labelled you by, or confined you with; or something you have simply grown up believing about yourself....

Gently resting his left hand on your head, Michael asks you to see and understand what lies beneath what you see, using his support to identify any perceptions or beliefs that are false or outmoded.... and, as you consider his words, you feel yourself bathed in a cool Light; and you find that it is surprisingly painless to sift through the thoughts and beliefs you hold about yourself – and easier than you might have believed to identify something that is obviously not true....

After giving you enough time to isolate something, Michael asks you to take a little more time to examine it from as many angles as you can, in order to see and understand how that thought or belief has affected your life: then (armed with that understanding) to decide if you are ready and willing to release it from your reality....

Time passes as you contemplate and consider this: then Michael gently touches the tip of his sword to the point where he knows the restriction is rooted – and, as he does so, your energy Body momentarily flares and flickers with silvery-blue light and is flushed through with waves of cool blue and green fire, before gradually settling into a new – and more comfortable – state of balance....

Eventually, after allowing all sensation to settle, you open your eyes and know that your prior belief is no longer a part of you – and realise that you feel lighter and freer as a consequence. Recognising this, Michael tells you that you may always call upon him if you wish to make any more changes, before sheathing his sword and taking you back to your seat. Here he gives you a bladed crystal that is a deep shade of indigo-blue, and tells you that it is **Indigo Kyanite**, his first Crystal Champion – explaining:

> *"Indigo Kyanite has a natural 'bladed' formation that will help you link directly to my Sword of Truth, and so may be used to cut through and clear away negative energies, effectively removing the 'old' to make way for the 'new'. Despite its apparent darkness, Indigo Kyanite vibrates to a surprisingly high frequency, and can provide a protective shield to both ground and protect you: this is because its indigo colour unites blue Light with black, thus attracting the energies and environment that allow only honest and truthful communication and manifestation to take place. Additionally, as a carrier of the Indigo Ray, Indigo Kyanite can open your brow chakra and align it with your Universal and Soma centres, whilst stimulating the neural pathways in your brain that activate your connection to the Cosmos and its multidimensional Universal 'databanks': if used with focus and intent these can provide you with profound insights when accessed through meditation, journeying, dreaming or astral travel, serving to awaken you to the reality of yourself as a much greater Being than the 'you' in this human embodiment – and to the realisation that you can only ever be dis-empowered by ignorance or fear; whilst showing you the relative 'smallness' of your world, when seen against all that comprises the vastness of the Universe."*

With a smile, Michael affirms that Indigo Kyanite may therefore help you work with his Sword of Truth, so that you may see yourself *and* your world in a new light!

All of a sudden a large snow leopard appears as if from nowhere, and comes to lie trustingly at his feet: directing your attention to its dense white coat marbled in dark spots and clouds, Michael explains that this allows it to remain hidden and camouflaged in the shadows and crevices of its mountain habitat; whilst its powerful shoulders and long tail enable it to move and balance on very steep slopes. As the magnificent animal rolls over to sprawl contentedly on its back, Michael lifts one of its huge paws, showing you its large furred pads, and adds that these also help it move safely over icy or difficult terrain: hence **Snow Leopard** can teach you how to move with confidence and purpose, regardless of the situation you find yourself in; or show you how to keep your focus and balance when endeavouring to reach a difficult or elusive goal; whilst its ability to survive in inhospitable environments may give you the inspiration, determination and resolve to 'keep going', even if times are hard or difficult. Gently stroking its soft belly, he says that you might also ask Snow Leopard to keep you shielded if you feel vulnerable or exposed; or to be your teacher if you want to learn the arts of concealment and/or silent or unobtrusive movement: furthermore, if you truly wish to make progress, Snow Leopard can help you reveal and admit your deepest (and possibly darkest) motivations and desires, by strengthening your trust in your own ability to deal with whatever you find; and giving you the courage to understand and accept *all* of yourself, including your shadow-side. After a little while the snow leopard rolls to its feet and silently pads away, at which Michael smiles and remarks that these great cats prefer solitude and remoteness: thus if Snow Leopard comes to *you* it is time to spend time in silent communion – for, as a protector and guardian of the Soul, Snow Leopard is gentle in spirit yet powerful in body, and will be your guide as you travel within to search for your inner Truths.

The Unicorns of Ultimate Purity and The Spiral of Contemplation:
Lifting a hand to touch the statue towering overhead, Michael remarks that most people consider unicorns to be mythical creatures – yet myth is often founded in fact, for unicorns *do* exist: furthermore, although their starry home is far away, it anchors the Light of Divine Purity for this Galaxy, so that true purity is never too far away. Michael tells you that unicorns use their horns to assess Light resonance and gauge purity, and to channel the pure White Light of Source – stressing that you should *never* touch one without their permission, or *ever* seek to ride upon their back. He explains that this is because all unicorns embody the pure attribute of innocence, and so to do either would besmirch their purity – unless your heart is entirely pure: even so, from time to time a unicorn may approach *you*; and will test *your* purity and intent by looking into your Soul with its deep-indigo eyes, and touching your heart with the tip of its horn.... then (if you 'pass muster') you may be invited to run with them – perhaps through the virgin-white forests of their home, where you can experience some wondrous things!

Taking your attention to the spiralling pathway laid out on the plateau, Michael says that he often walks its spiral, as he finds that it aids clear and focused contemplation and facilitates a profound meditative process that enables him to become As One with the Highest Truths of the Heart and Mind of The Divine. He explains that the black cobbles are rainbow obsidian – the Black Light of the obsidian having the power to take you within, grounding you to your True Self; whilst the white cobbles are rainbow moonstone – the White Light of the moonstone having the power to align you with your centre, promoting purity and balance of mind and emotions, body and spirit. With a smile, he adds that the diamond patterning of the adder aids and promotes clarity, transformation and change – especially within the mind and its thought processes – and so he knows you will find it helpful to connect with the Truths of your heart by walking the spiral too!

After leading you to the adder's head at the outer end of the spiral, Michael takes your hand and asks you to close your eyes – explaining that he will talk and guide you down the spiral: all you need to do is pay attention to whatever thoughts arise as you listen and walk.... and so you begin – hesitantly at first....

Soon you relax, and begin to walk with more confidence – and, recognising this, Michael asks that you take things (literally) one step at a time; and begin by allowing yourself to recall a time in your life which you found painful or traumatic – adding that whatever you need to look at now will simply 'pop' into your mind. Gently squeezing your hand, he prompts you to allow yourself to review the event *and* its consequences in your mind without fear – assuring you that his Light will help you see and understand your thoughts and feelings from a balanced and detached perspective....

Knowing that you have his strength at your side, you have the courage to do as he asks – and, having isolated something you need to review, you examine it carefully: as you start to do so, Michael asks you to think about how the event shaped or affected you at the time *and* (bearing in mind that your emotional and logical interpretations may now differ) look at what the event and its consequences taught you from the viewpoints of both 'then' and 'now' – and consider if the thoughts, beliefs or expectations that you acquired then still hold true now....

As you start to think, you feel your mind sharpen and your emotions still; and you find that you can begin to see exactly what the event contributed to your learning, then and now.... eventually, you understand how *everything* that you encounter and experience in every moment of every day shapes the person you are; and realise too that it is your *actions* and *reactions to* every experience that define who you are – and not the actual experience itself....

Having considered this for some time, you sense that the spiral of the pathway is tightening, and realise that you must be nearing its centre: slowing his pace, Michael asks you to now look with compassion at *everyone* connected with the event you have been thinking about (including yourself) – forgiving where forgiveness is due; and being truly thankful for all that you learned.... and, when he knows you have reached this point of recognition and acceptance, he asks you to open your eyes....

Smiling at you, Michael affirms that each day creates a new reality that serves to teach you more about self-mastery and balance – then, turning to face you, he plucks the dagger from his boot. He shows you its slim white spiralling blade, and explains that this was gifted to him by the unicorns, who asked that it be paired with black obsidian and bound in silver – thus holding White Light and Black Light in balance, so that it may catalyse change within all that is made manifest. He adds that the emerald it holds links with the one on his sword, generating an intrinsic connection that enables each to carry aspects of the other – hence, the dagger brings Light to the darkest of places, in order to illuminate the Truth and reveal negativity; and will promote and uphold the Right and balanced use of Power, through pure and unconditional love and compassion.

Michael tells you that (because he has been sanctioned to use the unicorns' purity to aid clearing, healing and balance) he will now wield his dagger to clear and cleanse your heart of anything that still holds you back or prevents you from being all that you want to BE, which in turn will strengthen your determination, and give you the courage to stay true to your Self, as you confront and conquer past traumas and pains. Turning to face you, he gently touches the tip of his dagger to your heart, declaring:

"May the Purity of Source, and the Healing it brings, clear and cleanse your heart of any erroneous beliefs or judgements that you have brought to Light, so that you may BE at peace within the pure Light of Grace, knowing and valuing all that you were; all that you are; and all that you will become."

At his words, a cool energy like crystal-clear water passes through you; and you know that the unicorns are playing an important part in clearing your heart.... you know too that you have connected with your personal Power, and can understand the benefits of using it wisely and with compassion to address and resolve the 'demons' of your past....

This done, Michael returns his dagger to his boot, and gives you a dark-blue stone that is dappled with royal-blue and white, telling you that this is **Sodalite**, his second Crystal Champion – explaining:

"Sodalite appears in varying shades and proportions of bright-blue, indigo-black and white – the amounts of each indicating whether that particular stone's focus is towards the darker or paler end of the Blue Ray's application (although each holds aspects of all its attributes – Indigo and Blue – making Sodalite usefully multipurpose!) Those that are mainly bright- or pale-blue offer particular support to your throat chakra, helping you communicate your thoughts and feelings to others with greater clarity and conviction, and aiding you in BEing 'your own person'; those that are mainly dark-blue or indigo offer particular support to your brow chakra, aiding and stimulating intuitive thought and helping you connect with your Higher-self and sources of Higher Guidance with greater clarity and ease; whilst those that are balanced in both may also awaken your Soma and Universal centres, helping you to connect with Universal / Cosmic knowledge and Truths – promoting greater insight and enabling you to embrace new (and possibly radical) thoughts and concepts. Nonetheless, working with any *Sodalite can help you expose contradictory patterns that will enable you to separate your own true thoughts and beliefs from those 'given' to or placed upon you by others – those with black and white aspects offering a particularly balanced and well-grounded clarity and depth that will aid focused and dispassionate self-evaluation, whilst giving you the determination to make fundamental changes to whatever no longer serves your purpose, even at the risk of upsetting or challenging others."*

Smiling, Michael affirms that Sodalite may therefore help you clear the energetic residue of whatever outdated thoughts or beliefs are no longer an aspect of *your* personal Truth, leading to more effective healing on all levels.

Taking your attention to the head of the unicorn statue, Michael points to the small wreath of ivy and white hellebore that encircles its horn and garlands its brow, where a slender pale-green insect is resting on one of the ivy leaves. He tells you that this insect is a praying mantis, chuckling as he adds that it is well named, for 'prayer' is simply a state of meditative contemplation (such as you have just experienced), whereby you still your mind and take your focus within to connect with your personal Power, which IS both the Light of Source *and* that of your own Divinity. Michael observes that, thus, you may call upon **Praying Mantis** to help you understand how (when you are centred and focused) you own the Power that comes from standing in the Light of your own Truth; or to teach you how to connect with your inner Light and take control over your Self and your actions, in order to 'be' or do whatever ensures the most positive and productive outcome for your needs at that time. With a wry smile Michael adds that the reproductive act of the mantis often ends in the death of the male, and so Praying Mantis can also bring you the courage to undertake any programme of self-improvement or change that requires an act of surrender or sacrifice – yet through which you may be recreated or reborn anew in body, mind and/or spirit; or to show you how to 'subdue' your 'masculine' side if you need greater balance – or if it is time for your 'feminine' side to take the lead. Suddenly, the mantis takes a flying leap and springs off to a new resting place – at which Michael chuckles, and observes that you might also call Praying Mantis to help you appreciate the virtues of inner stillness *and* of outer movement, and show you how to harness your body and mind to accomplish either one as appropriate; or to give you the impetus you need if it is time to take a 'leap of faith' and/or move on to 'pastures new'!

The Gift of The Sapphire Flame of Divine Expression:
Asking you accompany him back to the outer end of the spiral, Michael unfurls his magnificent wings, sweeping them upwards and out, before curving them around in front of his body to show off their beautiful iridescent feathers, which hold the full spectrum of blue – from aquamarine and turquoise, right through to royal-blue and indigo. At the edge of the plateau he asks you to turn so that your back is towards him, and steps forwards – wrapping his wings around you, so that you are completely enfolded in their soft brilliance. Looking out over the clouds below, you can feel and sense the strength and safety of his loving embrace; and, as you relax into his energies, Michael explains that his wings of Light provide a powerful cloak of protection that allows the passage of only that which is True and Pure, which is always at the heart of his endeavours. He reminds you about the gem that rests at the centre of his pendant, stressing that Truth is fundamental to the Sapphire Ray on which he serves, and hence to its core Divine state of Purity, Innocence and Love. With a smile in his voice, he points out that when you are innocent, truth is easy – simply because you know nothing else(!) – adding that *this* is why he always seeks to cut you free of all that binds you to your lower ego-self, or keeps you separate from the *ultimate* Truth: which is the realisation that YOU are Divine; and that The Divine is simply Love – uncorrupted, innocent and pure....

After a while, Michael furls his wings and leads you back to the unicorn statue: here he lifts up his pendant, and (pointing to the gem at its centre) tells you that the Sapphire Ray encompasses the Blue *and* Indigo Rays, the latter of whose functions are concerned with the transmission and interpretation of Cosmic Wisdoms held within all Universes and Planes of Dimension – past, present and future. Tapping the pendant's layered discs, he explains that these create a device that enables him to expand his awareness and 'BE' in multiple locations, Times and Planes of Dimension simultaneously. With a grin he reveals that he is one of the Lords of Time (a 'Time Lord', you might say!) and, as such, he can help you access deep memories of knowledge and wisdom acquired by your many Selves throughout all your existences, where this affects (or is relevant to) your current embodiment. He adds that this may aid you in uncovering more of your personal Truths; and in re-addressing the healing, clearance and resolution work you are undertaking in this lifetime, in order to become whole and complete – which in turn will increase the purity of your heart (and perhaps attract the attentions of the unicorns, who may choose to assist you further with your healing).

Drawing his dagger from his boot again, Michael touches its spiralling white tip to the blue sapphire on his pendant: at this a small sapphire-blue flame leaps from the gem to the point of the dagger; and Michael gently touches this to the base of your throat.... after a moment you realise that the (surprisingly cool) blue flame is being transferred into your throat chakra – and you are suddenly struck dumb, unable to speak or utter a sound, as Michael says:

"My Gift of The Sapphire Flame of Divine Expression has been placed within your throat chakra. Allow its Fire to clarify and reinforce every word that you speak, and every thought that you convey by touch, glance or gesture; and give you the courage, endurance and strength that you need in order to clearly, concisely and precisely speak your Truths at all times. This is your Gift from me: so let the love that is within your heart, aided and tempered by that Power, henceforth guide your thoughts, your deeds and your actions; and may everything that you do be imbued with the Light of Truth."

As his words fade, you find your voice has once more returned to you, and know that you will now be able to express yourself with greater clarity and purpose.

Sheathing his dagger, Michael waits to allow the Flame to settle; and explains that his Gift incorporates the Blue Ray of Communion and Truth and the pure Madonna-blue Light of The Divine Feminine, which shines through falsehoods to aid clear sight and understanding. He tells you that these are the twin architects for the foundation and birth of all things visible and invisible: for the Creation of everything begins with a pure and focused thought, made manifest through the Logos – the Power of the Word. With a smile, he adds that he has therefore placed his Gift within your throat chakra, so that it may help you in finding your own Truth (whatever it may be) and in choosing the words you use to convey or share whatever it is without corruption – thus expressing (and Creating) something that is both positive and pure.

Settling at your side, Michael gives you a transparent royal-blue crystal, telling you that this is a **Blue Sapphire**, his third Crystal Champion – explaining:

"Blue Sapphire holds the most refined aspects of the Blue and Indigo Rays, and will aid and support you in working with those Rays at the Highest level. Touching the Power of the Sapphire surrounds you in the Light of Truth, where you cannot hide from the truth or conceal anything from yourself or others! This is of great help when determining the truth behind what you read or see within others or within a situation – yet means that you too are fully revealed in all *your Glory! Thus, Blue Sapphire encourages you to carry out a transformative karmic review, stripping away layers that conceal your pure*

Inner-self and removing falsehoods and untruths to reveal your true core; and then resolutely dissolving the veils that promote the illusion of being separate from your own Divinity. Furthermore, because Blue Sapphire works with the Element of Air, it allows the freedom of movement that supports open-minded thought, and (sometimes) unusual methods of addressing issues that require resolution. Blue Sapphire may also help you in healing and/or assimilating fragments of your Self that have become disconnected or separated from you, perhaps through trauma, pain or fear: however, this need not be a distressing process, as Blue Sapphire has a cool, calm clarity and lucidity that will both reassure and comfort you – body, mind and spirit."

With a smile, Michael affirms that Blue Sapphire may therefore help you connect with (and use) his Gift, linking you with the timeless Power of the Sapphire Ray and its Light of Truth – and guaranteeing you his constant Love and protection!

Looking up, Michael whistles to a large black crow perched on the rock face high above you: at this the bird flies across and settles on his left shoulder, where it cocks its head and regards you with a bright intelligence in its eyes. Gently scratching it under its chin (at which the crow gives a soft 'caw' and hoods its eyes with pleasure) Michael tells you that crows are wise and loyal birds, who help monitor and protect the Sacred Cosmic and Spiritual Laws that govern and regulate the Universe: accordingly, you may call upon **Crow** if you need to monitor or improve whatever practices you use to promote your personal energetic clarity and integrity – or implement some if you do not currently undertake any (in which case Crow can also help you find a practice that is comfortable and right for your needs); or to help you make or refine plans that require a sound and principled or ethical foundation; or to guide you through any legal complexities involved in schemes where integrity and/or trust are an important aspect of the situation. With a smile, he adds that crows' wisdom and loyalty makes them good travelling companions, and so you may ask Crow to accompany you if undertaking a long or difficult journey: furthermore, because Crow mirrors his own ability to travel the hidden paths that span Time and Dimension, Michael says that you may also ask Crow to help guide and teach you if you need to recognise and understand any lessons that have their roots in past, present or future life experiences or existences; and/or to use his clear and far-sighted vision to help you see the patterns that underlie *all* your existences. With a final 'caw' the crow flies back to the rocks – and Michael chuckles, suggesting that it is a good idea to keep your eye out for the presence of crows, for if one comes to *you*, it may be a sign that you need to check your personal motivations – or the motives of those around you – for honesty and/or truth.

The Greenwood Guardians – Holly and Larch:

His *personal* mentoring complete for now, Michael affirms he is always available to aid and support you: you need only bring him to mind and ask for his presence, and he will attend you. Furthermore, he tells you that two great Tree Beings of the Plant Kingdom have also asked to support you in addressing his Theme of 'KNOW YOUR TRUTHS', adding that you need only request *their* presence, and they will be with you.

He explains that the first of these Greenwood Guardians is the Feminine essence of

Holly, who has asked to overlight and help you ground whatever work you undertake within *any* aspect of his chapter. The second is the Feminine essence of Larch, who has specifically asked to help you understand and assimilate his Gift of The Sapphire Flame of Divine Expression (if you have chosen to accept it).

When you are ready to connect with Michael's first Greenwood Guardian, you need simply call for the presence of **Holly** (*) .... Holly envelops you in a deep gold Light, and the Feminine spirit essence of Holly speaks to you, saying:

"I am the Light of Truth and Divine Expectation, strong in my support, secure in my protection. In even the darkest of days I maintain my Light, which fills me with delight in Be-ing and grounds me to the Wisdoms of both Earth and Sky. So rest with me now, and allow my energy to fill and saturate your Being, offering you the stability that empowers you to stand tall – safe and secure in the knowledge of your own Light.... Then let me align you with the Highest powers that make life not only bearable, but joyous; and show you the true beauty of sacrifice! For then, as you recognise my Light at your heart, you may see your wings unfurl, creating a wondrous sight that heralds the grounding of another immortal Master of Creation to the Earth and her bounteous goodness, whilst aligning all that may be made manifest by your hand with the Highest and most perfect of visions and ambitions...."

(* Jet and Carnelian will help you ground and connect with the energies and wisdom of Holly, if you wish to enhance your experience using crystals.)

If you have chosen to accept and work with Michael's Gift, and when you are ready to connect with his second Greenwood Guardian, you need simply call for the presence of **Larch** (*) .... Larch envelops you in a pale green Light, and the Feminine spirit essence of Larch speaks to you, saying:

"I channel the bronze Light of Expansion and Dissolution, enabling and facilitating transformation and change: thus you may regard me as an arboreal Master of Alchemy, for I offer you the energies of Void Potential and the crucible of my heart, in order that you may fashion your life as you desire it to be so.... So stand with me now, and see how choice offers you freedoms that are beyond compare; and look to find your inherent strengths that will not tarnish or wear, so that you may recognise and accept that you always have the power to fight against your own folly, and hence transform yourself into whatsoever you seek and desire.... Know too that I will always aid you and support you in this with my infinite love – for through me you will see your path in its fullness and entirety – recognising the beginning of your journey home; and knowing too the positivity and balance of the NOW, which will allow you a foretaste of the things yet to come at its joyous conclusion...."

(* Bronzite will help you ground and connect with the energies and wisdom of Larch, if you wish to enhance your experience using crystals.)

ARCHEIA MIKAELA

'WALK THE LABYRINTH WITH ME'

CRYSTAL CHAMPIONS:

Labradorite ♥ Azurite ♥ Blue Chalcedony

CREATURE COMPANIONS:

Tiger ♥ Cobra ♥ Bat

GREENWOOD GUARDIANS:

Myrrh ♥ Weeping Willow

*I have absolute faith and trust in my path.
I am as ONE with Divine Mind
and All That IS.*

MEETING MIKAELA

It is late in the afternoon, and you find yourself walking along a dusty road that is winding its way through a dry jungle wilderness. The fierce heat of the day is cooling as the sun lowers and loses its strength, and as you walk your nostrils are filled with the rich scents of sun-baked earth and moist vegetation, with subtle overtones redolent of exotic flowers and spices. The road meanders through a forest of very tall trees, whose leafy branches are festooned with hanging vines and garlanded with wild orchids – the ground below their lofty canopy dotted with dense thickets of thorny-leaved shrubs and stands of slender grasses laden with silvery-gold seed heads.

As you move deeper into the jungle the road widens and the undergrowth thins – and you notice how the trees' lengthening shadows fall in stripes across your path, so that you pass through shadow then light.... shadow then light.... shadow then light. You also realise that the forest around you is never silent – and as your hearing sharpens, you find that you can isolate and discern the sounds of a variety of insects and birds, interspersed with the occasional calls of animals you cannot see or identify: then suddenly you find that you can also hear the sound of fast-flowing water, and curiosity spurs you to move more quickly....

At long last you round a sharp bend and find you have arrived at an open clearing of sun-baked ochre earth, where an ancient temple stands bathed in a soft golden light. The temple is in rather an advanced state of decay – its crumbling blocks of golden sandstone semi-covered with vines and creepers, which are slowly absorbing it back into the jungle wilderness. The far side of the temple has in fact completely collapsed, its fabric strewn across the ground and tumbling into the river whose sounds led you here: this has caused the river to deepen and change course; leaving a shady pool in the temple's lee, where a small grove of sandalwood trees has created an oasis of tranquillity. Here a tall woman, gowned in white, is waiting for you: this is Archeia Mikaela. She steps forward to greet you, declaring:

"I am Mikaela, the Lady Faith – Keeper of the Blue Heart-Flame of Divine Will and Power, Guardian and Defender of the Faith, twin-flame and beloved of Michael. Know that I carry Michael's sword in my heart, and would do likewise for you – indeed, all that I am I offer to you now, that you may know companionship and joy as we travel life's paths together. So let not the clouds obscure your view – but see clearly and with delight the winding of the road leading ever inwards to the centre of All That Is, which is like a jewel set in the Crown of Life; and take advantage of my knowledge, faith, protection and guidance. Then, when your goal is reached, so you will discover that the road leads out again – for as your consciousness expands you will find that you gain a fresh perspective: one that is somehow greater, somehow more, than you had before. And thus, you may know the benefits of always travelling with a mind and heart that are open and free; and appreciate the delights to be found when you can simply BE."

Mikaela then guides you to a sandstone block beneath a sandalwood tree, and invites you to rest and take time to study her, so that you may accustom yourself to her energies.

As you settle, you observe that Mikaela is tall and elegant, with strikingly beautiful features and an hour-glass figure that is shown off to perfection by the long white gown she is wearing: this seems to be made of some sort of finely-woven silken fabric, which is reflecting the light of the evening sun. You cannot help but think that 'white' is not a very practical colour for such a dusty environment – yet nothing appears to adhere to the material, and the gown is spotless and pristine. Its bodice moulds itself to her form – its scooped neckline revealing pale flawless skin, and drawing attention to her long slender neck and womanly figure; whilst its full-length puffed sleeves mould her upper arms, before flaring out to drape softly around her hands and wrists. The skirt of the gown is very full, gathering snugly at the waist and then billowing out to brush the ground around her feet: these are slim with long slender toes, clad in dainty Indian-style sandals that are just visible beneath the hem of her gown. The tops of these are made of white leather, and have been tooled in gold using a labyrinthine design that looks like a four-leaved clover, in the very centre of which there is a single tear-drop-shaped diamond.

At this moment you notice that Mikaela is holding something in her left hand; and realise this to be the ends of a narrow belt-like girdle, which is knotted around her waist: this is made of the same white material as her gown, and so was almost invisible when seen against its whiteness. Closer scrutiny shows that the large and complex knot sits on her left hip, from where its cordlike ends hang free – and, noting your interest, Mikaela lifts her hand to show you that both ends of the cord have been intricately knotted into three web-like spheres: each is a different size; and each is evenly spaced a hands-width apart – the smallest being closest to her waist, the largest being near the cord's end.

Shifting your gaze up to Mikaela's face, you are immediately drawn to her arresting gentian-blue eyes, which are calmly surveying you in return: these are set beneath dark arching brows in a fair-skinned and delicate heart-shaped face; and are framed by thick nut-brown hair, which she wears swept back over her ears, like a pair of glossy bird's wings. She turns her head to show you how her hair has been twisted into a French pleat at the back of her head, where it is covered and secured in a net-like snood fashioned like a spider's web: this has been woven from fine silky white threads, and is studded with tear-drop-shaped faceted diamonds that catch the light as she moves her head, making them sparkle like the morning sun on snow.

Mikaela is also wearing a close-fitting gold necklace, whose pattern is based on a square labyrinthine 'Greek Key' design: as you look at it more closely, you note that it is glowing with a warm golden Light, which gently (and hypnotically) pulses in and out of the centre of each tiny square section, as it cycles around the base of her neck.

After pondering this, your gaze is drawn to Mikaela's right hand, which is cupped over something in her lap. Her middle finger bears a plain and simple gold ring, which is set with a large oval cornflower-blue sapphire, whose faceted depths wink and spark with an inner fire: this gem affirms Mikaela's role as co-overseer of the Sapphire Ray; and is the gem that links her with Michael, her twin flame. Lifting her hand, Mikaela reveals that it was concealing a labradorite sphere, whose highly-polished surface is filled with constantly shifting clouds of royal-blue and gold Light. Smiling, Mikaela slowly tilts it from side to side, showing you how the colour-play within the stone cycles through different hues of royal blue, turquoise, moss-green, violet, bronze and gold, depending on the angle and intensity of the light in which it is being viewed.

MIKAELA'S TEACHINGS
The Circle of Life – the Labyrinth and the Maze:

Mikaela observes that Michael is very direct in how he deals with misdemeanours and misdeeds: however, she prefers to employ the 'smoke and mirrors' (camouflage and confusion) technique so perfectly exemplified by the mineral of her sphere. Holding it out so that you can see it more clearly, she explains that labradorite reveals the metamorphic qualities of light: therefore, contemplating what is revealed within (and/or by) it may lead you to question what is real and what is an illusion; and to consider if you too create your own realities and illusions – and so have the power to transform any aspect of your Self or your existence into something new or different at will. Smiling again, she tells you that all Magi (light-magicians, if you prefer) understand how focused thought and intent can alter how reality is perceived; and *know* that everything that has been created has become so through directing Light by means of thought and intention: then, at a wave of her hand, the labradorite sphere vanishes; and the sandy earth of the clearing lifts and begins to spin, as if being stirred by a whirlwind....

After swiftly closing your eyes to protect them, you feel the fine grains start to swirl madly about you, whispering against your skin and ruffling your clothing and hair.... then, just as suddenly as it began, everything goes quiet and still.... Opening your eyes, you are amazed to see that the temple is no longer in ruins – its sandstone now like new; its square crenellated form flawlessly complete; the clearing itself paved in immaculate white marble. You also observe that the same pattern you saw on Mikaela's footwear has been etched onto the marble in gold to create an intricate labyrinth, whose winding path traces its way through eleven concentric circular 'layers' (arranged in four quadrants); the heart of which opens into a central space shaped like a six-petalled 'flower'.

Lifting her hand to touch her necklace, Mikaela remarks that this too represents a labyrinth – although of a much simpler (yet equally profound) design. She explains that the Ancient Greeks used this 'key' design to represent the myth of the 'Minotaur and the Labyrinth' – an allegorical tale about humankind's endeavours to rise above their 'lower' nature through mastery of the four Elements and the seven primary aspects of their subtle body, in order that they might finally transcend the wheel of death and rebirth.

Mikaela observes that the labyrinth in the tale was actually much more complex, incorporating many mazes through which the hero was led by a silken thread (signifying light and wisdom) as he strove to find the exit (signifying enlightenment and freedom from the cycle of rebirth). Stressing that a labyrinth and a maze are very different, she explains that a *maze* presents you with a choice of many routes, only one of which will lead you towards your goal (hence some paths lead to dead ends, requiring you to retrace your steps – hopefully learning which led you the wrong way so that you do not make the same mistake over and over!); whereas a *labyrinth* only has one route to follow (although its single path often appears to lead you in all directions and never directly to your goal – which may, in its own way, be equally as confusing or frustrating!)

With a wry smile Mikaela says that navigating each lifetime is a little like walking the Minotaur's labyrinth, with many 'mazes' that offer you different (and maybe testing) choices of lessons and directions designed to impart a wide range of learning experiences (some of which you might end up repeating many times!) – yet always leading you on to something new that will help you gain fresh insights and understandings about yourself and your world. Likewise, (when viewed holographically from the perspective of your Higher-self) the same applies to your Soul's entire journey back to source (the labyrinth), and to each of your Soul's lifetimes or existences (the maze) that comprise it.

Lifting her necklace, Mikaela rotates it so you can see how it forms an unbroken circle without beginning or end, and asks you to see how the golden line is unbroken, and how the pattern constantly repeats – leading in to the centre and then out again, before moving on; and to see how every change of direction gives a different perspective on what went before, and what is still to come. She explains how it therefore defines the many and varied cycles of Life, depicting the twists and turns of a single lifetime; as well as showing how every lifetime or existence is a part of the Soul's entire journey of exploration, as it seeks to return to Unity with its Source. Then, swiftly circling the whole necklace with her finger, she smiles and reiterates that, nonetheless, both have a common and ultimate goal – that of Unification (becoming One) with *all* that you ARE.

Getting to her feet, Mikaela now leads you to the labyrinth imprinted on the marble paving. She tells you that visitors to the temple sometimes walk this intricate labyrinth (which is similar to one laid out at Chartres Cathedral) as a meditative tool or instructive practice – much as you experienced with Michael's Spiral of Contemplation; and asks you to walk the path with her while she tells you a little more about it....

As you begin, Mikaela says that all labyrinths reflect the flow of Life and all things timeless and eternal, and define the infinite cycle of life, death and rebirth: however the four quadrants of this labyrinth *also* represent the four Elements of earth, water, air and fire and the four lower Bodies of the embodied human (the body, emotions, mind, and spirit). She asks you to see how the path you are walking cycles through each quadrant – moving inwards towards the centre and outwards again; and stresses how this is also true of the path you travel throughout every embodied lifetime: for, as you navigate inwards to your centre (to recognise your lessons and your motivations through inward-directed contemplation, and to find balance and understanding through your heart) *and* outwards (to recognise your place in the greater world and to know absolute balance from a Divine perspective) you will experience everything in multiple ways and on multiple levels – physically, emotionally, mentally and spiritually.

After a while you begin to appreciate the labyrinth's layout and design; and as your steps become more sure you understand how each quadrant supports you in seeing and reviewing your path with a different focus: one highlighting your physical senses and physical presence; one your intuitive thoughts and emotional feelings; one your logical thoughts and its processes and conclusions; and one that 'sees, feels and thinks' with heart-centred dispassion and compassion. Recognising this, Mikaela smiles, and says that the focus offered through the archetypal lesson of 'walking the labyrinth' is always useful: for if you wish to truly understand, reconcile and resolve problems, it is good to view them from a fresh or altered perspective – emphasising that the key to successful navigation is to BE in the moment, 'keeping your eyes on the prize', and have faith in yourself and the path, regardless of where it seems to be leading you....

Eventually you reach the six-petalled shape at the labyrinth's heart – and here Mikaela traces out two interlocking triangles in gold Light to link the six petals, before drawing the same pattern over your chest.... as she does so, she reminds you that your heart is *your* centre: the balance point, where Earth meets Heaven; the place where the 'lower-self' of the mind and body merges with the 'Higher-self' of the Spirit; and the place where you may find stillness and focus, clarity and peace!

Stepping back, Mikaela gives a low whistle – at which a magnificent white tiger with ice-blue eyes pads silently from the jungle, and immerses itself in the pool by the temple. As you watch, Mikaela observes that tigers' love of water shows their affinity with this Element, and shows that **Tiger** can be asked to help you understand, clarify and balance your emotions when their imbalance mars your judgement or perception; or to aid you with cleansing and clearing any aspect of your Self – body, mind or spirit – from anything that clouds your eyes and conceals the Truth. She tells you that tigers fiercely defend both family and territory, moving on their huge, yet sensitive, feet with stealth and grace – their subtle markings and silent ways allowing them to move through light and shadow unseen: thus, Tiger can teach you a great deal about how to perfect this art, whilst also offering you his protection; and/or to help you energetically shield your home and your family, if you feel you are under threat. Furthermore, as tigers prefer travelling the hidden pathways of the jungle, you may also ask Tiger for guidance and support if you need help to find a safe route through the perils of your own personal jungle; or need to choose the direction that is the most appropriate for your needs at that time. Mikaela adds that white tigers, like this one, are also Guardians of the Inner Light – guarding and guiding all who are genuine Seekers on the Path, and defending and protecting the many winding pathways that may be walked by the Soul: thus, the presence of a *white* Tiger might be a sign that the path you are on requires more detailed scrutiny, and that he is offering you his additional power and support if you require it.

Giving you a polished sphere that is a smaller version of her own, Mikaela tells you that this is **Labradorite**, her first Crystal Champion – explaining:

"Labradorite's constantly shifting Light offers useful camouflage and protection as you walk the labyrinths and mazes of your Life, promoting the magician's illusion of 'smoke and mirrors' and helping you manage your fears in order to take appropriate control of a situation: this makes it a powerful ally if you feel unsafe or ill at ease, or if you are confronted by darkness or danger. Furthermore, as it is sometimes necessary to present a false impression for your own safety, Labradorite can help you keep your energies strong and pure by enabling you to BE unseen. Labradorite can also help you pierce the 'veils of illusion', enabling you to confront and question the nature of reality, and making it easier to pinpoint what is realistic, relevant and important (and what is not!): this can help you look more dispassionately at the heart of any matter to see how your life (or something in it) can be freed in order to help it flow more easily and effectively, which in turn will bring about greater inner balance. Labradorite with blue and gold colour-play in particular supports your solar plexus and throat chakras, enhancing all mental processes and communication, and balancing your heart-flames of Wisdom and Will; whilst Labradorite with green and gold colour-play in particular supports your

solar plexus and heart chakras, enhancing all heart-centred thought processes, and balancing your heart-flames of Wisdom and Love."

With a smile, Mikaela affirms that Labradorite may therefore aid you in understanding more about the nature of Light, and the infinite ways in which Light may be wielded.

The Holographic Universe and the Multifaceted Nature of Divine Truth:

Mikaela now asks you to accompany her to the entrance to the temple: this is tall and narrow, and is flanked by two shoulder-high hexagonal sandstone pillars, each of which is engraved with a bird – one depicting a stork; the other a green plover. A large spectacled cobra is coiled on the top of each pillar, and you suddenly realise that you will have to pass these snakes if you wish to enter the temple! Noting your concern, Mikaela reassures you that, with her at your side, you will always have safe passage.... holding out the skirts of her gown, she adds that she may appear delicate and 'girly' – but looks can be deceptive, for the fabric of her gown is made of spider silk and white Light, and is impervious to destruction: hence, she will both guide *and* protect you – giving you the courage to conquer your fears, and the faith to find a way through the darkness.

Reminding you that *all* snakes are Masters of Creation, Mikaela tells you that the ones you see have the task of guarding the Powers and Wisdoms that are held within this temple – for cobras have a special affinity with the Elements of both earth and fire; and so have been tasked with directing the development of the energies of the Kundalini, and the safe awakening of its associated psychic abilities. She adds that cobras have an appropriately fearsome reputation, which is not misplaced: this is because they have the wisdom to understand that energy (which *is* Light) can be directed and applied with both 'positive' and 'negative' intent – and so may be used, or misused. With another smile, she says that (if you have the courage to ask) you will find **Cobra** to be a judicious, if strict, teacher, who will oversee and direct your personal and spiritual growth, which includes awakening your Kundalini, with both wisdom and care: she emphasises that this process must never be forced or rushed, as the Kundalini fires may not be brought to full power until your 'lower' chakras and ego-self are suitably mastered – although Cobra may then be asked to guide you through your mastery of your Higher chakras, as you work towards your Ascension. Mikaela adds that Cobra is always happy to be your teacher, *as long as* you are willing to work hard: for you need to be spiritually aware and well-disciplined to use Light (and the Kundalini's fires) in the positive and constructive manner Cobra will require of you. She explains that Cobra will therefore ask you to learn and understand how 'energy' feels in its different states (including its quantum, quality and frequency); and to practise controlling your baser desires, thoughts and impulses – the keyword being *'control'*: hence, Cobra might not come to you until you are truly ready, although its presence will always be a sign that focus and effort are required! Stepping forwards Mikaela leads you between their pillars – at which the cobras rise up and open their hoods, displaying their distinctive markings: at this she chuckles, and adds that the presence of Cobra in dreams or when journeying signals that a time of all-embracing and profound personal or spiritual growth is about to begin – and indicates the need to scrutinise or examine whatever you encounter or see closely, and with extra care.

Having passed the cobras, you enter the temple, which is cool and dark; and follow Mikaela closely, as she moves along a series of twisting passageways with assurance and ease: as you walk, your eyes adjust to the light, and you realise that the temple is larger inside than its outside appearance would suggest.... you realise too that the light level is slowly increasing – and eventually, after a few more twist and turns, you emerge into a large square chamber, the walls and ceiling of which are clad in snow-white quartz veined with translucent seams of gentian-blue crystal. The centre of the room is occupied by a tall hexagonal crystal of blue sapphire, which is emitting an intense blue Light; whilst the rest of the chamber is illuminated by flickering masses of clear blue and white flames, which are all burning in white unicorn horns that are attached to the walls of the chamber with silver brackets, like old-fashioned torches.

A simple bench sits below a torch on the far side of the chamber, where Mikaela invites you to sit at her side as she tells you more.... once you are settled, she lifts one end of the girdle that is knotted around her waist, and directs you to inspect the three white web-like spheres knotted into its end: this allows you to see that each one is formed from intricate layers of open knot-work – their loose multilayered structure allowing you just a glimpse of a crystal at its heart. Mikaela tells you that each sphere holds a holographic pattern of the Consciousness of the Universe, and embraces the principle of microcosm and macrocosm. She explains that each knot is basically composed of multiple layers of Light: these determine the resonance and frequency of the Diamond Light that is being channelled through the diamond crystals at their heart; whilst defining the Dimensions within which that Light is to be made effective. Mikaela reminds you that every diamond begins life as a soft and brittle carbon element – gradually clarifying and hardening over time through the actions of heat and pressure, before finally evolving into a resilient and brilliant crystal. With a smile, she observes that, as a carbon-based life-form, *your* body, mind and spirit may likewise be exposed to 'heat and pressure' that will help you grow and evolve; and assures you that you may always call upon her presence to support you, as you seek to become the diamond you were meant to BE.

Lifting the other end of her girdle, Mikaela shows you that she carries six diamonds in total: she explains that she uses one set of three to monitor the *existing* resonances of Diamond Light; and the other to establish the actual resonances *required,* by channelling the Diamond Light through the complex knot that ties the girdle at her waist. This knot holds a flawless blue sapphire crystal at its heart – thus sustaining the Blue, Indigo and Sapphire Rays multidimensionally across space and Time; and enabling her to regulate the Diamond Light that IS within *all* aspects of the blue spectrum on both an individual and Cosmic level, ensuring that its resonance and degree is of the Right magnitudes in and for every situation.

Touching the smallest spheres, Mikaela informs you that these have the smallest number of layers; and hold flawlessly clear diamonds: these channel the Diamond Light through the Crystal Ray, which enables her to *intensify* the Sapphire Ray's resonance, making its essence deeper and more focused and still; and augmenting its power to strip away all that is false – thus removing anything that has the potential to disassociate Souls from their Divinity, and facilitating the expression of their *Inner Truths*....

Touching the medium-sized spheres, Mikaela says that these have more layers than the first; and hold perfect opalescent-white diamonds: these channel the Diamond Light through the Pearlescent-white Ray, enabling her to *refine* the Sapphire Ray's resonance, making its essence more open and multidimensionally aware; and augmenting its power to allow Souls access to Higher information and Divine knowledge by enabling it to be simply 'known' – thus facilitating the expression of their *Outer Truths*....

Touching the largest spheres, Mikaela says that these have the largest number of layers; and hold pure white opaque diamonds: these channel the Diamond Light through White Light, enabling her to clarify the Sapphire Ray's resonance, making its essence fully clear and complete, so that the resonances of 'blue' that accentuate inward focus, and the resonances of 'indigo' that accentuate outward focus, are more easily defined; and augmenting its power to reinforce the Soul's profound and innate sense of Unity with All That Is, whilst (nonetheless) enabling it to experience self-identity and separation – thus facilitating the expression of its *Divine Truths*....

With a gentle smile Mikaela says that she realises these are profound concepts to absorb; and allows your thoughts a few minutes to settle.... she then gives you a deep blue crystal, telling you that this is **Azurite**, her second Crystal Champion – explaining:

> *"Azurite carries the Blue Ray with great clarity and command – surrounding you in its inimitable light, so that you may experience its purity and know its power: this will aid you in developing your 'logical' and 'intuitive' skills, whilst teaching you to have inner focus and mental self-discipline. Azurite is also calming and cooling, helping you to let go of your extraneous thoughts and feelings (which is another form of self-mastery and discipline!) so that you may simply relax your mind and extend your senses to BE in its energy, whilst taking the opportunity to understand yourself (and the world – seen and unseen) on all levels of body, mind and spirit. Because Azurite supports Truth through the throat and brow chakras and the Universal and Soma centres, it may also help you review and release anything that does not truly serve your purpose; and will cast a clear blue Light that may provide additional clarity whenever you channel or commune with your Higher Teachers and Guides. Moreover, if you think you are being deceived or led astray (in* any *situation), you may hold Azurite to your heart and ask it to help you discern the true and complete picture in whatever you see, hear, or are being told."*

Smiling, Mikaela affirms that Azurite may therefore help you discern the subtleties held within the Blue spectrum of Light, and understand their uses and their application.

The Gift of The Blue Flame of Divine Will and Power:

Asking you to accompany her deeper into the temple, Mikaela touches the wall to your right, at which a tall opening appears: beyond this you can see a long white corridor, whose high ceiling and mirrored walls create a sense of infinite space (although its full extent is hidden by a curtain of sparkling cobalt-blue Light that obstructs the way ahead). Reassuring you she will stay close to you, Mikaela asks you to walk down the corridor, and step through the Light.... as you comply, you are relieved to find that this is easy to do – even though you know that the masks or disguises you wear to veil or hide the real 'you' from others (perhaps through pride, fear, shame or guilt) are being stripped away....

Mikaela asks you to now turn and look closely at yourself in the mirrored wall; and see how your inner beauty, Light and integrity shines forth – saying:

"Be not untrue to your Self in order to satisfy others fears, or so that (through you) they may justify their own failings. You are who you have chosen to be, made manifest in flesh, with these thoughts; these emotions; and this body – for, in your wisdom, you made it so...."

As her words fade, so too does your reflection; and so you turn to move on, only to find that another curtain of Light (this time an iridescent royal-blue) obstructs the way ahead.

Again Mikaela asks you to go forwards and walk through it; and, this time as you do so, you know that all the pointless expectations, burdens and obligations that you or others have placed upon your shoulders are simply dropping away....

Once more Mikaela asks you to turn and look closely at yourself in the mirrored wall; and this time see how your innate wisdom, strength of mind and sense of Higher purpose now shines through – saying:

"Live not by the creeds of others, who fail to see the reality that is you because of their own fears and doubts. You have experience beyond measure – and the wisdom of the ages is reflected in your eyes for those that would look and choose to truly see...."

Again, as her words fade, so too does your reflection; and you turn again, and find that this time a curtain of shimmering blue-white Light obstructs the way ahead.

Once again Mikaela asks you to go forwards and walk through it; and this time you know that you are shedding all the remnants of ego that you hold in your consciousness – and your heart and mind expands to encompass ALL that you are....

Again Mikaela asks you to turn and look closely at yourself in the mirrored wall; and this time see how the Divine Light that IS the core truth of you shines forth with brilliance and Power: she then walks to stand behind you and rests her hands on your shoulders – saying:

"This is YOU! Is what you see not a fitting reality for one who holds a spark of The Divine, and is a true warrior for the Light? This, then, is a Truth: what you see IS your reality, without the need for encumbrance, artifice or disguise – and it is time for you to step forwards with pride, and declare (and show) yourself for who and what you truly are...."

As her words fade, so too does your reflection; and you turn again to see (at last) the end of the corridor, which opens into a six-sided chamber that has white chalcedony walls. Guiding you within, Mikaela leads you to the centre of the chamber, where a waist-high hexagonal pillar of crystal-clear quartz bears a bowl made of silvery-grey metal, within which a fire is blazing: each of the flames is a different shade of blue, and you are aware that all are emitting an oddly cool heat.

Asking you to stand to one side, Mikaela reaches into the fire and selects a single royal-blue flame: then, turning to face you, she touches the ring on her hand to the centre of your chest.... at this, your heart chakra becomes one with your High Heart centre.... the protective outer layer of the Lotus of your Heart opens.... and its pink petals unfurl to reveal a tightly closed blue bud within....

Mikaela now gently touches the blue flame she has selected to this bud, at which the blue petals of your Heart Lotus open and absorb the flame – flushing through with its fire, until each has a tiny replica of the flame flickering at its heart.... Noting this, Mikaela tells you that this is her Gift of The Blue Flame of Divine Will and Power, which she has given so that you may have the courage to follow your Highest Truths; and the strength to use its power to embrace all that is of the Highest Light. She then rests her hands on your shoulders in Blessing, and waits for the flames and petals to settle to an appropriate state of balance: this done, they close around their centre, and are enfolded in their outer layers – your heart centres likewise closing and finding equilibrium....

When she is happy that you are in the appropriate balance, Mikaela guides you to the far side of the chamber, where another narrow opening leads to a wider passageway beyond: this seems to be in darkness – but as you walk forwards, you realise that it is actually filled with a deep indigo-blue Light. Producing a dim light to guide you further, Mikaela leads you down the passage, before pausing to point out a roost of horseshoe bats that are clinging to the roof with their tiny claws. Awakening to your presence, one of them drops down and swoops around you; at which Mikaela explains that bats 'see' in the dark by using a type of sonar: therefore you may call upon **Bat** to guide you if you need to navigate through literal or figurative darkness; or if you wish to develop senses other than your physical sight; or if you are lost and want to find your way 'home'. She muses that Bat is said to be a symbol of rebirth and regeneration, and thus may support you through intense periods of transformation; whilst its reputation as a guardian of the underworld means that Bat can also be asked to guide and protect you when you are journeying or travelling out-of-body. Mikaela adds that Bat's presence may be a sign that it is time to let go of the 'old' to make way for the 'new', which might indicate that you need to undertake some form of trial or initiation – perhaps requiring you to confront your fears; and/or surrender something that no longer supports your spiritual or personal growth; and/or consign anything that prevents you from achieving your full potential to the Fires of your Higher-self – thus releasing you to be reborn anew. If any of these situations apply to you, Mikaela assures you that Bat will not only be the messenger, but will also be your wisest teacher, where its affinity with the Element of air can help you figure out the best way to achieve effective change, and aid you in dealing with whatever you need to address in the most logical and appropriate way. Suggesting that you now ask the bat to help you find the exit of the temple, Mikaela walks behind you as you follow the fluttery sounds of its flight – the light levels slowly increasing (indigo fading to deep and then pale blue).... until eventually you make your way back to the outside, where you find the temple once more a ruin; the white labyrinth no more.

Appearing at your side, Mikaela gives an enigmatic smile and gives you a pale-blue stone, saying that this is **Blue Chalcedony**, her third Crystal Champion – explaining:

"Blue Chalcedony works in a way that is gentle yet profound – cooling and calming, and stilling and balancing the mind and emotions, making it less painful to explore deep or long-standing issues that require resolution in order to move on. Blue Chalcedony also promotes serenity and peace, attracting the loving energies of The Divine Feminine to help you clarify and embrace your Soul's purpose, whilst retaining inner calm and

equilibrium. Thence, by clarifying your Self through healing your mind, body and spirit, you will be able to hold a finer quantum of Light, and more clearly ground the insights and wisdoms of your (Higher) Cosmic-self. Furthermore, because Blue Chalcedony supports the throat and Soul Star chakras, it may help you communicate with integrity, whilst still maintaining a clear connection to Universal Wisdom. You may also discover that Blue Chalcedony has a purity that resonates with a child-like innocence; and this may help you connect with your Inner Child, whose innate simplicity and naivety may give you the faith to find simpler solutions to problematic situations from a more basic, honest and less complicated viewpoint. This also makes Blue Chalcedony an excellent choice for all those who need more simplicity (and the peace it brings) in their life."

Smiling, Mikaela affirms that Blue Chalcedony may therefore bring you inner peace and help you move forwards with faith and trust, even when the way is hard or uncertain.

The Greenwood Guardians – Myrrh and Weeping Willow:

Her *personal* mentoring complete for now, Mikaela affirms she is always available to aid and support you: you need only bring her to mind and ask for her presence, and she will attend you. Furthermore, she tells you that two great Tree Beings of the Plant Kingdom have also asked to support you in addressing her Theme of 'WALK THE LABYRINTH WITH ME', adding that you need only request *their* presence, and they will be with you.

She explains that the first of these Greenwood Guardians is the Feminine essence of Myrrh, who has asked to overlight and help you ground whatever work you undertake within *any* aspect of her chapter. The second is the Feminine essence of Weeping Willow, who has specifically asked to help you understand and assimilate her Gift of The Blue Flame of Divine Will and Power (if you have chosen to accept it).

When you are ready to connect with Mikaela's first Greenwood Guardian, you need simply call for the presence of **Myrrh** (*) .... Myrrh envelops you in soft rainbow-black Light, and the Feminine spirit essence of Myrrh speaks to you, saying:

"I help heal the wounds of life's sweet sorrows old and new, giving of my red-gold blood to bring riches and joy to an otherwise harsh world. Though of barren ground, my bounty blesses the might of Kings – and thus may it bathe you too in regal goodness and mercy. So stand with me and surrender yourself body, mind and Soul to the darkness; and let the blackness fully embrace you, opening your heart and mind to the potentials that life offers.... and then let me show you the light at my heart, its iridescent rainbows inspiring you to greatness and total fulfilment – for I truly know that the Divine Light is eternally present, even in times of hardship or despair.... In this way, may that light and my love guide you ever onwards and upwards, that you may travel all the myriad paths of your life with faith and trust; and revelling in the exhilaration of all that your encounters and experiences teach you: for thus will you truly know the worth of sacrifice, and thus too will you truly understand the great gifts that the Light in ALL its manifestations offers you...."

(* Rainbow Obsidian will help you ground and connect with the energies and wisdom of Myrrh, if you wish to enhance your experience using crystals.)

If you have chosen to accept and work with Mikaela's Gift, and when you are ready to connect with her second Greenwood Guardian, you need simply call for the presence of **Weeping Willow** (*) .... Weeping Willow envelops you in a pale pink Light, and the Feminine spirit essence of Weeping Willow speaks to you, saying:

> *"Know that, although I weep, my tears (as with yours) may be of joy or sorrow – yet* all *tears are of the waters of the Soul, bringing clarity.... bringing balance.... and bringing healing. Hence, within my loving embrace you have the opportunity to know the wisdom that lies within you, enabling you to let go of anything that does not fully resonate with the pure and Divine Truth of your Being. So rest at my feet and allow my branches to create a canopy of Light that has the power to replenish your energy reserves, or heal your Soul if you are weary or sick; and know that I am the soft touch on your brow, as you go within to find both solace and peace.... Know too that I am the kind shelter that keeps you safe; the gentle voice that lulls you sleep when daylight seems far away; and the flexible strength that allows you to bow to the winds of ever-changing fortune without damage or harm.... Then allow your gaze to rest upon the abundant riches of silver and gold held within my leaves, and know that as long as you have faith you will always be provided for.... See too the perfect structure of every part of me, and allow yourself to likewise recognise the innate perfection of your own Be-ing – and then look for the Light that shines through all that I am, and simply open yourself to accept the support that is freely given by all those that truly love you –* knowing *that it is always possible to find purpose and strength in every moment of every day...."*

(* Blue Lace Agate and White Selenite will help you ground and connect with the energies and wisdom of Weeping Willow, if you wish to enhance your experience using crystals.)

ARCHEIA LUCIDA

'FIND THE CHRIST WITHIN'

CRYSTAL CHAMPIONS:

Tiger Iron ♥ Natural Citrine ♥ Tree Agate

CREATURE COMPANIONS:

Egret ♥ Jaguar ♥ Tree Creeper

GREENWOOD GUARDIANS:

Pomegranate ♥ Fig

*I accept and acknowledge
the Christ that I AM.*

MEETING LUCIDA

It is noon on a fine day in autumn, and you find yourself standing at the edge of a meadow bordering a dense forest of mature deciduous trees: their towering presence is stately and commanding; and when you tilt your head back to marvel at their height, you catch a glimpse of the golden sun in the clear blue sky above them, and feel its warmth filtering through the canopy to kiss your face and bless the ground beneath your feet. Everywhere you look nature's beauty and magnificence is captured within the forest's colours, shapes and forms – for the trees are in the process of withdrawing their life-force in preparation for their annual winter retreat, and many have already changed colour and are dropping their leaves. A sudden breeze causes those that have not yet fallen to flutter and dance, dappling everything in a silvery-gold light that shifts and shimmers all around you: then, as you stand admiring the scene, your eye is caught by a sudden movement, and a majestic russet-coated stag with a magnificent set of antlers appears from within the depths of the forest. Meeting your gaze, he seems to be commanding you to follow him, and so – as he turns back into the forest – you decide to go with him....

The narrow track he leads you down winds ever deeper into the trees, and as you follow in his footsteps you marvel at the wealth of textures, colours, shapes and sounds that are manifest in everything around you, each of which seems to awaken your senses in a different way. The red, gold, orange and bronze leaves that have already fallen are accumulating in layers and drifts, and these rustle and crunch beneath your feet at every step.... Here and there you spy fallen acorns, nestling in tiny dimpled cups; or find toffee-brown hazelnuts enfolded in their brittle papery husks – or prickly-coated chestnuts and glossy conkers spilling from their spiny shells.... In damper spots you find a wealth of fungi of all shapes, colours and sizes – some secreted in mossy hollows among the roots of the trees, or layered like lacy fairy platforms upon their trunks.

Eventually the track opens into a woodland glade that is open to the sky. This is ringed by a circle of ancient beech trees that offer some shelter and shade – and, as you pause on the threshold, you realise you have been led to one of Earth's natural cathedrals: a place of great sanctuary and peace, which glorifies the splendour of the natural world, and pays tribute to the Divine hand that creates all things. The glade's floor is carpeted with velvety green mosses and strewn with copper and bronze beech leaves that reflect the sunlight like a scattering of fallen stars; and in the very centre of the glade is a pool of still water, framed by a circle of ivory marble slabs speckled with silver lichens. To one side of this stands a woman clad in a many-layered rainbow robe: this is Archeia Lucida. She is small and slender, with lined and weathered skin – yet despite her obvious age, she has an authoritative and upright posture and stance that conveys a sense of unassailable inner and outer strength. Smiling, she thanks the great stag for his aid in guiding you here, and steps self-assuredly forwards to welcome you, declaring:

"I am Lucida, the Lady Clarity – Keeper of the Yellow Heart-Flame of Divine Wisdom, Guardian of the Light of Christ-consciousness, and twin flame of Jophiel. The Absolute Light of The Divine shines out through my Being in Rays of Rainbow Light, that it might fill your Soul with all possible potentials and offer you the means to become whole, complete, perfected and fulfilled. So stay with me a while, that my clarity may help you

find the wisdom that lies at the heart of who you are; and my love aid you in revealing the beauty of your Soul. For I would help you define anything in your life that you no longer need (and so might discard and leave behind); and aid you in finding the mercy and justice, love and peace you seek, as you search to find the meaning of Life and know your reason for BEing. And then, as you recognise in truth what you are, you may gain the courage and determination to grow to be the Master of your Being – rejoicing in all that you are and all that you have achieved, and taking up the mantle of your personal Christhood with honour and humble pride."

Offering you her hand, Lucida leads you to the side of the pool: here she conjures up two simple wooden chairs and, settling her robe around her, sits – inviting you to join her, so that you may take some time to examine her and become accustomed to her energies.

As you settle you meet Lucida's tranquil jade-green eyes, at which she smiles again, highlighting the laughter lines that are deeply scribed in her weathered mahogany skin. Her oval face has the proud features, sharply-defined nose and high angular cheekbones of a Native-American elder, although the strong lines of her face are somewhat softened by stray wisps of her surprisingly dark conker-brown hair. As she turns her head to allow you a different view, you can see that these have escaped from a golden net that secures her upswept hair in a neat bun at her crown. The net is made from fine strands of gold wire that have been fashioned into something that resembles an intricate spider's web: this anchors a dark-coloured sphere in the hollow at the bun's centre – closer inspection of which shows you that the sphere is a polished piece of rainbow obsidian, which is the stone that links her with Jophiel, her twin flame.

Your attention is next captured by Lucida's full-length robe, which is eye-catching, colourful and complex in its design: by rights it should look garish, yet it is actually breathtakingly beautiful. It has been fashioned from an ultra-fine light and silky material in a wrap-around style; and has a high 'V' neck and long flaring sleeves that drape softly around her wrists. The robe is multi-layered, having eight layers in all – the seven inner layers of material each displaying one of the colours of the visible spectrum of light (starting with red at the innermost layer, through to violet at the seventh). Each of these layers creates a rainbow of colour that is visible at the neck, cuffs and hem of the robe; and each is secured at the 'V' of the neck by a round bead polished from a crystal of the appropriate colour – ruby, fire opal, citrine, emerald, aquamarine, indigo sapphire and amethyst respectively. The topmost layer of the robe is multi-hued, blending all seven colours in three deep bands to create a triple (tertiary) rainbow from hem to neck, and shoulder to cuffs. A simple plaited and bound cord made from long threads of black silk secures the robe around Lucida's waist and knots at the front – where she appears to have tucked a deep-red rose bud that is on the verge of coming into bloom.

Lucida's long robe pools around her feet, which are shod in soft white moccasins. The tops of these are embellished with beaded ornamentation, and noting your interest, she lifts a foot to show you how tiny beads of rainbow obsidian (secured with knots of black silk thread) form a pattern that defines three concentric circles superimposed on a four-armed cross – in the centre of which an intricate knot of gold thread secures a large spherical bead of clear lemon-yellow citrine, so that it sits at the very heart of the cross.

Your gaze lastly moves to Lucida's square and capable hands, which are resting in her lap, and you note that she wears a ring on the middle finger of her right hand that holds a large tear-drop-shaped faceted amethyst: this is set in a simple mount on a wide silver band; and as you inspect the gem more closely, you see its incredible depth and clarity; and realise that it holds a tiny amethyst flame, which is flickering steadily in its heart. Her left hand, meanwhile, is cupping a plain and simple wooden bowl, whose red-brown patina has been polished smooth through years of constant handling – its beauty simply expressed through the natural pattern and colours of its grain.

LUCIDA'S TEACHINGS
The Grounding of The Christ-Light through the Cedar and the Rose:

Noting that your observations are complete, Lucida tells you that the wooden bowl she is holding was carved from the heartwood of an ancient cedar tree. As you admire its simple beauty, she explains that the rings and whorls within its grain hold the history of the tree's seasons, years and lifetimes of growth. With a smile, she says that she sees this as a metaphor for the human condition – each ring serving as a reminder of how each lifetime and experience is another opportunity to grow in wisdom and understanding, in order to 'grow straight and tall' within the Light of The Divine, and (ultimately) *know* immortality through merger with the Christ within.

Lucida emphasises that it is important to understand that the word 'Christ' does not refer to a specific person or set of religious beliefs or practices, but originates from a word that means 'anointed': this refers to an act of sanctification and purification that confers the potential for Divine transfiguration – hence a 'Christed One' is one who has been purified and Blessed by the absolute Light of The Divine; and designates *anyone* who has achieved oneness with their Christed-self. With another smile, she explains that 'Divine transfiguration' is the same thing as 'Ascension'; and adds that anyone who has attained their Christhood might also be referred to as an Ascended *or Illumined* Master – the title of 'Master' indicating that they have achieved Mastery of themselves, and not implying mastery over others!

Gently tapping her bowl, Lucida informs you that some ancient civilisations used cedarwood to build temples or other sacred structures, believing that its unique properties would help ground the many sacred wisdoms that hold the fundamental truths of life and immortality, and define the core principles that govern the right and proper application of Divine Light. She points out that grounding wisdom and Light must (by definition) incorporate recognising and developing your spirituality, for your Christed-self embraces the true identity of your Soul – which (although perhaps perceived as being 'above' and therefore separate from you) is, in fact, anchored within you throughout all your earthly embodiments, in order to inspire and direct your spiritual journey back to Unity with the Divine Light.

Smiling again, she lovingly reminds you that – as an 'apprentice Illumined Master' yourself – you have planned and designed all of your life's learning experiences so that *you* may ground sacred wisdoms and understand the nature of Divine Light, by practising mastery of your body (physical Self), mind (thinking Self) and emotions (reactive Self).

She emphasises that, therefore, every moment of every day brings endless opportunities that enable you to practise addressing, understanding, resolving and mastering the widest range of issues you can possibly imagine, so that you may eventually accomplish your transfiguration (or Ascension). With another gentle smile Lucida tells you that, as you continue to practise extending your focus and behaviours *away* from the impulses of your (lower) ego-self and *towards* those of your (Higher) Christed-self, you will increasingly make your choices with full awareness and understanding of the causes and effects of all your actions; and begin to live your life solely from the perspective of Love, which is the mark of a true Master!

As you start to think about what Lucida has been saying, you sense a movement behind you – and suddenly a snow-white egret swoops past you to land on the far side of the pool: delicately lifting its long slender legs and feet, it steps carefully into the water and stands motionless – observing the watery depths with a keen eye. Lucida draws your attention to the contrast between the white of its feathers and the blackness of its long bill and slender legs, whose long-toed yellow feet are being employed to stir up the muddy potential at the bottom of the pool; and remarks that you may ask **Egret** to show you how to use *all* your senses of touch and sight to locate, identify and observe anything that might be hidden below the surface of an issue or a situation, in order to know if it will support your forward progress; or to help you practise discerning the true nature of something by touch alone. Pointing to its yellow feet, Lucida remarks that Egret may also help you use the attributes of your Solar Plexus and mental (thinking) Body to look at anything you 'stir up' – including any associated emotions generated by their processes; and to utilise the Element of water and its cleansing properties to address what you find. As you watch, the egret pauses with one leg suspended in the air, and Lucida adds that Egret's mastery of balance can also support you in any healing or clarifying process that requires your body, mind and emotions to be more in balance with each other: moreover, its ability to maintain a sure footing within the murk and mire means that Egret will help keep you safely grounded throughout all processes of transformation and change. Slowly the egret takes another step, before returning to statue-like stillness – at which Lucida says that Egret's tranquillity may prompt you to spend more time in inner contemplation, which will help you attain and maintain a state of inner calm; whilst its elegance, even in flight, may show you how to move through life with grace and flow, dealing serenely with any obstacle in your way. At this, the egret takes to the air – and Lucida adds that Egret may also come to support you on his wings when you experience an extreme event, so that you may understand more about the essential nature of Light, and everything that defines wholeness and balance.

As the egret disappears from view, Lucida brings your attention back to the pool, where it seems the egret may have stirred something in its depths – for a lotus flower now floats on its surface. The lotus has butter-yellow petals, fading to creamy-yellow at their base – and, as you look more closely, you realise that each perfectly formed petal is also veined and tipped with gold. Lucida explains that this pool holds the waters of Divine Wisdom wherein grows the Lotus of Divine and Illumined Wisdom, so that all who are touched by its Light may know clarity and peace.

Taking her cedarwood bowl, she dips it into the pool.... holding this out to you, she says that you may use the water that it holds to wash your hands *if* you are ready to commit to a programme of self-transformation: then, if and when you are done, Lucida places her bowl aside, and takes the red rosebud from her belt.... She tells you that she bears this flower as a reminder of the Love that makes her One with the Divine Light; and as a sign of the everlasting and infinite love and compassion that she, in turn, holds for humankind. Lucida then lifts the rosebud to the sky – and, as it catches the sunlight, teardrops of dew (like rainbow-filled diamonds) start to form on its unfurling petals; and the slowly blossoming rose begins to radiate a deep crimson light that is flecked with sparks of copper and gold. She tells you that this rose carries and holds the Light that inspires the Passion of the Christed Ones – the Light of The Divine Masculine forever held within the heart of The Divine Feminine; and adds that calling upon the Light of this Rose will help you connect with the Angel of the Presence – the One who unites Creation and Transformation, and who *knows* that 'Love is all there IS'.

Tucking the rose back into her belt, Lucida says that she pledges to bring you a rose like this the very moment you are ready to accept the presence of its Light within you, and when you are ready to commit yourself to working consciously towards embodying your Christed-self. Smiling, she adds that she will gladly bring her bowl with the waters of Divine Wisdom whenever you ask for help in cleansing and clearing any thoughts, feelings, emotions, beliefs or attitudes that you are ready to release from your life.

Giving you a polished stone that has many layers of red, yellow, brown and silver; Lucida tells you that this is **Tiger Iron**, her first Crystal Champion – explaining:

"Tiger Iron unites red and yellow jasper, tiger eye and hematite in a single adaptable and multi-purpose stone, which has the ability to strengthen, align and balance your three lower chakras and auric Bodies, whilst simultaneously linking your Christed-self and your physical body. Thus, Tiger Iron can powerfully ground all *that you are to the Earth (Higher-self and lower-self; Soul and ego); helping you to view all that you experience from a Higher and more detached perspective, and enabling you to deal with any issues that are restricting or preventing your growth in a balanced and appropriate manner, which will allow you to resolve them with less fuss and more speed. The tiger eye and yellow jasper elements within Tiger Iron carry the Light of Christ-consciousness and the Gold Ray of The Divine Masculine, which will aid and support all mental reasoning and logical thought processes – particularly anything that concerns planning and structure. This is balanced by the hematite, which carries the Silver Ray of The Divine Feminine to aid and support intuitive processes, inspiration, creativity and flow – offering greater flexibility to whatever you do; whilst the addition of red jasper brings the fire and passion of the Red Rays to boost your enthusiasm, and give you the courage, energy and strength you need to move forwards with commitment and determination."*

With a smile, Lucida affirms that Tiger Iron may therefore help you in your process of self-creation and transformation, by freeing you to move into a new state of Being with positivity and faith in the productive process of change – *knowing* that Love truly IS all there is!

The Gift of The Yellow Flame of Divine Wisdom:
Removing one of her moccasins, Lucida says that she wants you to understand a little about the significance of the design that adorns it.... She begins by tracing out the four-armed cross, and explains that this represents the four Elements of earth, air, fire and water; and the four cardinal directions of north, south, east and west. Pausing on the pale yellow bead at the centre of the cross, she adds that each arm meets here – the nexus of 'Heaven' and 'Earth' (above and below) and the place of balance within, where the Element of ether inspires the Soul's awakening. Lucida continues by tracing out the three concentric circles, explaining that these represent the three Flames that fire and inspire the Lotuses of the Heart and Soul; the three pillars of the Kabbalistic Tree of Life, which create a spiritual 'map' to guide the Soul 'home'; and the three Great Suns that govern and direct evolution in accordance with the Divine plan.

Once again she rests her finger on the bead in the centre, and stresses that *this* is the focus point: the point that exemplifies the paradox that individuality and separateness can (and do) exist within oneness and unity – the one within the many: the many within the one. With another smile, Lucida says that she and her twin flame epitomise this concept, for whereas *he* (Jophiel) holds and directs the complete and undifferentiated White Light of The Divine, *she* holds and directs that same Light in its individual constituent parts – and so *as one* they hold the absolute Light in both diversity *and* unity. Gently tapping the bead at the centre of the design again, Lucida emphasises that you have to maintain focus and balance if you want to direct the Divine Light effectively: hence, this bead has been polished from a crystal of natural citrine, which not only acts as the balance point and focus for the cross and circles, but also grounds the Yellow Ray (which she and Jophiel hold) throughout all that it sustains.

Smiling, Lucida remarks that you might wonder why then, if her task is to ground and direct the Yellow Ray, she is robed in all the colours of the rainbow! Running her hand down the front of her robe, she says that the human eye may 'see' light in this form when it passes from one medium to another that is of a different density – for example from air to water, such as is found in a raindrop. She expounds that the three principles that underlie this phenomenon – refraction, dispersion and reflection – are each relevant to how she carries out her duties, and can be summed up in just three words: focus; scrutinise; and consider. Hence, she utilises the manifold attributes of the Yellow Ray to help her *focus* on the task at hand.... to *scrutinise* all the facts with dispassion.... and to *consider* all past, present and future options from *all* angles and perspectives.

With a chuckle Lucida says that you might do the same if you have a problem or issue to solve or resolve – for the Yellow Ray can awaken your innate curiosity; motivate your need to understand things fully; and inspire you to seek out answers and solutions (which may demand you to be willing to accept and 'know' something without logical rationale). She suggests that you apply her three-step decision-making process (focus; scrutinise; consider) in three stages: the first stage addressing the matter on hand.... the second stage addressing how you plan to resolve the matter (so you understand exactly what your plan involves, having considered it from all possible angles).... and the third stage reprising stage two from a Higher perspective, by addressing it through your heart!

Returning her moccasin to her foot, Lucida gives a whistle – at which a large tawny-gold jaguar emerges from the forest, and pads across to lie at her feet. Pointing out its sleek coat, which is randomly marked with black spots and cloudlike rings that outline deeper patches of amber and gold, Lucida explains that jaguars' colouring enables them to become invisible in their surroundings – for their role includes protecting the ancient and profound wisdoms of the sacred places that are hidden deep within the forests, and guarding the power and potential held within darkness and shadow: accordingly you may ask **Jaguar** to be your guide – as long as you are prepared to follow wherever he may lead you, with trust in *his* ability to find the path that is right for you, and with faith in *your* ability to confront and conquer your fears. Resting one hand on the jaguar's head, Lucida encourages you to do the same – inviting you to feel the strength and power that he is holding in check.... she then asks you to seek out the same strength and power that lies within you – adding that Jaguar can teach you how to hold and channel this power wisely and lawfully (or reclaim your personal power if you have given it away to others); or help you understand how to increase the amount of energy you can hold and control (physically, mentally or spiritually); or show you how to replenish your energy reserves after a period of illness or debilitation. With a smile, she observes that the jaguar is at home on the ground and in the water, and is also an agile climber who understands the joys and challenges of different – and sometimes difficult – types of terrain: accordingly you may ask Jaguar to help you master skills that require speed and dexterity, patience and stillness, perseverance and determination; or to aid and support you during any period of inner retreat that requires you to undergo a programme of self-knowledge, self-growth, and/or self-healing.

Lazily the jaguar rolls onto his back, revealing a teardrop-shaped golden-yellow crystal of exceptional clarity, which hangs from the snugly-fitting braided golden collar encircling his neck: reaching down, Lucida frees the crystal from his collar; and then turns to face you and touches the crystal to the centre of your chest.... at this, your heart chakra becomes one with your High Heart centre; the protective layers of the Lotus of your Heart open; and its layers of pink and blue petals unfurl, revealing a tightly closed yellow bud within....

Suddenly, the crystal flares with a bright yellow light; and the yellow bud of your Heart Lotus flushes through with an intense golden fire, before slowly unfurling its yellow petals – each of which now holds a tiny flickering yellow flame.... With a smile, Lucida tells you that she has given you her Gift of The Yellow Flame of Divine Wisdom to help you connect with the Highest aspects of your Being, and *know* the Wisdoms of the Highest Light: she then returns the crystal to the jaguar's safekeeping, and takes your hands gently in hers.... Slowly but surely all the flames and petals settle to an appropriate state of balance and close around their centre; and are then enfolded within their outer layer of protection, as your heart centres likewise settle, close and find equilibrium....

Sitting back, Lucida tells you that her Gift rests at the heart of the Pink and Blue Flames of Divine Love and Will for good reason – for knowledge and wisdom gained should *always* be applied with compassion and understanding, and in alignment with the best and Highest of intentions. Giving you a transparent pale-yellow crystal, Lucida tells you this is **Natural Citrine**, her second Crystal Champion – explaining:

> *"Citrine is a form of quartz that owes its colour to the presence of iron. In its natural form it can be found in hues ranging from the palest to the deepest golden-yellow, and it is the natural form of which I speak now. Natural Citrine is a useful tool for enhancing mental clarity, focus and concentration when studying – but its ability to expand and enhance focus and awareness is also valuable during journeying or meditation, when it can be of great use in helping you access and ground your experiences and knowledge more fully: this means that any information gained from such exercises is potentially of more tangible use, and can be more easily applied to your life in a logical and productive manner. As Natural Citrine holds the Higher frequencies of the Yellow Ray, it may not only enable you to become more open and receptive to any and all sources of information and knowledge, but may also help you to retain the appropriate degree of discernment and perspective throughout. Natural Citrine works especially well with the Hara centre of the Unified energy Body, helping you develop the inner wisdom that will enable you to recognise and value the lessons imparted by your family and friends; and encouraging you to appreciate and accept the greater reality of your Self that IS immortal – thus aligning you more fully with your Christed-self."*

With a smile Lucida affirms that Natural Citrine may therefore help you align your heart, mind and Soul, and be more open to the Highest forms of knowledge and understanding.

The Art of Balance through Focused Self-awareness:

After thinking for a while, Lucida says that the words 'balance' and 'equilibrium' are often used in texts on personal and spiritual growth – sometimes interchangeably, as both mean much the same thing: however, she prefers to use the term 'balance' when referring to the 'lower' aspects of the Self (the body, mind and emotions); and the term 'equilibrium' when referring to the 'Higher' aspects of the Self (the whole Spirit and the Soul). She tells you that the ability to attain and maintain either within and between your body, mind and spirit – regardless of what is happening to, or around, you – is a skill you will need to practise *if* you want to progress (particularly if you wish to accomplish your Ascension).

Lucida says that it may be helpful to first understand what 'balance' is: this entails knowing what being balanced feels like; recognising when (and why) you may have gone *out* of balance; and (if this is the case) knowing how to return to balance – adding that recognising the 'why' is particularly important, as this often enables you to know the 'how'! With a wry smile she adds that the concept of retaining balance in (and between) your body, mind and spirit is simple, but its execution can be hard: however, she is here to give you guidance and support, so that you may begin to understand how to master it.

Leading you over to the trees, Lucida makes use of a few pieces of fallen wood to build a simple seesaw: assuring you that it is quite safe, she helps you to stand on one end, and encourages you to walk along its length to the other end, which lowers to the ground with a bump as you do so.... with a smile, Lucida asks you to walk back to the middle of the seesaw, and straddle the central point with one foot on either side, and then close your eyes....

She now asks you to shift your weight onto one foot, and feel the balance change; and then to repeat this to the other side.... asking you to keep doing this, she suggests that you think about how only a small movement away from the centre upsets your balance; *and* see how – if you want to move safely – you only have two directions to choose from.... In due course Lucida asks you to open your eyes, and helps you down from your perch – pointing out that, as you have found, it is quite easy to stay upright and balanced when you focus solely on being still and on holding the midpoint: but as soon as you shift your attention towards one end or another, the harder it is to keep yourself centred and steady!

With a smile Lucida tells you that being 'upright and still' is, however, not always desirable – for without movement there is stagnation: hence 'being in balance' is more about understanding how to be in a state of dynamic potential, where your *physical* body is grounded and balanced and your *subtle* Bodies are centred and focused – enabling you to make quick decisions and rational judgements, with your mind's logical and intuitive sides working in tandem. She expounds that mastering the art of balance is, therefore, rarely about being still; but is about being able to maintain a state of *flexible* stability that is instantaneously responsive to surrounding or internal conditions – thus, if your actions, thoughts and feelings are appropriate for the occasion or circumstance, you probably *are* in balance; if they are inappropriate, you are probably *not*.

Reminding you that *everything* has an opposing or polar aspect, Lucida says that life is not meant to be 'black or white'; and 'extremes' are there for a reason: indeed, you are designed to experience both happiness *and* sadness; sickness *and* health; deprivation *and* excess; anger *and* serenity – the crux of the matter lies not in the experience itself, but in how you choose to act and react to it, *and* in the appropriateness of those actions and reactions. She adds that the nature of Life is such that 'choice' is rarely as simple as black or white, but more like many shades of grey: however, even though having more choices open to you may make it harder to make a decision, it also means there is less risk of finding yourself vacillating between two extremes and becoming unbalanced.

Lucida suggests that it may therefore be more useful to picture balance as being three-dimensional – perhaps as a point within a sphere – rather than two-dimensional, like a point on a line (or you on the seesaw!). In order for you to have a taste of this, she conjures up a large round table that has three legs; and explains that this offers the best stability where the ground is uneven. She then helps you climb onto it, and asks you to stand in its centre and close your eyes as you did before....

Assuring you that she will make sure you do not get too close to the edge, she asks you to shift your weight from one leg to the other, like before, and see how it feels.... she then asks you to take a small step in one direction.... then in a different direction.... and then another.... As you hesitantly do as she asks, Lucida asks you to sense how moving in different directions neither affects the stability of the table nor upsets your balance – as long as you do not get too close to the edge.... After a while, she asks you to imagine the auric field of your energy Body as being a large sphere around you.... and then imagine your pranic core extending down into the ground, before repeating the exercise – sensing whether you consequently feel any difference in your focus, balance and/or stability....

After a while longer, Lucida tells you to open your eyes, and helps you down from your perch – pointing out that it is always easier to maintain stability when you have a firm footing (or grounding) that allows you to keep your mind focused firmly on the task at hand. With a smile, she adds that you may also have discovered that it is easier to stay in balance when you have a strong and stable centre, for this enables you to maintain a state of multidimensional awareness of *everything* that is around you: furthermore, being in this state opens your mind to all possible choices and viewpoints, making it simpler to see (and test out) the many different shades of grey that, in truth, exist in any decision-making process; and helping you to know if, when and why you need to be still in order to plan, reflect or assimilate – or why, how, where and when to move – in order to make progress with the minimum of pain and struggle.

Leading you over to sit with her in the shelter of a beech tree at the forest's edge, Lucida touches you gently over your heart, and tells you that the Lotus of your Heart is a centre of balance, and as such is fundamental to your movement and growth, stating:

"Without love there can be no harmony; without wisdom there can be no structure; and without power there can be no direction.... And when the right balance is reached, all will be in accord – yet understand that 'balance' does not mean that all parts must be equal, for the weight of each part must have freedom to shift, according to need."

Smiling again, she explains that when you are able to balance *Will* (the impulse to move forwards positively and actively, whilst owning your Power and following the path that you have chosen for your Highest progress) with *Wisdom* (the ability to see truly, whilst considering the consequences of all your actions as you plan your optimum growth) and with *Love* (the willingness to always act with compassionate consideration for yourself and others, so that your growth is not at the expense of others, but is in harmony with the Divine Plan) you will have conquered the art of balance *and* equilibrium!

Lucida now gives you a small opaque white stone that is veined with dark green, and tells you that this is a piece of **Tree Agate**, her third Crystal Champion – explaining:

"Tree Agate is a green-veined form of opaque white quartz that is serene and content, with an independent spirit that may help you understand that 'being on your own' is not the same as 'being alone'. This particular agate carries the rooted stability of the great tree-Beings, and can support you in achieving steady, sustained and (most importantly) balanced *growth through their grounded wisdoms. Tree Agate is therefore not just a means of hearing and understanding their wisdoms with greater clarity, but is also a reminder of how the 'Lower' Worlds support the World of humankind – instilling you with a sense of grateful wonder in the Grand Design of all the Kingdoms of Earth and opening your awareness to all that supports you, enabling you to* know *your eternal connection to All that IS. Tree Agate's veins also show how progress and growth rarely happens in a 'straight line', and will help you adapt your balance when you need to change course – their pure white spirit offering you a stabilising Light that can help you truly see where your imperfections and imbalances lie. Then as you progress, they may offer you the healing you need as you undertake the inner (and outer) work that has the greatest potential to clarify and strengthen your Inner Light. Tree Agate may then help you respond appropriately and effectively to what you find, and aid you in resolving any*

ongoing problematic issues or situations, by giving you the focus and determination you need to remain well-balanced in body, mind and spirit; and the stability to acquire and maintain a sense of centred and well-rounded completeness with ease and grace."

With a smile, Lucida affirms that Tree Agate may therefore help you acquire and refine the skills that will help you to *know* balance, so that you may rejoice in the still-point *and* the path; the road to Enlightenment *and* its conclusion.

Drawing your attention to the tree to your right, Lucida points out a small brown-striped bird that is holding fast to the fine-grained bark with long-clawed feet. Together you watch it spiral its way around and up the trunk, seeking out tiny seeds and insects in the grooves of the bark with a slim curved beak. She tells you that this bird is (very aptly) called a tree creeper, and has very distinctive behaviours – living wholly on the trunks and branches of trees, and even roosting in hollows it sculpts in the bark. With a smile she says that **Tree Creeper** can teach you a great deal about how to cling to the 'Tree of Life' in order to benefit from the fruits of the 'Tree of Knowledge': his quiet tenacity and organised behaviours helping you to find ways to manage your time effectively and productively; his upward spiralling habit giving you the determination to keep moving onwards and upwards; and his subtle camouflage and quiet ways inspiring you to be unobtrusively 'at one' with all that surrounds you, without feeling the need to prove yourself by indulging in showy or arrogant behaviours. As the little bird reaches the top of the trunk, you watch him flutter down to the base of the next tree and begin again, at which Lucida asks you to watch how his long forked tail is helping him keep his balance and remain in firm contact with the tree. With a chuckle she says that Tree Creeper can, therefore, show you how to keep *your* balance – even if your world has been turned upside down – and motivate you to keep a grip on your mind and emotions if they seem to be spiralling out of control: furthermore Tree Creeper's straightforward and simplistic philosophies may encourage you to avoid wasting precious time and energy coveting something unrealistic or unobtainable, and instead work to achieve something to be proud of by using the tools you've got!

The Greenwood Guardians – Pomegranate and Fig:

Her *personal* mentoring complete for now, Lucida affirms she is always available to aid and support you: you need only bring her to mind and ask for her presence, and she will attend you. Furthermore, she tells you that two great Tree Beings of the Plant Kingdom have also asked to support you in addressing her Theme of 'FIND THE CHRIST WITHIN', adding that you need only request *their* presence, and they will be with you.

She explains that the first of these Greenwood Guardians is the Masculine essence of Pomegranate, who has asked to overlight and help you ground whatever work you undertake within *any* aspect of her chapter. The second is the Feminine essence of Fig, who has specifically asked to help you understand and assimilate her Gift of The Yellow Flame of Divine Wisdom (if you have chosen to accept it).

When you are ready to connect with Lucida's first Greenwood Guardian, you need simply call for the presence of **Pomegranate** (*) .... Pomegranate envelops you in a deep pink Light, and the Masculine spirit essence of Pomegranate speaks to you, saying:

> "The sweet sharpness of my fruits that nestle tightly together within their protective shell hold the infinite and eternal love and passion of The Divine, and these I offer to you now – for only love will enable you to confront your deepest and darkest fears. Know that this may be the love you have for yourself or for another, or the love that another has for you (including, of course, the love of The Divine, whose Love for you should never be discounted!) For it is only by confronting your fears and bringing all that you are into the Light that you will truly grow in spirit, and reach the heights you need to become the Illumined Master that is your goal.... Know then that I am also here to help you realise that without darkness there could not be Light; and to understand how the light cannot be complete without the dark. So let me guard and protect you as my strength gives you courage; and let my roots ground all that you know and are – and all that you are yet to know and be – whilst aiding you in addressing and assimilating whatever needs to be known and understood, in the fashion and degree that is right for you now...."

(* Rose Quartz and Garnet will help you ground and connect with the energies and wisdom of Pomegranate, if you wish to enhance your experience using crystals.)

If you have chosen to accept and work with Lucida's Gift, and when you are ready to connect with her second Greenwood Guardian, you need simply call for the presence of **Fig** (*) .... Fig envelops you in a curtain of rippling green Light, and the Feminine spirit essence of Fig speaks to you, saying:

> "Know that I have elected to be the guardian of the womb of your consciousness: barren ground giving way to the fertile growth of the newly arisen. So stand with me, and feel the healing waters spring forth from the earth around my feet and flow through your body and mind, heart and spirit – cleansing and clearing; healing and balancing every iota that is a part of you, so that the sweet fruits of our labours may then spring forth, bursting with bountiful goodness that tells of the wonder of Life and Creation; and overflowing with infinite Divine potentials that make any and all things possible.... Then let all those that have faith and believe in the ultimate and eternal Goodness and Grace of the Highest Universal Power be a part of your healing journey, reviving your own faith and belief in the great Wisdoms that you carry within, so that you may spread the seeds of your knowledge with a free and open hand – thus sharing the many riches with which you have been so righteously endowed; and shedding your own bright Light upon the path to Illumined Enlightenment for All...."

(* Kambala Jasper and Clear Quartz will help you ground and connect with the energies and wisdom of Fig, if you wish to enhance your experience using crystals.)

ARCHANGEL JOPHIEL

'SHINE YOUR LIGHT'

CRYSTAL CHAMPIONS:

HT Citrine ♥ White Phantom Qtz ♥ Ametrine

CREATURE COMPANIONS:

Locust ♥ Kestrel ♥ Wolf

GREENWOOD GUARDIANS:

Sweet Chestnut ♥ Bamboo

*I open my heart
and willingly share
my knowledge and skills.*

MEETING JOPHIEL

It is a fine afternoon in summer, and you find yourself standing on an old-fashioned flagstone path that is meandering its way through an old and rather dilapidated walled garden. The flags have been hewn from pale ivory-coloured sandstone; and the crevices between them are all overflowing with springy masses of white-flowering chamomile, which softens and blurs their edges. You are intrigued to observe that *everything* growing here – the trees, shrubs, flowers and even the grass that flanks the path – is white, with just the merest hints of green in the branches and stems. It looks almost as if everything is enveloped in frost: but when you reach down to touch the grass, you realise this is not so. Above you the sky also lacks colour, being a deep silvery-grey – like the sky before a thunderstorm: yet, even so, the garden seems to be illuminated in a soft white light, and the air around you feels comfortably warm and temperate.

As you begin to wander around, you discover that the garden is surrounded by very high walls made from blocks of the same pale ivory stone as the path: most of these are cracked and fragmented by age; and some have begun to crumble and collapse, adding to the sense of dilapidation – yet, nonetheless, they are still managing to support tumbling masses of rambling and climbing plants. Snowy clematis and ivory scented honeysuckle intermingle with trailing tendrils of 'old man's beard' and climbing white hydrangea, all softening the walls' profile and adding to the atmosphere of wild tranquillity. Everything is peaceful and still – and although the lack of colour *seems* odd, the sense of profound calm you feel as you stroll about is heightened by the massed banks and drifts of pure-white plants and shrubs that fill the deep flowerbeds fronting the walls. Drawn to inspect the beds more closely, you find that they hold many plants that would not normally be in season at the same time – yet here they are: lilies-of-the-valley with chrysanthemums; snowdrops with buddleia; marguerites with narcissi; camellia with snowberry; and tall and slender silver birch with blowsy white cherry and sweetly-scented amelanchier, all incongruously – yet harmoniously – in full and perfect bloom.

Suddenly, out of the corner of your eye, you see a flash of golden light appear amongst the whiteness, and you turn to see a tall slim figure brightly haloed in pale-gold light walking towards you down the path: this is Archangel Jophiel. Your attention is immediately captured by his splendid golden wings, which extend above him to frame his head and shoulders, and sweep down to brush the ground behind him. You sense that he is restraining them, holding them quite close to his body, but even so you are almost dazzled by their fiery brilliance – and by the flashes and sparks of gold and bronze light that he leaves in his wake. As he draws closer, Jophiel folds his wings tighter – veiling their intensity so that you can see him more clearly, and allowing you to see that he is clad in a simple flowing saffron-gold robe, which is skimming the ground around his bare and slender feet. The robe has a close-fitting neckline and long loose sleeves, and is unbelted and unadorned: from this you deduce that his manner is likely to be direct and down-to-earth – although you can also sense the Power that underlies his calm collected manner. Recognising your thoughts he smiles at you in welcome, declaring:

"*I am Jophiel – Keeper of the Golden Flames of Illumined Wisdom and Joy, Archangel of the Christos, and twin flame of Lucida, the Lady Clarity. Here, in my garden, be calm and be at peace.... Feel its gentle purity embrace you, dissolving your cares and your worries – for the tranquillity of this place enables the mind and the emotions to still, and offers the ideal space in which Creation can begin. Thus everything you picture, think or do here may (with forethought and design, focused intent and care) make real whatever you desire to be – so BE with me now and have faith in your own capabilities, your own innate wisdom. For thence you may understand that all that is here simply awaits the hand of The Divine (which is within you, as it is within me) to encourage it to evolve with joyous grace. You* have *the greatest teacher within! But I am also here, to guide your hand and gently steer you where need be, ensuring that whatever is done – and whatever you create – will be as you intend, and in accord with Divine Law."*

As soon as he has finished speaking, a white dove flutters down and settles on his right shoulder – and with another small smile Jophiel asks you to walk with him....

Strolling at your side, he guides you down the flagstone path until you reach a wide circular courtyard (paved in pale ivory stone, like the path) at the far end of the garden. The courtyard is encircled by eleven tall white pillars linked by simple yet elegant arches, which are laden with cascades of scented white jasmine and pure-white climbing roses. It also has a round three-tiered marble fountain at its centre, whose design is very plain and simple. The marble (once snow-white like the pillars) is now spotted with silvery lichens: even so, you can see that clear and sparkling water is flowing from the fountain's head – spilling down through the tiers and into the circular pool at the bottom, where nine pure-white water lilies (some in bud, some in full bloom) float upon its crystal-clear waters. Five curved white marble benches are set equidistant around the perimeter of this pool, upon one of which rests a large white linen satchel – and it is here that Jophiel leads you, suggesting that you take a little time to accustom yourself to his energies, and examine him more closely.

Asking you to sit facing the fountain, he plants his pale-skinned feet firmly on the ground, and settles at your side in a very upright posture, with one hand resting on the linen satchel and the other in his lap. This enables you to see that his equally pale and slender hands and fingers are unadorned – and then you suddenly realise that *all* his skin is strangely white and translucent, making it appear as if a brilliant light is shining on or through it. You also see that his skin is clear and unlined – although you have the feeling that he is much older than he appears. At this Jophiel gives an enigmatic smile, which draws your gaze to the azure-blue intensity of his eyes, whose compelling depths convey both ancient wisdom and vast intelligence. These sit beneath arched white eyebrows over a long slightly hooked nose, which is centred in an oval face that has well-proportioned and neat features. These are framed by a dense mane of wavy white hair, which has been pulled back and tightly bound at the nape of his neck with a simple leather thong – its snowy mass springing out to mantle his shoulders like a cloud.

Your examination of his features complete, Jophiel reaches into the satchel at his side, and takes out a small dagger that is about a hand's length long. Holding it balanced on the palm of his hand, he shows you that one end of the slim, smoothly-rounded black hilt holds an elegantly tapering blade that has been forged from silver; whilst the other is surmounted by a ring made of solid gold encircled by a realistic-looking vine of ivy that has been intricately carved from green moss agate. He then reaches up to the close-fitting neck of his robe and draws out a golden chain made of tiny interlocking ovals of gold, which was previously hidden from view: and, with a quick movement threads the chain through the ring – securing the dagger securely around his neck, so that it sits point down over his sternum. Once in place, the black hilt shimmers and gives off multi-coloured sparks of light – enabling you to see that the hilt is made from rainbow obsidian, which is the stone that links him with Lucida, his twin flame.

Once more reaching into the satchel at his side, Jophiel brings out a large book that has a dark brown embossed leather cover, and rests it in his lap: this enables you to see that the edges of the cover are bound with gold, and that its pages are locked shut with a gold clasp ornamented with a polished oval cabochon of orange-gold citrine. Secured into its spine is a bookmark made from a plaited ribbon of rainbow-coloured silk, the end of which is weighted with a large egg-shaped polished bead of deep purple amethyst – and noting your interest, but knowing that you have seen all you need to for now, Jophiel places the book to one side.

JOPHIEL'S TEACHINGS
The Gift of The Golden-yellow Flame of Illumined Wisdom:

Sitting back and relaxing, Jophiel tells you that inner contemplation is the key to the peace of his garden, and all it holds. Taking your attention to the stones that border the pool, he points to some script engraved on the surface of the one immediately in front of you, and explains that this translates as 'enlightenment'. With a smile, he adds that *all* the benches have an inscription set before them – the others translating as harmony, respect, purity and tranquillity – each of which serves as a point of focus when he has something (or nothing!) he wishes to contemplate. After listening to the waters cascade into the pool for a while, Jophiel stresses that this is a place of great Power, because the waters hold the absolute purity of the Diamond Light – enabling the pool to reflect only the truth to whoever gazes upon its surface; and the waters to cleanse and clarify whatever they touch: this means that they have the power to ignite the Inner Light that IS within you, by encouraging the blossoming of your Lotus of the Heart, and by rousing your Lotus of the Soul, if and when the time is right for its awakening.

Directing you to kneel by the pool, Jophiel asks you to cleanse your hands in the water, and then cup a little in your hands and apply it to your heart and brow – for this will help clarify, enhance and balance your heart and mind.... He patiently waits while you take time to do so; then suggests that you return to your seat to allow yourself time to appreciate (and enjoy) the benefits offered by the cool purity of the waters....

After a while, Jophiel gets to his feet and plucks a water lily bud from the waters at the base of the fountain: cupping it reverently in his hands, he watches as it slowly opens out into full and glorious bloom; before turning and reaching out to gently hold it in front of your heart centre, where it simply dissolves into Light and is absorbed into your energy Body: as this happens, you feel your spirits lift; and you sense your heart and mind coming into full alignment.... and then you gradually become aware that the Lotus of your Heart is soaking up the Light, like a sponge absorbing water....

Somehow it seems that all your senses are sharpening: and when you take your focus to the garden around you, you find that you can see every exquisite detail and hear every tiny sound.... yet as your awareness expands you do not feel uncomfortable, for you recognise that to be in this state is to be filled with Divine Bliss – whereby you are connected to everything, but still possess the inner peace that lets you simply BE....

Jophiel smiles as he recognises what you are feeling, and turns to select a second bud – plucking it and holding it in his hands as before: again he watches it slowly open, each layer of snow-white petals peeling back one-by-one to finally reveal their centre, which is filled with a cluster of tiny golden stamens.... Lifting the flower to his lips, Jophiel breathes on the stamens – at which the heart of the water lily bursts into a mass of bright golden-yellow flames: then, holding the flower carefully in his left hand, Jophiel detaches his dagger from the chain that secures it, and gently touches the tip of the blade to the flames....

Isolating a single golden-yellow flame, he gently transfers this from the flower to your brow, where it is slowly drawn into your energy field – eventually coming to a rest at the root of your brow chakra.... As it settles, you become aware of a gentle warmth gradually filling your head; and you hear Jophiel say:

"My Gift of The Golden-yellow Flame of Illumined Wisdom has been placed within the very heart of your mind, so that it may illuminate your path and be your guide as you move forwards. Let it shine for you when times are dark, or when you have difficulty finding your way; and let its Light show you how to transform all that you learn into true wisdom. For Wisdom IS Power – and, when used in the Highest Light, it offers by Divine Grace the greatest of all Blessings."

Jophiel then rests his hand on your head in silent benediction, as he waits for the Flame to find balance; before restoring his dagger to its place over his heart and returning the water lily to the pool, where it slowly closes its petals around the golden-yellow flames and reverts to its bud-like form....

Retaking his seat at your side, Jophiel says that it is a little known (but relevant) fact that the Yellow Ray that he and Lucida direct and oversee has a fundamental connection with the Indigo Ray, which sustains intuitive notions and inspirations through the brow chakra, which is where his Gift has been placed. Explaining that this connection will be significantly enhanced by his Gift, Jophiel advises you that this may catalyse flashes of instantaneous awareness and insight, as it will generate a channel of Light to connect his Gift to the Yellow Flame of Divine Wisdom (the Gift of Lucida, his twin flame), which is held within the Lotus of your Heart. Smiling, he adds that this may help stimulate your recall of 'All That You Are' – motivating your Soul to remember its true (and Divine) nature.

Giving you a crystal that is a very deep golden-yellow, Jophiel tells you that this is a heat-treated **(HT) Citrine**, which is his first Crystal Champion – explaining:

"It has been discovered that subjecting amethyst to intense heat alters its molecular balance and turns it golden-yellow, mimicking the processes that take place naturally within the earth and so giving HT Citrine similar properties to its natural cousin.

Because of its deep golden-yellow colour, HT Citrine works well with the sacral and solar plexus chakras and with the associated emotional and mental Bodies of the aura: thus it can help in balancing and aligning the functions of your right and left brain; your intuitive and logical processes; and your emotional reactions and reasoned thoughts. HT Citrine's most effective quality, however, comes about as a result of its own journey, whereby it has been subjected to the fires of transformation, which have endowed it with a level of spiritual understanding that can only be acquired by undergoing the deepest (and often darkest) of experiences: hence HT Citrine can offer you the Light of Higher Wisdom, whilst supporting you as you endeavour to understand and resolve life's more difficult lessons, enabling you to shine your Light more clearly."

With a smile, Jophiel affirms that heat-treated Citrine may therefore help you connect with your innate and intuitive Wisdom, giving you the courage to align yourself with your Highest potential.

Stepping to the pool, Jophiel selects a third water lily and lifts it from the water: once again he cups it in his hands; and once again its pure white petals unfurl – but this time they open to reveal that a small round white pearl is nestling in its heart. Lifting his dagger, Jophiel lightly touches its tip to the outer shell of the pearl, which slowly hinges open to reveal a many-layered iridescent interior; and tells you that this beautiful and lustrous pearl has taken years to form – each perfect and shiny layer being produced as a consequence of an instinctive response to an irritant that triggered its innate ability to defend its purity and reclaim inner harmony. With a compassionate glance, he says that you too may have discovered that life can be painful – yet it is a Universal Truth that the most difficult and distressing events or experiences have the potential to teach the most valuable and significant lessons: hence, those who choose to undergo the harshest lessons in Earth's great 'University of Life' will be rewarded with the finest 'Pearls of Wisdom', to both honour their courage, and celebrate their achievements and growth. Jophiel then touches the point of his dagger to the pearl again, which immediately hinges closed; and returns the water lily to the pool, before retaking his seat at your side.

Suddenly a small ivory and green insect leaps from the ground onto your knee, and Jophiel chuckles as he tells you that this is a locust – reassuring you that there is only one of them here! He comments that many regard locusts as unwelcome guests: yet, although it is true that in vast numbers they are able to strip a field of crops in the blink of an eye, locusts have much wisdom to share – especially if you view things from their perspective. He points out that a 'plague' of locusts only occurs if their environment has become out of balance, when they may gather in huge groups to seek plentiful food sources that will enable them to gorge beyond satiation: hence **Locust** can teach you some important lessons about abundance and excess, greed and need (from both a personal and planetary viewpoint); and/or help you understand how you never require more than is sufficient to satisfy your needs at that time. Drawing your attention to the locust's strong back legs, which can propel it long distances in a single jump, Jophiel says that you may also call upon Locust if you need to move forwards very quickly; or to support you if you have to take a blind leap of faith; or to give you some encouragement if it is time to do something that means undertaking a significant (and possibly daunting) change of direction – or if you simply want to understand how to live 'in the now'. With a smile, he adds that Locust may also appear to *you* if you need to work with others in a productive and cooperative manner, in order to accomplish something vital to your own (or others) benefit; or if your 'wants' are getting out of balance with your 'needs', and it is time for you to exercise some restraint; or if you are being asked to accept that the Earth has abundant bounty for all, *as long as* it is used and shared with wisdom: what is more (because locusts are a valuable food source in their own right) Locust may come to feed your Soul – especially if your cup is 'half-empty' and it needs to be 'half-full'!

The Circle of Learning – the Jasmine and the Rose:
Detaching his dagger from its chain so that you can see it more clearly, Jophiel tells you that its component parts are both purposeful and symbolic: firstly, its silver blade can cut through ignorance and peel away falsehoods to reveal the wisdom and truth beneath; whilst its rainbow obsidian hilt channels rainbow-black Light to generate the space and the means within (and through) which creation and evolution, change and transformation may occur.... and secondly, the gold ring holds the Circle of Learning, which (as you can see) has neither beginning nor end – thus illustrating the fact that there is *always* more to learn(!); whilst the moss-agate ivy that entwines it grounds, stabilises and binds in place whatever is learnt, so that it may be properly assimilated and fully understood.

Lifting the book that he had set aside earlier, Jophiel places it in your lap and asks you to feel the warmth and texture of the leather cover and its bindings; the smooth coolness of the polished citrine; the intricacies of the gold metallic clasp; the silkiness of the ribbon; and the shiny surface of the amethyst bead it holds.... As you explore how the exterior of the book feels beneath your hands, Jophiel tells you that this is *your* 'Book of Life', which contains knowledge and information of all kinds – being both a record of all that you have already learnt and understood in all your many existences, as well as all that you have yet to learn, know or experience. He adds that the ribbon always marks a place that holds knowledge that is relevant at a time of need – stressing that you may not attempt to read more than the page indicated by the rainbow marker, because to see all of your past, present and future would interfere with your Free Will....

Explaining that the flowers garlanding the courtyard help to keep the pool and its waters clear and in balance, Jophiel walks over to one of the pillars and cuts a white rose blossom and a stem of white jasmine with his dagger.... Retaking his seat, he lifts his left hand (which is holding the jasmine) and tells you that Jasmine is regarded as the 'King' of flowers – its fragrance becoming more intense after dark, when its masculine character balances the feminine energies of the moon; and its starry petals reminding all those who enjoy its bounty under a night sky to look up and survey the wondrous vastness of the Universe, and so know that they are never alone. He then lifts his right hand (which is holding the rose) and tells you that Rose is regarded as the 'Queen' of flowers – its scent becoming deeper and sweeter during daylight, when its feminine character balances the masculine energies of the sun; and its velvety petals reminding all those who enjoy its bounty in the clear light of day of the beauty and perfection that can be found in even the meanest and humblest of places.

Passing you the rose, Jophiel says that its gentle purity can help you to release any feelings of sadness or grief that you hold within: he then asks you to close your eyes and relax, and to deeply inhale its scent – and, as you do so, to bring to mind any sadness or grief (old or new) that may be affecting your life and making it hard for you to grow or progress.... After allowing you plenty of time to connect with the essence of the rose and consider what he has asked, Jophiel asks you to inhale the scent of the rose again – and this time allow the myriad strengths of your feminine side to bring your emotions into an appropriate state of balance with your mind and spirit, so that you can release your past sorrows and let them go....

Once you have released all that you can, Jophiel takes the rose from you, and touches the tip of his dagger to the citrine mounted on the clasp that seals your Book – at its touch, the clasp releases and the book falls open at a page indicated by the bookmark: Jophiel explains that you can absorb what is penned there by simply resting your hand on the page, and allowing any understandings you have *ever* gained from experiencing sadness or grief to filter into your mind.... As you do as he suggests, he emphasises that it is not necessary for you to have any *conscious* awareness of what is written and what you have learned – because that knowledge and understanding may make itself known in many ways (now *or* in the future), perhaps through words, visions or dreams, or through 'chance' happenings or meetings yet to come....

When he knows you are ready to move on, Jophiel closes your Book and passes you the jasmine, explaining that its warm vitality can boost your self-confidence and rekindle your sense of self-worth, giving you the courage, strength and determination to overcome any doubts and fears: he then asks you to close your eyes and relax, deeply inhaling its scent, like before – and, as you do so, to bring to mind any doubts you have about your capabilities, and any fears you have about the future.... After allowing you more time to connect with the essence of the jasmine and consider what he has asked, Jophiel asks you to inhale the scent of the jasmine again – and this time allow the myriad strengths of your masculine side to bring your mind into an appropriate state of balance with your emotions and spirit, so that you can release your doubts and fears and move forwards with positivity and determination....

Once you have released all you can, Jophiel again touches the tip of his dagger to the citrine mounted on the clasp that seals your Book – and again the clasp releases and the book falls open at a page indicated by the bookmark: Jophiel asks you to absorb what is held there by resting your hand on the page again, and allowing any understandings you have *ever* gained from experiencing self-doubt or insecurity to filter into your mind (reminding you that it is not necessary for you to have *conscious* awareness of what you have learned, as knowledge and understanding can make itself known in many ways)....

After a while, when he knows you have seen and done enough, Jophiel closes your Book: then, as the clasp locks shut, he takes the jasmine and the book away and places them in his satchel with the rose. With a smile, he informs you that *any* of the trees and flowers in his Garden of Eden can aid your healing and growth – you need simply ask him for what you require, and he will be your guide: furthermore, (if you accepted his Gift) you may open your Book to its marker at any time – beginning by clearing and grounding yourself and making sure you are centred, calm and still; and then focusing on the Golden-yellow Flame that he has empowered within your brow, until both the Flame and the Book are 'real' to you. Jophiel adds that if you are not able to achieve this (or if you did not receive his Gift) you may ask him to open your Book to the marked page and help you find the clarity that will enable you to understand whatever you find there.

Jophiel then gives you a clear quartz crystal that has white inner layers that mirror the shape of the crystal's termination, saying that this is **White Phantom Quartz**, his second Crystal Champion – explaining:

> *"Any crystal that contains 'phantom' layers shows the history of its growth, the layers marking times when its growing conditions changed in some way. This creates a permanent record within the crystal's structure, and highlights that it has a gift for helping you deal with any issues that are multilayered or buried in your psyche. The purity and absorbent qualities of this Phantom Quartz's white layers make it especially useful for drawing out (and then clearing) any 'negative' energies that are released as a consequence of any processes of self-healing or self-exploration – especially those to do with addressing episodes of sorrow, grief or depression. The clear quartz element offers additional power to the procedure, providing a clear Light that enables you to see things with greater clarity, whilst also offering you a 'light at the end of the tunnel' that brings positivity and hope. Additionally, just as the layers reveal the crystal's growth history, so too they may reveal your own patterns of growth – in this lifetime and/or in others: this makes White Phantom Quartz a useful aid in identifying repeating patterns of behaviour ('positive' and/or 'negative'); and in helping you to understand how to reinforce those habitual behaviours that are beneficial – and change those that are not. White Phantom Quartz can also help you access other Planes of reality or Dimension when meditating, journeying or dreaming; and can then support you in interpreting and understanding any information so obtained with greater clarity and positivity."*

Smiling, Jophiel affirms that White Phantom Quartz may therefore help all processes of self-review whereby you focus within, in order that you may embrace and honour your imperfections (*and* the imperfections of others); and may be a reminder that appreciating *all* that life teaches you is an important step on the path that leads to Enlightenment.

Drawing your attention to a russet bird that is hovering in the sky above you, its eyes fixed on the ground beneath, Jophiel tells you that this is a kestrel – a small falcon, whose keen eyesight can spot the smallest movement from a long distance away: this makes **Kestrel** a useful ally if you want to examine something in greater detail, or need to become more watchful or alert for changes happening within or around you. He adds that Kestrel is a master of the art of being still *and* observant, and so can be called upon to support you if you want to sharpen your focus or concentration; or increase your attention span if you find yourself flagging: moreover Kestrel's fine eye for detail can help you work on the finer points of whatever you are addressing, whilst retaining the broader and/or higher view of the bigger picture, so that you fully appreciate the wider implications of what you are seeing or doing. Jophiel remarks that a kestrel's ability to hover and fly in all sorts of weather conditions and environments demonstrates superior mastery of the air, thus you may ask Kestrel to teach you how to master your logical skills and thought processes if you need to make quick and accurate decisions; or to show you how to move through life with greater dexterity and grace by using your skills and talents more effectively; or to advise you if you need to 'check-out' an issue or situation so you can communicate your ideas, thoughts or feelings to the greatest effect. With a chuckle he says that a kestrel is always a sign of his (Jophiel's) presence – at which times it will be helpful to open yourself to receive any signs or messages that may be important to your growth and/or understanding at that time.

The Secret Garden and The Gold Flame of Joy:

Getting to his feet, Jophiel leaves his satchel on the bench by the pool and asks you to join him as he walks to the other end of the path.... As you stroll, he muses that Free Will may be seen as both a blessing and a curse: yet without it, it would not be possible to experience 'being human'. He remarks that some people (knowingly or unknowingly) have their Free Will heavily curtailed, which greatly restricts their freedom; whilst other people (usually with greater power) allow themselves too much, and do exactly as they please without regard to anyone else! With a wry smile he adds that it can be quite hard to choose between an existence that offers absolute freedom, where the full spectrum of behaviours ('good' *and* 'bad') is open to all; or an existence that allows no freedom at all, where only one kind of behaviours is permitted: yet, on balance, the Freedom that enables you to learn by experiencing the Divine Light in *all* its expressions IS a blessing.

Reassuring you that, regardless of your choices, he will always support you if you wish to learn with him, Jophiel gives a whistle – at which a large grey wolf with a creamy neck-ruff and ice-blue eyes appears. Jophiel calls it to him, remarking that **Wolf** is a great teacher, and adding that a wolf's presence is always the sign of a spiritual teacher's wise and illumined protection and support: therefore you may call upon Wolf if you need help in learning or understanding any lesson; or if you are undertaking a course of study and need support and encouragement to see it through. Reminding you that wolves hunt and live as a pack, Jophiel points out that they understand how to maintain order and discipline, whilst also ensuring that every member of the pack is appropriately supported and cared for: hence you may ask Wolf to support you if you are organising or planning to lead or teach a group of people; or if you find yourself in a group scenario that requires speedy and tactful intervention to resolve a problem. Jophiel recalls that the Illumined Master, Djwhal Kuhl, taught that wisdom is a wheel, and knowledge a circle: thus as you learn, so do you teach; and as you teach, so do you learn.... He explains that this makes it clear how important it is that all insights are shared, in order to improve and extend *everybody's* knowledge and understanding – not just because hoarding knowledge and information serves no-one; but because everyone experiences and understands life's lessons in different ways, and so may offer a fresh (even unexpected) viewpoint that may solve an issue or problem that you (or someone else) is experiencing. With a chuckle he says that this is why Wolf is often with those who teach or lead groups, for they may need reminding that neither teacher nor student can exist without the other: furthermore, Wolf encourages the sharing of all assets (including knowledge), knowing that the needs and strengths of the many *always* outweigh the needs and strengths of the few!

As he walks on with the wolf at his side, Jophiel observes that being outside in the natural world (or some similarly peaceful place) will always help recharge your batteries, enabling you to 'return to the fray' refreshed and restored. He adds that many places in the world are well suited for this purpose, stressing that it is important to find somewhere that resonates with your Soul, and where you feel calm and at ease – perhaps at a natural spiritual site (although you should ensure that its energies are pure); or somewhere with an abundance of trees, rocks or water; or even in a sacred space that you have created in your own home or outdoor space. Whatever you choose, he says that it is important to regard relaxation as an essential part of your day, and to spend regular time in a 'sacred' place restoring your inner harmony and balance. With another smile, Jophiel adds that you are always welcome to come to his garden in meditation or visualisation – especially if you want to think or plan, and/or need to restore your inner peace.

Having finally reached the other end of the path you find yourself at a wall: here a small wooden door lies partially hidden behind a tangle of ivy; and, with a smile, Jophiel tells you that this leads to his 'secret garden' and opens the door.... He leads you through, and into a small circular garden that sits in the shelter of a tall and dense hedge of yew, whose dark-green depths offset the brightness of the deep flower borders below. These are crammed with hundreds of sunflowers (all in full and perfect bloom), through which a narrow path of pale-yellow cobblestones leads to the centre, where a circle of lawn sits open to the sky. In stark contrast to the whiteness of the other garden, everything here is either green, yellow or gold; and you are drawn to immerse yourself in its warm and welcoming atmosphere....

Noting this, Jophiel guides you to the centre of the emerald lawn, and places his hand on the ground: at his touch, a large seven-sided sun-yellow crystal rises up through the grass, filling the space with a soft golden glow. The apex of the crystal stands level with his shoulders, and with a smile Jophiel invites you to draw closer: this allows you to see that a small circular depression has been hollowed into the crystal's termination; and (touching this with the tip of his dagger), Jophiel ignites a tiny flame that steadily grows bigger and brighter. It makes the crystal look like a huge golden candle – and recognising your thought Jophiel laughs, and tells you that this is the Gold Flame of Joy, which 'does exactly what it says on the tin'!

Inviting you to step forwards, he directs you to cup your hands around the Flame, which is now burning brightly at the apex of the crystal.... and as you do as he asks, you are surprised to find that the flame is cool and gives off no heat: and yet you are filled and surrounded with a comforting warmth that is like the gentle kiss of the Sun on a warm summer's day.... Little by little your body relaxes, and your heart expands and overspills with happiness – and you find yourself filled with bliss at the perfect wonder of the moment, at which Jophiel says:

> *"Ponder this: for all to know truth, all must know joy; for all to know joy, all must know truth – yet you don't have to be wise to be joyful; although one who is joyful is wise! And so I share my Joy with you; that you too may know the Joy of walking your path in Harmony and at Peace with your Soul."*

After allowing the Flame to burn for a few more minutes, Jophiel touches his hand to the crystal, and you watch as the Flame is drawn back into its depths.... Stepping back, he gives you a polished stone that is partly a golden-yellow colour, and partly a very clear purple, and tells you that this is **Ametrine**, his third Crystal Champion – explaining:

> *"Ametrine is a rare and harmonious natural blend of amethyst and citrine quartz that illustrates symbolically how spiritual endeavours can lead to greater mental clarity and insight – joining logic and intuition, and uniting mind and spirit in perfect balance. As Ametrine holds the Amethyst and Yellow Rays, it can help open, clarify and align your brow, crown and Higher chakras, whilst concurrently stimulating and clarifying your sacral and solar plexus chakras: then, as all comes into balance, they may all connect through your pranic core, providing the energies and opportunities that can expand your mind and consciousness, and help you access the Highest Universal and Cosmic Wisdoms. Ametrine can also support all learning and study, by strengthening focus and concentration whilst relaxing the mind, making it easier to assimilate difficult or complex information (from the most basic level all the way up to graduate level – and even beyond!); and helping you grasp how apparently disparate strands, concepts or theories interlink – thus it is a good choice for students of all ages and abilities. Last but not least, Ametrine brings the gift of logic and wisdom to all 'psychic' endeavours, so that you always know the difference between that which is real and that which is not; whilst bringing the gift of insight and Higher Wisdom to your daily life, so that all that you* thought *to be worldly and mundane may BE something so much more."*

With a smile, Jophiel affirms that Ametrine may therefore help align your mind with the Highest of your Spiritual potentials and Truths, so that you may truly know Joy.

The Greenwood Guardians – Sweet Chestnut and Bamboo:

His *personal* mentoring complete for now, Jophiel affirms he is always available to aid and support you: you need only bring him to mind and ask for his presence, and he will attend you. Furthermore, he tells you that two great Tree Beings of the Plant Kingdom have also asked to support you in addressing his Theme of 'SHINE YOUR LIGHT', adding that you need only request *their* presence, and they will be with you.

He explains that the first of these Greenwood Guardians is the Masculine essence of Sweet Chestnut, who has asked to overlight and help you ground whatever work you undertake within *any* aspect of his chapter. The second is the Masculine essence of Bamboo, who has specifically asked to help you understand and assimilate his Gift of The Golden-yellow Flame of Illumined Wisdom (if you have chosen to accept it).

When you are ready to connect with Jophiel's first Greenwood Guardian, you need simply call for the presence of **Sweet Chestnut** (*) .... Sweet Chestnut envelops you in a pale pink Light, and the Masculine spirit essence of Sweet Chestnut speaks to you, saying:

> *"I am the red within the green; the pink within the white. Through me you may learn to draw upon the wisdom, purity and balance of the Earth, enabling you to find the treasures that lie at the heart of the most thorny of experiences.... For I can show you how courageous sacrifice may lead to greater healing and balance, and will show you*

how heart-centred love can make the darkest of times seem light. So stand with me now, and feel my ancient wisdoms fill your heart and mind, whilst my understanding of true balance holds you steady.... then allow my compassionate mercy to flow through you, bathing you in the sweetness of Divine Love; whilst my Light surrounds you in a shield of knowing protection.... For thus you may find the strength to release all that is within you that confines or restricts your joy, or holds you back from partaking in the fullness of Life – for all that I AM is given to aid the growth and wisdom of all, that the world may uphold the Highest ideals of the Light, in full and complete understanding of the challenges – and merits – of evolution, change and growth...."

(* Ruby in Fuchsite will help you ground and connect with the energies and wisdom of Sweet Chestnut, if you wish to enhance your experience using crystals.)

If you have chosen to accept and work with Jophiel's Gift, and when you are ready to connect with his second Greenwood Guardian, you need simply call for the presence of **Bamboo** (*) .... Bamboo envelops you in a dark brown Light, and the Masculine spirit essence of Bamboo speaks to you, saying:

"I am empty mind.... I am flow.... I am elegance.... I am humble belief in the power of silent BEing.... So walk through the deep forest of my heart, feeling and sensing the natural world that sustains and upholds you on every level; and then stand with me, and know the patient and resilient flexibility that enables you to be strong within and yet yielding without: for the wisest of men knows that pure, calm and balanced energies provide the best support, and offer the most comprehensive and complete potential for Be–ing 'in the moment'.... Know that through me you may come to accept the worth of living in the NOW, and allow life to simply flow. So be at peace, and let the worries and cares of the day fall away.... Accept all that you have learnt, but do not waste your energies by living in the past.... Acknowledge all that you have yet to learn, but do not sap your energies by worrying about the future.... For yesterday is always gone, and tomorrow never arrives. So simply BE.... at peace...."

(* Yellow Jasper and Cappuccino [Bruneau] Jasper will help you ground and connect with the energies and wisdom of Bamboo, if you wish to enhance your experience using crystals.)

ARCHEIA ANNUNCIATA

'HOPE SHINES THROUGH'

CRYSTAL CHAMPIONS:

Pearl ♥ Fire Opal ♥ Rainbow Moonstone

CREATURE COMPANIONS:

Stork ♥ Whale ♥ White Dove

GREENWOOD GUARDIANS:

Linden ♥ Magnolia

*I fill my heart with hope and joy,
and willingly shine forth
the Guiding Light of Divine Spirit.*

MEETING ANNUNCIATA

You find yourself standing alone in a darkened desert on the cusp of night and day, just before dawn. A cool breeze caresses your skin, bringing with it the subtlest hint of the heat yet to come; and lifting small grains of sand to whisper about your feet. In the west a crescent moon is slowly sinking below the horizon, its thin silvered curve outlined against the indigo and purple hues of the still night-dark sky; whilst in the east the sun is just awakening, its first rays starting to gild the crests of the undulating dunes that span the horizon as far as the eye can see. Little by little the sun continues its inexorable rise – and as the light levels increase, you realise that a massive square structure stands a few hundred metres away from you to the west. This is very palely highlighted against the dark dunes and night sky behind it – but, as night turns into day, it starts to reflect the radiance of the rising sun, and begins to dominate the landscape.... Gradually it acquires more definition, enabling you to see that it has sheer walls made of snow-white stone and is shaped like a cube, with a very tall minaret rising up from each corner: these soar into the sky far above the tops of the walls – each slender tower crowned with a long tapering conical spire that appears to be clad in gold.

Eventually the sun tops the horizon – its light reflecting off the shiny surfaces of the walls and spires, creating shifting patterns of gold and white light that dance all around you; and making the sands glint and sparkle, as if strewn with countless diamonds. As you stand in wonder, enraptured by the sight, the wind picks up and the desert sands around your feet suddenly stir.... and then you hear a soft voice declare:

"I am indefinable and insubstantial.... You might recognise me by my absence rather than by my presence. For (like the air) I surround you at all times.... Yet with my love I uphold you; with my compassion I comfort you; with my Light I guide you; with my breath I offer you life – and my touch is so familiar, that you are often unaware of my Being.... All that is around you is an aspect of who I AM. And this is how it feels to be surrounded by the Love and Light of The Divine: borne aloft on wings of hope, at peace and unfettered – free to fly or to simply drift, as your own needs and wishes dictate. So allow hope to announce its presence and become real for you, that you may truly know the infinite and joyful possibilities that it brings; and let me take form so that you may know me better: for I am the Keeper of the Pearl-white Flame of Hope, Guardian of the Pearls Beyond Price and twin flame of Gabriel. I am Annunciata, the Lady Hope...."

As the words fade, the air shimmers – and a tall and slender woman with long white-blonde hair appears before you: this IS Archeia Annunciata.

The sun has risen further and the air is now getting hotter – so, suggesting that you accompany her inside her retreat where you can be more comfortable, Annunciata leads you across the flat sandy plateau on which the building sits.... As you approach its walls, you note that they are windowless and sheer; and that the only way in is through the pair of high arched ironwood doors (which are silvered with age, and bound and hinged with thick struts of blackened iron) located in the centre of the wall in front of you. The doors are set in a deep arched surround constructed from alternating square blocks of white and gold-leafed marble assembled in a three-dimensional chequerboard effect, whose seven stepped layers (each a hands-length or so in depth) reveal the thickness of the walls.

A small access gate has been built into the right-hand door – and it is through this that Annunciata guides you.... Glad to be out of the sun, you are taken by surprise at the stark simplicity of the structure's interior, which comprises little more than a pure-white marble floor and a high timber-clad ceiling. The ceiling is unusual, having four quadrants that are supported on two rows of tall white marble pillars running north-south/east-west through the centre of the building: this leaves a wide cross-shaped opening in the ceiling, and divides the floor into four equal squares. This interesting design shelters and shades a good proportion of the marble floor below; whilst the large cross-shaped area (which is open to the sky) lets in light, and promotes the circulation of cooler air throughout the lower level. Each corner is spanned by a curving wall, which you assume to be the lower part of the round minarets you saw before; and each wall has a tall arched opening, which gives access to a stone spiral staircase and (presumably) the upper part of the minarets.

Leading you towards one of these openings, where four huge cushions have been laid on the floor, Annunciata invites you to choose where you would like to sit, and take your ease whilst you examine her and become accustomed to her energies. The cushions have tapestry tops depicting various scenes of the natural world – one a regal white stag standing in a forest glade; one a young elk drinking at the shore of a mountain lake; one a stately grey heron standing tall on a reed-clad river bank; and one a cluster of shiny black beetles sifting through a drift of golden sand: so making your choice, you sit and relax....

You have already seen that Annunciata is tall and girlishly slender, with long white-blonde hair that is very fine and straight: this falls from a side-parting to her waist like a veil of white silk, which she brushes casually aside as she makes herself comfortable on the cushion beside you. As she settles, your eye is drawn to the simple silver circlet that threads through her hair and encircles her brow, which holds a thumbnail-sized fire opal cabochon in an intriguing silver mount: the mount has been crafted to create a pointed ellipse, and has been engraved to portray a vertically aligned eye that spans her brow from hairline to nose, with the vibrant orange opal (which forms the eye's pupil) centred over her third eye.

Shifting your focus, you see that Annunciata has delicate and youthful features set in an ovoid face with a softly rounded chin; and note that her skin is unusually pale and luminous, glowing with an inner light that gives her an etheric, somehow other-worldly, appearance. As with her hair, her brows are white-blonde and thus barely visible – although her long lashes have a golden tint that frames and enhances her wide-set gentian-blue eyes. These seem to draw you in – and you feel yourself momentarily held in a penetrating gaze that seems to see deep within your very heart and Soul.

Lowering your gaze to Annunciata's attire, you note she is wearing a simple yet elegant sleeveless gown made from white silk. It has a softly draping scooped neckline, and is loosely held in gathers around her slender waist by a long tasselled cord made of twisted strands of golden thread, from where it flows down to the floor and pools around her feet. Over the gown she wears a short cape of soft white velvet, lined with golden silk: the cape drapes around her shoulders, and fastens with a short tasselled cord that matches the one around her waist. Noting your interest, she removes the cape so you can examine it more closely, which enables you to see and admire the (barely-visible) line of white stitching that trims its edges, which comprises a series of raised pyramidal shapes linked by circles and loops in a complex and intriguing multi-layered three-dimensional pattern.

Retrieving her cape, Annunciata shakes it out and places it aside, which draws your eye to her long arms, which (despite their willowy appearance) are well-muscled; and to her delicate hands, whose surprisingly callused palms lead you to believe she is stronger than you thought. Furthermore, although the rest of her attire is softly feminine, her feet are shod in utilitarian boots – albeit made of supple white leather; and she has a pair of stiff white leather guards laced tightly around her forearms. Again noting your interest, she holds her arms out to show that the guards are armoured and reinforced with curved plates of silvery-gold metal, whose utilitarian nature is relieved by exquisite engravings of a pair of intertwined serpentine dragons, which have tiny (yet perfect) pearls for eyes.

Lastly your gaze is drawn to the large pendant resting over Annunciata's heart. Both the pendant and its chain are made of the same metal as her arm-guards; and the round disc of the pendant has also been engraved – this time with a design that replicates the labyrinth at Chartres. You also see that a series of six overlapping circles has been etched in its centre, to surround a small round cabochon of polished rainbow moonstone that is glowing with an iridescent blue sheen: this is the stone that links her with Gabriel, her twin flame.

ANNUNCIATA'S TEACHINGS
The Knowledge of Perfected Balance and The 'I' of The Pearl:

Passing you her pendant, Annunciata reminds you that the labyrinth symbolises the Path of Life that you travel in your quest for the Light of your Inner-self, as you seek to find your place within the vastness of the Divine Universe. She asks you to look closely at the six overlapping circles surrounding the rainbow moonstone at its centre, and tells you that all curved shapes (spheres, circles and spirals) are regarded as 'feminine' – for they allow both movement and expansion to occur, and give birth to form, which is the structure of all things. Pointing to the stone at the centre, she informs you that this covers a seventh (inner) circle that completes the pattern known as the 'Seed of Life', which is an ancient esoteric symbol that defines the beginning of life, and holds all the blueprints required for evolution and growth. Gently tapping the moonstone Annunciata adds that here, at the very centre of the Seed, is where you will find the eye – the 'I' that shines your Inner Light: your Divine spark; the eternal and infinite 'you'; your 'I AM' Consciousness, which affirms you as being a part *of* – not apart *from* – The Divine, and which embraces All That Is. She stresses that it is only by travelling the Path of Life (and developing spiritual strength, and accruing understanding and wisdom) that you will be able to increase the quantum of Light that you can hold – which in turn will determine the Planes of Dimension within which your awareness can 'BE', as you seek out your 'I'. With a smile, she further reminds you that *every* Path of Life is therefore a unique design that holds boundless possibilities within an infinite range of experiences, providing many opportunities for you to acquire greater self-knowledge and understanding through trials and tribulations, peace and joy – and all things in between.

Annunciata tells you that she and Gabriel 'as one' embody the Crystalline Clarity of Divine Consciousness and carry the Rainbow Light of Manifestation, so that the entire spectrum of experience is accessible to all. She explains that, as such, her tasks include preparing all sentient life-forms to receive the Pure Light of Spirit, so that they may learn to embody the Truth of their Being; and require her to facilitate balance within all the Rays of the spectrum, while at the same time ensuring that the core ratio and quantum of Divine Light remains constant. Smiling, she says that this entails maintaining a state of equilibrium and balance that will allow polar extremes to be created and held, in order to facilitate Universal learning throughout all Planes and Dimensions. She expounds that this is achieved through her understanding of Black and White Light, which together hold both the potential for Creation *and* the reality of Manifestation as One – for neither may exist without the other. She stresses that 'Black' and 'White' (and light and dark) are therefore simply polar aspects of the One Light – each having purpose and design, even though they may be 'seen' in very different ways: but it is important to understand that all are simply definitions of the manner in which Light may (through Free Will and choice) be applied, and are *not* a definition of the Light itself, which IS fundamentally and essentially neutral.

Standing, Annunciata pulls you to your feet and leads you into the minaret closest to you, where she guides you to the top of the spiral staircase: here a tall arched opening gives you access to one quadrant of the upper floor, which is tiled in horizontal rows of alternate black and white squares like a giant chessboard. Looking up, you see that the walls that surround this space are at least four times your height, and that the peaks of the minarets tower a good three times higher than that – making you feel very small. From this angle you can also see that the walls of each minaret have a series of rectangular openings just below their spires, at which Annunciata explains that the minarets act a little like the pipes of a church organ, through which air is channelled to create different resonances, which your ears may translate as sounds.

Taking your attention back to the floor, Annunciata explains that each quadrant is tiled with designs or patterns that support and sustain Earthly equilibrium from different perspectives – the one on the opposite corner being black and white like this one, but set on the diagonal rather than the horizontal. She says that each represents The Divine Light and its myriad potentials for transformation and enlightenment, the ones of this quadrant relating (in very simple terms) to Earthly reality; the ones opposite to Divine existence: then, informing you that the core principle of this quadrant is *'Perfected Balance'*, Annunciata asks you to go and lie down somewhere on its chequered floor....

Once you have chosen a spot and settled down, the wind lifts and a warm breeze begins to swirl around you – and, as the air moves through the openings in the minarets, you start to hear a series of musical notes and tones.... As you listen, Annunciata asks you to relax and just allow the notes to embrace and fill you, simply accepting that you can absorb the resonances they carry – explaining that these will catalyse and promote whatever healing and/or balancing is the most appropriate for your needs at this time, in order that you may better understand the greater purpose for your human life and all your Earthly life-experiences....

After allowing you time to absorb and assimilate everything she knows you can, Annunciata points to the sky, where a white stork is flying towards you with a bundle dangling from his long beak! This is such a cliché that you feel rather bemused – but Annunciata chuckles, remarking that what you see is often used to symbolise a birth or new beginning: hence **Stork** can be called upon whenever you need to make a fresh start; or if you want help to plan out a new project; or if you require guidance to oversee the development, birth and growth of something completely new. Landing in front of her, the stork passes its burden to Annunciata, who thanks it, and opens the wrappings to reveal a baby within.... Cradling it in her arms, she tells you that here, through Love, innocence is made manifest: the union of Divine Mother and Divine Father resulting in this Divine Child – an innocent babe born of Love and Light and imbued with the Purity of First Creation. She emphasises that (as the offspring of The Divine) *this* is the true source of your Power and the rock of your foundation: the hope, faith and trust that carries you ever onwards to find the true Light of your own Being! Directing your attention back to the stork, who is now resting on one leg in the shade, she says that Stork can teach you how to hold a core state of stability and outer balance as you attain the inner balance that will aid calm reflection, regardless of what is happening to (or around) you: in turn this will help you address and understand issues that might otherwise upset your balance with more clarity and equanimity. Pointing out its long beak she adds that Stork can also help you 'dig around' for hidden wisdoms; or help you probe and unravel the intricacies of life's conundrums to extract whatever information or knowledge you might need in order to understand your past (and clarify your future) as you travel the Paths of Illumination. With a smile, she says that Stork may also come to *you* if you need to look for the child within and reconnect with the purity, innocence and joy that is at your heart.

Helping you to your feet, Annunciata leads the way back down the spiral staircase, and lays the baby in the nest of cushions so it may continue its peaceful sleep in safety: then, lifting an arm and touching the engraving on its arm-guard, she tells you that this depicts the dragons who guard the 'Pearls Beyond Price' that embody the Divine Light of every 'I AM' Self , and gives you two perfect pearls (one white, the other black). She tells you that **Pearl** is her first Crystal Champion – explaining:

> *"The Pearl is a natural creation and great gift from Mother Earth, combining the Elements of earth and water to help you ground your awareness and understanding of your Self and your world in perfect clarity and balance. They embody the infinite Light that embraces* all *things and is your 'I AM' Consciousness and the Truth of your own Divinity: hence, if you allow it, these Pearls can help you rediscover who and what you are, in truth – their Light revealing your true and pure beauty, which eclipses all else, and illuminating all the many and diverse aspects that comprise your Being. The Black Pearl also asks that you now have the courage to confront the darkness within, using its strength and potential to create a new reality that is wiser and greater.... and the White Pearl asks that you use its purity and purpose to ensure that whatever you do (and whatever you create) is always accomplished with the purest and Highest of ideals. Moreover, both Pearls can help you respect and appreciate Life's countless irritations and difficulties that have (and will) beset you as you experience human embodiment,*

and will show you how to absorb their imprints and their wisdoms into your Soul: for only in this way will you progress, and truly know freedom."

Smiling, Annunciata affirms that Pearl may therefore remind you that your True Self does not know limitation: for the Pearl of your I AM Presence knows only magnificence!

The Knowledge of Perfected Creation and The Songs of the Whales:

Guiding you to the minaret to the right of the one you had just climbed, Annunciata leads you up the spiral stairs, telling you that it is good to have high expectations of life – not for things just to be 'OK', but for them to be amazing and brilliant. With a smile, she adds that it is important never to allow small-mindedness to diminish you, but to allow yourself the freedom to make the impossible possible, by always thinking 'greatness' *not* 'smallness': after all, why only ask for the sun if you can have the stars too! Stepping aside, she reveals that you have reached another quadrant of the upper floor – this one being clad in a repeating pattern of decorative tiles that are predominantly bright-blue on white with deep red and gold highlights. This is very pleasing to the eye (and a complete contrast to the structured starkness of the last one); and as you examine the tiles more closely, you see how each one bears a very intricate and beautiful stylised flower motif. Annunciata tells you that this quadrant glorifies the natural world and honours the munificence of Creation – the blue colours signifying the sky and the vastness of Divine Mind; the red signifying the earth and the fires of Divine Passion; the gold signifying the Sun and the riches of Divine Manifestation; and the white signifying the Moon and the purity of Divine Potential – hence, this quadrant's core principle is *'Perfected Creation'*.

Once again Annunciata asks you to go and lie down somewhere on its patterned floor.... and when you have chosen a spot and settled down, the wind lifts again – and, as the air again moves through the openings in the minarets, you start to hear a fresh series of musical notes and tones.... As you listen, Annunciata asks you to relax and just allow the notes to embrace and fill you, simply accepting that you can absorb the resonances they carry – explaining that these will catalyse and promote whatever healing and/or balancing is appropriate for your needs at this time, in order that you may truly *know* the love and purpose of ALL that surrounds you....

After allowing you enough time to absorb and assimilate everything she knows you can, Annunciata comes to sit by your side.... Reminding you of the engraving on her arm-guard, she informs you that the Dragons of the Rainbow Realm aid her in administering the Pearlescent-white Ray – for they are highly advanced Beings that know all there is to know about the composition and direction of Light. With an enigmatic smile she tells you that dragons were very involved in Earth's first founding – and, removing the silver circlet from her head, she asks you to look closely at the gemstone that adorns it....

As you stare into the fire opal's translucent orange depths, you suddenly feel its fire embrace you: and you find yourself strengthening as your heart opens and becomes filled with a deep and abiding love for Gaia (your Mother Earth).... As this humbling feeling sweeps through you, you realise how absolutely and unconditionally the Earth supports you; and you are completely overwhelmed by the breadth of her wisdom and the depth of her commitment to her part in the Divine Plan.... recognising how you feel, Annunciata smiles, and affirms that Gaia (like *all* the Solar and Planetary bodies) is a sentient Being in her own right. She explains that each of these Bodies has a particular affinity with one of the Ten Sacred Rays – Earth's being the Orange Ray, which is grounded through this gemstone; and which sustains the environment that best facilitates humankinds' lessons and experiences (which focus upon the emotions, feelings and reactions governed by the sacral chakra and emotional Body of the human energy field), as directed through the Flames of Divine Will, Wisdom and Love held within each 'Lotus of the Heart'.

Annunciata now touches the fire opal to your brow – asking you to close your eyes and open your mind, and listen to the sound of the Earth.... as you do as she asks, you feel your focus shift – and you suddenly hear a deep and resonant heartbeat, overlaid by hauntingly evocative whale-song.... slowly you find your awareness expanding; and you feel yourself connected to the heart of the planet and *all* the many life-forms she supports by an even greater love than you felt before.... As you marvel at this, Annunciata declares that *this* is the core sound of Gaia, your Earth Mother – her heart held in resonant accord with the reverberations of the songs of the whales, whilst they work to harmonise the collective resonance of all sentient planetary life.... and, as you continue to listen you feel your energies shift – and little by little you find yourself filled with renewed optimism and hope for the future....

After a while Annunciata lifts the fire opal from your brow, explaining that this gem also links Earth with the star 'Canopus', which is the true home of the whales that inhabit Earth's oceans. Returning the circlet to her own brow, she observes that (lamentably) not everyone understands or recognises the importance of these great oceanic cetaceans, who are the Keepers of Earth's history *and* the Singers of the Songs that sustain the resonant balance of the planet, and keep the Earth in harmony with the Greater Spheres of Earth's Solar System and Galaxy – the ultimate aim of which is alignment with the heartbeat of the Universe, and full connection to what the whales call 'Universal Mind' (or that which you know as The Divine).

Taking your hand, Annunciata observes that the whales of Earth's oceans will assist your healing journey and growth, if you ask – for they understand the resonant forces of sound and vibration that affect the planet, and know how to work with the cycles and rhythms that sustain Earthly life: thus you may choose to call **Whale** if you want to learn how to work with the healing powers of sound to restore and balance your energy Bodies (especially those of your physical body and your emotions) – perhaps by means such as singing or toning, playing an instrument, or simply listening to music; or by exploring the potentials of rhythm through movement or dance. Annunciata adds that whale-song also has the power to awaken dormant codings within your DNA, stimulating your recall of past or ancient knowledge associated with utilising resonance and sound for healing or creation: thus you may also ask Whale to help you recall past lives or existences where you have worked with such powers – thus (very importantly) enabling you to address and redress karmic issues if perhaps you had misused or abused those powers; and/or to understand how you might use those powers today on the side of the positive forces of Light. Then suddenly (and very unexpectedly) you realise you understand snatches of the songs the whales are singing as they commune over vast distances, hearing:

"...Sky above, sea below: together we can achieve that which must be done... Sea below, sky above: in pleasant harmony we work... Some hunt us, yet we will prevail: for us, all things are possible... All together onwards travel: for we must be as one together... Sea of blue, sky of white: we see all through day and all through night... Sky of blue, sea of green: as we journey all is seen... Riding the waves and diving to the deepest depths, we travel the Earth and to the stars: knowledge to share, freely given so all may learn..."

With a squeeze of her hand, Annunciata assures you that the whales fully accept the role they have elected to play to further humankind's appreciation of (and compassion for) Earth and the Animal Kingdom – adding that Whale will be your greatest teacher if you want to *really* understand the meaning (and value) of sacrifice and surrender for the Common Good.

After allowing you a while to return to 'reality', Annunciata assists you to your feet and leads you back down the spiral staircase: here she gives you an orange gem that you recognise as a **Fire Opal**, saying that this is her second Crystal Champion – explaining:

"Fire Opal is the Jewel of the Earth, aligning Earth's innate resonance with the Orange Ray and holding both in balance with the whole spectrum of Light and the other Sacred Rays of the Solar System. Fire Opal combines the Elements of earth, fire and water to help you fully ground your awareness of your Self as an emotional and *spiritual Being, thus promoting selflessness and encouraging you to have compassion for* all *life forms. Fire Opal also supports all creative and artistic endeavours, and its connection with the whales of Canopus can supply strength and passion to your sacral and throat chakras, encouraging you to use your voice constructively through speech or song: furthermore, its inner Fire can boost your energy, courage and confidence – providing you with an uncomplicated sense of excitement and optimism about whatever you are planning, or doing. When the time is right, Fire Opal also has the power to initiate and sustain the awakening and activation of your kundalini energies, promoting the raising of your consciousness through your primary chakras and energy centres to connect you with the Highest aspects of your Self – resulting in heightened awareness and clarity, and thus promoting the state of Enlightenment."*

With another smile, Annunciata affirms that Fire Opal may therefore aid you in your search for inner balance and healing; and may help you find the 'threads' that connect apparently disparate thoughts, feelings or beliefs, in order to more fully understand and reconcile them. She then muses that sometimes navigating life can be like trying to do a jigsaw puzzle that is missing some pieces *and* which has no picture on the lid: your initial impulse may be confusion – and then frustration – as you seek to make sense of it... but the trick lies in realising that this is *your* jigsaw; and in recognising that Free Will allows you to create whatever pieces you need to complete (and even modify or entirely change) the picture as you choose: therefore you do not have to confine your hopes and wishes to the small or the mundane, but can plan for as much magnificence as you can conceivably imagine – and create something truly amazing!

The Gift of The Pearl-white Flame of Hope:

Guiding you to the minaret opposite the one you had just climbed, Annunciata leads you up the spiral stairs, where (as before) an opening allows access to another quadrant of the upper floor: this one is tiled in black, with tiny inlaid gold tiles that portray a stylised 'sun'. The 'body' of the sun surrounds the base of the minaret, and has ten V-shaped 'rays' that extend to the two open edges of the floor – and, as you examine these more closely, you can see that the gold tiles are studded at random intervals with round cabochons of pure white moonstone, which sparkle and flash with a silvery fire as they reflect the sunlight.

Annunciata explains that the sun signifies the Sun that IS at the heart of the Solar System and at the core of the Universe – the gold defining the perfected structure and form that underlies all Creation, through the principles of the Divine Masculine; the white moonstones supplying the Purity of White Fire to ensure everything Created is flawlessly fit for purpose, through the principles of the Divine Feminine. Explaining that this quadrant's core principle is *'Perfected Manifestation',* Annunciata directs you to choose one of the sun's golden rays and lay down on it, ensuring that your head is nearer the base of the minaret....

Once you have chosen a spot and settled down, the wind lifts and a warm breeze begins to swirl around you – and, as the air moves through the openings in the minarets, you start to hear a fresh series of musical notes and tones.... As you listen, Annunciata asks you to relax and just allow the notes to embrace and fill you, simply accepting that you can absorb the resonances they carry – explaining that these will catalyse whatever healing and/or balancing you need at this time, in order that you may recognise and own the tremendous power and potential you have within – and with which you can fashion and shape your Self (and your Life) however you desire....

After allowing you enough time to absorb and assimilate everything she knows you can, Annunciata comes to kneel at your side.... Removing her pendant, she places it over your heart, and asks you to rest your finger on the smooth dome of rainbow moonstone set on the circle at its centre.... as you do as she asks, you feel yourself become balanced and calm – all your energies fully aligned and grounded.... and then you feel your energy field expand, clarify, and fill with Light – and your heart becomes filled with pure and joyful anticipation....

Reaching out, Annunciata rests her hand over yours so that it covers her pendant and your heart – and at this your heart becomes as one with your High Heart, and opens to reveal the bud of the Lotus of your Heart, nestled within its protective outer layer of petals.... Leaning over, Annunciata lifts her hand and tells you to remove your finger: she then gently breathes on the rainbow moonstone, which bursts into an iridescent mass of white flames that instantaneously surround the bud of your Lotus, and flush through with pastel hues of rainbow Light.... slowly these are absorbed by the bud's outer protective petals, transforming them into an impenetrable layer of pearl-white petals that close up to enfold the bud within – and, with a gentle smile, Annunciata returns her pendant to her neck, saying:

"My Gift of The Pearl-white Flame of Hope carries the Pure High frequencies of Hope and Joy to aid you in finding the Divine within, that you may know the Truth of your Being as both Master and Creator. Here it will also protect and inspire the three-fold

Flames of the Lotus of your Heart, so that whatever you give out to the world manifests in its purest form; and so that you may know the joy of living, loving and learning whilst Illuminated in the Pure White Fire of Spirit..."

Then, as your heart centres close and find equilibrium, Annunciata once more rests her hand over your heart, declaring that *this* is where she always dwells – to clarify, inspire and empower the Lotus of your Heart; and keep all its aspects in purity and integrity, whilst holding it at all times within the Unified Light of The Divine: therefore it is true to say that Hope is *always* in your heart!

Helping you to your feet, Annunciata gives you a small white semi-translucent stone that shines with a blue iridescence, telling you that this is **Rainbow Moonstone**, her third Crystal Champion – explaining:

"Rainbow Moonstone carries the full spectrum of the Rainbow Rays and highlights the vibrant blue energies of the Goddess and all that is an aspect of The Divine Feminine: hence, it has an innate purity that is protective and clarifying; and an innocence that knows only truth and joy. Thus, Rainbow Moonstone can restore and enhance feelings of positivity, hope and joy within you; whilst also promoting inner peace, stability and balance – aiding you in seeing 'the light at the end of the tunnel' if you are despairing, lost or confused. Rainbow Moonstone can also help bring any and all of your chakras into the most appropriate state of openness and alignment – its cool Light calming and refreshing you in body, mind and spirit; and aiding you in gaining (and retaining) a clearer perspective on 'the issues of the day'. Indeed, you may find that opening yourself to a more detached state of awareness, whilst flooding your energy Body with Rainbow Moonstone's full-spectrum Light, can also help align you through your heart and pranic core, so that you may become more focused and at ease with the world about you: in turn this can help strengthen and stimulate your intuition, and help you ground all that you see, sense, hear and know with greater clarity and accuracy. Rainbow Moonstone also wishes to remind you that it is a stone for all *– enabling you to embrace and honour your ' feminine side' and all its aspects and qualities with calm and balanced acceptance; and so helping you more easily identify and understand the purpose behind* everything *that Earthly life asks you to experience."*

Smiling, Annunciata affirms that Rainbow Moonstone may therefore help you find the Light of Hope within you – wherever you are, and whatever you are doing; and tells you that its aligning and balancing effects can be enhanced if you visualise (imagine) yourself touching it to each of your seven primary chakras in turn (from base to crown), and then resting with it over your heart chakra.

Tasks complete, Annunciata guides you back down the spiral stairs and leads you back to the cushions, suggesting that you rest awhile.... She is just settling at your side, when a white dove flutters down through the cross-shaped opening in the ceiling and alights on her shoulder: with a smile, she carefully lifts it into her lap, where it nestles down between her hands, softly billing and cooing. Remarking that this is one of the sounds that reflects inner contentment, Annunciata says that doves impart the same sense of deep peace and calm she finds when she enters the 'inner silence' – and, likewise, you may find **Dove** to be a useful companion if you need help finding a calm centre for the purposes of journeying, meditation or lucid dreaming; or even if you simply need help to 'switch off' and relax. Gently stroking the dove's head, she tells you that all doves carry and ground the pure essence of The Divine – adding that these beautiful and elegant birds also carry blessings between the Heavens and the worlds of Spirit, and are Universally regarded as symbols of simplicity, purity, love, fidelity and peace: accordingly, you can ask Dove to be your go-between if you wish to make 'Higher' and/or clearer connections with the unseen worlds around you; or if you need any of the aforementioned attributes to manifest more effectively (or powerfully) within your life. With a smile, Annunciata reminds you that it is dove who holds the olive branch of peace and hope – thus you may also call upon Dove for courage and support if you have had a disagreement or argument, and it is time to 'mend fences' or make-up with family or friends; or if you need help to release and heal the residue of any past emotional hurts or disharmony; or if you want to understand how to 'let go' of *anything* that prevents you from living a life filled with peace, harmony and joy. Remarking that a white dove is always a reminder of your true pure nature, Annunciata adds that if dove comes to you – in reality *or* in spirit – its presence indicates that you need to connect with your inner guidance through your heart, in order to look at and address a situation or issue you are involved in from a Higher (and more compassionate) perspective.

The Greenwood Guardians – Linden and Magnolia:
Her *personal* mentoring complete for now, Annunciata affirms she is always available to aid and support you: you need only bring her to mind and ask for her presence, and she will attend you. Furthermore, she tells you that two great Tree Beings of the Plant Kingdom have also asked to support you in addressing her Theme of 'HOPE SHINES THROUGH', adding that you need only request *their* presence, and they will be with you.

She explains that the first of these Greenwood Guardians is the Feminine essence of Linden (Lime), who has asked to overlight and help you ground whatever work you undertake within *any* aspect of her chapter. The second is the Feminine essence of Magnolia, who has specifically asked to help you understand and assimilate her Gift of The Pearl-white Flame of Hope (if you have chosen to accept it).

When you are ready to connect with Annunciata's first Greenwood Guardian, you need simply call for the presence of **Linden** (*) .... Linden envelops you in a pale red-gold Light, and the Feminine spirit essence of Linden speaks to you, saying:

"In every moment I draw upon the rich wisdom and strength of the Earth, which fills me with all that I need to enable me to grow and reach high into the Heavens. If you look at my heart-shaped leaves, you may understand why my Light binds me to the earth, giving me the ability to understand and know the truth in all that I encounter and see. So let me share this gift with you, for your path will become ever brighter and more clear when you have the benefits of a strong connection to the earth below your feet **and** *to the unseen world about you.... So stand in my shade and press your back to my trunk, and feel my solidity and strength – knowing that I can support you through life's ups and downs, by offering you stability and reassurance whenever you need a guiding star....*

then become aware of the sap rising within me, and listen to the contented humming of the bees that come to me for nourishment – for generosity of spirit and love for all is in every sweet drop of bounty that I provide; and you too may share in my abundance so freely given.... So relax into my embrace, and let me calm your mind, uplift your heart, strengthen your spirit, and inspire you to shine your Light – so that you can become the best you can be."

(* Bronzite and Smoky Quartz will help you ground and connect with the energies and wisdom of Linden, if you wish to enhance your experience using crystals.)

If you have chosen to accept and work with Annunciata's Gift, and when you are ready to connect with her second Greenwood Guardian, you need simply call for the presence of **Magnolia** (*) .... Magnolia envelops you in a rippling curtain of pink Light, and the Feminine spirit essence of Magnolia speaks to you, saying:

"In this Life I embrace the Grace that is given by the Benevolence of the Divine Light. Thus, as the darkness of winter comes to an end, my flowers herald the coming of spring with the promise of new life – replenishing the faith and love that IS the foundation of all things, through the pure creamy-white perfection of their blossoms. So see their glorious hearts of pink; and watch me dance in the joy of new beginnings – for all that I hold dear is born of Love, and held in every aspect of my Being.... Then sit beneath my outspread wings, and let the passion that encourages me ever onwards and upwards to greater undertakings and accomplishments fill you with its strength and power.... and feel the roots that ground me offer you the succour and support that will keep your centre strong and your mind open, so that you may always know the profound Love that is forever around you.... Then let me apply the balm of my loving kindness to all your wounds, and help you release your fears – so that you may move forwards into the future with a clear and balanced heart that is forever filled with the clear white Light of Hope and Joy...."

(* Snow [White] Quartz will help you ground and connect with the energies and wisdom of Magnolia, if you wish to enhance your experience using crystals.)

ARCHANGEL GABRIEL

'JOYFUL JOURNEYS'

CRYSTAL CHAMPIONS:

Herkimer Diamond ♥ Lapis Lazuli ♥ White Selenite

CREATURE COMPANIONS:

Honeybee ♥ Golden Pheasant ♥ Griffon

GREENWOOD GUARDIANS:

Hornbeam ♥ Horse Chestnut

*I joyously affirm the child that I AM,
and delight in the gifts
of love, life and laughter.*

MEETING GABRIEL

It is the end of a fine spring day, and you find yourself standing on a low rounded hill that is set in the middle of a wide grassy meadow. The air is cooling after the tender warmth of the day, and all is peaceful, calm and still. Looking around, you note that all the fields beyond the meadow are filled with cherry trees, each richly clad in a billowing profusion of white blossoms; and see that the emerald grass carpeting the ground around your feet is strewn with masses of tiny four-petalled white flowers. As dusk begins to fall the sky slowly fades from pale china-blue to a soft silver-grey, and each delicate star-like flower closes its petals in sleep – flushing through with a soft pink light as the setting sun anoints the feet of the clouds above you with molten gold, setting them vibrantly aflame in hues of apricot, pink and red. A single golden finger of light seems to be marking out a path that leads through the meadow towards the cherry-trees – and so, deciding to follow its route across the meadow to reach their shelter before night falls, you begin to hurry down the hill....

You have just reached its foot, when everything around you is suddenly illuminated in a bright white light; and, seeking its source, you look up to find that there is an Angel hovering above the place where you had just been standing: this is Archangel Gabriel. He looks exactly as you might imagine an Angel to look; for he is dazzlingly robed in white, and has magnificent white swan-like wings! As you acknowledge his presence, he flies down to join you, landing in front of you and embracing you in his Light, declaring:

"I am Gabriel – Divine Awakener, Overseer of the Temple of the Divine Light and Guardian of the Crystal Prism, and twin flame of Annunciata, the Lady Hope. You are my positivity, my pride and my joy! All that I am I owe to you, and in return I would show you the beauty, Light and Grace of my Being, so that you may recognise my radiance and – in its Light – likewise know the great Soul that you are. Know that now and for all time my ever-present Light is by your side, to awaken, guide and enlighten you: so open your eyes wide, and let my Light flood in.... sharpen your hearing, that you may hear my Light sing.... take a deep breath, and feel my Light fill your lungs.... and then open your heart, and let it give voice to the note that is uniquely yours, and by which your Soul is truly known – and let it blend in harmony with my own to awaken all that you can BE.... For thus may you find yourself in me: one heart; one Soul, travelling the roads of life and all that comprises Divine existence – and in that awakening, and in that journey, you may come to know where my true delight in Being lies."

Asking you to follow him, Gabriel folds his wings close to his body and strides off across the meadow, with his long robe brushing the grass around his bare feet.

Hurrying after him, you note with astonishment how everything that his Light falls upon instantly awakens and comes gloriously to life – the flowers opening their petals again; the grass growing longer and more lush. You can also hear a melodic low-pitched humming, and realise that a cloud of honeybees and tiny hummingbirds are trailing in his wake, each taking turns to hover amongst the awakened flowers and feed on their nectar. As you skirt round them, you have a good view of Gabriel's knee-length linen over-robe, which is open-fronted and slightly shorter in the sleeves than the cotton robe beneath it: although both are snow-white, their starkness is offset by the image embroidered down the back of the over-robe, which depicts a stylised flame. This has been featherstitched in deep royal-blue silk, with intricate stitching in fine gold thread adding depth and detail – so much so that the flame appears to flicker, almost as if it is real.

After a while, absorbed in your musings, you reach the edge of the meadow: here Gabriel pauses.... then, at a gesture of his hand, the cherry trees shimmer and shift to reveal a long tree-lined avenue, which leads towards a distant area bathed in a soft light. Asking you to walk at his side, Gabriel begins to pace down the avenue – at which point you notice that he is now carrying a long staff (curiously fashioned in the form of a tall and slender calla lily) in his left hand. With every stride he firmly taps the ground with the base of this staff, which charges the cherry blossoms with a soft white light that spills into the gathering gloom to light your way; until (eventually) you reach the end of the avenue of trees, and stand before a wide circular dais of white moonstone. This has been polished to a softly glimmering sheen, and is illuminated by a ring of six clear-crystal torches – each of which holds a translucent crystalline flame radiating a clear white light. In the centre of the dais there are two high-backed cherry-wood chairs – and, taking a seat in the one on the left, Gabriel invites you to make yourself comfortable in the other, so that you may study him and accustom yourself to his energies.

As you settle Gabriel smoothes down the front of his robe, enabling you to observe that he is very slim and lean; with pale skin and long thin fingers that are mirrored in his pale and slender feet, which are crossed casually at the ankles. Taking the opportunity to examine his over-robe more closely, you see that its edges and cuffs are embellished with a barely-visible band of raised white stitching, which creates an intriguing multi-layered pattern, comprising a line of four-sided pyramids linked by a complex series of loops and circles. In contrast his long-sleeved under-robe is very plain and simple – its soft folds gathered in at the waist by a belt woven from strands of pure white cotton, which is tied in a neat and simple knot, leaving its long fringed ends hanging loose.

Your eye is then taken by the unusual pendant that Gabriel is wearing: this rests over his heart, and hangs from a fine silvery-gold chain of electrum. The body of the pendant is also made of electrum, and has been fashioned in the shape of a dragon's foot – the claws of which are clasping a sphere of rainbow moonstone that is glowing with an iridescent blue light: this is the stone that links him with Annunciata, his twin flame.

As this appears to be his only adornment, you turn your attention to Gabriel's face, and are mildly surprised by his creamy-white skin and golden-lashed cornflower-blue eyes, which are set below inward-slanting gold eyebrows. His neat and delicate (almost feminine) features are well defined and arranged in a lean and somewhat angular heart-shaped face; and are framed by his long and wavy wheat-gold hair, which he wears swept back from his face and over his shoulders, from where it ripples halfway down his back: this style exposes a pair of slightly pointed ears, giving him a rather elf-like appearance – and he smiles with amusement as this thought passes through your mind.

Your gaze finally comes to a rest at Gabriel's hands, and you note that he is still holding his staff in his left hand – but the other now rests palm-down in his lap. Noting your interest he turns this hand over and opens his fingers, revealing that he is holding a large and perfectly clear crystal that is pulsing with a strong, clear Light – and, with a gentle smile, Gabriel tells you that this is a Herkimer diamond. Holding it out, he invites you to rest your hand on top of it – and as you do so, you are surrounded in a clear white Light.... Gradually you feel all your worries and cares drop away; and, as the Light and Power of the crystal fully embraces and fills you, you become aware only of yourself and the space that the crystal is holding for you.... Here, all is still; all is safe; all is serene: and as you let go and allow yourself to simply BE, your heart, mind and Soul are set free; and you understand that here – in this space, and in this state – you may find inner peace at last.... then, in your mind, you hear Gabriel say:

> *"Dwell not upon what might have happened yesterday, for you can do nothing about what has gone before. Know instead that you* always *have the power to shape today – and what comes tomorrow.... For at all times, even in the depths of the darkest hours of your Soul, I am there to aid and guide you."*

After waiting a moment for you to assimilate his words, Gabriel sets the crystal aside and allows you time to return to normal focus, with your mind now calm and clear.

GABRIEL'S TEACHINGS
The Crystal Ray and The Staff of Awakening:

Pointing to the intricate raised knot-work pattern that embellishes the edges of his over-robe, Gabriel explains that the pyramids (which represent the 'Pyramids of Rebirth and Resurrection') are made of white strands of spider silk, and cover and shield small, yet perfect, Herkimer diamond crystals. He remarks that you may have seen the same detailing edging his twin-flame's cape – although, in Annunciata's case, each pyramid covers and shields a perfect pearl. Resting a finger on one of the pyramids, he explains that the crystals that lie at the heart of these pyramids hold the Crystal Ray, which is an elemental emanation of the Diamond Light, and the primary Ray that he oversees and directs: hence he quite literally carries the Light for the World, and holds and sustains the Divine Spark of each 'unawakened' Soul, until all are awake (and satisfactorily able) to hold and embrace it for themselves.

Gabriel expounds that *all* processes of 'awakening' quicken this Spark – catalysing the reactions that encourage each person to take responsibility for the Light of their own Spirit; and gradually enabling his charge over it to be released. Pointing to the loops and circles linking the pyramids that border his robe, he adds that these symbolise the many choices that are open to you as you travel the Path of Life; and the myriad wisdoms you may embrace as you come to know Unity – furthermore, when examined from a Higher perspective, they show how *all* spiritual paths and choices are fundamentally connected; and how all lifetimes and existences are simply a part of a much Greater Whole.

He then gives you a small clear double-terminated quartz that is similar to the one you experienced earlier, and tells you that this is a **Herkimer Diamond**, his first Crystal Champion – explaining:

> *"Herkimer Diamond is a unique form of clear quartz – and one that is a little 'harder' than the norm, with an excellent clarity and a clear and high, yet stable, energy. It often grows in interconnected groups, where large and small crystals have bonded together through different planes of growth – thus exemplifying the aforementioned principle,*

whereby the many may become one. Herkimer Diamond has the power to channel a great deal of Crystal-clear Light into your non-physical and physical bodies and then hold and ground it there, so that all you think, say and do can become filled with a Higher resonance of Light: this will not only energise and strengthen you on all levels, but may also enable you to more clearly remember (and express) who and what you truly are. The Light carried by Herkimer Diamond is also very cleansing, and so it can be used to help you clear negativity from any aspect of your body, mind and spirit: in turn this makes it easier to release anything that you no longer need to carry, or that no longer serves your awakened Self. Then, as you clear out the old to make way for the new, Herkimer Diamond can help you refine your thoughts and emotions, supporting the integration and grounding of new concepts, thoughts and ideas that can aid your assimilation of a greater quantum of Light: as you work towards 'enlightenment', this has the potential to increase your conscious awareness yet further, whilst motivating and filling you with joyful enthusiasm for all that you learn, and all that you do."

Smiling, Gabriel affirms that Herkimer Diamond may therefore help you gain the clarity to see your path clearly; and give you the strength to share the joy you find in following the promptings of your own heart and Soul with those who are not yet fully awakened to the Truth of their own Divinity – thus adopting the role of 'an awakener' yourself, as you help others to find and reveal the Light that they seek within the deepest recesses of their Being – adding:

"Know that this journey is for every Soul to take for themselves – for in so doing they gain the wisdom and understanding they need to find their Self, and know the ultimate joy that this brings! Yet companionship and support on the path is both needful and welcome.... so use your heart to see your own path clearly – feeling and knowing the joyful rightness of what you do resonating deep within your Soul; then BE a Light to your World, stepping out from all that is familiar and leaving that which is safe and known behind, travelling with simply the Light that is at your Heart to illuminate your way.... Then explore what you do not know; what you do not understand: for there, amongst the dust and chaos, do diamonds lie – and as they bring value to your life, humbly and willingly share them with others, that they too may gain the courage and strength to look beyond the mundane and all that they currently hold dear and safe."

Sitting back, Gabriel now passes you his staff, and encourages you to examine it more closely.... As you run your fingers down its pale spring-green shaft, which is as long as you are tall, you find that it has a cool, slightly waxy, feel; and, when you gently tap it with a fingernail, you also find that it rings with a high clear tone, like that made by fine crystal or glass.... The shaft seems to be about the width of a thumb, and is topped by a white trumpet-shaped head that looks like the flower of the arum lily: this has highly polished curves that feel icy-smooth and glassy to the touch; and an arching golden calyx at its heart, which feels metallic and rough in contrast. Concluding that, as a whole, the staff appears to be an enigmatic blend of functionality and beauty; fragility and strength, you pass it back to Gabriel....

Stroking the glassy curves of the flower, Gabriel tells you that he chose to build his staff in this form because the arum lily epitomises purity and love more than any other flower he knows: thus, whenever he uses his staff to transmit, channel or regulate energy, it holds *and* magnifies the intention that anything passing through it be in its purest possible state – the fundamental energy that IS of Divine Source. Gently tapping the golden calyx, Gabriel explains that it feels as it does because it is made of layers of intermeshed strands of gold wire, which have been studded with dodecahedral crystals of iron pyrite, and tiny cubic crystals of brilliantly-clear diamonds. Gently touching a finger to one of these, Gabriel explains that calyx is there to channel and ground the Diamond Light, so that he might adjust its resonance and give it form, as appropriate for each situation. Running his hand down the stem-like shaft, he explains that this is hollow, and has three layers made from elemental matter fused by natural processes, which creates a material similar to a tektite or fulgurite – although it is, in effect, 'solidified' Light: the innermost layer is crystal-clear, and grounds the Light of First Consciousness.... the middle layer (which extends beyond the 'stem' to form the head of the flower) is white, and is saturated with the Light of Absolute Purity.... whilst the outer layer is pale-green, blending emerald-green and white Light and ensuring effective balance within unlimited potential.... furthermore, because each 'layer' has no specific crystalline structure, he is allowed total freedom in how the staff can be used or applied.

Reminding you that one of his prime callings is that of 'Divine Awakener', Gabriel chuckles as he remarks that it is also not coincidental that his staff looks like a very long trumpet, for it is often used to give a loud wake-up call to those who need it – rousing their Soul and awakening the pure essence of their Higher-self; and offering a subtle reminder to those Souls who have lost their way, or only need a gentle prompt. Stressing that this 'awakening' is not a call to a *specific* spiritual path or way of life, Gabriel explains that it is simply a *catalyst* that prompts anyone who has become dis-spirited, or (perhaps) become mired in materialism and/or the mundane realities of everyday life, to reconnect with the truth of who they truly are. With a smile he remarks that, for some, this 'ah-ha!' moment may manifest in a big way – perhaps as a consequence of a life-changing event or a challenging or (literally) awesome experience; whilst for others such realisations may come in small degrees – for few people are fortunate enough to be born with the desire and ability to redefine their life's purpose on a Higher spiritual level fully embedded within their conscious awareness! He asks if you can recall what set *you* on the path you are on, or prompted you to acknowledge your spiritual nature, or reconnect with your Divine Light within..... and if there had been just one thing, or a series of things, that led to your own realisation that 'there must be more to life than this'....

After allowing you a little time to contemplate this, Gabriel reclaims his staff and draws your attention to the clusters of white blossoms that festoon the branches of the cherry trees around you. He tells you that the trees symbolise hope and new beginnings, adding that the beauty and sweet scent of their flowers always fills him with delight: helping you to your feet, he leads you to the nearest tree, and as you inhale the heady aroma for yourself, you see a honeybee land upon a nearby blossom and begin to gather pollen.... As she moves from flower to flower, Gabriel remarks upon her industrious single-mindedness, saying that a bee can teach you a great deal about working hard and having focused concentration – hence you could call upon **Honeybee** if you need help to focus or re-focus your mind (especially if you get easily distracted); or if you have lost your sense of purpose, and/or have become sidetracked from your goal; or if you want to find satisfaction – and even joy – in doing mundane everyday chores and/or tasks. He explains that a bee's waggling dance conveys the location of this bounty to her sisters, showing that the honey-bee understands that communal effort and a common goal creates a colony that survives and thrives: hence Honeybee can help you find the 'sweetness' in life, whilst teaching you how to share willingly with others; or encourage you to see the advantages of working in harmony with others towards a common goal; or show you how to value your own (or others') innate gifts and talents that support a Higher purpose. Drawing your attention to the bee's proportionately small wings, and to the tiny hairs that cover her body, Gabriel adds that all bees contravene logic, because (aerodynamically) they should not be capable of flight – therefore you could also call upon Honeybee if you need encouragement to accomplish the 'impossible'; or want to have greater faith in the ultimate triumph of hope over adversity; or if you need a reminder of the advantages of keeping an open mind as you learn how to 'fly'! Observing that bees are also known to be scrupulously clean, he adds that you might also call upon Honeybee if you need help to keep your energy Bodies free from negativity; or if you want to learn appropriate clearing and/or protection techniques that will enable you to stay steadfast and strong.

The New Dawn Flame and the Baptism of Fire:
Returning you to your chair on the dais, Gabriel says that it may be useful to offer you his definitions of 'Spirit' and 'Soul' at this point, both being terms used (sometimes interchangeably) when referring to the aspects of your Self that are immortal: hence both are often embraced by the term 'Higher-self'. He adds that, for him, 'Soul' and 'Spirit' have similar, but fundamentally different, interpretations: your 'Spirit' being one and the same as your Divine-self – the pure spark of Light that lies reflected within, which is the aspect of you that IS Divine (and which will be all that remains when all your journeys of Self-exploration are complete); your 'Soul' being one and the same as your Christed-self, which is the Higher aspect of your Self that plans and guides all your lives whilst you are separate from your Spirit. Smiling again, Gabriel further adds that your 'ego-self' (or 'lower-self'), which might also be defined as your 'personality', comprises the embodied aspects of your Soul that have Free Will and choice, and which may therefore *choose* to accept *or* reject the guidance of your Higher-selves – or indeed that of anyone else!

Taking your hand, Gabriel says that once you fully awaken to the truth, beauty, power and consciousness of your Inner Light, you may come to embrace the true identity of your Soul, and realise that you *can* only follow the Way of kindness, gentleness and open-hearted love. He stresses that this understanding will become obvious as you truly grasp the reason for all of life's experiences – which *is* full and complete knowledge of the nature of Free Will and the consequences of choice. Raising his eyebrows, Gabriel then looks you in the eye and questions why anyone would *choose* unhappiness over joy; despair over hope; hate over love; or restriction over freedom – pointing out that *you* are always in control of your own destiny, and when you think and act in total accord with your Christed-self you can know only joy!

Reminding you that the word 'Christed' defines one who has embraced the true identity of their Soul, Gabriel tells you that he sometimes has the responsibility of being an overlighting influence (a guiding conscience, if you prefer) for an advanced Soul who has chosen to 'descend' and take Earthly embodiment through increasing their energetic density – usually because of a need to catalyse radical change: hence he has worked with prophets like Elijah and John the Baptist, who both embodied in order to awaken people to the reality of their Spirit and the existence of their Christed-self. Gabriel adds that this 'awakening' often included a symbolic cleansing (physical baptism) with water, in order to prepare the way for their spiritual baptism through the transformative fires of the Holy Spirit – the 'Breath of The Divine', which knows and speaks the Words of Creation.

Just then a hen-sized bird with a very long barred tail strolls onto the dais – his red and gold plumage startlingly bright against the whiteness. Gabriel tells you that this is a golden pheasant – a cousin of the peacock, its red and gold colours marking him as a bird of the Sun: hence you can call upon **Golden Pheasant** to promote and inspire structured and intelligent thought and/or logical or intuitive creativity; or to help you increase your energy levels if you are tired, weak or lethargic; or if you need aid reclaiming or owning your personal power, and/or assuming the mantle of your true identity. As it reaches his side, Gabriel points out how its feathers embrace *all* the colours of the spectrum – but especially the fiery red, orange and yellows, saying that Golden Pheasant can also show you how to use your personal powers for manifestation, whilst keeping your mind and emotions and your logic and intuition in effective and appropriate balance – thus helping you attain and retain equilibrium within and between body, mind and spirit as you seek to know your Self on a Soul level. Smiling, he adds that the hues of blue and green may also support you in integrating your lower- and Higher-selves with greater understanding and ease, as you endeavour to be 'at One' with every aspect of your Being. Observing that golden pheasants nest on the ground, and hence are familiar and comfortable with both the Elements of earth and fire (although not so much with flight and the Element of air!), Gabriel says that Golden Pheasant can teach you how to remain strongly focused, grounded and stable whilst you work to achieve self-transformation through the 'fires of your spirit'; or show you how to use your intuition and associated skills in a manner that is in harmony with the world of reality.

Suddenly the golden pheasant gives a shrill cry – at which the cherry trees shimmer and shift again, this time revealing a pathway that leads to a tiny white alabaster pyramid: fluttering towards it, the bird somehow simply vanishes through its walls; whereupon the pyramid pulses with light and begins to grow, until eventually its apex towers high above you.... Asking you to join him, Gabriel leads you to the pyramid, where you find an inset entryway barred by a golden door covered with decorative panels, which portray cherry blossoms in different stages of bloom: at a touch of his staff the door opens, revealing a long white corridor, down which Gabriel guides you to its end....

Here another door (this one clad in lapis lazuli) opens into a small square chamber clad in white marble, which has a large six-pointed star inscribed on the floor in bright white Light: in the centre of the star you can see a square white pillar bearing a round bowl made of clear crystal, within which blazes a mass of brilliant blue and gold flames.

You realise that these are exactly the same colour as the blue and gold flame on the back of Gabriel's over-robe – and at this he smiles. He tells you that the flame he wears is a ceremonial insignia, which portrays the New Dawn Flame and marks him as the Knight Commander of the Order of John (a Divine Order that exists to promote and advance the art of self-mastery through inner transformation); and explains that the primary purpose of this Flame is to illuminate and aid profound processes of honest and compassionate self-examination, in order to bring about greater self-awareness, self-understanding and self-acceptance. With another smile, he adds that this Flame may *also* be used to bring about the resolution of all inner and outer disharmony, with the ultimate aim of enabling the ego-self and the Christed-self to be fully reconciled and held in perfect equilibrium – the two that were once thought to be unconnected and separate *finally* reunited and recognised as ONE – through the accomplishment that some know as Ascension.

Directing you to enter the star and stand before the bowl of fire, Gabriel places his staff aside, and moves to stand opposite you.... Explaining that the flames you see hold the many aspects of the New Dawn Flame, he reaches into the bowl.... scooping out some of the flames (and showing you that they are safe to hold) he then lifts his hands and takes the flames to his solar plexus, brow and heart chakras in turn – pausing for a moment at each.... He then asks you to likewise take some of the fire in your own cupped hands, saying:

> *"With compassionate mercy may the New Dawn Flame be applied.... Let it bathe your body, mind and Soul in its transformative fires, that you may once more recognise and accept all, that in Truth, you are..."*

and asks you to begin by taking the flames to your solar plexus chakra – at the same time affirming your willingness to resolve any inner and outer disharmony that prevents you from *knowing* self-awareness....

This done, he directs you to next take the flames to your brow chakra – this time affirming your willingness to resolve any inner and outer disharmony that prevents you from *knowing* self-understanding....

This done, he instructs you to finally take the flames to your heart chakra – lastly affirming your willingness to resolve any inner and outer disharmony that prevents you from *knowing* self-acceptance....

Once he is satisfied that the Flames have initiated whatever you are ready to address at this time, Gabriel moves to your side and takes the flames from your cupped hands, before returning them to the bowl: he then places his hands gently on your crown in Blessing, declaring:

> *"Through the fires of the New Dawn Flame, may the purity and freedom of your Inner Light be restored, that you may know yourself in Truth – your ego-self and Christed-self fully reconciled and held in perfect equilibrium, reunited and recognised as ONE."*

Taking you aside, he gives you a stone that is deep royal-blue and streaked with golden specks and tells you that this is **Lapis Lazuli**, his second Crystal Champion – explaining:

> *"The deep blue of Lapis Lazuli, with its golden inclusions of iron pyrite, grounds the resonance of the Fire, Light and Illumination of the New Dawn Flame, and can be used*

to catalyse and support radical and self-empowering change. Lapis Lazuli's colours make it an excellent support for the solar plexus, third eye and throat chakras, which can help balance your left and right brain whilst strongly activating your intuitive mind and extrasensory abilities. Lapis Lazuli can also help you align and balance your Higher energy centres, facilitating connection to the inspiration and Wisdom of your Higher-self, and helping you access past-life information, understanding or knowledge that may be of use at that time: Lapis that has plentiful golden pyrite is especially useful for this, as it will help adjust and regulate Higher Cosmic energies, promoting greater clarity and making it easier to receive, ground and understand whatever information or knowledge is attained. Furthermore, all *Lapis Lazuli are reminiscent of the night sky, and so can connect you to the starry realms from which humankind originates – but particularly to the Wise Ones of the ancient Cosmic races that were amongst the early inhabitants of Earth. Thus Lapis Lazuli may help you contact the Teaching Masters associated with those times, including those that founded and Guided the civilisations of Ancient Egypt and Sumeria, who will – if asked – help guide you through a further process of spiritual growth that may help you recognise and claim your true destiny."*

Smiling, Gabriel affirms that Lapis Lazuli may therefore help you use the Power of the New Dawn Flame, and courageously embrace all your spiritual 'baptisms of fire'.

The Gift of The Crystal-clear Flame of First Consciousness:

Taking up his staff again, Gabriel leads you to the far side of the chamber: as you approach, the wall shimmers and a silver door appears – its surface embossed with a large shield-like panel that bears the image of a rearing griffon. At a touch of his staff the door opens, revealing a small round antechamber whose gold-clad walls are studded with diamonds. In the centre of the chamber a low plinth bears a statue made of white selenite (satin spar) that looks just like the griffon on the door. Gabriel chuckles and says that griffons are said to be mythical beasts – yet, nonetheless, they are perfectly real (and visible) to those who have the wit and will to see! He adds that a griffon's primary task is to guard the 'gold' of the Enlightened Soul, for they are extremely powerful guardians of all hidden wisdoms: hence one is most likely to appear if you are being asked to prove your trustworthiness or competence at a time that is of great importance to your spiritual quest. Pointing out that griffons have the body, legs and mane of a lion; and the head, wings, feet and talons of an eagle, Gabriel touches the eagle-aspects of the griffon in turn and explains that – as a wise and skilled Teacher and Guide – **Griffon** may mentor you on (and might test you upon!) your capabilities and skills pertaining to: the grasp and assimilation of knowledge; mental flexibility and the making of insightful, discerning and decisive judgements, choices and decisions; and/or the mastery of the challenges of transformation and growth – both personal and spiritual. He then touches the lion-aspects of the griffon in turn, and explains that Griffon may also mentor (or test you!) on your capabilities and skills pertaining to: stamina, strength and courage of mind, body and spirit; the moral codes that govern the protection and preservation of all that is innocent and pure; and/or the fair dispensation of justice through the liberating powers of mercy and forgiveness. With another smile, he observes that, although this may all sound very daunting, you will find Griffon to always be a scrupulously fair and non-judgemental Teacher, who fully understands the joys and pains of the path to Enlightenment! Then, with a respectful bow to the statue, Gabriel asks for permission to pass....

A hidden door swings open beyond the statue, allowing you entry to a very large pyramidal chamber, whose wide square floor and steeply sloping sides are clad in deep blue lapis lazuli, making it feel almost as if you are suspended in outer space.... In the centre of the floor a three-sided pillar of rainbow moonstone bears a totally clear crystal tetrahedron within which a single flame is burning: this flame is so bright and transparent that you only know it is there because of the faint rainbow-tinted shimmer that hangs in the air around it, like a heat-haze. Leading you a little closer, Gabriel asks you to look at the words engraved on the three sides of the pillar – at which you find that each bears a single word lettered in gold: one reads 'Law'; one 'Formation'; and one 'Experience'....

Gabriel explains that these three words define the fundamental manifestation of The Diamond Light (more commonly known as 'thought' 'word' and 'deed'); whilst the Flame you see within the crystal prism is a condensation of the crystal-clear Ray that carries the pure essence of Source. Lifting his staff, he reminds you that you were born in perfection – innocent in your hopes and expectations, and with the joy of Being in your heart: he then touches the head of his staff to the crystal tetrahedron and draws forth a single crystal-clear Flame....

He touches this to your Hara centre, and you feel a subtle coolness as the Flame is absorbed into your energy Body and slowly moves deeper within, before finally coming to a rest at your Seat of the Soul centre: stepping back, Gabriel lifts his staff and declares:

"My Gift of The Crystal-clear Flame of First Consciousness holds the Divine Pattern of the perfection of your Christed-self. It is given to regulate and focus the Divine Light and hold the immaculate concept for your evolution within the pure Light of Truth, maintaining all that you are – and all that you can become – in an unsullied and constant state; and ensuring that (as you awaken, open, clarify and embrace your Christed and Divine Selves) all your actions are precisely as your eternal Spirit intends.... Remember that through hope life *is born – a life everlasting that merely changes its form as it moves from one world to another, until finally reaching its joyous conclusion, which is Unity with the ONE."*

Moving closer, Gabriel gently rests his hands on your shoulders in silent Blessing.... then the chamber shimmers; and you find yourself back in your chair on the dais....

Retaking his seat at your side, Gabriel tells you that you can always call upon his Gift if you ever need to address, understand, reconcile and/or deal with the consequences of any misuse of power (whether your own or another's); or when it is time for you to master the Right and *proper* use of Power – which includes dealing compassionately with all those irritations, angers and fears that prevent you from allowing yourself (and/or others) to be joyful and happy! Giving you a small white crystal that somehow feels soft to the touch, Gabriel tells you that this is **White Selenite** (satin spar / gypsum), his third Crystal Champion – explaining:

"White Selenite (satin spar or gypsum) is a joyful carrier of the full spectrum of White Light. Despite its soft and rather plain exterior White Selenite has an inner strength that

can quickly and safely activate, open and align all your chakras through your pranic core, flooding your energy Bodies with high-frequency Light and energy: this makes it especially useful for clarifying and charging all the cells of your physical body, reminding them of their innate purity and perfection, and catalysing any healing that is not of a karmic nature, or associated with any unresolved life-plan. Despite its water-solubility, White Selenite is very much at home with the Element of water: this can help you understand its many states that allow an infinite breadth of movement, flow and stillness to be embraced; learn ways of keeping your energy Bodies clean and clear; and/or find and keep emotional balance in an effective and positive manner. Because White Selenite is related to the stone known as alabaster (which was used in sacred structures of Ancient Egypt to represent 'Potential' or 'Becoming'), it also has symbolic links with the varied processes of Ascension – and to the fifth Element of ether and the Forces that lead to Creation and Manifestation, making it a useful champion to aid and support all projects involving new beginnings and/or structured plans for personal and spiritual growth."

Smiling, Gabriel affirms that White Selenite may therefore help you reconnect with the pure Essence of your First Birth, by shining a Light that has the power to illuminate the true heart of all you are.... taking your hand, he adds that you may find it educational to observe how young children and animals spontaneously and artlessly play and interact with those that share their world; and reminds you that your child-self – your inner-child; your child within – is with you throughout *all* your lifetimes: thus, if you discard your burdens, cares, worries and woes and allow yourself to rekindle your state of childlike innocence, you will understand how to live joyfully in the moment. Stressing that *this* is your true birthright, he adds that cherishing your child within (who is intrinsically kind, gentle and free) can show you how to live life more simply – knowing how to find joy in even the smallest of things, and enabling you to see everything you strive to own, be or do from a less worldly perspective, which may help you determine its true use or value.

The Greenwood Guardians – Hornbeam and Horse Chestnut:

His *personal* mentoring complete for now, Gabriel affirms he is always available to aid and support you: you need only bring him to mind and ask for his presence, and he will attend you. Furthermore, he tells you that two great Tree Beings of the Plant Kingdom have also asked to support you in addressing his Theme of 'JOYFUL JOURNEYS', adding that you need only request *their* presence, and they will be with you.

He explains that the first of these Greenwood Guardians is the unified (Masculine and Feminine) essence of Hornbeam, who has asked to overlight and help you ground whatever work you undertake within *any* aspect of his chapter. The second is the Masculine essence of Horse Chestnut, who has specifically asked to help you understand and assimilate his Gift of The Crystal-clear Flame of First Consciousness (if you have chosen to accept it).

When you are ready to connect with Gabriel's first Greenwood Guardian, you need simply call for the presence of **Hornbeam** (*) .... Hornbeam surrounds your aura in a citrine-yellow Light whilst filling your energy field with purple Light, and the unified Masculine and Feminine spirit essence of Hornbeam speaks to you, saying:

> *"As I draw upon the ancient wisdoms of the Earth, I project my consciousness out to the Cosmos, knowing that the stars still shine for me, whether it be night or day. Thus, the blessings of the deep dark earth, and the pure transparency of her waters, each fill and empower every fibre of my being, giving me the clarity to hold myself in perfect balance – always in tune with the movements of the planets, and in harmony with the heartbeat of the Earth. In my Soul I know both spiritual and intellectual wisdom and reason, aligned with the perfection of the Plan that oversees All That Is: so stand with me now, for it is my joy and my honour to share this with you, giving willingly of both my inner peace and my outer strength to keep you tranquil and calm whilst the turbulence of human life spirals all around us.... And then, like me, you may learn to draw upon the Purity and Power of the Earth's Inner-Light to align yourself to the wonders and forces of Creation – and so keep every aspect of your Spirit in a state of balanced Truth. Then you may, in your turn, share the peace and joy your find with any who seek out your comfort and your aid...."*

(* Ametrine will help you ground and connect with the energies and wisdom of Hornbeam, if you wish to enhance your experience using crystals.)

If you have chosen to accept and work with Gabriel's Gift, and when you are ready to connect with his second Greenwood Guardian, you need simply call for the presence of **Horse Chestnut** (*) .... Horse Chestnut envelops you in an intense white Light, and the Masculine spirit essence of Horse Chestnut speaks to you, saying:

> *"When daylight fades from all that is around me, I remain resolute in my knowing that I have been filled with the absolute Light of the Divine Sun, which spills from my heart to light your way in the darkness.... I know too that, throughout those dark hours before daybreak, I am always held and sustained by the purity and love of The Divine Mother, who blesses me with the gifts that enable me to know and share the innocent joy of first breath.... Thus, as you share the sweetness of my seeds that offer the Power that fires your Soul, know that my power, passion and strength are always here for you – to fire and inspire all that you are, and help you persevere in your personal testament that endeavours to embrace hope and joy, regardless of what assails you.... So stand with me, and BE at all times held in a gentle state of Grace that has the power to clarify, heal and refresh your body, mind and Soul – giving you the ability to fill yourself with the innocence and love that will allow you to shine like a diamond in the night...."*

(* White Selenite will help you ground and connect with the energies and wisdom of Horse Chestnut, if you wish to enhance your experience using crystals.)

ARCHANGEL URIEL

'CREATE WHAT YOU DESIRE'

CRYSTAL CHAMPIONS:

Amber ♥ Green Jade ♥ Red Jasper

CREATURE COMPANIONS:

Phoenix ♥ Swan ♥ Spider

GREENWOOD GUARDIANS:

Mulberry ♥ Sycamore

*I create my reality in every moment,
and align myself with infinite abundance.
I choose to grow with positivity and grace.*

MEETING URIEL

It is a cool morning in late autumn, and you find yourself on a stony pathway halfway up a wild and windy mountainside. In front of you the trail climbs onwards and upwards, following a series of steep slopes and shallow steps that have been roughly cut into the flanks of the stark grey granite; whilst behind you the path snakes downwards in a series of vertiginous switchbacks, which vanish into a steep-sided valley that is densely wooded with blue-green cedar trees. Although it is getting colder you know that you have to continue climbing, and so you turn and move steadily onwards, one step at a time.... After climbing a little further, you are dismayed to find a few flakes of snow swirling around you: then *more* snow starts to fall – softly and gently at first, then with escalating strength, until everything around you is completely obscured in a disorientating blizzard of whirling white. Unsure of the path, you are frightened to move – yet you are equally afraid of staying still, for you are slowly but surely becoming chilled to the bone. So – feeling desperate – you cry out for help, even though you are doubtful that anyone will hear you.... then suddenly, and miraculously, you hear the sound of a dog baying in the distance, and so call out again and again....

To your relief a large and dense-coated Saint Bernard dog eventually emerges from the heart of the snowstorm and forges a path to your side. He is wearing a strong harness around his shoulders to which a large bundle is fastened – and assuming this is for you, you unwrap it as quickly as your increasingly numb fingers will allow.... Inside you find a long thick hooded cloak, a large pair of sheepskin-lined gloves, and a flask of clear liquid: hurriedly you don the cloak, drink a little of the restorative waters, and – thankful to feel warmer and stronger – put on the gloves and take a firm grip on the dog's harness, trusting he will guide you safely to your destination. Unconcerned by the whiteout the dog turns and pads confidently away – and, trudging at his side, you follow....

It seems as if your journey will never end, but eventually the incline levels out; the snowstorm abates; and the skies clear – revealing that you have arrived at a deep ledge that is partially sheltered by a rocky outcrop, over which the mountain towers to a peak in a near-vertical wall of dark grey striated rock. Tugging you forwards, the dog leads you towards a narrow wedge-shaped opening in the rock face, beyond which all seems dark: even so, he does not hesitate; and so you follow him through the opening and allow him to lead you a little further – glad to have finally reached some sort of shelter. Although you can see nothing, you can hear the soft plinks of slowly dripping water echoing all about you; and you sense that the space beyond is vast and deep: then, with a satisfied 'woof' the dog halts and sits at your feet. You are thankful for his reassuring presence as your eyes slowly adjust – then all of a sudden the inky darkness is pierced by a dazzlingly bright light emerging from the depths of the blackness beyond....

As this light approaches, your vision slowly adjusts – revealing the source of the light to be a tall figure seemingly cloaked in brilliant white Light: this is Archangel Uriel. He has long and gloriously luminous snow-white wings that are folded to frame his body, arching over his head and sweeping the ground around his feet like a long feathered cloak – the intensity of their light clearly illuminating his features as he draws closer, and revealing a face that bears the marks of age and noble wisdom. As he comes to a halt in front of you, Uriel stoops and removes the dog's harness, thanking him for his aid; and, with a low gruff bark in acknowledgement, the Saint Bernard shakes out his fur and pads silently off into the darkness. Uriel then steps forwards and greets you with a welcoming smile, declaring:

> *"I am Uriel, Keeper of the Flames of Resurrection and Rebirth, Architect of the Divine Light, and twin flame of Rainbow Aurora, the Lady Grace. Well met, my friend! You have been safely guided here to learn and understand much: for here, within this place that resonates with the heartbeat of the Earth, may be found many wonders and delights, such as might feed the Spirit and comfort the Soul – thus satisfying all inner needs and desires. So follow me, and let us rest awhile in peace whilst the fires of my consuming passion for the eternal Love and Light of The Divine surround and envelop you in their transformative yet tender embrace – for thus you may come to realise and appreciate the myriad secrets that are hidden within the sacred darkness of the Earth; and recognise too the rewards of exploring your own hidden depths, wherein lies the glorious gem of your Inner Light, which radiates such brilliance that it outshines even the diamond herself!"*

Then, asking you to accompany him, Uriel leads you deeper into the cavern....

Together you follow a winding path that has been worn smooth by the forces of nature over many hundreds of years, passing soaring pillars and hanging curtains of creamy calcite, which have formed in breathtaking arrays of stalagmites and stalactites. Their waxy surfaces seem to absorb Uriel's light as you pass, so that they glow with a luminosity that illuminates the space all around you, helping you find your way with more ease and enabling you to see into the nooks and crannies of the cavern's walls – many of which are crammed with clusters of quartz crystals: interestingly, each cluster emits a different coloured light, bathing you in a rainbow of colour that strengthens and warms you as you pass.

Eventually you reach the far end of the cavern, and here Uriel pauses: then, at a gesture of his hand, a low arched opening materialises in the wall, revealing that there is a large octagonal-shaped chamber beyond. As you step within, you are vaguely aware of the opening closing behind you – but your attention is on the generous central hearth and the wide rose-gold bowl that graces it, which is crammed with masses of tiny gold and scarlet flames. This is obviously the focal point of the chamber, as there are eight chairs spaced around it – each of which has been polished from a huge hexagonal ruby crystal that glows with a deep crimson inner fire. The chamber itself has been hewn from the mountain's granite core with great precision, its graphite-grey surfaces all polished to a matte-black sheen and bare of any ornamentation – apart from the wall directly opposite you, where a polished disc of opalescent white quartz hangs in a simple silver frame.

Gesturing to the ruby chairs, Uriel invites you to warm yourself by the fire whilst you take a little time to examine him more closely and become accustomed to his energies. Folding his wings closer to his body, he then settles on the chair beside you, stretching out his legs and loosely crossing his ankles as he does so: this reveals a pair of ruby-beaded leather moccasins that are laced snugly around his feet and lower legs – and realisation slowly dawns as you take note of his high angular cheekbones, deeply lined mahogany-coloured skin and hawk-like face with its prominent aquiline nose, which are all classic features of a Native American elder: moreover, his starkly sculptured face is typically framed by straight black shoulder-length hair, which is parted in the centre and bound with leather thongs to either side of his face. The smallest of smiles passes over Uriel's face as he notes your understanding – then, as his gaze meets yours and calmly regards you, you find yourself being drawn into the depths of his chestnut-brown eyes; and you feel the steadfast strength of his deep and abiding love for the Earth and *all* sentient life (including yourself): and at this your heart slowly opens and expands – enabling you to connect with him on an even deeper level.

Once he senses your acceptance, Uriel releases your gaze, freeing you to study his attire. This comprises a very plain and simple full-length white linen robe that has a closely-fitting round neckline and long wide sleeves that hang past his wrists; and a wide oxblood-red sash woven from raw silk: this wraps twice round his waist and knots behind him, its colour somewhat relieving the starkness of the robe. A large gold ring has been threaded onto the sash, securing a bunch of old-fashioned keys (each of which appears to be made of a different type of metal) over his right hip; whilst a rolled scroll of creamy parchment with a brown-and-white goose-feather quill (tied together with a gold ribbon) is tucked through the sash on his left side.

Your scrutiny ends at the hollow just below Uriel's right collarbone, where his only visible personal adornment (a brooch holding a large and perfect diamond, which is the gem that links him with Rainbow Aurora, his twin flame) has been pinned. The diamond has been cut and faceted into an octagonal shape, and is mounted in a solid gold setting crafted to resemble the foot of a phoenix, whose talons are grasping the gem and holding it securely in place.

URIEL'S TEACHINGS
The Sacred Flames of Resurrection and Rebirth:

With a smile, Uriel takes your hand and asks you to look into his eyes again: as you do so, you feel and *know* his spiritual strength and steadfastness – and a tranquil peace envelops you, clarifying your thoughts and calming your emotions..... As he senses you relax, Uriel reminds you that every trial and difficult situation you undergo is another opportunity to learn and grow – for, just as iron is tempered within the fires of a forge, every time you brave the fires of tribulation and suffering you will emerge from those experiences stronger and wiser. With another smile, he reminds you that being ready and willing to undertake, embrace and learn from everything that physical life has to teach you helps you acquire wisdom and understanding, enabling you to practise and perfect the art of self-mastery, and (ultimately) transform yourself into a Being of absolute and unlimited Consciousness.

Releasing your hand, Uriel gestures at the fire burning in the hearth and tells you that what you see are the Flames of Resurrection. He explains that these blend the Ruby and Gold Rays together as One, thus focusing the power of Divine Love through the wisdom of Divine Mind: the former supplying the munificent strength that understands and knows the paramount needs for perfect evolution; the latter knowing the precise and optimum parameters required to structure something so that it is unequivocally fit for purpose. Uriel emphasises that the transformative fire of the Resurrection Flames is a Sacred gift, given that through loss may come renewal.... that through death may come life.... and that through each simple, yet courageous, act of sacrifice or surrender may come something better – something greater: at this the fire flares up into a towering mass of deep crimson flames flecked with gold – and Uriel tells you that opening yourself to (and accepting) their power will allow you to truly *know* understanding, growth and evolution – and ultimately completeness....

He then plucks a single flame from the fiery mass and shows it to you, enabling you to see that (interestingly) it looks more like a feather than a tongue of fire – and as you reflect on this, Uriel very gently touches the feathery flame to your brow chakra; and asks you to bring to mind *any* doubts or fears you have that hold you back, or prevent you from moving forwards in your life....

As you consider his words, Uriel asks you to have the courage to surrender and let go of whatever you identify (consciously or subconsciously) – and as you ready yourself to do as he asks, you know that the flaming feather is being effortlessly absorbed into your mind.... Gradually you allow yourself to surrender to its power – and as you do so, you feel all self-doubt and fears about your abilities and about your future being somehow lifted from you; and your mind clarifies and slowly comes into a new state of positivity and balance....

Reaching out again, Uriel plucks a second feathery flame from the bowl: this time he gently touches it to your heart chakra, asking that you now look into your heart to recognise and see *anything* that stops you from giving or receiving love, or prevents you from allowing others close enough to see or know the real (and true) you....

As you ponder this, Uriel asks you to again have the courage to surrender and release whatever you identify (consciously or subconsciously) – and as you prepare yourself to do as he asks, you know that the flaming feather is being effortlessly absorbed into your heart.... Gradually you allow yourself to surrender to its power – and as you do so, you feel all your fears of rejection being removed; and your heart slowly opens to embrace a new reality of infinite love and compassion....

Reaching out for a third and final time, Uriel plucks a last feathery flame from the bowl: he gently touches this one to your solar plexus chakra, and asks that this time you examine your sense of Self, and look at how, where and why *any* lack of self-confidence, self-esteem or self-worth causes you to hold yourself back, or not fully value yourself....

As you consider this, Uriel asks that you once more have the courage to surrender and release whatever you identify (consciously or subconsciously) – and as you ready yourself to do as he asks, you know that the flaming feather is being effortlessly absorbed into your Hara centre.... Gradually you allow yourself to surrender to its power – and as you do so, you feel your mind, emotions and spirit align and your confidence rise; and as positive beliefs about yourself gradually take precedence, you are finally able to see and acknowledge your true worth....

Recognising the shifts that have now taken place within you, Uriel takes your hands and holds your gaze, saying:

"You now understand how the Resurrection Flames aid and support all acts of sacrifice or surrender, bringing you the opportunity to live anew by stripping away what, in truth, does not serve you. Some of your life experiences may have put you through the fire: but I hope that you now know you may either choose to fear the fire and its pains (and do all you can to avoid it) or simply trust and accept it – joyously accepting the cleansing actions of the flames and revelling in their transformative power, which will enable you to arise renewed, refreshed, and restored."

Then, satisfied that you have understood, Uriel releases you from his hold – and, still looking deep into your eyes, adds that he may also make his presence felt if (for any reason) you stray from your true Path and there is a need to illuminate the Truth, saying:

"Know that then my presence will Light every fibre of your Being, re-empowering you with the vibrant Flames of Resurrection and the remembrance of your immortality. Remember: Free Will is like fire – tamed it may be your finest servant; wild it may be your greatest enemy. For it is only when you make your choices with full and complete understanding – knowing the consequences of ALL – that your choices will be wise."

Releasing your gaze Uriel sits back, stares into the fire and gives a soft whistle.... at this the flames die back, and a large hawk-like bird with unusual fiery orange, gold and red plumage and a long plumed tail emerges from within the fiery depths. He flies to perch on Uriel's shoulder, and regards you with bright and intelligent eyes as Uriel explains that this legendary bird is a phoenix, who embodies both the light of the physical Sun that lies at the heart of the solar system *and* the Light of the spiritual Sun that lies at the heart of the Universe (which guides and directs All That IS). He chuckles as he points out that a phoenix powerfully demonstrates the lesson of rebirth through fire, whereby the flames that consume it leave an egg of potential within its ashes, which will then hatch to begin life anew. Suddenly, the bird gives a soft call and flutters over to sit on your shoulder.... you are surprised to feel that it is surprisingly light and that it gives off a gentle, yet warming, heat – at which Uriel laughingly remarks that fire always burns at the heart of a phoenix! With a smile, he tells you that this fire has the power to heal the root of all ills: hence, you may ask **Phoenix** to bring its gift of healing to you – *if* you are truly willing to accept it. He explains that, once requested, you simply need to hold out your hand to catch the droplet of fire the phoenix will produce for you; and then simply use or apply it *anywhere* you sense it needs to be used within your physical body and/or subtle energy Bodies. Uriel emphasises that Phoenix is always happy to answer your call if you need his aid to heal your body, mind or spirit; and/or to help you identify and address the root cause of any issues that are affecting (or interfering with) your balance or health in any way. He adds that you may also choose to call Phoenix whenever you need aid or support to make a transition from one state to another (including moving on from your physical body); or to mentor you when you are undertaking work that involves a fundamental change; or if you need the courage, impetus or determination to overcome difficulties or obstacles; or if it is time to identify and transform *anything* that is stopping you from achieving whatever you wish to do – or becoming whatever you wish to be.

Giving a last soft call, the phoenix leaves your shoulder and flies back to the fire, where he vanishes into the flames – dropping a shiny orange droplet in Uriel's lap as he passes, which immediately solidifies into a light waxy stone that is a clear golden-orange in colour. Uriel chuckles and gives this to you, saying that this is **Amber**, his first Crystal Champion – explaining:

> *"Amber is one of the foods that may be consumed by the phoenix, for as fossilised tree resin it contains the essence of the Light and Power of the Sun. Thus, Amber carries energies that are both warming and healing, and which have cleansing and purifying properties that may be used to clear, transform and increase the resonance of any of your subtle energy centres or Bodies – especially those directly connected with your physical body and your mind and emotions. Amber has a comforting presence that is both loving and reassuring, and so is useful to hold (or wear) if you are suffering from a lack of love or comfort in your life. You may also find Amber to be especially supportive if you are recovering from an illness, or are feeling tired or energetically low, when it can provide a powerful, yet stable, source of easily accessible energy. Through its resonance with the trees from which it was born Amber also offers a connection to the ancient knowledge and wisdoms of the Earth and the natural world, which may aid in your understanding and healing, and support you in becoming more securely rooted. Amber may appear in various colours – the green form being particularly healing and balancing; the red form being very grounding and energising. However, this golden-orange form resonates with the Gold and Orange Rays, and so can powerfully facilitate and support all acts of self-knowledge and self-transformation by imparting, inspiring and strengthening your wisdom, courage, determination and perseverance."*

Smiling, Uriel affirms that Amber may therefore help you start to shape your future, by supporting you in freeing yourself of any negative conditioning or influences that might otherwise hinder your progress; and by aiding you in addressing anything that might be preventing you from growing and evolving – especially if any aspect of your life is out of step with your Divine plan and/or is affecting your physical, mental or emotional well-being or balance.

The Keys of Understanding and The Scroll of Akasha:
Settling back in his chair, Uriel takes out the parchment scroll that was tucked through his sash, and holds it out to you on the palm of his right hand, the thumb and index finger of which are heavily stained with black ink. He explains that this scroll keeps an account of all the lessons you have already learnt and mastered in this and other lifetimes and existences; and holds a record of everything your Soul has expressed a desire to know and understand, both now *and* in the future: accordingly, it is the means by which your Higher-self records all your achievements and maps your potentials, enabling you to plan and review the options and opportunities that will allow you to gain the maximum benefit from all your embodiments. Gently tapping the scroll Uriel emphasises that it is *you* who is fully and solely responsible for planning and directing your own life – and it is *you* who pens the sacred records held within your scroll (albeit under the guidance of your Soul and with the scrutiny of Angelic overseers like himself). Ensuring the ribbon securing the scroll and its quill is in place, Uriel tucks it away again, adding that the scroll also forms what is known as an Akashic Record, for it meticulously

(and honestly) records details of all karmic debts owed and due. With a smile, he says that these are factors your Higher-self takes into account when planning and determining your life experiences – hence owning responsibility (and being accountable) for all your actions is vital, if you truly wish to progress towards absolute self-mastery.

Getting to his feet, Uriel strolls over to one of the matte-black walls of the chamber and touches it lightly with his hand: at his touch the wall turns white, and begins to emit hundreds of tiny beams of light.... slowly these coalesce, creating a transparent three-dimensional map of a human form with its etheric energy structures highlighted in strands of electric-blue light, a bit like an architectural blueprint. Pointing to the conical energy centre that extends downwards from the base of the spine, Uriel tells you that this is the base (or root) chakra of the human energy Body, whose primary focus is physical and bodily survival and fundamental material existence; but which also encompasses the ability to manifest and meet all personal needs. He explains that it is through this energy centre that humans construct their reality: but in order to do so effectively, they must be ready and willing to accept *and* impose both limitations and discipline. This is because *without* boundaries an idea, thought or concept cannot be contained – and if it is not contained, it cannot materialise or take form.

Uriel stresses that, nonetheless, it is perfectly possible to manifest anything you desire, *as long as* you give it the boundaries that will allow it to have substance: this means having a very clear understanding of exactly what it is (and what it entails); taking time to clearly focus on and very precisely identify everything you need to do (or have in place) in order to achieve it; and then (drawing upon your aforementioned knowledge) planning clearly and mindfully the steps required to bring it about. With a smile, he remarks that without self-discipline it is very easy to focus on (and as a consequence manifest) the things you don't want, instead of the things you do (!): the *key* is to clearly understand the difference between what you have already got; what you *think* you 'want'; and what you *actually* 'need'.

Returning to your side, Uriel says that he is a Keeper of the Keys of Understanding, which have the power to open and unlock many doors – some of which conceal secrets or 'hidden treasures' that are (as yet) not known or understood. Detaching the bunch of keys from his sash, he tells you that these are the ones he has determined to be relevant for your needs at this time; and invites you to select one – advising you to seek out one that resonates particularly well with your base chakra, explaining:

> *"The key you choose will help you understand or master something important for you to know at this time. It may unlock a tool to help you change or create something as you grow and progress; it may disclose a map or plan for the next steps of your journey; or it may reveal a guide that will help you understand your spiritual and physical needs at this time: but whatever key you select, it will be pertinent and relevant for you now."*

Once you have chosen the right key, you will find that it slips easily from his key-ring.... as it does, Uriel suggests that you put it somewhere safe until you have time to examine it properly – reminding you that its colour, shape and form will have symbolic significance, the defining of which may help you determine your true desires; identify what resonates with your heart and Soul; and/or unlock a door that will show you the way forwards.

Returning the remaining keys to his sash, Uriel emphasises that inward reflection is a vital part of understanding the key you have chosen – for you have already learnt that it is the desires of your Higher-self that define your path, and hence your life can only truly flow when you move *in accordance with* the desires of your Soul. Asking you to join him, Uriel walks over to the wall that bears the silver-framed plaque, and invites you to look closely at the disc of opalescent white quartz that it holds.... as you step forwards its surface shimmers, revealing a delicate etching that depicts a swan floating serenely on the surface of a tranquil lake. With a gentle smile, Uriel reverently touches his fingers to the head of the swan – and, at his touch, the plaque and the wall slowly dissolve into nothingness; and reveal the presence of another cavern beyond....

This cavern is filled with a soft white light that illuminates a wide underground lake set beneath a drusy canopy of iridescent white quartz crystals glimmering with a rainbow luminescence. A snow-white swan is resting in the centre of the lake, and as Uriel leads you to its shore, she glides across to greet you, leaving barely a ripple in her wake.... As she approaches, Uriel says that **Swan** exemplifies the Divine attribute of Grace, whereby the ego-self surrenders absolutely to The Divine (whose innate and perfect wisdom is, of course, *within* – and *not* above you!) He adds that 'Being in a state of Grace' can only come about if you have the courage to 'let go' and accept with absolute trust: yet Swan can and will guide and support you when you need to simply surrender to Divine Will, giving you the faith and patience to affirm and accept that all will happen if and when the time is right – for it is a (sometimes painful) fact that you waste more time and energy in struggling against the tide than you would expend by just giving in and going with the flow. Smiling again, he tells you that a great deal of stamina and strength lies beneath the surface of a swan's elegant serenity; whilst their loyalty and courage means they are very protective of their family: accordingly, Swan is a good choice of companion if you feel as if you are 'swimming against the tide' and need to boost your determination to carry on; or if you need to be the 'calm voice of reason' when dealing with family situations where there has been a rift or a split; or if you want to create a stronger sense of unity and purpose within *any* group, including family, friends and those with whom you work. Furthermore, because swans unwaveringly protect and defend their young, you may also call for Swan to guard you and those you care for when you are travelling; or to guide you through 'stormy waters' if you are journeying – alone or in a group, physically or etherically, within or without.

As the swan finally reaches the bank, Uriel kneels down and gently strokes her pure white wings (which are very like his own), and reminds you of the tale of the 'Ugly Duckling', which tells of a cygnet who hatched in a duck's nest, and (consequently) was perceived as 'different' and scorned and rejected by all he met, but who later grew into a beautiful white swan. He points out that Swan offers this tale as a metaphor for the magnificent transformation that is possible when you allow your life to be touched with the pure Light of The Divine, imbuing you with the gift of Grace that is your birthright, whilst providing a salutary reminder to never take anything at face value. With a smile, he adds that this includes learning to look beyond the surface in order to see the truth and beauty that IS in all things – and to have the courage to see your own glory within, which will grow and blossom as you learn to conquer all that you endure.

Noticing a glimmer of something green nestled in the downy feathers of the swan's back, Uriel reaches out and plucks up a small polished stone. Giving this to you, he tells you that this is a piece of **Green Jade**, his second Crystal Champion – explaining:

> *"Green Jade powerfully grounds the Green Ray, and is in harmony with all the realms of nature that can help you connect with the heart of the Earth: this will support you in being fully balanced and grounded as you seek out your truths, and aid you in taking positive action to bring your dearest hopes and desires to life. Green Jade is also very supportive to the heart centres, with a balancing energy that can offer your body, mind, emotions and spirit both healing and strength. It also has a simple honesty that can help you appreciate all the gifts that life brings,* whatever *form they take – and, in so doing, Green Jade encourages you to count your blessings, and recognise that the Universe is as magnificently abundant as you can accept it to be. Understand that it is only when you truly appreciate this for a fact that you will realise that limiting and destructive emotional reactions such as envy, greed, selfishness and jealousy have no place or value in your world (and so can choose to free yourself of them): then Green Jade will help you find heart-centred balance, showing and proving that freedom from such fears truly enables you to have and BE whatever you wish!"*

With a smile, Uriel affirms that Green Jade may therefore help you awaken to the infinite abundance of the Universe, and embrace the attribute of Grace in all you plan and do.

The Gift of The Divine Templates of Creation:

Getting to his feet, Uriel asks you to follow him to the far end of the lake, where two sets of stalactites and stalagmites have fused to create a pair of slender stone pillars. A large spider-web spans the gap between them, and you can see its maker (a black and white spider) sitting to one side of it: she is keeping her legs in contact with the delicate strands of spun silver that she has woven – and (drawing your attention to the multitude of fine hairs that cover her body and legs) Uriel explains that these enable her to perceive even the slightest of changes in the vibrations in her web and in the air around her: thus you may call upon **Spider** to teach you how to sense and interpret subtle changes in the energies around you, and so react quickly and appropriately to them; or to help you feel your way around obstacles, or navigate problematic situations with greater delicacy or dexterity; or if you would like to learn how to 'see' energy using your sense of touch or clairvoyant sight. Pointing out her eight legs and the figure-8 shape of her body, Uriel says that Spider is said to be a symbol of the Cosmic Order and Universal Unity that embraces Infinity: hence, you may ask Spider to teach you about the multidimensional workings and wisdoms of the Universe (material and/or ephemeral); or to advise you if you need help to determine what is 'real' and 'unreal' when journeying in meditation or in the world of dreams; or to help you identify, analyse and interpret thoughts, feelings and/or emotions with greater insight and accuracy. With a gentle movement of his hand, Uriel traces the web's framework of straight lines, and the spiral that connects them, and explains that Spider's affinity with the formation of the spiral (symbolising Universal Energy and the interconnectedness of all things), can help you acknowledge and integrate the *seemingly* disparate parts of your Self, showing you that in truth there is no such thing as past and future, but only the infinite NOW: furthermore, the perfection of the web tells him that Spider is a Master Weaver who understands the sacred geometry that underlies all Creation; and who understands the delicate art of bridging and balancing the myriad polarities that comprise that world – black and white, positive and negative, past and future, physicality and spirit. Smiling, Uriel adds that, perhaps most importantly, Spider's keyword is 'Create' (a theme very close to his heart!), and reminds you that, as the weaver of *your* web, *you* are the creator of your reality – hence you may also ask Spider to help you see the entire pattern of your 'web of life', so that you know if and how to change any parts of it that do not conform with what you truly desire.

Detaching the octagonal diamond from its setting on the breast of his robe, Uriel asks you to watch, and places it carefully in the very centre of the spider-web: sensing a change in the vibrations transmitted by its silver strands, the spider carefully approaches the diamond, and gently touches it with her long front legs.... after a few moments she begins to draw out strands of deep indigo-blue silk from the spinnerets on her belly – at which Uriel reclaims his diamond, restoring it to the clawed setting on his breast.

In the meantime the spider has begun to weave a new web on top of her silver one – starting by laying down a single circle at the centre, and then adding six more around that, creating seven circles in total.... as she weaves them together, Uriel tells you that she is outlining the Seed of Life – explaining that this sacred shape symbolises the beginning of Life, from which the Tree of Life (which directs the innate spiritual growth and natural evolution of all things) may take root, flourish and grow....

Meanwhile, the spider has laid down another six circles on the perimeter of the Seed of Life, creating thirteen circles in total.... and as she weaves them all together, Uriel explains that she is now outlining the Fruit of Life (which links all Dimensions of Consciousness; and symbolises the Way of Ascension through Illumined Awareness)....

Without pausing, the spider adds a further six circles to the perimeter of the pattern, and encloses it within two large concentric circles.... as she weaves these final ones into a single pattern, Uriel explains that she is completing the Flower of Life (which defines the Alpha and Omega, that IS both the beginning and the end of the Infinite Now; and which forms the matrix that defines all matter)....

After a short pause the spider begins to weave again – and you watch in amazement as she overlays the indigo-blue Flower of Life with a complex series of triangles, squares and pentagons; until (finally) she retreats to the edge of her silver web, having completed her task.... Thanking her, Uriel reaches out to carefully extract the indigo-blue web she has woven for him – and, lifting it to his lips, he exhales a gentle breath.... at this the web expands.... becomes three-dimensional.... and fills with a deep blue light....

Uriel explains that what you are looking at is known as 'Metatron's Matrix': this is the blueprint that holds the Divine multidimensional templates he has already spoken of, along with the five Platonic Solids (which define the building blocks of all creation) and the Star Tetrahedron of the Merkaba (which defines your Lightbody). Holding it up, he states that *this* is the foundation of the perfected patterns of Divine construction through which ALL things are made manifest – for it resonates with all the Cosmic and Universal

Forces and energies, and holds the blueprints for all that is, was and ever will be.

He then holds it to the diamond on his breast, at which it slowly shrinks down to the size of a ping-pong ball; and guides this carefully down through the centre of your pranic core, all the way to the root of your base chakra. Uriel then rests his hands lightly on your shoulders as your energy field adjusts its balance and absorbs his Gift, declaring:

> *"My Gift of The Divine Templates of Creation contains all the blueprints you could ever need or want, enabling you to create and make manifest all your wishes and desires as you grow and progress. For it holds the maps and plans that can help you form every single aspect of your journey (both now and in the future) as you return to Unity and to Source. Moreover, my Gift may help you more fully understand your Self and your place in the Universe – for it holds knowledge (both ancient and arcane) that defines and explains the mysteries of the Cosmos: hence it may require years of dedicated and focused study, if you are to fully understand even the smallest part; and must be used with consideration and discernment, if you are to truly know its value and worth...."*

Stepping back, Uriel reminds you that it is *always* possible to express and 'live' your spirituality in everyday life, thus demonstrating how matter, abundance and spirituality can (and should) coexist harmoniously. With a reassuring smile he tells you that he will always be there if you ask for help to master the sometimes painful business of living in the material world; and will be both your teacher and guide whenever you want his aid to design and plan your future with clarity and purpose.

Giving you a small chunk of an opaque brick-red stone, Uriel tells you that this is a piece of **Red Jasper**, his third Crystal Champion – explaining:

> *"Red Jasper contains a large amount of iron, whose deep red-orange is the life-blood of the Earth; and has a special affinity with the base chakra, which may aid you in connecting with (and understanding) my Gift. Although Red Jasper's resonance is not as high and fine as some crystals, it is a perfect companion when you need to keep your feet firmly on the ground and BE in the real world: remember, only those who are fully grounded to the Earth truly have the power to call-down and then clearly interpret and utilise the Higher knowledge that will enable them to change earthly-life for the better – for themselves and for others. Furthermore, because Red Jasper is aligned with the Fire at the heart of the planet (and hence to the Diamond at her core), this makes it a stable yet powerful means of increasing your energy, passion and zeal whilst you work upon any act of self-transformation – especially those that ask or require you to have the courage and determination to be proactive in making changes that you know in your heart you need to make, if you want to progress and BEcome the Star that you are."*

Smiling, Uriel affirms that Red Jasper may therefore help give you the courage and Will to unify matter and Spirit, so that your Light shines brightly upon everything you do as you work to make manifest the future you truly want and desire.

The Greenwood Guardians – Mulberry and Sycamore:

His *personal* mentoring complete for now, Uriel affirms he is always available to aid and support you: you need only bring him to mind and ask for his presence, and he will attend you. Furthermore, he tells you that two great Tree Beings of the Plant

Kingdom have also asked to support you in addressing his Theme of 'CREATE WHAT YOU DESIRE', adding that you need only request *their* presence, and they will be with you.

He explains that the first of these Greenwood Guardians is the Masculine essence of Mulberry, who has asked to overlight and help you ground whatever work you undertake within *any* aspect of his chapter. The second is the Masculine essence of Sycamore, who has specifically asked to help you understand and assimilate his Gift of The Divine Templates of Creation (if you have chosen to accept it).

When you are ready to connect with Uriel's first Greenwood Guardian, you need simply call for the presence of **Mulberry (*)** .... Mulberry envelops you in a silver-violet Light, and the Masculine spirit essence of Mulberry speaks to you, saying:

> *"My life is devoted to sustaining and maintaining the flow of energy that pervades the vessels and veins of the earth upon which I grow – and over countless lifetimes I have provided comfort and succour through my heart-shaped leaves, which allow those that spin the Web of Life to create with clarity and strength; and through the fruits of my flowers, which offer a bitter-sweet bounty that speaks of the pains and joys of existence. If you would stand with me I will show you the treasures of spiritual knowledge and understanding that are to be found within the canopies of stars that bless my resting places.... I will share with you my passion and zest for living, and show you how to burn away all that holds you back or prevents your undertakings from flowing with grace and ease.... and I will help you understand how to open your heart in order to balance and align your body, mind and spirit – that you too may become a Beacon for the Light that lies at the heart of ALL....."*

(* Bulls [red tiger] Eye and Hematite will help you ground and connect with the energies and wisdom of Mulberry, if you wish to enhance your experience using crystals.)

If you have chosen to accept and work with Uriel's Gift, and when you are ready to connect with his second Greenwood Guardian, you need simply call for the presence of **Sycamore** (*) .... Sycamore envelops you in a rippling gold Light, and the Masculine spirit essence of Sycamore speaks to you, saying:

> *"I am the masculine presence that is at the heart of the Dark side of Creation.... I am the presence that knows Unity, and understands the nature and essence of duality.... I am the one that constantly supports the Affirmative actions of The Divine Feminine, as she seeks to create new life and sustain evolutionary balance throughout the natural world.... Know then that I stand steadfast and upright throughout all that might beset me – so stand with me and lean against my trunk, and allow your body to feel the sanctuary and strength of my presence, whilst the essence of your Spirit learns to know and mirror my own... For All that I AM is Blessed and encompassed by the Divine Light that forms, enlivens and sustains the very fabric of life; and which has the wisdom to know (through the wonders of Creation) that ALL is Divine, and ALL is perfect in the moment – and* that *is the simple knowing that rules my heart, which I would share with you now, and always...."*

(* Natural Citrine will help you ground and connect with the energies and wisdom of Sycamore, if you wish to enhance your experience using crystals.)

ARCHEIA RAINBOW AURORA

'OPEN YOUR HEART'

CRYSTAL CHAMPIONS:

Morganite ♥ Preseli Bluestone ♥ Rainbow Aura Qtz

CREATURE COMPANIONS:

Snowy Owl ♥ Rose Dragon ♥ White Stag

GREENWOOD GUARDIANS:

Sycomore Fig ♥ Mimosa

*I open my heart,
and am as ONE
with the heartbeat of the Earth.*

MEETING RAINBOW AURORA:
You find yourself standing in pitch darkness, with no idea where you are – although you think you must be outdoors, for you somehow sense that there is open space around you, and you can feel the soft caress of a cool breeze on your skin. Despite the blackness you feel quite safe, although it seems wiser to stand still until you are more sure of your surroundings: so you simply close your eyes, extend your awareness, and listen.... At first you can only hear the whispers of leaves being stirred by the same swirling currents of air that brush your skin – but then, as you listen more carefully, you can just make out the soft tinkling sound of wind chimes toning in subtle harmonies, as they too are moved by the breeze....

After a while you decide to open your eyes, and find that you can just about see the outlines of what appear to be rocks and large rounded boulders; and can pick out the shadowy forms of branching trees and the delicate tracery of slender-stemmed foliage – all silhouetted against a graphite-grey sky. Gradually the darkness continues to lift, and as night gives way to day your surroundings acquire more and more definition – the deep intensity of the indigo sky above you fading into a soft blue-grey, and slowly filling with thin layers of silvery clouds highlighted with metallic streaks of copper and gold. As the light builds further, everything around you increasingly gains clarity and colour – finally revealing that you are standing at the entrance to a Japanese-style garden: this occupies a massive bowl-shaped hollow that has seemingly been scooped out of the surrounding landscape, which (in complete contrast) looks to be an arid wilderness of rock-strewn scrubland and steep-sided canyons, sparsely dotted with trees. Taking your attention back to your immediate surroundings, you see that you are standing at the end of a flagstone path edged with low rounded cobblestones: this circles the sloping sides of the garden in a smooth and seamless spiral – beginning where you stand at the rim, and culminating at the edge of a small lake, which occupies its centre. The waters of the lake are calm and still, their mirror-like surface reflecting the sky above – and you somehow know that this is where you need to go....

The garden is so tranquil that you feel no need to hurry, so you slowly wend your way towards the lake, taking time to absorb the simple beauty of your surroundings. The path flows with Zen-like order through raw ground that has been painstakingly planted with tall stands of slender bamboos and deep masses of arching grasses, bearing feathery seed-heads in multiple hues of bronze and gold; and past stunning lace-leaved red and copper ribbon-barked maples and low cedars and pines, whose deep green needle-clad branches have been meticulously clipped to resemble puffy layers of cloud. It also leads you through moss-clad rocky hollows, where simple sculptures reflect upon nature or the elemental world; and alongside open areas where solitary rocks and boulders sit in beds of white shingle, which have been painstakingly raked into clearly-defined patterns.

Eventually you reach the edge of the lake, where the path ends below a cedar-wood arch, which has two tall side pillars and an upward-arching lintel: a set of wind chimes made of waterfalls of crystal hangs at the centre of the arch – and as these are caught by the breeze they catch the rays of the rising sun, showering you in whirling rainbows of light; and their high sweet chimes ring out in perfect harmony. Then suddenly the chimes fall silent, and you hear the sound of footsteps: turning, you see a petite woman dressed in the style of a Japanese Geisha stepping gracefully towards you – this is Archeia Rainbow Aurora. She halts and bows to you in welcome, declaring:

"I am Rainbow Aurora, the Lady Grace – Revealer of the Universal Keys of Light, Guardian of the Divine Seal of Embedded Creation, and twin flame of Uriel. In the glow of my Light – there at dawn; there at sunset – I paint the world with the palette of Love, holding the balance of each day, each Life and each Soul cradled in the passion of my heart. All that I am I would share with you now, for all that I know is yours if you will but ask: so open your heart and – through the Grace of the outpourings of Divine Love and the pure arts of Creation – let the majesty and wonder that surrounds us fill you.... then simply allow yourself to find peace, secure in the knowledge that there is beauty in each new beginning – and *in each ending. For here we may enjoy the simple beauty of the natural world and all that adorns it, whilst I help you find the beauty and Grace within you, that it may flower to bathe your Soul in its Light and so set you free! For when you are at ease and aligned with the deepest desires of your heart and Soul thus will inner peace be borne, and you will find that the art of life is yours to master and enjoy: and then, as you revel in the beauty of whatsoever you create, so your Light will fall like rainbows upon the ground – Blessing ALL that it touches."*

With a gentle smile, Rainbow Aurora steps to your side, and – at a wave of her hand – a small circular island rises out of the lake, and a low arched cedar-wood bridge appears as if from nowhere, presenting you with a way onto the island. Asking you to accompany her, Rainbow Aurora steps through the arch and daintily crosses the bridge – and as you follow her, you realise that the perfect circle of the island has been paved in rounded cobbles to make a yin-yang symbol: one side is cobbled with white stones, and bears a large shallow bowl made of black granite in which a low fire is burning; the other side is cobbled with black stones, and bears a large shallow bowl made of white alabaster that is filled with crystal-clear water. An arching magnolia tree (in full and glorious bloom) stands on the S-shaped cusp of white and black in the very centre of both the symbol and the island – its trunk encircled by a bench that has been polished from a blue-grey stone that is flecked with white – and it is to this that Rainbow Aurora leads you....

Taking a seat and sitting gracefully erect, she neatly arranges her kimono and tucks her hands into her sleeves – inviting you to join her, so that you may examine her and become accustomed to her energies. In her guise as a Geisha, Rainbow Aurora's delicate heart-shaped face and long slender neck are painted chalk white; and, even though she appears to be quite young, her poise and composure suggests she is older and more worldly-wise than you might assume. Her silky jet-black hair is dressed in traditional 'kanzashi' style on top of her head, where it is secured by two long slender chopstick-like 'kogai' made of ebony and tipped with gold – its upswept form revealing a pair of small neat ears and the delicate nape of her neck, which is left bare of paint, enabling you to see that her skin is actually pale and smooth. Her elegant features are defined and painted in traditional fashion – her rosebud-shaped lips outlined in cherry-red; her dark ebony eyes outlined in black – and as she calmly surveys you, you sense that she is seeing deep within you, and know that nothing is hidden from her: recognising this, she gives you a gentle smile that implies she already understands a great deal about you, and that she is untroubled by what she knows.

Shifting your gaze to Rainbow Aurora's traditional wrap-around kimono, you see that it is made from a deep ruby-red silk that has been embroidered with tiny long-tailed birds: on closer inspection you recognise these to be phoenixes, and note how each has been delicately stitched in scarlet, gold, bronze and copper thread; and how each has tiny round faceted rubies for eyes. The edges of the kimono and the cuffs of the wide sleeves have been finished with deep bands of oxblood-red raw silk, which has also been used to fashion the wide sash that wraps tightly around her tiny waist, and ties in the traditional 'obi' (bow) in the small of her back.

Rainbow Aurora's tiny feet are just peeping out from beneath the draping hem of her kimono, enabling you to see that they are clad in a pair of traditional blocky 'geta': these are an unusual creamy colour and, noting your interest, she explains that they are made from ivory that was given to her by the elephants – adding that this was a great honour, for elephants bear the ancient wisdoms of all earth-dwelling creatures, and they have chosen to share this through the material that now supports and sustains her.

Lastly your gaze is drawn to Rainbow Aurora's only visible adornment – a fabulous pendant, which hangs from a fine gold chain so that it lies over her heart. The body of the pendant has been crafted in gold to resemble the foot of a phoenix, whose long claws are grasping a large octagonal cut and faceted diamond that is flashing with rainbow light: this is the gem that links her with Uriel, her twin flame.

RAINBOW AURORA'S TEACHINGS
The 'Tao' of the Open and Balanced Heart:

Once your inspection is complete, Rainbow Aurora gestures to the path that guided you through the garden, and explains that this represents the 'Tao': the indefinable 'way' that cannot be taught, but can only be experienced. She tells you that its spiralling route symbolises many things, including the perpetual movement of Universal Energy, which embraces and sustains all that you are in the world of physicality as it moves through the pranic core and chakras of your Linear Energy Body (and throughout the toroidal energy field of your Unified Energy Body). She adds that where you sit – here, at its heart – is the centre of the spiral that holds the balance between the Worlds of Spirit and Form; the point that bridges and connects the Higher and lower aspects of the individualised Self; and the place where duality and polarity are held in constant equilibrium, as signified by the image of the yin-yang – black at the heart of white; white at the heart of black. With a smile she says that *here* may be found the Divine Force that forms and inspires all things, sentient and non-sentient; and the Divine Power that regulates all natural processes, and promotes harmony and balance within and between opposing forces.

Reaching up to the magnolia tree that arches over you, Rainbow Aurora plucks a stem bearing a single flower that has just come into bloom.... She shows it to you so that you can see its perfect pale pink heart and magenta-pink pollen-bearing stamens, which are surrounded by a spiral of waxy white petals delicately veined with green, and tells you that this flower, her 'lily of the air', has many qualities in common with the calla lily and the amaryllis – and gently touches it to your crown: she then circles it over the front of your body to draw a spiral in the air that passes over, and links, your seven primary chakras (crown; base; brow; sacral; throat; solar plexus; heart).... Finishing at the centre of your chest, she touches the blossom to your heart chakra – at which your mind calms, and your thoughts settle and clarify.... you then feel your heart begin to open, gradually releasing ancient stresses and traumas that it has held within for so long; and bringing you to a place of centred contentment and peace....

In this moment you simply know that your body, heart, mind and spirit are joined as one in perfect balance, harmony and accord – freed to act and BE at ease.... you know too that, in *this* state, you are able to see things that trouble you more clearly, enabling you to understand their true value and purpose so that you may release whatever you do not need to bear – and assimilate and enjoy what serves you well....

Recognising what you are feeling, Rainbow Aurora allows you time to process what you need to, explaining that an open and unburdened heart enables profound connections to be made between your Earthly and Spiritual Selves, because your heart is your centre of balance: thus the *clearer* your heart chakra is, the clearer your link with your Higher-selves will be; the *stronger* your heart chakra is, the stronger your grounding to your lower-self and the Earth will be – both of which will enable you to identify and address any decisions or choices you need to make more clearly and effectively.... Giving you the magnolia blossom, Rainbow Aurora then retakes her seat at your side, adding that having a whole and balanced heart will then help you more plainly see and evaluate the potential consequences and effects of the decisions or choices you are considering – for yourself, for others *and* for the world.

Sitting back, Rainbow Aurora gestures at her attire and tells you that a 'Geisha' acquires the esteemed qualities of grace and serenity as a consequence of hard work and discipline, spending many years studying and mastering a wide range of skills and accomplishments in the spheres of music, dance, entertainment, art and conversation – many of which take a ritual form: hence all their aspects have to be carefully learnt, and must be executed in a very precise and disciplined way. Suddenly the garden blurs – and you see a theatre stage that is filled with rows of ballerinas dancing a piece from 'Swan Lake': then (just as quickly) the scene vanishes – and the garden is there again. Rainbow Aurora tells you that this ballet not only exemplifies the complex nature of the world of duality, but is also one of the most physically demanding to perform. She stresses that the extreme fitness and flexibility required can only be met through years of single-minded determination and disciplined practise – often entailing great physical hardship and pain: yet the audience sees only the poise, grace and elegance and the evocative creation that is the result. Smiling, she adds that it would therefore be wrong to assume that 'living' in serene and constant balance is easy – for you can only truly 'be in the flow', knowing instinctively why, when and how to act, when you are open and aligned with the Tao on *all* levels (and thus fully in tune with the Universe): yet *when* you succeed you will know that it has been worth every hard-won moment – for at this point Universal Energy flows without restraint, bringing the perfect clarity, infinite inspiration and boundless vitality that will enhance your creativity and make all constructive endeavours possible.

Although it doesn't seem possible that you have been here all day, all colour around you suddenly fades – and as dusk falls, a large broad-winged owl appears on the horizon and ghosts over the garden to perch on the bench at your side. The owl's face and breast are pure white, whilst her wings and back are barred with black spots; and as it surveys you with bright yellow eyes, Rainbow Aurora chuckles and tells you that this is a snowy owl. She adds that the snowy owl symbolises wise and pure knowledge, and is extremely patient – understanding how to judge when the time is right to move, or stay still: hence you might call upon the wisdom of **Snowy Owl** to show you the prudence of conserving your skills and energies until they are truly needed; or to teach you the art of perfect timing; or to help you find your centre and acquire the stillness that will enable you to link more clearly with your intuition and Inner knowing (and/or other reliable sources of Higher guidance). Drawing your attention to the owl's markings, Rainbow Aurora tells you that Snowy Owl also understands the nature of polarity, and can also aid you in identifying those polar aspects of your thoughts and emotions that require your acceptance or reconciliation, in order that you may know and love yourself fully and completely. Pointing towards the owl's large black talons, which are just visible under its densely-feathered legs, she adds that snowy owls are fiercely protective of their family – yet understand that *real* strength is never hurtful, harsh, overbearing or forceful; but is loving, gentle, honest and true: thus if you need to understand how to be open-hearted *and* strong (particularly in tricky situations that involve interpersonal relationships of any kind) Snowy Owl will always answer your call. Suddenly the owl takes to the air and flies away as swiftly and silently as it arrived – and, watching it go, Rainbow Aurora remarks upon how, despite their apparent bulky and cumbersome size, snowy owls have an effortless and majestic elegance: therefore Snowy Owl may show you how to move quickly and stealthily if you need to do or achieve something without drawing unwanted attention to yourself; or teach you how to move through life with greater ease and flow, whilst recognising and appreciating the intrinsic grace and elegance that is at the heart of everything and everyone – including yourself.

As the owl disappears over the horizon dusk becomes day once more, and all colour returns to the garden: indicating the place where the owl was perched, Rainbow Aurora invites you to take the pale pink transparent crystal that the owl has left for you, telling you that this is **Morganite**, her first Crystal Champion – explaining:

"Morganite is a pale pink form of the Emerald. It carries the Pink Rays of Divine Love and Compassion that can intensely, yet lovingly, clear you of anything that is not of that same frequency: as a result, Morganite can help you release burdens and heal traumas and pain (particularly those connected with an abusive or soured relationship) where a lack of understanding concerning the fundamental and true nature of love (and/or an abuse of power) has led to damage, dis-ease or disorder. You may also find that, in the process of healing such wounds, you will be attuned to Morganite's innate vibration of compassionate action, which may promote the review and resolution of even older karmic issues, enabling and allowing a positive and effective spiral of spiritual growth and refinement to ignite. Morganite also resonates powerfully with the Angelic Realms, ensuring that their love and support is always present whenever you use it – which can

facilitate profound spiritual healing that will benefit not only you, but also those around you – and the planet on which you dwell: although this may require you to undertake a programme of deep inner work, you may be assured that Morganite's gentle strength will provide the courage and motivation you need; whilst illuminating (and reminding you of) the enduring state of heart-centred equilibrium and inner peace that is your ultimate goal."

With a smile Rainbow Aurora affirms that Morganite may therefore help you to open and clarify your heart, *and* support you in gaining the focus that will allow you to extend the art and practice of healing and balance to embrace *all* of your chakras and energy centres.

The Seal of Embedded Creation and The Dragons of the Rainbow Realm:

Opening her arms as if to embrace her garden, Rainbow Aurora tells you that everything you see around you, from the smallest leaf on a tree to the sun in the sky, has been created in accordance with Divine Law – and upon very specific geometries that embrace many things, including number, shape and form. She stresses that this applies to *everything* that has been naturally created; adding that even the colours and patterns you see in nature have both purpose and design. Revealing that her role includes embellishing the fundamental design of all that is created, Rainbow Aurora smiles and asks you to imagine the fun to be had in giving definition, pattern and colour to something like a butterfly or a flower, whilst simultaneously envisaging and understanding how to augment its innately perfect design and construction so that it is absolutely fit for purpose. She muses that, just as the hard work and effort behind every artistic endeavour is often unrecognised, so too it is with the wonders of the natural world – adding that taking time to *really* see and sense every detail of the world around you, whilst being both physically and intuitively open and aware, may teach you a great deal!

Asking you to relax with your eyes closed, Rainbow Aurora directs you to focus on your base chakra, and connect with the stone of the bench beneath you.... and then focus on your Earth Star chakra, expanding it so that it connects securely with the earth beneath your feet.... She now asks you to imagine that your feet have roots like those of a giant oak, and allow them to extend and grow, as if they are seeking out the nourishment deep within the ground....

When she is satisfied that you are well-rooted, Rainbow Aurora asks you to open your mind, and allow yourself to sense the heartbeat and pulse of the Earth – *knowing* her life-force and accepting that she, too, has sentience and Spirit....

Once she is happy that you have made that connection, Rainbow Aurora asks you to open your heart, and allow yourself to feel the heart and essence of the Earth embracing you in return – *knowing* her love and accepting that she, too, has wisdom and Soul....

After a while, Rainbow Aurora asks you to simply allow your energy field to BE in whatever balance is right for you now, using your connection with the consciousness of the Earth to establish the state that best meets your needs at this time – commenting that creating a solid foundation in this way will help you understand much about structure, stability and balance; and allow you to benefit from what this understanding might bring.

Once she is happy you have reached equilibrium, Rainbow Aurora tells you to open your eyes: reaching into a small pouch secreted beneath her sash, she brings out an object that looks like a stamp or a seal. Cupping it in her hands, she holds it out to show you that its top has been carved from deep-green jade in the form of a sleeping dragon, which lies curled (like a cat) atop a squat pillar of polished ebony. Tilting her hands, Rainbow Aurora shows you that the pillar has a circular cast-bronze disc affixed to its base that is embossed with the complex and sacred design known as 'Metatron's Matrix', which holds the blueprints from which all things are created and made manifest. Gently tapping the jade dragon, she remarks that a great deal of knowledge and understanding about the true nature and purpose of dragons has been lost over the ages: yet they are ancient and wise Masters of Creation, who were instrumental in the creation of many of the stars and planets – including Earth. With another smile, Rainbow Aurora reveals that the dragons oversee the fifth Element of ether (one of the fundamental Forces of the Universe that IS at the point at which Creation begins), and hence understand – and work with – *all* the Forces of creation and dissolution; and with the Elements and Elementals of earth, air, fire and water; *and* with the Divine Light in all its frequencies and forms. She stresses that dragons are therefore not simply creatures from ancient myths: indeed, those known as Master Dragons truly exist (although 'beyond' what you might understand as the Dimensional Planes), in a 'place' that she calls the Rainbow Realm – which IS within, without, and around *everything*.

Rainbow Aurora now gently strokes the back of the jade dragon – at which it stirs; looks you in the eye; and breathes out a soft fiery breath.... at this, you find your eyes begin to close; and you hear these words form in your mind:

"Our breath helped form the morning – for Dragon's breath is Sacred fire, and IS the Fire of Creation. Know that our breath can burn away all that is not truly of the Spirit, so that it may more easily be seen, and so that you may come to know and understand its Truth, when you are ready to see. For, just as we hold and guard the secrets of Creation, so we hold and guard the Seed of Light that lies at the heart of your Being: for we possess strength and knowledge that you do not, and we know paths you cannot see. Thus, we are your eyes and ears – and your strength when yours would fail...."

As these words resonate within your heart and mind, you open your eyes to find that the jade dragon is asleep again – and that there is now a large rose-pink dragon sitting in front of you! Noting your surprise Rainbow Aurora chuckles, and explains that there are many types of dragons – each of which may choose its form and colour according to the needs, energies and experience of the one with whom they wish to link: in this instance, the rose dragon has presented itself to you as her Creature Companion. Smiling, she says that it is probably best if **Rose Dragon** tells you directly how it may aid you – and, once again, you find your eyes closing; and hear these words form in your mind:

"I teach balance through the heart, which is the centre of your Being and at the still point of All, whence comes Life. Know that without Love at the heart of all Creation, nothing could exist. For it was through love that the impetus and desire for living was born; and it is through the finest and truest love (that which is freely given, without boundaries or conditions) that The Divine shows itself to BE at the heart of all that IS. Know too that I monitor and guide; measure and channel that Love, so that it is a part

of all things that exist. To some people (and in some things) it may be sorely hidden – buried from sight, shielded or restrained: yet at Unity it will be revealed for what it is; for Union and a return to Grace is not possible without opening and surrendering to the Love within. Remember: the Seed of Light that lies at the heart of your Being is eternal; and I hold it illuminated in my Fire, which has the power to burn away all that seeks to cloak or confine it. So let me offer you the guidance you truly wish for as you move onwards on your path, helping you understand that you always *have the choice to BE in your heart and let your inner fires and passions burn free – enabling you to connect to the heart of All, in freedom and in Love;* or *to turn aside and deny its existence – even though denial serves no purpose but to bind your Spirit, and delay the time when Unity and Peace may be found and known throughout all Times and all Dimensions...."*

Once again these words resonate within your heart and mind, and when you slowly open your eyes again, you find that the Rose Dragon has vanished.... Rainbow Aurora smiles, and warns you that you must have a clear and open heart and be prepared to work hard with integrity if you choose to call upon Rose Dragon (or *any* dragon for that matter); for dragons are demanding and exacting teachers who will not come to any who think to Master them without respecting and understanding their true Power and nature!

Giving you two stones (one a dark blue-grey, one a deep green-grey – each lightly speckled with creamy-white flecks), she tells you that these are both **Preseli Bluestone**, her second Crystal Champion – explaining:

"Preseli Bluestone recalls the Dragons who created the Earth and gave your ancestors life: thus, it may help you link with the Dragons whose spiritual Light still remains deep within the Earth in the Ancient grounds of its birth. Preseli Bluestone may also enable you to become more in tune with the natural world that surrounds you; and help you to connect with the nature spirits and Elementals that are native to different regions of the world – the blue-grey form aiding contact with those that are spiritually 'older and wiser'; the green-grey form with those that are more grounded and environmentally aware. Because Preseli Bluestone also carries the wisdom of the Dragon Masters who once worked with the etheric fabric of the Earth and the regulation and flow of her 'life-blood' by means of the ancient 'dragon lines' (leys) that were designed to maintain energy balance within the natural world, this stone may be of use to Earth-workers, Grail Knights and Shamans (who must *remain separate from their ego when initiating* any *work connected with the planet's etheric construction and/or spiritual evolution) by assisting them in clearing blockages – and/or in addressing and redressing energetic imbalances – that stifle the natural flow within those lines. In aeons long past Preseli Bluestone connected Earth to the Cosmos, acting to convey information and knowledge to and from the planet for the benefit of humankind and all sentient life: so too might it be used today by those whose hearts and minds are open and wise enough to know its Truths and its power – aiding all those who are without ego to clearly and accurately read, interpret and understand the histories and records that are held within standing stones, or other such ancient markers, that define such sacred places of Power."*

With a smile Rainbow Aurora affirms that Preseli Bluestone may therefore help draw the Dragons of the Rainbow Realm (and all who aid Earth's healing and evolution) closer.

The Gift of The Rainbow Key of Light:

Asking you to join her on the white half of the yin-yang symbol, Rainbow Aurora leads you over to the black granite bowl, and asks you to look into the fire that is burning within it.... as you do, she reaches down and plucks out a single flame (showing you that it has a ruby-red core surrounded by a mass of feather-like plumes of crimson and pink) and then touches it gently to your brow, saying:

> *"I ask you now to remember why you are here; remember why you were born.... Know that you can choose to align yourself with the Buddhas of The Light, and accordingly freely bear and give the Light to all – so see only the Truth that is there...."*

After a pause, Rainbow Aurora adds that *all* who choose to walk the path of the Buddha (or the Christ) face challenges: but emphasises that – even in the face of the most intense anger, hatred, disdain, fury, fear or darkness that might be projected against you – it is *vital* to hold love in your heart, if you wish to retain and increase the brilliance of your Light.... Then, after waiting a while longer to allow you time to absorb her words, she lowers the flame and rests it against your heart, saying:

> *"Make your peace with The Divine that is within you and within All, by allowing your heart to fill with strength tempered with compassion; resolve tempered with forgiveness. Seek out that which is sweet, not bitter, and feel the thoughts of it nourish and refresh your Soul.... and then, as your heart gains in strength, simply allow anything that stops you from BEing your Buddha-self to pass through your heart without resistance...."*

Reminding you that being fully aligned with your Higher-self and with the Earth allows you to move in harmony *with* the forward directional impulses of Cosmic Law (choosing to have positive intent), rather than working or standing *against* them (choosing to have negative intent) Rainbow Aurora adds that she will always attend you if you have turned away from – or rejected – the 'positivity' of Divine Love; or if it has been concealed, hidden or distorted – or taken from you – by others. Then, once she knows you have had plenty of time to absorb her words, she returns the flame to the bowl....

Turning away, she gives a whistle – at which a white stag with a magnificent pair of shining silver antlers appears at the top of the spiralling path: as he makes his stately way to join you, Rainbow Aurora tells you that the white stag is a powerful totem animal of the Light, who is the acknowledged leader of all the creatures that make the forests and glades, mountains and moors their home – and, as such, is an important intermediary between 'Earth' and 'Heaven'. She adds that **White Stag** is a great judge of character, and can be called upon whenever you need help to recognise your own flaws and merits: having done so, he will help you find your perspective, and show you how to modify your thoughts or behaviours in order to bring about a more appropriate state of inner balance. Explaining that White Stag customarily walks the secret pathways of the Earthly and the etheric Realms, Rainbow Aurora tells you that he can help you find the Light if you have lost your way in the darkness, or are unsure of the right direction to take – and that he may sometimes appear to you in dreams, journeying or meditation to suggest or recommend a way forwards that you had previously dismissed or not considered, or a path that is new or unknown to you. Cocking her head, Rainbow Aurora listens for a moment, and conveys to you that White Stag tells her he is also prepared to help you seek out the knowledge and wisdom of other creatures or Beings that inhabit the forests and ways that he walks, if they are willing to come to your aid.

Eventually the stag reaches the end of the path and crosses the bridge to stand in front of you: at this, Rainbow Aurora observes that White Stag sometimes comes to test the purity of your heart and/or your intent – reassuring you that he does not judge, but simply seeks the truth within.... she then asks that you meet his gaze – and as he bows his head and looks deep into your eyes, you somehow know he is seeing the very essence of your heart and Soul....

After a while the stag steps back and lifts his head, revealing that he wears a collar studded with pearly iridescent crystals: detaching one, Rainbow Aurora gives it to you and tells you that this is **Rainbow** (aka Angel or Opal) **Aura Quartz**, her third Crystal Champion – explaining:

> *"Rainbow Aura Quartz is a form of clear quartz that has been bonded with elements of platinum and silver, thus holding the energies of the Pearlescent-white, Platinum and Silver Rays. It can be used to purify and cleanse any of your energy Bodies and chakras, whilst fortifying your determination and resolve – for it holds and emits a pure High frequency that promotes greater clarity and self-empowerment. Thus Rainbow Aura Quartz can also help you identify and connect with The Divine within you, and so stand in your Truth as a Co-Creator and Master of your own Reality. Rainbow Aura Quartz has a multidimensional (and timeless) nature, which brings a sense of expansion and of being drawn 'up' through the Dimensions, whilst simultaneously facilitating moving 'down' – thus enabling you to gain a profound sense of Unity with All; and potentially guiding you towards the attainment of true Cosmic Enlightenment. Hence Rainbow Aura Quartz can also help you connect more closely with your Enlightened Buddha-self, enabling you to see things from multiple and broader perspectives, which will help you face life with more serenity and equilibrium. Furthermore, the pastel rainbow colours that play across its silvery surface may also teach you about the joys of being whole and in balance, reminding you of the awesome prospect of inner peace that can be found through union with the vastness of your Self and the Universe."*

With a smile, Rainbow Aurora affirms that Rainbow Aura Quartz may therefore help you embrace Universal Consciousness, and BEcome a Rainbow Warrior for the Light.

Asking you to join her on the black half of the yin-yang symbol, Rainbow Aurora now leads you over to the white alabaster bowl, enabling you to see that it is filled to the brim with crystal-clear water.... Reaching up, she plucks another magnolia blossom from the tree, and dips it into the water: then (after shaking it clear of all the water droplets save one) she lifts her diamond pendant and holds it up towards the sun, like a prism.... and, as its rainbow Light falls upon the single dew-like droplet, she says:

> *"See before you a single droplet of The Diamond Light, sparkling with the Light of a thousand Suns! All that you are, and all that you can become, is bestowed in this Divine Light by the gentle mercy of the gift of Grace: so connect with the Divinity of your Spirit and feel the Wisdom of the ages and the serenity of your Soul encompass you, and let all be at Peace.... For the Key IS Light – and this is all you are, and all you need...."*

With these words Rainbow Aurora touches the magnolia blossom with a finger – and the water droplet transforms into a thin crystal of clear quartz that is encrusted with hundreds of tiny seed crystals.... Plucking the crystal from the flower, she declares:

> *"This is my Gift of The Rainbow Key of Light. May the Divine Light that it holds Illuminate and Awaken you to the Wisdom of Universal Mind, that you may learn to embody the Absolute Truth of the Universe in which you have chosen to BE."*

She then rests her left hand gently on your crown, and holds the crystal to your Universal centre at the base of your skull with the other hand – at which you feel a gentle warmth filling your head, as the crystal 'key' is slowly absorbed into your energy Body....

As it comes to a balance within, a brightly-coloured swallow-tail butterfly settles on your shoulder – at which Rainbow Aurora gives a gentle smile. She advises you that it will take time to fully assimilate her Gift and all that you have experienced here in her garden, but assures you that you can always call upon her if you need aid in mastering what you have discovered; or if you simply need encouragement to keep going if times are hard – for she understands all the difficulties you might face as you leave the safety of your cocoon behind and transform into a beautiful 'butterfly' like this, as you work to become all that you can BE.

Gift given, Rainbow Aurora steps back and bows to you in acknowledgement, before leading you back across the bridge to stand beneath the crystal wind chimes: there, at a wave of her hand, day instantly becomes night – and everything goes dark.... then all of a sudden the indigo-black sky above you is filled with radiant curtains of neon-green, pink, purple and gold light, which dance, sweep and swirl across the darkness of the sky in waves, as if moving to music that you cannot hear.... With another smile, she says that what you see is a natural phenomenon that has been created by highly refined emanations of Divine Light, which have been Blessed by her so that they may unite Heaven and Earth in this amazing (and grace-full!) outpouring of electrical energy, light and colour: and thus you simply stand at her side and watch the luminous beauty of the spectacle unfold, until eventually the colours fade – and then die away to nothing....

The Greenwood Guardians – Sycomore Fig and Mimosa:

Her *personal* mentoring complete for now, Rainbow Aurora affirms she is always available to aid and support you: you need only bring her to mind and ask for her presence, and she will attend you. Furthermore, she tells you that two great Tree Beings of the Plant Kingdom have also asked to support you in addressing her Theme of 'OPEN YOUR HEART', adding that you need only request *their* presence, and they will be with you.

She explains that the first of these Greenwood Guardians is the Masculine essence of Sycomore Fig, who has asked to overlight and help you ground whatever work you undertake within *any* aspect of her chapter. The second is the Masculine essence of Mimosa, who has specifically asked to help you understand and assimilate her Gift of The Rainbow Key of Light (if you have chosen to accept it).

When you are ready to connect with Rainbow Aurora's first Greenwood Guardian, you need simply call for the presence of **Sycomore Fig** (*) .... Sycomore Fig envelops you in a honey-gold Light, and the Masculine spirit essence of Sycomore Fig speaks to you, saying:

> "She that gave life to the world gave life to me – and thus I hold the pure mind of The Divine Mother within, that through her wise counsel you may know both sweetness and strength; and understand the Higher purpose that fires your heart and inspires your mind.... Those who know and acknowledge my true worth will find clarity in me as they stand well-rooted in the waters that are illuminated by the diamond heart of the Earth, with their heads touching the starry canopy of the Gods that gave birth to the Universe. For knowledge and understanding of the myriad Arts of Creation are at the heart of my presence, which has the power to fill all that you are, and all that you may become, with the Rainbow Light of its waters.... So let me nourish you with my bounty, that your Soul may become sated and refreshed by its sweetness; and offer you a resting place that will shield you from the heat of the day, and keep your heart safe and warm as you sleep beneath the stars...."

(* Clear Optical Calcite and Honey Calcite will help you ground and connect with the energies and wisdom of Sycomore Fig, if you wish to enhance your experience using crystals.)

If you have chosen to accept and work with Rainbow Aurora's Gift, and when you are ready to connect with her second Greenwood Guardian, you need simply call for the presence of **Mimosa** (*) .... Mimosa envelops you in a pale lemon-yellow Light, and the Masculine spirit essence of Mimosa speaks to you, saying:

> "To truly know clarity, you must be cleansed of all that stains the Truth of who and what you are – and I know well the healing and restorative powers of the Earth that is my home, whose loving fortitude and merciful strength fill me at all times: so let me share this with you now, that you may have the courage to open yourself heart, mind and Soul, and bring all that you are out into the Light for honest inspection.... Then I may assist you in identifying what you need to do in order to ensure the Light that you carry within grows and evolves with compassionate grace: so stand with me, and allow me to teach you how to purify and care for your body.... stand with me, and allow me to help you order and clarify your mind.... stand with me, and allow me to show you how to balance and harmonise your emotions.... For together we may hone and refine every part of you, that your ego-self may understand its place in the world.... that your heart may become open and strong.... and that your Soul may return to the pristine innocence that was yours at first birth...."

(* Green Fluorite will help you ground and connect with the energies and wisdom of Mimosa, if you wish to enhance your experience using crystals.)

ARCHEIA SHEKHINAH

'LOOK FOR ME WITHIN'

CRYSTAL CHAMPIONS:

Hematite ♥ Zircon ♥ Magnesite

CREATURE COMPANIONS:

Dolphin ♥ Magpie ♥ Cat

GREENWOOD GUARDIANS:

Juniper ♥ Amelanchier

*I delight in discovering
all the worlds that I am.
I AM a Unity of Light.*

MEETING SHEKHINAH

It is a cool autumnal morning, and you find yourself standing in a wide dew-clad meadow that spans the floor of a densely wooded bowl-shaped valley. It is not long after daybreak, and the dawn chorus is in full voice – the birds that make this place their home carolling a welcome to the day, as the pale watery sun slowly rises in a silvered sky. The trees that cloak the gently-sloping valley sides have mostly all turned colour: their red, bronze, orange and gold leaves falling, drifting and spiralling through the air, blanketing the earth round their feet in a fiery shroud as they ready themselves for their winter sleep. All is still; all is calm: then, suddenly, a stiff breeze rouses the leaves; the air around you stirs; and a white mist appears as if from nowhere – drifting low over the meadow, and winding around the trunks of the trees in soft gauzy veils. As you watch, the gossamer strands accumulate at the forest edge, gradually coalescing into an ethereal Angelic form that is as tall as the tallest of the trees before which it stands – the feathery wisps of its wingtips brushing the ground like trails of silvery-grey smoke; and its diaphanous robes sparkling, as if strewn with hundreds of tiny silver stars. Then, as the Angel glides slowly towards you, its appearance shifts and shimmers, revealing a tall and very slender woman completely veiled in white, who is crowned with a coronet of pale silvery-blue stars: this is Archeia Shekhinah. She greets you, declaring:

> *"I am Shekhinah, the Lady Patience – Vessel for The Divine Light, Guardian of Individuated Universal Consciousness, and twin flame of Sandalphon. I am beauty; and I am Light. Substance and form are as nought to me, for with every breath you take I become yet more insubstantial, as your own Divinity takes shape and form within you. Thus I am the ephemeral nothing that pools within your consciousness and becomes manifest through thine own hand, as you draw the outline of my form and hold the patterning of my Being. Know that I hold all that is Divine within you, just as you hold The Divine within me – hence all that I am and all that I own is yours, for we share the Light of The Divine that rests eternally within the heart of 'All That Is' as ONE."*

Words spoken, Shekhinah fades from sight – and you are immediately enveloped in a dense white mist....

Before you even have time to wonder what is happening, the mist disperses – and you find yourself standing in an old-fashioned cottage garden that obviously belongs to someone keen on self-sufficiency. Behind you there is a large and well-tended orchard that boasts a wide range of fruit trees and bushes, amongst which you can see a number of bee-hives; and an immaculately-kept vegetable plot that is mostly cleared and readied for the winter. In front of you a red-brick pathway winds its way towards a low thatched whitewashed cottage that lies at the other end of the long garden – so, escorted by a pair of blackbirds (who have unusual red and gold tails), you decide to make your way along it. Initially the path follows a wide burbling stream, which meanders cheerfully down the slight incline, before spilling into a duck pond framed by feathery-headed sedges and tall bronzed bulrushes; or leads you alongside neatly-edged flower beds, which are mainly bare, given the season. Yet signs of life remain in beds of late-blooming chrysanthemums and wallflowers, and in the rowan and holly trees – and the evergreen hedges of yew that surround and enclose the garden – which are all brightly jewelled with berries.

Shekhinah

Eventually the path ends at a large octagonal herb garden planted with a wide range of medicinal and culinary herbs, their beds defined by neat lines of low box hedging; and by a shingle-roofed well, which sits near the cottage close to the back door – the top half of which is open.... Hearing a warm and welcoming voice inviting you inside, you let yourself into a low beamed kitchen that has a grey flagstone floor and roughly plastered lime-washed walls that have aged to the colour of clotted cream. Two wide deep-silled windows admit daylight from the front and back of the cottage, enabling you to see the layout and details of the room, aided by a soft golden light supplied by oil lamps that hang from metal hooks set in the beams.

The door through which you just entered is by the rear window, which sits over a deep stone sink and a wooden draining board; whilst the front window is bracketed by pine shelves lined with assorted pots and utensils to one side, and the cottage's wooden front door on the other. The outer wall to your left is spanned by an old oak dresser laden with bright blue and white dishes and plates; whilst the wall opposite it has a door that (presumably) leads to another room, but is otherwise filled by a deep inglenook fireplace: this houses a gleaming black range and neatly stacked cords of wood, all ready to feed the flames glowing beneath the burnished copper kettle that is simmering on its grate. The range is fronted by two generously proportioned oak rocking-chairs, which sit on a colourful hand-crafted woollen rug – their bright patch-work cushions proffering a cosy and welcoming haven. Between the chairs you can see a wicker basket, where a sleek silver and black spotted cat is nursing a contented tumble of tiny kittens in the warmth of the fire; whilst above the range an ancient oak beam, garlanded with aromatic bunches of drying herbs, is studded with hooks that hold an assortment of fire-blackened pots and pans. Rather oddly, there are two niches set into the wall above the beam – one of which holds a life-like carving of a family of meerkats; the other a small sculpture of a silver gecko, whose body is studded with lime-green peridots and black opals.

A well-scrubbed oak table (bracketed by two kitchen chairs) dominates the centre of the room; and it is here that you find Shekhinah, who has now adopted the persona of a country goodwife, busily making bread. Glancing up, she invites you to make yourself comfortable in a rocking chair, so that you can examine her and accustom yourself to her energies whilst she works: so you choose a seat, settle down, and watch as she efficiently kneads and shapes the dough....

The first thing you note is that her capable hands are lightly wrinkled, with square palms and surprisingly slim fingers that are unadorned; you also see that her movements are very deft and quick – even though she is rather round and short of stature (some might say dumpy!) Her face too is round, with soft creamy skin and plump rosy cheeks that blend subtly into what appear to be the dimpled creases and wrinkles of age, making it hard to tell how old she really is – and recognising your thoughts, she looks up with a smile, revealing a pair of startlingly clear and bright forget-me-not-blue eyes that sparkle with lively humour.

Shifting your gaze to her apparel, you see that Shekhinah wears a voluminous white cook's apron that covers a full-length plain black dress that has a slightly iridescent green sheen. The dress is made of bombazine – its bodice having a high round neckline, and fitting snugly over her matronly bosom to her waist, where a stiff waistband gathers its generous skirts in soft folds that skim the floor around her feet. The close-fitting sleeves end just above her wrists, revealing the plain white cuffs of a simple cotton under-shift – although this rather austere attire is alleviated by the fact that her slender feet are shod in silver slippers encrusted with diamonds – rather like Dorothy's ruby slippers in the film 'The Wizard of Oz'!

Turning your attention to Shekhinah's hair, you note that she wears it swept up into a bun on the top of her head, where it is partially covered by a white cotton mob cap that has a chain of forget-me-nots embroidered around its edge in pale blue silk. The hair that remains visible at her nape and temples enables you to see that (apart from two silvery streaks that sweep back from her temples to curve over her ears like birds wings) it is mostly dark, like her eyebrows; with a faint iridescent green sheen that echoes the colour of her dress.

Task finally complete, Shekhinah puts the loaves she has been making into the proving oven and bustles around the table clearing up – allowing you to lastly appreciate the delicate necklace that fits closely around her neck, almost like a collar: this has been crafted to depict a chain of forget-me-nots – each of the tiny five-petalled flowers having been intricately carved from a natural blue topaz crystal (which is the gem that links her with Sandalphon, her twin flame). At the heart of each flower you can see a tiny round cut and faceted sparkling diamond – and this theme continues at her earlobes, each of which bears a silver earring ornamented with a single blue-topaz and diamond forget-me-not that matches the ones on her necklace, along with a single dangling magpie feather – one of which is black, the other white.

SHEKHINAH'S TEACHINGS
The Gift of The Holon of Universal Balance:

Once your inspection is complete, Shekhinah removes her mob cap and apron and lifts two forest-green hooded cloaks from a peg on the back of the front door: asking you to follow her outside, she leads you out through a timber-clad porch, which appears to be home to a number of woodlice and small brown crickets; and takes you into the front garden, where a pair of deckchairs have been arranged on a sheltered patch of lawn. Wrapping herself in her cloak, Shekhinah chooses one and makes herself comfortable, inviting you to do likewise in the other: as you settle, she tells you that she and her twin flame, Sandalphon, often sit here looking at the stars – and no sooner has she spoken, than day instantly becomes night. When you look up, it seems almost as if the sky has become an ocean of the deepest indigo – the stars dancing like spume on the waves, and all of the heavens arrayed in glittering splendour before you – and so you simply relax at her side and enjoy the marvellous spectacle.... After a while, Shekhinah points out some of the constellations, and then draws your attention to an exceptionally bright star that is almost overhead: she informs you that this star is called Sirius, although it is also known as the 'Dog Star' because it lies in the constellation of Canis Major; and tells you that it has a special bond with the sea-mammals known on Earth as dolphins. She then gives a wave of her hand, and momentarily everything shimmers.

As your vision clears you can see that four of the stars that surrounded Sirius have vanished, and four huge dolphins – two silver; two gold – have taken their place: then, at a gesture from Shekhinah the dolphins swim off through the heavenly ocean towards a bright gold-white star.... as they travel, she tells you that they are seeking the star called Polaris, which is also known as the Northern Pole Star because of its position over the Earth. She explains that this star is the location of a Higher-Dimensional portal through which the Gold Ray enters this part of the Galaxy – and you see how (having found the star) the dolphins draw on its Light to build four triangles and a square from long strands of gold, before finally weaving them together into a large four-sided golden pyramid.

Once the golden pyramid is complete, the dolphins tow it across the firmament until they reach a bright silver-white star: drawing on its Light as before, they build another four triangles and a square (this time from long stands of silver), before weaving them together into a large four-sided silver pyramid.... as they work, Shekhinah tells you that this star is called Canopus, although it is also known as the Southern Pole Star because of its position over the southern ocean: with a smile, she adds that it too is the location of a Higher-Dimensional portal – this one giving the Silver Ray an entry point to the Galaxy.

Once the silver pyramid is complete, the dolphins align the two pyramids base-to-base, and weave them together to create a gold and silver octahedron: then everything shimmers as night becomes day once more – and the octahedron falls from the sky into Shekhinah's outstretched hand.... It does not seem possible that something that seemed so huge in the sky could be so small in her hand – yet nonetheless, there it is! Shekhinah smiles as she sees your puzzled expression, and explains that the dolphins have made you something called a 'Holon', which is an etherically constructed shape that has the ability to affect consciousness in a specific manner – in this case, by providing an etheric tool that will help you maintain stability and balance. She adds that this is to be the 'vessel' that contains her Gift – for it will enable you to *allow* change, rather than resisting or avoiding it.

Turning the Holon in her hands, Shekhinah says that the octahedron is one of the 'Platonic Solids' that are to be found within Metatron's Matrix: as such, it represents the Element of air, and also symbolises the union of 'male' and 'female' in perfect balance and harmony. She explains that it has been created from *Gold Light* in order to sustain your awareness of the power, process and potential of the alchemy of change and transition; and from *Silver Light* to inspire you with a remembrance, reconciliation and reconnection of (and to) the Universal Light that IS within you – and within ALL.

With another smile she tells you that its structure will help you to reason and think more clearly and logically; whilst its composition will benefit your body, mind *and* spirit, by helping you keep your mind and emotions in balance as you work to understand and assimilate the many and diverse aspects of *all* that you are, and by helping you stabilise and integrate your physical and spiritual Bodies during times of personal and/or planetary upheaval or change. With a chuckle, she reminds you that when you allow yourself to BE in balance you connect more strongly with the Divine within you, enabling you to access (and master) what has been called 'Christ-consciousness' more easily – and thence speed your 'Ascension' to the next Dimensions.

Shekhinah now stands, and asks you to stand in front of her: she then draws a strand of water-clear energy from her heart, and fills the octahedron with its Light (which has a quality like liquid moonlight), turning the gold and silver translucent.... She explains that she has now placed the essence of her consciousness within the Holon, saying:

> *"'Shekhinah' has been given many interpretations: it has been called the feminine aspect of The Divine; and it has been described as a vessel for the Divine Source – and it* is *as a vessel I come.... Know that around me rotate the Sun and the Moon, for I am at the centre of your Universe, and am an aspect of your Universal Soul.... indeed, I AM your potential and your memory; I AM all that you have been, are now, or ever will be: I AM the womb for your consciousness* and *your Divine Light – which IS* everything.*"*

Shekhinah now cups the Holon in her hands, at which it shrinks down until it is about the size of a large egg: then, reaching down, she places this gently within your Hara centre, so that your Inner Light (or Divine Spark) is held within its heart – telling you that this is her Gift of The Holon of Universal Balance....

Gently resting her hands on your shoulders in Blessing, she explains that her Gift will help you open to the Light within you, so that you *know* the Higher Light, Wisdom and Consciousness of the Universe and all that IS within it; and will enable you to remain stable and balanced, as you explore the nature and purpose of both. Reminding you that *everything* is simply energy – Light – presenting itself as 'information' and 'knowledge', she adds that (because Light IS a holographic image of the entire Light of the Universe) your Inner Light and consciousness, which are but aspects *of* that Universe, are infinite: so it is true that *all* you could ever need to know or understand is *already* within you!

Stepping back and giving you a small (yet heavy) silvery polished stone, Shekhinah tells you that this is **Hematite**, her first Crystal Champion – explaining:

> *"Hematite is a powerful grounding stone that resonates strongly with the Earth and her core, and with the heart of your Being. Its silvery reflective surface can act like a mirror that will show up any polarities or seeming contradictions you hold within, including your loves and hates; joys and sorrows; hopes and fears; satisfactions and frustrations. At the same time it will provide whatever inner strengths and abilities you require to enable you to examine each aspect in detail, in order to see and appreciate the benefits and constructive qualities that each polar part brings you; and (as part of this exercise) will then help you identify, dissolve, resolve or balance any part or aspect that, after due consideration, you decide you no longer want or require. Hematite has a unique side that is rarely recognised, for its vibrations can connect you to Higher-frequency planetary and Cosmic energies (remember – energy* is *information and knowledge!); whilst at the same time helping you to fully ground and integrate whatever 'energy' you access: Hematite may therefore allow you to acquire an understanding of all the many Universal aspects of your Self that exist throughout all Times and Planes of Dimension, so that you may assimilate all knowledge consequently gained into a cohesive and rational whole that may further your own – and others' – development and growth."*

Smiling, Shekhinah affirms that Hematite may therefore help you to admit, accept and embrace the need for change; and support you as you endeavour to ground your absolute potential to your incarnate flesh.

Inviting you to rest in the deckchair and allow yourself a little assimilation time, Shekhinah settles at your side and points to the sky again: two dolphin-shaped clouds are 'cavorting' in the blue, and with a chuckle she says that dolphins often accompany her as she travels near and far, for their joy and zest for life is a constant source of inspiration and pleasure: accordingly you may call upon **Dolphin** if you want to connect with the gentle or joyful aspects of your Being, if for some reason you have forgotten how to 'be' either; or if it is important to be more light-hearted (or light-handed) in what you do – appreciating that a fine line exists between taking things seriously and taking them *too* seriously! She adds that you may also call Dolphin if you wish to experience and explore the myriad joys of the night skies – in body or in spirit; or if you need guidance to find a calm passage through life's stormy waters. Reminding you that *all* cetaceans understand how to live in perfect harmony with the oceans, tides, patterns and rhythms of the Earth, Shekhinah says that you may also ask Dolphin to show you how to be more in tune with your own natural cycles, and/or in closer – and more comfortable – harmony with the world (and Universe) in which you live. With a smile she says that dolphins prefer to live in close-knit communities and are great communicators, so Dolphin may also help you to heal, restore or create relationships between colleagues, family or friends, by teaching you how to express your needs, feelings and emotions more eloquently – and honestly. Moreover, because dolphins are air-breathers *and* masters of the waters of Earth's oceans and rivers, Shekhinah says that Dolphin can teach you how to balance the Elements of air and water – and hence your mind and emotions – by supporting you as you discover the healing power of water (which can be utilised in many ways!); or by encouraging you to work with the breath and/or with sound – perhaps through yoga or meditation, or through singing, chanting or playing a wind instrument.

Gradually the 'dolphin clouds' dissipate; whereupon Shekhinah leads you indoors; relieves you of your cloak; and encourages you to settle in front of the fire to get warm.

The Diamond Light that IS Within and Without:
Settling in the chair opposite you, Shekhinah lifts her feet to show you her diamond slippers: she says that they hold the Diamond Light, which IS the infinite undifferentiated Light of The Divine – the Pure Light of Source that *is* 'All that is, was and ever will Be'; and explains that, as such, they support and sustain her whilst she grounds, guards and upholds the Divine Spark of every incarnate Soul, as they seek (and eventually learn) to embody their Christed and Divine Consciousness for themselves. Shekhinah reflects that people can spend many lifetimes looking *outside* themselves for the source of their Light (and the peace and fulfilment it offers), perhaps relying on the words, wisdoms, guidance and Teachings of others in their quest: yet – although this may serve a purpose when you are first finding your way – the spiritually mature seeker understands that they need look no further than their own consciousness, which is anchored *within*....

Reaching over to gently touch your Hara centre with her fingertips, she observes:

"You may think that your consciousness 'occupies' a small space within your physical body – yet it may 'be' vast or minute, and you may therefore 'see' it contract or expand throughout a minuscule – or infinite – quantum of distance. For your consciousness is

everywhere *at all times and can* never *be restricted by Time, space or Dimension – as none of these truly exist: they are merely Divine constructs that allow you to experience events in linear form, and so gain full understanding of the nature of cause and effect."*

Smiling, she says that only when you extend your awareness *beyond* the confines of your physical body can you truly appreciate the smallness of your human existence, and so discern the rationale behind the restrictions that physical embodiment places on your Soul – and thus understand the greater purpose behind all that you experience and do.

Telling you that she wants to help you to understand a little more about the vastness of your consciousness and the Diamond Light, Shekhinah stands and moves behind you: resting her hands gently on your shoulders, she asks you to close your eyes and shift your awareness to connect consciously with her presence; and then allow her to help you to centre, focus and go within to find the core of your Being – and your Divine Spark....

As you relax, your awareness expands – and you *know* that you are surrounded in a brilliant white light.... you then hear Shekhinah instructing you to use all your senses to connect with the resonance of the Light around you.... and then seek out its counterpart within you.... Slowly you feel your whole body fill with the Light that embraces you; and your heart is filled and strengthened by a deep and abiding sense of faith and trust.... All that you Are is illuminated in Shekhinah's pure Light – and as you find your centre, you feel her touch your head in Blessing, and you decide to allow yourself to simply go with the experience – opening your mind, and directing your awareness within....

At this point Shekhinah advises you that, *if* you accepted her Gift of the Holon of Universal Balance, you should look for it at your Hara centre and use your imagination to make it grow big enough to encompass your whole body – so that the upper (gold) point of the octahedron touches your Soul Star chakra, and the lower (silver) point touches your Earth Star chakra: this will offer you greater stability and balance; and allow you to sense and know even more.... and so, if you accepted her Gift, you follow her advice....

After a while, and with Shekhinah's support, you easily recognise and connect with the Divine Spark that is held at the heart of your Lotus of your Soul; and touch your mind to the holographic reality of all that it is, and all that it holds – and, at that instant, your energy field expands in a magnificent explosion of Light; and you simply *know* that you are fully and consciously connected to the Love and Wisdom of the Divine Light that inspires and sustains the Universal Web of Life....

Momentarily you are overwhelmed by a wonderful feeling of perfect completeness, awe and bliss: and, as the significance of what you feel sinks in, you hear Shekhinah say:

"A spark of The Diamond Light is always within your Seed of Original Consciousness, and its essence is reflected through your heart. Yet only those who travel with an open mind and a compassionate heart in the Light of Grace and with the Truth of their Divine nature encompassing their Being can utilise this Light in all its Glory. For to know and fully understand this Light in its completeness is to know All – the knowing of which releases the Seed to BE once more a part of All That IS...."

For a while longer she allows you to revel in being at One with Universal Consciousness, *know*-ing all and *be*-ing all.... then leans over your shoulders to rest her hands over your

High Heart and Hara centres; and instructs you to contract your holon (if applicable) so that it returns to how it was before, *and* to hold the intention of fully grounding yourself and bringing your consciousness back to your centre.... When she is happy that you have done this, Shekhinah moves to stand in front of you and affirms that she is always there to help you connect with the magnificence of your Being and with the Enlightenment of the Universe, before giving you a small reddish-brown octahedral crystal. She says that this is **Zircon**, her second Crystal Champion – explaining:

"Zircon is a highly energising and stimulating stone, especially to the base and sacral chakras (and so to your physical body and to your emotional / feeling Body) – although it can *energise* any *sluggish energy Body, chakra or centre. Although not much to look at, this powerful little crystal is also very capable of grounding high-frequency energies through your pranic core into your Earth Star chakra, enabling perfect balance to be attained between the spiritual world and the mundane: this feature of Zircon may be of practical use if you tend to be spacey, or need help grounding, during* or *after meditation, journeying or channelling. Furthermore, Zircon is a powerful cleanser and detoxifier, and extremely effective results can be attained if you place one crystal on each of your seven major chakras to awaken, clear, energise and align them (but don't overdo it!) If you have chosen to accept my Gift, Zircon will also support you in visualising, maintaining, expanding and/or contracting your holon – thus aiding you in retaining your balance and increasing stability (on any and all levels) during times of personal or planetary energy shifts and/or upheavals."*

With a smile Shekhinah affirms that Zircon may therefore help you ground and rebalance your lower energy centres – and aid you in using your holon, if and as applicable.

Moving back to her seat, Shekhinah gives a whistle – at which a magpie flies in through the open door and alights on the arm of her chair, observing her with keen eyes: a moment later, it is then joined by another, who sits companionably opposite it – and, wittily reciting 'one for sorrow; two for joy', Shekhinah tells you that the magpie is one of her favourite birds, for it is bold, intelligent and relentlessly curious about everything! She adds that their determination and adaptability helps them thrive in any environment: hence **Magpie** can teach you how to adapt your work/life balance to suit your particular circumstances – maybe by changing direction or 'drawing a line' if you need to readdress something; or to give you extra support and encouragement if you need to complete a task that you find hard to finish; or to remind you of the many 'jewels' to be found when exploring yourself and your world as fully and deeply as you can. She explains that Crow (who teaches about Divine Law) is a cousin to black and white Magpie, who also teaches about Law – but from the viewpoint of unconditional acceptance, wholeness and balance of (and in) all things: thus Magpie can help you recognise the value of *all* knowledge, regardless of its nature – and irrespective of whether you choose to utilise it or not. With a smile she says that this can be useful if you need to find the 'gold' within the 'dross'; the 'good' within the 'bad'; or the 'positive' within the 'negative' (or vice versa): what is more, Magpie makes a wise 'devil's advocate', who may come to *test* you if you do not have a whole and balanced viewpoint of a problem or a situation; or to *guide* you if you ask for dispassionate and unbiased advice to help you weigh up the 'pros' and 'cons' of a choice or opportunity. With another smile, she adds that Magpie understands that *making* changes and *assimilating* shifts and changes (both in personal and planetary energies) takes time, and so may appear if you need reminding of the virtue of 'stillness' and/or of planning (patiently) for the future, so that your path runs more smoothly.

The Light of Universal Consciousness and The Holon of Infinity:
As the birds fly away, Shekhinah settles down and says that she wishes to return to the concept that your consciousness *is* everything; and tells you that you may find it helpful to see The Divine (in all its magnitude) as a hologram that has been shattered into inestimable fragments – each of which contains the complete paradigm of *everything*, of which 'you' are always a part.... Drawing an upright '8' in the air between you, using translucent rainbow Light, she tells you that this is another holon, which she calls the 'Holon of Infinity'. She explains that its shape may be used as a *concept* that defines how two (or more) apparently disparate parts are ONE; and/or as a visual prompt or *'tool'* that helps the mind – and the awareness – affirm that connection. She asks you to observe it closely, and see how the rainbow-light is constantly flowing and never motionless – thus highlighting the fact that this holon is both infinite and limitless....

Smiling, Shekhinah says that you may find the 'Holon of Infinity' useful in helping you link (and focus your attention on) specific aspects of your energy Body when you are working on your self-improvement or self-understanding – adding that (if you accepted her Gift), you should always first expand your Holon of Universal Balance in the way she showed you earlier (gold point *up*; silver point *down*), as this will help keep your energies balanced and stable as you work on whatever you are addressing.

Shekhinah tells you that she wants to start by showing you how to use a Holon of Infinity to help you fully ground your consciousness and have a clearer understanding of 'you' as a holographic particle of the Whole.... she reminds you to expand your Holon of Universal Balance (if applicable) exactly as you did before – and then visualise or use your imagination to 'pull' the Holon of Infinity she has just created towards you; and 'move' it into your energy field so that the upper half loops around your Divine Spark, and the lower half loops around your Earth Star chakra – explaining that this will help ground your Divinity to the Earth and your physical presence....

Once you have completed this, Shekhinah explains that every Divine Spark is like a transmitter, continuously 'sending' and 'receiving' information to and from the Universal Web in the form of energy (Light): accordingly all that 'you' (and everyone else!) learns is instantaneously accessible by ALL. After waiting a while to allow you to think about what this connection can therefore offer you, Shekhinah says that she wants to show you how to create and use a second Holon of Infinity to help you balance the wants, needs and desires of 'who' you *think* you are, with all that you *are*!

She now instructs you to see, imagine, feel or sense yourself drawing out a nice round figure '8' in translucent rainbow Light.... and then position it within your body so that the lower loop passes round your Hara centre, and the upper loop passes round your High Heart centre – reminding you to keep the first Holon of Infinity she made (*and* your Holon of Balance, if applicable) firmly in place as you do so....

After waiting until everything is correctly positioned, Shekhinah tells you to focus on the rainbow Light that is flowing through the Holon of Infinity you have just created (which links your Divine Spark and your heart), and allow your heart to align with your Soul; and your awareness to connect with the Universal Consciousness that is within *and* without you.... As you 'focus' and 'allow', Shekhinah observes that the first steps in becoming one with the Light of your True Self entail self-acknowledgement and self-acceptance: because being blind to *any* aspect of your Self is being blind to your own Light and the full truth of your Divine nature. Her words give you the courage to expand your awareness further and further.... until you are finally able to acknowledge the vast magnificence of all that you truly are – in all your disparate, yet glorious, parts....

After allowing you time to grasp this, Shekhinah asks that you now allow the Holon of Infinity you just created to dissipate, whilst keeping the other two holons in place – stressing that if you ever need aid to understand and assimilate 'all that you are' you can always call upon her. She then gives you a small slightly knobbly ivory-white stone, and tells you that this is **Magnesite**, her third Crystal Champion – explaining:

> *"The Spark at the centre of your Being recalls your past and your future, which has been veiled in forgetfulness for the purposes of this lifetime. It is a holographic particle of the Whole that IS Source – and as such contains the sum total of all that The Divine knows and experiences in the eternal and infinite NOW. Magnesite can help you ground that consciousness and Light to your physical body (literally bringing Heaven to Earth); and will support you in going within to connect with this knowledge and understanding, so that you may more easily recall all that your past and future Selves have learned – aiding you in understanding your 'now'; and helping you plan more effectively for your future. Know that full alignment with your Highest Self is possible with Magnesite's aid, for it will help you merge your Inner and Outer Light as one, supporting you in attuning your own specific frequency to the Universal Web of Light – whilst opening your mind to understand the Highest sources of wisdom and guidance that are appropriate for your needs at that time."*

Smiling, Shekhinah affirms that Magnesite may therefore help you to expand your mind and your awareness, so that you may align your Soul with your 'I AM' presence.

Sitting back in her seat, Shekhinah says that she lastly wants to show you how to use a Holon of Infinity to help you understand your spiritual roots – and appreciate your life-plan from a new perspective. She then draws a *downward*-pointing silver triangle in the air between you, explaining that this defines the multidimensional 'space' within each human female that holds their Divine Light and individual spiritual quintessence.... she then draws a gold *upward*-pointing triangle, explaining that this does likewise for every human male.... Moving them so that one lies on top of the other, she explains that, during acts of procreation, they merge into a multidimensional Star that contains copies of both arrays of Light-data: then, if a child is conceived, specific spiritual *and* physical information is transferred along with their DNA – thus passing on their multidimensional spiritual *and* ancestral genetic inheritance. With a smile, she remarks that therefore 'who you are' (and what you know) includes what you have learned 'by osmosis' from your birth-parents and ancestors – which will pass in turn to *your* children, if you have any.

Shekhinah tells you that this may make more sense if you experience it – and asks you to create another Holon of Infinity, exactly as you did before – but this time position it so that the lower loop passes round your Hara centre and the upper loop passes round your brow chakra.... as you do as she asks, she reminds you to keep your other holon(s) firmly in place – and waits until everything is in the correct location.... She instructs you to focus on the rainbow Light that is flowing through the holon you have just created, and allow your Soul to align with your Intuitive Wisdom; and your awareness to connect with the Tapestry of Life of which you are a part, so that you may seek out, examine and explore a few threads of your genetic, ancestral and spiritual inheritance that underlie the patterns of your current lifetime on Earth.... As you 'focus' and 'allow', Shekhinah waits – and then places something in your hand, suggesting that you research its symbolism later: for it represents a core attribute or gift that has been handed down through your spiritual and genetic ancestry and woven into your energy blueprint as an aspect of your own personal tapestry – and so it may help you to understand why you have incarnated here, and now. She then asks you to allow both your Holons of Infinity to dissipate; and instructs you to contract your Holon of Universal Balance (if applicable) so that it returns to its resting place in your Hara centre, *and* to hold the intention of grounding yourself and bringing your consciousness fully back to your centre....

This done, Shekhinah reaches into the basket by the range and lifts out one of the tiny spotted kittens: she remarks that in time this little cat will become fully independent, having learned from its mother all it needs to survive and thrive and grow into a sleek and efficient hunter. Tickling it under its chin, she says that cats seem to spend a lot of their time asleep – but they are often using this time to journey out-of-body and walk between the worlds: hence **Cat** may come to guide you in your dream state to help you gain greater inner (and outer) awareness; or teach you how to meditate or journey more effectively (which may include showing you how to free yourself from irrelevant or unwanted thoughts or external influences); or help you learn techniques that will enable you to become more self-aware in body, mind and spirit. With a laugh she adds that cats just know how to relax, have fun and go with the flow: indeed, they have no concept of 'should be...' or 'ought to be...' or 'must...'; and simply do not understand the concept of feeling guilty about doing nothing, or about doing something simply for the pleasure of it. Accordingly, Cat can also show you how to find inner peace by teaching you the *true* meaning of being self-ish(!) – inspiring you to create your own safe space in which to concentrate on your self-healing and balance (and to simply BE your Self as you review each day), enabling your thoughts and feelings to become clear and ordered in your mind, and helping you gain the clarity and perspective you need to address any difficult or problematic issues promptly, rather than letting them accumulate and 'fester'.

The Greenwood Guardians – Juniper and Amelanchier:

Her *personal* mentoring complete for now, Shekhinah affirms she is always available to aid and support you: you need only bring her to mind and ask for her presence, and she will attend you. Furthermore, she tells you that two great Tree Beings of the Plant Kingdom have also asked to support you in addressing her Theme of

'LOOK FOR ME WITHIN', adding that you need only request *their* presence, and they will be with you.

She explains that the first of these Greenwood Guardians is the Masculine essence of Juniper, who has asked to overlight and help you ground whatever work you undertake within *any* aspect of her chapter. The second is the Feminine essence of Amelanchier (Snowy Mespil), who has specifically asked to help you understand and assimilate her Gift of The Holon of Universal Balance (if you have chosen to accept it).

When you are ready to connect with Shekhinah's first Greenwood Guardian, you need simply call for the presence of **Juniper** (*) .... Juniper envelops you in a brick-red Light, and the Masculine spirit essence of Juniper speaks to you, saying:

> *"Clarity and perfect integrity are what I offer you, that through my passion you know what the sacrifices of Earthly embodiment are worth to you now.... My habits are many and varied – and thus I may show you the myriad ways there are of BEing in the world; that you may appreciate how, no matter what your path, and no matter who you have chosen to be,* you *are a vital part of the great tapestry that comprises human reality.... Remember: no one person is any greater than another; and* all *are essential to the Plan: thus, without your presence, the lines upon which the Divine Light is writ – and the glorious patterns that define the Universe – would not be the same. So hold your head high, and allow your heart to open with every word you speak; every deed you do; and in every minute that passes in the precious world of life and existence! Sit with me now, and inhale my essence.... and let your heart and mind be purified and filled with the clarity that enables you to see yourself with greater kindness, inspiring you onwards to grow into the true vastness of your Soul, being certain of your Self, above* all *else...."*

(* Carnelian and Bloodstone will help you ground and connect with the energies and wisdom of Juniper, if you wish to enhance your experience using crystals.)

If you have chosen to accept and work with Shekhinah's Gift, and when you are ready to connect with her second Greenwood Guardian, you need simply call for the presence of **Amelanchier** (*) .... Amelanchier envelops you in a rainbow-black Light, and the Feminine spirit essence of Amelanchier speaks to you, saying:

> *"Those who know and understand true balance understand that it embraces* all *– the darkness, and the light; the hope, and the disappointment; the joy, and the sorrow. For without knowing all things, there cannot be understanding.... without experiencing all things, there cannot be true choice.... without appreciating all things, there cannot be freedom.... Thus I have come to be the sounding board that allows you to judge yourself in the full and complete Light of your heart.... to be the anchor that keeps all that you are firmly rooted in the reality of the Universe.... to be the rainbow in the darkness that offers you solace and cheer in even the bleakest of hours.... and to be the perfect yet honest balance that allows you to see things exactly as they are, without embellishment or lies. And, as you learn to appreciate my gifts, so you will find the magician that is within you – the one from whom nothing is secret.... from whom nothing is hidden.... and for whom ALL things are possible...."*

(* Black Tourmaline and Rainbow Obsidian will help you ground and connect with the energies and wisdom of Amelanchier, if you wish to enhance your experience using crystals.)

ARCHANGEL SANDALPHON

'BALANCE AND GROWTH'

CRYSTAL CHAMPIONS:
Petrified Wood ♥ Tourmalinated Qtz ♥ Gaia Jasper

CREATURE COMPANIONS:
Turtle ♥ Crane ♥ White Peacock

GREENWOOD GUARDIANS:
Oak ♥ Coconut

*I am creating a magnificent future
that is filled with beauty,
with joy, and with peace.*

MEETING SANDALPHON

It is a fine morning in mid-summer, and you find yourself standing beneath a turquoise sky in a wildflower meadow that is lavishly strewn with masses of gloriously ripe grasses and flowers of all possible kinds. It is as if a giant hand had cast their seeds at random without worrying about where they fell – for even the tallest and most vibrant stands harmoniously beside the smallest and most delicate; and everything around you is delightfully pleasing to the eye. Here all is peaceful and calm; and as you relax – the sunlight warm upon your face – a soft breeze caresses your skin, causing the stems of the grasses to ripple in silvery waves and the heads of the flowers to nod and sway, as they too feel its touch. Looking beyond the meadow, you see that it lies at the foot of an alpine mountain, blending seamlessly into sloping emerald-green pastures that merge into the tree-line where a mixed woodland of deciduous trees, backed by serried ranks of evergreen larches and towering pines, rises ever more steeply upwards. Beyond that, the forest is forced to give way to steel-grey expanses of scree-covered slopes, which cloak the ground below the stark crags of the peaks above them, whose soaring snow-capped wonders are elegantly silhouetted against the clear blue sky.

Just as you are marvelling at their imposing and majestic splendour, the peaks are haloed in a deep green light that rapidly increases in brightness and intensity: transfixed by the sight (and wondering what is happening), you watch as the light expands and rises – and then a tall winged figure, robed in a green Light that is so deep it seems almost to be black, seemingly rises out of the very heart of the mountain.... It begins to fly towards you on massive wings of vibrant orange, red and gold, which look as if they are made of fire – drawing swiftly closer with every wing beat; until eventually it alights at the edge of the meadow and strides towards you.... Its appearance changes with every step – the brilliant fire of its wings dimming and fading, and the black-green Light enrobing it diminishing – finally revealing a short stocky man wearing a knee-length forest-green cape: this is Archangel Sandalphon. He meets, and greets, you declaring:

> "I am Sandalphon – Archangelic Anchor of the Light on Earth, Guardian of the Seven Kingdoms of Souls, and twin flame of Shekhinah, the Lady Patience. I am both great and small – for my heart and hands are with The Divine, whilst my feet are buried deep within the ground upon which I stand: thus I connect Heaven and Earth through many spheres of Cosmic Wisdom – grounding Divine Mind and Inspiration, and bringing the consciousness and creative impulses of their own Divinity to all things. This world is my delight and my joy! For in all things that have been created I find beauty and solace; and we are eternally joined in faith, love and in hope: so judge me not by what you see, yet by what I do, for I am IN all things and capable OF all things.... Know that from the rarest atmosphere to the depths of the planet's core, I am there.... from the highest mountain peak to the deepest valley, I am there.... from the tallest tree to the smallest grain of sand, I am there. Indeed, wherever there is need – and whomever should call upon me – I am there."

Then, with a smile, Sandalphon invites you to walk with him, so that you may examine him more closely, and become accustomed to his energies – then turns and strides away, his hooded cape billowing out behind him....

Sandalphon

As you hurry to join him, you see that his cape is made of densely-woven wool that has been dyed a lovely deep shade of green – and, although it looks rather shabby, you can imagine that it is probably very warm and practical. It fastens at the neck with a short length of gold chain, which is the only aspect of his apparel that is even remotely opulent – for (in complete contrast to his previous form) everything Sandalphon wears looks very plain and simple, home-spun and rustic. Under the cape he is clad in a rough and ready fawn coloured shirt that has elbow-length sleeves and a slit 'V' neck: this is tucked into a pair of well-worn dark brown trousers, which are held up with a short length of knotted rope, and worn rolled partway up his calves to reveal sturdy tanned legs and broad bare feet that are deeply ingrained with dirt and dried mud. Both shirt *and* trousers are made from a coarsely-woven linen that has softened with wear, adding to your impression that his only concern is that what he wears is comfortable and fit for purpose – rather than being worn for show or effect.... you also cannot help thinking that, all things considered, he looks a bit like a hobbit – and as this passes through your mind, he flashes you a quick grin that shows he is fully aware of your thoughts!

Having reached the end of the meadow, Sandalphon guides you on up the hillside, following the dried-up bed of a pebble-lined stream that runs down through the pasture from the forest beyond. Just before you reach the tree line, the terrain flattens – and here you find a shallow bowl-shaped hollow that was previously hidden from view: this holds a crystal-clear pool of mountain melt water, which (if full) would feed the currently dry stream. The pool reflects the single oak tree that stands sentry at its side, and Sandalphon invites you to join him on the wooden bench set square beneath its spreading branches....

As you settle at his side, you see that a bright emerald and blue dragonfly has just landed on his head! You also see that his cape has attracted a host of flying insects such as butterflies, ladybirds, bees, wasps and flies; whilst the ground around his feet is dotted with flightless insects such as ants, spiders and beetles: however, as he is not bothered by them, you decide to likewise ignore them – and continue your scrutiny by turning your attention to his face. This is rather square, with a cleanly-shaven jaw-line that is firm and strong; and with a long straight nose that juts sharply from between dense eyebrows that, in turn, sit below a wild mop of unkempt (and somewhat shaggy) conker-brown hair. Sandalphon's ruddy cheeks and weather-beaten skin might fool you into thinking that he is older than he is – yet his twinkling eyes are outlined by deeply creased 'laughter' lines, and are a clear and vibrant emerald-green. Realising that he is surveying you in turn, you see his full lips curve in amusement as you spot the vine that is twining itself through his hair. This vine is obviously (and bizarrely) alive – its evergreen leaves and tendrils home to clusters of tiny pale blue forget-me-nots that, on closer inspection, prove not to be real: instead they have been fashioned from gemstones – their petals intricately cut from sky-blue topaz, which is the gem that links him with Shekhinah, his twin flame; their centres each adorned with a tiny round crystal-clear faceted diamond.

A wide leather strap passes over Sandalphon's left shoulder and crosses his body to his right hip, where it secures an open-mouthed pouch made of stiff sacking: noting your interest, he dips his left hand into the pouch and brings it out to show you that it holds a multitude of seeds – each one a different shape, size and colour. You somehow know that these have the potential to grow into any and all possible varieties of plant, tree, flower or crop – and then, as you look more closely, you see tiny crystals amongst the seeds (again of all shapes and colours) and realise that they too are 'seeds', which have the potential to grow within the Earth and produce infinite types and varieties of crystalline mineral.

Returning the seeds to his pouch, Sandalphon holds out his left hand to show you that he wears a silvery-gold ring on each of his fingers and thumb: each ring looks to be a graduating thickness and width – the smallest and finest encircling his smallest finger, the largest and thickest his thumb; and as you look more closely, you see that each ring is densely covered with lines of symbols and script – none of which you recognise. With an enigmatic smile Sandalphon taps his other broad and capable hand (which is resting in his lap) to make sure you notice that the digits on this hand are likewise adorned: then, turning this hand over, he shows you that it was covering a four-sided obelisk made of multicoloured layers of sparkling aventurine – green at its base, rising through hues and tones of yellow and blue, and culminating in deep red at its pyramidal apex.

SANDALPHON'S TEACHINGS
The Alignment of The Lotus of the Heart with the Linear Bodies:
Now that your inspection is complete, Sandalphon tells you that many of the more common crystal 'families', such as the calcites, tourmalines and aventurines, are found in all, or many of, the colours of the rainbow. He explains that each crystal 'family' that displays 'rainbow' characteristics is of great practical use in harmonising and aligning the intrinsic Light frequencies of your Linear chakras and auric Bodies, using red at your base chakra (and so on) and ending with violet, clear or white at your crown chakra. He expounds that this is because each 'family' has a common fundamental resonance, which means they are harmonious and balanced as a whole; yet – depending on their colour (which is determined by the trace elements they contain), each will address the needs of the corresponding chakra and energy Body from a fundamental perspective that is either more 'physically' or more 'spiritually' orientated.

Lifting the obelisk he is holding, Sandalphon says that aventurine can help the cells of the physical body adjust to (and harmonise with) the energetic changes and shifts that influence and affect the Earth: for it is innately attuned to the ever-changing frequencies of the Divine Light that drive Cosmic transformation and evolution. Running a finger up a side of the obelisk, he adds that this particular shape helps ground these shifts because it defines the 'Axis Mundi' (the 'World Tree' that links 'Heaven' and 'Earth') and holds the five Elements of earth, air, fire, water and ether in balance. Pointing to the rainbow bands of colour, he explains that *this* colour combination promotes mastery of the mind and emotions through inward (and outward) directed communication; drives and inspires the transformational spiritual fires grounded within; catalyses the desire for (and the acquisition of) knowledge and understanding; and promotes heart-centred equilibrium and balance. Touching the apex of the obelisk, he adds that (at a 'Higher' level) it ignites, strengthens and empowers the pink, blue and yellow petals of the Lotus of the Heart, promoting the desire to accept and fully embrace the Divine attributes of Love, Will and Wisdom – which has the potential to result in profound spiritual transformation.

Reminding you that balance and groundedness are an important part of all processes of transformation and growth, Sandalphon reaches down and picks up a tiny acorn that has fallen from the tree, and places it in the palm of your hand: he touches it gently with a finger, remarking 'from tiny acorns do great oak trees grow' – at which it separates into two parts – the rounded cup, and its oval seed. Asking you to choose a site a reasonable distance away, Sandalphon now directs you to go and bury the seed in the ground.... and having done so, you return to his side.

Together you watch as a green shoot appears and starts growing at a phenomenal rate, as if time itself has been speeded up: almost in the blink of an eye the sapling oak moves through hundreds of seasons and years of growth, until it finally stands proud and tall – its broad leafy canopy shading the ground beneath.... Telling you that what you see is only half the picture, Sandalphon explains that you could only see the growth that was happening *above* ground: yet an equivalent amount of growth was also happening *below* ground – perfectly illustrating the axiom 'as above, so below'. With a smile, he says that (for paramount stability) an oak will only grow as high and wide as its roots are broad and deep – illustrating how important it is to be firmly rooted when reaching 'upwards' to spiritual heights and/or coping with 'the winds of change': likewise it is important to ensure that you too are well-grounded, if you wish to embrace *your* Highest potential.

Standing, Sandalphon asks you to sit up straight, with your legs slightly apart; your feet flat on the ground; and your hands on your knees.... He explains that it is important that you know how to balance, charge and align your seven Linear chakras, so that you may grow and evolve with your body, mind and spirit in perfect balance – and asks you to call to mind the 'Holon of Infinity' taught to you by his twin-flame, Shekhinah.... he then directs you to see, imagine, feel or sense yourself creating one now, with the lower loop of the figure '8' passing around your Earth Star chakra; the upper loop passing around your Soul Star chakra; and with the crossing point at your heart....

When you have managed this, he moves to stand behind you and rests his left hand gently on your crown: Sandalphon now gently touches his aventurine obelisk to the back of each of your chakras in turn – brow.... throat.... heart.... solar plexus.... sacral.... base.... Gradually you feel your crown chakra open to the Light of the Cosmos; and you know that every chakra he has touched is being flooded with the Highest Light that you can assimilate at this time – aligning them through your pranic core, and bringing your body, mind and spirit (ego-self and Higher-self) into greater harmony and balance.... Somehow you know that this Light is also permeating every part of your body – saturating and aligning every cell with the Divine Frequencies that are now grounded within the Earth's own energy field – and, with this realisation, you understand that this will help you to release any 'old' energies that might be restricting or blocking your growth; and enable you to move forwards in closer harmony with the heart of the planet on which you live....

After allowing plenty of time for the Light to be absorbed, and for your chakras to settle into a comfortable state, Sandalphon moves to stand in front of you, and gently touches the apex of his aventurine obelisk to your heart centre: at this all the petals of the Lotus of your Heart slowly unfurl; and each layer of petals draws upon the Light that the obelisk channels and holds – first the pink petals of Divine Love, whose ruby-red veins flush through with its fire.... then the blue petals of Divine Will, whose sapphire-blue veins brighten and intensify.... and lastly the yellow petals of Divine Wisdom, whose golden veins fill with a Light that is like liquid gold.... Once all the petals have been fully fired and inspired, Sandalphon holds the base of the obelisk to the very centre of the Lotus of your Heart, encouraging all the petals to align with the Emerald held at its core; and enabling it to settle into an appropriate state of openness and balance: then, when he is satisfied that all is in order, he places the obelisk aside and directs you to allow the Holon of Infinity that you created to dissipate, and then relax....

As you do so, he retakes his seat at your side and gives you a small polished stone that exhibits bark-like striations in mottled earthy hues of brown, cream and tan. He tells you that this is **Petrified** (Fossilised) **Wood**, his first Crystal Champion – explaining:

"Petrified Wood can help you connect and commune with the Ancient Beings of Earth and their wisdoms, especially those connected with the woodland realms of the gnomes, dryads and other Devic Beings. Each piece holds the wisdom of an ancient Tree-being who helped ground the Light of Heaven into the planet many thousands of years ago; and, as such, they can do likewise for you now – as long as you are willing to open your heart and mind. Petrified Wood's energy is also incredibly stable and robust, offering you a steadfast and reliable source of companionship and guidance that will oversee and support you through all programmes of personal and spiritual growth: note that, although transformation under the guidance of Petrified Wood may be slow, it will be steady, proving that true wisdom and worthwhile accomplishment comes through taking the time to recognise, understand, assimilate and value all *of Life's lessons fully and completely! Accordingly Petrified Wood may also help you realise the importance of the passage of Time as an aspect of Earth's learning opportunities; and help you see how linear events – often set over many lifetimes; and often karmic – are connected: indeed, silicified material like this whose markings clearly show its origins has an affinity for supporting journeying into the past, or for working on past-life or early-life lessons that require balance or resolution in this lifetime. Moreover, Petrified Wood may also help you appreciate the interconnectedness and interdependence of* all *life-forms that share your world, from the microscopic to the massive; the mundane to the marvellous!"*

With a smile, Sandalphon affirms that Petrified Wood may therefore help you to become 'grounded and strong, like the oak', whilst offering you its ancient and wise counsel.

Taking your attention to the mountain pool, Sandalphon points to a flat rock at the edge where a turtle is warming itself in the sunlight: he tells you that some traditions regard turtles as a symbol of Mother Earth and as a sign of The Divine Feminine, who engenders all life – adding that, because of this it is a totem often attracted to those who are Earth-workers or shamans. Hence if **Turtle** appears to you, it may be a sign that you are being asked to connect more closely with nature, and pay greater attention to the natural energies around you. With another smile, he points out that, even though turtles move quite slowly on land, they have the stamina to cover vast distances – hence illustrating the lesson that faster does not always equal better, and is not always the best way to accomplish your goals: accordingly Turtle can be called upon to show you how to move steadily and deliberately with determined focus, especially during periods of physical- or emotional-based shifts and changes; or to encourage you to have greater patience with yourself or others, accepting that change takes time; or to teach you to value the virtues of rest and stillness, which refresh the mind and enable you to move more decisively and proactively when the time is right – all of which promote the ability to 'go with the flow'. Remarking that its shell is tough enough to shield it from most predators, Sandalphon says that Turtle can also be called upon to show you some practical and effective ways of keeping your physical and non-physical energies stable and strong; or teach you how to ground yourself more securely for greater inner / outer stability and balance; and/or to help you find and identify the strengths that lie within you. Having enjoyed the sun for a while, the turtle slides into the water – at which Sandalphon chuckles, adding that its affinity with the Elements of earth *and* water means Turtle can help you find the right balance between your physical and emotional needs; and – as it is equally at home on the ground and in the water – can be asked to assist you in cleansing and clearing your body, mind and/or spirit of anything that hampers or prevents your transformation and growth.

The Alignment of the Heart of the Lotus with the Unified Body:
Settling back, Sandalphon reminds you that your 'Linear' chakra system is designed to support physical existence in the third-Dimensional Plane, enabling human life to be experienced through the 'cause and effect' of karmic functioning. He observes that it does this predominantly through your lower three chakras and their associated subtle energy Bodies (your physical Body and its survival processes; your emotional Body and its feeling/reactive processes; and your mental Body and its logical thought processes). Reaching out and resting his hand over your heart, he reminds you that your heart chakra is your centre of balance – which, as the Earth evolves to embrace the fifth- and sixth-Dimensions, becomes empowered to adopt a state of Higher (Divine) functioning that will allow it to govern the other six chakras. Gently tapping your heart, he explains that this empowerment will prompt all your other chakras to begin operating at a Higher level as well – thus catalysing a shift from the *Linear* chakra system to ONE *Unified* Chakra and Body, centred *here*, at your heart. With a smile he adds that this will align and unite all your chakras and auric Bodies and their functions, and promote the development and activation of your fifth-Dimensional Lightbody: then (explaining that he wants to guide you through the process of opening into the Unified Chakra aspect of your Unified Body, so you can know how it feels), Sandalphon walks to stand behind you; and rests his hands lightly on your shoulders....

He begins by asking you to imagine, feel or sense that (with each in-breath) you are drawing Light in through your heart chakra – front *and* back – until its conical 'funnels' (which connect at your pranic core) open at their roots, and merge to create one single ball of Light that fills the centre of your chest....

After waiting a while for this to happen, he directs you to continue drawing Light in through your heart, using each in-breath to expand the ball of Light until it encompasses your throat and solar plexus chakras – seeing or imagining that their conical 'funnels' likewise open at their roots, until they too are fully incorporated in the ball of Light....

Once again he waits for this to happen, before instructing you to continue drawing Light in through your heart until the ball of Light has expanded yet further – this time to incorporate your brow and sacral chakras in the same manner as before.... After another pause, he directs you to continue expanding the ball of Light – this time incorporating your crown and base chakras, once again in the same manner as before....

When he is satisfied that you have united your seven primary chakras, Sandalphon lifts his left hand so that it hovers a hand-span above your crown; and lowers his right hand so that it hovers a hand-span below the base of your spine: as he does, he explains that these two points mark the locations of the Alpha and Omega centres of your Unified Body, which anchor and stabilise the inner core of your Unified Chakra, and anchor it to All That IS.... He then asks you to create another 'Holon of Infinity' – and this time see, imagine, feel or sense the lower loop of the figure '8' passing around your *Omega* centre and the upper loop passing around your *Alpha* centre, once again crossing at your heart....

When you have managed this, Sandalphon instructs you to draw in Light as before, until the ball of Light encompasses and incorporates these two centres.... and, as soon as you have done so, he directs you to send a silver cord of Light UP from your Alpha centre, and connect it *with intent* to your Divine-self.... and send a golden cord of Light DOWN from your Omega centre, and connect it *with intent* to the core of the Earth....

When he is happy that you are fully connected up *and* down, Sandalphon returns his hands to your shoulders, telling you that he will hold your Unified Body stable, whilst you experience how 'being in' Unified Chakra feels for a little while longer....

Eventually Sandalphon judges it is time for you to shift back to 'be' in your Linear energy Body, and asks you to firstly allow your Holon to dissipate.... and then remove your hold on your Unified Chakra by returning your awareness to your Linear chakras – placing your focus on each of your chakras in turn, starting at your crown.... and moving down to your brow.... throat.... heart.... solar plexus.... sacral.... and base – before lastly reinforcing your Linear grounding by taking your attention to your Earth Star chakra and the soles of your feet – *with the intent* of being fully grounded in your Linear Body....

When he is satisfied that you are grounded, Sandalphon returns to sit at your side, and tells you that the quartz 'family' may help you to remember the stages of moving from 'Linear' to 'Unified' Chakra.... Giving you a Smoky Quartz crystal, he reminds you that the core of your Unified Chakra is held at your heart, saying:

> "Smoky Quartz embodies the Body and Heart of the Earth. The iron core of the Earth is a part of its fabric, and thus it carries the vibration of earthly Life itself – for from the core does all spring forth, and to the core will all eventually return. Thus, through this crystal you may ground to the heart of the Earth and the heart of yourself, which IS both your centre and the root of all that you are...."

Giving you a Citrine crystal, he reminds you that your Unified Chakra next incorporates your solar plexus and throat chakras (reasoning and communication), saying:

> "Citrine embodies the Mind of the Earth. It is structure; it is Creation, shaping all in order – the antithesis of chaos. It connects body to mind – and all to the Mind of the Cosmos, collating information and knowledge so that all may access it. For the mind IS

all-knowing; all-seeing – reaching out to the Infinite Universe from the Heart of All...."

Next giving you a Rose Quartz crystal, he reminds you that your Unified Chakra next incorporates your brow and sacral chakras (intuition and emotion), saying:

"Rose Quartz embodies the Emotion of the Earth – her heart-felt love and gentleness, which fills every atom, every cell; and illuminates all thoughts, words and deeds. Love IS the Fire of Creation that sparks to Life all that is made manifest; and is the pure love of the Creator in its most vibrant and potent form: for while Mind Creates, it is Love *that animates and gives life to all that has been made...."*

Now giving you an Amethyst crystal, he reminds you that your Unified Chakra next incorporates your base and crown chakras (physical-self and Spiritual-self), saying:

"Amethyst embodies the Spirit of the Earth. It inspires the inner knowing that is beyond what the logical mind perceives, by awakening the Light within that exists throughout infinity and spans all Times and Dimensions. It knows all that was, is and will be – and thus its Light empowers the Spirit to have faith in the infinite Plan of the infinite Creator, giving all hope in the certainty that all IS Divine...."

Next giving you a transparent Clear Quartz crystal, he reminds you that your Alpha and Omega centres connect you to the full spectrum of Light, which IS all things, throughout all Space, Time and Dimension, saying:

"Clear Quartz embodies the Soul of the Earth. It holds awareness of Infinite existence, and knows the multiplicity and vastness of your True Self – for it is the Recorder of the Universe, existing on many Planes and Dimensions in service to all Divine outpourings and Creations. To all things, animate and inanimate, it brings the Light of Source – the essence and Love of Creation, that all *may find and know their reality: thus, as you live within your self-imposed isolation and smallness, know that it offers you a window of clarity through which you may touch the true substance of your Being. So let the rainbow of its knowing fill your heart, mind and Soul with the certainty of your immortal Life – in all its varied and infinite Wisdoms...."*

Finally, Sandalphon gives you a Clear Quartz crystal that contains a number of fine black needle-like inclusions, telling you that this is **Tourmalinated Quartz**, his second Crystal Champion – explaining:

"Tourmaline is often found in association with quartz and is a common inclusion. When black, as here, it creates a powerful stone that is effective at grounding and balancing energy fields and energy centres, and excellent at absorbing and clearing the energy field of negativity – or anything that seeks to cloak or hide the pure Love and Light of Divine Source. Hence you will find Tourmalinated Quartz especially useful to help you ground and assimilate whatever you experience and learn on your spiritual journey, whilst offering you the clarity and sound judgement that will help you find the Truths that lie at the heart of all your encounters."

With a smile, Sandalphon affirms that Tourmalinated Quartz may therefore help you to ground and assimilate the wisdoms offered by the whole quartz family; *and* support your understanding of the construction of your Unified Chakra.

Hearing a sudden sound, you both look up to see a beautiful long-legged grey and black crane emerge from the forest: as it steps elegantly towards you, you marvel at the pale blue-grey colours of its wings and back, and the darker feathery plumes of its neck and head, which has a white cap and a swept-back mass of white plumes at its nape. Sandalphon observes that cranes are revered as symbols of long-life and immortality, and admired for their balance and grace – in this case, the plumes that grace this demoiselle crane's head and neck point to a pure and astute mind that can be both ruthless *and* kind. With a smile, he says that, accordingly, you may choose to call upon **Crane** if you need to more clearly see the truth behind a situation encountered in real life (or when in dream state or journeying); or reach a dispassionate conclusion or decision that is truly right and appropriate for you at that time. Adding that dreams are a gift of your subconscious mind that often offer a means of investigating and understanding past-life learning experiences that you have brought forwards (perhaps unresolved) into your current embodiment, Sandalphon tells you that Crane can also help you recall, interpret and understand the significance behind what you encounter in your dreams, and will aid you in addressing whatever is revealed: this will potentially enable you to balance karmic issues and/or make more sense of your life-plan and/or life-purpose. As the crane approaches him, Sandalphon (rather bizarrely) stands and bows to it – and then begins to dance and sway as if waltzing in time to an invisible orchestra! At this the crane sweeps open its delicate grey and black wings and begins to partner him in a graceful dance – and Sandalphon laughs approvingly, observing that mastering 'Life' doesn't always have to be hard work; and (as you can see) having Crane as a partner will help you dance more easily through life with balance, elegance and grace.

The Gift of The Sacred Seeds of Limitless Potential:
Dance over, Sandalphon bows to the crane in thanks, and gives a low whistle: this summons a raven, who flies down to perch on his right shoulder.... Lifting his hand to stroke the pure black glossy feathers of its back, he tells you that ravens aid and support all those who work with natural forces and laws – for they understand how to utilise them to bring about change and growth. Kneeling in front of you, he holds out his hands for you to re-examine the rings he wears – explaining that they are made of electrum, which is an alloy of silver and gold that holds The Divine Masculine and Divine Feminine virtues of structure and formation; inspiration and animation in perfect balance. He tells you that the script etched into each ring gauge and convey complex calculations of sacred number, form and measure: this helps him 'sow the seeds' of new possibilities and potentials – thus initiating, facilitating and stabilising the evolution of all things in accordance with Sacred and Divine Law. Lifting his right hand, he says that he uses *these* rings to interpret and discern precisely what is needed to bring about balance, harmony or growth; whilst (lifting his left hand) he uses *these* rings to identify and dispense whatever is required to fulfil those needs from within his bag of 'seeds'.

Reaching forwards, Sandalphon places his right hand over your heart – reminding you that this is the location of The Lotus of your Heart (which knows all that you are, and all that you need in this lifetime); and closes his eyes.... After a moment, he reaches into his seed pouch with his left hand and withdraws five seeds – three of which are plant seeds; two of which are seed crystals; then, sitting back on his heels, he places them in his right palm and shows them to you, asking you to look carefully at what you see.... Smiling, he says that each of them has been chosen as being especially useful for you to 'sow' now – the plant seeds being specifically chosen to meet the needs of your heart, mind and spirit (one for each); the seed crystals to meet the needs of your Linear Body and Unified Body (again, one for each): accordingly, each has a particular meaning or use (which might be literal or symbolic), and therefore you will find it useful to identify each seed and explore their meanings through research, using both logic *and* intuition.

Asking you to close your eyes, Sandalphon now reaches out and gently plants the five seeds in your Hara centre, so that they lie within your Holon of Universal Balance (the Gift of his twin flame, Shekhinah), saying:

"My Gift of The Sacred Seeds of Limitless Potential has been given to reinforce your Soul's expression of your True Self in this incarnation. Each of the seeds has been specifically chosen to supply you with an asset or attribute; situation or event that will help your current growth, learning and development – guided by and based upon what you have learnt from prior life experiences, both in this lifetime and in others. What has been planted will be nurtured and fed by your inner wisdom and consciousness – and as each seed grows, they will offer you a myriad of new opportunities and choices. Note that (even though all have been sown together) each seed may ripen or fruit at different times, in order to take account of your progress – whilst still anticipating your future needs. You should also be aware that the growth of the seeds may also act to stimulate the awakening of seeds planted long ago by the Elohim and the Angelic Hierarchy, with particular regard to the unfolding of the plan for Earth's Spiritual evolution – of which you are, of course, a part."

As soon as his Gift has been given, the raven flies off, and Sandalphon stands and gives another whistle – at which you hear the rattling of tail feathers. Opening your eyes, you find a pure white peacock standing in front of you.... and, with a laugh, Sandalphon tells you that he and Metatron (his 'brother-in-arms') share a Creature Companion – although Metatron's is (of course!) brightly coloured. He adds that this 'sharing' is not accidental, as they also share tasks concerning the distribution of the Divine Light – Metatron measuring, ordering and balancing the *individual* aspects of Light (the spectrum Rays); whilst he, Sandalphon, holds, focuses and grounds the Absolute – Unified – Light.

Taking your attention back to the white peacock, he points out how the beautiful patterns in its plumage, and the intricate 'eyes' and markings in its tail feathers, are still discernable despite its whiteness – illustrating that pattern and design are always present, even when the Light is both absolute *and* ONE. Therefore you may choose to call upon **White Peacock** when you are practising being 'in' Unified Chakra or Body; or when you simply need to hold or focus upon the purity and integrity of the Divine Light – perhaps if you find yourself in darkness (literal or figurative), or have lost your way and need a reminder of the 'light at the end of the tunnel'; or if you need to clear or cleanse yourself of any negativity (for which the tail feathers are particularly useful); or if you need to see something through the pure eyes of Truth. As the peacock draws closer Sandalphon says that the other difference between their Companions is that Metatron's peacock holds the masculine Light of the Sun; whereas his carries the feminine Light of the Moon, which is more nurturing: yet, when brother meets brother the two combine – Sun with Moon – in a pure and Sacred Marriage that has the potential to quicken the Christed-self within every embodied Soul. Hence you may also call for White Peacock to teach you how to nurture the gifts and attributes that may best help you to embody and BEcome your Christed-self; or to help you bring your masculine and feminine aspects into appropriate balance in and for each situation; or to show you how to embrace the powers and skills of intuition and creativity that will best aid and support your personal transformation and spiritual growth.

Reaching down to the peacock's back, Sandalphon lifts a multi-coloured stone that was resting there, and gives it to you. He says that this is **Gaia** (Polychrome) **Jasper**, his third Crystal Champion – explaining:

"Gaia Jasper is a joyful and well-grounded stone that resonates with the fundamental spiritual essence of Mother Earth – land, sea and sky. Gaia Jasper is a celebration of the great diversity and potential of the planet, both as a physical geological and spiritual entity; and as home base for the vast range of sentient life forms that inhabit her lands, oceans and skies. Although Jaspers do not, as a rule, resonate to a high frequency, Gaia Jasper has the unique ability to assist you in tuning-in to the full range of the Earth's natural resonances, whilst also strengthening your connections with the inner workings of the planet – and ultimately, of course, to the Cosmos. Thus Gaia Jasper may speak to you of the innate strength and spirit of the Earth and of all that connects and sustains her, as she dances through the vastness of space; and of the wondrous artistry and loving care of the Creator that is shown in the formation and beauty of each and every particle of her Being (remember – as it is with the planet, so too is it with you!) Through Gaia Jasper you may also connect more effectively with the fundaments of the planet – the Elemental Forces and Elements, and all those that work with them, including the Elementals and the Elohim – the Divine Architects responsible for the formation and structure of all the great Bodies of the Cosmos, including those of the Earth and the Solar System."

With a smile, Sandalphon affirms that Gaia Jasper may therefore help you appreciate the magnitude and diversity of nature's gifts that 'membership of planet Earth' allows you!

The Greenwood Guardians – Oak and Coconut:

His *personal* mentoring complete for now, Sandalphon affirms he is always available to aid and support you: you need only bring him to mind and ask for his presence, and he will attend you. Furthermore, he tells you that two great Tree Beings of the Plant Kingdom have also asked to support you in addressing his Theme of 'BALANCE AND GROWTH', adding that you need only request *their* presence, and they will be with you.

He explains that the first of these Greenwood Guardians is the Feminine essence of Oak, who has asked to overlight and help you ground whatever work you undertake within *any* aspect of his chapter. The second is the Masculine essence of Coconut, who has specifically asked to help you understand and assimilate his Gift of The Sacred Seeds of Limitless Potential (if you have chosen to accept it).

When you are ready to connect with Sandalphon's first Greenwood Guardian, you need simply call for the presence of **Oak** (*) .... Oak envelops you in a silvery reflective Light, and the Feminine spirit essence of Oak speaks to you, saying:

> *"Above all things, I know balance. It is my crowning glory, and all that holds and sustains me, enabling me to BE in this world for centuries of learning and growth, channelling the Divine Light into the core of the planet, that she – and all that live with her – may know the Love which that Light brings. Thus, I know well how to withstand the seasons and changes that affect the environment in which I grow; and have learned to adapt and adjust myself to BE, regardless.... So stand with me, and feel my regal grace surround you; be sheltered in my arms, and let me relieve you of the pressures that modern life may send to test you; lean against me, and allow my strength and wisdom to fill you with faith and trust, whilst stiffening your backbone and increasing your resilience and capability to live and learn from all that you experience.... For you are unique – just as every oak tree is; yet you are* also *the same at heart as all others that inhabit your world. Remember: our bark may be different; our leaves may not be the same – but we have the same sap running through our hearts and veins, which supports and maintains all that we are, that we may all be a reflection of The Divine...."*

(* Bloodstone and Green Aventurine will help you ground and connect with the energies and wisdom of Oak, if you wish to enhance your experience using crystals.)

If you have chosen to accept and work with Sandalphon's Gift, and when you are ready to connect with his second Greenwood Guardian, you need simply call for the presence of **Coconut** (*) .... Coconut envelops you in a pale green Light, and the Masculine spirit essence of Coconut speaks to you, saying:

> *"It is rare that one such as I may be of such infinite and varied service to those that rely on me for their needs – for, although I may not appear the most beauteous of trees, my bounty is glorious, and knows no bounds.... From the bark that shields me; the fronds that crown me; and the sweet white purity of my fruits that adorn me, I have been created to provide. So allow me to feed you and shelter you; nourish you and refresh you, that you may realise and accept that the Creator knows all needs – and would never stint on supplying them. All you need do in return is accept and be thankful, appreciating and recognising the abundance and wonder that surrounds you at all times: thus, open your eyes and truly see.... open your ears and truly hear.... open your mind and truly know.... open your heart and truly love – yourself, and* all *things.... For in that absolute state of wise and perfect love you will understand what should be valued – and what, in truth, is of no consequence at all!...."*

(* White Moonstone will help you ground and connect with the energies and wisdom of Coconut, if you wish to enhance your experience using crystals.)

ARCHEIA MAREIA

'RETURN THE LIGHT TO YOUR LIFE'

CRYSTAL CHAMPIONS:

Seraphinite ♥ Scolecite ♥ Turquoise

CREATURE COMPANIONS:

White Eagle ♥ Puffin ♥ Hummingbird

GREENWOOD GUARDIANS:

Baobab ♥ Yew

*I fill myself with the Light of The Divine.
I have the potential for all things
within me.*

MEETING MAREIA

It is a fine summer's evening, and you find yourself standing under wide open skies on a deserted sandy beach at the point where land meets sea, the sand stretching out to either side of you in a long curving crescent of pale sun-kissed gold. The apricot orb of the setting sun shimmers as it slowly slips below the horizon where silvered sea meets graphite sky; and, as you watch it drop from view, the sky slowly darkens and starts to fill with tiny pinpricks of light as the stars begin to emerge. Gradually the heat of the day gives way to the cool air of night, and you find yourself relaxing as you listen to the hypnotic tumbling hiss of the waves as they tirelessly advance and retreat, relentlessly curling onto the shore and then withdrawing in phosphorescent sheets of silken water. Time passes.... then suddenly (and rather bizarrely) a snow-white cloud, outlined in a radiant light as if its edges have been dipped in liquid gold, appears on the horizon: this drifts steadily through the night sky until it is high overhead – its billowy whiteness a stark contrast against the flat blackness of the heavens beyond. Then, as you watch, a small feathery white cloud detaches itself from the larger mass and drops rapidly towards you, its features gradually becoming more and more distinct the closer it gets, until you finally realise that what you had thought to be a cloud is in fact a huge white eagle.

With every powerful beat of its wings the eagle flies ever closer, eventually landing in front of you and mantling its wings. Hunkering down, it surveys you with intelligent eyes that are a deep and clear blue – at which you somehow know that it is inviting you to climb onto its back: so you carefully scramble up and make yourself comfortable, tucking your legs in front of its wing joints and settling down on its shoulders. Then, as you gently grasp the deep ruff of snowy feathers that graces its neck, the eagle lifts its head – and with one giant bound it leaps from the ground, every mighty wing-stroke lifting you higher and higher. Looking up, you realise that your destination is the cloud from whence it came, which is now even whiter and brighter than before, as if it is being illuminated from within; and, as a few more strong wing beats brings you closer still, you feel dwarfed by its size, which is much greater than it seemed from the ground now far below you.... Finally you reach the fringes of the cloud, and an opening appears – presumably leading deeper into its interior – and waiting for you here stands a tall and elegant lady robed in periwinkle-blue: this is Archeia Mareia. As the eagle alights on the cloud-clad ledge in front of her, she holds out her arms in welcome, declaring:

"I am Mareia, the Lady Virtue – Keeper of the Emerald Key of Divine Resonance and Balance, Joint Overseer of the Universal Star of Infinity, and twin flame of Raphael. Through the Temple of my Being, which lies twixt Heaven and Earth, you may see that all paths are open to those that walk with peace in their hearts: for with perfect peace comes perfect balance, just as with perfect balance may be found perfect peace. Thus, to be in harmony with your Self and all around you is to be at one with all – and to be at one with all is to know and understand the effortless rhythm of life, as it was meant to be. Understand that ALL that falls from the hand of the Creator is Blessed with the inner knowing of how to walk in peace, for all was founded with love! So feel my peace surround you, and allow the purity and innate goodness of your heart and Soul to rise to the surface and be fully with you, and thus in this world.... then allow yourself to feel

the love that is always with you, and cease all struggle: for to simply accept and BE in the flow is to be truly at ease; and then, as you walk freely with balanced footsteps, life's burdens will be nothing, and your transformation may be easy and without pain."

After thanking the eagle Mareia invites you to dismount, and so, with great trepidation, you climb down – and, discovering that the 'cloud' beneath your feet is in fact amazingly solid, you realise that this world is probably not what it seems to be on the surface!

Acknowledging your thought with an enigmatic smile, Mareia enters the opening in the cloud and leads you down a long tunnel-like passage, which in due course winds its way into a wide bowl-shaped arena that is open to the night sky above. The walls of the arena are made of deep drifts of feathery white clouds, which are constantly moving and shifting so that they form and reform a series of ethereal images and scenes – those to your left currently depicting a galloping herd of white horses; those to your right, a flock of white doves in flight.... The floor of the arena is illuminated in a soft white light, revealing it to be crisscrossed by white marble pathways laid out in a 'spider-web' pattern: these delineate neat rows of flowerbeds crammed with lilies-of-the-valley, whose spear-like emerald leaves shelter and support their gracefully arching stems of white bell-shaped flowers; and draw the eye towards the very centre of the garden, where a pure white lilac tree (in full and perfect bloom) stands sentinel amidst silvery-white drifts of slender-stemmed honesty. The arching branches of the lilac tree shelter a white alabaster bench that sits between a pair of white marble pillars, and it is here that Mareia leads you – settling her gown around her as she sits, and inviting you to join her so that you may take your time to examine her and become accustomed to her energies.

As you make yourself comfortable, you see that each pillar that flanks the bench bears an engraving – one portraying a sleeping mouse; the other a coiled-up blind-snake: observing your curiosity, Mareia merely smiles, surveying you with eyes that are the cool clear colour of the finest ice-blue topaz. These are set below finely arched eyebrows in a delicate oval face that has small and dainty features and a slightly pointed chin. Her skin is clear and milk-white; whilst her long chestnut-red hair is the exact colour of a freshly shelled conker: she wears this with a centre-parting, and drawn straight back from her face to mantle her shoulders, from where it cascades to her waist in glossy undulating waves. Her hair is anchored at temples and nape with a simple silver circlet that sits over her Soma and Universal centres, twisting once at her brow to form an elongated oval loop that points backwards over the centre-parting of her hair.

Your examination of her features complete, you survey Mareia's attire starting with her medieval style gown, which is made from deep periwinkle-blue velvet – the nap of which holds many subtle hues and tones of violet and blue. It has a rounded neckline that sits just below her collarbone; and long flowing sleeves that drape loosely to her wrists – the hem, neckline and cuffs being embroidered with silver thread in a complex repeating pattern of concentric round and oval loops: closer examination shows these to be grouped in sets of six – each set overlapping its neighbours, and having a common root at the edge of the fabric. The bodice of the gown is corseted, fitting closely to Mareia's upper body and waist, from where its generously-full floor-length skirt falls in soft folds to pool around her feet, which are shod in slippers made of the same velvet as the gown – their tops embroidered in silver thread, using a simple design of four oval loops connected at a common centre, like a four-petalled flower.

As Mareia shifts and folds her hands into her lap, the light catches a ring that adorns the third finger of her left hand: on closer inspection, you can see that this bears a large polished oval cabochon of white scolecite, secured in a simple claw-setting on a plain, wide, silver band. This leads your attention to her right hand, which is holding something that has a simple silver handle, similar to that of a corkscrew, but which is shaped like a flat infinity symbol (∞). Opening this hand, she allows you to briefly see that whatever it is has a plain silver shaft that is embedded in a short triangular pillar, from which three small and slender silver prongs (or tines) extend downwards, one from each corner.

As she closes her hand again, your eye is lastly drawn to the wide silver bracelet that snugly encircles her right wrist: this bears a small silver cube surmounted by two entwined short and slender silver pillars, which hold and support a small circular plate of hammered silver. Looking at this more closely, you can see that two small circles have been cut from this plate – taking a round 'bite' out of the circle on opposite sides, and so creating a shape that is like an arcing double-bladed axe: each of these curved halves bear a small cut and faceted oval yellow sapphire in their centre; whilst a large oval faceted purple amethyst (which is the crystal that links her with Raphael, her twin flame) bridges the 'bites', spanning the centre of the plate.

MAREIA'S TEACHINGS
The Emerald Key of Modification and Balance:

Recognising that your scrutiny is complete, Mareia gestures at the arena's walls: with a smile she tells you that she sees clouds as Elemental messengers from Heaven, for they hold many symbolic 'nuggets of wisdom' in their ever-changing patterns and forms. She explains that this is because clouds comprise the primary Elements of air and water (the Elements that relate to the mind and the emotions), and can form pictures designed to fire and inspire the imagination – serving as a reminder that all things are possible through the infinite flexibility of Free Will, which allows life to be lived without limits: furthermore, whatever their observer interprets within the patterns they form often has relevance to something that requires their attention or consideration at that time – with particular regard to the thinking and reactive processes concerned with *making* a choice or decision and/or *experiencing* the consequences of a choice or decision.

Taking your attention to the open sky above you, Mareia waves her hand, at which night instantaneously becomes day – and you watch in fascination as wispy white clouds gather and mass in the turquoise sky, shifting and morphing (as clouds do) into a series of formations that remind you of different animals: each one is only there for a moment before changing form – unicorn.... wolf.... bear.... bull.... monkey; and, as each in turn forms and fades, Mareia explains that these are animal totems, which each embody a set of qualities of mind that may help you master her Theme of 'Return the Light to your Life' – in this case the attributes of 'purity'; 'learning'; 'introspection'; 'strength' and 'ingenuity'.... As the clouds you have been observing begin to thin and dissipate, Mareia expounds that this might then be interpreted as: having a clear (*pure*) mind will aid in your *learning* and understanding, and *self-review* will strengthen your *determination* and sense of purpose, helping you to be open-minded and *flexible* in all you think and do.

Reminding you that the possibilities open to you are infinite, Mareia tells you that this is because Free Will allows you access to the complete spectrum of the Divine Light. With a smile, she says that she helps balance and fine-tune the infinite resonances and frequencies *of* that Light by means of the Emerald Ray – the Ray that she and Raphael oversee and direct: she then lifts the silver tool from her lap, and shows you that there is a superbly clear emerald (which has been cut and faceted in a 'trillion' cut) embedded in its triangular-shaped end. She explains that she uses this tool like a 'tuning key' to make very fine and precise adjustments to the frequencies of red, blue and green Light (the three primary resonances of White Light), each of which is assessed by one of the three silver tines jutting from its end: to do so, she focuses the Emerald Ray through the gem at their core; and uses it to determine and establish the appropriate ratios of each required in (and for) each situation being addressed.

After thinking for a moment, Mareia points to one of the tines of the 'tuning key' and says that (basically) *green* Light holds, supports and contains all things in a state of constant equilibrium, and maintains the frequencies required for Free Will to function.... pointing to the next, she says that *red* Light supplies the energies of fundamental nurture at its most basic and necessary level, providing the sound foundation that allows and enables consequent impulses to emerge, thus inspiring learning and growth.... pointing to the other, she says that *blue* Light facilitates all actions to do with communication and hence Creation – for all things are made manifest through the Logos (the 'Word' – the controlling principle in the Universe, which might be defined as 'Divine Wisdom made manifest in the Creation of All That Is').... Mareia lastly rests a fingertip on the emerald, and says that the catalytic energy of the Emerald Ray of Profound Truths and Potential sparks with pure Power – constantly defining and redefining the creative potential of Divine Mind: the infinite and vast awareness that IS both all *and* nothing! Smiling again, she adds that *this* is what assesses and determines, fires and inspires the 'fine-tuning' that is required.

Putting the key to one side, Mareia muses that Light can be perceived in many different ways – both directly, through its sound, colour, wavelength, resonance and vibration; and indirectly, through observing the behaviours its actions engender. With another smile, she adds that (luckily!) it is not necessary to *understand* Light in order to know its effects, for it is with you at all times: indeed, your subtle-energy system innately knows how to draw upon different frequencies of Light in order to survive and grow – hence, at times of doubt or uncertainty it is always a good idea to pause, step back, relax and BE; and then simply allow yourself time to view and consider things (subconsciously and consciously) from different and Higher perspectives.

Asking you to close your eyes, Mareia invites you to immerse yourself in the peace of her garden – opening your mind and your senses to everything that surrounds you; and simply accepting that your body instinctively knows how to find balance.... as you close your eyes your awareness shifts, and you feel a cooling breeze softly caressing your skin, and hear the papery whispers of the seed-heads of honesty as they sway and shift in the gentle wind.... then gradually the sweet scent of lilac envelops you and fills your senses, and your breath slows and deepens – all your subtle senses awakening and sharpening; your chakras instinctively and effortlessly aligning and coming slowly into balance, until you feel centred, focused and alert – yet unexpectedly peaceful and calm....

Resting her hand gently on your knee, Mareia says she knows that focusing your mind on an issue that requires your attention can be hard to do if you feel under pressure or out-of-sorts – but reminds you that closing your eyes and slowing your breaths will help you to relax and ground yourself, so that you can find your centre: then, by slowing your breath still further until your body and mind become fully calm and still, your energies can gently align without effort or stress – helping you to isolate and understand what needs addressing; and enabling you to shape and refine an effective and practical plan that will help you to achieve the most positive outcome.

After allowing you a few more moments of peace, Mareia asks you to open your eyes: giving a high-pitched whistle, she calls to the eagle that brought you to this place, who quickly answers her – passing low over the garden, before landing softly at her side. Stroking its pure white plumage Mareia tells you that this regal eagle carries and grounds the profoundly refined energies of the White Light of The Divine *and* the Gold Light of the Christ: hence **White Eagle** is always willing to bring the wise and compassionate mercy of your Higher (Christed *and* Divine) Selves to bear upon *any* situation or issue you need guidance upon – perhaps helping you understand and assimilate a particularly difficult or traumatic 'life-lesson'; or aiding you in reviewing and considering all your options if you have reached a turning point or a new stage in your life. Reminding you that – as with clouds – the many experiences and challenges you encounter in life often take different forms (each of which will have something new to teach or show you) she says that White Eagle can also teach you to master the art of balance from many different viewpoints and perspectives; or assist you in visualising and refining the next steps of a plan or scheme that will help you heal, grow or progress on any level. With a smile, she adds that clouds exemplify the transient nature of life, demonstrating that the Universe – of which you are but an aspect – is never static, but is constantly changing and evolving: hence White Eagle may also be asked to lend you his clear and penetrating vision if you wish to track and review the patterns of your own evolution with greater insight and clarity; or if you need to see beyond the surface of something in order to identify what *truly* lies beneath. She remarks that this may be especially helpful if you are not in good health (physically, mentally, emotionally *or* spiritually), when calling for White Eagle's wise and dispassionate viewpoint may help you firstly identify and understand the root cause of whatever besets you; and then secondly show you the most appropriate path to follow, in order to bring about change and resolution for the better.

With a sudden cry, the eagle takes to the sky again, dropping a deep green stone marked with feathery silver swirls into your lap: with a chuckle, Mareia tells you that this is a gift of **Seraphinite**, her first Crystal Champion – explaining:

> *"Seraphinite holds the Light of The Divine Feminine and the Angelic Realms, restoring the whole and balanced Light of Spirit to matter by means of the Silver and Emerald Rays: thus Seraphinite is a powerful catalyst for personal and spiritual evolution – its*

clear and compassionate strength radiating in spiralling waves of joyous peace that envelop you in an embrace that is both calming and reassuring, negating all cares and worries, and supporting self-understanding by opening, balancing and aligning your primary chakras and energy Bodies. Seraphinite may then flood all that you are with Light to engender self-healing and positive health and wholeness throughout all levels of your Being – it's high-frequency energies assisting you in releasing anything that is not of the Highest order within your emotional (reactive) and mental (thinking) Bodies, whilst reminding your physical body of the true perfection of its innate blueprint, which is embedded within your DNA. This can aid your evolution on all levels, by freeing you to assume the form that is your birthright and true purpose for Being; whilst giving you the determination, self-will and mental flexibility to enable and allow yourself to do and become anything you truly wish or need to be."

With a smile, Mareia affirms that Seraphinite may therefore help you reclaim your inner balance and know true healing, by opening you to the truths that underlie your reason for be-ing, and helping you acknowledge and accept that everything happens for a reason.

The Evolution of Life and the Perfection of Divine Creation:

Mareia tells you that 'Archangels' *never* embody on the earthly Plane – but they do sometimes act as Divine overseers or Overlighting Influences if there is a need to guide (or energetically support) incarnated Souls who have taken on roles that are significant or important to Earth's spiritual evolution, especially if their tasks are designed to catalyse radical change: indeed, it was her charge – and her joy – to oversee, inspire and support the Lady Master who embodied as the Mother of the Christ, sustaining both her and her son (the Christed-one) throughout their time on Earth. Mareia explains that this was because – as an Archeia – her primary function is to maintain the perfected conception of whatever needs to be made manifest, by regulating and charging it with the appropriate resonances of Divine Light, whilst concurrently monitoring and anchoring the perfected (yet constantly evolving) blueprints for its *spiritual* development and growth. She smiles, and expounds that her duties therefore embrace the foundation, establishment and evolutionary design of *all* the spiritual processes that guide Life and all life-forms (from the tiniest plankton in the oceans, to the largest Galaxies in the Universe) – adding that this is always done in accord with her twin flame (Raphael)'s work, which embraces the anchoring, holding and overseeing of the perfected multidimensional blueprints of the *physical* presence of everything that IS, including their structure and its evolution.

Revealing that she uses three items (along with her Emerald Key) to accomplish her tasks, Mareia points firstly to the silver circlet she wears: she tells you that this enables her to isolate and examine each component part of something in great detail, so that she knows if, when, why and how it has strayed from the Divine ideal.... she next points to the silver ring on her left hand, explaining that the scolecite it bears holds a many-rayed star formed of pure White Light, which she can draw upon, focus and direct, in order to address whatever requires adjustment; and restore it to its approved design.... she lastly points to the construct surmounting the silver band on her right wrist, adding that this connects her to the templates of Creation, as defined by Divine Mind; and (if and where modification is needed) enables her to catalyse the requisite patterns of Light, by way of the Divinely-directed Will that moves and inspires *all* evolution. With another smile she expounds that *this* involves a two-way flow of information (remember, information *is* Light) by means of the Silver, Amethyst and Yellow Rays: the silver elements guiding and enabling all movement and flow.... the amethyst crystal ensuring that all the Light frequencies are spiritually pure.... the yellow sapphires aligning and balancing action, logic and individual will with intention, spiritual understanding and Divine Will....

After pausing for a while, appreciating that she has given you a lot of information to absorb, Mareia observes that sometimes you need to *experience* something in order to *understand* it – and with these words she moves to stand behind you, and gently places her hands on your shoulders.... Asking you to give her your trust, she explains that (in order for you to gain a sense of the process that fires evolution and change), she needs to merge her energies with yours, so that she may monitor and guide your experience: all you need to do is let go; relax; and allow yourself to 'become' a part of her energy.... So, reassured by her serene (and inspiring) presence, you relax and let go....

As you do, you feel your energy field expanding outwards – and little by little your awareness merges with Mareia's, who is embracing the consciousness of every living structure and life-form in the garden with a feather-light touch.... In a strange (yet deeply profound) way, it somehow feels as if everything that is 'you' and 'other than you' has merged, and then expanded – drawing apart to expose every particle *and* the 'space' between them to your view; and thus enabling you to objectively, yet compassionately, assess their spiritual wellness and balance.... Recognising what you are experiencing, Mareia explains that what you might think to be 'empty space' is *not* a vacuum: rather, what you are observing is Black Light – the counterpoint of White Light, which provides the means and conditions that allow and enable change and creative processes to occur.... Gently squeezing your shoulders, she reveals that *here*, through the actions of Divine Forces and the Light that is held and distributed throughout the Universal Matrix, exists the means for the manifestation of *any* and all potentials – and, as your mind absorbs her words, your vision suddenly shifts and begins to function on a different level....

Looking now with your inner eye, you watch a deep blue Light that is filled with sparks of silver energy slowly penetrate what you had thought to be 'empty space'.... With a sense of detached curiosity you observe how some of the silver sparks 'touch' some of the particles – enlivening, changing or modifying them.... whilst other silver sparks suddenly flare up and then seemingly vanish, leaving a brand new particle in their wake.... Suspended in the midst of it all, it feels as if you *are* both the observer and the observed – the sparks, the Light.... the space, the particles – old and new, timeless and infinite.... After allowing you to experience this for a few moments more, Mareia helps you contract your energy field – gradually redefining your awareness and realigning and reintegrating everything around you, until you are the 'you' that you are familiar with, resting on the bench in the middle of her garden....

Once she is happy that you are fully restored, Mareia lifts her hands and returns to your side, remarking that you have experienced just a small glimpse of the evolution of Life (as viewed from the Dimensional state within which you are currently embodied)!

Giving you a small glossy white striated stone that is like the one held in her ring, she tells you that this is **Scolecite**, her second Crystal Champion – explaining:

> *"Scolecite has a High pure energy whose serene stability emits an aura of peace and grace that will help you centre, relax and connect with the innate essence of your Soul: this will make it easier to expand your awareness and make profound connections across Time, space and Dimensions, which may greatly aid and further your insights into the art of co-creation, and enable you to gain a greater understanding of yourself and your place in the Universe. Scolecite also channels 'Liquid Light', which may be used to fill and charge all of your energy Bodies – nourishing and feeding your Soul and Spirit, and helping awaken your awareness of the innate perfection of your own design, and the reasons for it 'being' the way it is. Scolecite in this form holds the full spectrum of White Light, making it very useful for effectively clearing psychic debris that has accumulated through holding on to 'negative' thoughts or emotions, and for balancing the energies of any of your chakras. In its clear crystalline form Scolecite's Crystal Ray energy (which makes it particularly powerful, cleansing and penetrating) can be used to remove density from anywhere within your energy field: this is especially effective if combined with the power of the Violet Flame through visualisation and/or with the support of an amethyst crystal, thereby helping you clear yourself of 'negative' influences, and leading to greater clarity and enhanced spiritual health."*

With a smile, Mareia affirms that Scolecite may therefore help your spiritual growth, by enabling you to experience and learn from do-ing and be-ing many things.

Suddenly your eye is drawn to a splash of colour at the edge of your vision, and you watch in amazement as a puffin waddles down the path towards you. Mareia chuckles, and remarks that this little bird is a triumph of hope over adversity – for although its design seems to make no sense, it can fly (albeit not very far!), swim, *and* burrow in the ground: hence **Puffin** is familiar with the vagaries of the Elements of earth, air and water, and can be called upon to help you balance your physical body, mind and emotions with greater ease. Moreover, Puffin's mastery of the oceans can help you to navigate life's sometimes stormy seas with humour and grace, aiding you in controlling any self-destructive thoughts and emotions – especially those that concern things outside of your control, or the 'little things' that stress you out, but are *truly* not important. Pointing out its orange webbed feet, and the colourful red, orange and yellow markings on its bill and around its eyes, she explains that these reinforce Puffin's connections with the lower three chakras and associated auric Bodies; whilst the clearly-defined black and white of its stumpy body and wings shows that it understands how to use and balance Black and White Light with both humour and ease: accordingly you can ask Puffin to help you see the marvels in all the creatures that share your world – whether beautiful, ugly, gentle, fierce, highly-coloured or monochrome – so that you may appreciate how everything that lives is designed with purpose and care, thus enabling many different existences to be experienced and enjoyed. Mareia affirms that Puffin may also come to inspire *you* to uphold a philosophy or viewpoint that fosters greater respect and love for all of the natural world, understanding that all things are innately designed to evolve naturally over time, and that to change or destroy any part of it without thought (or through greed or the wrong use of power) upsets the innate balance that holds the world in order – which of course ultimately would have a negative impact on the Divine Plan for the growth and evolution of the third-Dimensional human experience.

The Gift of The Infinity Cross of Multidimensional Reality:

Recognising that you are ready to begin to understand what she now wishes to convey, Mareia removes one of her slippers to show you the design embroidered upon it: she tells you that this is a pattern known as the 'Infinity Cross', because it resembles two infinity symbols (which each embraces the concept of limitlessness) crossing each other at right angles through their centres. She encourages you to trace out its shape with your finger, first one '8' then the other.... and, as you do, she adds that the Infinity Cross may also be used as an aid to self-healing: you need only to physically draw or paint it (using whatever colours you are drawn to use at that time); and then meditate upon it....

Asking you to continue to trace the '8's, Mareia explains that the Infinity Cross is just a part of a much greater blueprint that holds the perfected designs upon which all life is founded – which is something called the 'Infinity Star': this bridges the concept of limitlessness both multidimensionally and multiversally – and so, in its many forms, the Infinity Cross *and* the Infinity Star are something both she and Raphael are very familiar with, because it is so closely linked with their work in anchoring the blueprints for the potential and perfection of every evolving life-form in the Universe throughout all Times and Planes of Dimension.

Returning her slipper to her foot, Mareia next explains that what you know as DNA is just part of the blueprint that holds all that is, was and ever will be required for your own foundation and growth – wherever and whatever form that takes.... She adds that (in the explanation that follows) she will continue to use the term 'DNA', because this probably has some meaning for you – although (in very simplistic terms) each strand of DNA is actually an aspect of the Universal Matrix that distributes The Divine Light throughout this Universe, and beyond. Sitting back, Mareia says that she knows this concept may be hard to take in, but it is important to have a basic understanding of the function of the Infinity Cross and the Infinity Star before she gives you her Gift....

Tracing out an Infinity Cross in the air in front of her, she begins by explaining that each of its four loops anchors one strand of your multidimensional DNA – *two* strands of which are detectable within the third-Dimensional *physical* world in which you currently live. She adds that, *very* basically the other two strands (plus four more) 'are' in the next Dimension – elucidating that, as your Light quotient increases and you begin to extend your awareness *beyond* the third Dimension, you will awaken your consciousness to your DNA 'strands' that exist in other Dimensions; and gain more understanding of 'yourself' beyond that which you currently recognise: indeed, by the time you have expanded your awareness to embrace and merge with your fifth-Dimensional Lightbody, you will have accessed and assimilated these eight strands *plus* a further four (making twelve in total)!...

After a pause to allow you enough time to process this information, Mareia smiles and says that this is, of course, not the 'end': for twelve more strands in this Universal

Plane anchor and bridge Dimensions six through to nine; whilst (ultimately) thirty-six Infinity Crosses connect a total of six Universes across forty Dimensions. She adds that these have a common core and comprise the 'Infinity Star' of your total Being, which anchors the energetic signature of your one-hundred and forty-four strand DNA – and embraces all that you are throughout *all* Universal Planes and Dimensions....

Having conveyed all she wishes to on the subject of the Infinity Cross for now, Mareia draws your attention to a tiny hummingbird that is hovering amongst the flowers of the lilac tree.... as you admire its delicate form and the beauty of its iridescent-purple head and throat and emerald-green body and wings, she tells you that this little bird feeds on the lilac's nectar and converts its sweetness into Light – its wings keeping up a steady hover, by constantly moving in a perfect figure '8' or (as you now appreciate) the symbol for Infinity: accordingly you may call upon **Hummingbird** if you seek understanding or answers from past, current or future life events; or if you want help to find or enhance the 'sweetness' in your life; or if you need to make delicate adjustments to your spiritual balance. Tilting her head, Mareia asks you to listen to the musical thrumming of its tiny wings, observing that Hummingbird knows how to use sound to adjust and fine-tune the different frequencies of Light in order to retain perfect balance – innately adjusting its speed and angle of approach, so that it may find the optimum sweetness in every flower: thus Hummingbird can be called upon to teach you how to utilise sound to support your self-healing or meditation practices, enabling you to improve your inner and outer clarity and balance; or to offer you encouragement when you are working hard to achieve your dreams or dearest desires; or to show you a fresh approach if you are encountering blocks or dead-ends. Musing that folklore says that hummingbirds die each night, and are reborn again each morning, Mareia explains that their metabolic resilience means that you may also call Hummingbird if you need to make significant changes in your life or direction, and have to understand how something needs to 'die' in order to give birth to something new; or to help you go within to find a new and greater perspective that can show you how your current existence and/or way of life is but a small part of a much greater (and even more exciting) whole that is crammed with sweetness, Light and potential.

Suddenly, the hummingbird drops down to hover over Mareia's outstretched palm, its wings a blur – before simply vanishing, leaving a pale silver Infinity Cross filling her palm.... Moving to stand in front of you, Mareia lifts her hands to hold the Infinity Cross so that it lies horizontally through your Alpha centre; and so that its centre is aligned with the pranic core of your Unified Energy Body.... she then sets the Infinity Cross gently spinning anticlockwise, so that it spirals down your pranic core to your Omega centre: here it pauses, before a touch of her hand sets it gently spinning clockwise back up your pranic core, finally returning to a rest at your Alpha centre....

Stabilising it here with her hands, Mareia says that her Gift of The Infinity Cross of Multidimensional Reality has been given to help you expand your consciousness beyond the restrictions of your human physical condition, so that you may connect with your Unified Self, and open your awareness to the vastness of your Being: then, surrounding and enfolding you in her energy, she asks you to relax and simply BE in a state of inner balance and peace....

For a timeless moment you are absorbed by the energy that embraces you, and you have a sense of the Infinity Cross settling into position.... as it does, you somehow *know* that it has been encased in Silver Light and filled with a crystal-clear energy that flows like water – at which you hear Mareia explaining that this energy carries the three Divine Expressions of thought, word and deed – those of Law, Formation and Experience, which together will help you access the crystalline clarity of your Divine Consciousness – and so see the world through new eyes that are open to the wonders and delights of Divine Co-creation and Manifestation....

When she is satisfied that the Infinity Cross is securely positioned, and your energy field is in appropriate balance, Mareia returns to your side: giving you a small sky-blue stone, she tells you that this is **Turquoise**, her third Crystal Champion – explaining:

> *"Turquoise connects the Yellow and Blue Rays, so that they may work in harmony to promote clear communication within and without, making it possible to receive and act upon the innovative thoughts, ideas and inspirations that fire your mental reasoning processes, and which drive you to comprehend and accept all that you are. The clarity of a summer sky is grounded through this stone, offering a store of hope, peace and calm that can aid you in accepting that everything you experience is simply an aspect of Divine Order: this does not mean that you have to lie down and accept everything that happens to or around you, but reminds you that being in touch with your True Self (who* knows *your path and destiny) allows you to see their purpose with clear vision. This enables you to know if the troubles, strife or worries that you face are something you need to deal with and master – or if they are signs that you need to stop, think and reassess: if this is the case, Turquoise will help you determine the reality behind what is occurring, and support you in making the changes you need to make. Know too that negativity can only arise if you are not fully aligned with your path and with the Way of Light – which is that of Love: thus Turquoise can also help you clarify and strengthen your energy field, empowering you to lovingly conquer your doubts and fears, and live at all times in harmony with your Highest purpose and Truths."*

Smiling, Mareia affirms that Turquoise may therefore help you gain the clarity and inner peace that will help you release your lesser-ego-based will and desires, and align with the Light that IS your greater (Divine) Consciousness and Will.

The Greenwood Guardians – Baobab and Yew:

Her *personal* mentoring complete for now, Mareia affirms she is always available to aid and support you: you need only bring her to mind and ask for her presence, and she will attend you. Furthermore, she tells you that two great Tree Beings of the Plant Kingdom have also asked to support you in addressing her Theme of 'RETURN THE LIGHT TO YOUR LIFE', adding that you need only request *their* presence, and they will be with you.

She explains that the first of these Greenwood Guardians is the Masculine essence of Baobab, who has asked to overlight and help you ground whatever work you undertake within *any* aspect of her chapter. The second is the Masculine essence of Yew, who has specifically asked to help you understand and assimilate her Gift of The Infinity

Cross of Multidimensional Reality (if you have chosen to accept it).

When you are ready to connect with Mareia's first Greenwood Guardian, you need simply call for the presence of **Baobab** (*) .... Baobab envelops you in an orange-gold Light, and the Masculine spirit essence of Baobab speaks to you, saying:

"You may think that all is lost when you are at your most vulnerable, fearing that the slightest knock will set you awry: yet, I tell you that it is at this time that you are at your strongest! So find your centre – and let your Will be strong.... find your core – and ground up and down, connecting every particle of your Being to the Power of the Universe.... find your heart – and blend it with mine, that you may know and share the Love that brings both beauty and peace..... Then BE with me: for I am Life, through the sun and stars in the sky above me and the living waters of the Earth that I hold within me, that is as Liquid Light is to your Soul.... I am Creation, through the bounty that nourishes all those who understand that even a desert can be a place of succour and plenty.... and I am Balance, through the roots that hold me to the earth and which, through my tenacity, keep me secure even when parched and dry.... Know then that, above all, I AM a Beacon of Light that can guide the lost and the lonely Home...."

(* Infinite Stone and Sunstone will help you ground and connect with the energies and wisdom of Baobab, if you wish to enhance your experience using crystals.)

If you have chosen to accept and work with Mareia's Gift, and when you are ready to connect with her second Greenwood Guardian, you need simply call for the presence of **Yew** (*) .... Yew envelops you in a crystal-clear Light that is filled with sparks of gold, and the Masculine spirit essence of Yew speaks to you, saying:

"Abundance and plenty lie at the end of the long road – its fringes scattered with the bones of our ancestors, which tell both of hardships and pains; joys and delights. Yet all this is inspired and fired by the passion that drives the Soul onwards to experience more; to learn more; to accomplish more.... For the Soul innately knows that until all *is done, and* all *is accomplished it will not truly know peace: yet (paradoxically) it knows too that peace is not enough – for its stillness and silence frets the Soul, and persuades it that stasis is not an option; understanding, perhaps, that it is only through the greatest of efforts and sacrifices that genuine riches can be found.... So seek out those brilliant and sparkling gems of wisdom and profundity, which are scattered across the blackness of space, whose inky void is dark and empty – yet full and vibrant with potential.... For there is where you will find ME.... and there too will you find your immortal Self...."*

(* Bloodstone will help you ground and connect with the energies and wisdom of Yew, if you wish to enhance your experience using crystals.)

ARCHANGEL RAPHAEL

'WHOLENESS THROUGH TRANSFORMATION'

CRYSTAL CHAMPIONS:
Pink Calcite ♥ Aventurine ♥ Watermelon Tourmaline

CREATURE COMPANIONS:
Little Owl ♥ Green Woodpecker ♥ Hornet

GREENWOOD GUARDIANS:
Yew ♥ Maple

I accept all that IS Divine potential, and am filled with the healing Light of Love and Compassion.

MEETING RAPHAEL

It is midday in summer, and you find yourself standing at the top of a grassy meadow that carpets the lower slopes of a cirque (a bowl-shaped glacial valley) set high in an alpine range. The golden-white sun overhead is dazzlingly bright in the cloudless blue sky, and the air is crisp, fresh and wonderfully invigorating – clearing your head with every breath you take, so that you feel mentally sharp and alert. Above you the upper slopes of the cirque are densely wooded – blanketed in a fusion of deciduous and coniferous trees, all leafed in multiple hues and tones of green; over which steel-grey crags rear high into the sky, creating an arc of majestic snow-capped peaks around you – their pure ice-white perfection glittering and sparkling like diamonds in the sun. Below you the emerald meadow leads down to a still lake that lies in the bowl of the cirque, its mirror-like surface perfectly reflecting the grandeur of the landscape behind you – the lip of the bowl curving gently upwards, creating a low ridge across the valley floor. Beyond this the mountainside falls sharply away towards meadows, lakes and dense green forests speckled with smoke-like drifts of cloud, which span the landscape so far below you that it seems as if you are suspended in a world of your own.

Turning your gaze back to the trees and the mountains, your eyes, mind and senses continue to absorb your surroundings – and little by little the tranquil atmosphere of this place frees you of all your stresses and worries, leaving you with a wonderful feeling of calm contentment that makes you wish you could stay here for ever.... then, out of the blue, you feel a cool and gentle energy envelop you in a cloak of perfect peace – and looking around you for its source, you see that a massive sphere of green and violet light has risen up from behind one of the mountain's peaks, and is now soaring through the air towards you....

As it draws closer, the light shimmers – revealing the outline of what you *know* is an Angel (even though, oddly, it has no wings to keep it aloft).... and then the light shifts and morphs, and a masculine human form robed in violet and white alights in front of you: this is Archangel Raphael. He smiles at you and declares:

> *"I am Raphael – Joint Overseer of The Emerald Ray of Profound Truths and Potential for Divine Manifestation, Master of Infinite Balance, and twin flame of Mareia, the Lady Virtue. To be wing-ed would confine me to the heights – and all cannot be sustained in balance if there is restriction or confinement, or an inflexible perspective that rigidly defines what is possible and impossible. Thus I have no limitations and can be all things to all people – for my Light is Universal, continually spiralling in and out of Divine Centre to enfold and enlighten all that it touches, and promote and support a state of continuous evolution. Through the Light that IS, I accordingly align all with the Truth and beauty of their essential nature – enabling and facilitating the flowering of The Divine within all sentient life, whilst ensuring that all is in perfect accord with the blueprints upon which the multidimensional Universe is founded. Hence to work with me may be challenging – for the Diamond point of crystal-clear Consciousness that is within all Beings can only be revealed through hard work and dedication: yet you may be assured that my constancy and support will always be there to encourage and sustain you, even in the darkest of times."*

Inviting you to walk with him, Raphael leads you up to the forest edge, where a winding pathway eventually leads you through the trees to a small clearing in the forest: the ground is carpeted with a dense layer of green and gold moss, in the centre of which you can see a small hexagonal pool that has been hewn from the steel-grey bedrock of the mountain, its waters reflecting the blue sky above. In the centre of this pool is what appears to be an emerald flame, which is burning with such a fiery intensity that it is hard to believe that it is floating on water – and, with an enigmatic smile, Raphael leads you to the far side of the clearing, where two high-backed chairs sit beneath the arched branches of a silver-fir tree: here he selects a chair and makes himself comfortable, inviting you to do likewise so that you may examine him and accustom yourself to his energies.

You have already observed that Raphael is of average height, with a loose-limbed, slim and rangy build that is mirrored in the relaxed – yet alert – way he sits in his chair; and have also seen that he carries a staff, which he is still holding in his right hand. This staff is as long as he is tall, and (rather oddly) looks as if it is a living sapling of hawthorn – having a twining mass of earth-clad roots for its foot; a straight and slender trunk for its shaft; and a head that is a compact mass of thorny branches, covered in small fan-shaped leaves and clusters of tiny pink and white flowers. Shifting your gaze, you note that his other hand is fisted loosely in his lap and – noting your curiosity – he turns his hand over and uncurls his long slender fingers, revealing that he is holding a large and perfect pink danburite crystal.

Placing his staff and crystal to one side, Raphael smoothes down his robes, drawing your attention to his clothing: this comprises a plain and simple floor-length white cotton robe, and a mid-length over-robe of violet linen, whose open front and wide three-quarter length sleeves reveal the long sleeves and high rounded neck of the white robe beneath. Raphael's feet are just visible beneath the hem of the white robe, and you notice they are tanned and slender, like his hands, and are shod in very simple rope sandals. As he shifts his hands, a metallic glimmer suddenly catches your eye – and, taking another look at his over-robe, you note that its edges and cuffs have been embroidered with silver thread to create a repeating pattern of concentric round and oval loops, closer inspection of which reveals them to be grouped in sixes – each set overlapping its neighbours, yet having a common root at the fabric's edge.

Your attention is then claimed by the light shimmering around the complex (and rather intriguing) pendant that hangs from a gold chain around Raphael's neck. This rests over his High Heart centre; and is made from a circular plate of hammered gold from which two small circles have been cut – taking a round 'bite' out of the plate on opposite sides, and so creating a shape that is like an arcing double-bladed axe: each of these curved halves bear an oval cut and faceted orange sapphire in their centre; whilst a large oval faceted purple amethyst (which is the crystal that links him with Mareia, his twin flame) bridges the 'bites', spanning the centre of the plate.

Your inspection of his attire complete, you lastly turn your attention to Raphael's face: this is a perfect oval, with tanned olive-complexioned skin that is clear and unlined, giving him a youthful appearance. All his features are neat and sharply defined, and are framed by a fall of long straight jet-black hair, which has been drawn back and tucked over his ears, so that it hangs in a silky curtain to his shoulders. His eyes are deeply set below a pair of arching black eyebrows over a long straight nose, and are a very clear and penetrating emerald-green; and then – as you meet his gaze – they suddenly widen, and you see his pupils fill with a clear emerald Light, which seems to reach out and connect with the very heart of you.... Mesmerised by their depths, you feel yourself relax; and a gentle warmth fills your heart as a benevolent strength encompasses your mind.... then, slowly but surely, all your thoughts, feelings and emotions calm and settle, and you feel a sense of positive anticipation, as your spirits lift and connect with an unspoken promise of wholeness and balance.

RAPHAEL'S TEACHINGS
The Key to Wholeness and Health – Self-awareness and Love:

Holding your gaze, Raphael remarks that you may not appreciate that you are a living miracle(!): yet every cell of your body has an intrinsic understanding of all that it should be, moving through a constant cycle of death and regeneration without the need for your conscious awareness or participation – each organism designed to be in absolute harmony and accord with all parts of itself, and in full and complete alignment with the templates that have been established for that existence. With a smile, he says that he knows this because he holds and anchors the flawless patterns for all life-forms, and so understands and *knows* your fundamental perfection – whilst also understanding and acknowledging your right to explore a *different* pattern within any aspect of your body, mind or spirit, if you so choose. Raphael explains that your right to choose means that your pattern may not *be* one of absolute perfection; but stresses that every complex aspect of your Self – body, mind, emotions and spirit – will be as it is for a reason, even if complete and perfect health is your true state of Being. He adds that it is therefore fundamentally important to be able to determine if the state of health and wellbeing you are experiencing is a part of your life plan (or not): this is because being in alignment with your planned patterns of Be-ing – which includes moving back to absolute health, if you so choose – can only be achieved through knowing and understanding if, when, how *and why* you have strayed from the path of perfection.

Settling back, Raphael observes that people are often drawn to work in the healing professions because of their own experiences of illness or pain – indeed, those who have personally suffered any of the ills and pains that can beset body, mind or spirit often make the best healers, because their experience and understanding enables them to have true empathy with others: even so (whether you work in a healing profession or not), it is important that you work on your own self-healing and 'fill your own cup' first, *especially* if you put others before yourself through lack of self-regard, or as a means of avoiding addressing and dealing with your own issues or pains. He expounds that this requires full awareness, honesty and commitment (if you wish it to be truly effective): however it will also have a two-fold positive effect: firstly, undertaking and perfecting your personal healing will develop your existing knowledge and skills, making you a more capable and effective healer (both for yourself and – if applicable – for others); secondly, it will melt away anything that confines your Light, enabling you to open your heart and expand into the perfection of your true nature, filled with the Light of Divine Love and Compassion. Raphael adds that *this* is the absolute and pure resonance of The Divine, which can flood each and every cell with its Power – enabling them to recall their perfect blueprint at Divine level; and re-calibrate to the resonance aligned with the plan designed for your current existence. With a smile he declares that, hence, where nothing but love is present, disharmony or negativity simply cannot exist: thus the key to your personal healing is simply 'self-love'!

Taking your hand, Raphael emphasises that self-acceptance and self-love are the bedrock of a healthy and happy life: moreover it is a fundamental truth that consciously undertaking a programme of self-growth and personal healing gradually fills you with Love's Light, which (once *you* are filled) overflows to spontaneously give comfort to others. With another smile, he adds that, thus, just as self-love enables *you* to transform and return to wholeness yourself; so too will the love you have for yourself shape others: indeed, as you move towards a heart-centred state of Being, you will come to realise that *whatever* you do to (or for) yourself, you do to (or for) others; and understand that by perfecting your Self, you will bring healing to the world.

Taking up the danburite crystal he had set aside, Raphael gently touches it to your base chakra, and asks you to allow the resonance of the crystal to show you anything you need to address that will aid you in returning to your rightful blueprint of physical (bodily) health and wholeness in this lifetime.... as you consider what he has asked, he reminds you that the path of perfection is always of your own choosing *and* your own making: thus, if you have learned all that you need to from your current blueprint, you can always choose to change it....

After allowing you time to consider what he had asked, Raphael raises the danburite crystal to your sacral chakra, and asks you to this time allow the resonance of the crystal to show you anything you need to address that will aid you in returning to your rightful blueprint of emotional (reactive) health and wholeness in this lifetime – once again reminding you that the path of perfection is always of your own choosing *and* your own making; and therefore, if you have learned all that you need to from your current blueprint, you can always choose to change it....

Once again, Raphael waits for you to consider what he had asked, before moving the danburite crystal to your solar plexus chakra. He asks that this time you allow the resonance of the crystal to show you anything you need to address that will aid you in returning to your rightful blueprint of mental (reasoning) health and wholeness in this lifetime – once again reminding you that the path of perfection is always of your own choosing *and* your own making; and therefore, if you have learned all that you need to from your current blueprint, you can always choose to change it....

Finally, after giving you time to consider what he had asked, Raphael touches the crystal to your heart chakra, and asks you to allow its Light to pour into your heart – filling it with the self-love, courage, strength and determination that will enable you to change what you can, and compassionately accept what you cannot; and charging it with the wisdom and self-understanding that will enable you to achieve your rightful state of health and wholeness within body, mind and spirit with greater ease....

Once the crystal's Light has stopped flowing, Raphael places the danburite crystal aside again, and gives you a pale-pink transparent rhomboid-shaped crystal. He tells you that this is **Pink Optical Calcite**, his first Crystal Champion – explaining:

"Pink Optical Calcite is similar to my pink danburite, in that it carries the clear Pink Ray of Divine Love and Compassion, and supports absolute healing on all levels. This is due to its kind and calming resonance that can aid relaxation and make it easier to open and 'let go' – helping you release 'negative' thoughts and feelings; and so freeing your body, mind and emotions, and thus facilitating their return to their natural state of internal harmony, perfection and balance. Pink Optical Calcite can also help balance and align your crown and heart chakras, strengthening your connection to your Higher-self, and empowering all that you think, say and do with unconditional love, whilst embracing you in its non-judgmental Light. This will enable (and help) you to have more care and compassion for yourself and for others, and to truly value and appreciate how all *your life experiences have made you the person you are, as well as making you the person you are striving to become – whole, healed and complete."*

Smiling, Raphael affirms that Pink Optical Calcite may therefore help you open yourself to Love's Light, so that you have love in your heart for your Self at all times.

Looking up, Raphael gives a low whistle – at which a small owl flutters down from the tree to perch on his right shoulder. There it regards you with a beady orange eye as Raphael explains that owls have excellent hearing, which they use like radar to support their night vision when they hunt – hence they can 'see' with ease using more than one sense, perceiving and locating things that might be hidden from others: therefore you may ask **Little Owl** to aid and support the development of your clairaudient and/or clairvoyant skills; or help you recognise or identify *anything* you need to see or know that will aid you in your self-healing: this may be something that is hidden or masked, or something concerning your shadow-self – maybe something you have chosen to forget because you are fearful of (or embarrassed about) remembering or addressing it, or that you have subconsciously buried, perhaps because of its traumatic nature. Here Raphael adds that, if you work in the healing professions, Little Owl may also come to help you more clearly see and identify the issues that are at the root of your clients' health concerns; and/or to offer you wisdoms that will help you to work proactively with your client, so that they may gain the insights required to achieve an effective resolution. With a smile he assures you that if you ever have any doubts about the validity of what you are being told or shown – in physicality, or in spirit – you may call for Little Owl to boost your inner wisdom and 'knowing' in order to reveal any deceits or untruths. Suddenly the owl bobs up and down, before flying off with an ear-piercing shriek: and with a chuckle Raphael remarks that, despite its size, Little Owl's call will always grab your attention if you need to heed any subtle signs or signals hidden within your dreams or meditations; or if you need to move or proceed cautiously, with greater care, stealth or secrecy.

The Mastery of Balance through the Still-point Within:
Reminding you that he holds and anchors the flawless patterns of the structure and formation of all things, Raphael asks you to look more closely at the pendant he wears

around his neck.... He explains that it has many features in common with the wrist-plate that his twin-flame, Mareia wears – thus allowing him to align his work with hers, and enabling the blueprints of physical formation to be 'overlaid' with those of spiritual evolution (optimally aligning them to function 'as a whole'). Gently touching the gold plate, he expounds that the keynote of the Gold Ray is Truth; whilst that of the Silver Ray (as in Mareia's pendant) is Knowledge: thus 'as one' they are aligned with Divine Heart and Mind – Love and Wisdom, together comprehending and creating the ideal, with the munificence that allows infinite evolution.

Touching the orange sapphires set into each side of the gold plate, Raphael explains that these hold the Orange Ray, which inspires personal Will to align with the resonance of the Sacred Heart: this enables those in human embodiment to recognise, identify and define themselves *as* a Soul in human form; and brings the passion and fire that will spur them on to explore and define their place within the Universe as an infinite and immortal spiritual Being, who has simply *chosen* to endure and master all that living in a third-Dimensional world entails. Smiling again, he adds that this alignment and Mastery will eventually reveal and release the esoteric jewel that is held at the centre of each Lotus of the Heart, which IS an emerald.

Lastly touching the amethyst at the centre of the pendant, Raphael reminds you that the Amethyst Ray transforms and refines energy, enabling everything to be attuned to its optimal state. With another smile he adds that it is not possible to attain or retain balance *without* constant transformation and refinement – for 'energy' (Light) by its nature has to be able to instantly modify itself in order to maintain its equilibrium. He expounds that this is because Light *as a Divine quantum* is itself constant: it cannot be increased or diminished, but can only shift the distribution of the totality of its resonance in accordance with the needs defined by Divine Mind.... After thinking for a moment, he explains that for example (in simple terms), today you might need to access a greater proportion of 'red' (fire, passion, energy); but tomorrow your needs might require you to have a greater proportion of 'blue' (cool, dispassion, calm) – and this is accomplished by (consciously or unconsciously) shifting the balance within the Light that you hold.

Next lifting his staff, Raphael lays it across his knees, so that you can see it more clearly.... He tells you that he carries it as a symbol of his station in the seventh Order of Melchisadek, which works with the Violet and Amethyst Rays: yet because his staff has an Emerald at its core (which is the only gem able to hold the entirety of the Divine Light in balance) it is specifically and uniquely linked to his duties as a Divine Overseer of the Emerald Ray. He explains that, as such, he is a Master of Balance, whereby he bridges the worlds of Higher Dimension and Form, whilst holding all of existence – the Circle of Life – in constant and perfect balance and equilibrium.

Placing his staff aside, Raphael explains that the prime reason for your existence in this lifetime is to experience and understand Oneness through conscious awareness and integration of polar 'opposites' – which basically means learning and mastering the art of balance. He tells you that the Infinity Loop (∞ – as spoken of by Mareia) also symbolises all possible actions of Free Will, each 'side' having an absolute pole of expression – an extreme: in their centre is their crossing point – the core or centre; and your ultimate goal is to be able to hold the energy (Light) of the Infinity Loop (i.e. *all* potentials and possibilities) *in its entirety,* whilst also keeping it stable. He explains that basically this entails you accepting *all* aspects of your Self and embracing *all* the expressions of your potential, whilst remaining balanced in your core or centre at all times. With a wry smile he reassures you that knowing, holding or embracing both poles – your darkness *and* your light – will not make you 'bad' or 'good', or mean that you have to act on all that you know or hold within your Self; but explains that, although it may seem impossible to imagine now, this is what it means to BE Divine: *knowing* all possible extremes.... *knowing* the true meaning of Free Will and 'choice'.... *knowing* the consequences of all the choices you could possibly make.... and then *making* or *allowing* those choices with nothing but Love in your heart!...

After waiting for you to take in all that he has told you, Raphael informs you that learning to keep your *internal* balance, regardless of what is happening to or around you, is a useful skill to acquire as you work to become whole and perfect. He stresses that 'perfect' does not mean 'flawless', but means being or doing the best you can at any given time; furthermore, 'balance' does not necessarily mean 'equal', but means holding your body, mind and spirit in the state that is appropriate for the circumstances or situation you find yourself in at that time. He then tells you that finding and retaining appropriate balance is easier when you focus through your 'still-point', which is a place of inner strength and calmness located within your Hara centre: reaching over, he gently touches a point just below your navel, explaining that taking your attention to the area situated about two fingers-width within your body at this location will aid you in being more objective and focused, centred and (appropriately) responsive.

Raphael now asks you to take your attention to your still-point, and practise holding this as your centre of balance – with your eyes open or shut, whichever you prefer.... as you do so, he advises you to keep your feet flat on the ground with your back as straight as possible, without holding any tension; and – if you feel your attention wavering at any time, to simply refocus on your still-point without stressing about it.... He says that it may also help to hold your right palm over your Hara, with your thumb by your navel – and tells you that, with practise, it will be possible to go to your still-point in an instant....

After a while, Raphael asks you to return your focus to him, and gives you a deep-green stone that has silvery sparkles within it. He reminds you that the Hara centre is also the location of the templates that hold your Soul's plans for the growth and learning experiences of your current embodiment; and tells you that this is **Green Aventurine**, his second Crystal Champion – explaining:

> *"Green Aventurine will help connect you to the rhythms of the natural world and enable you to find inner peace and stability, especially when you are in the company of living things that focus the Green Ray in nature, such as plants and trees. This is because its deep green colour supports your Heart centres and stimulates attainment of a state of balance that is lovingly rooted through the heart; whilst its silvery sparkles bring a zest for life and ground the Silver Ray energies, promoting change by catalysing the impetus to seek balance in any area of your life where it is lacking. The Silver Ray aspect can also help you connect more effectively with the aspects of your Soul that are rooted*

within your Hara centre, making stability within your still-point (and connection with your Higher knowing) much easier. Green Aventurine is surprisingly powerful for such a common stone, and can be used on any energy centre to stimulate and aid the release of old or outmoded patterns of beliefs or behaviours, whilst effectively supporting their healing and true balance – especially on the emotional and physical levels. It can also aid you in identifying and understanding the root causes or core issues that underlie illness or disease; and support you in completing whatever programme of self-healing you need to undertake, in order to become whole again. Furthermore, Green Aventurine is an ideal healing partner for seraphinite (Mareia's Crystal Champion) – 'earthing' its effects, and helping ground them fully in the physical third-Dimensional world."

With a smile Raphael affirms that Green Aventurine may therefore help you find balance through your still-point, so that you may gain the clarity you need to attain wholeness and balance within your Self *and* your Life.

As he finishes speaking, a bright green woodpecker flies out from the forest and drops to the ground in front of you, and starts hunting for ants amongst the grass. As he watches it, Raphael remarks that the industrious ant is the green woodpecker's favourite food: hence **Green Woodpecker** can show you the best ways to refresh and support your energies during periods of intense learning, study or growth; or be asked to teach you how to conserve or increase your energy during a period of illness or recuperation, self-healing or personal growth. Calling the woodpecker closer, Raphael explains that its vivid green plumage marks it as a carrier of the Green Ray of Balance and Harmony; whilst its bright scarlet cap indicates its ability to attract, magnify, ground and guard esoteric wisdom and knowledge: accordingly you may call upon Green Woodpecker to help you find and/or hold your still-point; or to teach you how to attain and retain balance if you are out of harmony in body, mind or spirit; or to aid and support you if you need help in communicating or understanding anything of a deeply profound esoteric or arcane nature. Pointing out its large stubby bill, Raphael adds that (because woodpeckers have very tough bills and skulls) Green Woodpecker can also guide you to the root of a thorny issue, and/or offer you his wisdom and understanding as you seek out the truth at the heart of a matter that requires your attention; whilst its skill in transmitting sound and vibration might help you choose the most appropriate vibrational therapy and/or select the most effective vibrational remedy for your own or others' healing or development.

The Gift of The Enlightened Lotus of Divinity:

As quickly as it arrived, the woodpecker flies back to the forest, dropping a large yellow and black bodied insect in Raphael's lap as it passes overhead: placing it on his palm so that you can see it more clearly, he tells you that this insect is a hornet – a large species of wasp that is both feared and respected! Pointing to its golden-yellow body and its black 'W'-shaped markings, he explains that hornets are profound esoteric symbols that represent mental balance – linking the Kabbalistic spheres of Binah and Chokmah (embodying understanding and wisdom); and promoting their equilibrium through the Element of fire: hence you may ask **Hornet** to show you how to increase or deepen your mental powers of reasoning, thought and rational intelligence; or to help you balance your intellect and inspiration, enabling you to reach true understanding; or to show you how to work with the breath to bring about transformation, healing and balance (perhaps through yoga or meditation). Raphael adds that hornet also carries both Black Light and the Gold Ray, which together enable and facilitate the foundation and structure of all things: thus you may also call upon Hornet to show you how to design, plan and map out the future you truly desire, so that it may BE all that you want it to be; or to guide you through the set-up of a new venture or project, so that it may stay firmly on track whilst still remaining open to new possibilities and potentials. Pointing to its strong jaws, Raphael informs you that hornets build multilayered nests from masticated tree-bark, creating a series of six-sided cells in which (through a strong hive mentality that has a single goal) its young are reared from larvae to adult: this entails them passing through five stages of metamorphosis, indicating that you may also ask Hornet to support you in working towards embracing the state of 'Unified Body', thus bringing both order and the concept of spiritual intent and manifestation into the physical Plane; or to help you experience true Unity with the world about you, whilst showing you the benefits of working with others towards a common goal; or to teach you how to hold and be all that you can BE, with all aspects of your Self in harmonious accord. Then, placing the hornet carefully in the tree behind him, Raphael asks you to accompany him to the hexagonal pool at the centre of the clearing.

Here he reaches into the water, and draws the Emerald Flame towards him: he then plucks a smaller Flame from its heart, and asks you to find and hold your still-point of inner balance.... Once you have done so, he stands in front of you and gently touches the Flame to your base chakra.... your sacral chakra.... your solar plexus chakra.... and finally your heart.... somehow you understand that this Flame is being absorbed by the Emerald that sits (shielded and protected) at the very core of the Lotus of your Heart – and then, as he gently rests his hand over your heart chakra, you hear Raphael saying:

> "Connect with the Divinity of your Being and know yourself as The Divine knows you. Feel the wisdom of the ages within – and let the serenity of your Soul encompass your thoughts.... Then let the centeredness of your mind encompass your feelings.... let the tranquillity of your emotions permeate your physical body.... and let all be at Peace.... For this is all you ARE; and all you will ever BE."

After allowing you a few moments to fully assimilate the energies of the Flame, Raphael reaches into the Emerald Flame again: this time he draws a sapphire-blue lotus bud from the Flame's very heart, and shows it to you....

He explains that the lotus flower embraces all the Elements – it has its roots in the mud (earth); its stem in water; its flowers and leaves in the air; and it takes its energy from the Sun (fire): hence it defines the harmonisation of the four Elemental qualities of practicality (earth); emotion (water); intellect (air) and creativity (fire). Gently touching the bud, Raphael observes that, on a spiritual level, the lotus generally signifies bliss or nirvana – whilst the *blue* lotus (like this one) was specifically regarded as a symbol of creation and rebirth, and revered as being the Origin of all Life. As an aside, he remarks that there is an etheric retreat in the Himalayas that carries its name; comprising seven vertically-aligned chambers, each of which is overseen by an 'Illumined One' who is devoted to teaching Mastery of one of the third-Dimensional subtle Bodies. With a smile, he adds that all those who wish to study here begin at the lowest level, which relates to the base chakra and its associated auric Body: this has to be mastered before ascending to the next level, which relates to the sacral chakra and its associated auric Body.... He adds that this pattern continues – observing that mastery of the middle level (that of the heart) is often the hardest, as from this point onwards all study is self-led and self-generated.

Gently holding the blue lotus bud between the tips of his fingers, Raphael informs you that this bud carries the etheric signature of the 'Retreat of the Blue Lotus'; *and* holds the template of your 'Lotus of the Soul', which you are not allowed to access until you have awakened and developed your 'Lotus of the Heart' to the appropriate degree of understanding and balance: this is because the Lotus of the Soul anchors intensities of Light that are usually only appropriate for Higher-Dimensional existences. Smiling, he tells you that, nonetheless, any embodied individual who demonstrates a high degree of competence and trustworthiness in their spiritual practice and understanding *can* be given this template when in 'lower-Dimensional' embodiments, and may then ask to study their personal Mastery with the Illumined Ones who oversee the Retreat of the Blue Lotus.

Raphael now lifts the sapphire-blue bud until it is level with your crown, and places it upon the very centre of the Infinity Cross that sits at your Alpha centre (which was the Gift of his twin flame, Mareia).... As it settles in place, the sapphire-blue bud *and* the Infinity Cross spiral slowly down your pranic core, and come to a rest level with your sacral chakra: here the lotus bud detaches from the Infinity Cross and settles within your Seat of the Soul centre; whilst the Infinity Cross spirals back up your pranic core to its starting position at your Alpha centre....

Resting his hands on your shoulders, Raphael directs you to take your awareness to the sapphire-blue lotus bud, which is gently glowing within you – and, when he knows that you can feel its gentle warmth pervading the area just in front of your sacrum, he places his hands on your head in Blessing, saying:

> "This is my Gift of The Enlightened Lotus of Divinity.... I ask only that you always travel with the innocence of a child.... that you see each new thing with the joyous eyes of a child.... and that you love ALL with the open heart of a child.... For remember, it is the child who carries the Grail...."

Once he is sure that you have fully assimilated his words *and* the sapphire-blue lotus bud, Raphael helps you back to your chair and retakes his seat at your side.... Here he reminds you that the lotus bud is only a template, and so as such it will remain inert until you are *truly* ready and able to work with it, which will not be until you have fully mastered the lower expressions (mind, body and emotions) of your embodied human existence: even so, his Gift *will* establish a link with your co-creative fifth-Dimensional (and Higher) Self – the 'you' that is already open to your Reality as a Divine Being of Light and an aspect of Divine Source; and *will* aid you in accessing the guidance and wisdom you require as you work towards your self-mastery.

Reaching out, Raphael places a polished disc of crystal (which has a ruby-red core and an emerald-green outer layer) in your hand. He tells you that this is a crystalline slice of **Watermelon Tourmaline**, his third Crystal Champion – explaining:

> *"Watermelon Tourmaline is one of the very best crystals for working with the heart and High Heart centres, and with all issues of healing, balance, self-love and compassion. It carries the Ruby, Red and Pink Rays that are closely connected with the Fires of your essential nature; and holds the Divine Love and Compassion that allows you to be who and what you are. If you let its Fire fill your heart, you will find that your dearest wish will be to BEcome aligned with the infinite Love and Light of The Divine, who knows and accepts all that IS in the world: this will help you to understand why, when and how to make effective shifts and changes that will enable you – and in turn your world – to hold the Grail and fully embody Love. Watermelon Tourmaline also holds the Emerald and Green Rays that are most closely connected with the balance of your heart chakra and the spirituality of your third-Dimensional embodiment; and understands the true nature of health, wholeness and balance across all Times, Planes and Dimensions. If you let its Light fill your Soul, you will understand how to embrace all that is, and learn how to release your grasp on your ego-based third-Dimensional existence, so that you may hold and shine a greater quantum of Light and* know *wholeness and balance."*

With a smile, Raphael affirms that Watermelon Tourmaline may therefore help you ready yourself to awaken the Lotus of your Soul, by fully developing and balancing the Flames of Divine Will, Wisdom and Love that comprise the Lotus of your Heart.

The Greenwood Guardians – Yew and Maple:

His *personal* mentoring complete for now, Raphael affirms he is always available to aid and support you: you need only bring him to mind and ask for his presence, and he will attend you. Furthermore, he tells you that two great Tree Beings of the Plant Kingdom have also asked to support you in addressing his Theme of 'WHOLENESS THROUGH BALANCE', adding that you need only request *their* presence, and they will be with you.

He explains that the first of these Greenwood Guardians is the Feminine essence of Yew who has asked to overlight and help you ground whatever work you undertake within *any* aspect of his chapter. The second is the Masculine essence of Maple, who has specifically asked to help you understand and assimilate his Gift of The Enlightened Lotus of Divinity (if you have chosen to accept it).

When you are ready to connect with Raphael's first Greenwood Guardian, you need simply call for the presence of **Yew** (*) .... Yew envelops you in a crystal-clear Light that is filled with sparks of gold, and the Feminine spirit essence of Yew speaks to you, saying:

> *"The gateway to the worlds beyond is the gateway within – and all that you are, and all that you know, may be found here. Know that I can aid you in this search by keeping your energies safely grounded to your current reality, secure in the understanding that Earth's heart is your home and your foundation: for I have both the fortitude and the endurance to stand alone, a lone warrior for the Light – who even so recognises the virtues of a Unified Spirit, and* knows *they are* never *alone.... So stand with me, and feel yourself become part of my essence.... feel yourself embraced in my timeless and infinite*

strength, which is at all times both light and dark; flexible and unyielding; merciful and without pity.... and thus you will know that (even though you may be bowed by forces that sometimes threaten to overpower you) you will always spring back to align with your True Self: complete and perfect, and made stronger by those forces that can never bend you to any Will other than that of your own Higher and Divine Self...."

(* Bloodstone will help you ground and connect with the energies and wisdom of Yew, if you wish to enhance your experience using crystals.)

If you have chosen to accept and work with Raphael's Gift, and when you are ready to connect with his second Greenwood Guardian, you need simply call for the presence of **Maple** (*) .... Maple envelops you in a swirling orange, red and bronze Light, and the Masculine spirit essence of Maple speaks to you, saying:

"The Love of The Divine is always present in my sap, which rises with my life-force to imbue all that I am with its sweet delights, feeding and nourishing the life that is within me and without.... So rest against my beribboned trunk, and allow its satiny coolness to bind and heal the wounds and sorrows that you bear, replacing their hurts and pains with a sweetness that warms and cheers.... Then stand and watch with me as a long year passes – seemingly in the blink of an eye: see the bright summer fade to a glory that embraces the respite and peace of autumn, and see the Passion of The Divine in my crown.... recognise the wisdom of evolution that empowers and enables me to shed all that I was, thus allowing me to transform and grow anew – restored, refreshed and ready to begin the new cycle of growth, which always follows a deep and dreamless sleep.... and marvel at the wonder of the Divine design that guides my seasons, knowing not only my own nature, but seeing all of which I am an insignificant – yet complex and infinite – part. For then you may come to understand the daily miracles of the love and wisdom that directs every cell that is an aspect of my Being; an aspect of this woodland I call home; an aspect of the world upon which I live; and an aspect of the Universe in which I exist.... Then deny, if you can, the Divine Order that underlies all that IS, which always knows my perfection – and likewise knows yours!...."

(* Gaia [Polychrome] Jasper and Amber will help you ground and connect with the energies and wisdom of Maple, if you wish to enhance your experience using crystals.)

ARCHEIA MAGDALENA

'THE BLESSING OF MERCY'

CRYSTAL CHAMPIONS:
Moonstone ♥ White Girasol ♥ Aqua Aura Qtz

CREATURE COMPANIONS:
Butterfly ♥ Ocelot ♥ Firebird

GREENWOOD GUARDIANS:
Hawthorn ♥ Eucalyptus

*I open my heart to the Light of the Rose
and am free from fear.
I am at Peace with All That Is.*

MEETING MAGDALENA

It is early morning on a fine day in late summer, and you find yourself strolling down a neatly trimmed path that is paved with rounded pebbles of creamy-grey flint. This flows through a verdant landscape of traditional English parkland, whose undulating meadows and well-tended lawns are crowned with rainbow-filled droplets of dew that sparkle with fire as they catch the first rays of the rising sun. The lush emerald swathes create a perfect setting for a variety of well-spaced copses and groves of trees, which fill gently rounded hollows or mantle grassy knolls, presenting a landscape that (owing to the diversity of shapes and forms, textures and colours) is both interesting and pleasing to the eye. Each group is perfectly matched with a contrasting backdrop of turquoise-blue sky or emerald grass; and each tree has been artfully positioned so that their majestic beauty can be accentuated by the sunlight as it filters through their branches and leaves, or be framed and enhanced by the ever-shifting shadows that circle around their feet.

As you walk on, the fresh morning air feels cool and slightly damp on your face; and with every breath you take, you realise that your senses – and your awareness of everything around you – are being heightened and enhanced. You find that everything you look at is in perfect focus, and can discern and distinguish every nuance of colour, hue and tone.... you can smell and identify every scent carried on the breeze, which shifts and changes with every step – some odours heavy and cloying, redolent with musk and spice; others damply earthy, or delicately sweet and fresh.... you can also isolate and hear the songs of different types of birds, and become aware of the more subtle sounds of the myriad winged insects that are flying around you.... Gradually you realise that what you perceive is within *your* control; and you discover that you can fine-tune or modulate your senses to dampen and/or amplify them exactly as you please – and so, as you walk on, you have fun practising adjusting your perception of the world around you....

Eventually, you find that the path has led you to the summit of a low hill, beyond which lies a lake shaped like an elongated hourglass: on its far side is a rugged limestone escarpment, which curves around the lake and towers into the sky, its wild and untamed heights a stark contrast to the softly rounded landscape you have just enjoyed. The lake itself is tranquil and still, reflecting the sky and everything around it like a mirror: where it narrows at its centre, it is bisected by a graceful, yet solidly built, arched bridge made of silvery-white stone – and waiting for you here is a tall and slender lady gowned in silver. This is Archeia Magdalena. She is holding a single white rose that is in full bloom, and beckons for you to join her – and as you reach her, she smiles in welcome, declaring:

> *"I am Magdalena, the Lady Mercy – Bearer and Guardian of the Grail, Sustainer of the purity of the Ascension Flame of Eternal Life, and twin flame of Azrael. Know that I hold the innocence and purity of new life, borne into the world on merciful wings of love. Hence, through me you may find the calm centre that holds the beauty of your true form, that you too may accept and bear witness to the peace and Bliss of your own pure Divinity; and with my aid you may learn to BE that infinite love, so that through the completeness and purity of your Soul all may know the truth of your Being. Understand that I do not ask you to surrender* to Love; *but rather that you surrender your fears to become* Love: *hence, I am here to teach you how to release all fears and set yourself*

free, becoming all that you can with a clear and open heart and mind, so that you may share the hopes and joys of the Light of Freedom with the world that is yours."

Gesturing to the path that leads over the bridge, Magdalena invites you to accompany her to the other side – and as you join her, you note (with some surprise) how white rose petals seem to fall around her feet with every step she takes, as if strewn there in Blessing by an unseen hand – and she acknowledges this thought with another small smile.

Reaching the other side of the bridge, you find that the ground has been paved in white limestone, creating a wide open terrace that fills the space between the lake and the cliff-like wall of the escarpment behind it. In the centre of this (aligned with the end of the bridge, and at the foot of the escarpment) you can see a small square-fronted Grecian-style temple: this has been cut into the rock-face behind it, and is garlanded with ivy and bedecked with leafy green ferns, so that only the low stepped threshold, fronted by four tall columns that support a wide triangular portico, is visible. In the centre of the terrace to either side of the temple (and overlooking the lake) are two curved stone benches: the one to the left of the temple is set beneath a tall statue of a griffon, which appears to be made of glossy black obsidian; whilst the one to the right of the temple is set beneath an arc of silver-birch trees, whose branches are veiling it in dappled shade. Inviting you to join her, Magdalena leads you to the latter – suggesting that you sit at her side and take a little time to examine her, so that you may become accustomed to her energies.

As you settle at Magdalena's side you are immediately drawn by the classic beauty of her face. She calmly meets your gaze, enabling you to look into her long-lashed eyes, which have dark brown irises set around hypnotically deep jet-black pupils: these seem to draw you in, simultaneously projecting an unexpectedly powerful strength, coupled with what feels like a profound and perceptive compassion, which somehow embraces and fills you with its unconditional love and power – and recognising this, you know that whatever you say or express in Magdalena's company will simply be accepted, and be considered with the utmost care and integrity.

As she senses your acquiescence Magdalena gives another small smile, and you feel at liberty to look at her more closely – observing both elegance and grace in her bearing and manner, and in her perfectly-proportioned oval face with its strikingly-defined bone structure. Her skin is lightly tanned a pale golden brown; whilst the eyes that had so captivated you are deeply set beneath arching dark eyebrows over a long straight nose. Her hair is the same deep brown as her eyes, with natural red and copper highlights that glint as they catch the sun: it is also obviously thick and curly, as she is wearing it piled up on the top of her head (in a classic Grecian style), where it is captured and held by a long twisting band of silvery-gold electrum, from which a few stray ringlets are escaping – adding a touch of casual informality to what is otherwise a rather formal appearance.

Your gaze is next drawn by Magdalena's floor-length gown, which is similarly in Grecian style. It has been fashioned from a finely-pleated silver material, which appears to have been woven from strands of pure spun silver; and is moulded to her slender body by means of two fine tasselled cords, which have been plaited from long threads of silver and white silk: these tie behind her, encircling her torso – one just below her breasts; the other around her waist. From here the gown flows to the floor like a waterfall of liquid silver, pooling around her long and slender feet, which are shod in a simple pair of silver satin ballet slippers. The hem of the gown is trimmed with tiny silver sleigh bells, which not only weight it down, but also emit soft tinkling chimes as she moves; whilst the tiny pleats at the top of the gown have been gathered to drape over her right shoulder, leaving her left shoulder and arm uncovered. The ends of the material are secured in the hollow just below her right shoulder with a clasp made of electrum, which has been fashioned to portray the head of a 'Green Man' – the eyes of which have been cut and faceted from deep green moldavite, which is the stone that links her with Azrael, her twin flame.

From here your gaze shifts to Magdalena's (mostly) bare arms, which are slender, tanned and well-toned. A slender torque, fashioned from silver in the form of a snake, spirals downwards around the bicep of her right arm; and has been fashioned in great detail, with each tiny scale upon its body clearly defined – and, as you examine it more closely, you can also see that it has intricately faceted tear-drop shaped eyes, which look to have been cut from water-clear diamonds. The spiralling torque leads your eye down to the rose Magdalena is still clasping lightly in her hands; and to her slender fingers, where you observe that the ring finger of her left hand bears a plain band of silvery-gold electrum that is set with a simple polished oval cabochon of silver-sheen obsidian.

MAGDALENA'S TEACHINGS
The Merciful Freedom of Living in The NOW:

Tucking the rose into the cord around her waist, Magdalena turns to face the silver-birch trees that shade the bench on which you sit: inviting you to do likewise, she asks you to select a tree, and use your senses to explore the features of its trunk, branches and leaves.... So, choosing a tree, and deciding to examine its slender trunk first, you slowly run your fingers over its satiny white bark, which is dotted with tiny ridges and markings; and carefully push against its trunk to test its flexibility: as you do, you can sense the strength that underlies the tree's delicacy; and become aware of the life-force pulsing within.... you also appreciate how the tree can bend or flex in response to external forces, and understand how this protects it, yet also makes its trunk stronger....

Reaching up, you next explore the tree's slender branches and twigs – noting how they dance and sway in harmony with the breeze, rather than resisting its touch; and feeling and seeing how their glossy brown buds and green toothed leaves ripen, unfurl and mature as they absorb the life-giving light and nourishment of the sun....

Standing, you decide lastly to rest your back against the trunk of the tree, and look up through its branches to the sky above – observing how the fragile twigs and leaves are delicately outlined against the blue of the sky; and watching the play of light and shadow as you (like the tree) feel the sun dot your face with its warmth and light....

As you enjoy your communion with the tree, Magdalena tells you that the silver-birch is one of her favourite trees – its delicate flexibility and grace, enhanced by its beautiful silvery-white aura, being both uplifting and calming; its generous and giving nature gladly offering healing, nurture and shelter to many other life-forms through its buds and bark. She smiles and says that you too are born with the innate understanding of how to live harmoniously (and generously) with the world about you, and so have the potential to BE like this tree: moreover, although (or perhaps because!) a silver-birch is relatively short lived, its nurturing wisdom will help you to recognise the pointlessness of expending precious time in constantly reliving or rehashing issues, situations or events that are in the past (especially if you are unwilling or unable to address or resolve them); whilst its unconditional spirit will show you the joy to be found in simply going with the flow and living life in the NOW.

With another gentle smile, Magdalena says she cannot emphasise strongly enough how holding on to futile, cheerless or judgmental emotions (such as regret, guilt, shame, jealousy, anger or hatred) blocks the free-flow of love within you – and as a consequence drastically impedes your growth – expounding:

> *"Loving yourself is about freeing your Self – first and foremost by releasing all fear-based patterns and responses that include any outward-directed energies that consist of* anything *other than love. For if you hold emotions such as blame, resentment, bitterness or suchlike within your heart you are holding onto ego-based fears, and are unable to fully embody love. Love IS all you need! So let go of anything that prevents you from seeing and loving the uniqueness of all: for in releasing your fears, your ego 'dies' and you are set free to simply BE – embracing, accepting and holding Love for your Self and for all things.... then, ultimately, when all hearts are filled with love and can join AS ONE, you will know Peace, and understand the Truth about Love."*

Magdalena adds that inviting the Light of silver-birch into your life can also help you see and appreciate the beauty and gift of each new day, encouraging you to gladly release the past and move forwards with your heart and Soul less burdened: then, explaining that you can ask the tree currently supporting you to help you to cease expending effort in maintaining the façade of your 'humanness', Magdalena suggests that you now bring to mind any fear-based patterns or responses that you wish to release and let go of....

After pausing to allow you time to think, she tells you to simply relax and surrender to the flow of Divine Light, which is an intrinsic part of your consciousness; and ask the silver-birch to help you break the cycle and release whatever is keeping you fixated on the pointless or the past.... As you do as she asks, you feel the trunk of the tree supporting your spine and strengthening your inner core.... and you slowly relax and find yourself seeing some of your long-held worries or grievances for what they truly are.... then, after a while, a gentle breeze begins to blow – and as you feel the tree's branches and leaves begin to sweep through your energy field, you hear the voice of the silver-birch in your mind encouraging you onwards, saying:

> *"Let me help connect you once more with your Divinity.... Truly embrace it.... Accept it, and accept your worth.... Allow yourself to honour each part of you for what it is; and know that everything you experience is simply one aspect of the energy that IS the Universe: for then you may come to understand that rejecting, denying or ignoring any one of them merely delays the ultimate advent of Oneness and Union...."*

As these words of wisdom sink in, you feel the silver-birch giving you the courage to let go – and slowly but surely you release your hold on whatever you had brought to mind.... With every breath you feel your energies lighten – your heart less burdened; your Spirit more free – until eventually you know you have released all you can for now.... Thanking the silver-birch, Magdalena helps you to disconnect your energies, soberly stressing that refusing to release (or learn from) the past denies your worth and denies yourself Divine Flow, which makes your life much harder – because, in truth, dealing with life is easy when there is no separation from The Divine, who knows only love.

Then, guiding you back to your seat on the bench, Magdalena reaches up and lifts a beautiful butterfly from a branch above her head: sharing with you her wonder at its elegant form and colour, and the perfect and delicate structure of every aspect of its wings and body – from each tiny iridescent scale upon its wings, to the fine downy hairs that clad its legs and feet, she observes that butterflies are truly wonderful insects, who go through many stages in their growth from egg to caterpillar to cocoon, before finally emerging in this beautiful form. With a wry chuckle she says that some of those stages may not appear to be as beautiful as the end result – yet each part has been designed with great care to suit its purpose perfectly: accordingly **Butterfly** symbolises the many varied phases of personal transformation, and so can teach you how to transform with more ease by showing you the stage of development you have currently reached; or by helping you to see, admit and accept all that you are (and all that you have learnt) at every stage; or by encouraging you to plan your future with clarity and order, endowing every step with beauty and grace. Returning the butterfly to the tree, she tells you that butterflies always remind her that the work of self-transformation never ceases, but is a constant cycle of development – ever changing and evolving according to your needs: hence Butterfly may also appear to *you* if you need encouragement to accept and embrace change, and/or keep moving forwards with positivity: furthermore, its delicate and ephemeral beauty will help you appreciate the blessing of every moment that has been given to you, helping you to recognise the fleeting nature of Time and preciousness of human existence; and enabling you to endure and overcome your trials and tribulations with serene acceptance – and with greater compassion for your Self and for others.

Sitting back, Magdalena gives you a slightly translucent glossy white stone and tells you this is **White Moonstone**, her first Crystal Champion – explaining:

> *"White Moonstone holds White Light in harmony with the catalysing power of the Silver Ray, offering the potential to bring about rapid change, transition and growth. Thus, if you feel like a butterfly that has become stuck in its cocoon, White Moonstone can give you the impetus to overcome stasis, and help you identify and understand the root causes of any thoughts, feelings or emotions that are restricting your growth or holding you back: then, if you are truly prepared to discard, refine or transform them, White Moonstone will reinforce your courage and Will to succeed, and support you through whatever comes. Paradoxically, White Moonstone has a calm and steady heart that can also provide you with a stable foundation, so that you may view both the merits and the disadvantages of the different ways in which you might move forwards; whilst giving you the courage and dispassion to view them from a balanced perspective, and then supporting you in taking the most appropriate (and heart-centred) action. Furthermore, White Moonstone's refined yet powerful resonance carries the Powers of The Divine Feminine and the Goddess, and so can help you clarify and purify your heart and upper*

chakras and associated energy Bodies, enabling you to benefit from clearer connections to your Christed and Divine Selves, and to all sources of Higher guidance – especially that of the feminine Masters and Illumined Ones."

Smiling, Magdalena affirms that White Moonstone may therefore help you identify and release old patterns and move forwards with a lighter heart – and thus grow and evolve with clarity and grace.

The Fearless Heart and The Glory of The Grail:

Asking you to accompany her, Magdalena leads you to the threshold of the temple: up close, you can see that its stonework is plain and unadorned, with the exception of the heads of the four columns that support the portico – each of which has been sculpted into the head of a bird: looking at these from left to right, you see a dove; then a jay; then (bizarrely) a kookaburra; and lastly a wild turkey.....

Inviting you to stand on the threshold of the narrow entryway, Magdalena moves aside and gestures you forwards: stepping up, you peer inside and find you are looking at something that looks like the interior of a big cube of pure white marble. All the surfaces have been polished to a soft sheen and are totally bare, with the exception of the floor – the centre of which has been etched with a six-pointed star, and inlaid with gold. In the very centre of this star stands a tall white marble pedestal, on top of which rests a simple silver chalice shaped like an upturned bell: this is emitting a very clear bright light that surrounds the chalice like a halo, enabling you to see that it is engraved with a design that depicts a stylised five-petalled rose set upon an equal-armed cross (+) within a circle....

After a while, you realise that the temple is resonating with a low-pitched humming, which sounds rather like a hive of industrious bees – and, with a gentle touch, Magdalena cautions you to go no closer. She explains that what you see and hear is the Light that *is* the innate essence of All Things – adding that some might call the chalice 'the Cup of the Grail', for its Light gives Life that brings sacrifice, yet also brings reward: for through suffering is borne the strength that empowers your quest to be one with the infinite Love, Light and Mercy of The Divine. With a soft sigh she says that the words 'sacrifice' and 'suffering' are often misunderstood and hence feared: yet immortality (which begins and ends each cycle of death and rebirth) can only be known by experiencing, understanding and accepting the nature of *all* things; and so it is the *Grail* that holds the Enlightenment that allows initiation into eternal life....

Drawing you back and away from the temple, Magdalena leads you to the bench in the shadow of the black griffon, where she encourages you to make yourself comfortable, before settling at your side.... Taking out the rose from the cord at her waist, she shows you the perfection of its form and the unsullied whiteness of its petals, each of which bears a single droplet of dew. She tells you that the rose symbolises the non-judgmental love that IS the eternal essence of The Divine (the Light of the Grail) – the open flower offering the template upon which every human heart is designed: furthermore, the *white* rose she holds perfectly symbolises the purity and passion of the Divine Mother, whose Light she joins in alchemical marriage with that of the Divine Father in order to quicken and bring forth the Christed-child that IS within each embodied Soul.

Holding the rose out towards you, she invites you to open yourself to its essence and inhale its sweet perfume; and allow it to remind you of the innate perfection of your consciousness and your connection with The Divine.... doing as she asks, you close your eyes and breathe deeply of the Light of the Rose – and, as your awareness expands, Magdalena directs you to feel the strength in your heart and accept what in truth you are, so that you may acknowledge the Christ within you and unite with your infinite Soul....

Slowly you feel your heart open – and all the 'walls' that you had (subconsciously or otherwise) erected around it as 'protection' fall away: yet you feel neither vulnerability nor fear; for you are instantly enfolded in a vast and compassionate embrace that fills you with such strength and positivity that you feel able to willingly release all your human frailties and fears – finally seeing and fully understanding them for what they are....

Gradually you begin to understand that the negative thoughts or feelings you hold about yourself or about others are nothing but lower ego-based reactions, which have clouded your heart and prevented you from moving forwards.... you recognise too that the walls you had placed around your heart, which you *thought* would protect you, have in fact only served to confine and limit you – preventing you from learning all you can, and holding you back from fulfilling your full potential....

Recognising that you are seeing yourself in a new light, Magdalena asks you to look through the eyes of your Soul, and *know* yourself AS a part of the Universe: without bounds or bonds that restrain or restrict, but simply as energy – an essence – that exists throughout all worlds, all Times, and all Dimensions....

Doing your best to do as she asks, you feel your heart expand as your infinite Soul embraces all that you are – and you realise that you would rather BE in *this* open-hearted state, than cling to the old patterns that immobilised and imprisoned you in a constant cycle of fear, recrimination or remorse.... and – recognising when you have reached this important point of realisation, Magdalena then very gently touches the rose to your heart: as you slowly ground yourself back into your body, this anchors your new understanding within you, whilst simultaneously ensuring that your heart is in an appropriate state for your needs at this time....

Once she is happy that you have found the right balance, Magdalena tucks the rose back into the cord at her waist, and gives you a small translucent white stone that has been engraved with the same symbol that you saw on the silver chalice in her temple. She tells you that this is **White Girasol**, her second Crystal Champion – explaining:

> *"White Girasol carries the pure Light of clarity and spiritual peace. In its soft, yet resolute, light you will* know *the freedom of an open heart, and know too the mercy that IS always within the Love that is borne there. Then, in the most gentle of dreams, White Girasol will help you envision the perfection that is at the heart of all things.... thence Hope may unite with Faith to show you the Truth that makes separation unbearable – and Unity possible. Furthermore, through its affinity with the Element of water, White Girasol may help cleanse you of negative or destructive energies, bringing clarity to your thoughts, feelings and emotions; and refreshing your Spirit and feeding your Soul with the life-giving properties of its essential nature. Above all, White Girasol carries the essence of the Grail, empowering you to surrender your fears so that LOVE can be*

born, by offering you a calm place of sanctuary that will hold you in a loving embrace, whilst providing a healing balm that has the power to return your Soul to its inborn state that knows only wholeness and Grace."

With a smile, Magdalena affirms that White Girasol may therefore help you truly *know* the Light of the Grail – and the Rose that lies forever at its heart.

Sitting back, she gives a call – at which a little spotted ocelot appears in the entranceway of the temple, and prowls over to settle contentedly at her feet.... As she affectionately fondles its ears, Magdalena observes that (as with all cats) the ocelot has perfected the arts of going within and journeying out-of-body: this teaches it to scrutinise and challenge apparent realities on many different levels of Dimension, and prepares it to make wise judgements before planning and taking action. She tells you that you might therefore choose to call upon **Ocelot** if you are finding it hard to make the time or space to think about what is going on in your life or in the world around you, and/or need help to attain a contemplative, introspective or meditative state; or if you want help reviewing, interpreting or analysing anything you encounter in dream state or when journeying; or if you are having difficulty seeing problematic issues with sufficient clarity or detachment. Indicating its dense and beautifully spotted coat, Magdalena tells you that this keeps the ocelot warm in winter and cool in summer, and also provides very good camouflage, which aids it in remaining unseen: hence Ocelot can also teach you how to keep your balance and ease when confronted with extreme situations; or show you how to travel lightly – unseen and unheard – in both physical and non-physical worlds. With a smile she adds that the Ancient Ones believed that the roar of the ocelot called the Sun into the sky: thus Ocelot's presence can also reinforce specific attributes connected with your 'masculine side', helping you to maintain your physical body and health, and strengthen your ability to focus upon (and manifest) anything required to maintain your physical and material survival; and to sharpen the logical thought processes that drive and maintain your personal evolution and growth, and strengthen your ability to focus upon (and integrate) the many and varied aspects of your 'lower' ego-self. Moreover, despite its comparatively small size, Ocelot has great courage and so can be called upon to guide, support and protect you whilst you seek out, confront and vanquish your fears – whatever their cause, and whatever their nature.

Presence made known, the ocelot pads back to the temple: then, gently taking your hand, Magdalena recommends that whenever you experience or recognise a 'negative' emotion, thought or feeling within you, you call for Ocelot to be present, and simply ask yourself 'what is it that I fear?' – posing this question to each of your responses, until you reach the point where there *is* no more fear to confront, expounding:

"For example, if you feel diminished, alone or afraid – what do you fear?.... If you seek to have power or control over others – what do you fear?.... If you feel the need to compare who you are, what you do, or what you possess with others – what do you fear?.... If you run away from, or deny, love – what do you fear?.... If you scorn your own or others beliefs, femininity, masculinity or sexuality – what do you fear?.... If you are unwilling to see or accept a particular aspect or characteristic of yourself, or of others – what do you fear?...."

Then, after holding your gaze for a moment, Magdalena gives your hand a gentle squeeze and sympathetically stresses:

> "Know that each time you deny your fears you are denying the Christ within.... Fear paralyses. It prevents you from moving forwards; it prevents you from opening to the abundance of Divine Love and BEing love! So remember this: if you hold Love in your heart – only *Love* – you can hold no fear."

The Gift of The Magdalene Flame of Innocence, Purity and Love:

Sitting back, Magdalena stretches out her left hand and invites you to look closely at the stone in her ring.... As the obsidian catches the light, you realise that there is a pattern within its silver sheen that looks like a slender long-tailed bird – and, with a smile, Magdalena lightly touches the ring to the silver torque on her right arm: at this, everything around you momentarily shimmers and fades from view; before being restored – somehow clearer and brighter than before.... then, as you look around you, your eye is drawn to a sudden flash of light; and you watch wide-eyed in wonder as a small bird that looks like a cross between a bird of paradise and a scarlet peacock soars over the lake towards you....

Landing on Magdalena's shoulder the bird surveys you with shining eyes that look like faceted diamonds – and you realise that this bird is like nothing you have ever seen before(!): its feathers are each formed of delicate filaments of copper, silver and gold; the long curling plumes of its tail are embellished with rubies, emeralds and sapphires; and the soft plumes that crown its head are adorned with tiny glowing white pearls. With a smile, Magdalena tells you that this bird is a firebird – mythical, yet real; and explains that its task it is to help weave the 'Tapestry of Life whose interwoven threads illustrate the essential nature of the Universe, and record every experience of all the aspects of the ONE that *is* All That Is. She adds that this means **Firebird** can show you the pattern of *all* your lives (past, present and future), and can help you see and understand all that you are throughout Time, space and Dimension: moreover, Firebird will offer you a view on Life that is both simple and straightforward, enabling you to put all your worries and fears into their proper perspective, by seeing them as simply one part of a much greater design. Lightly touching the gems that adorn its tail, Magdalena adds that the firebird carries the Rays of Light that hold the Awareness, Love, Truth, Wisdom, Inspiration and Reality of The Divine: hence Firebird may come to aid you in your quest to embody your Higher- (Christed-) self, helping you to accomplish your goals with greater selflessness, ease and grace, and enabling you to find the love and beauty (that *is* within and without), with which you can imbue and fill your world. With another smile she says that this will help *others* who follow in your footsteps learn from all *your* experiences – making their own journeys of self-growth and transformation less arduous and perplexing!

Running a finger lightly down the firebird's breast, Magdalena explains that each of its feathers are made of condensed Light: then, as a single tiny silver feather loosens and drops into her palm, she lifts it to show you how it flickers with silver Light, like a miniature living flame, before gently touching it to one of the sapphires on the firebird's tail – at which the feather turns a fiery silvery-blue....

With a chuckle, Magdalena tells you that what you see in this feathery flame is the Magdalene Flame of Innocence, Purity and Love, which holds the potential to return all sentient life-forms to the Divine state they once held before taking on the density of human third-Dimensional (and/or other) experiences. She reassures you that this Flame acts in perfect harmony with all belief systems and spiritual practices – for its primary purpose is to infuse all that it touches with the Purity of The Divine Mother and the Divine Light of Grace, thus reminding it of (and restoring it to) its innate state of absolute innocence: and this is to be her Gift to you.

Standing and turning to face you, Magdalena rests her left hand on your shoulder: then, with a cry, the firebird springs into the air and begins to fly counter-clockwise around you.... with every circuit he flies, his plumage grows brighter and brighter and your surroundings fade – gradually losing all definition, colour and form until there *is* nothing left but you and Magdalena....

Lifting the silvery-blue feather she has been holding, Magdalena positions it so that it sits just above your Soma centre – announcing that this is her Gift of The Magdalene Flame of Innocence, Purity and Love: at her words the feather flickers, then flares up into a brilliant silvery-blue flame, which rapidly expands to encompass your Alpha centre and your Soul Star chakra.... Resting both hands on your shoulders, Magdalena encourages the Flame to settle into balance, declaring:

> *"This Flame embraces the Light of the Rose, which bears the totality of Source through the Mercy and Love of the Divine Mother. May it remind you of your own all-embracing Light and of the truth of your Divine nature, which is both innocent and pure; and may it inspire all the sparks of your Soul-creation to recall what once was and will be again, so that you may move forwards with purpose and intent, and BE that all-encompassing and all-knowing state once more.... Understand, that in order to become pure Spirit through your Ascension, you must transform all traces of your mortality and release all that keeps you bound to the world of physicality and separation: know that this does not mean losing remembrance of what it is to be human and to have known the joys and trials of Free Will; but means learning to achieve absolute self-mastery and balance through merciful self-judgement and choice. Then – when you truly* know *what it is to be whole; and when you willingly accept suffering and pain, yet still act at all times from a place of loving compassion, forgiveness and mercy – you will have learnt all that human embodiment can teach you, and may choose to free yourself from the wheel of Life and Death...."*

While she has been speaking, her Gift has been assimilated into your energy Body – and so the firebird takes to the air again; this time flying round you in a clockwise direction.... Gradually both his plumage and your surroundings are restored to their original state; and then – once the process is complete, the firebird flies away; and Magdalena steps back and retakes her seat at your side.

She tells you that her Gift is an ideal tool to use after applying the Violet Flame, when it will refill and charge you with the fundamental essence of the Love and Mercy of The Divine Mother; and explains that to use it in your personal clearing process *after* applying the Violet Flame (as taught you by Tzadkiel), you need simply see or imagine drawing upon its fire until your heart is filled and surrounded in a sphere of silvery-blue Light.... and then slowly see or imagine that sphere expanding outwards, until your entire body and aura are filled with its Light.... Giving you an aqua-blue crystal that shines with a translucent rainbow iridescence, she tells you that this is an **Aqua Aura Quartz**, her third Crystal Champion – explaining:

> *"Aqua Aura Quartz is created by bonding atoms of gold with clear quartz, resulting in a profound merger of the Crystal and Gold Rays that embraces the attributes of* all *of the Rainbow Rays, thus reminding all that it touches of the essential purity of their nature: this makes it a highly useful crystal for addressing issues connected with disorders of the nervous system, cellular structure or DNA – where perhaps they need reminding of their fundamental design and formation, in order to know how to return to their correct state of order and balance. Aqua Aura Quartz may also strengthen, clear and balance your throat, brow and crown chakras and/or Universal and Soma centres; and can be used to enhance and support all modes and levels of communication (verbal, non-verbal, written or telepathic): in this respect, Aqua Aura Quartz is especially useful for helping you to make contact with the Highest Realms of the Angels, especially those who control the balance of the Universe and the manifestation of Divine Will – namely the Seraphim, (who inspire faith and enable you to embody Divine Love); the Cherubim, (who promote and uphold the free-flow of the subtle essence of Divine Knowledge, enabling you to embody Wisdom); and the Ofanim, (who inspire your trust in the Power of The Divine, and enable you to* know *and embody your True (and pure) nature."*

Smiling, Magdalena affirms that Aqua Aura Quartz may therefore help you connect with (and use) her Gift of the Magdalene Flame to reveal the Truth of your essential nature.

The Greenwood Guardians – Hawthorn and Eucalyptus:

Her *personal* mentoring complete for now, Magdalena affirms she is always available to aid and support you: you need only bring her to mind and ask for her presence, and she will attend you. Furthermore, she tells you that two great Tree Beings of the Plant Kingdom have also asked to support you in addressing her Theme of 'THE BLESSING OF MERCY', adding that you need only request *their* presence, and they will be with you.

She explains that the first of these Greenwood Guardians is the Feminine essence of Hawthorn, who has asked to overlight and help you ground whatever work you undertake within *any* aspect of her chapter. The second is the Feminine essence of Eucalyptus, who has specifically asked to help you understand and assimilate her Gift of The Magdalene Flame of Innocence, Purity and Love (if you have chosen to accept it).

When you are ready to connect with Magdalena's first Greenwood Guardian, you need simply call for the presence of **Hawthorn** (*) .... Hawthorn envelops you in a pale grey rippling Light, and the Feminine spirit essence of Hawthorn speaks to you, saying:

> *"In spring my blossoms offer hope, filling the hedgerows with a radiant beauty that transforms the dark stillness of winter with their promise of renewal.... in summer my shaded depths offer both protection and shelter, which enables new life to grow and thrive, free from harm.... in autumn my fruitful bounty offers joyful sacrifice, the scarlet*

and gold gifts of my being sustaining others whilst I prepare to slumber once more.... and in winter I rest and assimilate all that I have experienced, that I may grow in wisdom and in love.... And thus, I understand the cycles of life and death that drive this world; I know that beyond every horizon there lies yet another; and I live content with my purpose for Being inspiring my Soul, fully accepting of my place within the Plan of which all *are a part. Hence, if you would stand with me I will crown you with my thorns, which know the pains – and joys – of sacrifice and surrender.... I will fill you with the sweet scent of my flowers, which offer both clarity and balance.... and I will feed you with my fruits, which bear the plentiful seeds of mercy and trust, that you may satiate your Soul and BE a well-spring of Love that will replenish the Light of the world...."*

(* Tourmalinated Quartz will help you ground and connect with the energies and wisdom of Hawthorn, if you wish to enhance your experience using crystals.)

If you have chosen to accept and work with Magdalena's Gift, and when you are ready to connect with her second Greenwood Guardian, you need simply call for the presence of **Eucalyptus** (*) .... Eucalyptus envelops you in a sky-blue Light, and the Feminine spirit essence of Eucalyptus speaks to you, saying:

"In my darkness and in my Light I feed the fires of Illumination that light the path where only the fearless may tread, which lies between the Spheres that define the path to Enlightenment, and facilitate a return to the heart of the Divine Creator. Cut me down, and I will grow again – denser, deeper, and greater than before.... Touch my lifeblood, and know that it feeds the Fires that bring about enduring transformation, allowing for new growth to arise through death, and new life to arise through surrender to the lightning bolts of change.... Know then that in death I will greet you still, my Inner-self always alive with the sounds of the Universe, which resonate throughout all that I AM: so rest in my shade and listen – truly listen – and you will hear the wisdoms of the world, and know then the wisdoms of your heart.... then breathe deep of all that I AM, and you will find clarity and purity of mind – and find too the pure Breath of God that enlivens and inspires all that has been made, empowering and strengthening the heart and the mind, that they may respond to your Soul's yearning to reunite with the Father and Mother of ALL things that ARE...."

(* Sea-green Aquamarine and Blue Chalcedony will help you ground and connect with the energies and wisdom of Eucalyptus, if you wish to enhance your experience using crystals.)

ARCHANGEL AZRAEL

'CHANGE AND TRANSITION'

CRYSTAL CHAMPIONS:
Black Obsidian ♥ Clear Danburite ♥ Moldavite

CREATURE COMPANIONS:
Dragonfly ♥ Adder ♥ Raven

GREENWOOD GUARDIANS:
Gingko Biloba ♥ Corkscrew Hazel

*I willingly undertake and embrace
positive transformation and change.*

MEETING AZRAEL

It is a fine day in mid-summer, and you find yourself standing beneath a cloudless azure sky on a beautifully manicured lawn that winds its way down the middle of a long rectangular garden, like a slumbering emerald serpent. The garden is surrounded on all sides by neatly clipped evergreen hedges, which provide a tranquil contrast to the riot of colour on display in the well-tended flowerbeds that lie to either side of the path; and you can smell the sweet scents of sun-warmed grass and fragrant blossoms drifting about you, borne on a gentle breeze. You can also hear the melodious sounds of birdsong, and the soothingly hypnotic humming of insects and bees, all busily working in beds that are crammed with flowers in full bloom, which seem to have been planted in a rather random fashion – resulting in sweeping swathes and clusters of colour, which merge and blend all the hues and tones of the rainbow you could possibly imagine in glorious abandon.

As you look around, you note that the beds also host a fine assortment of specimen trees, each showing off the very finest of its colours; and realise that, logically, many of these plants and trees would not normally flower or leaf at the same time: yet here each leaf and bloom is at the absolute peak of its perfection and beauty – the fiery bronze-red autumnal colours of a maple blending harmoniously with the sweet perfection of a pale-pink cherry tree decked in its springtime finery.... hope-filled yellow and white heads of daffodils and ivory narcissi nestling at ease amidst blowsy blooms of wine-red peonies.... trailing tangles of purple violas and bright-blue speedwell lovingly entwined amongst tall leafy stems of scarlet and orange dahlias.... Indeed, everywhere you look it is plain to see that each tree, plant and flower has chosen to show itself at the peak of its perfection and beauty, uniting *all* in a startling, yet jubilant, celebration of the natural world.

As you are musing upon this, a tall figure of a man suddenly appears. Oddly, he is surrounded by clouds of multicoloured butterflies and iridescent dragonflies, and has a wild turkey at his side: this is Archangel Azrael. He smiles and greets you, declaring:

> *"I am Azrael – Overseer and Guardian of the Flames of Transition, Keeper of the Ways that bridge all Dimensions, and twin flame of Magdalena, the Lady Mercy. I welcome you to this garden – a place of great harmony and cheer, which has been created by my own hand! Here I work to bring forth the best that is within each living thing, whereby each is valued and aligned with their own perfection and that of everything about them; and presenting a place of glorious inspiration, where time may be made to contemplate things from all possible perspectives, and see everything (past and present) from many viewpoints. Know that, with me, you may safely lay your Self bare – and so appreciate and understand whatever in your life requires your forgiveness; atonement; acceptance or change: for it is only by so doing that you will truly grow and acquire wisdom, and return yourself to a state of Grace. Understand that to truthfully see and own all aspects of yourself without flinching or turning from any of them is to know and love yourself fully: so let me show you how to uncover the many secrets and treasures that are buried within your depths, in order that you may become the best you can be, whilst valuing all that you are."*

Then, asking you to accompany him, Azrael strides away down the grassy path with his hands clasped behind his back, leaving the insects and the turkey enjoying the garden....

As you hurry after him, you note that he is clad in a voluminous long-sleeved robe, which looks like an academic's gown: this hangs loosely on his lean form, billowing out behind him as he walks – and, as the fabric of the gown moves and catches the light, you notice that it is emitting sparks of silvery Light. Intrigued by this, you take a closer look and discover that its finely woven – yet dense – black material is sprinkled with hundreds of tiny water-clear diamonds, which seem to both absorb *and* reflect the light.

You continue to puzzle over this until you reach the end of the garden, where a pair of ancient yew trees form a shady arch over a wooden garden seat, whose curved back has been lovingly carved to portray a nesting pair of collared doves. The seat is bracketed by two simple waist-high stone plinths – the one to your left made of pure white marble, and bearing a football-sized sphere of polished jet-black obsidian; the one to your right made of dense black basalt, and bearing a huge crystal-clear diamond that has been cut and polished into a star-tetrahedron (two interpenetrating three-sided pyramids), which is glowing with an intense crystal-white Light. Settling down at the end by the white plinth, Azrael invites you to join him and make yourself comfortable, so that you may take time to study him further and become accustomed to his energies.

As you make yourself comfortable, Azrael sits back and relaxes, casually crossing his legs to reveal that beneath his long open-fronted gown he is wearing a pair of soft and velvety loose-fitting black trousers, which are gathered and tucked into calf-length black leather boots. His lean and lanky torso is draped in a loose-fitting silk shirt, which is a shade of purple so deep it looks almost black: this has long flowing sleeves that gather at his wrists; and a deep 'V' neck loosely laced with a simple black leather thong, revealing his throat and the top of his chest.

As he shifts to clasp his hands around one knee, your attention is drawn to Azrael's pale-skinned hands, which are long and elegant, with slender (almost delicate) fingers that are bare of any adornment. You are rather surprised that his skin is so pale – and as you raise your gaze to his face, you cannot help but note the contrast between the stark blackness of his shock of short dark hair and the almost white translucency of his skin, which seems to glow as if lit from within. As you continue to inspect his angular (and rather gaunt) face; you take in his long narrow aquiline nose and dense black eyebrows, which are set in a straight line over a pair of very deep and penetrating eyes: these are so black that the irises seem to merge with the pupils; and, as he calmly returns your gaze, you feel that he can see right into and through you – yet, despite his towering height and his dark rather saturnine looks, you find that you feel surprisingly at ease.

After a while you break your stare, and allow your gaze to drop to Azrael's only visible adornment, which is a large pendant fashioned from gold that hangs from a long golden chain to rest over his heart. This has been sculpted in fine detail to depict the head of a 'Green Man', with two brilliant emerald-green eyes faceted from moldavite, which is the stone that links him with Magdalena, his twin flame. Noting your interest, he explains that the head portrays a Celtic deity who was said to vanish each autumn and reappear each spring, thus symbolising the eternal cycles of life within the natural world; adding:

"I know the transience of life – for I have seen the passing of ages and civilisations far too numerous to count, and recognise and value the purpose of death and resurrection;

renewal and regeneration – glorying in the ability of every life-form to transcend their prior state of Being."

Then, turning the pendant over, he reveals that it bears the words 'We are ONE' – which serves as a constant reminder to him that diversity and Unity are not incompatible!

AZRAEL'S TEACHINGS:
The Obsidian Mirror – Truth, Trust and Transformation:

Gazing deeply into your eyes, Azrael asks you whether you fear him.... Your heart tells you that, despite his somewhat sombre presence, he emanates an honourable aura of calm, spiritual wisdom; and you somehow know that here, in his presence, you can think, say, do or be anything at all – and this will neither faze nor anger him. Recognising your thoughts Azrael smiles, remarking that some call him the 'Angel of Death' and fear him: yet he is, and can be, many things to different people – for he has many names and identities by which he may be known and experienced, including those of the 'Angel of the Akasha' and the 'Angel of Ascension'. He explains that his primary role is, however, facilitating *all* instances of change and transition (which is simply a transformation from one state of Being to another), in order to enable each Soul to hold a greater quantum of Light and move closer to The Divine – with the ultimate goal of absolute Unity with their Divine-self, and thence All That Is.

Reminding you that *everything* that exists is of the Divine Light and is beloved by the Creator, Azrael stresses that it is vital to understand that it is necessary to accept and assimilate *all* that you are, if you want to be at one with yourself and all about you. With a smile he explains that, as such, part of his role is to help you look truthfully at yourself in your entirety, which takes both honesty and courage – for unless you are prepared to see all that you are, including the 'darkness within', you will not be able to fully identify and understand your motivations.... and, without discerning exactly what defines you and 'makes you tick', you will not be able to recognise and fully appreciate your weaknesses and strengths. With another smile he adds that *only then* will it be possible to decide what you do (and don't!) want or need within your life, and so feel complete and be at peace.

Emphasising that 'want' and 'need' are very different things, Azrael observes that you are probably able to identify some ways in which you think or act that you dislike or are uncomfortable with – and which you may have chosen to disregard or disown, or pretend to be something they are not. Yet it is important to be able to look honestly and closely at anything you label in a 'negative' fashion; and identify its weaknesses *and* strengths, before deciding whether to accept, retain and assimilate it; modify, change and transmute it; or reject, discard and remove it: for example, you might define anger as a 'negative' emotion – yet anger has the power to motivate and energise in a very positive fashion, and so the issue is not the *emotion* itself, but about why and how it is *applied*. With a smile, he expounds that, therefore, anger can be a 'positive' emotion, as long as it is channelled in a constructive manner towards a goal that is beneficial for all concerned! After taking a moment to think, Azrael says that another example of a 'negative' emotion might be jealousy, which (on closer examination) may arise from having low self-esteem or a lack of self-belief; or in having a fear of scarcity or shortage – maybe of opportunity or material wealth: yet when you can clearly and honestly pinpoint its root (who or what you feel jealous of, and why); can acknowledge and truly value your own unique skills and talents; and – most importantly – can accept that you inhabit an infinitely abundant Universe, then any jealous feelings will become pointless and simply fade away!

Observing that it is easy to focus on the small blemishes and ignore the greater parts that are amazing in their Light and perfection, Azrael emphasises that it is important to see, acknowledge and honour the many positive aspects, gifts, skills and talents that you possess – as well as those that you think are not so 'positive': then, reaching out to the white marble plinth to his side, he takes up the black obsidian sphere that rests there, and asks if you have the courage to look within its mirror-like depths, and see ALL of your Self ('good' *and* 'bad') fully and completely....

As you consider his words, you know that you have the courage to see and understand whatever you need to – and, recognising that you have made your decision, Azrael passes you the sphere.... As you accept it, you look at your reflection in its deeply polished surface; and hear Azrael advise you to open your mind, and begin by simply being willing and prepared to accept whatever chooses to present itself to you as a first impression – for your Soul always knows the most important thing for you to recognise at the most appropriate time....

Suddenly, as you realise that you have the courage to be honest with yourself, the image you see morphs and shifts.... and then, as you begin to see certain character traits, thoughts, feelings or emotions within you that perhaps you feel uncomfortable about (or even dislike), Azrael asks you to identify the one that is strongest; and allow the obsidian mirror to help you trace back and isolate its root cause, so that you may see the validity – or otherwise – of what you uncover....

After allowing you plenty of time to closely examine what you see, Azrael tells you that (with conscious awareness and intent) you can choose to accept, modify, or discard whatever you have uncovered; and suggests that you firstly examine any misgivings or fears you have about doing so – reminding you that you gain a great deal of self-insight when you reason through your fears, and asking:

> *"What do you fear most about the process and outcome of change?... Do you perhaps fear the loss of something that you believe defines you (when in truth your Soul is your true reality, and your physical existence merely an illusion).... Do you perhaps fear the loss of something you love (when in truth Love is simply Light, which can never be destroyed).... Do you perhaps fear loss of face, or fear that others may think poorly of you if you choose a different path, or speak your own mind (when, in truth, by stifling your truths you are choosing to confine your Spirit and silence your Soul).... Do you perhaps fear there is not enough of something – such as wealth or love – to go around (when in truth it is your fear that* creates *that lack, by inhibiting the natural flow of abundance).... Or do you perhaps fear failure (when in truth doing nothing is more of a failing than if you were to try and not succeed)"....*

After allowing you a little while to mull over his words, Azrael continues, stressing:

> *"There IS nothing to fear, save fear itself: and therein is your dilemma. For, although it would be foolhardy to take an unconsidered risk, it is vital to have the clarity, honesty*

and courage to see your thoughts and fears for what they truly are, so that you can then boldly and decisively choose when and how to act."

Then, gently touching your hand, Azrael quietly adds:

"It is those who 'sacrifice' themselves who are strongest – and all change requires the sacrifice of something. For some the reward for that sacrifice may be clear, thus making it worthwhile – but sometimes there seems no obvious point or gain. And then you need to have the courage and strength to trust*; and the self-belief and* faith *to go ahead and make the change anyway!"*

Taking heart at his words, you allow yourself to accept the truth of what you saw in the obsidian sphere; and – as you decide how to deal with what it revealed – you know that Azrael will give you the inner strength to *change* what you can and *accept* what you cannot, enabling you to move forwards with clarity and purpose....

Once he knows your resolution is strong, Azrael returns the obsidian sphere to its plinth, and points to the large dragonfly hovering in the air above you: this has a vivid emerald and blue striped body, and four delicate lacelike wings that are shimmering with iridescent rainbow light. Smiling, he says that **Dragonfly** is a Master of Illusion, who may come to ask you to question the nature of what you think to be real; or to help you see through the 'veils of illusion' to the reality that lies below. He remarks that, as such, Dragonfly can aid you in identifying truths and falsehoods within what you think, hear or see; or in ascertaining the true nature of anything you encounter when travelling out-of-body, or journeying in dreams, meditation or visualisation. He adds that you may also call upon Dragonfly to show or remind you of the possibilities of the existence of other worlds and Planes of Dimension, and – if you need to be more tolerant or open-minded – Dragonfly may also appear to help you recall the different roles *you* have played in your many and varied lifetimes, not just here on Earth, but in other parts of the Universe too. Commenting how it is equally at home on the ground, on water, and in the air; Azrael says that Dragonfly can also teach you how to work with the Elements of earth, air and water to help you balance and master your body, mind and emotions (thus aiding the process of change or transformation) by doing activities like gardening, walking, singing, yoga, bathing or swimming – or less tangible things, such as inner journeying, meditation or guided visualisation. Lastly pointing out how this particular dragonfly carries the Blue and Emerald Rays, Azrael explains that *this* one has asked to help you balance your heart and throat chakras, so that you may have the courage to speak your truths and live your life in equilibrium and harmony with the Earth – and *all* that are a part of your world.

As swiftly as it first appeared the dragonfly suddenly vanishes, leaving a glassy black stone in your lap. Giving a chuckle, Azrael tells you that this is **Black Obsidian**, his first Crystal Champion – explaining:

"Black Obsidian is very protective and cleansing, having the advantage of being strongly grounding whilst simultaneously opening your awareness to all the levels, sides and facets of your Being. It has a power that can be strongly catalytic in its actions, and has the capacity to work deeply and relentlessly: yet, if you have the courage to look within, Black Obsidian will positively, actively and effectively aid and

support any and all forms of self-healing, as long as you are ready and willing to take full responsibility for yourself and your actions. Hence Black Obsidian's deep reflective brilliance may reveal your 'dark side', bringing everything fully into the light in order to highlight any negative thoughts, beliefs or attitudes that you may hold about yourself or others, which may have become evident through habitual or repeating patterns or behaviours. As a result, this may help you identify and understand their underlying cause: and then Black Obsidian will support you if you choose to accept and assimilate them, and/or empower and encourage you if you choose to change or transform them into something more positive and productive."

With a smile, Azrael affirms that Black Obsidian may therefore help you see yourself as you truly are – reminding you that it is only when you confront your darkness that you can find the absolute Light of your existence!

The Diamond Lantern – Surrender, Sacrifice and Self-mastery:

Azrael looks at you and says he knows very well the fears that the prospect of change or transition brings, but points out that true progress on the road to self-mastery is only possible when you are prepared to open and surrender yourself fully (heart, mind and Soul), and are willing to sacrifice all that you think you are, leaving everything that is not truly 'you' behind: therefore, if you wish to attain a state of absolute wholeness and balance, you must have the courage to strip yourself back to your core; *and* have the determination to confront and understand the nature, cause, and effect of your 'darkness' *and* your 'light'. He adds that this may mean facing some harsh, and maybe painful, realities – for the Valleys of Shadow are numerous, and have been constructed to teach the most difficult of lessons: yet when you are willing to see with clarity; and when you are willing to master and rise above the pitfalls of fear and doubt, you will behold the Light that shines over the horizon, and know that – in truth – there is no *requirement* to walk in the Valleys, merely the *choice*.

Reaching out, Azrael gently touches his fingertips to your heart and brow chakras, and tells you that (as your heart and mind open) you will understand that *all* paths are of Light, and thus know that the Valleys need hold no fears. With a soft smile he adds that, furthermore, all who have walked the Valleys are stronger for it – for the strongest Soul is the Soul that has been tested: this is because (in having passed through the fire, and having had its fiery imprint branded into its heart) it will have forged itself a core of gold that will provide a truly secure foundation on which to build its dreams.

Getting to his feet and walking to the black basalt plinth, Azrael reverently touches a finger to one of the diamond lantern's points, disclosing that it holds the absolute Light of Source: then, lifting the lantern from its resting place, he slowly passes his hand over it to reduce the brightness of its Light, before giving it to you to hold.... As you examine it, he explains that its shape (a star-tetrahedron) is created by the merger of two tetrahedrons (three-sided pyramids) – one pointing up, the other pointing down. He says that, in this way, the masculine and feminine aspects of the Element of fire merge 'as One', creating something that anchors and holds the Divine Light of Creation; *and* defines the Merkaba (and your Body of Light), which is unconfined by third-Dimensional physicality.

Azrael tells you that, therefore, if you shine the Light of his lantern onto whatever was revealed when you looked into his black obsidian sphere, you will see *all* sides of your nature clearly illuminated alongside your perfected (and Divine) Self: and then, if you choose to draw upon the lantern's catalytic Light, you will be able to initiate (and then undertake) a profound programme of self-transformation, progress and growth.... Then, placing a hand on your shoulder, Azrael asks you to now have the courage to allow the Diamond Light to shine upon you, proclaiming:

> *"Within the Divine Light ALL paths are open to you. I cannot undertake your journey or make your choices for you: for this is* your *journey, and it is only by testing each path that you will understand what each one gains you – or costs you. Understand too that to experience is to BE – and there may be parts of that experience that you choose not to repeat! But forget not what was learnt in the process, for every experience creates the weft and weave of your life, and may be seen in many lights.... Know too that you will walk most easily when you know what it is to be fearless: so* surrender *your fears, your heart and your Soul to the Light....* sacrifice *your illusions, your self-imposed limitations and your ego to the Light.... For only strength and self-belief will enable you to master the paths you walk, and give you the power to make or create a different reality: that which you perceive as being your current reality restructuring itself, redrawing and recreating every aspect of itself anew. What was – no more; what could be – now real."*

After allowing you time to assimilate his words and absorb his lantern's Light, Azrael tells you that you can call upon him if you need help to conquer your fears or understand the lessons offered by the Valleys of Shadow; or if you want him to bring his obsidian sphere and diamond lantern to aid you as you progress towards self-mastery. He then returns the lantern to its plinth, and gives you a perfectly clear striated crystal that has a wedge-shaped termination. He tells you that this is **Clear Danburite**, his second Crystal Champion – explaining:

> *"Clear Danburite is one of the best crystals for providing you with a clear and effective connection to the Angelic Realms, for its innate clarity is difficult to defile, and can help you forge coherent connections to your Higher-self and many Planes of Higher spiritual Guidance. Clear Danburite's innate strength and integrity is often overlooked, for it works in a very gentle and subtle way through a high and refined resonance that can be hard to sense: nonetheless, as it both calmly and gently helps open and activate your Higher energy centres, whilst simultaneously grounding you firmly in the reality of your physical existence, it can set up a flow of energy that establishes a permanent bridge to span all aspects of your Self (body, mind, spirit; past, present, future). Clear Danburite can then help you bring each part into sharp focus, to reveal whatever needs to be changed; and then aid you in addressing the issue from all perspectives to bring about long-lasting resolution. Last, but not least, Clear Danburite has a loving and supportive energy, whose clear Light will help you find the courage to embrace radical change, even if the prospect of this initially fills you with fear or self-doubt."*

Smiling, Azrael affirms that Clear Danburite may therefore bring the Illumination of Source closer, so you can see things more clearly – reminding you again that it is only by confronting your darkness that you will find the absolute Light of your existence!

Azrael

Drawing your attention to the foot of the black plinth, where a black and white adder is coiled up in peaceful sleep, Azrael reminds you that snakes are ancient and wise creatures that carry the knowledge of the processes of creation and evolution: hence they are powerful allies that understand the true nature of the interconnectedness of all things, one to another; and (because of their ability to shed their skin in order to grow) can teach you much about the benefits of undergoing change and transformation. He explains that **Adder**, with its diamond-shaped coppery-black and white markings, can teach you about balancing polar opposite or extreme states within your mind and thought-processes: thus you may choose to call upon Adder if you have outgrown something, or if life is getting uncomfortable and you are unsure why; or if you are in a mental or emotional quandary, and need rational input to return to balance. With a quick wink, Azrael then strips off his gown and shirt, before reaching down to offer his hand to the adder, who acknowledges Azrael's presence, and then sinuously winds its way up his right arm to spiral around his bicep: gently running his finger down its back Azrael remarks that serpents are ancient symbols of leadership, Kingship and Mastery – marking the bearer's wisdom, strength and ability to work with 'magic'. Smiling, he reminds you that *true* magicians work with the arts of creation and dissolution, by controlling and directing Light in accordance with the principles of Spiritual and Cosmic Law: accordingly Adder can also be called upon if you need to understand how to plan or create something new – or deconstruct something unwanted; and/or if you need its structured and balanced energies to support you as you learn to control your inner Powers (which entails understanding about wise judgement, balance, fairness, order and accountability) as you strive to arrive at an optimal outcome.

Reclaiming his shirt, Azrael strolls up and down as he dresses, explaining that (as a guiding conscience) he is profoundly linked to many Masters, Avatars and Founders of the world's Faiths (past and present) – including Ishmael and Yeshua, upon whom two of Earth's great religions, Islam and Christianity, were founded. He wryly muses that World Faiths and spiritual belief systems are born whenever there is need for people to change their perspective away from egotism and elitism towards unity – which, unfortunately, often leads instead to even greater disillusionment, narrow-mindedness and repression! He says that this is because it is often easier for humankind to hide paralysed in fear and self-conviction behind the barriers that they have erected – afraid to venture beyond what they *see* as safe and comfortable, but which, in truth, provides neither safety nor comfort for the Soul! With a gentle smile, he observes that (although humankind as a whole has some way to go before they allow themselves to accept the peace of absolute unity) every time a heart and mind opens to acknowledge similarity and celebrate diversity, the reality of that Unity draws closer: lifting his pendant, Azrael reminds you of the words on its back ('We are ONE'), and states that he remains convinced that eventually all *will* be in absolute accord, and peace and joy will mark the beginning of a glorious Age.

The Gift of The Merkaba of The Ascension:

Standing still, Azrael gives a whistle, and holds out his left arm – at which a raven flies down from the top of the yew trees and perches on his wrist. Lifting his other hand to stroke the glossy black feathers of its back, Azrael tells you that ravens aid and support all those who work with natural forces and laws, for they understand how to use them to bring about change and growth. With a smile, he adds that **Raven** guards all ceremonial magic, and is a teacher for all those who work with the transformative power of Black Light, as it understands how to utilise its infinite potentials to help bring about change and growth: hence Raven is a wise and powerful teacher, who can show you how to be more disciplined in your spiritual practice or programme of self-healing or self-growth; or help you understand the difference between 'darkness' and 'Black Light'; and/or teach you about the processes of alchemical transformation, on both a personal and spiritual level. Gently stroking the bird's massive beak, Azrael assures you that Raven's presence should never be feared, for it knows how to mine the darkest depths for the most brilliant gems: thus Raven will be your protector, teacher and guide when you journey into the darkness of your Inner-self or the blackness of the Void: for there, in void space or in the hidden depths of your Soul, Raven's magic and wisdom can give you the courage and strength to learn whatever you need to know or understand about your innermost fears and/or 'dark' side, in order to bring about cohesive and productive change in your Self and your life; or teach you to accept (sometimes devastating) change in order to create or bring about something that ultimately serves the 'greater good'. Azrael smiles, and adds that Raven's ability to shape-shift may also show the masks or disguises that you (and others) wear, so that you always see the truth that lies below; and can help you to make *gradual* changes that will enable you to embrace whatever new reality you choose to create with more ease – whilst its ability to manipulate Time may help you assimilate and master multidimensional energy-shifts (personal or planetary) with less difficulty or pain.

Suddenly, the raven gives a harsh 'caw' and hops up Azrael's arm to perch on his right shoulder: at this, Azrael takes his gown and gently places it around your shoulders, before helping you to stand and guiding you a few paces away from the trees. Then, with the raven still perched on his shoulder, Azrael starts to walk around you in counter-clockwise circles.... As he walks, you find that the Light around you (and the garden itself) slowly fades; and, little by little, you become immersed in an inky blackness that is darker than night – and hear Azrael's voice saying:

"My Realm is dark and empty, yet full and vibrant; without Light, yet blinding to look upon; silent, yet the merest whisper of it would deafen you: for I govern the Void that defines the polar aspects of The Divine, separating Spirit from non-Spirit; the real from the illusionary; the potential from the manifest...."

Time itself seems to stand still: and as everything around you finally loses all sense of shape and form, it feels as if you are both *nothing* and *everything*.... Now the only thing that penetrates your consciousness is Azrael's voice as he continues to speak, saying:

"Here you are as you are – just you, and you alone.... On some level this state may feel familiar to you, for you spend time like this between transitions: so this, then, IS the real you – your Spirit, your Soul, your Spark – withdrawn from all influences, so that you may have the opportunity to be at one with your Self, and so understand more of what it is to be pure energy – to BE pure Spirit.... So let this remind you of the transitory nature of Life; and be a remembrance of what has gone before and *will come again...."*

After what could be seconds or hours, you become aware that a solitary spark of pure crystal-white Light hangs in the blackness in front of you; and you watch as it is enclosed in a sphere of silvery Light, which slowly condenses into a tiny crystalline star-tetrahedron (merkaba).... This hovers for a moment, before rising up to come to rest in the space between your Alpha centre and your Soul Star chakra, where it is drawn into the heart of the Magdalene Flame that was the Gift of Azrael's twin flame, Magdalena.... As this happens, Azrael declares:

"This is my Gift of The Merkaba of The Ascension. Know that the merkaba holds the template of your Lightbody; whilst the spark it holds will become the Ascension Flame (the transformative Fire through which you will pass when *you are ready to Ascend), which carries the Light that catalyses reunion with your Christed-self and a permanent reconnection to your Divinity. At the point of your Ascension the merkaba will expand to surround your Unified Body; and the Ascension Flame will descend into your heart to merge with the twinned Lotuses of your Heart and Soul, so that you may be As One with the Flames of the Alpha and Omega, and embrace a new state of BEing...."*

Gift given, you sense Azrael circling you again – this time in a clockwise direction; and you feel his Gift settling into balance with (and within) your Magdalene Flame.... Slowly your surroundings and your sense of Self fully return – and as the garden becomes 'real' again, Azrael stops in front of you; takes his gown from your shoulders; and guides you back to the garden seat.

Here he gives you a deep green glassy stone that looks like half a shelled walnut, telling you that this is **Moldavite**, his third Crystal Champion – explaining:

"Moldavite is a rare and unusual stone that carries the energies of both the heart of the Earth and the Cosmos that gave it birth. It holds within it an energy that embraces the finer resonances of the seven main colours of the spectrum of Light, which have been grounded by The Divine Feminine through the constellation known as the Seven Sisters of the Pleiades: hence all those who have star-root or other connections with this particular star system may be especially drawn to this stone, which offers them a sense of comfort and sanctuary if they are unable (or unwilling) to accept the density and reality of Earthly existence. Its lack of crystalline structure means that Moldavite can also support and enable any and all transformative actions, which may be challenging to those who live in fear of change – for, through the emerald Light at its heart, it has the power to catalyse evolution and growth, whilst facilitating an opening of the heart and an illumination of the mind that knows *only wholeness and balance throughout the entire spectrum of human behaviours. Yet, above all else, Moldavite will support the courageous in developing their awareness and expanding their consciousness, as they walk the (often difficult, and sometimes shadowed) paths that will eventually lead them to achieving their personal Ascension."*

Smiling, Azrael affirms that Moldavite may therefore help you connect with infinite worlds, which you have yet to explore; and remind you of the glorious munificence of a Universe that allows and promotes all Life, all Light and all Love.

With another loud 'caw' the raven flies away, and Azrael retakes his seat at your side, replacing his cloak around his shoulders. As he settles, he expounds that the term

'Ascension' is sometimes taken to imply an event that simply occurs without conscious effort, or as an outcome of living a virtuous life – however, although this is partly true, a better reality is that Ascension happens as a consequence of achieving total self-mastery: this means reaching the point where you are 'master' of all aspects of your human physical Self – body, mind and emotions – regardless of what life throws at you! With another small smile, he adds that at that point you will have the ability to expand your consciousness and transcend Time and Dimension (which is what you are working towards as you learn to shift your awareness from Linear to Unified Body, and start to absorb new experiences from a 'Higher' viewpoint).

After thinking for a moment or two, Azrael reaches out and rests his hand on the black obsidian sphere to his side, adding:

"Know that I oversee the Realm in which the Kabbalistic sphere of Da'at exists; and represent all the pathways that are hidden – the invisible ways that can be found only through your own personal search for your own truth and reality. Da'at is the sphere of generation and regeneration that allows anything to come into existence and BE: the sphere that holds all knowledge outside of space, Time and Dimension – so containing all the potentials that you have to transform yourself and become pure Spirit...."

then, holding your gaze, he emphasises:

"All matters within your life that are unresolved or unfounded exist within this Realm, and you cannot cross it without all these things being fully resolved. Hence to traverse the realm in which Da'at exists you must be willing to walk my hidden pathways and give up all that you think you are, leaving everything behind that is not truly YOU. Remember: it is only by confronting your darkness that you can find the absolute Light of your existence; and I promise you now that you may be assured of my presence at the edge of the abyss – yet I will not take your hand, but would ask you to have the courage to simply step out and follow me across the great Divide that is between physicality and Spirit, in order to Become what you are meant to BE. Then, when we reach the other side, and you are in your transformed and perfect state, you *will see me as I am – and I will welcome you through the doorway with love and with joy."*

The Greenwood Guardians – Gingko Biloba and Corkscrew Hazel:

His *personal* mentoring complete for now, Azrael affirms he is always available to aid and support you: you need only bring him to mind and ask for his presence, and he will attend you. Furthermore, he tells you that two great Tree Beings of the Plant Kingdom have also asked to support you in addressing his Theme of 'CHANGE AND TRANSITION', adding that you need only request *their* presence, and they will be with you.

He explains that the first of these Greenwood Guardians is the Masculine essence of Gingko Biloba, who has asked to overlight and help you ground whatever work you undertake within *any* aspect of his chapter. The second is the Masculine essence of Corkscrew Hazel, who has specifically asked to help you understand and assimilate his Gift of The Merkaba of the Ascension (if you have chosen to accept it).

When you are ready to connect with Azrael's first Greenwood Guardian, you need simply call for the presence of **Gingko Biloba** (*) .... Gingko Biloba envelops you in a silvery-green Light, and the masculine spirit essence of Gingko Biloba speaks to you, saying:

"The roots of my Being link all that are of my ancestry throughout the world, regardless of Time or Dimensional experience. I have known death, and I have known life; I have known sorrow, and I have known ecstasy; I have known turmoil, and I have known peace, which understanding (through having grown in self-knowledge, and in certainty of my greater-purpose) I am enjoined to share with you now.... So be at one with me, and allow me to support you in living your Truth whilst grounding you in your own Great Enlightenment – knowing serenity, knowing grace, and knowing that you simply ARE – ever evolving; ever growing; and ever ennobling the Light that IS at your heart. Then, may you henceforth BE always at peace with the world, allowing and accepting change; and trusting always in the profound goodness of your own magnificent Spirit, which knows your true worth and conceives every lifetime and experience that you choose to embrace, explore and assimilate...."

(* Tiger Iron and Labradorite will help you ground and connect with the energies and wisdom of Gingko Biloba, if you wish to enhance your experience using crystals.)

If you have chosen to accept and work with Azrael's Gift, and when you are ready to connect with his second Greenwood Guardian, you need simply call for the presence of **Corkscrew Hazel** (*) .... Corkscrew Hazel envelops you in an indigo Light, and the Masculine spirit essence of Corkscrew Hazel speaks to you, saying:

"From the deep dark heart of the Earth I spiral upwards towards the Light of the Sun, who rules the day and guards the night: thus I know balance – within and without – for I hold the polar extremes of darkness and light, black and white; and the place where they meet, where BEing begins. I understand that to know and accept all that you are takes courage and strength – yet Life is *simple, if you let it be so – you need only connect with the Light within, which is fully innocent and pure, and you will see this to be true.... So stand with me, and I will help you in your quest to know yourself fully and completely – and then, if you have the will, wit and wisdom to do so, you may hear the songs that span all Times and Dimension, which tell of the Alpha and the Omega, the Beginning and the End.... and you may know the myriad wisdoms of the Universe and gain knowledge of the much Greater whole, which goes far beyond that which is yet known!..."*

(* Black Tourmaline and White Moonstone will help you ground and connect with the energies and wisdom of Corkscrew Hazel, if you wish to enhance your experience using crystals.)

ARCHANGEL RATZIEL

'OPEN TO THE LIGHT'

CRYSTAL CHAMPIONS:
Apache Tear ♥ Snowflake Obsidian ♥ Jet

CREATURE COMPANIONS:
Cheetah ♥ Ostrich ♥ Elephant

GREENWOOD GUARDIANS:
Maple ♥ Acacia

*I am a Master of the Infinite Light.
Perfect awareness is mine.*

MEETING RATZIEL

It is early evening, and you find yourself standing beneath open skies on the fringes of a desert, at the exact spot where its sun-bleached sands meld with the fertile lushness of a river's flood plain. To your left the fine pale sands stretch far into the distance, the wind-sculpted crescents of their low rolling dunes lightly veiled by a shimmering haze as the heat of the day submits to the cool of the night; whilst to your right the land appears less hostile, becoming progressively more verdant and green. You can hear the sound of flowing water: so, deciding to seek its source, you carefully pick your way bare-footed through a fusion of green, gold and emerald short- and long-stemmed grasses and crops – the soil dark, firm and moist (and much cooler than the desert sands) giving off earthy scents of loam and sweet new grass with every step you take.

After a while, you reach the banks of a wide river: here its margins are delineated by deep stands of silver-stemmed rushes and reeds – their feathery heads, bronzed by the lowering sun, whispering as they sway hypnotically back and forth in a cooling breeze. In contrast, the opposite side of the river is completely open – the water lapping against its gently sloping banks, where a dozen large crocodiles are dozing on the ochre earth and soaking up the last of the day's heat: these fearsome creatures are paying no attention to the tiny black and white birds perched on their backs – recognising, perhaps, that they are performing a service as they pick off and consume the insects and leeches that have attached themselves to the reptiles' tough leathery skin.

Appreciating that the crocodiles are favouring the other bank, you turn your back on the river and watch the sun continuing its slow descent through the sky, sinking to the horizon in a fiery ball of vermilion and orange: this tints the cloudless sky above your head in glorious hues of peach and pink; and bathes the distant desert landscape in a soft golden light, which contours the dunes and defines their rapidly darkening shadows – until, eventually, the landscape fades as the sky too darkens.... Overhead, the stars begin to emerge – and your attention is suddenly taken by one that glitters especially brightly: this appears to be growing in size.... then, a moment later, you realise that this is because it is rapidly drawing closer....

Just as you are wondering what it would be like to be hit by a meteor (!), it abruptly shimmers and vanishes – and a massive sphere of brilliant silvery-grey Light materialises on the ground some distance in front of you.... Blinking to clear your vision, you re-focus your eyes to see a tall platinum-winged Angel striding towards you, its towering form seemingly cloaked in black and silver Light: as it approaches, it furls its metallic wings, enabling you to see that it has taken the form of a powerfully-built ebony-skinned man wearing nothing more than a knee-length Egyptian-style kilt: this is Archangel Ratziel. Reaching you at last, he greets you – declaring:

"I am Ratziel – Divine Guardian and Overseer of The Word, Author of The Sublime Transcendental Mysteries, Light of Wit and Wisdom and twin flame of Jochara, the Lady Victory. I am he that sustains the Breath of Life, fired and inspired by the Wisdom that is beyond reason, that it may BE in accordance with the words of the World of Fire and Creation; and I am he that holds the fabric of the Universe, and allows the differentiation between what is and is not: thus all that I AM is of Divine contemplation;

and all that I do is of the Will of the Divine Light.... So attend me now, and I will show you the secrets of my world, if you would let me, and will open you to understand the many Truths of The Great Mystery, so that you may come to realise that there is much more to Heaven and Earth than you at first might believe."

Ratziel then turns and strides off, away from the river and towards the desert – and, as you hurry after him, you realise that he is heading for a tall cluster of date palms....

You quickly reach this little 'oasis', which stands within a circle of tall burnished brass lanterns: these are radiating a warm golden light, which illuminates the scene and casts a flickering light on a pair of fawn-coloured dromedaries resting in the shadows nearby. Leading you into the centre of the palm trees, where a colourful fringed carpet (weighted down by two wooden camel saddles padded with sheepskins and striped rugs) has been set out, Ratziel encourages you to make yourself at ease.... He then offers you a dish of dates and a glass of mint tea before settling himself on the carpet nearby – where (leaning casually back against one of the saddles) he invites you to take a little time to examine him and become accustomed to his energies.

Doing as he suggests, you note how the warm glow of the lanterns gives Ratziel's smooth and glossy ebony skin a coppery-red glow, and highlights his well-toned and powerful physique. What you can see of his hair (which he wears very closely cropped) is a silvery-grey, suggesting that he is not young: yet Ratziel's skin is unlined; and he possesses a commanding and very masculine aura of primal strength and power. This is emphasised by his broad shoulders and muscular chest, which tapers to a narrow waist; and by his long, loose, well-proportioned and muscular limbs – although his square and unadorned workman-like hands and rather large bare feet have surprisingly long and slender fingers and toes.

Ratziel appears very relaxed and at ease; and, as he observes you in turn, he meets your gaze with cat-like eyes whose extraordinary irises are a tawny amber flecked with gold: these are lushly lashed in black, and deep-set beneath prominent brows in a face that is square and somewhat flat, with a wide nose and generous mouth. His neck is short but muscular, and his well-shaped ears have uncommonly long lobes: these have been pierced to enable them to hold a pair of flattened oval platinum 'rings', whose elongated surfaces are engraved with a series of arcane sigils, none of which you recognise.

As you have already noted, Ratziel is only wearing a 'shendyt' – a wrap-around kilt that is flat at the front and pleated at the sides to allow for movement: this is made of plain but finely woven sand-gold coloured linen, and reaches from just above his navel to just above his knees – sitting higher at the small of his back, and lower at the front. It is secured around his waist by what looks like a tasselled length of rope, which is knotted to the right of his navel: intrigued, you lean forwards to examine it more closely, and realise that the 'rope' is actually the tail of a lion, and that the 'tassel' is its tufted tip. Meeting your questioning gaze, Ratziel smiles and merely states that this was gifted to him to honour his strength, courage, endurance and wise leadership.

Your eye is lastly drawn to Ratziel's adornments, starting with his crescent-shaped pectoral ornament: this appears to have been made from a large double-layered piece of dark brown leather, and hangs around his neck on a matching leather thong to cover the upper part of his chest. In the centre of the leather you can see a large rectangular cut and faceted pale-pink morganite (pink beryl), which is the gem that links him with Jochara, his twin flame: this gem is 'sandwiched' and held in place by the two layers of leather; and glints with rosy pink sparks as it catches the lantern-light. The only other item visible is a torque that has been fashioned from silvery-gold electrum in the shape of a long and slender lizard, which spirals up around his right bicep: on closer scrutiny, you discover that one of its eyes has been cut from a white diamond, which is sparkling with an inner fire; and the other from a black diamond, which is glimmering with hidden depths.

RATZIEL'S TEACHINGS
The Knowledge and Wisdom of The Ancient Ones:
Recognising that your inspection is complete, Ratziel stands and picks up a sturdy staff that was resting on the ground behind him: holding it in his right hand, with its base resting on the ground, you note that it is as long as he is tall; and can see that it has been made from the wood of an ebony tree, whose hard black wood has been polished into a plain round shaft crowned by two slender finger-length ebony prongs. These spiral round each other in a single double helix – and noting your puzzlement, Ratziel just gives an enigmatic smile, and asks you to accompany him into the darkness of the desert beyond.

As you leave the shelter of the trees and begin to stride out over the cooling (and now moonlit) sands, he draws your attention to the female cheetah resting in the forked branches of a nearby acacia tree – who (at his whistle) lifts her head, and drops nimbly to the ground. As she bounds over to pad along at his side, Ratziel reassures you that she will not harm you, adding that **Cheetah** is a clever and capable hunter who is both swift and economically agile in its movements: hence you may call upon Cheetah if you need a guardian to help you move swiftly through difficult or hostile terrain; or to teach you how to uncover and interpret the hidden wisdoms in signs or symbols that appear to you in dream state or when journeying; or to show you how to choose the path that will allow you to achieve your current goal in the least complicated way and with greater ease and grace. Resting his hand on her head, Ratziel remarks that a cheetah's loping gait enables it to cover great distances; whilst its quick reactions, flexible backbone and well-honed musculature allows it to show an impressive turn of speed if need arises: thus Cheetah can also help you analyse the energy and effort required to master something; or teach you how to assess your capabilities and energy levels, so that you learn to pace yourself appropriately in accordance with your needs and the situation at that time; and show you how to be more flexible (physically, *and* in your attitudes and thought processes). With a smile, he adds that Cheetah's keen senses are also multidimensionally aware; whilst its preference for peace and solitude allows it the liberty to move wherever need or impulse takes it: accordingly Cheetah can give you more confidence in your intuitive abilities, helping you develop your powers of clairaudience, clairvoyance and clairsentience with both discernment and discipline – thus helping you connect with your Higher-self (and with other Realms and Dimensional Beings) with greater clarity and ease; and enabling you to find the inner calm and focus that will enable you to instinctively *know* the 'right' path to take at all times.

As you continue your march across the sands, Ratziel tells you that he has seen the birth and development of many worlds and civilisations, and been a Guiding Conscience to many of the Great Avatars and Masters who were active in the foundation of Earth's Ancient Civilisations. He chuckles as he observes that humans like to think that they are alone in the Universe, yet this is far from the truth – for many myths are founded on fact; and those once titled 'gods' were regarded thus simply because humans could not explain their abilities or presence in any other way that made sense to their (somewhat limited) understanding of their own place within the Universe!

He goes on to tell you that in times long past in Ancient Egypt, one of these 'gods' (who was known as Osiris) was said to be the son of Ra (the Supreme Being): yet in fact 'he' was a Cosmic Master whose presence was to catalyse the foundation on Earth of what were called 'Mystery Schools'. With a smile he explains that these were to teach people how to attain Higher levels of conscious awareness within a spiritual reality that transcended normal reason, thereby helping them to understand and *know* themselves to be 'immortal' (and hence Divine) Beings of Light; and informs you that their teachings included fostering the ability to access the Higher Wisdoms of the Cosmos.

Drawing to a halt, Ratziel lifts his staff and conjures up a dome of soft golden light, illuminating a massive statue that has been sculpted from the desert's bedrock of golden sandstone: this has the body of a crouching lion with a human-like feminine face, whose head and shoulders are covered with a 'nemes' headdress (as worn by some pharaohs). Ratziel explains that the statue marks an aspect of Earth's past when Beings from beyond the Sun came to assist and support the growth and development of an Ancient civilisation that predated those of Ancient Egypt: these intergalactic Beings were human-like and very tall – yet with cat-like features, golden furred skin and a 'mane' of golden-brown hair like that of a lion. With a smile, he says that this statue is not unique in its purpose, for Earth has many such records sculpted in stone, each of which were used to hold or store knowledge and information – and *some* of which once provided the inhabitants of Earth with inter-dimensional gateways that allowed them access to other worlds.

As you approach the statue, you stop at the wide and shallow copper bowl (filled with a blazing mass of fiery golden flames) that rests in front of its outstretched 'paws': the fire sheds light over its face, and cast the sands around it into shadow – and, as you comprehend its true size and magnificence, you realise that you feel genuinely humbled in its presence. Here, at Ratziel's command, the cheetah settles contentedly on her belly with outstretched legs and tail so that she spans the gap between the statue's paws: then, asking you to give him your trust, Ratziel asks you to lie on the sand with your head resting on the cheetah's back, so that your feet are pointing towards the statue's heart....

As you do as he asks, you gaze up at the inscrutable visage towering far above you, and realise that the statue is in fact a sentry – guarding its knowledge, and watching and waiting with infinite patience: then, kneeling at your feet, Ratziel puts his staff to one side and lightly rests his hands on your ankles.... at this, you feel yourself being gently grounded, aligned and balanced.... and then, after waiting a few moments more, Ratziel directs you to be guided in your breathing by sensing the rise and fall of the cheetah's ribs beneath your head.... and so you simply relax, and allow your eyes to close....

At first you are only aware of the warmth of the cheetah's fur and of her gentle rumbling purr: but then, as you expand your awareness, you find that your breathing synchronises; and you begin to feel a circular pulsing in your head.... this appears to be clearing your airways and sharpening your mental clarity – and, as he recognises what you are feeling, you hear Ratziel say:

> "ALL is everything: everything is ALL.... Open yourself now to The Divine.... Know *you are everything.... for you ARE everything....*"

and then, as you absorb his words, you feel Ratziel's Light surround you; and know that it is safe to release your hold on what (until now) has been your rather limited view of reality.... Gradually you sense your awareness begin to expand beyond what you had thought of as YOU – encompassing all of the Earth.... and the Solar System.... and then the entire Galaxy, until it is as if you are connected to a vast Body of Consciousness....

Incredibly, it feels as if your energy Body is being filled with stars and light: then, out of the blue, you hear a single exquisite note sound in your mind.... this resonates through every part of you, and fills you with wonderment and indescribable joy – and, recognising this, Ratziel reminds you that what you think of as 'space' is neither empty nor silent. You can hear him smile as he explains that what you are hearing is the unique resonance that links *you* with 'The Divine': it is *your* note; *your* Divine expression – and, as you immerse yourself in the experience, you find that for a while you have no concept of space or time.... Eventually, however, Ratziel draws your awareness back to your human Self again, keeping his hands on your ankles and guiding you 'back' until he is sure that you are fully grounded in your earthly human reality....

Helping you to sit up, Ratziel reminds you that having the ability to connect with ALL is not about *disconnecting* from the Earth and disappearing 'up there'; but is about *expanding* your awareness to encompass the Earth Plane *and* beyond. With a smile, he stresses the importance of remaining well-grounded in your human reality throughout your explorations, if you want to fully recall and utilise what you learn; and emphasises the importance of looking to the energetic health and integrity of your human (Earthly) Self *before* looking to the rest of the Universe.

Thanking the cheetah for her help, Ratziel guides you across to sit and rest in front of the fire, where he gives you a small odd-shaped glassy black nugget. He tells you that this is **Apache Tear**, his first Crystal Champion – explaining:

> "*Apache Tear is a form of obsidian that is dark smoky-brown and semi-transparent. It is often found in natural nuggets, and – as with all obsidians – is a form of volcanic glass that has no specific crystalline structure, due to the rapidity with which it formed. This lack of structure is of great benefit if you wish or need to work without rigidly imposed boundaries, as it encourages freedom of thought; freedom of movement; and flexibility of purpose. Hence Apache Tear can support you in developing new projects using 'blue-sky thinking'; and in 'open-ended' journeying in meditation or visualisation – in which case you should always ensure that you have cleared and grounded your energy Bodies beforehand (which Apache Tear may also assist with), to be certain that 'unrestricted' does not mean 'unsafe' or ill-considered! You may also be drawn to work with the polished version of Apache Tear for extra clarity as you travel within and*

without – for, just as science seeks beyond the Earth to gain a clearer understanding of the nature of the Universe, Apache Tear can aid your personal healing and Ascension work by showing you other worlds and existences too numerous to mention – thus supporting you in 'reaching for the stars', both literally and metaphorically!"

Smiling, Ratziel affirms that Apache Tear may therefore help you to remain firmly and safely grounded in the Earthly Plane, whilst you explore other worlds in your quest to acquire and assimilate Higher knowledge and wisdoms.

The Book of Ratziel – Love, Light and The Word:

Unconcerned by the presence of the cheetah resting nearby, a small group of ostrich suddenly strolls out of the darkness of the desert: chuckling, Ratziel says that it seems impossible that ostrich are defined as 'birds', with their ridiculously long legs, huge feet and extravagantly plumed bodies – and their comical 'Donald-duck' beaks and big dewy eyes that are always so coquettishly framed with long lush lashes! Smiling, he says that some think ostrich are cowardly or stupid – yet they focus with enthusiastic curiosity on whatever crosses their path, and aggressively defend themselves if under attack – furthermore, ostrich wisely work harmoniously as a group, sharing the guardianship and rearing of their young, and demonstrating loyalty and patience with all of their extended 'family': thus you may ask **Ostrich** to teach you how to juggle family commitments and responsibilities, or support negotiations between parents, siblings or friends if a family member needs help in caring for a child or vulnerable adult; or to aid you in 'oiling the wheels' to restore harmony if certain individuals in your family or circle of friends do not get along; and/or to teach you how to have more patience or tolerance in dealing with a particular person or situation. As the ostrich come closer, Ratziel remarks that (uniquely) their plumy black and white feathers are perfectly symmetrical in their growth, because they are not needed for flight: indeed, like humankind, they have chosen to forgo flight for earthly existence – hence Ostrich may come to *you* to remind you of the many reasons there are for choosing human embodiment; or to help you in staying grounded, whilst you learn how being in physicality does not prevent you from flying on the etheric or spiritual level! With a wry smile, Ratziel observes that few people understand the part Ostrich plays in grounding Black Light and White Light and in holding polar opposites in harmony and balance (as was known and understood by the Egyptian 'goddess' Ma-at, who personified the Divine Laws of Truth, Justice, Balance and Order): nonetheless, you may ask Ostrich to help you embrace the mind-set of fairness, balance and accountability when you are working to address and clear unresolved karmic issues; or to support you if you need the strength and determination to remain true to yourself and your Highest Truths when you are under pressure; or to help you examine your own (or others) hearts for the truth that underlies your (or their) words or actions.

All of a sudden, one of the ostrich trots over and drops a small black and white stone (and a perfect black and white feather) on the ground in front of him, before loping off to rejoin its companions.... Picking both items up, Ratziel gives you the stone (which looks like a night sky dotted with tiny white snowflakes or stars), telling you that this is **Snowflake Obsidian**, his second Crystal Champion – explaining:

"Snowflake Obsidian is an opaque black obsidian that bears tiny white crystals of cristobalite, giving it more structure than might be present in other obsidians. Even so, it remains flexible in how it can work with you through a wide range of situations, helping you understand how and why you react to extreme situations in your life, whilst enabling you to look deeply within to find and establish an appropriate balance between your rational (thinking) mind and your intuition – this can be especially useful if you have a tendency to be indecisive, or to vacillate between viewpoints or polar extremes. Snowflake Obsidian resembles a star-studded night sky – and so meditating with it may help you gain a Higher perspective on your personal / work / family life, thus enabling you to isolate and appreciate the benefits and rewards each aspect brings, and so determine where your true priorities lie. Snowflake Obsidian can also help show issues more starkly in black and white, making it easier to see the truth in what is there, and so helping you to identify and appropriately address problematic issues: additionally, Snowflake Obsidian may assist you in recognising and accepting what all *sides and aspects of your own nature contribute to the sum total of your personality – teaching you the irrelevance of labelling* anything *as 'good' or 'bad', and offering the contrast and clarity that will help you see the motivations and reasoning that lies behind every action and response you (or others) choose to take or make."*

Smiling, Ratziel affirms that Snowflake Obsidian may therefore help you understand the 'extremes' in your life – and aid you in finding the most appropriate balance, as you explore your 'reason for being'.

Joining you by the fireside, Ratziel gives you the ostrich feather to hold and takes your attention to the torc spiralling around his right bicep: touching it with his left hand, he smiles as the silvery lizard comes magically to life and darts up to sit on his shoulder, explaining that this is a Fire Lizard, who has the ability and Power to unite the worlds of form and non-form through the Elements of earth and fire.

Telling you to watch carefully, he then stoops over the fire burning in the copper bowl, and encourages the little lizard to jump into the flames.... as you watch, you see the lizard circling the inside of the bowl – and you stare in amazement as the gold flames flare with a dazzling blue-white Light.... Slowly all the flames absorb this Light, steadily increasing and growing until eventually a tall column of fiery blue-white flames fills the bowl – at which Ratziel removes the lizard from the bowl and returns it to his arm, where it reverts to its previous form....

Explaining that the bowl is now filled with a substance that will clear, charge and protect you while you join him on a journey, Ratziel thrusts his hands into the blue-white flames to show you that they will not harm you, and then offers you his arm to help you climb into the bowl.... As you do, you are immediately immersed in a cool strong energy flow, and you know that this fully surrounds and protects you: then all of a sudden you feel your energies shift – and as your body begins to gently vibrate in harmony with the resonance of the flames that embrace you, you realise you are feeling much stronger and clearer.... Recognising this, Ratziel steps into the bowl and stands behind you, at which the flames die down, leaving a column of pale blue-white energy in their place that makes it appear as if you are both encased in polar ice (although you are not cold, and your movement is not restricted).... then Ratziel unfurls his wings – and, as he wraps them around you and enfolds you in their cool embrace, everything goes dark....

Time seems to stand still until Ratziel releases you from his embrace – whereupon you find yourself in a large rectangular chamber, which is lined with white alabaster and filled with a soft golden light. He informs you that you are standing in one of several chambers that can be accessed through the Power of the Lion-el; and explains that this is one of the places where the libraries of information that hold all the records of Earth's history (past, present and future – and the keys to human life and purpose) are kept. Then, at a wave of his hand, the light brightens – and you see that a gold rectangle (inlaid with black onyx and white marble tiles to create and define an elongated four-pointed star) has been inscribed on the floor in the centre of the chamber.

In the very centre of this star stands a tall pedestal made of gold – the top of which has been sculpted in the form of a long-tailed bird, whose outspread wings are supporting an open book that appears to be the source of the chamber's light. Ratziel explains that the bird you see (who is of the same lineage as the firebird and the phoenix) was revered by the Ancient Ones for its ability to channel the Light of the Sun and unite the five Elements of earth, air, fire, water and ether – adding that its presence was said to herald all Divine Acts of Creation and Animation, which, of course, only happen through the Power of Love, Light and The Word....

Gesturing to the open book, Ratziel tells you that some know this as 'The Book of Ratziel' – although you could, perhaps, also call it a text book on Creation! Reminding you that 'Time' is merely an illusion, and that 'Light' IS the foundation of all things (including all possible learning and knowledge), Ratziel explains that this book captures 'The Word' and records *everything* about the disposition of Light – its language; its composition; and its application in the Divine Acts of Materialization and Dissolution – which (basically) means that it holds everything that will ever be known or understood.

Asking you if there is something *you* would really like to know or understand now, Ratziel cautions you to remain outside the golden rectangle and walks over to the golden pedestal.... after giving you time to think, he lays a hand on the open book – at which the chamber begins to reverberate with sound, and you are bathed in waves of multicoloured Light.... Directing you to close your eyes and look within, Ratziel advises you to simply allow yourself to absorb the Light, and whatever you are experiencing – and, as you shift your awareness, you feel your body tingling; and you have the strange experience of 'seeing' all kinds of symbols and script pass before your inner eye.... You are unaware of the passage of time – but at some point you somehow know that you *know* the answer to whatever you wanted to know or understand, and open your eyes....

Seeing this, Ratziel lifts his hand from the book, and as the sound and colour slowly fade from the chamber, he tells you that it may take a while for you to assimilate and fully comprehend all that you need to – for The Light is not constrained by Time. Then, when the chamber is finally silent and still, he assures you that he will aid you in your understanding in dream-state or in meditation; and moves to stand behind you, enfolding you in his wings.... Just like before, everything goes dark.... and, when you are released from his embrace, you find yourself back in the desert, standing in front of the fire....

The Gift of The Black Light of The Alpha and Omega:
Retrieving his staff, Ratziel walks away from the fire until he is silhouetted against the desert sky: here, he raises his arm and points his staff at the sky – at which a fine shaft of pure white light shoots out of one of the prongs at its tip, and spirals up towards the stars. When he lowers his staff, the light dissipates; and as Ratziel returns to your side he smiles and says that it is not what you *saw*, but what you *did not* see that is important! He explains that, very basically, his staff channels White Light (which you *could* see) and its counterpart, Black Light (which you could *not* see). He emphasises that *both* are eternally present everywhere – stressing that White Light *needs* Black Light, as without it, it can neither function nor exist: this is because Black Light IS all possible potentials as yet un-manifest, from which *anything* may come into be-ing – but only through the application of White Light and its constituent parts. With another smile, he explains that (again, very basically), it is *his* task to use his staff to allocate and direct both Black and White Light in their appropriate measures; and it is his *twin flame's* task to use sound to blend them as required in (and by) each specific moment of creation and/or dissolution.

Having given you a brief overview of what you need to understand, Ratziel asks you to accompany him to the statue of the 'lion', and touches his staff to its heart: at its touch an opening appears in the sandstone, beyond which you can see a tunnel that is glowing with a soft golden light.... Helping you over the threshold, Ratziel leads you into the heart of the lion and along the tunnel, which follows a long but gently sloping incline, until you eventually reach what appears to be a dead-end: here an impressive statue of a bejewelled elephant blocks the way, its gold body and silver tusks inlaid with diamonds and pearls – even so, you have the distinct impression that it is guarding something even more valuable.

Smiling as he recognises what you are thinking, Ratziel reverently touches its trunk and tells you that a very long time ago the elephant was chosen to be the Earth's Record Keeper: however, it was later decided that human greed might lead to all elephants being wiped from the face of the Earth, and the task was passed on to an ocean-dweller – nonetheless, elephants still embody the three noble qualities of Divine Power, Wisdom and Love; and their great strength, heart and intelligence means that **Elephant** may help you to awaken and balance the three-fold Flames of the Lotus of your Heart; and then will mentor you in grounding and developing *any* of their attributes. Ratziel goes on to explain that the leader of a herd is always its most experienced female, who (as with the whales) holds the histories and wisdoms of their race, their heritage and their roots; and knows the invisible pathways that map their land, and the places that provide for and sustain them: accordingly Elephant can show you how to unearth your roots and value the inner and outer paths you have travelled (past, present and future); or help you to find the sources of inner and/or outer Guidance that are right for you, if you need to overcome obstacles or work through blocks (physical, mental, emotional or spiritual); or to give you a dispassionate overview of the consequences of the choices open to you, if you are at some sort of crossroads in your life. Adding that this 'gentle giant' experiences human emotions – including love, joy, grief and rage, Ratziel explains that Elephant can also help you consider and understand your reactions to events or situations in your life; or teach you how to listen patiently to others when they express their thoughts and feelings (*and* show you how to respond with appropriate empathy and tolerance!); and to support you, if you ever have to embrace – or dispense – 'tough love'.

Stepping aside, Ratziel asks you to find the ostrich plume he gave you earlier, and then touch it to the tip of the elephant's trunk.... as soon as the plume comes into contact with the elephant's trunk, the black parts of the feather slowly fade, until the whole of the plume is white.... then, in the blink of an eye, the elephant simply vanishes, revealing a space beyond that is pitch black and seemingly empty.... Taking the (now white) feathery plume from your hand, Ratziel steps forward and raises his staff, proclaiming:

> "All that is Light is dark; all that is dark is Light! Know that manifestation may only come about within the Void that IS at the cusp of White Light and Black Light, which is brought into being at every singular moment or instance of thought or inspiration.... Within it can be found the potentials for All Things – for that which appears to be hidden is simply not yet come into form, and is merely awaiting the enlightenment that allows the waters of Truth and Light to BE at one with the Word...."

He then strikes the ground with the heel of his staff three times – and the air shimmers, before clarifying – revealing that you are standing at the entrance of a large pyramidal chamber that is walled in white selenite....

Below the apex, in the pyramid's very centre, there is a knee-high cube of polished rainbow obsidian – and (after leading you into the chamber) Ratziel asks you to sit down on this, with your feet flat on the floor and your head erect.... Once you have done so, he stands facing you and declares:

> "All That IS and All That Will Ever Be IS Light.... In its fullness and majesty this Light, which is the BEing of The Divine, is known as the Diamond Light – a spark of which is held within your Seed of Original Consciousness; its essence reflected through your Heart.... This all-encompassing and all-embracing Light is held in balance through its twofold states of Being known as White Light and Black Light: and you now understand that, within the Black Light, unawakened and inert consciousness awaits awareness of its true nature; and awaits the spark that will act upon it to allow it to Become:"

then, lifting his staff, Ratziel touches it to a point just above your head; and a point just below the base of your spine.... He informs you that he has placed a sphere of condensed Black Light within the Alpha and Omega centres of your Unified Body – the one at your Omega centre being double the size of the one at your Alpha centre – explaining:

> "The Black Light of the Alpha and Omega is my Gift to you now.... I counsel, however, that you will only be able to fully connect with this Light in all its Glory when you have awakened, balanced and charged the Lotuses of your Heart and Soul, and attained full Unification with All that you Are: yet to know the Divine Light in its completeness is to know everything – and thus my ultimate Gift is that knowledge, for it holds the secret to All That IS, the understanding of which releases the Seed to BEcome ONE again."

Ratziel then bows to you in Blessing, before moving to stand behind you, where (resting his staff down the length of your spine) he waits until his Gift has settled within your Unified Body and energy field....

When he is satisfied that his Gift has been appropriately assimilated, Ratziel lifts his staff again – and in a sudden and eye-watering flash of light the chamber vanishes; and you find yourself sitting on the carpet beneath the grove of date palm trees, back in the desert.... Suggesting that you rest a while, Ratziel gives you a small light-weight black sphere that has been polished to a soft matte sheen; and tells you that this is **Jet**, his third Crystal Champion – explaining:

"Jet carries and holds the pure Black Light that offers and provides the space and infinite potentials that will allow you to restructure or recreate the future that your Soul needs, in order to BE the Diamond it is meant to be. Jet may help you accomplish this by enabling you to connect with the 'real world' through grounding you in a state of calm, dispassionate detachment: this makes it more comfortable to explore your Self and your motivations as you acknowledge both your shortcomings and (just as importantly) your strengths. This will enable you to recognise and value your own worth, whilst identifying and understanding whatever you need to resolve, heal or clear in order to strengthen clarify and enhance the three-fold Flames of the Lotus of your Heart. Jet may then aid and support you in releasing, transmuting, clearing or healing whatever you have identified that needs to be addressed, thus promoting discernment and positive growth – and, in turn, freeing you to hold more Love (most importantly) for yourself, and then for others; and empowering you to live your life with the Will and Wisdom to see and know ALL as simply travellers on the same difficult and demanding path to Enlightenment."

With a smile, Ratziel affirms that Jet may therefore help you recognise and understand the purpose of Black Light, and so truly come to know yourself (and the Light within) in *all* your Glory.

The Greenwood Guardians – Maple and Acacia:

His *personal* mentoring complete for now, Ratziel affirms he is always available to aid and support you: you need only bring him to mind and ask for his presence, and he will attend you. Furthermore, he tells you that two great Tree Beings of the Plant Kingdom have also asked to support you in addressing his Theme of 'OPEN TO THE LIGHT', adding that you need only request *their* presence, and they will be with you.

He explains that the first of these Greenwood Guardians is the Feminine essence of Maple, who has asked to overlight and help you ground whatever work you undertake within *any* aspect of his chapter. The second is the Feminine essence of Acacia, who has specifically asked to help you understand and assimilate his Gift of The Black Light of the Alpha and Omega (if you have chosen to accept it).

When you are ready to connect with Ratziel's first Greenwood Guardian, you need simply call for the presence of **Maple** (*) .... Maple envelops you in a swirling red, orange and tan Light, and the Feminine spirit essence of Maple speaks to you, saying:

"Although my body is slender and insubstantial, I embrace the world of healing with my fingers; and hold the Word in my heart. Thus I know well how to heal the pains that hold you in stasis – cold and empty, and in need of my touch, which delicately traces out all hurts, warming them with my love and releasing them to the Light – for I hold a

great passion within that can energise and inspire you, body, mind and Soul.... So stand with your back against my trunk, and feel the metal that strengthens all that I am – reaching up, reaching down, and reaching within; in order to find and join with the Power that comes from an ever-open mind and a loving heart.... Then shine forth with me the riches of your heart, and share them with the world; and know the great peace and love that IS within the Light that surrounds you at all times.... Allow it to expand all that you are, balancing your mind and your emotions, and reconnecting you with your Consciousness that IS both Universal and Infinite – so restoring your faith in Living and BEing.... HERE and NOW...."

(* Gaia [Polychrome] Jasper and Amber will help you ground and connect with the energies and wisdom of Maple, if you wish to enhance your experience using crystals.)

If you have chosen to accept and work with Ratziel's Gift, and when you are ready to connect with his second Greenwood Guardian, you need simply call for the presence of **Acacia** (*) .... Acacia envelops you in a rippling pale green Light that is flecked with black, and the feminine spirit essence of Acacia speaks to you, saying:

"My Spirit is such that I am never restricted or confined by my Earthly existence, for my mind and my awareness knows that I have the freedom to roam the Heavens, delighting in that which makes me so much more than I am.... Yet the part of me that is rooted to the ground is content to give of my bounty, providing sustenance and shelter for the myriad Souls that roam this land: for throughout my many lifetimes I have reached the understanding that knowledge shared is wisdom gained; and I have learned to welcome, sense and read the footprints of all those that have walked this land before: thus, if you would stand with me, I can tell you of the lives and histories of *all the Kingdoms of Earth – for their records are planted deep within the ground, and their resonance can be understood, if you have the will, wit and patience to do so. Know too that every step you* take leaves its own footprint upon the ground, which is recorded in Light for those that follow to know if they choose *– so choose the way you walk with care: for* everything *that you make manifest in this world creates the foundations upon which those that have yet to come will have to build!...."*

(* Jadeite and Green Aventurine will help you ground and connect with the energies and wisdom of Acacia, if you wish to enhance your experience using crystals.)

ARCHEIA JOCHARA

'SWEET SURRENDER'

CRYSTAL CHAMPIONS:

Aquamarine ♥ Tibetan Tektite ♥ Snow Quartz

CREATURE COMPANIONS:

Condor ♥ Mountain Goat ♥ Polar Bear

GREENWOOD GUARDIANS:

Rowan ♥ Date Palm

I surrender to the Power of Divine Love, and open my heart to align with the Gifts of the fundamental forces of Divine Creation.

MEETING JOCHARA

It is a fine morning in early summer, and you find yourself standing on a well-trodden path that is zigzagging its way up the steep sides of a 'V' shaped valley. A fusion of dark earth and small rough stones has resulted in a yielding, yet slip-proof, footing; and here and there you can see tiny imprints in the mud, indicating that the path is mainly used by animals. To either side of you the ground rises and falls sharply, yet the way is well-defined by a line of grey lichen-covered rocks, and is wide enough to walk without fear of falling. The valley is set high in a towering range of mountains, and falls away on your right-hand side towards a silver ribbon of water, which is just visible far below – the slopes becoming greener and more lush the deeper they plunge into the river's gorge. On your other side the slopes become more sparsely covered with vegetation the higher they rise – their rugged starkness randomly dotted with low spreading camellia bushes, whose dark glossy evergreen leaves and red, pink and white flowers provide welcome splashes of colour in an otherwise rather barren terrain. Somewhere in the high distance you can hear the crashing sounds of a waterfall in full spate – so, choosing to climb the path, you move on, stopping now and then to regain your breath and enjoy the view....

After walking steadily for some time, you near the crest of a ridge and what looks like the end of the path. Appreciating that your climb is nearly over, you take a final few steps and emerge on the rim of a deep oval plateau that cuts into the mountain, creating a natural amphitheatre that has spectacular views over the valleys and peaks below and beyond. The rocky face that curls around the plateau has sheer craggy slopes, which rear high overhead to culminate in a vertiginous peak that is liberally dusted with snow: this is the source of the waterfall you could hear before, which is cascading down from the mountaintop in a dense veil of white water, and pouring into a wide dark pool that (over time) it has sculpted and scoured from the bedrock of the plateau floor.

Nearby you can see a long curved bench made of polished black obsidian: this has been placed to overlook the pool at its widest point – and so, with nothing else to do, you decide to rest for a while. No sooner have you sat down, than the waterfall suddenly stops flowing – revealing a pair of soaring white pillars of polished snow-white quartz, which flank a high narrow opening that appears to lead into the mountainside beyond. A tall woman clad in a red sari (with a black fan-tailed bird sitting on her right shoulder) stands in the entryway: this is Archeia Jochara. As she lifts a hand in welcome, the bird flies low over the pool towards you; and a narrow arching bridge of grey granite rises up from the depths of the pool, creating a way across the water. Crossing this swiftly (with surprising grace, in view of her rather sturdy physique), she greets you, declaring:

"I am Jochara, the Lady Victory – Weaver of Sound and Light, Master of The Fundamental Forces of Divine Creation, and twin flame of Ratziel. Here, we stand on the very roof of the world, surveying all that is of the immensity and majesty of Divine Creation! In this place we are open to the sky, where we can feel the kiss of the sun and hear the wisdom of the Universe in the voices of wind and water; here too we may gain passage to the depths that lie within, so that we may hear the voices of earth and fire and understand the love and strength that underlies All That Is. Thus, as you dwell in physicality on the beautiful planet that you now call home, I ask you to have faith in me

and in yourself; and to give your trust willingly and openly, in the full knowledge that together we can connect with the very heart of the Earth: for then you may come to know her essence – and the forces that shape her – as well as I."

With these words Jochara joins you on the obsidian bench, and invites you to spend a little time examining her and accustoming yourself to her energies.

As she sits, Jochara crosses her ankles and relaxes – her hands cupping an olive-green drawstring bag in her lap. You note that her hands are square, with calloused palms and fingers – all short-nailed and bare, apart from the middle finger of her left hand, which bears an unusual gold ring. Closer scrutiny shows this to comprise a plain gold band bearing a tiny golden bowl shaped like the cup of an acorn: this holds a wonderfully clear rose-pink morganite crystal (the gem that links her with Ratziel, her twin flame), which has been intricately carved into the shape of a flower of clover. You also note that Jochara's skin is the rich colour of strongly brewed tea, and is smooth and unlined – and, although you sense she is much older than she appears, her strong and sturdy physique suggests that she is no stranger to hard work: furthermore, even if you might not describe her as classically beautiful, she has an unusual and arresting appearance that projects an aura of self-assured power.

Taking your attention to her features, you examine her square-shaped face, strong rounded chin and perfectly proportioned mouth and nose, which are framed by her dark-brown hair: this has been brushed back from her face to the nape of her neck (revealing a surprisingly small and delicate pair of ears), where it has been braided into a waist-length plait, and interwoven and bound with metallic strands of silvery-gold electrum. Shifting your gaze to Jochara's eyes, which are set beneath dark arching brows, you are surprised to find that they are a deep gentian blue: and, as their cool intensity holds your gaze, you become filled with a sense of determination that strengthens your inner resolve.... At that moment you feel as if you could achieve *anything* – and, as Jochara recognises what you are feeling, she gives a gentle smile.

With some difficulty you drag your eyes away to admire the vibrancy of Jochara's attire: this comprises a deeply-pleated sari of finely-woven cherry-red silk worn over a plain and simple cherry-red cotton underskirt, with a matching choli whose short sleeves and navel-length hem have been trimmed with a band of gold ribbon. Closer inspection reveals that the hems of the sari are likewise trimmed – and that they have been further embellished with a row of long-tailed golden birds, embroidered in gold thread.

Jochara's surprisingly small and slender feet (shod in gold open-toed pumps) are just visible beneath the hem of her underskirt, revealing that her toenails are painted cherry-red to match her clothing; whilst her muscular, yet well-toned, arms are bare – except for the narrow gold bangles encircling her right wrist. Scrutiny of these shows there to be twenty of them in total – each loosely connected to its neighbour by two pairs of intertwined strands of gold wire. The lowest bangle rests on the joint of her wrist and is slightly larger than the others – possibly because it has two gold loops attached to it, which extend slightly over the back of her hand.

Once more this leads your attention to the drawstring bag in Jochara's lap, which you can now see has a row of symbols embroidered around its opening in gold thread.

With a smile, Jochara shows you that a long cord of plaited black silk has been stitched to the bag's sides, enabling it to be hung crosswise over her torso so that it rests on her left hip and leaves her hands free: then, opening the bag (which is made of silk, and lined with felt to match its exterior) she shows you that it holds a small Tibetan singing bowl, whose polished interior reflects the light of the sun like a mirror. She then demonstrates how the bag is secured by a double-ended drawstring that has been braided from metallic threads of gold and silver – each end of which has been loosely woven into a tiny 'cage' that holds a small diamond sphere sparking with rainbow light.

JOCHARA'S TEACHINGS
The Fundamental Forces of Air and Water:

Returning the bag to its usual resting place over her shoulder, Jochara tells you that in order to 'create' *anything*, you need to understand the fundamental matter and forces that will shape it: this entails learning their purpose, and becoming familiar with how they function, so that you become able to direct and oversee their implementation with both wisdom and discernment. She explains that this place is a good spot to learn a little more about some of the forces that shape the world around you on a very physical level: those of the Elements of earth, air, water and fire. Reminding you that whatever you see around you is also within you, Jochara points out that you are *also* physically shaped by those same Elements, through the atoms that construct you; the air that you breathe; the water that permeates your cells; and the biological processes that fire you. She expounds that those same Elements also exert an influence at a more subtle level – for each has a particular affinity with one of the subtle energy Bodies that supports and sustains you throughout your physical embodiment: the Element of earth with your physical Body; the Element of water with your emotional Body; the Element of air with your mental Body; and the Element of fire with your spiritual Body. With a smile, she adds that therefore (if you choose to) you can use the virtues of the Elements to help you heal, clarify, energise and balance yourself on any level – body, emotions, mind and spirit.

Drawing your attention to the skies above the mountain peak, Jochara points to a large bird with a huge wingspan who is effortlessly riding the thermals, and gives a shrill whistle: at this the bird immediately swoops lower, arcing effortlessly through the air to show off its magnificent plumage – the underside of its wings and its tassel-like primary feathers, body and tail being a dense jet-black; the upper side of its wings and the deep white ruff that encircles its neck, like a feather boa, being pure snow-white. Jochara tells you that the bird is a condor, who is familiar with the Element of air in all its glory – its colouring indicating that it is also a master at balancing extremes: hence you may ask **Condor** to show you how to gain and/or maintain balance within your mental Body and thought processes; or to mentor you if you wish to learn how to work with Black Light and White Light to create something new, or to bring about change. Smiling, she adds that (because it is related to Vulture) Condor may also come to direct or guide you through the 'ending' or 'beginning' of something; or to help you understand and deal with any 'life-and-death' matter – literal or metaphoric. As you watch its skilful mastery of the currents of air that lift it once more high into the sky, Jochara remarks that you may also call Condor if you want a higher, wider or more detached perspective that can help you see the full and complete picture of an issue, situation, plan or concept; or if you need greater flexibility in your approach to resolving a problematic issue. Adding that some know it as a bird of the Sun, she tells you that Condor can also help you understand more about Faith and Trust, Truth and Light, by teaching you how to work with the Elements of both air *and* fire together – although you should take care if you choose to do so, as they can be a powerful, and sometimes unpredictable, combination!

Getting to her feet, Jochara tells you that the Element of air is the Vessel that holds 'Divine Mind' within you – and so it may be illuminating to see, sense and feel some ways in which it shapes your world (literally *and* figuratively).... After leading you to the edge of the plateau, she stands behind you with her hands on your waist to hold you steady and secure, and instructs you to shuffle slowly forwards until the tips of your toes are at the absolute brink of the precipice.... Reluctantly you comply – but as you look out over the distant mountain peaks and cloud-filled valleys below, all fearful thoughts about your precarious position suddenly vanish; and you find yourself relaxing – overwhelmed by such an unassailable sense of stillness and calm, that you begin to feel completely detached from the hectic and often complicated world of humanity....

Recognising the point when your mind and thoughts settle, Jochara explains that the Element of air inspires and directs the thoughts and Words that shape and define all Creation: then, asking you to close your eyes and trust her, she instructs you to begin clearing your mind by listening to the sounds of the wind as it moves through the valley below, and swirls around the plateau where you stand.... After a while she asks you to hold your arms out to your side, as if you are flying; and sense how the air feels as it passes over your skin.... presses against your body.... and sweeps through your aura.... She then tells you to take some long slow deep breaths; and discern how (as you take it within, and replenish the oxygen in your body) the air feels.... tastes.... and smells....

Eventually you find that your senses and your mind feel sharper and more alert; and now Jochara asks you to think if there is a particular thought process that you would like to have better control over; or any subject that you would like to understand more about on a logical or rational level.... As you consider this, she tells you to continue breathing steadily and deeply – and, as something comes to mind, to simply *allow* any thoughts, feelings or emotions associated with it to come to the surface, without attachment....

When Jochara senses this beginning to happen, she counsels you to open your eyes and watch how the wind changes and shapes the clouds in the sky above you, saying:

> *"Simply observe the patterns being created in the air in front of you by the Sylphs (the Elementals of air): then open yourself – heart, mind and Soul – and simply* surrender *everything to the Element of air.... For the Sylphs will help you clear and centre your mind; clarify and balance your thought processes; correct the root causes of erroneous judgements and beliefs; and help you connect more effectively with Divine Mind...."*

After allowing you time to consider and see all you can at this time, Jochara ensures that you are fully grounded and balanced: she then assures you that you may call upon the aid of the Sylphs and the Element of air at any time – adding that you may find it useful to carry or hold a piece of Blue Chalcedony, if you wish to draw the Sylphs closer to you....

Leading you back to the pool, Jochara tells you that the Element of water is the Vessel that holds 'Divine Will' within you – and so it may be illuminating to see, sense and feel some ways in which it shapes your world (literally and figuratively). She says that it is *this* Element that enables all that is Created to be refined and developed through trial, error and experience: then, asking you to kneel by the water and close your eyes, she suggests that you again begin by clearing your mind – this time by simply listening to the sounds of the waterfall (which is once more cascading down into the pool), and to the gentle lapping of the wavelets as they travel across its surface to break upon its lip.... After a while, she instructs you to lean over and place your hands into the water, and (keeping your eyes closed) sense how the water feels as you lift and lower your hands.... move them quickly, and slowly.... and sift it through your fingers.... She then tells you to take a little of the water to your lips, and drink; and discern how (as you take it within, and enliven and refresh your body) the water feels.... tastes.... and smells....

Eventually you know that your senses and your mind feel calmer and clearer; and at this point, Jochara asks you to think if there is a particular emotion that you would like to have better control over; or any subject that you would like to understand more about on an intuitive or emotional level.... As you consider this, she tells you to continue breathing steadily and deeply – and, as something comes to mind, to simply *allow* any thoughts, feelings or emotions associated with it to come to the surface, without attachment....

When Jochara senses this beginning to happen, she counsels you to sit back and open your eyes, and allow your gaze to rest on the water – observing it where it is calm and still, and where it is flowing and turbulent, saying:

> *"Simply observe the patterns being created in the water by the Undines (the Elementals of water): then open yourself – heart, mind and Soul – and simply* surrender *everything to the Element of water.... For the Undines will help you cool and calm your emotions; clarify and balance your reactive processes and feelings; identify and address the root causes of any inappropriately directed emotions; and help you connect more effectively with Divine Will...."*

After allowing you time to consider and see all you can at this time, Jochara ensures that you are fully grounded and balanced: she assures you that you may call upon the aid of the Undines and the Element of water at any time – adding that you may find it useful to carry or hold a piece of Blue Lace Agate if you wish to draw the Undines closer to you....

Helping you back to the seat, Jochara settles at your side and gives you a clear ice-blue crystal: she says that this is **Aquamarine**, her first Crystal Champion – explaining:

> *"Aquamarine has a clear and fine energy, which is clearing, calming and cooling to the mind, body and emotions – bringing a sense of peace and wise detachment that makes it a useful aid if you need to see or consider something from a less emotional perspective, or if you need to cleanse and clear your body, mind or spirit of stagnant or undesirable energies. Aquamarine has a natural affinity with the throat chakra, and can support and enhance clear communication on many planes – both with other people, and with your Higher-self, Guides and/or Spiritual Teachers: this offers the potential to extend your field of knowledge, enabling you to understand and* know *things on a deeper and more profound level. Aquamarine can also help you truly hear what is being communicated*

to you, bringing a clarity that enables you to identify anything that is hidden, or which lies beneath the surface; whilst its free-flowing nature can also help you free your mind – catalysing profound shifts in awareness that can help you recognise how apparently disparate thoughts, ideas or concepts are connected; and allowing you to clear away any restrictions that confine your thinking, enabling all your understandings to become greater and more complete."

Smiling, Jochara affirms that Aquamarine may therefore help you clarify, balance and refine your mental and emotional auric Bodies; your sacral and solar plexus chakras; and your mind, thoughts and emotions.

The Fundamental Forces of Earth and Fire:

Drawing your attention to the lofty peaks and crags high overhead, Jochara points to a herd of sure-footed goats, leaping agilely from ledge to ledge: all have long dense coats and thick ruffs; and most have fine pairs of long curving horns. She remarks that mountain goats are well-suited to living in difficult terrains like this; and, as you watch them move confidently about the vertiginous slopes, she says that you might therefore choose to call **Mountain Goat** to help you master difficult terrain, or survive in a hostile environment; or to teach you how to attain greater heights of understanding, or Higher states of Being; or to show you how to be more flexible or open-minded in your approach if your path is difficult, blocked or unclear; and/or to give you more certainty, confidence and determination if you have consequently become discouraged or dispirited. Pointing out how effortlessly they work with the Elements of both earth *and* air, Jochara says that Mountain Goat may also be of aid if you need help in balancing or extending the agility or scope of your physical body and/or mind; or if you need to be more grounded when journeying, meditating or otherwise accessing Higher knowledge, ensuring that whatever information you retrieve can be easily recalled and put to good use. Smiling, she says that Mountain Goat also knows the benefits of self-determination and freedom, tenacity and perseverance, and so can guide and support you if you have 'reached the end of your tether'; and/or need help to free yourself of *any* outside influence that is holding you back, and preventing you from BEing who or what you wish to BE.

Moving to stand behind you, Jochara once again asks you to trust her – and, as you sense a movement and shift in the air, you feel and see a huge pair of wings wrap around your body: paradoxically these seem to have form, yet be formless; to be transparent, yet utterly black.... then suddenly everything around you sparks with red and gold Light – and you somehow *know* that you have shifted into another Dimension; and realise that you are passing swiftly down through the Earth's crust and mantle, into her very core....

When you come to a stop, you find yourself in a large cavern that has rounded walls formed from white chalcedony. Strangely it is cool, and not at all dark or oppressive – for it is illuminated by a sphere of Light that is so bright you are unable to look at it directly: this floats in the very centre of the cavern, so that its light is both absorbed and reflected by all the surfaces, making everything within the space clearly visible.

Sensing your puzzlement, and your awe, Jochara materialises at your side: stepping forwards, she removes her singing bowl from its bag, and passes it through the sphere of

Light.... As she withdraws it, you note that it is now filled with flames that (rather oddly) are all opalescent white – although they flare and flicker as a burning fire would normally do.... Then, asking you to follow her, Jochara leads you through a low doorway into a smaller side chamber: this one has rainbow obsidian walls and a low domed ceiling, and would be completely dark, were it not for the bowl of flames she is carrying.

Placing the bowl in the centre of the floor, Jochara dims its light until the chamber is almost dark again, before asking you to lie down full-length on the floor.... She tells you that the Element of earth is the Vessel that grounds 'Divine Love' within you – and so it may be illuminating to see, sense and feel some of the ways in which it shapes your world (literally and figuratively). Once you are settled, she explains that the Element of earth provides the foundation that allows, sustains and maintains the integrity of all structure and form: then, asking you to again close your eyes, she suggests that you once more clear you mind – this time by listening to the sounds the fabric of the Earth makes, as it holds and surrounds all that you are.... After a while, she instructs you to run your hands over the ground where you lie, and see how it feels to your touch.... and sense how it supports every part of your body, as you allow yourself to relax into its embrace.... She then tells you to take some long slow deep breaths; and discern how (as you take the air within to help centre and ground you) this place feels.... tastes.... and smells....

Eventually you know that your senses and your mind feel focused and strong; and at this point Jochara instructs you to extend your awareness, and connect with the heart of the planet; and then think if there is any specific issue connected with your physicality that you would like to have better control over; or any matter concerning your physical health, growth or survival about which you would like to understand more.... As you consider this, she tells you to continue breathing steadily and deeply – and, as something comes to mind, to simply *allow* any thoughts, feelings or emotions associated with it to come to the surface, without attachment....

When Jochara senses this beginning to happen, she counsels you to open your eyes, and allow your gaze to rest on the chamber's domed ceiling – watching how the reflected light plays over the surface, creating shadows that constantly shift and change, saying:

> *"Simply observe the patterns being created on the ceiling by the Gnomes (the Elementals of earth): then open yourself – heart, mind and Soul – and simply* surrender *everything to the Element of earth.... For the Gnomes will help you strengthen and focus your mind; ground and balance your emotions; find the root causes of any physical ills, so that you understand how to heal them; and help you connect more effectively with Divine Love...."*

After allowing you time to consider and see all you can at this time, Jochara ensures that you are fully grounded and balanced: she then assures you that you may call upon the aid of the Gnomes and the Element of earth at any time – adding that you may find it useful to carry or hold a piece of Red Jasper, if you wish to draw the Gnomes closer to you....

Helping you to kneel in front of her bowl (which is still filled with flames), Jochara tells you that the Element of fire is the Vessel that guards and inspires the 'Divine Light' within you – and so it may be illuminating to see, sense and feel the many ways in which it shapes your world (literally and figuratively). She explains that the Element of earth is the means by which Word becomes Deed: then, asking you to close your eyes again, she suggests that this time you clear your mind by simply listening to the sounds the flames make as they flicker and flare in her bowl.... After a while, she instructs you to lean over and place your hands in the bowl – reassuring you that the flames will not burn you, so you need not fear them; and (keeping your eyes closed) see how they feel against your skin.... and then move your hands around, and see how they feel as you sift them through your fingers.... She then directs you to cup a little of the fire in your hands and take some long slow deep breaths, before holding the flames in front of your heart to discern how (as it clarifies and cleanses your heart) the fire feels.... tastes.... and smells....

Eventually you know that your senses and your mind feel purer and clearer; and at this point, Jochara asks you to think if there is a particular personal spiritual issue or situation that you would like to have better control over; or any spiritual topic that you would like to understand more about on a Higher level.... As you consider this, she tells you to continue breathing steadily and deeply – and, as something comes to mind, to simply *allow* any thoughts, feelings or emotions associated with it to come to the surface, without attachment....

When Jochara senses this beginning to happen, she counsels you to sit back and open your eyes, and allow yourself to gaze deeply into the flames – observing where they are gentle and calm, and where they are flickering and flaring, saying:

> *"Simply observe the patterns being created in the flames by the Salamanders (the Elementals of fire): then open yourself – heart, mind and Soul – and simply* surrender *everything to the Element of fire.... For the Salamanders will help you expand and concentrate your mind; clarify and restructure your emotions; fire and inspire your spirit, so that you may recall who you truly are; and help you connect more effectively with The Divine Light...."*

After allowing you time to consider and see all you can at this time, Jochara ensures that you are fully grounded and balanced: she assures you that you may call upon the aid of the Salamanders and the Element of fire at any time – adding that you may find it useful to carry or hold a piece of Carnelian if you wish to draw the Salamanders closer to you....

Returning her bowl to its bag, Jochara kneels behind you and rests her hands on your shoulders: once again, everything goes dark – and you *know* you are moving back through the Dimensions to return to the obsidian bench beside the mountain pool.... When you open your eyes, you find you were right; and with a smile Jochara makes sure you are settled, before giving you a slightly pitted and wrinkled waxy black stone. She tells you that this is **Tibetan** (Black)**Tektite**, her second Crystal Champion – explaining:

> *"Because it has no crystalline structure, Tibetan Tektite is very adaptable if you need to work in a more open or flexible manner; and is especially useful to support meditation, journeying or channelling for the purposes of 'outside' contact. Of course,* all *tektites have an innate ability to aid you in connecting with locations and civilisations other than Earth's; but* black *Tektites have the specific ability to strengthen and ground your energy Body, whilst simultaneously opening and aligning the channels that promote a clear and conscious connection with the Cosmic energies that exist both within* and *beyond the Earth. If you are an embodied Soul who is (consciously* or *unconsciously)*

aware of having lifetimes elsewhere, and find life on Earth hard-going, you may find solace in the energy of Tibetan Tektite – for it may offer you a 'sense of home' that makes human embodiment more bearable; and can be used to support multidimensional healing and energy adjustments for body, mind and spirit – as long as you are willing to remain open-minded about the nature of the process and its end results."

With a smile, Jochara affirms that Tibetan Tektite may therefore help you ground more fully to the Earth (and beyond), and balance your body, mind and spirit more effectively.

The Gift of The White Light of The Alpha and Omega:

Opening the bag that holds her singing bowl, which is now empty of flames, Jochara lifts the bowl into her lap and takes out a finger-sized tube made of black suede. Pushing this onto the index finger of her right hand, and connecting it to the hooks on her bangle using two strands of gold and silver thread plucked from the drawstring cord, she supports the bowl on the palm of her left hand, and shows you how she plays it with her gloved finger – circling and striking the bowl to create a series of ringing tones and bell-like chimes. She explains that she uses the resonance of sound to direct the Diamond Light in accordance with Divine Law – 'weaving' it to bring about structure and form; awakening and activating that which is made manifest, so that potential may BECOME; and reshaping and/or transmuting that which requires dissolution or change. Lifting her finger, she tilts the bowl so that you can clearly see your reflection, and tells you that it is made from the Seven Sacred Metals that carry the innate resonances of the Solar System – thereby ensuring that everything is regulated in harmonious accord with *all* the Bodies that ARE within the influence of the Sun: accordingly, she may also sound it to ease the effects of multidimensional shifts and changes initiated at Cosmic and/or Universal level.

Looking up, you find that the waterfall has again ceased to flow – and that a small golden-furred cat with large tufted ears is now sitting between the white pillars of quartz that bracket the way into the mountain. With a chuckle, Jochara asks you to follow her, and walks across the bridge – speaking softly to the cat and thanking it for its vigilance, before leading you through the opening into a high-ceilinged corridor that disappears into darkness. Here Jochara lightly sounds her bowl, creating a soft light that illuminates your immediate surroundings: this reveals that the black granite walls are completely covered with lines of writing in Sanskrit text; and that the passage leads steeply downwards – and so, as she walks on, you follow very carefully in her footsteps....

After walking for what feels like ages, you finally arrive at a tall door that is clad in silver and studded with pearls: lifting her bowl to illuminate it in more detail, Jochara shows you that the door bears a complex Tibetan mandala inlaid with gemstones that sparkle in the light, proclaiming:

"Through the Tenfold Power of the Kalachakra may be found that which is called Enlightenment: for herein dwells the Cosmic Buddha – that which embraces all Time and space, and knows both eternity and infinity. By its Light may you come to claim victory over all of your Self; and come to know the perfection of your consciousness and so truly comprehend that ALL is interconnected, and ALL is *but one single living entity of which we are all a part: above,* and *below; Creator,* and *that which is Created!"*

Then, at a single powerful strike of her bowl, the corridor resonates with sound; and the door swings open, revealing that you are standing at the entrance to a square chamber that is entirely clad in black rainbow obsidian.... In the very centre of the chamber there is a knee-high cube of polished white selenite – and (after leading you into the chamber) Jochara asks you to sit down on this, with your feet flat on the floor and your head erect. Once you have done so, she stands facing you and says:

> "Remember: *All That IS and All That Will Ever Be IS Light....* In its fullness and majesty this Light, which is the BEing of The Divine, is known as the Diamond Light – a spark of which is held within your Seed of Original Consciousness; its essence reflected through your Heart.... This all-encompassing and all-embracing Light is held in balance through its twofold states of Being known as Black Light and White Light – and you now understand that within White *Light lies awakened and active consciousness, which will allow and enable the realisation of the potentials of All Things:"*

Jochara then strikes her bowl again – and you watch in awe as a hand-sized sphere of pure sparkling White Light condenses in the base of the bowl.... Dividing this into two spheres of unequal size, she places the smaller one at the heart of the sphere of Black Light that Ratziel (her twin flame) placed within the Omega centre of your Unified Body; and the larger one to surround and embrace the sphere of Black Light that he placed within your Alpha centre, declaring:

> *"The White Light of the Alpha and Omega is my Gift to you now.... The Lights that now rest within your Alpha and Omega centres reflect the essence of your Soul that defines the Highest possible manifestation of that which is known as Divine Father and Divine Mother. As ONE they ARE the beginning and the end: but you will only be able to fully connect with this Light in all its Glory when you have awakened, balanced and charged the Lotuses of your Heart and Soul,* and *attained full Unification with All that you are."*

Holding her singing bowl in front of your heart, Jochara now begins to softly sound it: at this your heart expands, and you are surrounded in dancing rainbows of light: these all merge until you stand within a single sphere of crystal-clear energy – and (as Jochara continues sounding her bowl) you assimilate all the Light you can.... Once you have, she returns her bowl to its bag, and enfolds you in her wings to make sure your energies are fully balanced and grounded: then you sense a shift in the air, and close your eyes....

In an instant you find yourself back on the seat by the pool: here Jochara bows to you in Blessing, and gives you a polar bear figurine made of glossy white stone. She tells you that this is **Snow** (White) **Quartz**, her third Crystal Champion – explaining:

> *"Snow Quartz is the feminine essence of quartz, holding within its structure many tiny inclusions of air and water that turn it opaque. Thus you may find Snow Quartz of great benefit in helping you balance your thoughts and emotions, whilst bringing you the clarity you need to see underlying issues more fully and completely. At times it can be hard to own up to your own faults or failings – but Snow Quartz has a cool, calm and gentle energy that will prompt you to remember and acknowledge the benefits of bringing (perhaps) long-held issues or beliefs into the Light for review and resolution. This does not mean that Snow Quartz is not powerful, but its power is subtly contained*

and rarely confrontational, making it a very predictable and steady ally in the search to find your Self and live by your Truths: furthermore, because Snow Quartz holds the full spectrum of Light in a very accessible form, it has within it all possible resonances that you may require to aid and support your healing and growth on any and all levels of body, mind and spirit – with or without the aid of the Elementals!"

Smiling, Jochara affirms that Snow Quartz may therefore help you know the purpose of White Light, and truly come to know yourself (and the Light within) in *all* your Glory.

She goes on to explain that she has chosen to give you snow quartz in the likeness of a mother polar bear, in order to help you connect with the energies of this solitary and fearless female. Jochara tells you that all polar bears know how to exist in what appears to be hostile terrain, yet (as with all those who are familiar with the ways of the water shamans and work to hold the icy extremes of the planet in balance) the ice and snow holds no fears for this bear: for she holds the Pure Light of The Divine in integrity and power. With a gentle smile, Jochara adds that it is a little known fact that the polar bear was given the task of holding this Light for the Earth by the Unicorns, when it became clear that Earth was too hostile an environment for their super-pure essence: accordingly, you may call **Polar Bear** to help you clarify your subtle energy system (especially your heart) in order to hold more Love and Light; or to teach you how to navigate the pitfalls of an ego-based human existence that so often lead to abuses of power – usually because of fear-based actions and/or reactions; or to encourage you to stick to your path if times are difficult or dark. Touching the bear's head, Jochara remarks that, like all bears, polar bears spend time in hibernation, when they journey in search of wisdom and knowledge by following the Light that they hold within, which links them with All That IS: hence you can ask Polar Bear to teach you how to build up or improve your meditative or intuitive practices; or to show you how to make clearer and more effective connections with your Higher-self and/or other sources of Higher Guidance; or to guide and protect you as you search within yourself to discover who (and what) you truly are. With a smile, she adds that polar bears are gentle yet protective mothers, who need to teach their cubs how to survive in very harsh conditions: thus, if you find parenting difficult, or if you are struggling through hard times, Polar Bear may come to you, to show you how to raise, nurture and support your own children, so that they can grow up to become kind, capable and confident individuals in their own right.

The Greenwood Guardians – Rowan and Date Palm:

Her *personal* mentoring complete for now, Jochara affirms she is always available to aid and support you: you need only bring her to mind and ask for her presence, and she will attend you. Furthermore, she tells you that two great Tree Beings of the Plant Kingdom have also asked to support you in addressing her Theme of 'SWEET SURRENDER', adding that you need only request *their* presence, and they will be with you.

She explains that the first of these Greenwood Guardians is the Masculine essence of Rowan, who has asked to overlight and help you ground whatever work you undertake within *any* aspect of her chapter. The second is the Feminine essence of Date Palm, who has specifically asked to help you understand and assimilate her Gift of The White Light of the Alpha and Omega (if you have chosen to accept it).

When you are ready to connect with Jochara's first Greenwood Guardian, you need simply call for the presence of **Rowan** (*) .... Rowan envelops you in a rose-gold Light, and the masculine spirit essence of Rowan speaks to you, saying:

"At my heart is the rose of Eden, which knows full well the pains and joys of birth, growth and death – yet knows too the endless delight there is in living with a heart always full of love. When you are filled with the Light of Love you need no more protection than this – so, with a gentleness that is not just the preserve of the feminine, I will wrap you in a warm and tender embrace, and hold you steady as you experiment with all that 'being human' entails.... Feel the wisdom that is drawn from the ground through my roots, spreading like a comforting blanket of knowledge and understanding throughout your body, so that you may simply relax into acceptance, without further struggle or pain.... Feel too the fire in my sap, which inspires and empowers you to persevere, moving always onwards to conquer both heights and depths as yet unknown; and giving you the strength to test the bounds that have served only to keep you restrained and confined in smallness. For in my embrace, all is in perfect balance and harmony: all that is oft defined as 'male' or 'female' finally reconciled and united as ONE; and all apparent contradictions reconciled and seen for what they are in truth – opportunities to be valued, so that through experience you may know *wisdom...."*

(* Bronzite and Green Aventurine will help you ground and connect with the energies and wisdom of Rowan, if you wish to enhance your experience using crystals.)

If you have chosen to accept and work with Jochara's Gift, and when you are ready to connect with her second Greenwood Guardian, you need simply call for the presence of **Date Palm** (*) .... Date Palm envelops you in a deep brown Light that is flecked with silver, and the feminine spirit essence of Date Palm speaks to you, saying:

"Tall I stand – my simple elegance reaching to the stars, my slender trunk well-armoured, yet easy to ascend for those who seek the sweetness of my fruits and the shelter of my branches. Thus, through ages too countless to know, I have held the balance of the now parched desert in my hand, and drawn upon its dark and hidden depths to provide the sustenance that offers healing and nurture to both body and Soul. So stand with me now, and let us talk of new seasons, new growth and new beginnings – and of Lights never lost, but merely resting between worlds before rising again stronger and wiser! Partake of my fruits – and know the power and passion of the land that feeds and sustains me, that I may willingly share my wisdom and love with those that partake of my bounty – and sense then how the energy that runs within and around you is drawn down into the earth, grounding the Light that feeds and sustains you, that you may understand the Divine process of evolution and change that allows all Souls the opportunity to experience the miraculous cycles of life.... Then simply open your heart, and willingly trust in the process that will, eventually, guide you home...."

(* Cappuccino [Bruneau] Jasper and Seraphinite will help you ground and connect with the energies and wisdom of Date Palm, if you wish to enhance your experience using crystals.)

ARCHEIA OKINA

'WHAT IS CONSCIOUSNESS?'

CRYSTAL CHAMPIONS:
Cobalt Aura Qtz ♥ Pyrite ♥ Chrysanthemum Stone

CREATURE COMPANIONS:
Otter ♥ Scarab Beetle ♥ Skunk

GREENWOOD GUARDIANS:
Wych Hazel ♥ Elm

I am my past, my present and my future:
I am all that is; I am all that was;
I am all that will ever BE.

MEETING OKINA

It is an early morning in late summer, and you find yourself standing on the banks of a river that is coursing swiftly through a deep and craggy gorge. The water glints and glistens as it rushes over the rounded rocks that line its bed – its glassy surface broken by low ripples and waves that reflect both sky and gorge in a chain of constantly-changing fragmented images. On the far side of the river, the sheer sides of the gorge are footed by dense masses of bushes and trees, which hang over the water in banks of impenetrable vegetation, offering deep cover and shade to birds and fish alike: in contrast, the bank where you stand is more open and orderly, possessing a path of randomly spaced slabs of dark-grey granite and slate, set into a carpet of dew-laden chamomile and emerald and gold mosses. This path is wide enough for several people to walk side-by-side, and is partly shaded by the cliff-like wall that soars above you – its vertiginous ledges providing footholds for small ruby-berried rowan trees, whose branches are garlanded with rosettes of silvery-grey lichens; and offering roosting spots to pairs of grey collared-doves.

Somewhere in the distance up-stream you think you can hear the muted sounds of crashing water – and so, deciding to walk in that direction, you follow the river through a long snaking series of twists and turns: with every bend the sounds grow louder – the river-bed becoming deeper and the waters swifter and darker as the gorge narrows; until, eventually, a final bend reveals that you have reached the end of the path. Here (rather bizarrely) a small grey donkey is resting in an open-fronted stable, beyond which the gorge ends abruptly at a sheer cliff wall, which is split in two by a narrow fissure that confines the river in a high-sided chasm. Rough-hewn steps lead up to a rocky ledge that clings to the wall of the chasm and curves away out of sight above the turbulent waters, which are barrelling through its 'V' and tumbling out in a deafening roar – and, although you cannot see where the ledge is leading, something urges you onwards....

Carefully you access and negotiate the ledge, keeping your balance by holding onto the rocky wall, and follow it through another series of twisting bends.... with every turn the din of the rushing water lessens and, in the dense shade, the air is chill – but you keep moving steadily onwards, until at last the chasm opens out into a high circular canyon, where you are greeted by the sight and sound of a spectacular waterfall cascading into the deep crystal-clear pool at its foot.... Here the air is filled with a fine mist, and teeming with shimmering arcs of multicoloured rainbows generated by shafts of sunlight filtering through the trees edging the rim of the canyon; and the rocky walls are garlanded with lush arrays of orchids, ferns and creeping vines, all flourishing in the humidity – the tiny droplets of water that grace their leaves glittering and sparkling like diamonds, as they catch the sunlight and drop to the ground below.

Thankfully, you find that the ledge you followed now widens, sloping gently down to a line of stepping stones that lead across the pool (which spans the bowl of the canyon floor), on the other side of which some more steps give access to a curving path that vanishes from view behind the waterfall. Then, just as you are debating whether to move forwards, a petite oriental woman dressed in a dark indigo outfit and carrying a spear steps from behind the shimmering veil of water: this is Archeia Okina. She beckons for you to join her, and so you carefully cross the stepping stones and climb the steps to meet her on the other side, where she greets you with a bow and a smile, declaring:

> *"I am Okina, the Lady Liberty – Keeper of the Ray of Revelation, Guardian of the Cosmic Seeds of Light, and twin flame of Tzaphkiel. I am glad to welcome you to this place, to show you the secrets of the Universe that lie so close to my heart, and the mysteries that are a part of your Greater Self. Here all may be revealed to those that have the grace and courage to walk the boundaries between what is perceived as real and unreal, as together we survey space and Time and glimpse what it is to BE Divine. For all is so much more than you might think – and when you allow yourself to expand into the magnitude and wonder of all that is within* and *without you, then you will see and learn much. I see you as you truly are – yet doubt that you, as yet, have the least inkling what this is! Yet I tell you that you are a wonderful sight to behold indeed: for in you I witness The Divine, and understand exactly what has been wrought, and why."*

With these words Okina leads you along the path to the waterfall, behind which a wide opening gives access to a small domed cave: light from the canyon beyond filters through the curtain of water to softly illuminate the space, enabling you to see that a low platinum bowl (filled with a mass of deep-indigo flames) sits between two wooden meditation stools in the centre of the floor. As you move inside, you notice how the sound of the falling water becomes muted and dimmed – the air cooler and dryer, the energy settled and still, as if this place is disconnected from the environment outside – and with a smile Okina lays her spear aside, and settles on one of the stools in a relaxed (yet upright) pose, inviting you to take the other so you may inspect her and become used to her energies....

As you settle, you are aware that Okina is small and delicate in stature – yet she has an alert and arresting presence that conveys a great sense of controlled power and hidden strength. Her skin is the colour of jasmine tea, and she has a rounded face that bears the classic features of Ancient China, with rosebud lips set below a small and slender nose; whilst her wide almond-shaped eyes are emphasised by a pair of finely arched eyebrows and a fringe of long black lashes – and, as she serenely meets your gaze, you recognise the warmth in their deep brown irises and jet-black pupils, and begin to relax....

Okina's long straight silky hair is the blue-black colour of a raven's wing, and is worn drawn back from her face in a high ponytail: this passes through a short cylinder made of some sort of reflective black metallic substance, and twists around her crown in a loose coil, where it is captured in a net made of fine strands of the same black metallic material, which is strewn with water-clear diamonds that have been polished to resemble droplets of water – making it seem as if she is crowned with sparkling drops of dew.

Dropping your gaze, you note that Okina is wearing a jacket-like top and matching trousers made of deep-indigo-blue raw silk, which catches the light to reveal that it has lots of tiny chrysanthemum flowers embroidered all over it in indigo-black thread. The sides of the top overlap slightly at the front, and are secured with tiny buttons (intricately knotted from strands of the same black metallic material that secures her hair) that pass through braided loops of black silk. The top is short and quite 'blocky', with a narrow mandarin collar and wide straight sleeves: these end just above her wrists in deep cuffs of densely-woven matte-black cotton, edged and bound with black silk thread; whilst its hemline follows the contour of her rib-cage, curving down from the base of her sternum in the front to waist level at the back. The cut of the top bares Okina's smooth abdomen, drawing your attention to the large white pearl set in her navel: this pearl is the gem that links her with Tzaphkiel, her twin flame, and is glowing with a soft rainbow-white light. Lowering your gaze, you note that Okina's trousers have wide straight legs that fit snugly to her slim hips, where they fasten at the sides with buttons and loops that replicate those of her top; and have deep hems of matte-black cotton (like the cuffs of the top). These just skim her bare feet (which have toughened soles that suggest she rarely wears shoes), and reveal a plaited white silk thread strung with creamy spotted cowrie shells, which is tied loosely around her left ankle.

Suddenly, your eye is caught by a flash of light at the hollow of her throat, where a small seven-pointed star made of highly-polished silvery platinum sits in the opening of the mandarin collar of her top: this star is mounted on a narrow collar of platinum that encircles the base of her neck – and, as Okina lifts her left hand to touch it, you note that (rather oddly) she also has a black leather thong knotted around her wrist, which holds a small carving of a raven's skull that has been intricately fashioned from ivory.

OKINA'S TEACHINGS
The Ray of Revelation and The Mind of The Divine:
Noting that your scrutiny is complete Okina gives a high chirruping call, at which three young otters appear at the cave entrance and rush over to tussle and play around her feet. Laughing as she watches their carefree frolics, completely absorbed in their game, she says that water-loving otters revel in the joy of being alive, and make the most of every opportunity to have fun – even during the customarily serious business of hunting for food: accordingly, you may ask **Otter** to show you how to seek out the delights to be found in every moment of every day, and to teach you how to see life as a game to be enjoyed, rather than a burden to be endured. With a smile, she adds that even adult otters are curious and love to play – so Otter may come to remind you to reclaim your inner-child and rediscover the delights of exploring or doing something simply for the fun or wonder of it: in turn this will help you be more creative and spontaneous, and enable you to become more flexible and proactive in solving problematic issues and/or dealing with difficult situations as you encounter them in everyday life. Watching the cubs tumbling around the floor, Okina points out how otters are at ease on land, but are truly at home in water, where their fluid flexibility allows them to be 'in the moment' – hunting, playing, learning and exploring as need or desires dictate: hence Otter may show you how to live in the now by encouraging you to stop worrying about yesterday and tomorrow, and to let go of anything (tangible or non-tangible) that has become a burden or is holding you back – especially if this is having a detrimental impact on your emotional state, or is confining you in the pointlessness of a fear-based reality.

After one final tussle the otters dash off, and Okina gives another call: at this a pretty little ring-tailed lemur appears, jumping up to sit on her right shoulder, and curling its long tail around her neck.... Speaking softly to it, Okina strokes its fur and then points with her finger – at which the lemur leaps to the ground and scampers towards the back of the cave, giving out loud whooping calls as it darts away, tail held erect like a flag....

Somehow you know that the lemur is asking you to follow it – and Okina encourages you to do so, resting a hand lightly on your shoulder to reassure you of her presence as she follows you to the back of the cave: here a cleft in the rock reveals only pitch-blackness beyond, and you pause – but Okina tells you to follow the lemur's calls, assuring you that the floor of the cavern beyond is smooth and you can move without fear of injury....

At first your steps are hesitant, for it is so dark you can see nothing at all – in fact, trying to use your eyes makes it harder to focus your other senses, so you boldly decide to close them, and apply your hearing to pinpoint the direction the lemur is taking. Hearing his calls echoing ahead of you (suggesting that the cavern is high and wide), you begin to walk forwards with steadily increasing confidence – until, after a while, your spatial awareness warns you the space is narrowing....

Applying a gentle pressure to your shoulder, Okina tells you that you are about to enter a narrow corridor: then, placing your left hand against one wall and your right hand against the other, she bids you to use them both to guide yourself from now on – assuring you that their surfaces are smooth and free of hazards, and that the ceiling high enough to remain upright. A little nervous, you open your eyes – but, finding that it is still too dark to see, you quickly close them again and decide to use your hands to feel your way down the passageway, as the calls of the lemur encourage you onwards.... You start tentatively: but then, as the corridor follows a series of smoothly snaking curves and begins to slope downwards, you are suddenly overcome by a childlike feeling of excitement and begin to run faster and faster – until it almost feels as if you are flying.... Filled with exhilaration you race on, until you gradually become aware that the lemur's calls sound as if they are closer, and reluctantly slow your speed – finally coming to an abrupt halt as the walls you have been touching suddenly vanish....

Realising you have reached the end of the passageway, you open your eyes to find that you are on the threshold of a large square chamber that is flooded with deep purple light. Although the light does not offer much illumination, you can see that each of the walls has a high rectangular opening in its centre – one of which is where you stand: on closer scrutiny, you can see that the walls are all engraved with lines of an ancient script, and that each opening is bordered by a bas-relief sculpture depicting a trailing vine of ivy. Appearing at your side, Okina explains that the light in the chamber is the Light of the Ray of Revelation – the Ray that guides the development of your Consciousness in your studies as an apprenticed 'Illumined Master': then, directing you to the opening on your left, she asks you to step inside.... Here a short hallway leads to a door that bears a copper plaque engraved with a stylised rendering of a spider's web – and, with a smile, Okina instructs you to open the door and stand on its threshold....

Doing as she asks, you find that everything beyond is pitch-black, and you literally cannot see your hand in front of your face. You hear Okina reminding you that (if you truly wish to find Illumination) you must pass through the darkness of the Void – which demands that you have the courage to conquer your fears and face your demons! Moving behind you, she rests her hands on your shoulders and tells you that – in this instance, however – her objective is to show you a little about the nature of Divine Consciousness: and at this you sense her growing in stature, and feel her shield you with her wings....

Asking you to have the confidence to step out into the blackness that confronts you, Okina assures you that she will not let you fall – so, although apprehensive, you blindly take a step forwards.... then another.... and another, until you are moving courageously through a blackness that seems to have neither substance nor form: at this point, you hear Okina's voice in your mind, saying:

> *"When you understand the True nature of the Void that IS on the cusp between Black and White you will know that here you may behold Infinity!... For here you can see all points in all Times, places and Dimensions and from all perspectives.... Here you may touch the infinite and all-embracing Mind of The Divine, whereby Truth may be unveiled and transcendent wisdom be acquired.... And here too you may find the answer to the question: 'What IS Consciousness?'...."*

and, as her words die away, Okina opens her wings – and you know you have travelled beyond the darkness of the Void; for spread out before you is a truly mind-blowing vista! *Everywhere* you look you can see millions of stars and galaxies – one after another; a constantly changing mass of spiralling and swirling clouds of multi-coloured dust and Light painted onto the vast canvas of space – and as you gaze in awe at the vastness of it all, you have the strange feeling that *you* are seeing through the eyes of The Divine, and you begin to sense the astounding timelessness of the Miracle that is Creation.... Then you suddenly realise that somewhere out there Earth is spinning around its Star, the Sun; and you appreciate that you are smaller than the merest speck compared to the immensity of what you are seeing – yet, even so, you *know* that The Divine knows and cares about you; and know that *you* are important to the Divine plan: insignificant, yet significant! Then you hear Okina's voice in your mind again, saying:

> *"Divine Mind IS everywhere.... And with every thought born of Divine Mind, Divine Consciousness expands and more matter comes into being: Divine thought* becomes.... *Thus, if something exists, it IS a part of Divine Consciousness – for* without *Divine Consciousness,* nothing *exists! Know then that when your awareness expands beyond your ego-consciousness to fully embrace your Divine-Consciousness, you will truly BE an Illumined Master, and so understand the true meaning of the words 'I AM'"*

and with these words, Okina enfolds you in her wings – and you are momentarily once more shrouded in darkness....

Releasing her hold, Okina furls her wings and steps aside, revealing that you are once more back at your entry-point to the square chamber. Giving you a dark-blue crystal that has shimmering metallic highlights of magenta and gold, she tells you that this is a crystal of **Cobalt Aura Quartz**, her first Crystal Champion – explaining:

> *"Although sometimes mislabelled as Flame Aura Quartz, this crystal has a very deep and intense royal-blue base-colour, which should enable you to tell them apart. As you may expect, Cobalt Aura Quartz powerfully grounds the Indigo and Blue Rays, making it a superb support as you seek to attain Higher and Cosmic Consciousness: however, it is its* Magenta *Ray aspect that will enable you to connect with the profound Universal Intelligence and Divine Truths that underlie everything you see, hear or experience – the understanding of which (with the aid of its Gold Ray aspect) leads to the attainment*

and grounding of Divine Wisdom. This means that Cobalt Aura Quartz can help you merge with the greater reality of yourself, so that you may identify and understand whatever you need to address and resolve in order to move into (and claim) the fullness of your personal Power: furthermore, the clarity of the quartz that lies at Cobalt Aura's heart can help you recognise and deal with any unwanted influences that are revealed in your journey of self-discovery; and will heighten your powers of discernment, so that you may more clearly perceive the truth within whatever you see, hear or are shown or told when channelling, journeying or communing with other-Dimensional Beings."

With a smile, Okina affirms that Cobalt Aura Quartz may therefore help draw the Higher frequencies of Light closer, furthering your search for Illumined Knowledge and Truth.

The Gift of The Golden Halo of Universal Awareness:

Okina next directs you to the opening on the opposite side of the chamber, and asks you to step inside.... Here a short hallway leads to another door (this one bearing a gold plaque engraved with a stylised rendering of a scarab beetle), and with another smile she instructs you to open the door and stand on its threshold as you did before: again you find that everything beyond is dark – but this time you can (literally) see a light at the end of the tunnel. So stepping around you to lead the way, Okina guides you swiftly through the shadowy darkness, until you finally reach a small domed chamber that is floored in white quartz. You realise that this is the source of the light you could see – and as your eyes adjust to its brightness, Okina leads you to a low elm-wood stool that is set in the centre of the chamber, and invites you to sit down....

Once you are settled, she draws your attention to the ivory carving that she wears around her left wrist, and reminds you that the raven is the totem of all those who work with Magic. With a smile she says that the concept of 'magic' often frightens people – yet the Adept who works with High White Magic righteously bears the responsibility of mastering the Divine Forces that construct and deconstruct matter, requiring them to be fully proficient in the arts and principles that underlie science, mathematics and music. With a chuckle she adds that, in fact, a *true* Magician is one who knows and understands that everything is simply an illusion(!) brought about (quite literally) by (Divine) mind over (Divine) matter.

With a wave of her hand, Okina now takes your attention to the domed ceiling of the chamber, which has begun to glow with a deep indigo light and fill with a multitude of stars, as if you are sitting beneath a night sky.... After a moment it feels as if you are being drawn up into the indigo light – and you feel a strange mix of serenity and nervous anticipation: you then become aware that your throat and brow chakras are opening; and that the Universal and Soma centres of your Unified Body are awakening.... and as they all come into alignment and balance, you realise that the indigo light is moving through your whole energy field in waves.... For several minutes you experience moments of utter stillness and peace, followed by short bursts of energy that bombard your senses; and on some level you understand that the pulses of energy convey rapid downloads of information that will inspire and strengthen your inner knowing, and reinforce your commitment to your inner truths....

After a few more moments the pulses of energy diminish, and the indigo light fades, and everything around you becomes still.... Okina explains that the Indigo Ray offers a profound connection to 'Unity Consciousness' that allows everything that is discovered and known to be shared for the Enlightenment of *all*: this means that its Light has the power to catalyse a sense of profound Unity with all things, whilst still allowing each individual to retain a sense of self-identity and separation. Smiling, she adds that this offers *you* the ability to access deep memories of everything your True Self knows and understands throughout all Times and Dimensions – along with knowledge of all that comprises the Universe – thus placing *whatever* you need to know and understand within your grasp, as you walk the path of your own Enlightenment.

Asking you to sit up straight with your head erect, Okina moves to stand in front of you and plucks seven golden stars from the 'night sky' above your head.... she melds and shapes these into a golden ring that is about two handspans wide, and then holds this above your head, declaring:

"This is my Gift of The Golden Halo of Universal Awareness, which is given both as a sign of your commitment to the acquisition of Higher knowledge and insight; and to help you strengthen your connections with the Infinite Wisdom of the Universe...."

She then lowers the golden ring to rest level with your brow chakra, where she pauses for a moment; before tilting the ring on a forty-five degree angle so that it rests over the Soma and Universal centres of your Unified Energy Body, and pausing again.... After a few more moments, she lowers the golden ring to the base of your neck, level with your throat chakra, before pausing again.... Then, holding her hands steady (one to either side of your neck) Okina gently encourages the golden ring to shrink until it fits snugly around your pranic core, saying:

"May the Golden Halo of Universal Awareness promote and enhance your perception and interpretation of worlds both seen and unseen.... May it advance and sustain your progress, so that your heightened awareness will enable you to know the reality of ALL the Dimensions that comprise the Universe.... And may it support all endeavours that lead to your Highest spiritual evolution, that you may finally become Enlightened and BE as ONE with Unity Consciousness."

Stepping back, Okina bows to you three times as a sign of respect: she then gives you a small carving of a scarab beetle that has been fashioned from a nodule of golden pyrite.

She explains that the scarab is an ancient symbol of eternal life, which speaks of the nature of the resurrection and immortality of the Soul. Pointing to its divided carapace, she tells you that each side also symbolises the left and right sides of the human brain, which summon and direct your innate powers of reasoned thought and intuition: thus you may call upon **Scarab** to show you how to sharpen and perfect your perceptive skills *and* your logical thought processes so that both are as keen as they can be; and to teach you to recognise when (and understand how) to bring each side to the fore as appropriate for the situation you find yourself in – thus enabling your mind to BE in perfect equilibrium in every moment, making your path forward more clear. Touching you gently over your heart, Okina says that in Ancient Egyptian times a scarab was often placed here after death, in order to protect the heart (which was believed to hold the thoughts, feelings and experiences of the Soul) on its journey through the after-life: hence you may ask Scarab to help you remember the lessons you have taught or been taught in this or other lifetimes and to view them with dispassionate objectivity, so that you may address and clear any unresolved karmic issues and move forwards with your Soul less burdened. With a smile she adds that Scarab can also teach you a great deal about the purpose behind living and experiencing Time and Dimension through the widest possible range of possibilities and potentials; and/or support you in adjusting and adapting to energy shifts on both a cellular and energetic level as you – and the Universe – grow, evolve and transform to *know* both Immortality and Enlightenment.

Helping you to stand (and leading you back to the hallway and the square chamber beyond) Okina adds that, thus, **Pyrite** is her second Crystal Champion – explaining:

"Pyrite is sometimes called 'Fool's Gold' – yet although it is no fool, it does *hold gold within it in the form of the Gold Ray, which gives structure and form to the Universe, and holds the Fundamental Essence of the Reality and Potential of your Divine-self. Pyrite will work effectively and powerfully to ground this Ray within both yourself and the Earth – and if you no longer find 'traditional' grounding stones work well for you, you may find Pyrite to be the solution to your 'problem'. Pyrite's reflective surface also offers you a mirror, whereby you may see the reality of your Self and the world about you; whilst its iron core will boost your determination (and give you the stability and self-discipline you might need) to make whatever changes are necessary to enable you to increase the Light you hold. Furthermore, Pyrite can ground the intrinsic strength, munificence and understanding of the Diamond Light, which knows – and allows – the paramount and most appropriate direction for the perfect evolution of all of Divine Creation: for its prime task is to BE and hold the ideal space that allows movement, growth and change to take place, whilst helping* all *to hold greater joy in their heart."*

With a smile, Okina affirms that Pyrite may therefore help you ground the Wisdom of the Universe within your heart, whilst grounding you to the Earth and to the unconditional Love that constantly sustains you on this stage of your journey of Illumination and Hope.

The Magenta Ray and The Cosmic Seeds of Light:

Directing your attention to the opening that is on the right-hand side of the square chamber, Okina asks you to step inside: here another short hallway leads to another door (this one bearing a silver plaque engraved with a stylised rendering of a roosting bat), and with another smile she instructs you to open the door and stand on its threshold as before.... Beyond, the space feels vast – but the light is such a deep shade of magenta (the most intense combination of violet and crimson possible) that you find it hard to make anything out. Guiding you forwards, Okina says that this paradoxical place is both vast and minute – and, taking the pearl from her navel, she produces a light that dimly illuminates your immediate surroundings: this enables you to see that the ground around you is covered with hundreds of indigo chrysanthemum flowers, whose colour is so deep and intense that they almost appear black – yet, when you peer at one more closely, you realise that every single indigo petal is subtly tinged with the magenta light.

Warning you that you may watch, but must not touch, Okina reaches out and very gently touches a finger to the flower you are examining: at her touch the chrysanthemum slowly unfurls its petals, showing you that each is curled around a cluster of tiny seeds that glow with a golden Light.... It does this a layer of petals at a time, until eventually the very heart of the flower is revealed, exposing a marble-sized blue and white sphere that is gently pulsing with light: once you have seen it, Okina smiles and reverently touches the flower again, and the process is reversed – each tiny petal furling around the sphere and the golden seeds, until the chrysanthemum is restored to how it was before....

Okina tells you that you have just had the privilege of seeing the Seeds of Potential that are a part of Earth's multidimensional Universal Consciousness, which are shielded by the Highest possible Light of Divine Love. Guiding you into an open space a little distance away, she explains that each of the billions of flowers in this place holds the consciousness of a planet or star that is awaiting its birth or rebirth, together with the Seeds of Light that will catalyse its evolution and growth by disseminating information and knowledge (and initiating communication with the rest of the Universe), and thus enabling new civilisations to rise and prosper.

Moving behind you, she then rests her hands on your shoulders – stating that you can help plant the Seeds for the Earth, simply by opening your heart to the Magenta Ray, which will fill you with unconditional love and allow you to see the intrinsic beauty in *all* things *everywhere* (in turn, opening your mind to know and accept the Highest Truths): and, advising you to close your eyes, she once again enfolds you in her wings.... At this you are bathed in a Magenta Light that is so vivid you can see it even with your eyes closed – and Okina directs you to slowly open your heart to its power; and requests that you then consider each of her following three questions very carefully, asking:

> *"Firstly: are you willing to do your best to hold the Highest Light of Compassion within your heart?.... Secondly: are you willing to humbly open your mind and do your best to recognise the beauty that IS within all things?.... and Thirdly: are you willing to do your best to champion and defend the weak and the vulnerable everywhere, regardless of what may beset you?...."*

Time passes, and *if* you have decided that it is possible for you to answer 'yes' to each question, Okina directs you to allow the Lotus of your Heart to open, so that the Pink Flames of Divine Love may be charged with Magenta Light – augmenting and enhancing each 'petal' so that you may more closely embody the Love that does, indeed, 'pass all understanding'; and to then allow the Magenta Light to infuse your Hara centre, so that you may become fully awakened to the reality of your Self that embodies the ultimate expression of Divine Love....

After allowing sufficient time for the Magenta Light to infuse your Heart Lotus and Hara centre (if and as appropriate) Okina assures you that, regardless of your reply, she is always willing to bring the Magenta Light to inspire and illuminate your heart and mind: then once again everything around you goes dark – and, when you open your eyes, you find yourself back in the cave behind the waterfall....

Here Okina invites you to retake your seat by the fire, and (settling at your side) she gives you a palm-sized black stone that has been polished to reveal an inner pattern that resembles a many-petalled white flower. She says that this is a **Chrysanthemum Stone**, her third Crystal Champion – explaining:

> *"Chrysanthemum Stone is a rare and unusual gift of the Earth, for it carries Black and White Light in perfect – and beautiful – balance. The radiating patterns that you see are reflections of the many-layered petals that comprise the Lotuses of your Heart and Soul, given to remind you of the multifaceted reality of your Self as an infinite and immortal Being of Light; and are also representations of the feathers that comprise your Wings of Light, which are given to remind you that you always have the ability to fly! Thus, may Chrysanthemum Stone be a manifold blessing to you, bringing you both good fortune and joy; and reminding you that (in every moment of every day)* you *have the power to change your reality – simply by believing in your Self and embracing ALL that you are, with a mind that is open and a heart that is full of love. Know too that Chrysanthemum Stone can help you in attaining and maintaining balance in any aspect of your life – be this spiritual or mundane; and will support you throughout all your journeys of self-healing and exploration (body, mind and spirit) in order that you may ultimately find and know freedom, happiness and peace."*

Smiling, Okina affirms that Chrysanthemum Stone may therefore help remind you of the place that guards the Cosmic Seeds of Light, that you may recognise and appreciate the Greater Plan that IS at the heart of the infinite and compassionate Multiverse.

Opening her hand, she reveals that she is also holding three tiny golden seeds of Light.... she places the first so that it hovers in the air in front of your solar plexus chakra, and tells you that – if you choose to accept it – this seed will help any aspect of your (lower) ego-self that is 'non-aware' to become 'aware', which will enable you to more fully *identify with* your Highest Truths....

Next, she places the second seed so that it hovers in the air in front of your brow chakra, and tells you that – if you choose to accept it – this seed will help you 'tune in' to Divine Mind and Universal Consciousness with greater clarity, which will enable you to more clearly *know and understand* your Highest Truths....

Lastly, she places the third and final seed so that it hovers in the air in front of your throat chakra, and tells you that – if you choose to accept it – this seed will help you accept your Divine-self, which will enable you to more openly *communicate and convey* your Highest Truths, and so begin to create the reality that you truly desire...

Okina tells you that (if you choose to accept them all) the seeds will simply embed themselves in an appropriate place; or (if you choose not to accept them) they will return to the Earth.... As you make your choice, Okina reminds you that every thought you have is a Divine Thought; and that whatever you create is a Creation of The Divine: hence it is vital that you always acknowledge the responsibility of possessing such Power – and also demonstrate the humility to be trusted with it.

Gifts given, Okina gives a whistle – at which a small skunk appears from the depths of the cave and comes to snuffle around her feet: with a chuckle, she says that everyone knows of little black and white skunk's special 'talent' for self-preservation that reminds others to respect it at all times – thus allowing it to focus on its needs without wasting time or energy on pretending to be something that it is not: hence you may ask **Skunk** to show you how to enhance your subtle senses and augment your instinctive awareness so that you are always open to the subtle signs or signals that can alert you of the need to alter course or be more vigilant; or to help you accept yourself as you are, without ego or pretence, whilst teaching you how to walk your path with your head held high, respecting yourself and your choices, and respecting others' too – but without allowing yourself to be cowed or bullied from your course, or forced to become something you are truly not. With a smile she adds that you cannot expect others to respect you, if you do not respect yourself – and so skunk may come to call if you need reminding of this! As the little skunk continues to sniff around, Okina tells you that skunks are nocturnal animals that are highly attuned to the magic of the cycles of the heavens; and who understand the virtues and benefits of spending time in solitary and silent contemplation – both within the ground and under the stars: accordingly, Skunk can teach you how to journey or meditate with greater effectiveness; or show you how to move in closer harmony with the seasons and cycles of the Earth; and/or help you to align your energies with the Cosmic energies that guide the planets and stars of the Solar System and Galaxy, thus inspiring and catalysing the most positive outcome for whatever you choose to change or make manifest in your life. As the skunk vanishes into the darkness again, Okina adds that, on the topic of manifestation, Skunk may also help you understand more about the polar functions and properties of Black and White Light, because it knows how to keep them in the right and proper proportions and balance for that very purpose – and may also guide you as you practise defining, refining and creating the world (and reality) you truly need.

The Greenwood Guardians – Wych Hazel and Elm:
Her *personal* mentoring complete for now, Okina affirms she is always available to aid and support you: you need only bring her to mind and ask for her presence, and she will attend you. Furthermore, she tells you that two great Tree Beings of the Plant Kingdom have also asked to support you in addressing her Theme of 'WHAT IS CONSCIOUSNESS?', adding that you need only request *their* presence, and they will be with you.

She explains that the first of these Greenwood Guardians is the Feminine essence of Wych Hazel, who has asked to overlight and help you ground whatever work you undertake within *any* aspect of her chapter. The second is the Feminine essence of Elm, who has specifically asked to help you understand and assimilate her Gift of The Golden Halo of Universal Awareness (if you have chosen to accept it).

When you are ready to connect with Okina's first Greenwood Guardian, you need simply call for the presence of **Wych Hazel** (*) .... Wych Hazel envelops you in a glossy black Light, and the feminine spirit essence of Wych Hazel speaks to you, saying:

> *"Wholeness through wisdom I bring, the gentle yellow of my flowers in early spring signalling the return to life that heralds the start of a new year and a new season, and glorifying life reborn. Through the dark days of winter I sleep, dormant in my physical body, yet empowered with life and passion within, which gives my Soul the freedom to question the Light that fires and inspires the Universe, the understanding of which fills me with joy and wonder for all that I encounter. For even in darkness I understand that*

there is purpose and joy to be found within everything; and that which is hidden from view feeds and fills my heart with both passion and energy, and a simple and innocent peace – grounding my Soul to the Earth, and joining my Spirit to the wisdoms at her heart. So stand with me, for I may ease your spirits when you are weary or low – healing the wounds of life that leave you bloodied and torn, and giving you the strength and determination to seek out the diamonds that hide in the darkness of your Soul, so that your passion for living, learning and BEing may be restored.... and then, as one, we may rest at ease, safe and secure in the embrace of the Earth, whose munificent and wise consciousness allows us to understand – and thus create – the future we need...."

(* Black Tourmaline will help you ground and connect with the energies and wisdom of Wych Hazel, if you wish to enhance your experience using crystals.)

If you have chosen to accept and work with Okina's Gift, and when you are ready to connect with her second Greenwood Guardian, you need simply call for the presence of **Elm** (*) .... Elm envelops you in a very pale purple rippling Light, and the feminine spirit essence of Elm speaks to you, saying:

"Within me you will find mind and spirit joined as one – logic and intuition in perfect harmony and accord. For at my heart is a love and a passion that is so deep and profound that it is rare to find: yet this is what I offer you – the crystal-clarity of the Earth refined into Diamonds that are fit to crown the Consciousness of the Universe; with rainbows of hope, expectation and delight spilling over to surround you in a cloud of Glory! So stand with me and BE a Beacon of Light, shining forth your innate innocence, purity, love and wisdom to the world.... Stand with me, and be proud to carry that Light at your heart, in ever-joyous communion with that which lies at the Heart of All – that which begat the world; and that which will be its last triumphant farewell.... For I can show you the worlds that dwell within worlds, and teach you the wisdoms that link Times, Dimensions – and yes even Universes – as yet unseen, so that you may eventually come to understand and know *the infinite and eternal nature of your Consciousness...."*

(* Natural Citrine and Amethyst will help you ground and connect with the energies and wisdom of Elm, if you wish to enhance your experience using crystals.)

ARCHANGEL TZAPHKIEL

'KNOW YOURSELF – KNOW ALL THINGS'

CRYSTAL CHAMPIONS:

Hawks Eye ♥ Rainbow Obsidian ♥ Clear Qtz

CREATURE COMPANIONS:

Peregrine Falcon ♥ Octopus ♥ Sparrow

GREENWOOD GUARDIANS:

Cypress ♥ Baobab

*I align myself at all times
with the Light and Will of the Universe.
I AM Divine Light incarnate.*

MEETING TZAPHKIEL

You find yourself standing in the middle of a busy street, on what feels like the end of a long winter's day. The road is crammed with an endless queue of buses and cars, each edging aggressively forwards in belching clouds of exhaust fumes that assault your nostrils with their stench; whilst the pavements overflow with people frowningly intent on their own business, jostling and jarring you as they impatiently force their way past. Some are laden with glossy bags, and sweep by you leaving a tired scent of perfume and desperation in their wake; others have mobile phones glued to their ears, totally oblivious to those who share their space and seemingly wishing only to be somewhere else. It is also cold and beginning to get dark, and you have absolutely no idea where you are; but every time you try to stop somebody to find out you are wordlessly rebuffed – or simply ignored as if you don't exist.... After a while of getting nowhere, you start to feel anxious – and, as you begin to panic that you are stuck in some weird dream world of cacophony and chaos, your desperation peaks, and you call out for somebody – *anybody* – to help you.... slowly, with each pleading cry for help, the crowds around you fade.... and slowly an entirely different scene imposes itself on your reality....

It is still dusk, and still cold – yet your surroundings are in complete contrast to how they were before. The crowds have been replaced by a small flock of contentedly-grazing sheep; and the frantic city street has dissolved into an otherwise empty landscape, which is stark, yet peaceful and still. To your left the gently undulating curves of a grassy wind-swept plain lead the eye towards a distant arc of snow-capped mountain peaks, which are majestic in their isolated solitude; whilst in front of you the ground slopes up to the foot of a rocky escarpment that curves around to your right, its craggy face marked with the ravages of weather and time. Below it the ground forms a natural bowl, the centre of which is covered with mossy rocks and boulders – suggesting, perhaps, that at one time a massive waterfall cascaded over the cliff here. Then, all of a sudden, you spot something white moving down the slope towards you – which, as it draws closer, you realise to be the figure of an old man: this is Archangel Tzaphkiel. Oddly he is carrying a snow-white hare – yet the oddest (and most welcome) thing about him is the bright white light that is blazing from his chest like a beacon. As he reaches you, he greets you, declaring:

"I am Tzaphkiel – Divine Guardian of the Veils of Illusion, Archangel of Enlightened Awareness and Cosmic Truths, and twin flame of Okina, the Lady Liberty. In this place your Soul may be set free, as I help you release your frantic grip on the world that you mistakenly think to be your reality. For I fear you may have forgotten the fulfilment and joy to be found in simply being at one with yourself and the natural world about you.... in taking time to sit and dream, allowing yourself to freely wander the Realms of infinite possibility.... in taking time to gaze into the inky depths of a night sky, allowing the stars and the heavens to fill your heart and mind with their luminous light and wisdom.... Here you may simply BE with the pure essence of your Self – your Soul, your Greater Spirit.... Here you may find your centre and your Self, and so find ALL – without hold or compulsion; without need or necessity, and know the Truth and Power of your Light.... Then, in simplicity, and beyond the needless clutter with which you encumber your mind and your spirit, you will find peace."

Tzaphkiel

With a smile, Tzaphkiel asks you to join him, and leads you up the slope towards the rocks.... Despite his age he moves swiftly and surely, using the tall staff he is holding in his right hand for support, and you follow him as best you can, using his light to guide your footsteps. Eventually you reach the rocks – and, as you weave your way through them, you come across a pool of water in a low sheltered hollow, which was previously hidden from view: here a crystal-clear spring bubbles up through the ground, its waters feeding the pool to offer a shallow watering place for animals and birds (which is currently being enjoyed by some black and white avocets and a tall grey heron, who looks to be standing sentinel over its waters).

Tzaphkiel is waiting for you at the foot of the escarpment, at a place where the rock has been eroded away to create what looks like a low cave: here the welcome glow of a fire that is burning just beyond the entrance beckons you onwards – and, realising that you are getting cold, you need no further encouragement to join him.... With a smile, he guides you over the rough-hewn threshold to a simple wooden chair that rests beside the fire, and (after placing a rough woollen blanket around your shoulders for warmth) gently lowers the sleeping hare into a nest of dried grasses near the cave entrance. He then goes off to find another chair, and so you take the opportunity to gaze around – noting that the cave is clean, if sparsely furnished, with just a few simple baskets and homemade shelves to hold some basic living essentials. It is also deeper than you first thought – and as the firelight flares and casts its light further into the cave, you find that it reveals a series of ancient cave paintings that apparently chronicle events from the far-distant past, naively but brilliantly captured in earthy tones of red, orange, ochre and black.

Chair found, Tzaphkiel returns to sit by your side and invites you to take some time to inspect him and become accustomed to his energies. As you do, a part of you wonders if you are still in a dream-world, for he looks a little like Gandalf the Grey (in the Lord of the Rings films): recognising your thought, a swift grin lights his long thin face, and you are glad to find that he obviously has a sense of humour, for he has a very commanding presence that could be misread as forbidding or stern. Closer scrutiny shows his leathery wind-worn skin to be pouched and wrinkled with age – yet he has lively and penetrating steely grey eyes that are filled with compassion and ageless wisdom. These sit below a prominent furrowed brow and bushy grey eyebrows, and bracket a large hawk-like nose that dominates his features; whilst a windblown mass of long grey hair straggles over his shoulders to his waist, matched by a long wispy beard that trails down his chest to a point at his navel. His ears and mouth are both on the large side – but even though he is neither young nor handsome, he possesses an aura of controlled and focused power that makes you feel very secure in his presence.

Taking your attention to his apparel, you see that Tzaphkiel is clad in a floor-length grey robe, which is gathered round his waist with what looks like an old piece of rope. It is plain to see that what he wears is purely functional and of little importance to him, as the robe itself is made from rough homespun material that resembles sacking, with long dangling sleeves, and a round neckline that has been slit at the front for ease of dressing; whilst its ragged (and somewhat grubby) hem trails on the floor, giving you a glimpse of a pair of unexpectedly clean and slender feet shod in simple rope and leather sandals.

Shifting in his chair, Tzaphkiel crosses his ankles and rests his hands on his knees, enabling you to see that, unlike his feet, his age-spotted hands are ingrained with dirt – although his knobbly fingers look surprisingly supple, despite his obvious age. You are also surprised to see that the lower joint of his left thumb bears an incongruously large ring that has a wide silver band set with an oval white pearl, which is the gem that links him with Okina, his twin flame. The other odd, yet obviously significant, item he wears is a large pendant, which has been crafted from platinum in the shape of a seven-pointed star: this hangs round his neck on a platinum chain, which is long enough to hold it 'point up' over his solar plexus. Leaning over to look at it more closely, you find that each arm of the star is engraved with strange patterns, which as yet mean nothing to you; whilst its centre holds a large crystal-clear diamond that has been cut into a seven-sided heptagon – and you suddenly realise that *this* is what was giving off the bright white light that first drew your attention to his presence.

TZAPHKIEL'S TEACHINGS
The Alignment of Personal Will and Divine Will:

Observing that your inspection is complete, Tzaphkiel leans down and picks up his staff, which you now see serves a dual function as a spear, for its shaft is topped with a blade made of a silvery-grey metal. Reaching over, he rests it across your lap for you to touch and inspect more closely.... to your surprise you find that the shaft of the spear is 'D'-shaped, at which he smiles, explaining that his twin flame holds the other half of the same spear: for everything they do, they do As One – two halves in perfect union and accord, creating that which is whole and complete. Tzaphkiel tells you that the spear has many functions, but the most important of these (for you, here and now) is its ability to link Heaven and Earth throughout all possible aspects of Time, space and Dimension. He points out that this concept embraces just about anything you could imagine – including all aspects of the Cosmos and all aspects of every sentient life-form, from the tiniest atom and particle of multidimensional Light to the infinity that IS Divine Consciousness.

As Tzaphkiel encourages you to continue examining it, you test out the spear's oak shaft, which has acquired a soft golden sheen from many years of constant handling; and its surprisingly elegant heart-shaped platinum blade, which has sharp flattened edges and a raised centre etched with 'veins' to resemble the leaf of a linden tree.... As you lift it to assess its weight, Tzaphkiel points out that shaft and blade are perfectly balanced both in physicality *and* in essence – the masculine assertive power, wisdom and justice of the Oak blending with the feminine patience, compassion and mercy of the Linden, and both aligning the Earthly powers of Wood with the Cosmic powers of Platinum.

Smiling, he suggests that you close your eyes and open your awareness to sense the spear's energy.... as you do, you feel the wood thrumming with a subtle vibration that speaks to you of the wisdom and memory that spans Time and Dimension; and can hear the blade singing to you of the vastness of the Universe and its myriad mysteries.... Recognising this, Tzaphkiel remarks that whatever you are sensing may help you work out how the spear aids him in uniting the Higher- and Lower-Dimensional Worlds; and in aligning and balancing Cosmic Forces throughout the Universe with Divine Will....

After a while, Tzaphkiel tells you to open your eyes: then (at a wave of his hand) a football-sized sphere manifests in the air in front of you.... as you watch, this gradually acquires colour and definition, until it is as if you were surveying planet Earth from outer space.... With a smile, Tzaphkiel says that he often sees Earth like this: for, since the very beginning of Time, he has been actively involved in assisting stars and planets to take on shape and form; and in guiding them through their subsequent growth and evolution, as they move towards Higher-consciousness – which once included directing the Elements and Elementals as they created the basis and foundation of the world you know today.

Reclaiming his spear, he emphasises that the holographic nature of the Universe means that what IS within the 'greater' also IS within the 'lesser': hence your *Unified* Energy Body (which is toroidal in form) mirrors the Earth's energy field; just as *all* your energy Bodies mirror the energy structures (and associated functions and principles) that founded the Earth – and, indeed, every other Planetary, Galactic and Universal Body! After thinking for a moment, he says that your *Linear* Energy Body is atypical, because its chakras are designed to separate 'feeling' 'knowing' and 'doing' *specifically* for the purpose of living and learning on a third-Dimensional Earth: yet in order to understand his Theme ('Know Yourself – Know All Things') you need to be able to align your mind and emotions and learn to hold them in Higher balance AS ONE.

With a smile, he gets to his feet, and says that (as a High Magician of the Second Order of Melchisadek) he may offer you his spear to aid you in your self-understanding and self-mastery, and asks you to stand to one side of the fire.... Handing you his staff, he tells you to hold it upright with base resting on the ground between your feet, and moves behind you: resting his right hand on your right shoulder, he explains that the primary function of the chakras at the *back* of your body concern the alignment of your personal Will to your Divine Will, and so govern how you *act*, rather than how you think or feel.... Gently touching his left hand to the back of your sacral and solar plexus chakras in turn, he tells you that these two chakras govern actions connected with self-will, self-regard, self-belief and self-acceptance.... then, lifting his hand to gently touch the back of your heart, throat and brow chakras in turn, he says that these three chakras govern inward- *and* outward-directed actions connected with unconditional love, the acknowledgement and acceptance of personal truths, and the practical (and selfless) use and application of knowledge, concepts and ideas....

As you absorb this information, Tzaphkiel rests his left hand on your left shoulder – and, as his presence embraces and empowers you, you realise that all the primary chakras down the back of your head and spine are slowly opening and coming into balance.... you know too that you are being filled with a wise and compassionate strength that will allow and enable you to take positive steps to align your personal Will to that of The Divine....

After allowing your realisations to settle, Tzaphkiel grounds and centres you, before reclaiming his spear and guiding you back to your chair.... Retaking his seat at your side, he gives a whistle – at which a slender blue-grey falcon flies through the cave entrance, and comes to perch on his shoulder. Tzaphkiel tells you that this peregrine falcon is one of his favourite birds, for it is a swift and skilful flyer with a courageous heart and the dogged determination that enables it to fearlessly plummet single-mindedly through the air in order to take its prey: accordingly, you may ask **Peregrine Falcon** to give you the courage to overcome your fears and go whole-heartedly for your goals; or to show you the sheer joy to be found in mastering the Element of air and harnessing your powers of logic and reasoning (enabling you to grow in wisdom and strength of mind) and/or to determine what is and isn't practicable, as you hone in on the finer details. He adds that their astounding eyesight also enables peregrines to see clearly and in great detail from lofty heights, so Peregrine Falcon may also offer you a Higher perspective over issues or problems that are affecting your judgement or progress; or show you the greater picture when you are planning for the future, or reviewing past (or recent) events; or teach you how to view things on more than one level, especially when using and/or honing your intuitive or psychic skills. Smiling, he says that (like him) peregrines prefer to live in quiet and remote places, although they are extremely adaptable if they need to be: thus Peregrine Falcon can teach you how to be content with nothing but your own company; or show you how to find the quiet and still places within *and* without, enabling you to let go of the everyday world and relax – reducing your stress, and increasing your tolerance and patience; or be asked to guide you in your quest for wisdom and understanding by encouraging calm and honest introspection and rationalisation (which will help you act wisely, rather than react unwisely, to whatever is happening in your life); and/or to show you how to adapt your circumstances to suit your needs, so that you may find peace even amidst the noise and chaos of Earthly existence.

Giving a sudden shrill cry, the falcon flies off to his roost at the opening of the cave, dropping a small indigo stone that emits chatoyant flashes of silvery-grey in your lap as he passes. With a grin, Tzaphkiel says that this is **Hawks** (Falcons / Blue Tiger) **Eye**, his first Crystal Champion – explaining:

"Hawks Eye is a stone that is often overlooked – yet it holds and controls a powerful combination of Indigo, Black and Platinum Light that may promote the acquisition and grounding of Higher knowledge, and the harmonisation of the Higher powers of intellect and intuition. Thus, as it carries and grounds many Rays of Cosmic knowledge, wisdom and understanding, it resonates intensely with the brow chakra and the Soma and Universal centres of the Unified Body: hence Hawks Eye can support and enhance outward and inward directed journey-work and meditation, and may be helpful in any situation that requires focused, logical, and/or reasoned thought processes to be used hand-in-hand with intuitively derived or inspired input. Hawks Eye's power must never be taken lightly however, for in working with it you may open yourself to catalytic change that might be swift and radical: nonetheless, it is a great choice if you know you are 'more' than simply flesh and bone, and are ready and willing to sacrifice your lower-ego to align with the Truth of your Greater Self and 'soar' to new heights. In part, this is due to the fact that Hawks Eye is the precursor of Tiger Eye (one of the most powerful stones for attracting the Gold Ray and aligning with your Christed-self), and so has the potential to attract the situations that herald and support the coming of the Christ within."

With a smile, Tzaphkiel affirms that Hawks Eye may therefore help you see through the 'Veils of Illusion', enabling you to refine your Self and align *your* will with *Divine* Will.

The Gift of The Spear of Divine Enlightenment:
Sitting back, Tzaphkiel explains that his Gift is designed to BE as ONE with the Gift given to you by Okina, his twin flame. He tells you that it will help you strengthen and align your personal Will with that of your Christed- and Divine-self more fully and completely; and allow you to experience (and understand) the relationship that exists between your 'lower' ego-self and your 'Higher' Christed-self with more clarity. He adds that his Gift will be placed in the pranic core of both your Linear *and* Unified Energy Bodies (spanning the sacral and Soul Star chakras in the former, and linking the Hara centre of your Unified Energy Body with your Christed-body in the latter): this will also enable you to perceive how Okina's Gift likewise exists in more than one Dimension (being present around both the throat and brow chakras of your Linear Energy Body, *and* spanning the Soma and Universal centres of your Unified Energy Body).

Stating that he will be starting with your Unified Energy Body, Tzaphkiel asks you to sit as upright as possible, with your feet flat on the floor; and moves to stand behind you.... As he places his hands on your shoulders, the cave brightens – and you realise that the diamond in his pendant is once again radiating a brilliant Light: this simultaneously warms and relaxes you; and, as the Light continues to grow, you know that your Unified Energy Body is awakening and coming into balance.... Gradually the Light expands, until everything around you fades from sight – then all you are aware of is you; Tzaphkiel; and the Light surrounding you....

As this becomes your reality, Tzaphkiel takes up his spear and carefully lowers it down your pranic core, so that the foot of the spear is within your Hara centre, and its head is within the upper opening of the toroidal energy field of your Unified Body, about an arm's length above your head.... As it settles into place, you receive a swift mental impression of the imprint of Okina's Gift that spans your Soma and Universal centres; and realise that her Gift sits around the mid-point of the spear.... as you ponder upon the significance of this, the heart-shaped tip of the spear emits a shower of platinum sparks, which merge and blend with the Light around you; and slowly you feel yourself connect with the wisdom of the Universe – your appreciation of the enigma that is summed up in the tenet 'as above; so below' enhanced.... your awareness of your Self as an infinite and eternal Being of Light made more real....

Recognising the point of realisation you have reached, Tzaphkiel raises the foot of the spear to the root of your solar plexus chakra, and shortens the length of the staff so that its head rests within your Soul Star chakra: this time as it settles into place you receive a different impression of Okina's Gift, and see two imprints of it: a very faint one encircling your brow, and a brighter one encircling your pranic core at the root of your throat chakra.... you realise that the latter one sits around the mid-point of the spear – and as you again ponder upon the significance of this, the heart-shaped tip of the spear emits a shower of indigo-blue sparks, which merge and blend with the Light around you....

Explaining that he is now going to help you assimilate and balance the energies of the spear, so that both templates become an integral part of both your Linear and Unified Energy Bodies, Tzaphkiel moves to stand to one side of you, and rests one hand gently over your sternum and the other over your sacrum.... as soon as he does so, you find your focus shifts, and you become aware of a warmth growing beneath his hands.... then you feel your crown chakra open – and the Light that surrounds you floods your pranic core, clarifying and charging all your senses so that they are fully awake and alert.... Any worries or fears that you have instantly ease and diminish; and you recognise an enhanced feeling of self-confidence and belief in your innate abilities and skills filling you with renewed drive and positivity.... You also start to appreciate how being in an ideal state of balance between body and spirit, logic and intuition is helping your mind to open – revealing new thoughts, concepts and ideas that you had not considered before....

It almost feels as if you are a beautiful flower opening fully to the Sun for the first time – and as you bathe in its glorious Light you *know* the perfection of your world and your place within it.... Then suddenly you see the Greater picture; and can see everything that adversely affects you and confines you in your 'human-ness' – and as soon as you comprehend and acknowledge this, you find that you are finally able to disconnect your Will from the control of your ego-self, and align it fully with that of your Greater Self.... Amazingly you find that NOW you can accept and take control of your emotions and reactions; and you know that you can choose to clear yourself of whatever petty cares and concerns are holding you down.... and so you simply open your heart, and lovingly release them all into the Light – rejoicing in the fact that your mind is now free to acquire new knowledge and information that will aid your growth, rather than stifle it....

After allowing plenty of time for this to happen, Tzaphkiel removes his spear and fully centres and grounds you, helping you return to the reality that is the cave.... He then lightly rests his hands on your head in Blessing, declaring:

> *"My Gift of The Spear of Divine Enlightenment is given to Illuminate your Mind with the radiant reality that IS your True Self! So open yourself to the Universe, and feel its sound resonate through you, encompassing all that you are (heart, mind and Soul); and know that in that moment – in that perfect Peace – you will find your Self."*

Gift given, Tzaphkiel helps you back to your chair and settles at your side. Giving you a large polished disc of black stone that reflects the firelight in translucent bands of colour, he tells you that this is **Rainbow Obsidian**, his second Crystal Champion – explaining:

> *"Rainbow Obsidian has a superficial blackness that hints at its excellent grounding qualities – yet it will not ground you to the* Earth, *but to your* Self: *this is because it holds the full spectrum of Light within its darkness, which will fill you with a sense of confidence and purpose whilst offering a rainbow pathway that will guide you deep within. It would therefore be wrong to assume that Black Light has no range in its resonance – for Rainbow Obsidian attests that it mirrors the spectrum that is found within White Light, enabling you to know true balance and equilibrium, whilst retaining a strong connection with both your inner and outer-self. Thus, Rainbow Obsidian will shift and change when light is shone upon it, reminding and reassuring you that the Divine Light is always present, even within the darkest of life's most traumatic and painful moments; and may also serve to help you understand and value the lessons that such events present, which perhaps may not be experienced so completely or profoundly in any other way. Rainbow Obsidian also has an inner strength and adaptability that can give you the courage and determination to see whatever you need to address with*

greater honesty and clarity; and the flexibility to master or resolve it in the best way possible for yourself and all concerned: in turn this can lead to true and absolute healing through genuine acceptance and forgiveness of whatever you find – and to a much greater appreciation of your True Light and reason for Being."

With a smile Tzaphkiel affirms that Rainbow Obsidian may therefore help you reconnect with his Gift, if you need help to align yourself with its Enlightened Wisdom.

Asking you to turn the disc over, he points out how one side is engraved with a stylised depiction of an octopus, whose eight arms are spread out around its body like a many-rayed star: the disc catches the firelight as you tilt it, sending shimmering waves of green, gold and purple dancing over the arms and body, making it seem almost as if the octopus is spiralling through a dark ocean or sky. Tzaphkiel comments that few people appreciate the intelligence of the octopus, or understand its profound connections with the multitude of Galaxies that spiral through space: yet **Octopus** can teach you about the multifaceted structure of the Universe, and help you uncover the myriad Mysteries that rule Time and space, through experiencing and understanding the true nature of the Diamond Light in *all* its aspects. He adds that the ability of the octopus to radically alter its shape, form and texture enables it to adapt itself to its environment as each situation requires; whilst its ability to change its pattern and colour by expanding and contracting the pigment-containing cells in its skin enables it to hide or express and communicate its thoughts and emotions using the Language of Light: thus, you may call upon Octopus to surround you with an eight-pointed Star of Light if you need help to shift your resonant frequency, or need to increase or improve your shielding or grounding; or to show you how to adapt to working in different environments, by helping you recognise what will serve you best in each situation (understanding when and how to keep a low profile, as well as when and how to make your needs, thoughts or feelings very plain); and to give you the courage and determination to stand up for yourself and what you deserve when other people do not seem to be listening to what you are saying. Pointing to its eight tentacles, Tzaphkiel observes that octopi rely a great deal on senses other than sight, and are experts at feeling their way into and through mazes and other confined spaces: hence you may also ask Octopus to help you develop intuitive skills connected with sensing and knowing – especially on Higher and finer levels; or to guide and advise you if you find your path is hidden, unclear or excessively confining on any level.

The Enlightenment of The Platinum Star of Illumined Truth:

Putting his spear aside, Tzaphkiel lifts his pendant for you to see it more clearly.... He explains that this is The Platinum Star of Truth and Light, which holds a diamond at its heart so that it may direct and distribute the Light of Source and Divine Creation throughout the Universe by means of the Platinum Ray of Stellar Enlightenment and Illumined Truth, upon which he serves. He expounds that this Ray holds the Cosmic aspects of silver, black and indigo Light that promote Universal Christ-consciousness, whereby intellect and reason (mind) always dwells hand-in-hand with pure and selfless compassion (heart).... Pointing to the representation of the Earth that still hovers in the air between you, he emphasises that *everything* that exists is made of Divine Light, and so has some degree of consciousness – which, as far as Earth is concerned, *includes* all minerals and crystals, flora and fauna, as much as it does humanity. With a wry smile he adds that he therefore uses the word 'humanity' on purpose, as its definitions of kindness, benevolence, unselfishness, consideration and compassion are the principles and values to which *all* who have been granted dominion over others (human, animal, plant or mineral) should adhere!

Reaching out to gently touch the hovering sphere, Tzaphkiel reminds you that, just as *he* tends and guards his flock, *you* have the capacity to be a wise and loving guardian to all of Divine Creation: however, your ego-self will always struggle to embody the ideals he has just listed *unless* you expand your consciousness and fully align with your Christed-self. He counsels that this alignment can be simple if you use your powers of mental reasoning to master your emotional feelings and reactions; and work to balance intellect with inspiration – taking the knowledge that you acquire as you extend your awareness; and using your Inner Wisdom to reach a rightful understanding.... Touching a hand to his head, he adds that *here* is where you integrate your human and spiritual experiences, and allow yourself to align with the *concept* of those Higher principles and values; whilst *here* (touching his other hand to his heart) is where you truly *understand* what it means to be a member of humanity! With a smile, he says that he hopes that *your* humanity will enable you to share your Light with ALL that comprises your Earthly home – for it would be folly to assume that humankind are the only ones who seek to extend their awareness and refine their consciousness.

Suddenly you are interrupted by the sounds of chattering birds, and a small flock of gregarious sparrows flutters in through the cave to a ledge behind you, where they settle down to roost for the night. Tzaphkiel chuckles as he watches them bicker for position, observing that sparrows are the complete opposite of peregrines – loving company and confined spaces, and cheerfully sharing group responsibilities: accordingly you might ask **Sparrow** to teach you how to value the companionship of family and friends; or to help you acclimatise to crowded or cramped conditions, by adjusting your energies to adapt to the environment; or to give you greater confidence in your own value and self-worth – recognising when there is a time to be humble, and a time to 'blow your own trumpet' (whilst also appreciating that one does not preclude the other!) Tzaphkiel muses that it can be interesting to observe a flock of sparrows, for although they have no pretty song, they always declaim their presence vigorously and loudly: hence Sparrow knows that every voice is important and deserves to be listened to, and can always be asked to help you make *your* voice heard, empowering you to communicate your needs both firmly and effectively. With a smile he adds that in comparison to other birds a sparrow's plumage may also seem rather dull, yet it is excellent camouflage, and serves its purpose well: thus, Sparrow can help you be grateful for the personal attributes you have been given, accepting that there is always a good reason for their presence – or lack; and can teach you to appreciate the many advantages of keeping things simple, rather than making them needlessly complex – for simplicity will help you get to the heart of a matter (and achieve your goals) more quickly and efficiently than that which is more complicated, which often makes it harder to 'see the wood for the trees'!

Gesturing about the cave, Tzaphkiel says he has found simplicity to be fundamental to a fulfilling life, for he knows that *knowledge* is the key to contentment and happiness. With a smile he adds that neither can be bought or acquired through material trappings, which literally 'trap' you in an obstructive cycle of limitation; but may only be found by identifying your Soul's core desires. He says that in order to know what would *genuinely* fulfil you and make you happy, you may need to firstly consider just how happy, fulfilled and content you feel in your everyday life at present (and why), saying:

"Think about what gives you joy or makes your heart sing – then reflect if you could make joyful things a bigger part of your life, and contemplate how you might do so.... Ask yourself if there is anything you have always dreamed of doing, but have never had the courage, time or means to do – then think about how doing so might make you feel, and contemplate how (or what) you could change to make your dream real."

As you begin to consider this, he emphasises that you should disregard material or other such obstacles that prevent you from fulfilling your desires, and be as creative as you like – letting your imagination and deepest dreams and desires run wild and free!...

After you have taken as long as you need to muse and reflect, Tzaphkiel lifts his pendant so that it reflects the firelight.... You watch it slowly grow, until it fills the space between you – the diamond at its heart creating a mirror at its heart – then, directing you to gaze within it, Tzaphkiel asks you to allow yourself to see, sense or know whatever is holding you back from having more joy in your life, or preventing you from working towards, and/or fulfilling, your dreams.... As you stare at your reflection, the seven arms of the platinum star abruptly flare with a silvery Light, and Tzaphkiel counsels you:

"Allow the Wisdom of the Cosmos to provide the illumination you need to find the Truth behind what you are seeing; and then simply allow its Light to help you identify and recognise some ways in which your Soul's true needs may be fulfilled in this lifetime."

For several minutes the Light flickers and flares, and you know that a series of images are passing through the mirror (or materialising and disappearing in a sequence) – even if you are not yet able to identify or fully connect with them: then, with a final flare of Light the pendant returns to its original size, leaving a single flame (which is silver-white shot through with flashes of dark blue, gold and platinum) hovering in front of you....

Explaining that the Flame holds the Light of Illumined Truth, Tzaphkiel invites you to pluck it from the air and secure it within your heart.... As you do, he tells you that you may call forth its Light whenever you need to reinforce your personal Truths in order to live joyfully in accordance with your Soul's Greater purpose, saying:

"Place your personal truths within the Light of Illumined Truth, and see them burn as a single Flame.... Know that Truth will overcome all obstacles placed against you, and allow the Flame to guide you.... then speak your truth, and allow your truths to be seen by all – not tainted or influenced by your own ego, but expressed purely and clearly: for, as you are true to yourself and true to the ultimate Truth, you will merge with the Christed-Light and act for the good of all – and then all may become ONE once more."

Tzaphkiel then gives you a clear crystal, which looks as if two crystals have merged, one partly within the other, telling you that this is **Clear Quartz**, his third Crystal Champion, which has grown in the formation known as a 'sceptre' – explaining:

> *"Clear Quartz is truly King of the mineral Kingdom, being the most multi-purpose and adaptable crystal you will find. It grows in a huge range of shapes and forms, which all have their own special gifts and characteristics – and this particular crystal has chosen to take the form known as a 'sceptre', which is given to you now as a symbol of your personal Sovereignty: hence to work with it is to take ownership of your life and all that is within your control, and is a sign of your commitment to act from this point onwards with wisdom and kindness in all things. Be aware that it is no coincidence that the most powerful crystals on Earth – both now, and in the Ancient past – have been Clear Quartz, for it is a natural and powerful amplifier of Light, which many civilisations have prized for its wide-ranging attributes and virtues. These virtues and its capacity for 'memory' allow it to hold and retain ancient records and memories, for it is the only crystal that can be reliably programmed: thus this crystal may help you keep a history of all your journeys of self-discovery, providing an Illuminating record for those that follow in your footsteps in years yet to come. Know too, that in many ways Clear Quartz can BE whatever you want it to BE, which makes it a profound companion for your self-healing and growth, regardless of where you are on your journey...."*

With a smile Tzaphkiel affirms that this Clear Quartz may therefore be an honest and true companion, its multifaceted wisdom and Light aiding and supporting your endeavours. He then bows to you and steps back, arms outspread in silent Blessing, saying:

> *"Look to me now: simplicity in all its facets you see laid bare before you, and reflected in its Light you may see my face: calm and at peace, and content with all that I am.... Understand that life is what you choose to make of it. It is not about what others think of you or what possessions you have, but is about how you choose to live your life as you discover who you are through self-love, self-knowledge, self-acceptance and self-belief. Such wisdom cannot be bought, but can only be won through an honest heart and an open mind; and the truly wise person will understand that the greatest of all riches is knowledge – of your Self, and of all that is within and around you. Remember: the potentialities of all that you seek to become are within your grasp. So stand firm – sure and certain in the essence that is you; and may the riches of your heart and mind shine forth, to sparkle like a thousand gems upon your breast, and crown you with the Light of The Divine, that all who see you may henceforth know the Truth of your Being."*

The Greenwood Guardians – Cypress and Baobab:

His *personal* mentoring complete for now, Tzaphkiel affirms he is always available to aid and support you: you need only bring him to mind and ask for his presence, and he will attend you. Furthermore, he tells you that two great Tree Beings of the Plant Kingdom have also asked to support you in addressing his Theme of 'KNOW YOURSELF – KNOW ALL THINGS', adding that you need only request *their* presence, and they will be with you.

He explains that the first of these Greenwood Guardians is the Masculine essence of Cypress, who has asked to overlight and help you ground whatever work you undertake within *any* aspect of his chapter. The second is the Feminine essence of Baobab, who has specifically asked to help you understand and assimilate his Gift of The Spear of Divine Enlightenment (if you have chosen to accept it).

When you are ready to connect with Tzaphkiel's first Greenwood Guardian, you need simply call for the presence of **Cypress** (*) .... Cypress envelops you in a green Light that is filled with sparks of silver, and the masculine spirit essence of Cypress speaks to you, saying:

> *"The clarity that you will find within my embrace will fill your mind with astonishment that you did not realise you knew 'all this' before – yet the part of you that is eternally wise will know that it is merely the veil of forgetfulness and illusion that has prevented you from understanding the Truth until now! Thus I stand in still and silent vigil, aiding all those that seek my Light by offering healing and balance to the weary, and succour to those that have lost their way.... As you rest in my shade you will see me point the way ever onwards, ever upwards – through the stars of the heavens, and even unto the very centre of the Universe, where all things began. In my plain and simple presence you might overlook the Power that I hold within – yet know that the purest and kindest of things are to be found in the most humble of places; and I would teach you how to expand your heart and mind to recognise and accept this – and to realise that you too may grow to be a Guardian of the Divine Light: rooted in the darkness of the giving earth, yet nonetheless overflowing with the bountiful Light that brings the Gift of Grace to melt away karma, and purify all ills...."*

(* Green Aventurine will help you ground and connect with the energy and wisdom of Cypress, if you wish to enhance your experience using crystals.)

If you have chosen to accept and work with Tzaphkiel's Gift, and when you are ready to connect with his second Greenwood Guardian, you need simply call for the presence of **Baobab** (*) .... Baobab envelops you in a gold and orange Light, and the feminine spirit essence of Baobab speaks to you, saying:

> *"Infinite delight is held always at my heart, whilst the gift of the Sun crowns my brow: for all that I am knows only perfect balance, which feeds and sustains me through the many and varied seasons of my growth. Thus, if you stand with me, above all else I will teach you the art of going within, that you might connect with the Emerald Ray that carries the Light of Profound Truths and Potential for the Divine Manifestation of All That Is. For when you* know *this Light, this will be all you need, in order to BE who and what you wish to BE; and you will have found the courage and determination to explore the world of form and non-form that exists in stasis around you. This will enable you to seek out and find the Great and Ancient Wisdoms of the Cosmos, which rule the skies through which you whirl – oblivious to the vastness and splendour in which you are immersed. And then, and only then, will you* truly *know all there is to know.... and* then, *and* only then, *will you be free to Create your Life all over again...."*

(* Infinite Stone and Sunstone will help you ground and connect with the energy and wisdom of Baobab, if you wish to enhance your experience using crystals.)

REFERENCE MATERIAL AND INDEXES

AN OVERVIEW OF THE HUMAN ENERGY BODY

What follows is my *personal* interpretation and understanding (at 2016) of:

1: The Linear Energy Body (of the physical third-Dimensional human)
2: The Unified Energy Body – Unified Chakra / Body (moving towards Lightbody)
3: The Lotus of the Heart
4: The Lotus of the Soul

1: The Linear Energy Body and the Linear Chakras

The human physical body is constructed upon etheric templates that look a little like interwoven architect's blueprints: these give all the parts of your physical body structure and form; provide the energy constructs that nourish your physical and subtle bodies with Universal life-force energy (prana); and connect you with All that you Are throughout Time and Dimension. You are much more than the physical body you can see and touch!

The etheric (subtle energy) Bodies are intrinsically linked to the physical body, and are cleverly designed so that the body, emotions, mind and spirit can be distinguished and understood as separate functioning units. This 'separation' is achieved by structuring the energy Body in distinct parts that – nonetheless – have the innate capability to share information and understanding: this enables you to experience physical, emotional and mental survival and growth as individual aspects of your Being – allowing you to think thoughts and feel emotions, which may or may not be rational; react to things that 'push your buttons', and act appropriately or inappropriately; and experience your immortal Soul from the perspective of the human world of physicality, which also enables you to experience the consequences of Free Will and choice.

The typical human is designed to experience life in seven-year cycles – the main structures of the energy Body (the seven primary chakras and auric Bodies) facilitating this in stages, by supporting the development of the body, mind, emotions and spirit from a different perspective. Each of these chakras is shaped like a conical funnel, and rotates to facilitate the transfer of energy and information; and each has a key relationship with one of the seven primary auric Bodies (often referred to as 'layers' – although they are not wholly separate from each other) that surround and interpenetrate both the physical body *and* all the other 'layers' of the aura.

I call these seven chakras the **LINEAR CHAKRAS**, as they are ordered adjacent to each other in a line. Each penetrates the pranic core*, which runs through the centre of the body to span the 'soft-spot' on top of the skull and the perineum at the bottom (quite literally!) of the torso. Note: you may find that the names and perceived locations of the chakras mentioned below are different from this in other belief systems.
(* also known as 'the central column')

- ♥ **The base chakra** is located at the perineum, and is associated with the auric Body that lies closest to the skin. Both relate to your physical body and physical health, and to your ability to focus upon and manifest all the fundamental needs required to maintain your physical survival and material existence.

- ♥ **The sacral chakra** is located at the front and back of the torso level with the sacrum (the large triangular bone that sits at the base of the spine), and is associated with the second auric Body. Both relate to your emotions and emotional health; to all impulses and needs that drive your procreative survival and emotional evolution; and to the way in which you experience, feel and react to change and growth.

- ♥ **The solar-plexus chakra** is located at the front and back of the torso level with the diaphragm, and is associated with the third auric Body. Both relate to your mind and mental health; to all logical thought processes that drive and maintain your personal evolution and growth; and to your ability to focus upon, identify and integrate all the many diverse (and polar) aspects of your 'lower' (human) ego-self.
- ♥ **The heart chakra** is located at the front and back of the torso in the centre of the breastbone, and is associated with the fourth auric Body. Both relate to your spiritual health and spirituality; to all endeavours that drive and inspire your personal spiritual evolution and growth; and to your ability to give and receive love unconditionally.
- ♥ **The throat chakra** is located at the front and back of the neck level with the sternal notch of the collarbone, and is associated with the fifth auric Body. Both relate to your Higher awareness of your Self as a fully-conscious and sentient Being; to all endeavours that promote your Higher spiritual evolution, learning and growth; and to your ability to acquire information and knowledge, and share it with others.
- ♥ **The brow** (or third eye) **chakra** is located at the front and back of the head level with the centre of the forehead, and is associated with the sixth auric Body. Both relate to your interpretation of worlds visible and invisible to 'normal' sight; to all endeavours that promote clear perception through use of your Higher senses and your creative visualisation (imagination); and to your ability to see, using both your outer (physical) sight, and your inner (non-physical / 'clairvoyant') sight.
- ♥ **The crown chakra** is located at the head in the area of the fontanelle (the soft spot), and is associated with the seventh, and outermost, auric Body. Both relate to your links to Divine Mind and Divine Inspiration; to all endeavours that promote clear perception and enable you to 'know' your Divine-self; and to your ability to expand your awareness of your Self far beyond the limits of Time, space and Dimension.

There are also two more chakras that play a very important role in the Linear Body:

- ♥ **The Soul Star chakra** is located about one hand's length above the crown. It has strong links with the crown chakra, and connects your physical body and its seven primary chakras to the Higher-Dimensions: this offers you a gateway to your 'Higher chakras' (eight through to fourteen), and enables you clearer access to Higher sources of consciousness, through which you might come to recognise, accept and embody the reality of your Christed-self and Divine-self.
- ♥ **The Earth Star chakra** is located up to an arm's length below the feet. It has strong links with the base chakra, and acts to connect and ground your physical and Linear energy Bodies to the physical and non-physical aspects of the Earth, Galaxy and Universe. It also helps you ground and assimilate Dimensional shifts and changes – both global and personal.

2: The Unified Energy Body (the Unified Chakra and Unified Body)

The Linear Energy Body is designed specifically to support learning and growth in the third-Dimensional world of human physical existence and experience: however, as you learn more about Free Will, discernment and choice and begin to master your body, emotions, mind and spirit, you may become aware of the seven 'Higher' chakras that lie 'beyond' the crown chakra, and the seven auric Bodies that surround and interpenetrate the auric Bodies mentioned in the previous section. These are associated with Higher Dimensions and understanding, and there are different fields of thought about how these integrate with the Linear Bodies – but I favour the concept of the 'Unified Chakra' (whereby the seven 'lower' chakras merge into one) and the 'Unified Body' (whereby all fourteen chakras and auric Bodies become ONE).

The **UNIFIED BODY** is a fourth-Dimensional structure that acts like a 'stepping stone' to link the third-Dimensional physical body to the fifth-Dimensional Lightbody. It takes the form of a single toroidal energy construct centred on the middle of the chest, and is around twice the size of the aura of the Linear Body. My experience is that the Unified Body instinctively and naturally develops in tandem with the opening, activation and grounding of the seven 'Higher' chakras and their associated auric Bodies mentioned above – but it can also be experienced by deliberately merging your Linear chakras and auric Bodies through focused thought and intention: however, to do this requires you to have cleared and balanced your Linear chakras *and* activated your Alpha and Omega centres (see later), thus ensuring you cannot access your Unified Body and its 'Higher' energies until you understand how to master your Linear Body and its challenges.

When you are 'in' Unified Body, your Linear chakras (1-7), Higher chakras (8-14), and all their associated auric Bodies and templates become ONE, and begin to resonate with the frequency of Divine Love: this allows you to hold and ground a greater quantum of Light, and offers you a very different perspective on your thoughts, feelings, actions and reactions! Eventually you will be able to move in to and out of Unified Body at will and with full awareness, 'switching' or 'shifting' to 'BE' in 'Linear' or 'Unified' state, according to need – although in actuality (and in practise) I have found that both states exist within the same space simultaneously, and hence it is possible to have full and total conscious awareness of 'Being' in both states at the same time.

Within the Unified Body, there are certain centres that retain energy connections to the physical and Linear Bodies: these focus specific aspects of the Divine Light to enable you to begin to understand (and work responsibly with) Higher-Dimensional energies, as and when you become capable of doing so.

- ♥ **The Alpha centre** is located in front of the pranic core, about a hands-length above the top of the brow. It anchors your Linear Body to your Unified Body, and links your Unified Body to your Christed-self and Divine-self by means of a cord of silver Light.
- ♥ **The Soma centre** is located just above the brow chakra, level with the hairline. It helps sustain your Linear brow and crown chakras; and aids and enhances mental clarity and all enlightened forms of communication, perception and intelligence that sustain your forward progress. It also joins with your Alpha and Universal centres to

create a triangular portal of Light that aids your attainment of Higher-Dimensional states of awareness.

- ♥ **The Universal centre** (sometimes known as 'The Mouth of God') is located at the back of the head and at the base of the skull, in the region of the cerebellum. It has connections to the limbic system of the brain, and provides you with a connection to other Dimensions of consciousness, allowing you access to the Universal data banks (the etheric 'repositories' that store all information and knowledge, including your memories). It also aids and supports the exchange of telepathic communication with other sentient life forms, and is your primary focal point for all inter-Galactic and inter-Dimensional communication.

- ♥ **The Gaia centre** spans the region of the physical heart, thymus gland, heart chakra and the Lotus of the Heart (see section '3' that follows). It is aligned with Earth's physical and etheric energies, and with all the living and sentient life forms that inhabit her. When awakened and balanced it improves the efficiency and effectiveness of your immune system and 'light-ens' your physical body, leading to improved cellular regeneration and rejuvenation; and enables you to work more effectively with the principles of Creation and Manifestation.

- ♥ **The Hara centre** spans the area between the pubic bone and the diaphragm. It holds the patterns of your genetic lineage, as handed down by your parents at your physical birth; and the templates of the pure consciousness that you were prior to taking embodiment: this includes the immortal aspect of your consciousness that knows and remembers all the lessons and experiences of your past – and future – lifetimes.

- ♥ **The Seat of the Soul centre** is located just in front of the sacrum (the large triangular bone that sits at the base of the spine). It has links with the sacral and ninth chakras of your Linear Body, and hence with your Soul group and your awareness of your other Selves that exist throughout Time and Dimension. It also holds the multidimensional template of your Lotus of the Soul (see section '4' that follows); and inspires you to comprehend the principles of karma, duality and accountability, and the mechanics and responsibilities of all acts of Creation and Manifestation.

- ♥ **The Omega centre** is located behind the pranic core, about a hands-length below the end of the spine. It anchors your Linear Body to your absolute Consciousness through the toroidal energy field of your Unified Body; and connects you to the Earth's own Unified Body – and thence to the Planetary, Galactic and Universal Grids – by means of twelve grounding cords of golden Light. It works in harmony with your Alpha centre, maintaining stability of the core of the toroidal energy field of your Unified Body; and also encourages and supports the functioning of the 'Waves of Metatron'* that flow between your Alpha and Omega centres: these can sometimes be sensed as waves of energy moving up and down your pranic core – their primary purpose being to help anchor your fifth- and sixth-Dimensional energy templates into your physical body, and to clear, connect and 'fine-tune' the energetic circuitry of your Lightbody.
(*Metatron will help you recognise and experience these Waves if you ask him to!)

3: The Lotus of the Heart

The Lotus of the Heart is a multidimensional energy construct that holds and sustains the three-fold Flames of the Enlightened Heart, which support and inspire your Soul's experience of Earthly existence. It is located within the heart of the Gaia centre, and is so called because it resembles a lotus flower – each flame-like 'petal' being made of condensed Light, nesting in layers that open and close to reveal (or conceal) the bud at its core: this bud remains closed until you are able to embrace the Emerald at its heart, which meantime is kept sealed and protected within a 'Melchisadek Star of Light'. When it is fully awakened your Heart Lotus establishes a permanent and conscious connection with your Christed-self.

- ♥ The innermost layer of petals is butter-yellow, veined with gold – the tips of which are a deep golden yellow, fading to pale lemon at their base: these are the Flames of Divine Wisdom overseen by Lucida, the Lady Clarity.
- ♥ The next layer of petals is sky-blue, veined with sapphire – the tips of which are a deep royal blue, fading to pale blue at their base: these are the Flames of Divine Will and Power, overseen by Mikaela, the Lady Faith.
- ♥ The next layer of petals is sugar-pink, veined with ruby – the tips of which are a deep rose pink, fading to pale pink at their base: these are the Flames of Divine Love, overseen by Seraphina, the Lady Charity.
- ♥ These three layers, which comprise the three-fold Flames of your Heart, are enclosed within an outer (protective) layer of pearlescent-white petals: these are the Flames of Hope, overseen by Annunciata, the Lady Hope.

4: The Lotus of the Soul

The template of the 'Lotus of the Soul' is located between the root of the sacral chakra and the sacrum, within the Seat of the Soul centre near the base of the spine. This Lotus is usually only 'present' and accessible when you are experiencing Higher existences (Lightbody and beyond): however, once the Lotus of your Heart is fully awakened, opened and developed, and you are able to consciously maintain it in an appropriate state of balance, the Lotus of the Soul may be grounded into its template when you are in physical embodiment *provided that* you have proved competent and trustworthy in your spiritual practice. It should be noted, however, that your Divine-self determines and oversees its unfolding and activation, because of the necessity to act at all times with integrity and respect for the power and potential it holds. As with the Lotus of the Heart, the Lotus of the Soul IS condensed Light:

- ♥ The outermost layer of petals is crystal-white; and is overseen by Gabriel.
- ♥ The next layer of petals is sapphire-blue; and is overseen by Michael.
- ♥ The next layer of petals is emerald-green; and is overseen by Raphael.
- ♥ The innermost layer of petals is ruby-red; and is overseen by Uriel.

All the petals embrace your 'Pearl' at the core, which is not accessible until you are fully awake and consciously ready to embody your Reality as an aspect of Divine Source.

THE DIVINE LIGHT AND THE SACRED RAYS

The Diamond Light IS the infinite undifferentiated Light of the Divine – the Pure Clear Light of Source. It holds the Pure White Light of the Alpha and Omega and exists throughout all Dimensions and Planes of Reality, and is eternally present within all Rays and Flames (focused condensations of specific wavelengths of Light) in variable degrees. When I was writing our 'Ascension' course, Metatron said this about the Diamond Light:

"...The Diamond Light comprises White Light (which holds the fundamental forces and matter required for Creation), and Black Light (which defines the Void of Potential and enables the 'space' within which Formation may occur, as and when brought forth from the non-manifest possibilities of Divine Mind). Both are eternally present throughout ALL Dimensions and Planes of Reality – for without Black Light, White Light cannot 'Become'. Moreover, although The Divine is ONE – a true Unified Consciousness that knows no separation – it comprises two prime aspects that may be defined as 'feminine' and 'masculine'; and has two fundamental expressions: the Gold Ray – the 'masculine' manifestation of The Divine, which holds the essential space for Creation and allows the fundamental matter of Creation to take on shape and form; and the Silver Ray – the 'feminine' manifestation of The Divine, which enlivens and activates that which is Created... adding: *Please be aware that this is a very basic explanation – for 'Rays' are not simply Light: they are beyond your current understanding, which is still evolving..."*

Nonetheless, it is true to say that Light defines and constructs *everything* that exists – and because the Archangelics *are* 'Light made Manifest' they are (by intent and by design) intrinsically connected with its definition, distribution and administration:

- ♥ Ratziel and Jochara oversee the interaction of White and Black Light.
- ♥ Metatron and Sophia oversee the interaction of the Gold and Silver Rays with both White and Black Light.
- ♥ Azrael and Magdalena oversee the Void Space of Potential and direct the interactions of all aspects of the Divine Light and the Rays within that space. They perform some of their duties by utilising the energies of the (Higher Cosmic) Copper Ray of Solar Service and Solar Christ-consciousness, which provides a medium through which the un-manifest may become manifest.

The vibratory frequencies of the Diamond Light's constituent parts are regulated and distributed throughout the Universe by energy 'transformers' that monitor, adjust and 'divide' it as appropriate for need. To access Earth's Plane of Reality, the Diamond Light passes through 'The Temple of the Divine Light', which is an aspect of The Divine Feminine that acts like a Crystal Prism: this initially steps the Light down into four key aspects – the Crystal, Ruby, Emerald and Sapphire Rays, whose intensity can be refined, decreased and/or blended to create a 'rainbow' of Light whose constituent parts are then defined by concentration and colour, and named in accordance with what is generally perceptible within the visible spectrum of light.

- ♥ Shekhinah guards the Crystal Prism and holds its interface with the Diamond Light; whilst Sandalphon oversees the grounding of all the Rainbow Rays for the benefit of the Earth and all her many and varied life-forms.

- Gabriel holds the Crystal Ray and its interfaces with the Crystal Prism and the 'Pearl' (another aspect of The Divine Feminine), which 'gives birth' to the Pearlescent-white Ray: this holds the Higher, finer (and paler coloured) aspects of the Rainbow Rays 'as One', and is held and grounded by Annunciata, who also directs all its interactions with the individualised aspects of the base spectrum Rays, red through to violet.
- Uriel and Rainbow Aurora hold the Ruby Ray and its interface with the Crystal Prism; oversee the blending of all Light that contains the Ruby Ray, including orange, purple, violet and magenta; and ground the Ruby Ray through all its saturations and hues of red.
- Raphael and Mareia hold the Emerald Ray and its interface with the Crystal Prism; oversee the blending of all Light that contains the Emerald Ray; and ground the Emerald Ray through all its saturations and hues of green.
- Michael and Mikaela hold the Sapphire Ray and its interface with the Crystal Prism; oversee the blending of all Light that contains the Sapphire Ray; and ground the Sapphire Ray through all its saturations and hues of indigo and blue.

When we first began working with the concept of the Rays in 2006, Mark and I had been discussing how they related to Light and colour, when Metatron told us:

"...Visible Light breaks down into a spectrum which you choose to interpret as seven separate and distinct colours. But (if Light is defined as 'colour') the spectrum is in fact infinite, comprising many different hues, tones and shades without division. There are no black or white lines to break off or separate each one from the next: you 'see' and interpret it differently, because human eyes are simply not sensitive enough to pick up the differences. But whether you say there are seven, or seventy-seven thousand, or a million colours, the concept is what matters! It is perfectly acceptable to describe Light (and the Rays) in this way, because – as an aid to understanding – this gives Light a structure and order that may help you gain the knowledge that you seek..."

Archangelic twin flames hold one Rainbow Ray of the visible spectrum: the 'masculine' counterpart usually being responsible for the more intense (and deeper coloured) aspects; the 'feminine' the finer (and paler coloured) aspects:

- Tzadkiel and Amethystia hold the Violet Ray.
- Michael and Mikaela hold the Blue and Indigo Rays (*and see* Sapphire Ray above) assisted by Tzaphkiel and Okina, who administer the Higher aspects of the Indigo Ray by means of the (Higher Cosmic) Platinum Ray of Stellar Enlightenment and Illumined Truth, which is connected with Universal Service and Universal Christ-consciousness.
- Raphael and Mareia hold the Green Ray (*and see* Emerald Ray above).
- Jophiel and Lucida hold the Yellow Ray.
- Haniel and Maryllisa hold the Orange Ray.
- Chamuel and Seraphina hold the Red Ray, and also assist Uriel and Rainbow Aurora in grounding the Ruby Ray through all its saturations and hues of red, including pink.

INDEX OF CREATURE COMPANIONS:

Name	Archangel/Archeia	Page
Bat	Mikaela	152
Bee (Honey)	Gabriel	203
Butterfly	Magdalena	301
Cat	Shekhinah	251
Chameleon	Maryllisa	105
Cheetah	Ratziel	327
Cicada	Haniel	121
Condor	Jochara	341
Crab	Amethystia	35
Crane	Sandalphon	263
Crow	Michael	139
Deer	Amethystia	37
Dog	Chamuel	97
Dolphin	Shekhinah	246
Donkey	Metatron	53
Dove (White)	Annunciata	194
Dragon (Rose)	Rainbow Aurora	233
Dragonfly	Azrael	315
Eagle (Golden)	Haniel	123
Eagle (White)	Mareia	273
Egret	Lucida	160
Elephant	Ratziel	333
Falcon (Kestrel)	Jophiel	178
Falcon (Merlin)	Seraphina	78
Falcon (Peregrine)	Tzaphkiel	371
Firebird	Magdalena	305
Glow-worm	Maryllisa	108
Goat (Mountain)	Jochara	344
Goose	Tzadkiel	26
Griffon	Gabriel	207
Hornet	Raphael	290
Horse	Chamuel	93
Hummingbird	Mareia	278
Jaguar	Lucida	163
Jaguar (Black)	Haniel	118
Jay	Tzadkiel	21
Lion	Metatron	52
Locust	Jophiel	175
Lovebird	Seraphina	82

INDEX OF CREATURE COMPANIONS: continued

Name	Archangel/Archeia	Page
Magpie	Shekhinah	248
Mountain Lion (Cougar / Puma)	Sophia	67
Mouse	Amethystia	40
Ocelot	Magdalena	304
Octopus	Tzaphkiel	374
Ostrich	Ratziel	330
Otter	Okina	355
Owl (Great Grey)	Maryllisa	111
Owl (Little)	Raphael	287
Owl (Snowy)	Rainbow Aurora	231
Peacock	Metatron	49
Peacock (White)	Sandalphon	264
Pheasant (Golden)	Gabriel	205
Phoenix	Uriel	217
Polar Bear	Jochara	349
Praying Mantis	Michael	137
Puffin	Mareia	276
Rabbit	Sophia	66
Raven	Azrael	319
Scarab Beetle	Okina	359
Skunk	Okina	362
Snake (Adder)	Azrael	318
Snake (Cobra)	Mikaela	148
Snow Leopard	Michael	134
Sparrow	Tzaphkiel	375
Spider	Uriel	221
Squirrel	Sophia	63
Stag (White)	Rainbow Aurora	235
Stork	Annunciata	189
Swan	Uriel	220
Tiger	Mikaela	147
Tree Creeper	Lucida	167
Turtle	Sandalphon	259
Turtledove	Chamuel	90
Vulture	Tzadkiel	24
Whale	Annunciata	191
Wolf	Jophiel	179
Woodpecker (Green)	Raphael	290
Wren	Seraphina	78

INDEX OF CRYSTAL CHAMPIONS:

Name	Archangel/Archeia	Page
Agate (Blue Lace)	Sophia	69
Agate (Tree)	Lucida	166
Amber	Uriel	218
Amethyst	Amethystia	34
Ametrine	Jophiel	181
Angelite	Maryllisa	105
Apache Tear (Smoky Obsidian)	Ratziel	329
Apophyllite (Clear)	Haniel	119
Aquamarine	Jochara	343
Aventurine (Green)	Raphael	289
Azurite	Mikaela	150
Bronzite	Haniel	124
Calcite (Honey)	Amethystia	38
Calcite (Optical Clear)	Seraphina	77
Calcite (Optical Pink)	Raphael	287
Carnelian	Maryllisa	110
Celestite (Blue)	Haniel	120
Chalcedony (Blue)	Mikaela	152
Charoite	Sophia	66
Chrysanthemum Stone	Okina	362
Citrine (Heat Treated)	Jophiel	174
Citrine (Natural)	Lucida	163
Danburite (Clear)	Azrael	317
Girasol (Pink)	Seraphina	83
Girasol (White)	Magdalena	303
Hawks (Falcons) Eye	Tzaphkiel	371
Hematite	Shekhinah	245
Herkimer Diamond	Gabriel	201
Jade (Green)	Uriel	221
Jasper (Gaia – Polychrome)	Sandalphon	265
Jasper (Red)	Uriel	223
Jasper (Yellow)	Metatron	52
Jet	Ratziel	335
Kyanite (Indigo)	Michael	133
Labradorite (Golden)	Tzadkiel	27
Labradorite	Mikaela	147
Lapis Lazuli	Gabriel	206
Lepidolite	Tzadkiel	23
Magnesite	Shekhinah	250

INDEX OF CRYSTAL CHAMPIONS: continued

Name	Archangel/Archeia	Page
Malachite	Maryllisa	107
Moldavite	Azrael	320
Moonstone (Rainbow)	Annunciata	194
Moonstone (White)	Magdalena	301
Morganite	Rainbow Aurora	231
Obsidian (Black)	Azrael	315
Obsidian (Rainbow)	Tzaphkiel	373
Obsidian (Snowflake)	Ratziel	330
Opal (Fire)	Annunciata	192
Pearl (Black and White)	Annunciata	189
Petrified (Fossilised) Wood	Sandalphon	259
Prehnite	Seraphina	80
Preseli (Stonehenge) Bluestone	Rainbow Aurora	234
Pyrite	Okina	360
Quartz (Aqua Aura)	Magdalena	307
Quartz (Cobalt Aura)	Okina	357
Quartz (Flame Aura)	Metatron	49
Quartz (Rainbow / Angel / Opal Aura)	Rainbow Aurora	236
Quartz (Clear)	Tzaphkiel	376
Quartz (Haematoid)	Metatron	55
Quartz (Phantom – White)	Jophiel	178
Quartz (Rose)	Chamuel	91
Quartz (Snow / White)	Jochara	348
Quartz (Tourmalinated)	Sandalphon	262
Rhodocrosite	Chamuel	92
Ruby	Chamuel	96
Sapphire (Blue)	Michael	138
Scolecite	Mareia	276
Selenite (Clear)	Amethystia	39
Selenite (White / Satin Spar)	Gabriel	208
Seraphinite	Mareia	273
Sodalite	Michael	136
Sugilite	Tzadkiel	21
Tektite (Tibetan / Black)	Jochara	346
Tiger Eye	Sophia	64
Tiger Iron	Lucida	161
Tourmaline (Watermelon)	Raphael	293
Turquoise	Mareia	279
Zircon	Shekhinah	248

INDEX OF GREENWOOD GUARDIANS:

Name	Archangel/Archeia	Page
Acacia	Ratziel	336
Amelanchier (Snowy Mespil)	Shekhinah	252
Apple	Maryllisa	111
Ash	Seraphina	84
Aspen	Amethystia	41
Bamboo	Jophiel	182
Baobab	Mareia	280
	Tzaphkiel	378
Beech	Sophia	70
Birch	Chamuel	97
Cherry	Chamuel	98
Chestnut (Horse)	Gabriel	210
Chestnut (Sweet)	Jophiel	181
Coconut	Sandalphon	266
Cypress	Tzaphkiel	378
Elm	Okina	364
Eucalyptus	Magdalena	308
Fig	Lucida	168
Gingko Biloba	Azrael	322
Hawthorn	Magdalena	307
Hazel (Corkscrew)	Azrael	322
Hazel (Wych)	Okina	363
Holly	Michael	140
Hornbeam	Gabriel	209
Juniper	Shekhinah	252
Larch	Michael	140
	Tzadkiel	28
Linden (Lime)	Annunciata	195

INDEX OF GREENWOOD GUARDIANS: continued

Name	Archangel/Archeia	Page
Magnolia	Annunciata	196
Maple	Raphael	294
	Ratziel	335
Mimosa	Rainbow Aurora	238
Mulberry	Uriel	224
Myrrh	Mikaela	153
Oak	Haniel	126
	Sandalphon	266
Palm (Date)	Jochara	350
Pine (Chile – Monkey Puzzle Tree)	Metatron	56
Pine (Scots)	Amethystia	42
Pomegranate	Lucida	167
Poplar	Seraphina	84
Redwood	Metatron	56
Robinia (False Acacia)	Sophia	70
Rowan	Jochara	350
	Maryllisa	112
Sycamore	Uriel	224
Sycomore Fig	Rainbow Aurora	237
Tamarisk	Haniel	125
	Tzadkiel	28
Willow (Weeping)	Mikaela	154
Yew	Mareia	280
	Raphael	293

INDEX OF TEACHINGS: (The...)

Title	Archangel/Archeia	Page
The Alignment of Personal Will and Divine Will	Tzaphkiel	369
The Alignment of the Heart of the Lotus with the Unified Body	Sandalphon	260
The Alignment of The Lotus of the Heart with the Linear Bodies	Sandalphon	257
The All-seeing Eye and The Communion of The Grail	Tzadkiel	24
The Art of Balance through Focused Self-awareness	Lucida	164
The Blessing of Mercy and the Promise of Karmic Freedom	Chamuel	94
The Book of Illumined Truths and The Waters of The Diamond Light	Haniel	117
The Book of Ratziel – Love, Light and The Word	Ratziel	330
The Crystal Ray and The Staff of Awakening	Gabriel	201
The Circle of Learning – the Jasmine and the Rose	Jophiel	176
The Circle of Life – the Labyrinth and the Maze	Mikaela	145
The Crucible and The Alchemy of The Silver-Violet Flame	Sophia	64
The Diamond Lantern – Surrender, Sacrifice and Self-mastery	Azrael	316
The Diamond Light that IS Within and Without	Shekhinah	246
The Emerald Key of Modification and Balance	Mareia	271
The Enlightenment of The Platinum Star of Illumined Truth	Tzaphkiel	374
The Evolution of Life and the Perfection of Divine Creation	Mareia	274
The Fearless Heart and The Glory of The Grail	Magdalena	302
The Flame of Truth and Light and The Serpents of Creation	Haniel	120
The Fundamental Forces of Air and Water	Jochara	341
The Fundamental Forces of Earth and Fire	Jochara	344
The Gift of The Absolute Light of The Illumined Heart	Sophia	61
The Gift of The Amethyst Flame of Transformation	Amethystia	33
The Gift of The Black Light of The Alpha and Omega	Ratziel	333
The Gift of The Blue Flame of Divine Will and Power	Mikaela	150
The Gift of The Crystal-clear Flame of First Consciousness	Gabriel	207
The Gift of The Divine Templates of Creation	Uriel	221
The Gift of The Enlightened Lotus of Divinity	Raphael	290
The Gift of The Golden Halo of Universal Awareness	Okina	358
The Gift of The Golden-yellow Flame of Illumined Wisdom	Jophiel	173
The Gift of The Holon of Universal Balance	Shekhinah	243
The Gift of The Infinity Cross of Multidimensional Reality	Mareia	277
The Gift of The Lightning Bolt of Divine Inspiration	Metatron	50
The Gift of The Magdalene Flame of Innocence, Purity and Love	Magdalena	305
The Gift of The Merkaba of The Ascension	Azrael	318
The Gift of The Mirror of The Soul	Maryllisa	109
The Gift of The Pearl-white Flame of Hope	Annunciata	192
The Gift of The Pink Flame of Divine Love	Seraphina	81
The Gift of The Quill of Quetzalcoatl	Haniel	122

INDEX OF TEACHINGS: (The...) continued

Title	Archangel/Archeia	Page
The Gift of The Rainbow Key of Light	Rainbow Aurora	235
The Gift of The Rose-pink Flame of Divine Compassion	Chamuel	89
The Gift of The Sacred Seeds of Limitless Potential	Sandalphon	263
The Gift of The Sapphire Flame of Divine Expression	Michael	137
The Gift of The Spear of Divine Enlightenment	Tzaphkiel	372
The Gift of The Violet Flame of Transmutation	Tzadkiel	22
The Gift of The White Light of The Alpha and Omega	Jochara	347
The Gift of The Yellow Flame of Divine Wisdom	Lucida	162
The Grounding of The Christ-Light through the Cedar and the Rose	Lucida	159
The Healing Power of Love Without Limits	Seraphina	78
The Holographic Universe and the Multifaceted Nature of Divine Truth	Mikaela	148
The Key to Wholeness and Health – Self-awareness and Love	Raphael	285
The Keys of Understanding and The Scroll of Akasha	Uriel	218
The Knowledge and Wisdom of The Ancient Ones	Ratziel	327
The Knowledge of Perfected Balance and The 'I' of The Pearl	Annunciata	187
The Knowledge of Perfected Creation and The Songs of the Whales	Annunciata	190
The Light of The Star of Venus and The Beauty Within	Maryllisa	103
The Light of The Sun and The Sword of Truth	Michael	131
The Light of Universal Consciousness and The Holon of Infinity	Shekhinah	249
The Lyre of Light and The Charitable Heart	Seraphina	75
The Magenta Ray and The Cosmic Seeds of Light	Okina	360
The Mastery of Balance through the Still-point Within	Raphael	287
The Merciful Freedom of Living in The NOW	Magdalena	299
The New Dawn Flame and the Baptism of Fire	Gabriel	204
The Obsidian Mirror – Truth, Trust and Transformation	Azrael	313
The Power of the Rainbow and The Light Within	Metatron	47
The Ray of Revelation and The Mind of The Divine	Okina	355
The Rose of Peace and The Dynamic Duality of Absolute Balance	Maryllisa	106
The Sacred Flames of Resurrection and Rebirth	Uriel	215
The Sacred Purpose of Sigils, Symbols and Signs	Amethystia	38
The Seal of Embedded Creation and The Dragons of the Rainbow Realm	Rainbow Aurora	232
The Secret Garden and The Gold Flame of Joy	Jophiel	179
The Spiral of Transformation – Perspective and Choice	Amethystia	35
The Star-borne Hammer of Dissolution and Creation	Metatron	53
The Sword of Divine Justice and the True Meaning of Power	Chamuel	92
The 'Tao' of the Open and Balanced Heart	Rainbow Aurora	229
The Tau Key of Perfected Manifestation	Sophia	67
The Unicorns of Ultimate Purity and The Spiral of Contemplation	Michael	134
The Violet Ray and The Cloak of Immaculate Illumination	Tzadkiel	19

On wings of love we bear you up:
your courage, dreams and woes borne by us
and shown to the world as shining Lights of hope.
Open now to the presence of the One that is YOU; that is I:
a veil removed; a doorway opened,
to reveal the presence of the Shining Ones,
whose Light reflects your own.

Beloved, we love you, as you love us:
dear sister; brother; parent; child.
Born of the ONE true Light, filled with Grace
and in certainty of your Soul and Spark -
the essence of that which you call The Divine,
yet which is of you, as you are of it.

With your eyes you can see the Light of the Divine;
with your lips you can speak the sounds of Creation;
and with your ears you can hear the Wisdoms of the ages,
filling you with peace and the knowledge
that here - in this place - you are EVERYTHING.

(Given by Tamarenth – the Elohim of Beauty and Form – to herald the start of 2012.)